The Ethics of Public Health

The International Library of Medicine, Ethics and Law
Series Editor: Michael Freeman

Titles in the Series:

Death, Dying and the Ending of Life, Volumes I and II
Margaret P. Battin, Leslie P. Francis and Bruce M. Landesman

Abortion
Belinda Bennett

Health, Rights and Globalisation
Belinda Bennett

Health and Human Rights
Rebecca Cook and Charles Ngwena

Children, Medicine and the Law
Michael Freeman

Ethics and Medical Decision-Making
Michael Freeman

The Ethics of Public Health, Volumes I and II
Michael Freeman

Mental Illness, Medicine and Law
Martin Lyon Levine

The Elderly
Martin Lyon Levine

Genetics and Gene Therapy
Sheila A.M. McLean

Rights and Resources
Frances H. Miller

Organ and Tissue Transplantation
David Price

AIDS: Society, Ethics and Law
Udo Schüklenk

Women, Medicine, Ethics and the Law
Susan Sherwin and Barbara Parish

Legal and Ethical Issues in Human Reproduction
Bonnie Steinbock

Medical Practice and Malpractice
Harvey Teff

Human Experimentation and Research
George F. Tomossy and David N. Weisstub

Neuroethics
Paul Root Wolpe

The Ethics of Public Health, Volume I

Edited by

Michael Freeman F.B.A.

University College London, UK

ASHGATE

Published by
Ashgate Publishing Limited
Wey Court East
Union Road
Farnham
Surrey GU9 7PT
England

Ashgate Publishing Company
Suite 420
101 Cherry Street
Burlington, VT 05401-4405
USA

Ashgate website: http://www.ashgate.com

British Library Cataloguing in Publication Data
The ethics of public health.
Volumes 1 and 2. – (The international library of medicine, ethics and law)
1. Public health–Moral and ethical aspects. 2. Medical policy–Moral and ethical aspects.
I. Series II. Freeman, Michael D. A.
174.2'9444–dc22

Library of Congress Control Number: 2009924480

ISBN: 978-0-7546-2605-3

Mixed Sources
Product group from well-managed forests and other controlled sources
www.fsc.org Cert no. SGS-COC-2482
© 1996 Forest Stewardship Council
FSC

Printed and bound in Great Britain by
TJ International Ltd, Padstow, Cornwall

Contents

PART III THE HISTORICAL DEBATE

PART IV RESEARCH ISSUES

PART V PUBLIC HEALTH AND AUTONOMY

PART VI QUESTIONS OF GOVERNANCE

PART VII PUBLIC HEALTH AND HUMAN RIGHTS

PART VIII SURVEILLANCE AND PRIVACY

PART IX PREVENTION AND ITS LIMITS

PART X CONFINEMENT AND LIBERTY

Acknowledgements

The editor and publishers wish to thank the following for permission to use copyright material.

American Society of Law, Medicine and Ethics for the essays: Larry Gostin (1991), 'Ethical Principles for the Conduct of Human Subject Research: Population-Based Research and Ethics', *Law, Medicine and Health Care*, **19**, pp. 191–201. Copyright © 1991 American Society of Law, Medicine and Ethics; A.M. Capron (1991), 'Protection of Research Subjects: Do Special Rules Apply in Epidemiology?', *Law, Medicine and Health Care*, **19**, pp. 81S–89S. Copyright © 1991 American Society of Law, Medicine and Ethics; Carol Levine (1991), 'Children in HIV/AIDS Clinical Trials: Still Vulnerable After All These Years', *Law, Medicine and Health Care*, **19**, pp. 231–37. Copyright © 1991 American Society of Law, Medicine and Ethics.

Boston College School of Law for the essay: David W. Johnston (1992), 'Cuba's Quarantine of AIDS Victims: A Violation of Human Rights?', *Boston College International Comparative Law Review*, **15**, pp. 189–212. Copyright © 1992 Boston College School of Law.

British Medical Journal for the essays: Spencer A. Hall (1992), 'Should Public Health Respect Autonomy?', *Journal of Medical Ethics*, **18**, pp. 197–201. Copyright © 1992 British Medical Journal; Kelley Lee and Anne Mills (2000), 'Strengthening Governance for Global Health Research', *British Medical Journal*, **321**, pp. 775–76. Copyright © 2000 British Medical Journal.

Cambridge University Press for the essay: Charles Weijer (1999), 'Protecting Communities in Research: Philosophical and Pragmatic Challenges', *Cambridge Quarterly of Healthcare Ethics*, **8**, pp. 501–13. Copyright © 1999 Cambridge University Press.

John Wiley and Sons for the essays: Ronald Bayer and Amy L. Fairchild (2004), 'The Genesis of Public Health Ethics', *Bioethics*, **18**, pp. 473–92. Copyright © 2004 John Wiley and Sons; Mark A. Rothstein (2002), 'Rethinking the Meaning of Public Health', *Journal of Law, Medicine and Ethics*, **30**, pp. 144–49. Copyright © 2002 John Wiley and Sons; James F. Childress, Ruth R. Faden, Ruth D. Gaare, Lawrence O. Gostin, Jeffrey Kahn, Richard J. Bonnie, Nancy E. Kass, Anna C. Mastroianni, Jonathan D. Moreno and Philip Nieburg (2002), 'Public Health Ethics: Mapping the Terrain', *Journal of Law, Medicine and Ethics*, **30**, pp. 170–78. Copyright © 2002 John Wiley and Sons; Leslie P. Francis, Margaret P. Battin, Jay A. Jacobson, Charles B. Smith and Jeffrey Botkin (2003), 'How Infectious Diseases Got Left Out – and What this Omission Might Have Meant for Bioethics', *Bioethics*, **19**, pp. 307–22. Copyright © 2003 John Wiley and Sons; Nancy E. Kass (2004), 'Public Health Ethics: From Foundations and Frameworks to Justice and Global Public Health', *Journal of Law, Medicine and Ethics*, **32**, pp. 232–42. Copyright © 2004 John Wiley and Sons; Michael

J. Selgelid (2005), 'Ethics and Infectious Disease', *Bioethics*, **19**, pp. 272–89. Copyright © 2005 John Wiley and Sons; David Armstrong (1995), 'The Rise of Surveillance Medicine', *Sociology of Health and Illness*, **17**, pp. 393–404. Copyright © 1995 John Wiley and Sons; Marcel Verweij (2005), 'Obligatory Precautions against Infection', *Bioethics*, **19**, pp. 323–36. Copyright © 2005 John Wiley and Sons; Marcel Verweij (2001), 'Individual and Collective Considerations in Public Health: Influenza Vaccination in Nursing Homes', *Bioethics*, **15**, pp. 536–46. Copyright © 2001 John Wiley and Sons.

Lynne Rienner Publishers for the essay: Kelley Lee and Richard Dodgson (2000), 'Globalization and Cholera: Implications for Global Governance', *Global Governance*, **6**, pp. 213–36. Copyright © 2000 Lynne Rienner Publishers.

Massachusetts Medical Society for the essay: Ronald Bayer and C. Healton (1989), 'Controlling AIDS in Cuba: The Logic of Quarantine', *New England Journal of Medicine*, **320**, pp. 1022–24. Copyright © 1989 Massachusetts Medical Society.

Oxford University Press for the essays: E. Ziglio, S. Hagard and J. Griffiths (2000), 'Health Promotion Development in Europe: Achievements and Challenges', *Health Promotion International*, **15**, pp. 143–54. Copyright © 2000 Oxford University Press; Simon Szreter (1988), 'The Importance of Social Intervention in Britain's Mortality Decline *c*.1850–1914: A Re-interpretation of the Role of Public Health', *Social History of Medicine*, **1**, pp. 1–37. Copyright © 1988 Oxford University Press; Geoffrey Rose (2001), 'Sick Individuals and Sick Populations', *International Journal of Epidemiology*, **30**, pp. 427–32. Copyright © 2001 Oxford University Press; Dyna Arhin-Tenkorang and Pedro Conceição (2003), 'Beyond Communicable Disease Control: Health in the Age of Globalization', in Inge Kaull, Pedro Conceição, Katell Le Goulven and Ronald U. Mendoza (eds), *Managing Globalization*, New York: Oxford University Press, pp. 484–515. Copyright © 2003 Oxford University Press.

Springer Science and Business Media for the essay: Ronald Bayer and Amy Fairchild (2002), 'The Limits of Privacy: Surveillance and the Control of Disease', *Health Care Analysis*, **10**, pp. 19–35. Copyright © 2002 Springer Science and Business Media.

Taylor & Francis for the essays: Anita Goraya and Graham Scambler (1998), 'From Old to New Public Health: Role Tensions and Contradictions', *Critical Public Health*, **8**, pp. 141–51. Copyright © 1998 Taylor & Francis; Elihu D. Richter and Richard Laster (2005), 'The Precautionary Principle, Epidemiology and the Ethics of Delay', *Human and Ecological Risk Assessment*, **11**, pp. 17–27. Copyright © 2005 Taylor & Francis.

Temple Law Review for the essays: Scott Burris (2004), 'Governance, Microgovernance and Health', *Temple Law Review*, **77**, pp. 335–61. Copyright © 2004 Temple Law Review; Sofia Gruskin (2004), 'Is there a Government in the Cockpit: A Passenger's Perspective, or Global Public Health: The Role of Human Rights', *Temple Law Review*, **77**, pp. 313–33. Copyright © 2004 Temple Law Review.

The American Public Health Association for the essays: Daniel Callahan and Bruce Jennings (2002), 'Ethics and Public Health: Forging a Strong Relationship', *American Journal of Public Health*, **92**, pp. 169–76. Copyright © 2002 The American Public Health Association; Solomon

R. Benatar (1998), 'Global Disparities in Health and Human Rights: A Critical Commentary', *American Journal of Public Health*, **88**, pp. 295–300. Copyright © 1998 The American Public Health Association; Bernard D. Goldstein (2001), 'The Precautionary Principle also Applies to Public Health Actions', *American Journal of Public Health*, **91**, pp. 1358–61. Copyright © 2001 The American Public Health Association.

The Hastings Center for the essay: Jonathan M. Mann (1997), 'Medicine and Public Health, Ethics and Human Rights', *Hastings Center Report*, **27**, pp. 6–13. Copyright © 1997 The Hastings Center.

The Johns Hopkins University Press for the essay: Dan W. Brock (2000), 'Broadening the Bioethics Agenda', *Kennedy Institute of Ethics Journal*, **10**, pp. 21–38. Copyright © 2000 The Johns Hopkins University Press.

Every effort has been made to trace all the copyright holders, but if any have been inadvertently overlooked the publishers will be pleased to make the necessary arrangement at the first opportunity.

Series Preface

Few academic disciplines have developed with such pace in recent years as bioethics. And because the subject crosses so many disciplines, important writing is to be found in a range of books and journals, access to the whole of which is likely to elude all but the most committed of scholars. The International Library of Medicine, Ethics and Law is designed to assist the scholarly endeavour by providing in accessible volumes a compendium of basic materials drawn from the most significant periodical literature. Each volume contains essays of central theoretical importance in its subject area, and each throws light on important bioethical questions in the world today. The series as a whole makes available an extensive range of valuable material (the standard 'classics' and the not-so-standard) and should prove of inestimable value to those involved in the research, teaching and study of medicine, ethics and law. The twenty volumes together – each with introductions and bibliographies – are a library in themselves – an indispensable resource in a world in which even the best-stocked library is unlikely to cover the range of materials contained within these volumes.

It remains for me to thank the editors who have pursued their task with commitment, insight and enthusiasm, to thank also the hard-working staff at Ashgate – theirs is a mammoth enterprise – and to thank my secretary, Jacqui Bennett, for the enormous assistance she has given me in bringing the series from idea to reality.

MICHAEL FREEMAN
Series Editor
Faculty of Laws
University College London

Introduction

'Public health' is a term of art. It envisages a philosophy of intervention, the object of which is the protection and promotion of the health of a population. It is concerned more with prevention than care and treatment. An early and classic definition is Winslow's:

> Public health is the science and art of preventing disease, prolonging life and promoting physical health and efficiency through organized community efforts for the sanitation of the environment, the control of community infections, the education of the individual in principles of personal hygiene, the organization of medical and nursing services for the early diagnosis and preventive treatment of disease, and the development of social machinery which will ensure to every individual in the community a standard of living adequate for the maintenance of health. (1920, p.23)

The definition is all-embracing, and if this collection attempted to cover this range, it would require not only several volumes, but a dilution of focus.

Thinking ethically about public health is relatively new. But efforts to promote health and prevent disease were undertaken by some of the earliest civilizations (Rosen, 1993). Religion shared a common ground with medicine. Consider, for example, the following passage in Deuteronomy 28: 15, 21–22.

> If thou wilt not hearken unto the voice of the Lord thy God … the Lord shall make the pestilence cleave unto thee, until he has consumed thee from off the land; whither thou goest to possess it. The Lord shall smite thee with a consumption, and with a fever, and with an inflammation, and with an extreme burning, and with the sword, and with blasting, and with mildew; and they shall pursue thee until thou perish.

Certain illnesses were seen as God's punishment for sin. What is usually translated as leprosy (*Zara'ath*) is one example, found in Leviticus 13–14. There is archaeological evidence that other ancient civilizations, for example the Egyptians and the Incas, appreciated the significance of sanitation and urban planning (Inglis, 1965). There were further developments with the Greeks (Phillips, 1973). Hippocrates (in *Airs, Waters and Places*, which is usually attributed to him) tried both to explain ill health and to offer recommendations for avoiding disease. For example, he observed an association between marshland and malaria: that the Greeks failed to understand the causal relationship (they thought the disease was caused by drinking swamp water) is beside the point. The Romans too were aware of the health implications of the environment and they developed methods of purifying water supplies. Epidemics (smallpox, plague) nevertheless struck, most ferociously in the time of Justinian when 40 per cent of the population of Constantinople died (McNeill, 1976).

With the decline of the Roman Empire and the decay of its system of public health, the knowledge accumulated by the classic civilizations was lost. Eight hundred years separate the plague of Justinian and the Black Death of 1347–51. The latter probably originated in China and within a couple of years it had killed about a third of Europe's population (see Kelly, 2006 and the classic account of Ziegler, 1969, p. 230). According to Roy Porter,

> A Europe which had been relatively epidemic-free turned into a crucible of pestilences, spawning the obsessions haunting late medieval imaginations: death, decay and the Devil, the *danse macabre* and the Gothic symbols of the skull and crossbones, the Grim Reaper and the Horsemen of the Apocalypse. (1997, p. 123)

There were different views as to the cause, and responses depended upon the theory accepted. If it was God's punishment, then only prayer and fasting (and flagellation) could be effective. A common belief was that Jews were to blame: they had poisoned the wells. There was as a result much persecution of Jewish populations. In Basle, Jews were penned up in a wooden building and burnt alive; 2,000 were slaughtered in Strasbourg and 12,000 in Mainz. Flagellants (whipping was thought to propriate divine anger) led the burghers of Frankfurt into the Jewish quarter for a wholesale massacre (see Poliakov, 1974, vol. 1, pp. 107–22; Cantor, 2001, ch. 7; Benedictow, 2004, pp. 392–93; and also Brewer, 1988, pp. 144–49).[1]

Physicians put the emphasis on individual treatment. They had no power to effect public health measures: that was the magistrate's province. Venice tried quarantine methods: a committee of three nobles laid down burial regulations, banning the sick from entering the city and jailing intruders. In Milan, the council sealed in the occupants of affected houses, leaving them to die. Porter (1997, p. 125) notes that this may have worked because Milan's death rate (15 per cent) was lower than elsewhere. In Florence, a committee of eight was given dictatorial powers: they required the killing of cats and dogs – they did not know that the disease was being carried by rats.

Throughout Italy leper houses beyond city limits were established. In Ragusa (now Dubrovnik) a 30-day isolation period was instituted in 1377 for all arriving from plague-infested areas: this was subsequently increased in 1397 to 40 days.[2] Marseilles (in 1383), Venice (in 1423), Pisa (in 1464) and Genoa (in 1467) took similar action. Initially, these were the initiatives of ad hoc health boards of nobles and officials. But around 1410, in Milan, a permanent magistracy for the preservation of health was established. Bills of Mortality were initiated in Milan: these listed causes of death. The Board contained a physician, a surgeon, a notary, a barber, two horsemen, three footmen and two grave-diggers. Doctors were not full members but acted as advisers. The Milanese model was followed elsewhere in Italy. It became a common practice to close borders, extend quarantines and introduce health passes.

Although these approaches were not found in northern Europe, other public health measures had been introduced in northern cities even earlier. For example, in London regulations were introduced in the latter part of the twelfth and early thirteenth centuries to control a range of activities considered hazardous to health. There were rules, for example, on the slaughter of animals and regulations governing 'offensive trades'. Some European cities, such as Paris and Prague, took measures to improve the environment, paving streets to make them easier to clean. Municipal abattoirs were established as a way of preventing offal littering. And there

---

1 There are now suggestions in the Arab press that Jews are responsible for Asian flu.

2 Thus becoming a true quarantine (*quarantenaria* = 40 days). On why 40 days, see Wain (1970, p. 62).

were, apparently, severe penalties for those who infringed these rules and regulations (Rosen, 1993).

In the centuries following the Black Death there was rarely any systematic response to disease. A syphilis epidemic, such as that which attacked Europe in the late fifteenth century, might be responded to by the closing of brothels, the medical examination of prostitutes or compulsory 'treatment' for offenders. Only gradually were the causes of diseases examined, and this led to, or at least coincided with, public health interventions. The deleterious effect of the consumption of alcohol, in particular cheap gin,[3] was noted and led to the imposition of a high tax on gin and supposedly limited its availability.[4] James Lind (1716–91), a Scottish naval surgeon, noted that armies lost 'more of their men by sickness, than by the sword'. He demonstrated – using the world's first controlled clinical trial[5] – that scurvy was caused by an inadequate diet and could be prevented by issuing fresh fruit rations. Captain Cook adopted this finding – on his first circumnavigation in 1770 there was only one death – but it was not until the early years of the following century that the Admiralty implemented Lind's regime.[6] Sir John Pringle's analysis of epidemics in the army had a similar fate. His *Observations on the Diseases of the Army* (1752) was filled with advice on ways to prevent the most common disorders: typhus, dysentery, 'bilious' fevers, scabies and so on. His argument struck a chord with the Enlightenment concern for hygiene, public health and the value of life.[7]

But by the close of the eighteenth century (in England) public health was being taken more seriously. Some municipal corporations began to tackle problems like polluted water supplies. Manchester even established (in 1796) a Board of Health. The prison reform movement, led by John Howard, also awakened public health concerns. Howard concluded that filth and a close atmosphere were responsible for endemic conditions like gaol fever (typhus). It was around this time that Edward Jenner (1749–1823) discovered a smallpox prophylactic: cowpox vaccination (Fisher, 1991).

The stage had been set for the Victorian Revolution. Clearly, public health initiatives antedate the nineteenth century. Public health no more began than it ended with the Victorians (see Baggott, 2000, p. 18), but they did much to establish its infrastructure (Frazer, 1950; Smith, 1979). The great Victorian philanthropists did not show much interest in public health. However, as the public health movement developed, it reached an 'accommodation with the broader notion of "improvement", which was a major influence in the Victorian era … The public health movement became a moral crusade to eliminate the visible signs of filth, physical cleanliness and good health being viewed as a precondition for both social and spiritual progress' (Baggott, 2000, p. 27; see also Wohl, 1984).

The medical profession was not in the vanguard of public health reform. The medical colleges 'never gave an impetus', and the 'organised medical profession played a surprisingly secondary and desultory role in the vast expansion of Victorian state provision' (Porter, 1995, p. 59). Vested interests, business generally and water companies, were often resistant to public health reform. In Switzerland in 1831, for example, the local business community was so

[3] Satirized in William Hogarth's *Gin Lane*.

[4] See the Gin Act 1751.

[5] On board HMS Salisbury in 1754.

[6] But 'the delay was not that result of blind prejudice and ignorance on the part of the naval authorities', according to Langford (1989, p. 630).

[7] The military hospital was also his idea (see Porter, 1997, p. 295).

concerned about the impact of a possible quarantine on trade that they forced doctors to retract their diagnosis of cholera (see Longmate, 1966, pp. 27–32).

A key figure in the Victorian sanitary revolution was Edwin Chadwick (1800–90). He had spent time as Jeremy Bentham's secretary and his Poor Law bears the mark of Benthamism. But it didn't work: pauperism did not decrease. Chadwick concluded that much poverty was due not to fecklessness but to disease. Many of those who were compelled to enter workhouses were clinically sick or seriously disabled.[8] The social costs of sickness converted Chadwick to the 'sanitary idea': to prevention. Poverty could not be abolished but poverty which was the result of preventable disease could be. Chadwick used Poor Law medical officers' reports as data for his *Report on the Sanitary Condition of the Labouring Population of Great Britain* (1842).[9] This charted the prevalence of disease and poverty through maps, vital statistics and descriptions of streets, dwellings, refuse, privies, sewers, drainage and odours. Unsanitary living conditions and squalor were to blame for the ill health and shortened lives of the labouring poor.[10] Chadwick's work led to Britain's first Public Health Act in 1848. This created the General Board of Health. If 10 per cent of ratepayers in an area petitioned the Board, or if the death rate in the area rose above 23 per thousand, the town council had to set up a local board of health, responsible for sanitary supervision, drainage and so forth, and empowered to raise local rates. Within five years 103 towns had adopted the Act. But there was resistance from vested interests championing 'local autonomy' and supported by *The Times*, which, in 1848, had declared cholera to be 'the best of all sanitary reformers' (quoted in Porter, 1997, p. 412).

Chadwick was ousted and the General Board ceased to operate in 1854. His bureaucratic model was replaced by one based on medicine and run by a doctor. John Snow's cholera investigations in 1849 were a watershed. He argued that cholera was linked to contaminated drinking water. He was able to test this hypothesis when there was a major outbreak of cholera in Soho in late August 1854 (see Pelling, 1978). Better drainage and sewerage systems were gradually put in place. In 1854 Sir John Simon was appointed as Britain's first chief medical administrator. There was significant new legislation: the Local Government Act 1858 permitted compulsory purchase for sanitary purposes, the Sanitary Act 1866 gave local authorities new powers to provide clean water supplies and to regulate tenements, and the Vaccination Act 1867 increased penalties for failure to vaccinate infants.[11] There were anti-vaccination groups whose opposition was grounded largely on civil liberties considerations.[12] They prevailed. Compulsory vaccination was rescinded in 1909.

Similar battles were fought over communicable diseases. There was legislation permitting quarantine for those with specific contagious diseases such as smallpox. Sexually transmitted diseases began to attract critical attention in the second half of the nineteenth century. Its impact on the army at the time of the Crimean War stirred concern. The first Contagious

---

[8] The Poor Law medicine service which developed as a result may be seen as constituting the seeds of a National Health Service, a century later.

[9] The circulation of this was enormous (20,000 copies were sold within two weeks).

[10] In Bethnal Green (in London's East End) the average age of death of labourers was 16 (it was 45 for the better off).

[11] Compulsory vaccination against smallpox was introduced in 1853.

[12] A campaigning journal, Henry Pitman's Anti-Vaccinator, was launched in 1869. The National Anti-Compulsory Vaccination League was founded in 1874.

Diseases Act in 1864 targeted prostitutes working in the ports and garrison towns. They could be required to undergo physical examination: if found to be infected, they could be detained for up to three months and compulsorily treated. Further legislation provided for the regular inspection of 'known prostitutes'. There was opposition from civil libertarians and feminists as well as from the medical profession, and the legislation was short-lived (see Mort, 1987). It was repealed in 1886.

Tuberculosis also attracted public health legislation (see Smith, 1988). Bacteriology demonstrated that it was an infectious airborne disease. There were campaigns to stop spitting in public places and in the 1890s in Britain (and also in France; see Barnes, 1995) there were demands for the compulsory detention of contagious cases. This did not happen but the sanatoria which the poor were 'encouraged' to enter were custodial institutions in all but name: as Porter puts it, 'quasi-punitive, even if justified on medical grounds' (1997, p. 412). By 1910 there were 41 public sanatoria in England: these were run mostly through the Poor Law. There was coercion[13] but there was also financial support for the families of patients. Sanatoria taught the work ethic so that those who lived to leave their sanatorium were able to repay by work what the taxpayer had spent in restoring them to health. But most died in sanatoria (perhaps as many as three-quarters). To quote Porter again: 'nominally preventive or therapeutic, it was often terminal, a dustbin where the dying could never again infect family and workmates. Surreptitiously, the sanatorium functioned as "a segregative" institution, protecting society from the "degeneratives" within' (1997, p. 423).

Unsurprisingly, it didn't take long for medicine to expand its category of 'degenerates'. Nor was it long before the dangers of allowing such people to reproduce were perceived. The eugenics movement, the impact of which was felt for much of the twentieth century, was a misguided product of the nineteenth-century initiative to improve public health. It led to policies of forced sterilization in a number of countries, and not just Nazi Germany, the country with which it is particularly associated.[14]

The USA developed medically based immigration control. Between 1892 and 1954 over 12 million immigrants were medically inspected. The target, initially at least, was the infectious disease, but mental abnormality assumed increasing importance as eugenics established itself. And the US Supreme Court was prepared to legitimate this movement and its practices, including forced sterilization: Mr Justice Holmes was happy to proclaim that 'three generations of imbeciles were enough' in Carrie Buck's case.[15] Only about 2 per cent of those processed through Ellis Island (in New York Harbour) were denied entrance to the USA, but the perception of an immigrant threat and the use of public health powers to protect against it remained. The case of 'Typhoid Mary' illustrates this (see Leavitt, 1996). Mary was a cook who infected nearly 50 people with enteric fever in New York in the early years of the twentieth century. She was mandatorily detained in an isolation hospital but, after a habeas corpus suit, was released on condition she worked in a laundry. She reverted to cooking and, using an assumed name, got a job in a maternity hospital kitchen. Two more people died.

---

[13] And lives in sanatoria were highly regulated: no alcohol or tobacco was allowed and patients needed passes to go outside.

[14] On Britain, in particular, see Trombley (1988).

[15] *Buck* v. *Bell* 274 U.S. 200 (1927). See Kevles (1995, pp. 110–12). An interesting postscript to the case is found in Gould (1984, pp. 323–36).

Mary was sent back to Quarantine Island and detained there for life: in effect, as she put it, banished 'like a leper'.

Until the twentieth century, the health problems of the industrialized world and those of the rest of the world (which it had colonized) could be split. Colonialism had not been good for the health of the 'Third World' (see Arnold, 1993 and Watts, 1997). As Porter explains:

> 'Epidemiological link-ups between previously isolated regions, the movements of fleets and armies, of millions of slaves and indentured labourers, the spread of disease by ecological change and social dislocation, the misery bred by shanty-towns – all have been implicated in the hail of death that European rule brought. The good that western medicine did was marginal and incidental' (1997, p. 482).

The twentieth century brought new problems. One of the early effects of globalization was to bring health problems from different parts of the world together. This was seen strikingly in 1918 when the most mobile and lethal pandemic ever to strike the world[16] killed over 25 million people in six months, to be followed by an epidemic of encephalitis lethargica[17] and a further wave of killer influenza two years later. A side-effect of the Great War, it killed about three times the number who died in the war (see Kolata, 2000).

The flu pandemic was the worst pestilence since the Black Death, nearly 600 years earlier. And nothing of its intensity has happened since. Whether this is pure chance – and, as I write, some think luck may have run out with the onset of avian flu and now swine flu – or because of better medicine (antibiotics, vaccines) and better health measures is uncertain. Better international structures had been put in place after the cholera pandemics in the middle of the nineteenth century and International Sanitary Conferences were held.[18] It was at the seventh of these, held in Venice in 1891, that there was agreement on the quarantining of westbound ships with cholera on board. But by then cholera had virtually disappeared.

In 1907, 23 European countries set up the Office International d'Hygiène Publique (OIHP) in Paris.[19] This collected and disseminated information on a variety of diseases (cholera, plague, yellow fever, malaria, typhoid). It also served as a forum to discuss such issues as sanitation, inoculation and isolation. The League of Nations, established following the First World War, set up its own health body, the Health Organisation of the League of Nations. Since the USA was not a member of the League of Nations, the OIHP was not disbanded, and parallel agencies operated to further world public health goals. Initially, there was little cooperation between the two institutions but this improved in time. The League of Nations Health Organisation was able to establish commissions: one to target malaria, a second to target cancer.

The League of Nations collapsed with the onset of the Second World War and the Health Organisation ceased to function as a result. To avoid this happening again, when the World Health Organization (WHO) was set up after the Second World War it was given a status independent of its parent body, the United Nations. Its goal was 'a state of complete physical,

---

16 Now, of course, rivalled (if not overtaken) by HIV/AIDS.

17 An inflammation of the brain and spinal cord.

18 The first and second were in Paris (1851 and 1859), the third in Constantinople in 1866, the fourth in Vienna in 1874, the fifth in Washington in 1881 and the sixth in Rome in 1885.

19 Non-European nations including India and the USA joined later.

mental and social well-being and not merely the absence of disease or infirmity'. UNICEF was also established at this time, under the umbrella of UNESCO.

WHO initiated programmes for immunization for the world's children against diphtheria, polio, tuberculosis, tetanus, whooping cough and measles. It also promoted the training of para-health personnel, such as China's barefoot doctors.

The world health movement had some outstanding successes, notably the worldwide eradication of smallpox. When Bangladesh became free of the disease in 1974 the world's press was able to proclaim the end of smallpox, though ironically a British photographer caught and died of the disease in Birmingham four years later. Today, the virus only exists, at least officially, in two laboratories, though there is concern that it may constitute one of the biological weapons held in reserve by one or more irresponsible rogue states.

WHO has been less successful with other major childhood diseases. India manages to immunize only half its children born each year against measles and polio, and immunization rates in Central Africa are lower. It is also now recognized that diseases unknown in the developed world have been neglected or targeted inappropriately. An example is bilharzia, which went virtually unnoticed in the West until US personnel acquired it in the Philippines during the Second World War.

And war, poverty, famine and population displacement have aggravated the problem. So, for example, malaria has not been eradicated: indeed, more people are infected by it today than in 1960. And as Porter points out, 'the parasite changes its genetic makeup more rapidly than the pharmaceutical industry can produce new and tested drugs' (1997, p. 488). In addition, diseases once in retreat are returning – and not just in poor nations. Tuberculosis is becoming more common. It is on the increase in the USA and in Europe but the increase in prevalence in parts of Africa is much greater. More than 3 million people a year die from tuberculosis, 95 per cent of them in the developing world.

Cholera has also returned. It broke out in Indonesia in 1961 and spread through Asia and Africa, attacking 29 countries in two years. It reached Peru in 1991 and spread throughout South America, where 4,000 died of the disease. In 1993 a new strain erupted in India and Bangladesh and spread to South East Asia.

Old diseases re-emerge – diphtheria in the former Soviet Union and its empire is one example – and 'new' ones emerge. AIDS was first noticed in 1981 and the HIV virus was discovered in 1983 (see Grmek, 1990 and Garrett, 1994). It was AIDS more than any other disease that stimulated thinking about the ethics of public health. An early book was Ronald Bayer's *Private Acts, Social Consequences* (1989) (see also Bayer and Fairchild, Chapter 1 in this volume). In the early 1980s, before the cause of AIDS was uncovered, we were able to witness pronouncements reminiscent of biblical times: it was the 'wrath of God' wreaked upon 'the gay'. Even today, there are some – the former President of South Africa Thabo Mbeki is a prominent example – who deny the causal role of HIV.[20] Not surprisingly, conflict rages over the appropriate treatment, over the ethics of treating sufferers in particular ways,[21] over the policies of drug companies, particularly their impact on the developing world, where

---

[20] An early dissenting voice was Peter Duesberg, a Berkeley immunologist.

[21] There is controversy over the role of AZT: is it a prophylactic, a treatment or, as some claimed, 'AIDS by prescription'?

HIV and AIDS are most prevalent. Insights into this can be found in Udo Schüklenk's volume in this series (see Schüklenk, 2001).

Concern that there would be a worldwide AIDS epidemic forced governments to take sexual health more seriously. In Britain it was the Thatcher era: family values were preached, if not always practised, by members of her government and there was a reluctance proactively to promote sexual health (see Durham, 1991). It was 1988 before the dangers of AIDS were proclaimed in a national advertising campaign.[22] Things did improve: a Cabinet committee on AIDS was created, and the medical profession and public health experts were given the job of devising a strategy (see Berridge, 1996). But the Thatcher government opposed needle-exchange schemes to prevent HIV transmission among drug users: in time this policy was also reversed.

The Major government of the 1990s did not have a coherent policy on sexual health. HIV/AIDS was proclaimed as one of its target areas – and it adopted the more enlightened policy on drug users referred to above – but it also included within an Education Act (that of 1993) a provision that permitted parents to withdraw their children from sex education classes, and Major's Health Minister ordered the withdrawal of a booklet on sexual matters produced by the Health Education Authority. In addition, in 1994, the government scrapped a £2 million AIDS awareness campaign and, in 1996, cut funding for AIDS prevention and treatment.

During this period and thereafter HIV infection has continued to rise, though at a rate much less than was predicted in the early 1980s. According to the United Nations (UNAIDS, 2007), there are about 33 million people today living with HIV.[23] Two-thirds are in sub-Saharan Africa. The majority are women. In 2007, about 2 million people in the world died of AIDS: about one-sixth of these were children under 15. There are also large numbers of AIDS orphans.[24] In the years since the epidemic was discovered about 25 million people have died as a result of AIDS. Most people in developing countries who could benefit from AIDS drugs have no access to these drugs. We were warned recently that we may never find a vaccine for AIDS.[25] Questions have therefore been raised as to whether it might be better to focus spending on prevention (on safe-sex campaigns, for example) (see Pisani, 2008), on testing and on treatment. WHO designated 2006 the 'Year of Acceleration of HIV Prevention in the African Region', and made HIV testing its priority (see De Cock *et al.*, 2006). There is mandatory pre-marital HIV testing in Nigeria, Botswana and the Democratic Republic of Congo.[26] In the United States of America, two states, Illinois (see Turnock and Kelly, 1989) and Louisiana, imposed such a requirement but soon abandoned it when couples moved to neighbouring states to marry. It is also on Missouri's statute book.[27] In Europe, the only country to contemplate mandatory pre-marital testing (and prohibit marriage for those with HIV or AIDS) was Albania, but it caved in when many organizations, including international

[22] The initial advertisement was fought over and appeared in censored form (see Garfield, 1994).

[23] This number was revised downwards to take account of an overestimate in India. See also Hunter (2003).

[24] On the problems of whom, see Todres (2007).

[25] By David Baltimore, a leading authority on HIV, quoted in *Guardian*, 15 February 2008.

[26] On the Congo, see Rennie and Mupenda (2008).

[27] Missouri Revised Statutes, chapter 191, Health and Welfare, Section 191, 692. See further Closen, Gamrath and Hopkins (1994).

ones, voiced serious objections.[28] There are problems with treatment too: there is evidence that 40–50 per cent of patients do not comply with their treatment regime (see Kalichman and Rompa, 2003).

Ethical issues in relation to HIV/AIDS began to be debated as soon as the pandemic emerged (see, for example, Mohr, 1987; Bayer, 1989; O'Brien, 1989, Childress, 1991). The literature is now substantial: a previous volume in this series, edited by Udo Schüklenk, offers an excellent selection (as at 2001, when it was published). Only more recently, with the publication of the journal *Developing World Bioethics* in particular (but also other periodical literature) and with books such as Paul Farmer's *Infections and Inequalities* (1999) (see also Farmer, 2003), Sudhir Anand, Fabienne Peter and Amartya Sen's *Public Health, Ethics and Equity* (2004) and Michael Selgelid, Margaret Battin and Charles Smith's *Ethics and Infectious Diseases* (2006) have the issues in this collection come sharply into focus. A further catapult has been a proliferation of books and articles addressing health and human rights (see Cook, Dickens and Fathalla, 2003; Gruskin, Grodin, Annas and Marks, 2005).

This collection is divided into 20 sections, ten in this volume, the remainder in Volume II.

An Introduction

The 'Introduction' addresses the origins of public health ethics and the meaning of public health, examines some tensions and contradictions, and looks at some achievements and challenges.

In Chapter 1 Ronald Bayer and Amy Fairchild remark upon the fact that as bioethics emerged 'little attention was given to the question of the ethics of public health' (p. 4). This was surprising since the values and practices of public health offered 'a rebuke to the ideological impulses of bioethics' (p. 4). In particular they cite the emphasis in bioethics on the individualistic concept of autonomy (but see O'Neill, 2002). Bayer and Fairchild focus on a number of obvious areas, including HIV/AIDS, surveillance and privacy, and confinement and the limits of liberty to demonstrate that those involved in the practice of public health are committed to a set of values which are often in conflict with 'the autonomy-centred values of those who take an individualistic and anti-paternalistic stance' (p. 18). They see the challenge of public health ethics to be to formulate when public health paternalism is justified, but also 'to articulate a set of principles that would preserve a commitment to the realm of free choice' (p. 22).

Mark Rothstein, in Chapter 2, analyses different definitions of 'public health'. One can include within the sphere of public health everything that affects health. Of course, the list is then voluminous: war, poverty, over-population, civil rights and so on. Such an all-embracing definition is ineffective, counterproductive and impractical. An alternative, which is less expansive, is the 'traditional' (Baggott, 2000) conception of public health which focuses on the 'health of entire populations rather than individual patients' (p. 24). Rothstein identifies problems with this too. It would include 'the efforts of nonprofit organizations, commercial entities, and private citizens to promote healthy lifestyles' (p. 24), such as a cigarette company's programme to discourage smoking by children. Also, it fails to demarcate individual and public health. And it does not justify governmental coercive measures. The

---

[28] In particular Amnesty International (see Amnesty International, 2004).

conception of public health Rothstein advocates, 'government intervention as public health', involves 'public officials taking appropriate measures pursuant to specific legal authority, after balancing private rights and public interests, to protect the health of the public' (p. 25). But when? For Rothstein certain conditions must be met: the health of the population must be threatened (for example an infectious disease is rampant); the government must have 'unique powers and expertise' (p. 25) (this is exemplified by disease reporting and surveillance); and, third, such intervention should be more likely to produce an effective intervention (he cites newborn screening programmes).

In Chapter 3 Anita Goraya and Graham Scambler offer historical insights into the developments of public health (see also Part III of this collection). They distinguish the 'new' public health from the 'old'. The 'old' public health went through three stages, they point out. First, there was the 'sanitary' phase, developed in response to the industrial revolution. They cite the work of Chadwick, already discussed in this introduction (see p. xxviii). During this phase 'the role of the Victorian public health physician was broad but compatible with the functions of the state' (p. 30). The second phase began in the 1870s. It emphasized preventive services such as immunization and family planning, and the innovative provision of maternity services, health visitors and so on. The discovery of antibiotics and insulin led to the third phase, dating from the 1930s. Goraya and Scambler designate this the 'therapeutic' phase of public health. What is new about the 'new' public health is 'the rediscovery that influences on health are multifaceted and include economic, environmental, ecological, political and behavioural components, as well as the provision of, and equitable access to, medical services' (p. 32). They examine this 'new' public health through the prism of the public health physician and his/her roles as health strategist, health promoter, health expert, health advisor and health bureaucrat. The physician works, however, within a system where the commitment is to the health of individuals rather than populations, and where there is 'a lack of receptiveness to the now compelling evidence that the health of populations and unequal distribution of disease reflect broader political and structural features of British society' (p. 37). The authors raise the question as to where change can come from.

In Chapter 4 E. Ziglio, S. Hagard and J. Griffiths offer a developmental approach to European innovations in health promotion and situate these within the context of the changes which have been transforming European society. As they emphasize, 'political, economic, social, cultural, behavioural and biological factors are interwoven' (p. 47). They all have a part to play in determining and sustaining the health of a population. Although their essay focuses on Europe, their thesis applies to the developing world as well.

And Bioethics

Part II situates public health questions within bioethics. Bioethics paid little or no attention to public health issues until relatively recently. It was the appearance of AIDS in the 1980s which led those who had concentrated on doctor–patient issues to examine also population-wide concerns of public health (Smith *et al.*, 2004).

James Childress and his colleagues argue in Chapter 5 that the 'terrain' of public health ethics 'includes a loose set of general moral considerations – clusters of moral concepts and norms that are variously called values, principles, or rules – that are arguably relevant to public health' (p. 56). They illustrate this by reference to a screening programme. Is it likely to be 'effective'? Will its benefits outweigh the infringed general moral considerations (the question of proportionality)? Is the policy essential to achieve the goal (necessity)? Does it involve the least infringement possible consistent with realizing that goal (least infringement)? Can it be publicly justified? The authors address also the relationship between public health and human rights. They agree with Jonathan Mann that ultimately 'ethics and human rights derive from a set of quite similar, if not identical, core values' (p. 62, quoting Mann, Chapter 25, this volume, p. 379).

In Chapter 6 Daniel Callahan and Bruce Jennings examine the moral problems raised by public health that extend beyond the earlier boundaries of bioethics and require, they argue, their own form of ethical analysis. For example, 'Because of its public and governmental roles, public health has ethical problems unlike those of most other professions' (p. 69). There is a tension between individual health and rights and government obligations and population health. Also, 'the economic and social impact on communities of public health measures' (p. 69), which requires cost–benefit analysis, is another example where conflict may arise.

Dan W. Brock, in Chapter 7, also argues for a broadening of the bioethics agenda. He argues that when bioethics has addressed justice or equity it has been in relation to access to health care (how scarce resources should be allocated, for example),[29] and on justifying a moral right to health care, rather than concentrating on health itself. This, he maintains, has left bioethicists 'largely silent' on the issues raised when limited health care resources must be 'prioritized' by either public, government health care programmes or private health insurers or providers. And, 'the focus on health care rather than health fosters the assumption that differential access to health care is the principal inequity … and the principal cause of inequalities in health … But in fact differences in access to health care account for only a very small proportion of the differences in health between different groups in society' (p. 74). Other more significant social determinants of health should concern us as much.

In Chapter 8 Leslie Francis, Margaret Battin, Jay Jacobson, Charles Smith and Jeffrey Botkin tell us why, they believe, infectious diseases got left out of bioethical discourse, and what this omission might have meant for bioethics. Infectious diseases stand out because 'a patient may be both victim and vector' (p. 95). They thus remind us of our 'vulnerability to assaults from outside' (other humans or a mosquito, for example), but also place us in 'the position of putting others at risk' (p. 95). For this reason, the authors argue, the application of standard approaches (emphasizing autonomy and the harm principle)[30] is inappropriate. The traditional understanding of autonomous agency 'ignores our embodiment and relationality' (p. 105). They go on to show what this means for informed consent and distributive justice in health care. Thus, they ask, 'Is it a violation of agency, if the patient who has him/herself been a victim is required to consider how s/he might victimize others? Or if the ability of patients to enter clinical studies depends on both their own choices and the involvement of others to whom they might pose risks?'(p. 105) Questions of distributive justice also look different when 'providing a decent minimum of care world-wide may be critical to reducing everyone's vulnerability to disease' (p. 105).

---

29 But see, Daniels (1985), who as Brock acknowledges, did frame a right to health care within a theory of justice. See also now Daniels (2008).

30 As in J.S. Mill's *On Liberty* (first published in 1859).

Nancy E. Kass, in Chapter 9 (see also Kass, 2001), emphasizes how public health ethics has begun to be part of academic and professional discourse. She traces the stages though which this has gone, and looks to a future in which questions of global concern will become central. It is, she notes, in the context of global public health where the most significant, most preventable and most tragic of public health problems exist. This theme re-emerges in Volume II, in Chapter 19 in particular, and elsewhere in these volumes.

In Chapter 10 Michael Selgelid bemoans the lack of attention given to infectious diseases by bioethicists. He points to the importance of such diseases, and to the difficult ethical questions they pose. He cites surveillance, mandatory testing, mandatory vaccination or treatment, notification of authorities or third parties, isolation, quarantine and travel restrictions. Many of these issues are discussed in more detail elsewhere in this volume. He gives a third reason why we should be focusing upon infectious diseases: justice. As he observes, pathogens prey upon the poor: most deaths from infectious diseases occur in developing countries. What we designate 'tropical' diseases are not peculiar to tropical countries, but rather to poor developing ones. This essay also explores reasons for the neglect. Selgelid identifies a high-tech, wealthy-world slant to discussion in bioethics; the fact that bioethics emerged at a time of tremendous optimism in medicine; the fact that the diseases in question (particularly AIDS) affect 'the other' (or are thought to do so); to complexity; ironically, to a misperception that the questions raised are too easy; and to religious hijacking, bioethicists being pre-occupied by discussion of religious objections to such issues as abortion and cloning.

The Historical Debate

It was Hegel who observed that people and governments have never learnt anything from history. Those concerned with the pandemics of today can certainly learn from historical experience, the flu epidemic of 1918 now being a well-documented example (see Markel, 1997; Kolata, 2000; Barry, 2004).

This section offers two rather different historical essays. The first is by Simon Szreter (Chapter 11; see also Szreter, 2002, 2003). It engages with the debate engendered by the revisionist work of Thomas McKeown (1976). McKeown's thesis – fast becoming the new orthodoxy – hypothesized that the medical establishment (including the public health movement) played only a minor role in the decline in national mortality levels in the second half of the nineteenth century. McKeown argued that this decline was primarily explained by the 'invisible hand' of rising living standards, in particular the consumption of better food. Szreter shows the decline to be attributable rather to the leading role played by the public health movement in meeting the challenge of urban congestion created by industrialization. A lesson is that 'a significant life-saving "expansion in the health infrastructure" of a country does not *necessarily* require advanced "medical technology" nor necessarily require, at least initially, the political act of "creating a universal free health service"' (p. 175).

In Chapter 12 David Armstrong charts the rise of 'surveillance medicine'. This requires 'the dissolution of the distinct clinical categories of healthy and ill as it attempts to bring everyone within its network of visibility' (p. 179). Thus, for example, questions were asked about children, and categories of child ill-health emerged which had passed 'unnoticed' previously, including 'the nervous child, the neurotic child, the over-sensitive child'. Even normal childhood could be seen as 'potentially hazardous'. Medical surveillance left the hospital, and 'penetrated' the wider population (p. 180).

Each of these essays offers lessons for the future.

Research Issues

Part IV of this collection turns its attention to research issues (see also Farmer and Gastineau Campos, 2004, reproduced as Chapter 31 in Volume II). Ethical principles to protect human subjects in clinical research emerged after Nuremberg and are, of course, well established. Larry Gostin (Chapter 13) sets these out at the beginning of his essay. But what of population-based research? This is defined by Gostin to include 'all research and practice performed on, or which affects, groups of people or populations'. It includes 'epidemiologic research and surveillance, and intervention epidemiology, including field trials for drugs or vaccines' (p. 192). Gostin articulates five foundational principles to protect the dignity and integrity of all populations. These are (i) 'first do no harm' – that is protect the health and well-being of populations; (ii) respect for populations, in particular their right to self-determination; (iii) protection of vulnerable populations – the non-dominant, subservient, minority races, but also prostitutes, drug users, the gay population; (iv) protection of the privacy, integrity and self-esteem of populations; and (v) the equitable distribution of benefits and burdens to populations.

In Chapter 14 A.M. Capron is also concerned with the protection of research subjects, in particular with situations in which 'the consequence of an epidemiological study might be characterized as a wrong even though subjects' interests (material as well as physical) have not been harmed' (p. 205). Treating people solely as means to an end, an end not chosen by them, 'wrongs' them though it may not 'harm' them. Capron emphasizes the importance of informed consent which has, he argues, four functions: (i) it reminds us of the 'Kantian imperative' just referred to; (ii) it encourages better research (it may have a beneficial 'reflexive effect' (p. 206) on the research experiment itself); (iii) it allows 'the relationship of subjects and investigators to be brought within the norms of more typical social interactions' (p. 206); and (iv) it protects privacy.

Of vulnerable populations, children have always constituted one of the most obvious, despite having adults, including parents, to protect them. In Chapter 15, written in 1991, Carol Levine comments upon their vulnerability 'after all these years'. She explains why the problem is still with us.

Charles Weijer's essay (Chapter 16) focuses on the effects of research on particular communities. In addition to the usual ethical principles should we also recognize 'respect for cultures' (p. 225; first called for by Levine, 1982)? Weijer thinks so, and gives three arguments to support this: (i) community interests are separable from individual interests (he illustrates this by reference to studies on cancer genetics in Ashkenazi Jews); (ii) ethical principles also acknowledge 'the moral status of players' (p. 226); and (iii) this can be justified in the same way as other ethical principles have been. Weijer goes on to consider how this new principle can be implemented. He points to examples in Australia, Canada and the USA where research is conducted with first nation communities. Of course, respect for communities is not confined to first nations or Ashkenazi Jews. As Weijer rightly notes, it can include, for example, people with HIV/AIDS.

The final essay in this section is by Geoffrey Rose (Chapter 17). It offers an obvious, if neglected, insight. 'Case-centred epidemiology identifies individual susceptibility, but it may fail to identify the underlying causes of incidence' (p. 240). And he concludes that 'the priority of concern should always be the discovery and control of the causes of incidence' (p. 240). This important lesson may have been lost on many who have questioned research into (for example) infectious diseases.

Public Health and Autonomy

The significance of autonomy and its limits when public health is an issue has been referred to already in a number of the essays (particularly Chapter 7). The problem is stated tersely by Spencer Hall in Chapter 18. In Chapter 19 Marcel Verweij poses the question somewhat differently: if we have a duty not to infect others,[31] how far does this extend? He explores the foundation and scope of duties not to infect others. Do they go too far? Is there, in other words, an 'over-demandingness' problem? He argues that utilitarianism can largely avoid the over-demandingness critique, and that contractualist moral theory (as in Scanlon, 1998), while offering a more plausible ground for our obligations to avoid infection, yields moral requirements that are very demanding.

Questions of Governance

Modes of governance structure health in the world. Susan K. Sell notes, in an essay not included in this collection, that

> global governance means devising, implementing, and enforcing policies in a way that accommodates a broad range of stakeholders and publics. Challenges to effective global governance of public health issues include trade pressures, multi-layered governance (i.e., local, national, bilateral, regional, international), the complexity of health policy jurisdiction across multilateral organizations, the simultaneous development of hard and soft law in diverse venues with conflicting mandates, and values, economic coercion, and unequal access to resources and institutions. Among the central features of the quest for global governance in … public health are the blurring lines between public and private, the increasing role of the private sector in public policymaking, growing global inequality, constricted autonomy for the weak, and the inappropriateness of 'one-size-fits-all' policies for diverse contexts. (2004, pp. 363–64)

Scott Burris, in Chapter 20, emphasizes that governance is 'an overarching issue of concern to health from an ecological point of view' (p. 266). He offers a theory of 'nodal governance' to describe the management of events in social systems. Nodal governance 'focuses attention on how governance happens – how power is wielded – at specific points within a system, and thus raises essential normative questions about democratic decision-making' (p. 267). As Drahos explains, 'the idea of nodal coordination derives from recent theoretical approaches that make

---

[31] On which see Harris and Holm (1995).

networks and nodes the principal categories in theorizing about changes in governance' (2004, p. 404). As Burris notes, far from the state being the only force engaged in the government of conduct, it is clear that non-state actors have taken on the role of governing 'not just other private entities but the state itself' (p. 269). Burris uses the example of the 'weak' WHO which, during the SARS crisis, was able to exercise control over states merely by the use of press releases (travel warnings, for example). See also his account of the TRIPS agreement as the product of the regulation of states by corporate nodes (p. 275). It may have been engineered by democratically elected governments but

> If in fact Pfizer and a few other companies are to a considerable extent dictating the global availability of essential medicine, the description invites consideration of basic ideas such as the view that human rights obligations are directly binding only on states, or that the state is primarily responsible for ensuring the provision of a basic public good like disease control. (p. 276, citing Fidler, 2004, p. 249)

In Chapter 21 Kelley Lee and Richard Dodgson analyse cholera from the nineteenth century onwards as a case study of the links between globalization and health. They marry international relations and health fields because knowledge of the globalization process can be used to understand the nature of health issues better and because knowledge of health and disease can be used to understand better the nature of globalization. Cholera, they demonstrate, is 'a reflection of the ills of globalization itself' (p. 294). They show that the first six pandemics of cholera can be understood as closely related to socio-economic and political structures. It travelled 'the same routes around the globe as European imperialism' (p. 301). It was in this sense 'an integral part of ... the globalization process' (p. 301). The seventh pandemic (which began in 1961) is, the authors argue, a reflection of 'the contradictions of globalization in the late twentieth century' (p. 307). But, as with previous pandemics, the link between cholera and deprivation is close. And, they note, we need to understand globalization to explain the epidemiological profile of this pandemic: 'Through changes in human interaction spatially, temporally, and cognitively, cholera has become more geographically widespread and persistent over time. That the disease can "jump" across continents within hours, for example, poses new challenges for national health systems' (p. 307).

In Chapter 22 Dyna Arhin-Tenkorang and Pedro Conceição summarize international efforts to fight communicable diseases up to the middle of the twentieth century. They then describe the results of international cooperation on public health since the 1950s. Why have some communicable diseases been 'tamed' while others remain a problem? Their answer is that problems persist when the 'publicness' of the responses is limited. By 'publicness' they understand three inputs crucial for controlling disease: available and accessible medical knowledge, a national public health infrastructure and private household spending on complementary goods and services. They discuss in detail the first two of these inputs. They go on to explore the steps now needed to strengthen the publicness of efforts. These include tapping new sources of funding and increasing incentives for global health research. The authors conclude by proposing the deployment of rapid response task forces – for example the dispatching of international health teams to help countries control spreading diseases as quickly as possible. This, of course, opens up the debate about the limits of humanitarian intervention, recently in focus in Myanmar in 2008.

Kelley Lee and Anne Mills's brief essay (Chapter 23) puts the case tersely for strengthening governance in order to develop global health research. They argue that the countries which most need health research should decide what should be funded. Currently, diseases that affect large populations in developing countries are given comparatively little attention. This inequity, it is now generally accepted, needs to be redressed.

Public Health and Human Rights

It is significant that health long assumed a low profile in the thrust to recognize human rights. Thus, for example, the European Convention on Human Rights makes no reference to health as such. And so in 1998 the European Commission was able to hold that there was no breach of Article 2[32] when the Italian health service refused to pay for drugs which, it was argued, would improve the patient's condition.[33] The Commission did, however, recognize that there might be an obligation if the drugs were essential to save life. The Universal Declaration of Human Rights provides that everyone has the right to a standard of living adequate for the health and well-being of himself and his family including food, clothing and medical care (Article 25.1). Of course, what is meant by medical care is not defined, and the need for it varies widely.[34] WHO defines health as 'a state of complete physical, mental and social well-being, and not just the absence of disease or infirmity'.

It is as a result of the HIV/AIDS pandemic, as well as issues relating to women's health (reproductive rights, in particular) (see Cook, Dickens and Fathalla, 2003; Fisher and Syed, 2007) and the egregious violations of human rights in Rwanda, the former Yugoslavia and elsewhere that health has become a human rights issue (Gruskin, Grodin, Annas and Marks, 2005; Tolchin, 2008). Cloning, genetic manipulation and enhancement (Mehlman, 2003) offer further reasons why health is becoming seen inevitably as a human rights issue.

This collection offers three essays on public health and human rights. The first is by Sofia Gruskin (Chapter 24). She explores the ways in which human rights have come to be of relevance to global public health in the last two decades. She then reviews the ways in which the formal structures and systems of human rights and of global health have been set up. She goes on to survey the different approaches bringing human rights and health together. She concludes with a discussion of current challenges, in particular those concerning the accountability of non-state actors. These will become increasingly important, though the state must remain ultimately responsible for the promotion of public health (and human rights).

Jonathan Mann, in Chapter 25, makes the point that while 'medicine has chosen the language of ethics', human rights is 'a far more useful framework, vocabulary, and form of guidance for public health efforts to analyze and respond directly to the societal determinants of health' (p. 378). In his view the linkage between public health and human rights may be explored by considering three relationships: (i) the burden on human rights created by public health policies and practices; (ii) the understanding that human rights violations have deleterious health impacts (torture, for example); and (iii) the inextricable link between promoting and protecting human rights and protecting health. He notes that human rights should be respected 'not only for their instrumental value in contributing to public health goals, but for themselves, as societal goods of pre-eminent importance' (p. 379).

---

32 The 'right to life' provision.

33 *Scialacqua* v. *Italy* (1998) 26 EHRR CD 164. See also O'Sullivan (1998).

34 On the limits of medicine, see Stark (2006).

Chapter 26, by Solomon Benatar, is a terse analysis (as at 1998) of global inequalities in health and human rights. Benatar emphasizes exploitative global economic activities, in particular the irresponsible business practices of multinational corporations, as a cause of the widening gap between the 'haves' and the 'have-nots'. It is easy to assume inequalities can be explained by poverty but education, particularly of women, may be an important predictor of having a better mortality record than that predicted by gross national product (see Marmot, 2004, p. 46).

Surveillance and Privacy

There is just one essay in this collection on surveillance and privacy (though the issue emerges in many other essays). In Chapter 27 Ronald Bayer and Amy Fairchild focus on the US Center for Disease Control's determination in 1999 to require HIV case reporting. A debate had raged for years with angry exchanges between advocates of comprehensive public health surveillance and gay organizations and civil libertarians. As Bayer and Fairchild state 'medical privacy is not an absolute' (p. 392).[35] They locate case reporting in historical and contemporary contexts (discussing cases such as polio and cancer), and contrast US practices with European ones, where in the main (certainly in Western Europe)[36] notification is by code or without unique identifiers. The central ethical question posed by HIV name reporting is 'when do the claims of public health legitimately trump the claims of privacy and confidentiality …? A subsidiary question is: Do the claims of privacy carry sufficient weight to make reporting systems that are less accurate, but that are nevertheless adequate more compatible with ethical standards?'(p. 403). Of course, surveillance carries the risk that information may be 'inadvertently disclosed' (p. 404), however careful agencies are to keep it confidential.

Prevention and its Limits

Prevention is obviously preferable to cure. And most infectious diseases – there are exceptions like Ebola and SARS – are preventable. Of course, some individuals and some communities may not wish to take advantage of preventive measures. Their religious convictions may cause them to object to immunization. They may put these convictions above the risk of infection. Others may doubt – for genuine or maverick reasons – the actual effectiveness of immunizations. In developing countries, there is competition for resources, and education or industrial development or military defence may win over improvements in sanitation, the provision of clean water or the relief of poverty, measures which would all assist in the war against disease.

The precautionary principle is well established as a guide in all areas of public policy. It is, for example, a 'fixture in international environmental lawmaking' (Applegate, 2000, p. 413; see also Sands, 2000 and Applegate, 2002). Bernard Goldstein, in Chapter 30, maintains it is

---

[35] For discussions in case law, see *Tarasoff* v. *Regents of the University of California* 551 P. 2d 334 (1976) and W v. Edgell [1990] 1 All E.R. 835.

[36] Cf. the former Communist states where names are recorded.

applicable also to public health actions. For Elihu Richter and Richard Laster (Chapter 29) the major components of the precautionary principle are

> defining the risk to be prevented, shifting of the burden of proof from demonstration of risk to demonstration of absence of risk, reducing risk through substitute technologies or removal or modifying a hazardous technology exposure at the source, and promoting modal shifts and substitution, and using interventions proportionate in cost to the costs of the prevented hazards and risks. There is also emphasis on rigorous evaluation of the efficacy of interventions, in terms of benefits versus the risks, or the risks of doing something as opposed to waiting and doing nothing. (pp. 424–25)

But they contrast epidemiology and public health with mathematics: 'No human lives were lost because mathematicians required 300 years to solve Fermat's Theorem' (p. 425). Delays in recognizing risks from past exposures and acting on the findings – cigarette smoking and lung cancer is the best documented example – meant that millions of lives were lost which could have been saved.

In Chapter 28 Marcel Verweij justifies the practice of influenza vaccination in nursing homes for elderly residents who are not capable of giving their consent by reference to a common interest they all have that there not be an influenza outbreak. Such an outbreak would not only affect the health of residents but would be detrimental to their everyday social life as well, and the care that each receives.

Confinement and Liberty

The Cuban experiment with quarantining individuals infected with HIV not surprisingly attracted interest. This collection contains two essays on the subject. In Chapter 31 by David Johnston the question is raised as to whether the quarantine programme violates international human rights law. Johnston concludes that it does not. As Larry Gostin points out in Chapter 33, 'courts have been highly deferential to public health measures, including isolation and quarantine' (p. 485).

In Chapter 32 Ronald Bayer and Cheryl Healton address the logic of quarantine (in the Cuban context). They point out that it is viewed as 'an extension of the postrevolutionary health care system' (p. 465). In Cuba (as described in their essay) education was not the dominant element in the anti-AIDS stategy. It would seem that no coercion was necessary to effect a screening programme since 'all Cubans come into contact with the medical system in the workplace, at school or during treatment for disease' (pp. 465–66). And informed consent was deemed unnecessary. Of course, some false positives are generated and the consequence – quarantine – is grave. The quarantine regime is described in this essay. There is some difference of opinion as to how those who refused to enter sanatoria or escaped from them were dealt with: there is more than a suspicion that they were treated harshly.

In Chapter 33 Larry Gostin examines the issue more generally: should a person who risks AIDS transmission be subject to coercive state action? He concludes that the use of coercive powers would be counterproductive. He cites historical evidence to demonstrate that coercive powers have been almost exclusively used against 'unpopular targets such as prostitutes' (p. 509) and that compulsory powers have not altered the course of disease epidemics.

Although the three essays in Part X are specifically about HIV/AIDS, they are applicable to other public health concerns too (see further Musto, 1988; Bayer 1991, pp. 169–206).

References

Amnesty International (2004), *Albania: Disability and The Right To Marry*, London: Amnesty International.

Anand, S., Peter, F. and Sen, A. (2004), *Public Health, Ethics and Equity*, New York: Oxford University Press.

Applegate, J.S. (2000), 'The Precautionary Preference: An American Perspective on the Precautionary Principle', *Human and Ecological Risk Assessment*, **6**, pp. 413–43.

Appelgate, J.S. (2002), 'The Taming of the Precautionary Principle', *William and Mary Environmental Law and Policy Review*, **27**, pp. 13–78.

Arnold, D. (1993), 'Medicine and Colonialism', in W.F. Bynum and R. Porter (eds), *Companion Encyclopaedia of the History of Medicine*, London: Routledge, pp. 1385–405.

Baggott, R. (1998), *Public Health – Policy and Politics*, New York, St. Martin's Press.

Baggott, R. (2000), *Public Health – Policy and Politics*, Basingstoke: Macmillan.

Barnes, D.S. (1995), *The Making of a Social Disease: Tuberculosis in Nineteenth Century France*, Berkeley: University of California Press.

Barry, J.M. (2004), *The Great Influenza: The Epic Story of the Deadliest Plague in History*, New York: Viking.

Bayer, R. (1989), *Private Acts, Social Consequences: AIDS and the Politics of Public Health*, New York: Free Press.

Bayer, R. (1991), *Private Acts, Social Consequences: AIDS and the Politics of Public Health*, New Brunswick, NJ: Rutgers University Press (paperback edn).

Benedictow, O.J. (2004), *The Black Death 1346–1353*, Woodbridge: Boydell Press.

Berridge, V. (1996), *AIDS in the UK: The Making of Policy 1981–1994*, Oxford: Oxford University Press.

Brewer, M. (1988), 'The "Black Death" and Anti-Semitism', in S. Almog (ed.), *Anti-Semitism through the Ages*, Oxford: Pergamon.

Cantor, N. (2001), *In the Wake of the Plague*, New York: Simon and Schuster.

Chadwick, E. (1842), *Report on the Sanitary Condition of the Labouring Population of Great Britain*, London: Poor Law Commission.

Childress, J.F. (1991), 'Mandatory HIV Screening and Testing', in F.G. Reamer, *AIDS and Ethics*, New York: Columbia University Press, pp. 50–76.

Closen, M., Gamrath, R. and Hopkins, D. (1994), 'Mandatory Premarital HIV Testing: Political Exploitation of the AIDS Epidemic', *Tulane Law Review*, **69**, pp. 71–115.

Cook, R.J., Dickens, B.M. and Fathalla, M.F. (2003), *Reproductive Health and Human Rights*, Oxford: Clarendon Press.

Daniels, N. (1985), *Just Health Care*, Cambridge: Cambridge University Press.

Daniels, N. (2008), *Just Health – Meeting Needs Fairly*, New York: Cambridge University Press.

De Cock, K.M. *et al.* (2006), 'Unfinished Business – Expanding HIV Testing in Developing Countries', *New England Journal of Medicine*, **354**, pp. 440–42.

Drahos, P. (2004), 'Intellectual Property and Pharmaceutical Markets: A Nodal Governance Approach', *Temple Law Review*, **77**, pp. 401–24.

Durham, M. (1991), *Sex and Politics: The Family and Morality in the Thatcher Years*, Basingstoke: Macmillan.

Farmer, P. (1999), *Infections and Inequalities: The Modern Plagues*, Berkeley: University of California Press.

Farmer, P. (2003), *Pathologies of Power: Health, Human Rights and the New War on the Poor*, Berkeley: University of California Press.

Farmer, P. and Gastineau Campos, N. (2004), 'Rethinking Medical Ethics: A View from Below', *Developing World Bioethics*, **4**, pp. 17–41.

Fidler, D. (2004), 'Constitutional Outlines of Public Health's "New World Order"', *Temple Law Review*, **77**, pp. 247–89.

Fisher, R.B. (1991), *Edward Jenner 1749–1823*, London: André Deutsch.

Fisher, W.W. and Syed, T. (2007), 'Global Justice in Healthcare', *U.C. Davis Law Review*, **40**, pp. 581–678.

Frazer, W.M. (1950), *A History of English Public Health 1834–1939*, London: Ballière, Tindall & Cox.

Garfield, S. (1994), *The End of Innocence: Britain in the Time of AIDS*, London: Faber.

Garrett, L. (1994), *The Coming Plague*, Harmondsworth: Penguin.

Gould, S.J. (1984), *The Mismeasure of Man*, Harmondsworth: Penguin.

Grmek, M.D. (1990), *History of AIDS: Emergence and Origin of a Modern Pandemic*, Princeton: Princeton University Press.

Gruskin, S., Grodin, M.A., Annas, G.J. and Marks, S.P. (2005), *Perspectives on Health and Human Rights*, New York: Routledge.

Harris, J. and Holm, S. (1995), 'Is there a Duty not to Infect Others?', *British Medical Journal*, **311**, pp. 1215–17.

Hunter, S. (2003), *Black Death: AIDS in Africa*, New York: Palgrave Macmillan.

Inglis, B. (1965), *A History of Medicine*, London: Weidenfeld and Nicolson.

Kalichman, S.C. and Rompa, D. (2003), 'HIV Treatment Adherence and Unprotected Sex Practices among People Receiving Antiretroviral Therapy', *Sexually Transmitted Infections*, **79**, pp. 59–61.

Kass, Nancy E. (2001), 'An Ethics Framework for Public Health', *American Journal of Public Health*, **91**, pp. 1776–82.

Kelly, J. (2006), *The Great Mortality: An Intimate History of The Black Death*, London: Harper Perennial.

Kevles, D. (1995), *In The Name of Eugenics*, Cambridge, MA: Harvard University Press.

Kolata, G. (2000), *Flu: The Story of the Great Influenza Pandemic of 1918 and the Search for the Virus that Caused It*, Basingstoke: Macmillan.

Langford, P. (1989), *A Polite and Commercial People*, Oxford: Oxford University Press.

Leavitt, J.W. (1996), *Typhoid Mary: Captive to the Public's Health*, Boston: Beacon Press.

Levine R.J. (1982), 'Validity of Consent Procedures in Technologically Developing Countries', in Z. Bankowski and N. Howard-Jones (eds), *Human Experimentation and Medical Ethics: Proceedings of the XV CIOMS Round Table Conference*, Geneva: Council for International Organizations of Medical Sciences, pp. 16–30.

Longmate, N. (1966), *King Cholera: The Biography of a Disease*, London: Hamish Hamilton.

McKeown, T. (1976), *The Modern Rise of Population*, New York: Harcourt, Brace Jovanovich.

McNeill, W.H. (1976), *Plagues and Peoples*, Oxford: Anchor Press.

Mann, J.M. (1997), 'Medicine and Public Health, Ethics and Human Rights', *Hastings Center Report*, **27** (3), pp. 6–13.

Markel, H. (1997), *Quarantine! Eastern European Jewish Immigrants and the New York City Epidemics of 1892*, Baltimore: Johns Hopkins University Press.

Marmot, M. (2004), 'Social Causes of Social Inequalities in Health', in S. Anand, F. Peter and A. Sen. (eds), *Public Health, Ethics and Equity*, New York: Oxford University Press, pp. 37–62.

Mehlman, M.J. (2003), *Wondergenes: Genetic Enhancement and the Future of Society*, Bloomington: Indiana University Press.

Mohr, R. (1987), 'AIDS, Gays and State Coercion', *Bioethics*, **1**, pp. 35–50.
Mort, F. (1987), *Dangerous Sexualities: Medico-Moral Politics in England since 1830*, London: Routledge, Kegan Paul.
Musto, D.F. (1988), 'Quarantine and the Problem of AIDS', in E. Fee and D.M. Fox (eds), *AIDS: The Burdens of History*, Berkeley: University of California Press, pp. 67–85.
O'Brien, M. (1989), 'Mandatory HIV Antibody Testing Policies: An Ethical Analysis', *Bioethics*, **3**, pp. 273–300.
O'Neill, O. (2002), *Autonomy and Trust in Bioethics*, Cambridge: Cambridge University Press.
Pelling, M. (1978), *Cholera, Fever and English Medicine 1825–1865*, Oxford: Oxford University Press.
O'Sullivan, D. (1998), 'The Allocation of Scarce Resources and the Right to Life under the European Convention on Human Rights', *Public Law*, pp. 389–95.
Phillips, E.D. (1973), *Greek Medicine*, London: Thames and Hudson.
Pisani, E. (2008), *The Wisdom of Whores: Bureaucrats, Brothels and the Business of AIDS*, London: Granta.
Poliakov, L. (1974), *A History of Anti-Semitism* (5 vols), New York: Schoken.
Porter, R. (1995), *Disease, Medicine and Society in England 1550–1880*, Cambridge: Cambridge University Press.
Porter, R. (1997), *The Greatest Benefit To Mankind*, London: Harper Collins.
Rennie, S. and Mupenda, B. (2008), 'Ethics of Mandatory HIV Testing in Africa: The Case of Goma, Democratic Republic of Congo', *Developing World Bioethics*, **8**, pp. 126–37.
Rosen, G. (1993), *A History of Public Health*, Baltimore: Johns Hopkins University Press.
Sands, P. (2000), 'The Precautionary Principle: A European Perspective', *Human and Ecological Risk Assessment*, **6**, pp. 445–58.
Scanlon, T.M. (1998) *What We Owe to Each Other*, Cambridge, MA: Harvard University Press.
Schüklenk, U. (2001), *AIDS: Society, Ethics and Law*, Aldershot: Ashgate.
Selgelid, M.J., Battin, M.P. and Smith, C.B. (2006), *Ethics and Infectious Diseases*, Malden, MA: Blackwell.
Sell, S.K. (2004), 'The Quest for Global Governance in Intellectual Property and Public Health: Structural, Discursive and Institutional Dimensions', *Temple Law Review*, **77**, pp. 363–99.
Smith, C.B. *et al.* (2004), 'Are there Characteristics of Infectious Diseases that Raise Special Ethical Issues?, *Developing World Bioethics*, **4**, pp. 1–16.
Smith, F.B. (1979), *The People's Health 1830–1910*, London: Croom Helm.
Smith, F.B. (1988), *The Retreat of Tuberculosis 1850–1950*, London: Croom Helm.
Stark, A. (2006), *The Limits of Medicine*, New York: Cambridge University Press.
Szreter, S. (2002), 'Health, Class, Place and Politics: Social Capital and Collective Provision in Britain', *Contemporary British History*, **16**, 27–57.
Szreter, S. (2003), *Health and Human Security*, Cambridge, MA: Harvard University Press.
Todres, J. (2007), 'Rights, Relationships and the Experience of Children Orphaned by AIDS', *UC Davis Law Review*, **41**, pp. 417–76.
Tolchin, B. (2008), 'Human Rights and the Requirement for International Medical Aid', *Developing World Bioethics*, **8**, pp. 151–58.
Trombley, S. (1988), *The Right To Reproduce*, London: Weidenfeld and Nicolson.
Turnock, B.J. and Kelly, C.J. (1989), 'Mandatory Premarital Testing for Human Immunodeficiency Virus: The Illinois Experience', *Journal of the American Medical Association*, **261**, pp. 3415–18.
UNAIDS (2007), *AIDS Epidemic Update 2007*, Geneva, UNAIDS.
Wain, H. (1970), *A History of Preventive Medicine*, Springfield, IL: Charles C. Thomas.
Watts, S. (1997), *Epidemics and History: Disease, Power and Imperialism*, New Haven: Yale University Press.

Winslow, C.E.A. (1920), 'The Untilled Fields of Public Health', *Science*, **51**, pp. 23–33.
Wohl A.S. (1984), *Endangered Lives: Public Health in Victorian Britain*, London: Unwin Methuen.
Ziegler, P. (1969), *The Black Death*, New York: Harper Torchbooks.

Part I
An Introduction

[1]

THE GENESIS OF PUBLIC HEALTH ETHICS

RONALD BAYER AND AMY L. FAIRCHILD

ABSTRACT

As bioethics emerged in the 1960s and 1970s and began to have enormous impacts on the practice of medicine and research – fuelled, by broad socio-political changes that gave rise to the struggle of women, African Americans, gay men and lesbians, and the antiauthoritarian impulse that characterised the New Left in democratic capitalist societies – little attention was given to the question of the ethics of public health. This was all the more striking since the core values and practices of public health, often entailing the subordination of the individual for the common good, seemed opposed to the ideological impulses of bioethics.

Of what relevance is autonomy-focused bioethics for public health, with its mix of justifications including those that are either implicitly or explicitly paternalistic or that seek to impose strictures on individuals and communities in the name of collective welfare? To examine the deep divide between the central commitments of bioethics and the values that animate the practice of public health, we focus on a series of controversies implicating the concepts of privacy, liberty, and paternalism.

Recognising the role of moral values in decision-making was a signal contribution of bioethics in its formative period. Over the past three decades a broad array of perspectives emerged under the rubric of bioethics but individualism remains central. As we commence the process of shaping an ethics of public health, it is clear that bioethics is the wrong place to start when thinking about the balances required in defence of the public's health.

In the beginning there was bioethics. The 1960s and 1970s witnessed extraordinary challenges to the broadly understood authority of medicine. Perhaps most strikingly, the paternalistic authority of physicians was brought into question by a new medical ethics that gave pride of place to the concept of autonomy.[1] Paralleling the challenges to medical practice were those that involved the research enterprise. Against a backdrop of scandal and abuse, and haunted by the experience of the violations of human dignity that had occurred under the aegis of medical research in Nazi Germany, a new ethics of research took hold.[2] Informing that moral world-view was the basic belief that no individual should be required to participate in research endeavours – no matter how important for the public good – without his or her informed consent.[3] Thus, the ethics of clinical research and the ethics of medical practice were conjoined by a commitment to autonomy and individual rights.

Remarkably, as bioethics emerged and began to have enormous impacts on the practice of medicine and research – fuelled, to be sure, by broad socio-political changes that gave rise to the struggle of women, African Americans, gay men and lesbians, and the antiauthoritarian impulse that characterised the New Left in democratic capitalist societies – little attention was given to the question of the ethics of public health. This was all the more striking since the core values and practices of public health, often entailing the subordination of the individual for the common good, seemed to stand as a rebuke to the ideological impulses of bioethics.

Just how vast a gulf existed between the ethos of public health and the individualistic and antipaternalistic values of bioethics is given historical referent in the person of Herman Biggs. Biggs – a highly influential New York City health official who implemented a new set of public health interventions targeting the individual in the late nineteenth and early twentieth centuries – gave full expression to the moral foundations of public health: 'The government of the United States is democratic, but the sanitary measures adopted are sometimes autocratic, and the functions performed by sanitary authorities paternal in character. We are prepared, when necessary, to introduce and enforce, and the people are ready to accept, measures which might seem radical and arbitrary, if they were not plainly designed for the public good, and evidently beneficent in their effects.'[4] It was the spirit

[1] David J. Rothman. 1991. *Strangers at the Bedside: A History of How Law and Bioethics Transformed Medical Decision Making.* New York, NY. Basic Books.

[2] Ibid. pp. 96, 99, 185–197.

[3] Terrence H. Ackerman. 1996. Choosing Between Nuremberg and the National Commission: Balancing of Moral Principles in Clinical Research. In *The Ethics of Research Involving Human Subjects: Facing the 21st Century.* Harold Y. Vanderpool, ed. Baltimore, MD. Frederick Press: 83.

[4] Hermann M. Biggs. 1897. *Preventive Medicine in the City of New York.* New York, NY. Health Department: 28, note 2.

of Biggs that informed thinking during the Progressive Era – the formative period of American public health.

When, at the beginning of the twenty-first century, a systematic effort to articulate an ethics of public health began, the deep differences between bioethics and public health would draw immediate attention.[5] In 'An Ethics Framework for Public Health', Nancy Kass thus writes, 'codes of medical and research ethics generally give high priority to individual autonomy, a priority that cannot be assumed to be appropriate for public health practice.'[6] Similarly, Daniel Callahan and Bruce Jennings, in their effort to begin a broad engagement on the ethics of public health, argued, 'In early bioethics, the good of the individual, and particularly his or her autonomy, was the dominant theme, not population health.'[7] That formative perspective, which retained its grip, compelled Callahan and Jennings to acknowledge that their own effort had to confront an epistemological 'obstacle': 'the difference between the individualistic orientation of bioethics and the population and societal focus of public health.'[8] These challenges echoed the trenchant arguments made by Renee Fox decades earlier.[9]

Of what relevance is autonomy-focused bioethics for public health, with its mix of justifications including those that are either implicitly or explicitly paternalistic or that seek to impose strictures on individuals and communities in the name of collective welfare? To examine the deep divide between the central commitments of bioethics and the values that animate the practice of public health, we focus on a series of controversies implicating the concepts of privacy, liberty, and paternalism.

[5] James F. Childress, Ruth R. Faden, Ruth D. Gaare, Lawrence O. Gostin, Jeffrey Kahn, Nancy E. Kass, Anna C. Mastroianni, Jonathan D. Moreno & Phillip Nieburg. Public Health Ethics: Mapping the Terrain. *Journal of Law, Medicine, and Ethics* 2002; 30: 170–178. Public Health Leadership Society. 2002. *Principles of the Ethical Practice of Public Health.* Version 2.2. Public Health Leadership Society.

[6] Nancy E. Kass. An Ethics Framework for Public Health. *American Journal of Public Health* 2001; 91: 11.

[7] Daniel Callahan & Bruce Jennings. Ethics and Public Health: Forging a Strong Relationship. *American Journal of Public Health* 2002; 92: 169.

[8] Ibid. p. 170.

[9] Renee C. Fox. Advanced Medical Technology – Social and Ethical Implications. *Annual Review of Sociology* 1976; 2: 231–268. Renee C. Fox & Judith P. Swazey. 1988. Medical Morality is Not Bioethics: Medical Ethics in China and the United States. In *Essays in Medical Sociology.* Renee C. Fox, ed. New Brunswick, NJ. Transaction Books: 645–70. Rothman, *op. cit.* note 1, pp. 242–243.

FIRST ENCOUNTERS: EPIDEMIOLOGICAL RESEARCH AND THE LIMITS OF CONSENT

Epidemiology is the foundational science of public health. Regulations designed to protect the autonomy and privacy of research subjects would require modification in the face of public health-focused research, regardless of whether it was conducted by government agencies or academic entities. Beginning in the 1970s, a discussion began about whether the emerging rules and regulations for human subjects' research would apply to epidemiological studies. Was informed consent necessary when research involved the use of extant records? Would imposing consent requirements for the examination of data sets involving large numbers of people – many of whom would be difficult or impossible to locate – render epidemiological research virtually impossible?[10] 'The clash between the privacy rights of persons and the need for access to and disclosure of personal health-related information', noted one observer, 'is the most frequent ethical dilemma to confront epidemiologists.'[11] In 1981, the United States Department of Health and Human Services (DHHS) issued regulations for the protection of human subjects explicitly exempting epidemiological research involving already existing data from informed consent requirements provided the risk to subjects was minimal, the research did not record data in a way that was individually identifiable, and the research could not otherwise be conducted.[12] The concession represented a relaxation of the fundamental principle that individuals could not be conscripted into research without their consent, for it was clear

[10] L. Gordis, E. Gold & R. Seltzer. Privacy Protection in Epidemiologic and Medical Research: A Challenge and a Responsibility. *American Journal of Epidemiology* 1977; 105: 163–168. L. Gordis & E. Gold. Privacy, Confidentiality and the Use of Medical Records in Research. *Science* 1980; 207: 153–156. L. Gostin. Ethical Principles for the Conduct of Human Subject Research: Population-Based Research and Ethics. *Law, Medicine, and Health Care* 1991; 19: 191–201. A.M. Capron. Protection of Research Subjects: Do Special Rules Apply in Epidemiology. *Law, Medicine, and Health Care* 1991; 19: 184–190. C.I. Cann & K.J. Rothman. IRBs and Epidemiologic Research: How Inappropriate Restrictions Hamper Studies. *IRB: A Review of Human Subjects Research* 1984; July/August: 5–7. N. Hershey. IRB Jurisdiction and Limits on IRB Actions. *IRB: A Review of Human Subjects Research* 1985; March/April: 7–9. K.J. Rothman. The Rise and Fall of Epidemiology, 1950–2000 A.D. *NEJM* 1981; 304: 600–602.

[11] John Last. 1996. Professional Standards of Conduct for Epidemiologists. In *Ethics and Epidemiology*. Steven S. Coughlin & Tom L. Beauchamp, eds. New York, NY. Oxford University Press: 57.

[12] Code of Federal Regulations, Title 45, Public Welfare, Department of Health and Human Services, National Institutes of Health, Office for Protection from Research Risks, Part 46, Protection of Human Subjects (45 CFR 46).

that the benefits of records-based research were significant enough to trump the claims of the individual.

The tension between the claims of individual informed consent and the demands imposed by record-based epidemiological research was also confronted in other economically advanced democratic nations. How these tensions were resolved reflected the extent to which the rights of the individual were given priority, judgements about how significant a burden would be entailed by insisting upon consent, and the social value accorded to such retrospective record-based studies. The Australian National Health and Medical Research Council, for example, required ethical review of all epidemiological studies and the consent of subjects unless such a requirement would render it impossible to conduct the study. In 1991, the European Union likewise proposed that that all studies undergo ethical review.[13] However, the proposed directive gave such priority to privacy and consent that epidemiologists expressed alarm over the future of their efforts. In response to arguments that the directive would make epidemiological research unfeasible, a 1995 directive made provisions for research without consent in instances where confidentiality was adequately protected, obtaining consent was impracticable, and the research was of sufficient importance. France and Germany passed similar provisions a year before the European Union approved its final directive, though at the end of the 1990s, concerns remained, especially in Great Britain.[14]

The Council of International Organizations of Medical Sciences (CIOMS) also addressed the issues imposed by the use of existing clinical records as part of its broader analysis of the ethical issues posed by epidemiological studies. In its 1991 report, it acknowledged that prior efforts to provide ethical guidance for biomedical research focused on 'patients and individual subjects' were not sufficient for studies involving 'groups' of people. Thus, while emphasising the importance of the principles of research ethics first propounded in the Belmont Report, it recognised that their application in the epidemiological context would require flexibility. Most important, the CIOMS epidemiological guidelines, like those from nations that had addressed these issues before, noted that individual informed consent was not always practical in epidemiological studies, while asserting that individuals and their representatives should 'normally' be told that their

[13] Baruch A. Brody. 1998. *The Ethics of Biomedical Research: An International Perspective.* New York, NY. Oxford University Press: 57.

[14] Ibid. pp. 62–63.

medical records or stored tissue samples might be used for future epidemiological studies.[15] In the end it was the duty of researchers who sought to undertake such record-based studies 'to explain to an ethical review committee how the study would be ethical in [the absence of consent].'[16]

AIDS, PUBLIC HEALTH, AND ETHICS

The encounter over epidemiological research foreshadowed a more sustained and critical effort to enunciate an ethics of public health in the context of the AIDS epidemic, which began in the early 1980s. It is not surprising that when those schooled in bioethics first sought to address the ethical challenges posed by AIDS, they did so guided by the principles and values that had shaped the confrontation with medicine and the research enterprise.[17] Their efforts were informed by the intense concern of gay men about threats to privacy and civil liberties advocates fearful that AIDS would provide the occasion for the erosion of a set of substantive and procedural constitutional rights forged by the US Supreme Court. These concerns, in turn, were reflected in the posture adopted by public health officials in many cosmopolitan centres.[18]

Emerging from the complex mix of ideological, moral, and political forces was a commitment to treating AIDS differently from what the history of epidemic control might have suggested. In lieu of the compulsory tradition, that often involved mandatory case reporting by name, contact investigation, and where necessary the use of isolation, an 'exceptionalist' perspective took hold.[19] Focused on the centrality of education for mass behavioural change, the protection of the rights and privacy of people infected with HIV, and a rejection of coercive measures, the approach to AIDS was voluntarist at its core. A simple dictum emerged: no public health policy that violated the rights of individuals could be effective in controlling the spread of HIV. There was, therefore, no tension between public health and civil

[15] CIOMS. 1991. *International Guidelines for Ethical Review of Epidemiological Studies*. Guideline 3.

[16] Ibid. Guideline 2.

[17] R. Bayer, C. Levine & S. Wolf. HIV Antibody Screening: An Ethical Framework for Evaluating Proposed Programs. *Journal of the American Medical Association* 1986; 256: 1768–1774.

[18] R. Bayer. 1989. *Private Acts, Social Consequences: Aids and the Politics of Public Health*. New Brunswick, NJ. Rutgers University Press.

[19] R. Bayer. Public Health Policy and the AIDS Epidemic: an End to HIV Exceptionalism? *NEJM* 1991; 324: 1500–1504.

liberties. Indeed, the protection of civil liberties was critical to the public health.

This view informed decisions in virtually all advanced democratic nations and was reflected on an international level in the effort to forge a relationship between public health and human rights.[20] While recognising that, in principle, limits on rights could be justified by the claims of public health, the United Nations Office of the High Commissioner for Human Rights and the Joint United Nations Programme on AIDS concluded that coercive public health measures were counterproductive since they tended to 'drive away people most in need of services and failed to achieve their public health goal of prevention through behavioral change, care, and health support.'[21] It was thus possible to declare that 'public health interests do not conflict with human rights. On the contrary, it has been recognized that when human rights are protected, fewer people become infected.'[22] Perhaps the most extreme formulation of this commitment to the protection of the rights of individuals was given voice by Jonathan Mann, who more than any other individual was responsible for seeking to embed public health in a human rights framework. He recognised the tension between public health and human rights, but in so doing, restated the conflict in a new way: 'For the present, it may be useful to adopt the maxim that health policies and programs should be considered discriminatory and burdensome on human rights until proven otherwise.'[23]

While AIDS provided the starting point, those committed to a health and human rights perspective saw the new articulation as having broad implications for public health more generally. If there were to be an ethics of public health, it would have to reflect in fundamental ways the values that gave birth to bioethics. Writing about the jurisprudential foundations of public health, George Annas challenged the relevance of *Jacobson v Massachusetts*, a 1905 case in which the US Supreme Court upheld mandatory smallpox vaccination, employing language that would serve

[20] David Kirp & Ronald Bayer, eds. 1991. *AIDS in the Industrialized Democracies.* New Brunswick, NJ. Rutgers University Press. Lawrence O. Gostin & Zita Lazzarini. 1997. *Human Rights and Public Health in the AIDS Pandemic.* New York, NY. Oxford University Press: xiv.

[21] Office of the United Nations High Commissioner for Human Rights and the Joint United Nations Programme on HIV/AIDS. 1998. *HIV/AIDS and Human Rights: International Guidelines.* New York & Geneva. United Nations: 37.

[22] Ibid. p. 10.

[23] Jonathan M. Mann, Lawrence Gostin, Sofia Gruskin, Troyen Brennan, Zita Lazzarini & Harvey V. Fineberg. Health and Human Rights. *Health and Human Rights* 1994; 1: 16.

as the basis for the broad exercise of public health powers in the twentieth century: 'Today, almost one hundred years after *Jacobson*, both medicine and constitutional law are radically different. We now take constitutional rights much more seriously, including the right of a competent adult to refuse any medical treatment, even if life-saving treatment.'[24]

SURVEILLANCE AND THE LIMITS OF PRIVACY

Since the end of the nineteenth century, surveillance has served as a critical element in the practice of public health. Central to the effort to monitor and intervene in the face of threats to the public health, surveillance has imposed on healthcare institutions and especially physicians the duty to report cases to confidential registries. Almost always such reports have included the names of the afflicted. Hence surveillance has represented a striking example of the ways in which the claims of public health could intrude upon the privacy of the clinical relationship. For most of the twentieth century such practices, *once established*, went unchallenged. AIDS provided the context for an assault on the privacy-limiting features of surveillance activities.

Soon after the first cases of AIDS were reported by the Centers for Disease Control in June 1981, state health departments in the US began to require that physicians and hospitals report by name each newly diagnosed case.[25] Once the capacity to test for the presence of the antibody to HIV became possible in 1985, it was only a matter of time before some public health official would seek to extend to HIV infection the reporting requirements that were in place for AIDS. The rationale for such reporting drew upon the history of public health: reporting would alert public health officials to the presence of individuals infected with a lethal infection; would allow them to counsel infected individuals about what they needed to do to prevent further transmission; would permit the authorities to monitor the incidence and prevalence of infection. Alert to concerns about privacy and confidentiality, health officials underscored the existence of administrative, regulatory, and statutory protections for reported names. There was no reason to believe that state health departments would fail to protect the identities of those with HIV when they

[24] George Annas. Blinded by Bioterrorism: Public Health and Liberty in the 21st Century. *Health Matrix* 2003; 13: 47.

[25] Bayer, *op. cit.* note 18, pp. 101–136.

had protected those with AIDS, tuberculosis, and other reportable infections.[26]

To these propositions, gay community-based antagonists to name-based reporting and civil liberties advocates retorted that AIDS was different: social hostility and AIDS-related hysteria could lead to changes in policy, legislatively imposed, that would permit for breaches that would never occur with other conditions.[27] And then those in registries would lose their jobs, their housing, and perhaps their liberty. These were arguments that impressed many health officials in states with relatively large AIDS caseloads. Reporting, they came to believe, would be counterproductive; it would drive people away from testing and counselling – essential control measures in the public health campaign against AIDS in the United States and elsewhere. It did not matter that public health departments had an exemplary record in protecting name-based reports.[28] If those most at risk for HIV had fears about what would happen to them, then that was all that mattered.

As therapeutic advances began to emerge in the late 1980s, fissures began to appear in the relatively broad and solid alliance against name-based reporting. The traditional values of public health began to reassert themselves against the privacy-based concerns that had prevailed during the epidemic's first decade. At the end of November 1990, the CDC declared its support for HIV reporting, which it asserted could 'enhance the ability of local, state and national agencies to project the level of required resources' for care and prevention services.[29] The House of Delegates of the American Medical Association endorsed the reporting of names as well, thus breaking with the traditional resistance of medical practitioners to such intrusions on the physician-patient relationship.[30] In 1991, New Jersey became the first high-prevalence state to require HIV-case reporting by name.[31] In the

[26] Ronald Bayer & Amy L. Fairchild. The Limits of Privacy: Surveillance and the Control of Disease. *Health Care Analysis* 2002; 10: 19–35.

[27] Bayer, *op. cit.* note 18.

[28] L.O. Gostin, J. Ward & C. Baker. National HIV Case Reporting for the United States: A Defining Moment in the History of the Epidemic. *NEJM* 1997; 337: 1166.

[29] Centers for Disease Control and Prevention. Update: Public Health Surveillance for HIV Infection – United States, 1989 and 1990. *MMWR* 1990; 39: 861.

[30] R. Bayer, *op. cit.* note 19: 1501.

[31] Intergovernmental Health Policy Project. Reporting in the States. *Intergovernmental AIDS Reports* 1989; November/December.

following years, the CDC continued to press for named reporting of HIV cases, an effort that assumed the dimensions of a campaign.

Although most, if not all, AIDS-service organisations as well as civil liberties advocates remained adamantly opposed to name reporting, arguing instead for the use of unique identifiers that could protect the privacy of people with HIV infection, the public health community, with the CDC in the lead, concluded that such an approach would simply impede the adoption of an effective system of surveillance. Nevertheless, marking the extent to which concerns for privacy continued to shape decision-making in public health, the CDC, in its 1999 recommendation for nationwide HIV case reporting, reluctantly opened the way to the use of unique identifiers in those states that preferred a reporting course that did not entail the use of names.

The debates that occurred over name-based reporting in the context of the AIDS epidemic would inevitably raise questions about the practice of surveillance itself as advocates of privacy, to the astonishment of public health practitioners, suggested that the warrant for the violation of privacy in the early twentieth century no longer deserved unquestioned obeisance.

CONFINEMENT AND THE LIMITS OF LIBERTY

Isolation and quarantine represent the most plenary exercise of the state's authority in the name of public health.[32] Historically, the imposition of isolation and quarantines to control infectious threats was bounded by few procedural protections. The rights of the individual were viewed as subservient to the judgements of those with public health authority. As the pattern of morbidity and mortality underwent an epidemiological transformation in the twentieth century, as chronic conditions replaced infectious diseases as the pre-eminent threat, the role of quarantine and isolation became marginal to the practice of public health in the United States. There were lingering threats that called forth the

[32] Although the terms are often used interchangeably, isolation is the separation of individuals known to be infectious. In contrast, quarantine is the restriction of the activities of healthy individuals or populations exposed to a communicable disease. A.S. Benenson, ed. 1995. *Control of Communicable Diseases Manual.* Washington, DC. American Public Health Association. J. Barbera, A. Macintyre, L. Gostin, T. Inglesbury, T. O'Toole, C. DeAtley, K. Tonat & M. Layton. Large-Scale Quarantine following Biological Terrorism in the United States: Scientific Examination, Logistic and Legal Limits, and Possible Consequences. *JAMA* 2001; 286: 2711–2717.

exercise of the power to confine – tuberculosis, for example – but they were relatively uncommon.

The worldwide threat of Severe Acute Respiratory Syndrome (SARS) in 2002 posed starkly the question of when, in the name of public health, individuals and communities could be deprived of their liberty. In several respects, SARS took society back to a pre-therapeutic era: no definitive diagnostic test, a non-specific case definition, and no effective vaccine or treatment.[33]

Countries used one of the oldest public health tools in response to the first outbreak of SARS: isolation and quarantine, underscoring the tension between liberty and the imperative to protect the public's health. During the first SARS outbreak, public health authorities implemented isolation and quarantine in countries with diverse socio-political and constitutional traditions, ranging from China, Hong Kong, Vietnam and Singapore, to Canada and the United States.[34]

Confinement of individuals with disease and those exposed raised questions about the level of risk that justified loss of liberty. Frank cases needed to be isolated, but when a case was unconfirmed or when the individual had simply been exposed or was suspected of being exposed the justification for restricting liberty was problematical. Uncertainty about how wide to cast the net of quarantine for exposed, asymptomatic individuals was framed by the absence of a diagnostic assay that could rapidly distinguish between the infected and merely exposed with high specificity. But very broad quarantines were viewed as justifiable because of the uncertainties of risk.

Most jurisdictions confined patients in their homes or general hospitals, but others considered the construction of special infectious disease hospitals.[35] In Asia and Canada, authorities ordered mass quarantines or closures for schools, hospitals, factories, hotels, restaurants, places of entertainment, and residential buildings.[36] Some countries, particularly the United States, sought

[33] J.L. Gerberding. Faster . . . but Fast Enough? Responding to the Epidemic of Severe Acute Respiratory Syndrome. *NEJM* 2003; 348: 2030.

[34] B.R. Bloom. Lessons from SARS. *Science* 2003; 300: 701.

[35] Hong Kong Economic and Trade Office Tokyo. Press release. Available at: http://www.hketotyo.or.jp/english/news_sars030605_e.html (accessed 14 July, 2003).

[36] J.B. Kahn. Quarantine Set in Beijing Areas to Fight SARS. *New York Times* 25 April, 2003: A1. Centers for Disease Control and Prevention. Severe Acute Respiratory Syndrome – Singapore 2003. *MMWR* 2003; 52: 40–41. K. Bradsher. The SARS Epidemic: Economy; Outbreak of Disease brings Big Drop-off in China's Economy. *New York Times* 28 April, 2003: A1. A. Wayne. In Singapore, 1970s Law becomes Weapon Against SARS. *New York Times* 10 June, 2003: F4.

voluntary separation of exposed patients,[37] but others used more intrusive forms of enforcement. In Singapore, where thousands were subjected to quarantine, authorities used thermal scanners, web cameras, and electronic bracelets to enforce quarantine, supervised by a security agency.[38] In Hong Kong, the police department's electronic tracking system was used to enforce quarantine.[39] While recourse to compulsory measures posed few challenges to the underlying values of authoritarian regimes, officials underscored the extent to which the threat of SARS justified resort to coercive measures even in liberal democratic societies. In Canada, a high school was closed and 1500 students ordered to home quarantine because of a single case involving a student with symptoms of SARS; Ontario's commissioner of public health warned those who violated the home quarantine that he had the authority to hospitalise those who failed to adhere to the order.[40]

In the fall of 2003, as the international community braced for the possibility of a resurgence of SARS, it became clear that the isolation procedures used during the initial outbreak had been far too stringent. The CDC reported that individuals quarantined after contact with an asymptomatic SARS patient 'had no detectable risk' of infection. Moreover, there were no cases in which an individual transmitted the disease to his or her contacts while under quarantine. Thus, the CDC concluded that 'Focusing only on persons who had contact with an actively ill SARS patient would have reduced the number of persons quarantined by approximately 66 percent, without compromising its effectiveness.'[41] The CDC then elaborated a finer range of surveillance and quarantine recommendations, these included: passive monitoring on the part of the individual with no activity restrictions; active monitoring by healthcare workers either by phone or in person (which might or might not include explicit quarantine restrictions); working quarantine (for people, such as healthcare

[37] M.H. Cooper. Fighting SARS. *CQ Researcher* 20 June, 2003.

[38] World Health Organization. Severe Acute Respiratory Syndrome – Singapore, 2003. *Weekly Epidemiogic. Record* 2003; 78: 161.

[39] World Health Organization. 2003. *Severe Acute Respiratory Syndrome (SARS): Status of the Outbreak and Lessons for the Immediate Future.* Geneva. World Health Organization.

[40] D.L. Brown. Sick of Quarantine in Toronto; After School's SARS Scare, Teens Bored by Week in Isolation. *Washington Post* 3 June, 2003: A20.

[41] Centers for Disease Control and Prevention. Efficiency of Quarantine during an Epidemic of Severe Acute Respiratory Syndrome – Beijing, China, 2003. *MMWR* 2003; 52: 1039. See also: WHO. SARS – Epidemiological Findings, Clinical Picture, and Case Management. Available at: http://www.wpro.who.int/sars/docs/interimguidelines/part2.asp (accessed 9 February, 2004).

workers, who provide essential services); focused measures (such as building closings or event cancellations) to increase the social distance among members of a group where transmission was believed to have occurred; and community-wide or regional measures (such as school closings and transportation system shut downs) to increase social distance in areas where extensive SARS transmission occurred, where there was a lack of clearly identifiable epidemiological links between cases, and where restrictions on known contacts was deemed insufficient.[42]

PATERNALISM AND THE LIMITS OF AUTONOMY

For government to impose restrictions on those who represent a risk to others falls clearly within the broadly accepted exercise of state power in liberal societies and in principle entails no fundamental problem for the autonomy-focused perspective of bioethics. Problems emerge where the risk to others is uncertain. It is here that an important divide emerges between the judgements of those committed to autonomy and those whose first priority is the public health. It is a divide characterised by complex questions of what moral weight to give to the *likelihood* and *severity* of harm. However these matters are resolved, they raise issues that are fundamentally different from those posed by behaviours that represent primarily a threat to individuals themselves. It is here that the spectre of paternalism emerges, and that the tension between public health perspectives and autonomy-focused bioethics is positioned in its boldest relief.

Tobacco consumption represents the single most important cause of morbidity and mortality in advanced industrialised societies. It thus serves as an object lesson in the ways in which the antagonism towards paternalism has both shaped and limited public health policy.

In 1964, when the Office of the US Surgeon General issued the first report on the hazards of tobacco use, 50% of men and 35% of women smoked cigarettes.[43] This meant there were millions of smoking adults whose health and lives were imperilled. But as the American campaign against tobacco took its first halting steps in

[42] Centers for Disease Control and Prevention. Public Health Guidance for Community-Level Preparedness and Response to Sever Acute Respiratory Syndrome (SARS). Version 2; Appendix D1: Interventions for Community Containment. 8 January, 2004. Available at: http://www.cdc.gov/ncidod/sars/guidance/D/index.htm (accessed 9 February, 2004).

[43] US Department of Health and Human Services. 2000. *Reducing Tobacco Use: A Report of the Surgeon General*. Washington, DC. Government Printing Office.

the context of fierce resistance from the tobacco industry and its political allies, it avoided the taint of paternalism, the suggestion that the state was seeking to impose its preferences on those who smoked cigarettes.

Three broad sets of policies were adopted to confront the challenge posed by tobacco over the next four decades: restrictions on advertising; the imposition of taxes; and limits on public smoking. In each case, a public warrant for the measures adopted sought to demonstrate that it was third parties, innocent victims, or children that were the object of protective measures. Only insofar as warnings about tobacco, weak as they were, were posted on cigarette packages, did public health efforts direct themselves to those who bore the full burden of cigarette-related suffering, disease, and death.

Efforts to limit tobacco advertising, a complex matter in polities that accord protection to commercial speech, almost always focused on the claims of children. It was they who were vulnerable to the manipulations and seductions of advertising. If in order to protect them, it was necessary to limit advertising that could be viewed by adults – proposals in the US to ban outdoor advertising within 1000 feet of any school effectively meant a ban on all outdoor advertising in many communities – that was a price that had to be paid.

As public health officials came to recognise that cigarette consumption was price-responsive despite the addictive nature of nicotine, the possibility of facing the threat of tobacco-related disease by raising taxes became increasingly appealing. But the public justification of such taxes was almost always that either increasing the price of cigarettes would render them too costly for adolescents or that those who smoked cigarettes imposed healthcare costs on the non-smoking population.[44] Such externalities could be internalised by raising taxes on cigarettes. Indeed, fairness dictated the imposition of such burdens on smokers.[45] If such taxes also discouraged those who smoked from continuing their habit, that was simply an added advantage to a policy directed at the protection of non-smokers and those, who because of age, were an appropriate target of paternalistic interventions.

Finally, virtually from the dawn of the public health campaign against cigarette-related morbidity and mortality, the effort to

[44] Thomas A. Hodgson. Cigarette Smoking and Lifetime Medical Expenditure. *Milbank Quarterly* 1992; 70: 81–125.

[45] Kenneth E. Warner. Cigarette Taxation: Doing Good by Doing Well. *Journal of Public Health Policy* 1984; 5: 312–319.

restrict smoking in public settings has played a central role.[46] Such efforts *preceded* the first evidence that side-stream smoke posed a hazard – at least in enclosed environments – by more than a decade. By the end of the twentieth century, a radical transformation had occurred. Smoking, which was an integral dimension of the social world, was increasingly relegated to the private domain.[47] Debate over how far to press such restrictions ultimately had to confront the question of whether bans on outdoor smoking could be justified in terms of annoyance abatement rather than disease prevention. An antismoking activist declared, 'Even if outdoor environmental tobacco smoke were no more hazardous than dog excrement stuck to the bottom of a shoe, in many places laws require dog owners to avoid fouling public areas. Is this too much to ask of smokers?'[48] Not all antismoking activists shared this view. Said the editor of *Tobacco Control*, 'We need to ask whether efforts to prevent people from smoking outdoors risks besmirching tobacco control advocates as the embodiment of intolerant, paternalistic busy-bodies, who, not content at protecting their own health, want to force smokers not to smoke.'[49]

Despite such concerns, by the end of the twentieth century, the willingness to embrace explicitly paternalistic justifications for antismoking policy was becoming more evident, no doubt facilitated by the emergence of a sharp social gradient in cigarette consumption – those who are educated smoke less and less, those at the bottom of the social ladder continue to smoke.

The most dramatic reflection of the willingness to embrace paternalism was to be found in measures seeking to 'denormalise' smoking. We typically do not think of health promotion campaigns as paternalistic. But when they go beyond the provision of information and systematically seek to transform the very desires and preferences of those to whom they are directed, they assume a fundamentally different character. Indeed, the use of social marketing techniques to undercut smoking behaviour must be

[46] Ronald Bayer & James Colgrove. 2004. Children and Bystanders First: The Ethics and Politics of Tobacco Control in the United States. In *Unfiltered: Conflicts over Tobacco Policy and Public Health*. Eric Feldman & Ronald Bayer, eds. Cambridge, MA. Harvard University Press.

[47] Allan Brandt. 1998. Blow Some Smoke My Way: Passive Smoking, Risk, and American Culture. In *Ashes to Ashes: The History of Smoking and Health*. Stephen Lock, Lois Reynolds & E.M. Tansey, eds. Amsterdam. Rodopi Press.

[48] J. Repace. Banning Outdoor Smoking Is Scientifically Justifiable. *Tobacco Control* 2000; 9: 98.

[49] S. Chapman. Banning Smoking Outdoors Is Seldom Ethically Justifiable. *Tobacco Control* 2000; 9: 95–97.

viewed as paternalistic in impulse as well as practice. In a 1998 report, California's tobacco control programme openly advocated a social norm change designed to protect 'generations who have already reached adulthood.'[50] When New York City sharply increased tobacco taxes in 2002, the justification was not that smokers imposed costs on others, but rather that hefty prices might help force smokers to quit. The mayor of New York City saw this as an effort to save the lives of smokers themselves.[51]

TOWARD AN ETHICS OF PUBLIC HEALTH

What the foregoing discussion has demonstrated is that those involved in the practice of public health embrace a set of values that are often, if not always, in conflict with the autonomy-centred values of those who take an individualistic and anti-paternalistic stance. But ethos is not ethics. When bioethics first emerged it confronted a tradition of medical practice and research within which paternalism still commanded both loyalty and impassioned defence. It was that dominant world-view that bioethics sought to overturn. In the context of public health, the question that needs to be addressed is whether paternalism and subordination of the individual for the good of the commonwealth should serve as the foundation for an ethics of public health or whether the perspective derived from the dominant autonomy-focused and anti-paternalistic currents in bioethics should serve as a point of departure for a thoroughgoing challenge to the fundamental values and practices of public health.

We begin with the conviction that at the core of public health practice is the charge to protect the common good, to intervene for such ends even in the face of uncertainty. This stance may, we believe, necessitate limits on the choices of individuals on grounds of communal protection against both hazard and paternalism. It is in this regard that this article may be distinguished from other recent efforts to articulate a set of moral considerations for public health, which have commonly focused on the centrality of social justice for public health.

During the twentieth century, public health interventions were often justified by an explicit or implicit invocation of the harm

[50] California Department of Health Services. 1998. *A Model for Change: The California Experience in Tobacco Control.* Sacramento, CA. California Department of Health Services: 4.

[51] Michael Cooper. Cigarettes Up to $7 a Pack with New Tax. *New York Times* 1 July, 2002: B1.

principle. First enunciated by John Stuart Mill, that principle provides the standard for judging liberty-limiting acts of government.[52] It would be hard to imagine a set of ethical arguments that could challenge this posture. Indeed, limitations on the rights of individuals in the face of public health threats are firmly supported by legal tradition and ethics.[53] All legal systems, as well as international human rights, permit governments to infringe on personal liberty to prevent a significant risk to the public.[54]

Nevertheless, there are limits to the application of even the most central of precepts. In recent decades, efforts to bind the harm principle have focused on employing the least restrictive or intrusive alternative that could protect the public health against significant risk. But what constitutes a least restrictive/intrusive alternative and how the significance of risk is to be judged are only in part empirical matters. More important, moral judgements are involved. In fact, the tension between autonomy and public health perspectives is reflected in all such judgements. We believe that the standard appropriate to public health cannot be derived from the basic assumptions of a bioethics dominated by individualism.

The case of tuberculosis makes this clear. When individuals fail to complete the course of treatment they run the *risk* of reactivation and of developing multi-drug resistant strains of mycobacterium tuberculosis, which can be difficult and costly to treat, even deadly. The risk posed by any individual for such developments may not be judged 'significant.' But more important, when non-compliance characterises large numbers of individuals – as was the case in the US in the early 1990s – there is no question but that the threat to public health attains significance. It is therefore the *collective* hazard that provides the warrant for intervention even when the threat posed by any individual may not attain the standard of significance.[55] This is, of course, a point suggested by Geoffrey Rose in his now famous formulation of the ways in which

[52] John Stuart Mill. *On Liberty* quoted in: *The Philosophy of John Stuart Mills.* 1961. M. Cohen, ed. New York, NY. Modern Library: 185–319.

[53] Lawrence O. Gostin. Public Health Law in an Age of Terrorism: Rethinking Individual Rights and Common Goods. *Health Affairs* 2002; 21: 79–93.

[54] United Nations Economic and Social Council (ECOSOC). The Siracusa Principles on the Limitations and Derogation Provisions in the International Covenant on Civil and Political Rights. UN Doc. E/CN.4/1985/4, Annex. Available at: http://www1.umn.edu/humanrts/instree/siracusaprinciples.html (accessed 7 July, 2003).

[55] Ronald Bayer & Laurence Dupuis. Tuberculosis, Public Health, and Civil Liberties. *Annual Review of Public Health* 1995; 16: 320–322.

small benefits to individuals from public health interventions may produce quite significant collective goods.[56]

The global outbreak of SARS discussed above provides an example of how in the face of grave threats a public health perspective may mandate interventions even when it is unclear whether such threats may become significant. The precautionary principle provides a starting point for the ethics of risk management. The principle stipulates an obligation to protect populations against reasonably foreseeable threats, even under conditions of uncertainty.[57] First articulated in the context of environmental hazards, the precautionary principle seeks to forestall disasters and guide decision-making in the context of incomplete knowledge. Given the potential costs of inaction, it is the failure to implement preventive measures that requires justification. Proponents of the precautionary principle explicitly defend their position by noting that entities that threaten the environment are best able to bear the burdens of regulation. Opponents warn that the imposition of such burdens may stifle economic progress and scientific innovation.[58] In general, the principle has only recently been explicitly invoked in the context of epidemic threats where pre-emptive actions may burden individuals and impose limits on their freedoms. Nevertheless, the precautionary principle has implicitly guided public health interventions designed to limit or forestall epidemic outbreaks.

The challenge to the precautionary principle is illustrated by quarantine in the case of SARS. Health officials had to act without full scientific knowledge about the nature of disease transmission. To avoid catastrophe, they took action that proved unnecessarily extensive. The only safeguard against the misuse of authority is transparency and an open acknowledgement that new evidence may necessitate a reconsideration of policies.

In the end, a focus on population-based health requires a population-based analysis and a willingness to recognise that the ethics of collective health may require far more extensive limitations on privacy, as in the case of public health surveillance, and on liberty, as in the case of isolation and quarantine, than would be justified from the perspective of the autonomy-focused

[56] Geoffrey Rose. Sick Individuals and Sick Populations. *International Journal of Epidemiology* 2001; 30: 427–432.

[57] J. Applegate. The Precautionary Preference: An American Perspective on the Precautionary Principle. *Human and Ecological Risk Assessment* 2000; 6: 413–443.

[58] J. Morris. 2000. *Defining the Precautionary Principle. Rethinking Risk and the Precautionary Principle.* New York, NY. Butterworth-Heinemann: 1–21.

orientation of the dominant current in bioethics. Compulsion and, indeed, coercion – so anathema to this tradition of bioethics – are central to public health. Nevertheless, it is important to recognise that while mandatory measures and recourse to coercion may be necessary, efforts designed to elicit the voluntary co-operation of those at risk for acquiring or transmitting infectious diseases are preferable and, indeed, may be more effective. From an ethical perspective, such efforts are desirable because they enhance the public's health without gratuitously burdening privacy and liberty. From a pragmatic perspective, such efforts reduce the necessity of invoking the coercive power of the state that may provoke resistance at a juncture when co-operation is essential. Thus, while a public health perspective will not privilege liberty and privacy, it does not follow that it should be insensitive to the importance of protecting individual rights.

More challenging is the question of the role of paternalism in public health. Mill's anti-paternalism has struck a powerful cord in American political culture, as we noted in our discussion of tobacco policy. Animated by a broad utilitarianism that seeks to maximise communal well-being, public health has embraced measures that go far beyond the very limited recognition of justifiable paternalism in conventional bioethical accounts.

In a striking example of the effort to justify paternalism in the context of occupational health regulations, Norman Daniels argued that the protection of workers against hazardous workplace exposures *that they themselves* might choose to risk could be justified because of the 'quasi-coercive' economic context within which workers were forced to choose.[59] But such a defence of paternalism is too limited. The central commitment to collective well-being requires a much more robust embrace of paternalism – one that goes beyond interventions designed to protect those whose choices are limited by lack of knowledge or understanding. We ought, for example, to protect motorcyclists from the hazards of unhelmeted riding not because they may impose costs on the community in the event of accidents or because they are too young to appreciate the hazards entailed, but because we are morally bound to prevent avoidable suffering and death.

It is not surprising that among the most forthright defences of public health paternalism has come from Robert Goodin, a utilitarian: 'We do not leave it to the discretion of consumers, however well informed, whether or not to drink grossly polluted water,

[59] Normal Daniels. 1985. *Just Health Care*. New York, NY. Oxford University Press: Chapter 7.

ingest grossly contaminated foods, or inject grossly dangerous drugs. We simply prohibit such things on grounds of public health. That appeal is justified, in turn, most standardly by recourse to utilitarian calculations . . . To a very large extent . . . the justification of public health measures, in general, must be baldly paternalistic. Their fundamental point is to promote the wellbeing of people who might otherwise be inclined cavalierly to court certain sorts of diseases.'[60] The challenge, we believe, for public health ethics is to define those moments when public health paternalism is justified and to articulate a set of principles that would preserve a commitment to the realm of free choice.

The effort to shape public health policy in liberal societies will require a forthright acknowledgement of the tensions and trade-offs that will inevitably arise when the claims of public welfare and well-being intrude on privacy, individual choice, and liberty. Recognising the role of moral values in decision-making was one of the signal contributions of bioethics in its formative period. To be sure, over the past three decades a broad array of perspectives has emerged under the rubric of bioethics. Dissatisfaction with the historically dominant commitments to individualism has been reflected in communitarian claims, feminist perspectives, and now even in explicitly politically conservative formulations. Nevertheless, individualism retains its hegemonic status. It is thus that bioethics cannot serve as a basis for thinking about the balances required in the defence of the public's health. As we commence the process of shaping an ethics of public health, it is clear that bioethics is the wrong place to start.

Ronald Bayer
Amy L. Fairchild
Center for the History and Ethics of Public Health
Department of Sociomedical Sciences
Mailman School of Public Health
Columbia University
New York, NY 10032
USA
rb8@columbia.edu
alf4@columbia.edu

[60] Robert E. Goodin. 1989. *No Smoking: The Ethical Issues.* Chicago & London. The University of Chicago Press: 30–31.

[2]

Rethinking the Meaning of Public Health

Mark A. Rothstein

Public health is a dynamic field. Outbreaks of new diseases, as well as changing patterns of population growth, economic development, and lifestyle trends all may threaten public health and thus demand a public health response. As the practice of public health evolves, there is an ongoing need to reassess its scientific, ethical, legal, and social underpinnings. Such a reappraisal must consider the disagreement among public health officials, public health scholars, elected officials, and the public about the proper role of public health and the distinctions, for example, between public health and clinical care, and public health and health promotion.

In this article I will attempt to characterize the main points of contention as well as offer my own views regarding the proper scope of public health. Greater clarity and consensus on the meaning of public health are likely to lead to more efficient and effective public health interventions as well as increased public and political support for public health activities.

Alternative Definitions of "Public Health"

Human rights as public health

There is a growing trend to include within the sphere of public health all the societal factors that affect health. This is a very long list, including war, violence, poverty, economic development, income distribution, natural resources, diet and lifestyle, health-care infrastructure, overpopulation, and civil rights.[1] There is much to recommend viewing the sources of health broadly — in other words, considering health as more than the absence of illness and disease. Yet the conceptual value of considering the health of a population in light of a wide array of factors does not necessarily translate into a practical framework for implementing policy. The term "public health" is a legal term of art, and it refers to specifically delineated powers, duties, rights, and responsibilities. Even beyond its legal usage, public health applies to specific institutions and individuals, such as public health departments and public health officials.

The "human rights as public health" definition has been applied both internationally and domestically. According to Morris Schaefer: "The health of most people in the world depends less on access to medical services than on efficient farming, distributive justice, ensuring 'domestic tranquility,' and broad-based, sustainable development of natural and built environments."[2] Similarly, on a national level, William R. Breakey has written: "We should be as much concerned about the thousands of people who are homeless in American cities and the thousands of children in residentially unstable families as we are when there is an epidemic of an infectious disease affecting a few hundred people, and we should respond with the same urgency."[3] Schaefer and Breakey are certainly right in their assessments. Nevertheless, just because war, crime, hunger, poverty, illiteracy, homelessness, and human rights abuses interfere with the health of individuals and populations does not mean that eliminating these conditions is part of the mission of public health.

It is understandable why knowledgeable and caring health professionals would want to improve the health of individuals and communities by focusing on the root causes of illness and disease. Analyzing political, economic, and social issues in a scientific manner is appealing by providing essential data and more rigorous methodology. It also seems to help make the concerns more objective and their remediation more achievable. Unfortunately, labeling so many activities as public health does little if anything to eliminate the problem of poor health. "Even if we claimed that poverty is the root cause of all disease, which it surely is not, we would hardly be closer to solving the problem — just as we were no closer to eliminating the threat of nuclear war after pointing out that Armageddon would interfere with physicians' treatment of their patients."[4]

Ilan H. Meyer and Sharon Schwartz refer to the transformation of social issues into health issues as the "public healthification" of social problems, which they consider analogous to the medicalization of individual social problems.[5] In their view, public health provides too narrow a perspective to be effective. "In the case of many social problems, public health research questions as currently conceptualized are less complex than the social and political issues (conflicting interest groups, conflicting value systems, power relationships) that need to be resolved for interventions to be successfully applied."[6]

In a recent article, Larry Gostin describes three main reasons the all-inclusive notion of public health is not only ineffective but counterproductive.[7] First, the field of public health lacks precision if it includes such disparate areas of concern that have as their only commonality causing adverse effects on health. Second, as the field of public health expands well beyond its core area of expertise, it can claim no special abilities to end wars, modernize agriculture, or restructure economies. Third, by becoming involved with economic redistribution and social restructuring, the field becomes highly politicized.

The human rights definition of public health also raises practical problems. What curriculum could possibly train public health professionals on all the various root causes of poor health? What political system or public health budget will support far-ranging interventions by those charged with protecting public health? What effect will such seemingly quixotic activities have on the ability of public health professionals to combat traditional public health problems, such as infectious diseases and poor sanitation, as well as new threats, such as bioterrorism?

Individuals trained in public health should not give up the noble struggle to ensure that every person has a minimum standard of living to support a healthy life. But this battle must be fought together with people from all disciplines and all walks of life and without using the self-defeating strategy of annexing human rights into the public health domain.

Population health as public health

A somewhat less expansive, but still broad definition is the one traditionally used in public health. Under the traditional conception, public health focuses on the health of entire populations rather than individual patients. According to Dan Beauchamp and Bonnie Steinbock: "Whereas in medicine, the patient is an individual person, in public health, the 'patient' is the whole community or population. The goal of public health is to reduce disease and early death in populations."[8]

One of the most commonly cited definitions of public health in this vein comes from the Institute of Medicine (IOM) report *The Future of Public Health*: "Public health is what we, as a society, do collectively to assure the conditions for people to be healthy."[9] Although I would place this definition in the traditional category, it is a vague definition that fails to indicate the primary objective or scope of public health. Unlike most other definitions of public health, it does not explicitly state that public health is concerned with the health of the population rather than individuals.

The IOM report also makes public health the responsibility of everyone, although it gives primacy to government efforts: "The mission of public health is addressed by private organizations and individuals as well as by public agencies. But the governmental public health agency has a unique function: to see to it that vital elements are in place and that the mission is adequately addressed."[10] In contrast to this government-centered approach, a more expansive definition of public health cited in, but not necessarily endorsed by the IOM report is the following: "It's anything that affects the health of the community on a mass basis."[11] Under such a view, efforts to improve access to health care as well as more general measures to prevent injury and illness and reduce morbidity and mortality, such as advice to use sunscreen and eat healthy foods, would be considered public health. I term this conception of public health the "population health as public health" model.

There are three important characteristics of the "population health as public health" model. Each characteristic, however, raises concerns. First, this version of public health is the province of both the public and private sectors. Thus, public health would include the efforts of nonprofit organizations, commercial entities, and private citizens to promote healthy lifestyles. A beer company's "drink with moderation" campaign, a cigarette company's program to discourage underage smoking, and a religious organization's promotion of abstinence to reduce teen pregnancy would all be considered public health efforts. With such a broad approach, there is a risk that the urgency of public health will become diluted, and the public will have an increasingly difficult time in distinguishing public health from public relations.

Second, "population health as public health" fails to establish any meaningful lines of demarcation between individual health and public health. Under the "population health as public health" approach, when individual health measures are performed on or addressed to an unspecified but sufficient number of individuals, then this becomes public health. For example, when primary care physicians adopt as the standard of care a new type of screening test or treatment modality, the result may be to improve the health of numer-

Volume 30:2, Summer 2002

ous individuals. But it is unclear at what point cumulative individual health measures become population health. It is also unclear when responsibility for such a health measure shifts from the individual health-care provider to a public health official.

Third, unlike traditional public health measures, such as infectious disease control, the failure to undertake population health measures, such as a treatment or preventive measure for a person who is sick or at risk, does not place the health of other individuals in jeopardy. Consequently, when population health is based on multiple individual health actions, it may not justify coercive measures on the part of the government. Responsibility for these interventions would lie with individual health providers, non-governmental organizations, and government agencies acting in their non-coercive, population health role. The "population health as public health" approach is thus ill-defined, with diverse actors pursuing widely divergent strategies to deal with the same health problems, tackling health problems of varying severity, and often pursuing their own agendas with little coordination or accountability. Furthermore, it is ill-advised to adopt a definition of public health that mixes government with non-government initiatives, coercive with non-coercive measures, and harms that affect individual health with those that affect the health of the public.

Government intervention as public health

The third conception of public health, and the one I advocate, is more limited in scope. "Government intervention as public health" involves public officials taking appropriate measures pursuant to specific legal authority, after balancing private rights and public interests, to protect the health of the public. These measures may be coercive. The existence of a public threat demands a public response, and in a representative political system it is the government that is authorized to act on behalf of the public.[12] The police power is the constitutional authority on which public health measures are based. According to the U.S. Supreme Court:

> According to settled principles, the police power of a state must be held to embrace, at least, such reasonable regulations established directly by legislative enactment as will protect the public health and the public safety.... There are manifold restraints to which every person is necessarily subject for the common good. On any other basis organized society could not exist with safety to its members.[13]

The moral and political authority (and duty) of the government to mandate public health actions, including quarantine, isolation, immunization, contact tracing, property seizures, and environmental regulation, derives from one of the following three conditions. First, the health of the population is threatened. The paradigmatic public health threat is an infectious disease, where the threat to the public is through the horizontal transmission of infection. Other health threats may have a public health effect because they involve common resources and because the failure to control the problem at the source will lead to adverse health consequences to many people. Thus, person-to-person transmission is not necessary to have a public health threat. Food safety, sanitation, water fluoridation, insect and vermin control, and pollution control are examples of public health measures to address health threats to the public.

The second type of condition to justify a public health intervention occurs when the government has unique powers and expertise related to an essential aspect of public health. Disease reporting and surveillance illustrates this category. Legally mandated reporting of certain types of health conditions, such as some infectious diseases, occupational diseases, cancers, sexually transmitted diseases, gunshot wounds, child fatalities, and suspected cases of domestic violence, are all important to the collective health of the community. Reporting allows for data aggregation and analysis as well as more direct intervention to prevent additional cases. Without mandatory reporting, important cases would be lost, and only the government has the authority to mandate reporting. Moreover, government public health agencies have access to the trained professionals needed to interpret the data.

The third type of condition to justify a public health intervention occurs when government action is more efficient or more likely to produce an effective intervention. An example would be newborn screening programs, which are mandated by law in every state. Public health programs to identify inborn errors of metabolism and other heritable disorders offer uniformity in standards and reporting. In addition, screening programs are often tied to publicly financed follow-up and treatment.

The key element of public health is the role of the government — its power and obligation to invoke mandatory or coercive measures to eliminate a threat to the public's health. Without a threat to the public, it is much more difficult to make a case for the use of coercive powers; in the absence of such legal authority, the participation of individuals in health-enhancing activities ordinarily must be voluntary. Applying these principles to the three sources of moral and political authority for governmental public health activity, the justification for activity goes in descending order from (1) population-wide health threat; to (2) unique governmental powers and expertise about an essential aspect of public health; to (3) the need for more efficient and effective governmental action in ensuring public health. Public health activities in this third category may overlap with population health measures. Consequently, newborn screening for phenylketonuria (PKU), congenital hypothyroidism, and other disorders; school-based medical screening for scoliosis, tuberculosis, vision and hearing problems, dental caries, and other conditions; and broad health promotion activities may be considered in varying degrees by different jurisdictions to lack the urgency and public health effects necessary to require universal participation.

Under this narrower definition of public health, a "public health clinic" providing primary care is *not* engaged in public health; it is a public entity providing individual health care. In the United States, because there is no guaranteed access to health care, the responsibility for providing health care to uninsured individuals often falls to public health agencies. One effect of this allocation of responsibility is that providing primary care services tends to be commingled with, and to crowd out, other public health functions. As a result, many health departments lack the resources to engage in core public health functions, such as epidemiology, disease surveillance, and environmental regulation.

Dr. Barry Levy, former president of the American Public Health Association, observed that 97 percent of those questioned in a Harris poll did not know what public health is, and that a substantial number of the respondents said that public health is health care for the indigent.[14] According to Dr. Levy: "It should therefore not surprise us that many of our elected officials believe that when you move so-called indigent people into private-sector managed care programs, there is no need for public health anymore."[15]

In support of a narrower definition

There are five reasons I believe it is desirable to embrace a narrower definition of public health. First, health-related activities that trigger the coercive power of government raise the most serious and complex legal and ethical issues; only activities falling within a narrow definition of public health can justify the use of this power. Second, the narrow and more specific classification of public health activities indicates the outer limits of coercion for government programs. Third, the classification scheme helps in allocating responsibilities for public, population, and individual health among the private, public, and not-for-profit sectors. Fourth, classifying possible government activities according to public health roles helps in setting priorities. Fifth, because public health has been the justification for some overreaching or even reprehensible prior government activities, ranging from eugenics to unethical research on human subjects, a narrow definition of public health will help steer public health officials away from activities that are inappropriate for the government.

This last point is illustrated by the recent emphasis on public health genetics.[16] Public health involves government action, coercive powers, and societal interests taking precedence over individual rights. In genetics, the dominant values are autonomy, reproductive freedom, and privacy. Thus, public health genetics seems paradoxical, thereby strongly suggesting that any undertaking in the field must be approached with great care. Any government activity is of particular concern when applied to genetics and reproduction. After all, paternalistic, coercive, government efforts to improve the nation's health through genetic intervention were the hallmarks of the eugenics programs adopted in the first third of the twentieth century. Public policy in genetics has yet to recover from this debacle of mixing public health powers with the scientific means to achieve ostensibly desirable social objectives. Accordingly, those who would advocate a broad view of public health genetics beyond proven measures, such as newborn screening, should have to demonstrate that government action is essential and that detailed measures have been taken to protect individual rights.

Public health genetics also must draw clear distinctions with clinical genetics and clinical medicine. For example, hereditary hemochromatosis is a recessively inherited disorder of iron overload. It can cause serious organ damage if undetected, but it is relatively easy to test for presymptomatically using a genetic test, and it is easy to treat through periodic phlebotomies. Is reducing the morbidity associated with hemochromatosis a public health issue or a clinical issue that can be resolved through genetic testing by primary care providers in the course of regular medical examinations? I would argue that it is an individual health issue that, collectively, may become a population health issue, but it is not a public health issue.

Public Health Professionals, Schools, and Agencies

The taxonomy I am proposing may seem threatening to some public health professionals who may view the classification scheme as unsupportive of their work, misguided, naïve, dangerous, or callous. I believe that such views would reflect an inaccurate interpretation of my proposal. I unequivocally support all of the health-related activities under the categories of individual health, population health, and public health. I also support even the broadest aims of the "human rights as public health" model. What I oppose is the use of the term "public health" as an open-ended descriptor of widely divergent efforts to improve the human condition. It surely will not hasten the elimination of disparate forms of human privations to call them public health issues.

A return to a narrow definition of public health should not have any effect on the curricula of schools of public health, although it might be appropriate to change their names to schools of public and population health. Even though aspects of health promotion, health education, health policy, health services, health research, and health law may be outside the "government intervention as public health" model, these and similar subjects are an essential part of the public (and population) health curriculum. So, too, are epidemiology, biostatistics, toxicology, sanitation, occupational and environmental health sciences, and all of the other methodology and basic science disciplines on which public health is

Volume 30:2, Summer 2002

based. For educational purposes, it does not matter whether particular methods and skills belong to population health or public health, and it does not matter whether the students subsequently work in the public, non-profit, or private sector.

The narrow definition of public health may have an effect on setting the priorities of public health agencies. The top priorities should be those matters requiring mandatory interventions and therefore falling within the narrow definition of public health. In theory, the issues described as population health, including health promotion and health research, would be the next priority. This allocation of responsibilities, however, assumes that the public health agency is not responsible for providing basic medical care, such as prenatal and well-baby care, and other services. To the extent that these are health department responsibilities, then they will need to be integrated into the second level of priorities, after those measures that directly and immediately affect the health of the population.

The Ethical Foundations of Public Health

According to the definition I have suggested, public health invariably involves a balancing of individual and group interests, or private and public interests. Viewed in terms of bioethics, the conflict is between autonomy and paternalism. Decisions about where to strike the balance are not static, and they are influenced by varied and often changing value systems — on an individual, group-wide, and population-wide basis. This fact suggests several necessary responses by public health officials. First, public health interventions must be culturally sensitive and take into account a range of values on issues such as privacy, autonomy, liberty, and dignity. Second, because public attitudes change over time, public health officials must continually justify public health interventions, even longstanding measures of proven efficacy. Third, public health officials and their allies in the public and private sectors must be vigilant. For example, according to the Centers for Disease Control and Prevention report *Public Health's Infrastructure: A Status Report*: "Complacency about the need to maintain vigilance against public health threats has allowed the costly resurgence of many nearly eliminated diseases, including, most recently, tuberculosis and measles...."[17]

A few examples will demonstrate the balancing of group versus individual and public versus private interests. Immunization requirements have been a keystone of public health practice since the early part of the twentieth century. Within the last ten years, however, there have been a number of efforts in state legislatures to increase the statutory exemptions from mandatory immunization. In many states, parents have long been permitted to raise religious objections to immunizations. Some advocates would extend the grounds for exemption to include general personal beliefs about the safety or efficacy of immunization. Broad exemptions, however, raise the distinct possibility of a resurgence of vaccine-preventable disease.[18] Thus, in terms of public health policy, it is necessary to recognize the objections to immunization among growing segments of the population and to demonstrate the current safety, efficacy, and importance of mandatory immunization. Without such documentation, policy development in the legislative arena may afford greater weight to individual liberty interests and asserted parental rights than to public health.

In some instances, public health policy development involves the balancing of two competing private interests. For example, occupational and environmental health are traditional areas of public health activity. New research has established that individuals vary in their risk of illness from occupational exposure based on genetic factors. Should an employer be permitted to use genetic tests to exclude from hazardous exposures individuals who have a genetically increased risk of occupational illness?[19] From a scientific standpoint, numerous factors must be considered, including the absolute risk, the relative risk, the severity of the risk, the latency period, and whether the condition is treatable.[20] Assuming that it made sense from a scientific standpoint to reduce the exposure of at-risk individuals, this would only be a starting point for the policy analysis. The interests of the employer in productivity and profitability (as well as the public interest in preventing illness) would still need to be balanced against the privacy and economic interests of the individual. Here, the conflict between autonomy and paternalism involves primarily private interests, but the government's role in public health (as well as in civil rights and employment policy) is to strike the proper balance.

Conclusion

In common parlance, "public health" is now a general, descriptive term and not a term of art. It is incongruous to embrace the broadest meaning of public health at the same time that our legal system and public health infrastructure are based on a narrow definition of public health jurisdiction, authority, and remedies. Moreover, the boundless conception of public health now gaining in popularity not only may fail to achieve its goal of alleviating the economic and social roots of ill health, but it may actually impede the ability of public health officials to provide traditional public health services.

The moral and political power of governments to act in the realm of public health devolves from the existence of a serious threat to the public. Coercive public health measures are justified by the natural law principle of self-preservation applied on a societal basis. Indeed, modern public health traces its philosophical roots to nineteenth century utilitarianism.[21] The broad power of government to protect public health includes the authority to supersede individual liberty and property interests in the name of preserving the greater public good. It is an awesome responsibility, and therefore it cannot and must not be used indiscriminately.

According to the definition I support, only public health officials can undertake public health actions because their coercive powers are firmly grounded in constitutional provisions and enabling legislation. In my view, public health does not include providing basic health services or population health measures, such as health promotion, and it does not include private actors undertaking similar individual or population health measures. The distinctions among the definitions of public health and their various applications are more than semantic. A clearer understanding of the role of public health helps to allocate responsibilities, set priorities, and avoid inappropriate government activities.

Acknowledgments

Gabriela Alcalde of the Institute for Bioethics, Health Policy and Law at the University of Louisville School of Medicine contributed to this article.

References

1. See, e.g., B.C. Amick III et al., eds., *Society and Health* (New York: Oxford University Press, 1995); S.P. Marks, "Jonathan Mann's Legacy to the 21st Century: The Human Rights Imperative for Public Health," *Journal of Law, Medicine & Ethics*, 29 (2001): 131–38; M. Marmot and R.G. Wilkinson, eds., *Social Determinants of Health* (New York: Oxford University Press, 1999).

2. University of Washington School of Public Health and Community Medicine, Department of Heath Services, *Public Health & Related Definitions, at* <http://depts.washington.edu/hserv/research/phdefinitions.shtml> (last revised Apr. 13, 1998) (statement of Morris Schaefer).

3. W.R. Breakey, "It's Time for the Public Health Community to Declare War on Homelessness," *American Journal of Public Health*, 87 (1997): 153–55, at 153.

4. K.J. Rothman, H-O. Adami, and D. Trichopoulos, "Should the Mission of Epidemiology Include the Eradication of Poverty?," *Lancet*, 352 (1998): 810–13, at 812.

5. I.H. Meyer and S. Schwartz, "Social Issues as Public Health: Promise and Peril," *American Journal of Public Health*, 90 (2000): 1189–91, at 1189.

6. *Id.* at 1191.

7. L.O. Gostin, "Public Health, Ethics, and Human Rights: A Tribute to the Late Jonathan Mann," *Journal of Law, Medicine & Ethics*, 29 (2001): 121–30, at 123.

8. D.E. Beauchamp and B. Steinbock, "Population Perspective," in D.E. Beauchamp and B. Steinbock, eds., *New Ethics for the Public's Health* (New York: Oxford University Press, 1999): at 25.

9. Committee for the Study of the Future of Public Health, Institute of Medicine, *The Future of Public Health* (Washington, D.C.: National Academy Press, 1988): at 19.

10. *Id.* at 7.

11. *Id.* at 37 (quoting unidentified interviewee).

12. See L.O. Gostin, "Public Health Law in a New Century Part I: Law as a Tool to Advance the Community's Health," *JAMA*, 283 (2000): 2837–41.

13. *Jacobson v. Massachusetts*, 197 U.S. 11, 25, 26 (1905).

14. B.S. Levy, "Creating the Future of Public Health: Values, Vision, and Leadership," *American Journal of Public Health*, 88 (1998): 188–92, at 189.

15. *Id.*

16. See M.A. Rothstein, "Genetics and Public Health in the 21st Century: Using Genetic Information to Improve Health and Prevent Disease" (book review), *N. Engl. J. Med.*, 343 (2000): 1580.

17. U.S. Department of Health and Human Services, Centers for Disease Control and Prevention, *Public Health's Infrastructure: A Status Report* (2001): at 12, *available at* <http://www.phppo.cdc.gov/documents/phireport2_16.pdf> (last visited Mar. 21, 2002).

18. C. Feudtner and E.K. Marcuse, "Ethics and Immunization Policy: Promoting Dialogue to Sustain Consensus," *Pediatrics*, 107 (2001): 1158–64.

19. See M.A. Rothstein, "Genetics and the Work Force of the Next Hundred Years," *Columbia Business Law Review*, 2000 (2000): 371–402.

20. See M.A. Rothstein, *Medical Screening and the Employee Health Cost Crisis* (Washington, D.C.: Bureau of National Affairs, 1989): at 132–40.

21. A.H.M. Kerkhoff, "Origin of Modern Public Health and Preventive Medicine," in S. Doxiadis, ed., *Ethical Dilemmas in Health Promotion* (New York: John Wiley & Sons, 1987).

[3]

From old to new public health: role tensions and contradictions

ANITA GORAYA & GRAHAM SCAMBLER
University College London, Medical School, UK

ABSTRACT *This paper reviews the three primary phases of the 'old' public health in Britain, and considers its displacement by the so-called 'new' public health since the 1970s. It identifies and explores the core aspects of the role of the new public health physician—as 'health strategist', 'health promoter', 'health expert', 'health adviser' and 'health bureaucrat'—and the tensions and contradictions associated with them. It concludes by discussing the* location paradox *facing public health physicians committed to achieving the kinds of change necessary if the public health is to be improved and issues of health inequality effectively addressed.*

Introduction

This paper focuses on the role of the public health physician in Britain, a matter of wide, vigorous and renewed debate since the change of government following the 1997 general election. After briefly tracing the three phases of activity associated with the 'old' public health, which supplies the background context for recent developments, we concentrate on the growing references to the 'new' public health over the last quarter of a century, its distinctive philosophy, and the opportunities and prospects available to public health physicians to translate theory into practice. Our contention is that there are such unresolved tensions, even contradictions, implicit in the diversified and demanding role of the new public health physician as to undermine any consistent application of the new public health philosophy. The concept of a *location paradox* is introduced to help account for this problem.

The old public health

Three phases of public health activity over the last century and a half in Britain have been identified.[1] The first, termed the *sanitary* phase, developed in response to the industrial revolution and the concomitant poverty and overcrowded and insanitary living conditions of the new urban workers. Epidemics of the 'fevers' afforded this population little respite. The prevailing theory of miasma held that fevers were caused by foul air deriving from the putrefaction

Correspondence to: Graham Scambler, PhD, Visiting Professor of Sociology, Department of Sociology, Emory University, Social Sciences Building, 1555 Pierce Dr, Atlanta, GA 30322, USA.

of organic matter and waste. The remedy, as advocated by sanitary reformers such as Chadwick, lay in the provision of effective drainage systems and supplies of running water to flush away the causative filth. The pioneering public health activists of the day, such as Duncan and Simon, were party to both theory and solution. The sanitary reforms embodied in the public health legislation of 1848, 1872 and 1875 were purely environmental in scope, leaving unaddressed and undisturbed underlying social and economic structures; indeed, this legislation coincided with a tightening of social control over the poor through the poor law abolition of outdoor relief and worsening conditions in workhouses to serve as a deterrent against their utilization. Significantly, then, the role of the Victorian public health physician was broad but compatible with the functions of the state.

The second or *preventive* phase of public health engagement began in the 1870s. The germ theory of disease, and scientific advances in bacteriology permitting the identification of the specific organisms causing disease, led to a redefinition of the type of intervention appropriate for public health. As Lewis points out,[2] once it was realized that dirt *per se* did not cause infectious disease, the mandate of public health physicians narrowed, no longer vesting authority to deal with all aspects of environmental sanitation, housing and poverty as the means to reduce disease. The emphasis switched to germs, and therefore to the susceptibility of the individual. This led to personal preventive services such as immunization and family planning, and to the innovative or extended provision of maternity services, infant welfare centres, health visitors, pasteurized milk stations and school medical and nursing services, together with the health education of the individual recipients of these services. Public health physicians adjusted to work within this narrowed remit and justified their endeavours as 'applied physiology'. The traditional role of 'community watchdog' was effectively ceded at this juncture to a new generation of pressure groups (e.g. the Committee Against Malnutrition, the National Unemployed Workers' Movement). The endeavours of such groups and other social investigators provided the foundations upon which the academic discipline of social medicine was built in the 1940s. The Institute of Social Medicine was founded in 1942 at Oxford, with John Ryle as its first professor. He defined social medicine as 'clinical medicine activated in its aetiological inquiries by social conscience as well as scientific interest' (quoted by Lewis[3]). However, in its efforts to attain academic credibility, social medicine emphasized its links with clinical medicine and epidemiology at the expense of those with social science and health policy, and a damaging rift developed between the academic specialists on the one hand, and the service providers and practitioners of public health medicine on the other.

Meanwhile the discovery of sulphonamide antibiotics and insulin heralded the third or *therapeutic* phase of public health, dating from the 1930s. The beginning of this era coincided with the apparent demise of infectious disease and the development of organized medical treatment services. Scientific and medical advances occurred rapidly and the concept of the 'magic bullet' gained credence. When the National Health Service (NHS) was introduced in 1948 it was strongly oriented toward hospital treatment, in keeping with the prevailing orthodoxy that future improvements in health would be accomplished primarily through medical means. Public health physicians, remaining within local authorities, became 'administrators with medical knowledge', whose function was to manage and coordinate the hospital and non-hospital 'community' services; but they had neither the opportunity nor any explicit mandate to investigate the health status of their populations and to plan services accordingly.

The concept of the community physician had its antecedents in both the schism between academic specialists and providers/practitioners and the NHS reorganization of 1974. The community physician was to be responsible for 'community diagnosis' and for providing 'the intelligence necessary for the efficient and effective administration of the health services'.[4] The main emphasis was on prevention through the individual, based on a multicausal epidemiological approach and close liaison with clinical medicine. Public health departments were to come under health authority control, thus separating the community physician from environmental health and social work services. With the replacement of consensus by line management under the rubric of enhanced individual accountability in 1983, however, it seemed that the community physician's general task of rationalizing resource allocation might progressively be lost to professional managers.

The 1970s also saw growing scepticism about the medical model of health. Escalating medical costs were not being matched by corresponding improvements in health status. McKeown showed that the decline in mortality and morbidity from infectious disease occurred because of limitations in family size, an increase in food supplies and a healthier physical environment, with specific preventive and therapeutic measures contributing only minimally.[5] The highly influential 'Lalonde Report' released by the Canadian Government in 1974 openly acknowledged that health services are only one—and not the most important—factor in determining health status, stressing the contributions of human biology, environment and lifestyle.[6] In the wake of an increasingly forthright rejection of the ideology which had dominated the therapeutic phase of the old public health, there developed the beginnings of the *new public health.*

The new public health

Public health has been often and variously defined of late, examples including:

> The science and art of preventing disease, prolonging life and promoting health through organized efforts of society (p. 1).[7]
>
> The organized application of resources to achieve the greatest health for the greatest number (p. 8).[8]
>
> What we, as a society, do to assure the conditions for people to be healthy. This requires that continuing and emerging threats to the health of the public be successfully countered. These threats include immediate crises, such as the AIDS epidemic; evolving problems, such

> as the ageing of our population; and the toxic by-products of a modern economy, transmitted through air, water, soil or food (p. 19).[9]

What is 'new' is the rediscovery that influences on health are multifaceted and include economic, environmental, ecological, political and behavioural components, as well as the provision of, and equitable access to, medical services. The multisectoral potential for improving health has thereby been recognized, so that a plurality of agents—medical and non-medical professionals, voluntary and community workers, single-issue groups, and so on—are implicated in the active fostering and maintaining of health. The concept of public health has expanded too, into a philosophy that posits health as a universal and pre-eminent goal; and this (largely implicit) evaluation promises to widen the legitimate scope of public health to scrutinize the activities of the food and tobacco industries, energy, defence, transport and the media, and the departments and policies of national governments. Vested interests threatening the public health may need to be exposed and/or collaboratively enjoined to alter their practices. Every individual and corporate body potentially influences health.

How, then, is the role of the contemporary public health physician in Britain best understood? And what is the relation of philosophy to practice as new public health threatens to displace old? In responding it is convenient to consider in turn the public health physician as *health strategist*, *health promoter*, *health expert*, *health adviser*, and *health bureaucrat*.

Health strategist

Public health physicians, as opposed to most other health activists, work within the health service. While recognizing that medical services are but one discrete influence on promoting health, therefore, they have a key role in the strategic and rational allocation of resources. According to the 'Acheson Report' in 1988,[7] a central task of the Director of Public Health (DPH) was 'to provide epidemiological advice to the District General Manager and District Health Authority on the setting of priorities, planning of services and evaluation of outcomes'. The concept of health strategist therefore incorporates that of specialist adviser, administrator and coordinator. The advice offered should be rationalized towards the best allocation of resources and is to be based on the commissioning and analysis of epidemiological studies.

Clearly the criteria dictating what is 'best' or 'rational' are variable, political and under constant negotiation: they may, for example, involve considerations of equity, equality, comprehensiveness, cost effectiveness and political expediency. Klein has contended that priorities tend to emerge in practice from pluralistic bargaining between different lobbies, modified by shifting political judgements made in the light of changing pressures.[10] He argues that while no technological fix, scientific method or philosophical prescription exists for determining priorities, the debate can be further rationalized by expanding the plurality of participating voices, that is, by creating a situation in which there is open and accessible dialogue during which arguments can be tested against the evidence and conflicts between different values or preferences explored. He seeks to direct attention to the *structure* of decision making at all levels of organization—from the Department of Health to purchasing authorities to clinicians—and the nature of the interrelationships between these different levels. Public health physicians are organizationally situated and theoretically charged to help make this decision-making process explicit and to ensure that open and comprehensive dialogue does occur. The public must be involved in such dialogue, not only to provide accountability for the spending of public money, but also as a precondition for generating a truly multisectoral enterprise.

In this vein, the Oregon Health Plan has been an innovative enterprise; it was initiated by primary care physicians to enable local citizens to decide collectively how their health care should be financed, and who, and most importantly what, should be covered by such a plan.[11] Crucially, there was a consensus at the outset that the objective of the plan was to 'improve, maintain or restore health', and that while cost reduction and improved access to medical services might be means to this end they were not ends in themselves. While many serious and valid criticisms have been made of the methods used,[12,13] the project was nevertheless a genuine attempt to involve the public, recognized advocacy and other health care interest groups as well as health care professionals, and has since entered the state legislature.

Similar projects were initiated soon after in Solihull, City and Hackney, Mid-Essex, Oxfordshire, Southampton and South West Hampshire and Wandsworth.[14] Problems encountered included the absence of information to guide priority setting, the difficulty of meaningfully comparing different services, and the methodological implications of the wording of questions and the effect on results of providing respondents with information about local health needs and outcomes. It has also been pointed out that most local voices have so far had little significant impact on decision makers, and indeed that purchasers are not penalized in any way if they fail to consult and listen to the public, thus reducing the incentive for them to do so. The role of the public health departments in encouraging this approach to community participation is vital. This once again emphasizes the public health physician's role of coordinator between the health authority, general practitioners (GPs), consultants, social services, environmental health, health promotion units and the local community.

Health promoter

This refers to the public health remit to 'develop and evaluate policy on prevention, health promotion and health services....' (p. 28).[7] It includes activities such as immunization, screening, family planning and the provision of health information.

Health promotion and disease prevention also became a formal responsibility for GPs for the first time with the new GP contract of 1990. Health promotion with individual patients by GPs, and with whole populations by public health physicians, must develop as integrated and complementary approaches, ultimately under the rubric of primary health care. GPs target specific high-risk individuals within the population, but an effective public health strategy for disease prevention must be targeted towards the entire population if risk is widely diffused throughout it, as it is for cardiovascular disease for example. The aim is to shift the whole distribution of risk factors and exposures in a favourable direction. This results in what Rose has called the *prevention paradox*, namely that while the overall benefit to each individual in adopting a behaviour which slightly lowers risk is by definition small (e.g. a 2 or 3 nm Hg reduction in diastolic blood pressure), the effect on the whole population burden of disease will be large.[15] This paradox has unfortunate implications for health education directed at persuading the population to modify its behaviour. Furthermore, since the prevalence of individuals at high risk depends on the mean value of risk, society as a whole may be judged responsible for these individuals; and indeed the problems of the conspicuous minority may be solvable only when society as a whole is reformed. Rose's approach is a far cry from the *Health of the Nation* and governmental approaches, which still have difficulty coming to terms with social inequalities in health, recently preferring to focus on 'variations'.[16]

The population approach to prevention points beyond medicine and towards economic and social policy. Health promotion therefore also embraces health protest by legal, fiscal and political measures.

Health expert

The specialist in communicable disease and infection is a public health expert who fulfils a service function by undertaking "the surveillance and coordinated management of outbreaks of communicable disease and infection".[7] The Acheson inquiry was precipitated by the inadequate control of two such outbreaks in the mid-1980s, and the Report recommended an urgent revision of the law relating to infectious diseases. However, a subsequent paper has shown that there is still lack of clarity about the statutory responsibilities of local and health authorities, and has made several recommendations, including the assembly of new regional and sub-regional teams with colleagues from clinical medicine and microbiology.[17] The employment of some communicable disease consultants by hospital provider units has been interpreted by some authors as indicating the potential creation of an autonomous speciality, making generalist public health physicians more expendable.[18]

Health adviser

The independent advisory function of the old Medical Officer of Health (MOH) was seen as an integral part of the role. The MOH could not be dismissed without Ministerial consent, thus giving statutory support to his or her freedom to speak out against local vested interests operating against the public health. The 'Acheson Report' makes a distinction between advisory and advocacy functions, and explicitly rejects the latter: "We ... reject the view ... that public health doctors, employed in the public sector, have a duty or a right to advocate or pursue policies which they judge to be in the public interest independently of any line of accountability. In the extreme this would place them in a position above Parliament" (p. 32).[7] It contends that the supposed role of the MOH as an independent advocate for public health has been much misunderstood, and that "it did not confer some 'divine right' to ruffle political feathers by commenting with impunity on the public or political issues of the day ..." (p. 91, Annexe 6).[7]

The MOH presented his or her arguments to the Council who decided the matter, and thenceforth the duty of the MOH was to implement that decision. The 'Acheson Report' concludes that the same procedure is applicable today, and points to a Faculty of Community Medicine newsletter which suggests that instances where community physicians were disciplined or criticized for speaking out arose precisely when those physicians had not "pursued the professional point of view appropriately"[19] (e.g. by publicizing their opinions to the media without health authority approval). An earlier joint statement from the Faculty of Community Medicine and the Royal College of Physicians, however, states that "the primary responsibility (of community physicians) is to their patients, and they must be free to be critical of NHS management and policies where their professional judgement requires this".[20]

The post-1974 alignment of public health departments within the health authority, and the more recent corporate responsibility resulting from the executive membership of DPHs in the health authorities, has been deemed a necessary trade-off of independence for influence.[21] The significance of this with regard to the DPH's annual report has elicited some debate.[18,22] On balance, it may be that the influence gained by working within the system is greater than would have accrued had public health physicians stayed on the outside in the name of free speech. This may be especially so given the heightened public and media awareness of public health risks in recent years, epitomized by the growing alarm at environmental issues, the political viability of the green movement in some European countries, and the advent of 'popular epidemiology' (e.g. litigation initiated by the community against industries perceived to be causing ill-health, based on the lay collection of data about exposure and symptomatology).[23,24] This is not necessarily to affirm the Acheson stance, but merely to point out that a tactical willingness to exert influence at the centre may have a greater return than a principled activism at the periphery. The point remains that the primary allegiance of the public health physician must be to his or her population and not to the health service *per se*.

The wider concept of advocacy as a means of empowering individuals has been less well debated until recently. Ashton still seems to represent a minority when he suggests that "the new public is about giving away knowledge, power and skills; it is about enabling individuals and communities to take control of their own health.... In the new public health, professionals should be on tap, not on top."[25] Examples of exceptions include the involvement of the Dublin public health department in the community mothers' programme, based on the Bristol early childhood development programme; this uses specially trained experienced volunteer mothers to support deprived first-time mothers during the initial year of the child's life.[26] The study showed that, while difficulties in evaluation remain, the study mothers and children did significantly better in a variety of outcome measures than did the randomized control mothers and children. Its authors conclude that the empowerment of the new mother from the community, and the sharing of experience rather than the transmission of advice, significantly improves health outcome and raises the self-esteem and confidence of the new mother in her role as a parent. They point out that this philosophy accords with the Alma Ata approach to community-based health care.[27] Similar projects have also been started in Nottingham and Tilbury.[28] The health advocacy schemes for women from ethnic minority groups using maternity services, as in City and Hackney, are based on a similar philosophy. Both initiatives have met with some professional hostility—from physicians, midwives and health visitors[29]—but support has been forthcoming from others who see advocacy projects as complementary to their profession.[30,31] In an ideal world each individual would be sufficiently skilled to act as his or her own advocate, but in its absence the socially disadvantaged with correspondingly poor health status may continue to benefit from additional support.

Health bureaucrat

While bureaucracy is not a function of public health medicine *per se*, the involvement of most of its practitioners in the NHS, it has been argued, amounts to an effective assimilation in this role.[18,32] One paper has suggested that production of the DPH's annual report may be too laborious and time-consuming to justify its putative use in purchasing decisions, and that there may be other more effective ways of achieving the desired goal.[32] It provocatively commends the option of not producing a report at all for some years providing this is an informed and positive decision. Another paper emphasizes that public health physicians must shed the baggage of involvement in the actual day-to-day preparation of corporate contracts and the negotiation process, leaving this to managers.[33] More controversially, a self-proclaimed 'heretical' paper has warned that public health physicians are in danger of being seduced into over-involvement in administration, and that their energies are thus being diverted away from 'real' health improving activities: they may become mere 'technical assistants' to purchasing teams in health authorities.[18] The public health role is thereby being diminished to needs assessment, which not only makes the public health specialist potentially expendable, replaceable by managers, but represents a goal displacement from improving health to improving health services. This, the authors conclude, is inimical to a conception of public health founded in McKeown's hypothesis that public health crucially needs to evaluate the effectiveness of medical services, thus justifying the public health interest in the purchasing role.[34,35]

Beaglehole and Bonita too stress the effects of public health physicians' insinuation into the managerial culture associated with the internal market: "it appears that assessment of the health of the population is focusing on health care needs, and promoting health is becoming equated with 'purchasing for health gains', a process which down plays the role of the social and economic determinants of health".[36] DPHs, they add, are increasingly involved in the organization of medical services, to the detriment of broader public health activities.

Conclusion

This paper began with a short characterization of the 'sanitary', 'preventive' and 'therapeutic' phases of the old public health in Britain, spanning nearly a century and a half and being superseded by an identifiably new public health only slowly and haltingly since the 1970s. Five aspects of the evolving and still contested role of the new public health physician were then noted, namely, 'health strategist', 'health promoter', 'health expert', 'health adviser' and 'health bureaucrat'. A brief inspection of each of these clusters of tasks, and of the continuing and politically charged debates around how they are to be interpreted, revealed considerable dissensus in the public health community. It was apparent too that there exist seemingly intractable tensions, and perhaps contradictions, within and between clusters of tasks, a recipe for acute role strain.

Inevitably the role of the new public health physician is compromised. "The important public health function, to promote and maintain the health of the nation, cannot be achieved through purchasing alone because the major determinants of health lie outside the health services; public health medicine must continue to focus attention on these social, economic and political issues."[36] According to what we shall here call the *location paradox*, the public health physician is employed within a health care system in which, unexceptionally, there is a commitment to the health of individuals rather than populations, and a lack of receptiveness to the now compelling evidence that the health of populations and unequal distribution of disease reflect broader political and structural features of British society. This individualistic approach is likely to be consolidated with the current switch to 'primary care led purchasing'.[37] Moreover, public health physicians firmly located 'inside' the health care system are arguably deterred by their management-oriented roles and by inter-professional rules of procedure and conduct from the *effective* pursuit of precisely that political and structural change 'outside' the system which is a precondition for improved public health and reduced health inequality.[24] Nor has government—at least, up to the 1997 general election—generally been willing to support potentially significant local initiatives by national action; and the radical reduction of funding for the Health Education Authority for England in 1994 sent clear signals. However, as mentioned earlier, had public health physicians been further removed from health service decision making, outsiders rather than insiders, they may well had have even less influence. It seems that the new public health physician, possessed of an effective agenda, has no effective location to implement it.

It does not follow from the location paradox that public health physicians cannot effect change. In a recent paper three types of change are distinguished in relation to health promotion: *operational*, *political* and *structural*.[38] Operational change, ranging from health education and prevention programmes to more accessible and user-friendly medical services, can be negotiated from within the health care system. Political change cannot be accomplished from within the health care system, but rather requires government support and national action, for example, legislative or fiscal innovation. Structural change, similarly, is beyond the compass of those within the health care system, requiring action from without; in the case of structural change, however, even government action may be relatively ineffective in the face of deep and enduring social structures, for example, around class, gender and ethnicity. It may lie within public health physicians' sphere of influence to negotiate operational change, but even the most ardent and radical can be little more than catalysts for the kinds of political and structural change required by a new public health geared to emulating the scale of accomplishment of the sanitary phase of the old public health. Public health is not a means for transforming contemporary society.[39,40] If the quest for such change is serious, however, it must be acknowledged by public health physicians that the most likely agents may be lay activists with potential to mobilize the public, namely, given the loss of salience of the old class-based politics, members of salient single- or multi-issue pressure groups of social movements. The extent of their willingness, and capacity, to explore alliances here might be considered a measure of the perceived seriousness of their quest.

References

1. Kickbusch I. Health promotion strategies for action. *Can J Public Health* 1986; 77:321–26.
2. Lewis J. The origins and development of public health in the UK. In: Holland W, editor. *The Oxford textbook of public health.* Vol. 1. Oxford: Oxford University Press; 1991.
3. Lewis J. *What price community medicine?* Brighton: Wheatsheaf Books; 1986.
4. Morris J. Tomorrow's community physician. *Lancet* 1969; 11:811.
5. McKeown T. *The role of medicine—dream, mirage or nemesis.* London: Nuffield Provincial Hospitals Trust; 1976.
6. Lalonde M. *A new perspective on the health of Canadians.* Ottawa: Government of Canada; 1974.
7. Department of Health. *Public health in England: the report of the Committee of Inquiry into the Future Development of the Public Health Function (Acheson Report).* London: HMSO; 1988.
8. Brotherston, quoted in Draper P, editor. *Health through public policy: the greening of public health.* London: Green Print; 1991.
9. Institute of Medicine. *The future of public health.* Washington, DC: National Academy Press; 1988.
10. Klein R. Dimensions of rationing: who should do what? *BMJ* 1993; 307:309–11.
11. Kitzhaber J. Prioritizing health services in an era of limits: the Oregon experience. *BMJ* 1993; 307:373–7.

12. Oregon Health Services Commission. Prioritization of Health Services—*A report to the governor and legislature*. Oregon: Health Services Commission; 1991.
13. Geller R, Cooper R. On the Oregon trail in Solihull. *Public Health Physician* 1993; 4:3–4.
14. Ham C. Priority setting in the NHS: reports from six districts. *BMJ* 1993; 307:435–38.
15. Rose G. *The strategy of preventive medicine*. Oxford: Oxford University Press; 1992.
16. Secretary of State for Health. *The health of the nation*. London: HMSO; 1991.
17. O'Brien J, O'Brien S, Geddes A, Heap B, Mayon-White R. Tempting fate: control of communicable disease in England. 1993; 306:1461–64.
18. Whitty P, Jones I. Public health heresy: a challenge to the purchasing orthodoxy. *BMJ* 1992; 304:1039–41.
19. Rue R. The community physician. *Newsletter of the Faculty of Community Medicine* 1987; 11.
20. Faculty of Community Medicine and Royal College of Physicians. Joint Statement: Health service management and the community physician. *Lancet* 1985; 291:1144.
21. Gatherer A. Being executive. *Public Health Physician* 1991; 2:2.
22. Watt I, Ibbotson S, Nicholson C. Annual Reports of Directors of Public Health. *BMJ* 1993; 306:1282–83.
23. Popay J. Involving local people in health gain: the contribution of lay epidemiology. *HFA/2000 News* 1992; 19:5–6.
24. Scambler G, Goraya A. Movements for change: the new public health agenda. *Critical Public Health* 1994; 5:4–10.
25. Ashton J. Acheson—a missed opportunity for new public health. *BMJ* 1988; 296:231–32.
26. Johnson Z, Howell F, Molloy B. Community mothers programme: a randomized controlled trial of non-professional intervention in parenting. *BMJ* 1993; 306:1449–52.
27. *Lancet*. Declaration of Alma Ata. *Lancet* 1978; Nov: 111040–41.
28. Jackson C. Community mothers: trick or treat? *Health Visitor* 1992; 65:199–201.
29. Ni Brolchain C, Lawton D. Child development programme challenged? *Health Visitor* 1991; 64; 92.
30. Suppiah C. No substitute. *Health Visitor* 1991; 64:171.
31. Ashdown S. Deluded health visitors. *Health Visitor* 1991; 64:171.
32. Shanks J. The Annual Report—monstre sacre? *Public Health Physician* 1991; 4:1.
33. Eskin F. Contracting—key role or baggage? *Public Health Physician* 1991; 4:1.
34. Bhopal R. Public health medicine and purchasing health care. *BMJ* 1993; 306:381–82.
35. Cochrane A. *Effectiveness and efficiency: random reflections on health services*. London: Nuffield Provincial Hospital Trust; 1972.
36. Beaglehole R, Bonita R. *Public health at the crossroads: achievements and prospects*. Cambridge: Cambridge University Press; 1997.
37. Iliffe S. The retreat from equity: implications of the shift towards a primary-care led NHS. *Critical Public Health* 1995; 6:36–42.
38. Scambler G, Scambler A. Social change and health promotion among women sex workers in London. *Health Promotion Int* 1995; 10:17–24.
39. Hamlin C. State medicine in Great Britain. In: Porter D, editor. *The history of public health and the modern state*. Amsterdam: Editions Rodopi BV; 1994.
40. Scally G. Public health medicine in a new era. *Soc Sci Med* 1996; 42:777–80.

[4]

Health promotion development in Europe: achievements and challenges

E. ZIGLIO[1], S. HAGARD[2] and J. GRIFFITHS[3]
[1]*World Health Organization Regional Office for Europe in Copenhagen, Copenhagen, Denmark,* [2]*London School of Hygiene and Tropical Medicine, London, UK and* [3]*Health Promotion Wales, Cardiff, UK*

INTRODUCTION

Fifteen years ago, a set of possible concepts and principles for health promotion was put forward for discussion by the WHO Regional Office for Europe WHO (WHO, 1984). Those concepts and principles informed and underpinned the Ottawa Charter 2 years later (WHO, 1986) and have provided the basis for the many health promotion innovations emanating from Europe ever since. These have included projects, e.g. Healthy Cities, Health Promoting Schools, Health Promoting Hospitals and, more recently, the Investment for Health approach to implementing health promotion. All have had their origins in the European Region (Ashton, 1992; WHO, 1991; WHO, 1992; WHO, 1994b; WHO, 1996b; WHO-EC-CE, 1992; WHO-EC-CE, 1997).

However, there is evidence that the overall impact of these innovations has been relatively limited in the region [see, e.g. (De Leeuw, 1989; Tsouros, 1990; Grossman and Scala, 1993; Jensen and Schnack, 1994; Sidell *et al.*, 1997; Pelikan *et al.*, 1998; Ziglio, 1998)]. At the same time, the European Region has changed dramatically since the endorsement of the Ottawa Charter—geopolitically, economically and in terms of social development—with new challenges emerging all the time (Ziglio, 1993; Ziglio, 1998).

In this light, rather than give an overview of health promotion in Europe, this paper takes a developmental approach to European innovations in health promotion, in the context of the remarkable changes which have been transforming European society. It considers the kind of health promotion strategy likely to be most effective in Europe in the future and concludes that it is vital to reassert the centrality of health to human and social development. This implies revisiting approaches to sustaining and improving health, and recognizing, implementing and sustaining effective measures. The authors emphasize the importance of an intense focus:

- on the key underlying processes which create health; and
- on the systems and capabilities that need to be developed to ensure effective, sustainable action.

TAKING STOCK OF PROGRESS—THE OVERALL PICTURE

Since the Ottawa Charter, much health promotion activity has taken place and the practice of health promotion within a number of countries has developed considerably. The implementation of a wide range of health promotion initiatives has generated much collective experience within Europe and added considerably to both knowledge and progressive change. Specific segments of the population, e.g. older people, young people, women, migrants, disabled and chronically ill people, have been involved in a variety of activities aimed at improving or gaining more control over their health (WHO, 1998b). Programmes and projects have been conducted in a variety of regional and social settings, e.g. cities, schools, workplaces and health care organizations.

At the same time, the European Union (EU) —comprising 15 member states with a combined population of ~300m, and having 10 applicant countries in various stages of membership negotiation—has steadily enlarged its role in public health in the 1990s, through the Treaties of Maastricht and Amsterdam. Some international projects, e.g. the WHO/Council of Europe/EU (European Commission) 'Health Promoting Schools', have provided for health promotion development to be systematically planned on a multi-country basis, implemented with strong sharing of experience, and monitored, evaluated and developed step by step. In their turn, such projects have helped to stimulate moves in some countries towards a more strategic approach to programme development and a more ecological approach to health through intersectoral action and community development at the local level (WHO-EC-CE, 1992; WHO-EC-CE, 1997; WHO-EC-CE, 1998).

In the last few years, some European countries (e.g. Switzerland, Austria, Estonia) have been setting up Health Promotion Foundations (WHO-HEA, 1998). These foundations have provided funding for organizations and NGOs to develop programmes of health promotion that addressed specific issues related to lifestyle and behavioural factors. These programmes have provided valuable contributions to climate building and the dissemination of health promotion thinking. Such development still has to prove, however, to what extent it can tackle the real health determinants prevalent in European countries today. So, although the foundations are instrumental in sustaining many of the organizations involved in health promotion in countries, they may lack the power to steer the policy agenda towards major issues related to the social and economic determinants of health (e.g. inequities, healthy public policies). Unless this strategic approach to health promotion is present in foundation-funded programmes, their impact and scope may be rather limited. An effective approach might be to use foundations to move the thinking of organizations by issuing terms of reference demanding that programmes are created to address health determinants relevant to the country/region the programme will be launched in. For foundations to operate effectively they need to be part of an overall infrastructure where the three functions of health promotion (enabling, mediating and advocating) are properly developed. This is a condition which is still rarely met in Europe and elsewhere.

However, in a number of countries, health promotion has been reduced to a service function —to be purchased, rather than planned as a collective good crucial to human development (Beauchamp, 1997; WHO-HEA, 1998). The implications of this for health promotion at a population level can be considerable. The reasoning behind the move to commissioning in health care is readily understood. Its main intention is to clarify the relations between inputs and outcomes, and to establish and manage accountability for the use of resources, thus allowing contracts for specific clinical or supporting services to be drawn up, costed and agreed. However, applying this approach to health promotion exposes a number of weaknesses, as most of its work is not susceptible to slicing into discrete packages and managing in this way. In particular, being treated as a 'service' to be bought—more often than not from providers operating wholly within health care—fails to recognize that the promotion of health cannot be left to the health sector alone.

It is also likely that the commissioning process reduces the opportunities for partnership and alliance building. By setting tightly defined outcome measures, against which success or failure are measured, health promotion activity can be reduced to an easily deliverable, easily measurable set of activities which do little to resolve the underlying causes of poor health and which may even increase rather than reduce inequality in health. A further potential danger comes from having many locally based commissioners, all with their own priorities and programmes. This can result in a fragmented approach, the duplication of effort and the lack of a co-ordinated strategy at a national level.

While the concept of accountability—in which the providers are accountable for the service they provide and the commissioners are accountable for commissioning the most appropriate service —is critical to the appropriate use of resources, the case of health promotion poses the following important questions which need to be answered.

- Are the activities being commissioned the most appropriate activities?
- Will these activities lead to an improvement in health at the population level?
- Is the commissioning based on democratic principles?

- Are the determinants of health being addressed through the commissioning process?
- Is the commissioning process taking place in the context of long-term investment for health?

If the answer to each of these questions is 'yes', then the commissioning of health promotion is a process which could result in major health benefits. If, however, the answer to one or more of the questions is 'no', then the commissioning process may be acting detrimentally to the health and well-being of individuals, and of society as a whole. In the last decade these questions have been the subject of debate in many European countries.

Determinants of health: knowledge and action

Since the Ottawa Charter our knowledge of health determinants has been increasing rapidly. Our understanding of the importance of socio-economic resources has expanded (McKeown, 1976; Fitzpatrick, 1982; Blane *et al.*, 1993; Evans *et al.*, 1994; WHO, 1995a; Blanc *et al.*, 1996; Wilkinson, 1996; Bartley *et al.*, 1997; WHO, 1998a). The role of social and cultural resources, e.g. social networks, social capital, social integration and cohesion, and the interplay of these assets with psychological resources for coping with change is beginning to be more widely recognized. However, the balance of research effort is still tilted towards disease rather than health creation or salutogenesis (Badura and Kickbusch, 1991). There is no doubt that we still need to learn much more about the relationships between different determinants and how to measure these, and about the methodologies that address the complexities of social system change. By contrast there has been a huge plethora of work on lifestyles that has been developed in association with the predominant mode of action, which is still about individual behaviour (Whitehead *et al.*, 1998). However, while the messages of lifestyle and personal behaviour have been taken on board by much of the population, and there is correspondingly greater awareness of the need for personal responsibility for health, the ability of many people to act upon this knowledge and understanding is generally severely limited by the absence of a conducive cultural, social and economic environment.

Oversimplified approaches

Despite an apparent widespread acceptance of a socio-ecological model of health amongst people working in health promotion, most health promotion activity has continued to be issue based or else has focussed on only one determinant at a time. Rhetoric has largely failed to become reality. Thus, much of the change that has actually happened has been first-order change, involving relatively small-scale and minor adjustments, and without any major impact on the determinants of health or policy development (WHO, 1998c). Second-order change, which involves a paradigmatic shift leading to new structures, processes actions and outcomes, has barely begun to happen. It will not happen until the starting point for action is the creation of health, not an issue or problem, a disease or death, but health itself. Nor can it happen until it is accepted that social systems are complex and interwoven, and their interconnections are crucial to the creation of health.

Infrastructure deficits

Correspondingly, while the multifaceted concept of health underpinning the Ottawa Charter is much more in keeping with people's experience and understanding in their everyday lives, such a holistic approach is still not reflected in institutional structures, organizational decision-making and policy actions. The latter continue to be mainly issue or sector based, rather than focused on the complex inter-relationships among sectors. Many programmes have not been properly supported by appropriate funding and infrastructures (WHO-HEA, 1998). There remains an almost universal failure to operationalize those aspects that emphasize health as a social and collective good.

Lack of healthy public policies

This explains the difficulty of finding outstanding examples of healthy public policy—a principal objective of the Ottawa Charter and target 13 of the HFA strategy for Europe (WHO, 1991a; WHO, 1991b). Target 13 aims to support the development of healthy public policies to promote and sustain health in the European Member States of WHO. In order to achieve this target, intersectoral policies and health promotion programmes should be in place at both national and sub-national levels of policy-making and

Box 1: Recent developments in Healthy Public Policy.

Health promotion strategies need to be based on the firm and stable foundation provided by healthy public policy. It is encouraging to see that such developments are beginning to occur with the following examples drawn from newly published public health documents in the UK.

- 'At the local level, each of the determinants of health affected by public policy—environment, housing, access to leisure, health and social care, education and other services—should be considered together rather than as separate policies, taking into account their potential impact on health. One way of achieving this would be the introduction of Health Impact Assessment, ... All policies impact on people's lives, some to a greater extent and with more immediacy than others. The health experiences of a population at national or local level, can reflect the impact of such policies, ... Health Impact Assessment is designed to be supportive but critical, and to inform the policy-making process'.
- 'Health improvement and narrowing of health inequalities between social groups is likely to be achieved primarily by economic, social environmental and public health policy rather than by medical or other personal health care services'.
  (Better Health, Better Wales; Welsh Office, Cardiff, 1998)
- 'A fresh approach is necessary—a public health strategy which addresses the root causes of our health problems. Improving lifestyles must continue to be rigorously tackled, but within a framework which recognizes, and focuses on, the underlying social, economic and environmental circumstances which influence health'.
  (Working Together for a Healthier Scotland; The Stationery Office, Edinburgh, 1998)
- 'Tackling inequalities generally is the best means of tackling health inequalities in particular'.
- 'The national contract recognizes that the Government can create the climate for our health to be improved. It pledges to deliver key economic and social policies. It places requirements on local services to make progress in improving the public's health.'
- 'The Government and national players can, ... Ensure that policy-making across Government takes full account of health and is well informed by research and the best expertise available.'
- 'The Government has already taken two key steps to ensure that health is a central theme of Government policy.
- First, for the first time ever in England the Government has appointed a Minister for Public Health to ensure coordination of health policy across Government, not just in the Department of Health. The Government has set up a dedicated Cabinet Committee of Ministers from 12 different departments, to drive the policy across Government.
- Second, the Government will apply health impact assessments to its relevant key policies, so that when they are being developed and implemented, the consequences of those policies for our health is considered. The Department of Health has already published guidance, called *Policy Appraisal and Health*, and if necessary this guidance will be revised in the light of experience.'
  (Our Healthier Nation, A Contract for Health; HMSO, London 1998)

administration. Commitment to healthy public policy varies between member states. In this respect, the development in the UK is very interesting and worth noting (see Box 1). Without doubt, in many countries there has been a growing awareness that the promotion and maintenance of people's health cannot depend upon the health care sector alone. This awareness, however, has not corresponded with systematic action and reviews of the legislative, financial, organizational, managerial and educational potentials necessary for a structured approach to health promotion. When progress has been made, it has often been fragmentary and half-hearted (WHO, 1998c).

Legislative, financial, managerial, educational and administrative support to health promotion should have been strengthened, and investment for health increased, far more than has been happening in the majority of European countries

(WHO-HEA, 1996; WHO-HEA, 1998). Participatory practices could have been more widely introduced at country, regional and local level to involve people in policy-making, implementation and evaluation (WHO, 1998c).

In Europe, there is still a great awareness deficit among policy-makers of the impact of their policies on health, though the European Union has begun to introduce measures to subject policy initiatives in other fields to health impact assessment (EC, 1997). This needs to be extended and widely adopted throughout Europe. The opportunities for investment for health, the social benefits of having strong health promotion infrastructures, and the funding and supportive mechanisms for promoting health, have not yet found their correct and necessarily high position in the debate and policy-making of most European countries.

Summary of trends

Reports from member states and specific country surveys carried out by the Health Promotion and Investment Programme of WHO/EURO (WHO, 1996a; WHO, 1996b; WHO, 1996c; WHO, 1996d; WHO, 1998a; WHO, 1998b; WHO, 1998c) reveal both negative and positive developmental trends in progress towards a structured approach to health promotion. Box 2 summarizes the main positive and negative developmental trends of the 1990s.

SUSTAINING THE VISION BUT REVISITING THE MEANS

Social and political difficulties

Since the early 1990s, the promotion of health and adoption of healthy lifestyles have often been hampered by social and political difficulties in many European countries. Drastic reduction of social welfare, diminished scope of social policy, economic scarcity and fiscal upheaval risk eroding progress even further in many member states in both western and eastern Europe. In many instances, countries' economic and political priorities are often inconsistent with, and even militate against, progress towards the achievement of health promotion objectives. The evidence demonstrates that in Europe the development of healthy public policy remains an elusive HFA target.

Ottawa Charter principles

The principles underlying the Ottawa Charter still stand. However, this review points to the need to revisit the means by which its vision of health promotion can be realized, especially in view of the many changes which have occurred in Europe in the last decade. On one hand, the philosophy underpinning the Ottawa Charter has come to be accepted more widely, which indicates a gradual change in consciousness. For example, the European Charter on Environment and Health, in emphasizing the relationships between health, well-being and the environment, explicitly identifies the need for governmental and public action at all levels in the interest of health (WHO, 1994c). Its principles, priorities and strategic elements also draw attention to the relationship between social and economic development, health and well-being. The Charter advocates that a higher priority should be given to individual and community health rather than to a simple definition of economic growth. It also advocates research to support policy development. The Charter has led to a strong implementation process in the majority of European Region member states. Similarly, Agenda 21 also underlines that development must be equitable in order to be sustainable, and needs to be intersectoral with a recognition of community interdependencies. Agenda 21 has been widely taken up at a local level in the European Region.

Hastening policy change

On the other hand, this growing consensus on values has been inadequately reflected in policy development. This is not altogether surprising as it is well known that radical change and shifts in policy take upwards of 20 years. Transformation is dependent on a change in consciousness, a paradigm shift. To understand how such change is to be brought about, we need to focus on how we can encourage people to develop new ways of working, and design processes and infrastructures able to operationalize the broad vision of health promotion. This requires a shift in emphasis to the policy level, aiming to establish health promotion as central to human development. The challenge is to demonstrate convincingly to policy-makers that health and development are related in a virtuous circle, just as Marmot has argued in the case of work and health (Marmot, 1998). Health leads to development and development leads to health.

Box 2: Developmental trends in public policy in the 1990s.

POSITIVE TRENDS

- There is an increasing awareness of the need to develop a modern health promotion strategy in keeping with the concepts and principles of the Ottawa Charter and HFA policy.
- There is more interest and action in member states in developing settings-based health promotion programmes. Many countries are investing in intersectoral co-operation between the education and health sectors with the aim of establishing health-promoting schools. Activities in the workplace and health care settings are also on an upward trend throughout the European Region.
- There are a growing number of health promotion initiatives by bodies outside the health sector, e.g. labour unions, education sector, voluntary organizations, self-help and consumer organizations, and industry.

NEGATIVE TRENDS

- The role given to health promotion in health care reform processes has been minor or insignificant in many member states.
- The budget allocated to, and utilized specifically for, health promotion is far too small. On average it is much less than 1% of the health budget of member states—far too little for sustainable action.
- In the great majority of member states, institutional arrangements for health promotion policy development and implementation are very weak or inappropriate. Some countries have established intersectoral and interministerial arrangements which could be highly instrumental for creating the appropriate policy development infrastructure for healthy public policy. However, in practice such arrangements have produced only limited progress, mainly because their mandates have not been clearly designed, nor have they appropriate and sufficient technical assistance for their roles. Without a clear mandate for health promotion, they tend to remain at the periphery of government policy-making.
- Although several member states have established national and, in some instances, also subnational, centres or agencies for health promotion, most have a remit too limited to enable them to be strong players for implementing effective and sustainable action in the five action domains identified by the Ottawa Charter.
- Programmes are often *ad hoc*, issue based, and use health education as the main, if not the only, means of implementation. A comprehensive, credible, well-designed strategy and implementation measures, properly supported by financial, infrastructure and other development means, are absent in most member states—north, south, west or east in the European Region. Programmes tend to be weak or limited in scope and time, resources and staffing.
- Modern training in health promotion is available in only very few member states.

Investment for health

This implies a new dialogue with those who govern expenditure and policy throughout Europe, to engage their interest in the consequences of their actions for health and the corresponding implications for long-term social and economic development. Positive strategies can be adopted to reach an understanding of different value systems, find common ground and seek change (Levin and Ziglio, 1997; Ziglio, 1998). With well-planned, concerted and sustained action in many societies over many years, the principles and values that underpin health promotion might be progressively brought to the forefront of public policy. By this means, the determinants of health might be influenced in the long term, which could have a significant impact on the quality of life of European people and their ability to realize their full potential. That is a long-term social investment issue not a series of short-term financial tactics.

STRATEGIES TO ENCOURAGE INVESTMENT FOR HEALTH

Meaning of investment for health

The Jakarta Declaration states that current investment for health in many countries is inadequate and often ineffective. This statement is true for many, if not all, European countries. If health is truly regarded as a crucial social and individual resource, and therefore an investment, health promotion can be considered an investment strategy in social and economic terms, as well as for health. In that case the definition of health promotion needs to be extended thus:

the process of enabling individuals and communities (people) to increase control over the determinants of health and thereby (and to) improve their health.

[new words underlined, deleted words (in parentheses)]

It follows that health promotion strategies then become investment strategies, i.e. they are strategies which maintain and create health equitably and are integral to sustainable social, economic and human development policies. Three key questions then become the focus in the identification of appropriate policies for health (Kickbusch, 1997), in line with human rights.

- Where is health promoted and maintained in a given population?
- Which investment strategies produce the largest population health gains?
- Which investment strategies help reduce health inequalities?

Policy-makers and health planners in Europe do not yet place these questions at the centre of their thinking. (WHO, 1996d; Ziglio, 1998).

Influencing policies towards investment for health

To help policy-makers at different levels grasp this new paradigm, both conceptually and operationally, WHO/EURO has, since 1994, been undertaking a number of innovative demonstration projects which address these three questions. These are summarized in Box 3.

The outcomes of these projects show that there is great capacity for innovation and change at the various levels of decision-making: national, regional and local. The projects have identified both potential barriers to change and also the most effective strategies to achieve change. All confirm that individual health promotion programmes and projects can only achieve their health objectives if there are appropriate comprehensive strategies at the relevant policy level. Otherwise, they underperform or fail. A critical success factor is keeping in view the bigger picture, and the interconnections between policies, when dealing with individual decisions in particular areas.

As the Jakarta Conference declared, the development of knowledge and practical expertise in this area demands further work, conducted through partnerships at different levels of decision-making.

The main lessons learnt from these demonstration projects are shown in Box 4.

CONCLUSIONS: LESSONS LEARNT AND PRIORITIES FOR FUTURE ACTION

Within the European Region, health promotion will need to respond to the challenges and seize the opportunities of an increasingly dynamic and technologically changing continent, with its complex and growing international interdependencies. Health promotion efforts are essential and must be intensified. These require an integrated approach able to link with, and influence, social, economic and human development. There is a pressing need for ensuring that health promotion is positioned at the heart of (healthy) social and economic development.

The principle of intersectoral working, which is the basis for health promotion, is generally accepted in theory. In order to make progress in practice, there is a need to modernize institutional arrangements in both Western Europe and in the countries of Central and Eastern Europe. The current organizational, legislative and institutional mechanisms in the great majority of member states are not conducive to intersectoral action for the promotion and maintenance of health. There are few signs that countries are yet willing and committed to introducing the required structural innovation for systematic health promotion programmes and policies.

Political, economic, social, cultural, environmental, behavioural and biological factors are interwoven, and all play a role in determining and sustaining the health of a population. There is growing recognition that the ways in which

Box 3: Summary of innovative investment for health demonstration projects in the European Region of WHO.

AUDITING INVESTMENT FOR HEALTH OPPORTUNITIES

The Ministers of Health and the Presidents of the Parliaments of Slovenia and Hungary invited the Investment for Health Programme of the European Office of the World Health Organization to undertake an in-depth audit of the national approaches, and new opportunities to promoting the health of the citizens. The auditing was to include relevant aspects of policies and programmes, both public and non-governmental, along the strategic principles described above.

To deliver this service, it is crucial to have access to necessary descriptive and analytic data, and also to have access to the opinions of a variety of involved groups including consumer groups, health professionals, administrators, and political leaders at local and national level. This international auditing conducted by WHO/EURO aimed at providing the following outputs.

- A unique opportunity for mutual learning during the process.
- A consensus-building exercise within the country requesting the audit.
- A strategy for investment in health promotion designed to provide the Parliaments and Ministries of Health with recommended priorities for discussion, debate and action.
- An advocacy tool for the field of health promotion.
- Greatly enhanced European visibility for the countries requesting the audit in the field of health.

DEMONSTRATION PROJECTS ON INVESTMENT FOR HEALTH

So far, three demonstration projects have taken place: one in the autonomous provinces Trento and Bolzano, one in the autonomous Region of Valencia and one in Chemnitz, Saxony. These projects have been organized around local expertise supported by a WHO Project Team and additional resources when needed [see (WHO, 1994a; WHO, 1995b; WHO, 1996a; WHO, 1997)].

Box 4: Lessons learnt from European Investment for Health Demonstration Projects.

A strategy for health promotion in the European region needs to achieve the following.

(1) Further develop political and managerial understanding of the determinants of population health and foster a focus on health rather than engagement in health care issues.
(2) Affirm the place of health promotion at the heart of social, economic and human development, and influence such development to optimize health, equity and sustainability.
(3) Encourage the establishment of infrastructures that create the capacity for sustainable intersectoral action at national, regional, local and international levels.
(4) Develop tools to assist countries and regions to assess the potential for investment in key sectors and to identify the channels of accountability for population health in those sectors.
(5) Identify incentives which would encourage all the stakeholders who are related directly or indirectly to the promotion and maintenance of the quality of life of populations to come together to work for health.

society fosters the economy, regulates employment, provides education, assists its members in times of economic or other difficulties, sets up strategies to counteract poverty, crime and drug abuse, and stimulates equitable and sustainable economic and social development have a decisive impact on health.

The consequences for health of relative social disadvantage are now well documented. So too is the impact of sudden and huge economic shock

(Levin *et al.*, 1994; Makara, 1994; UNICEF, 1997). The demographic and mortality crises in the east of the region parallel those suffering famine or war. Between 1989 and 1994, both birth and marriage rates fell by up to 40% in several Eastern European countries. Over the same period, male death rates in Russia doubled from such causes as cardiovascular disease and violence, while life expectancy declined to below retirement age. Several of the worst affected countries have now stabilized, demonstrating the existence of social and cultural capital which has provided the resources and abilities to deal with the shock of economic change (Whitehead, 1994; Cornia and Paniccia, 1995; Cornia, 1997). This points to important lessons for investment considerations and approaches.

An innovative, collaborative approach is required to ensure that a wide range of health promotion initiatives, programmes and policies are planned and implemented in an integrated manner. It is increasingly confirmed through practical experience that 'Health promotion demands coordinated action by all concerned: by governments, by health and other social and economic sectors, by non-governmental and voluntary organizations, by industry and by the media' (WHO, 1986). In Europe, we are fast learning that health promotion programmes and policies can be better implemented when countries recognize that they are capable of both producing health outcomes and of contributing strongly to healthy social and economic results. In a nutshell, this is what WHO/EURO puts forward as the Investment for Health approach to the development of health promotion.

Investment for Health should increasingly be seen by countries as an approach, at all levels of policy-making, for optimizing the health-promoting impact of a wide range of policies. These policies include, e.g. education, income maintenance, health care, labour, housing, agriculture, transport, tourism, energy, communication. The approach involves identifying relevant policy attributes; considering factors that may enhance or inhibit policy change; assessing change options that offer benefits both to health goals and the primary intent of a specific policy sector; and planning the political process of achieving the necessary legislative, regulatory, financial, organizational or educational changes.

During the 1990s, European governments, faced with the escalating costs of a producer-driven high tech health care system, have pursued health care system reforms. These have tended to focus on the production of, rather than the demand for, health care. Currently, some 90% of the European member states are undertaking health care reforms, often simply aiming at a reduction of costs, and not taking into account the broader picture. As the Ljubljana Charter points out, this is a severely limited downstream approach [(WHO, 1996c); see also (Saltman and Figueras, 1997)]. This severe limitation needs to be recognized and the illusion of control, through short-term technical responses, needs to be abandoned, because such responses deal only with the margins of the central issue, which is the creation of health.

Experience in the European region increasingly suggests that this important aspect of health care reforms necessitates paying attention to national and local management arrangements for health promotion, and that these are likely to be at risk if they are not explicitly considered as part of the reform process. Success is most likely to be founded on:

- creating and sustaining a national centre and/or regional centres for health promotion, as part of the general arrangements for public health, to act as a focus for analysis and action, to run country-wide and/or regional programmes, and to lend support to the development of local expertise and the implementation of local programmes;
- establishing and sustaining local expertise in health promotion and appropriate organizational arrangements, and in acting as a local focus for intersectoral motivation, support and action;
- defining the skills and expertise needed, and setting up appropriate training programmes;
- enhancing capacity in relevant research disciplines and information systems.

In Europe, considerable change has taken place since the development of the original vision which was incorporated in the Ottawa Charter. Political, economic, social and technological change have generated new health challenges, not least the challenge of dealing with rapid change itself. Whereas 10 years ago European societies were based on the provision and purchase of goods and services, societies today increasingly exchange information and knowledge. All this is resulting in constantly evolving patterns of everyday life, evolution in how people work, relate to each other and spend their leisure time. In under 7 years, the European region of WHO has expanded its official membership from 32 to over 50 countries, as the former Eastern Bloc has been geo-politically transformed. The changes have taken place at a very rapid rate and people have varied in their ability to respond to the change.

The impact of economic globalization of the economy, the domination of multinational corporations and the primacy placed on private profit and company shareholders at the expense of the majority of people, all highlighted in the Jakarta declaration, have been especially painful in Europe, where there had been a long period of stability. The additional strains of transition among the former Eastern bloc states have created high levels of uncertainty and anxiety about the future. In the whole of Europe, unemployment has affected a wide sweep of people who have never before experienced joblessness or underemployment. These include skilled workers, technicians, sales people, managers and administrators. At the same time, those in work are experiencing stress from work overload and have a fear of job insecurity. Fear of an uncertain future rather than of the present reality is the key. Research indicates that, while many people are experiencing short-term unemployment, the vast majority find new work. It is the core of the long-term unemployed who are experiencing the most problems. The nature of work is changing to their disadvantage. The absolute amount of work has not diminished but there is inequality in the distribution of the means of earning a living. Thus, there are widening inequalities between people within countries and the already socially disadvantaged are hardest hit.

In line with the outcome of the Jakarta Conference, in Europe we have learned that the commitment to health promotion demands an approach that emphasizes consultation, negotiations and more opportunities to put health high on the agenda of policy-makers. Governments continue to play a major role in health. But health is also influenced greatly by corporate and business interests, non-governmental bodies, community organizations and single individuals. Their potential for preserving and promoting people's health should be encouraged, and alliances forged to provide the impetus for health action. Promoting health is going to need to take on a more assertive role across the range of policy reforms under widespread review in many European member states.

Address for correspondence:
WHO Regional Office for Europe
8 Scherfigsvej
DK-2100 Copenhagen
Denmark

REFERENCES

Ashton, J. (1992) *Healthy Cities*. Open University Press, Buckingham.

Badura, B. and Kickbusch, I. (eds) (1991) Health Promotion Research. World Health Organization, Regional Office for Europe, WHO Regional Publications, European Series, No. 37, Copenhagen.

Bartley, M., Blane, D. and Montgomery, S. (1997) Socio-economic determinants of health; health and the life course: why safety nets matter. *British Medical Journal*, **314**, 1194–1196.

Beauchamp, D. (1977) Lifestyle, public health and paternalism. In Sidell, M., Jones, L., Katz, J. and Peberdy, A. (eds) *Debates and Dilemmas in Promoting Health*. MacMillan Press, London.

Blane, D., Brenner, E. and Wilkinson, R. G. (1996) *Health and Social Organization—Towards a Health Policy for the 21st Century*. Routledge, London.

Blane, D., Smith, D. and Bartley, M. (1993) Social selection: what does it contribute to social class differences in Health? *Sociology of Health and Illness*, **15**, 1–15.

Cornia, G. A. (1997) Labour market shocks, psychosocial stress and the transition's mortality crisis. *Research in Progress Number*, Vol. 4, October. United Nations University, WIDER, Helsinki.

Cornia, G. A. and Paniccia, R. (1995) The Demographic Impact of Sudden Impoverishment: Eastern Europe during the 1989–1994 Transition. Unicef, International Child Development Centre, Unicef, Florence.

De Leeuw, E. (1989) *The Sane Revolution: Health Promotion: Background, Scope and Prospects*. van Gorcum, Assen.

Department of Health (England) (1998) *Our Healthier Nation*. HMSO, London.

European Commission (1997) Public Health in the European Community. Health Promotion Programme (1996–2000). European Commission, D.G.V., Luxemburg.

Evans, R. G., Barcer, M. L. and Marmot, T. R. (eds) (1994) *Why are Some People Healthy and Others Not?* Aldine De Gruyter, New York.

Fitzpatrick, R. M. (1982) Social concepts of disease and illness. In Patrick, L. D. and Scambler, G. (eds) *Sociology as Applied to Medicine*. Baillier Tindall, Eastbourne.

Grossman, R. and Scala, K. (1993) Health Promotion and Organizational Development. European Health Promotion Series, No. 2. World Health Organization, Regional Office for Europe, Copenhagen.

Jensen, B. B. and Schnack, K. (eds) (1994) *Action and Action Competence*. Studies in Educational Theory and Curriculum Volume 12. Royal Danish School of Educational Studies, Copenhagen.

Kickbusch, I. (1997) Think Health: What Makes the Difference? Address given by Dr Ilona Kickbusch at the *4th International Conference on Health Promotion*, Jakarta, Indonesia, 21–25 July 1997. World Health Organization, HPR/HEP/4ICHP/BR/97.3, Geneva.

Levin, L., McMahon, L. and Ziglio, E. (eds) (1994) Economic Change, Social Welfare and Health in Europe. World Health Organization, Regional Office for Europe, Copenhagen.

Levin, L. and Ziglio, E. (1997) Health promotion as an investment strategy: a perspective for the 21st century. In Sidell, M., Johns, L., Katz, J. and Peberdy, A. (eds) *Debates and Dilemmas in Promoting Health.* MacMillan Press, London.

Makara, P. (1994) The effect of social changes on the population's way of life and health: a Hungarian case study. In Levin, L., McMahon, L. and Ziglio, E. (eds) *Economic Change, Social Welfare and Health in Europe.* World Health Organization, Regional Office for Europe, WHO Regional Publications, European Series No. 54, Copenhagen.

Marmot, M. (1998) Improving the social environment to improve health. *Lancet*, **351**, 57–60.

McKeown, T. (1976) *The Role of Medicine: Dream Mirage or Nemesis?* Nuffield Provincial Hospital Trust, London.

Pelikan, J. M., Garcia-Barbero, M., Lobnig, H. and Krajic, K. (eds) (1998) *Pathways to a Health Promoting Hospital.* G. Conrad, Health Promotion Publications, Gamburg, Germany.

Saltman, R. and Figueras, J. (1997) European Health Care Reform, Analysis of Current Strategies. World Health Organization, Regional Office for Europe, WHO Regional Publications, European Series No. 79, Copenhagen.

Scottish Office (1998) Working Together for a Healthier Scotland. The Stationery Office, Edinburgh.

Sidell, M., Jones, L., Katz, J. and Peberdy, A. (eds) (1997) *Debates and Dilemmas in Promoting Health.* MacMillan Press, London.

Tsouros, A. (ed.) (1990) *WHO Healthy Cities Project: A Project Becomes a Movement.* FADL/Sogess, Copenhagen/Milan.

UNICEF (1997) Children at Risk in Central and Eastern Europe: Peril and Promises. Unicef, International Child Development Centre, Economies in Transition Studies, Regional Monitoring Report, No. 4, Florence.

Welsh Office (1998) Better Health, Better Wales. Welsh Office, Cardiff.

Whitehead, M. (1994) Counting the human costs: opportunities for and barriers to promoting health. In Levin, L., McMahon, L. and Ziglio, E. (eds), *op. cit.*

Whitehead, M., Dahlgren, G. and Diderichsen, F. (1998) Social Inequalities in Health: What are the Issues for Health Promotion? (Unpublished Working Document for the European Committee for Health Promotion Development.) World Health Organization, Regional Office for Europe, Health Promotion and Investment Programme, Copenhagen.

Wilkinson, R. G. (1996) *Unhealthy Societies.* Routledge, London.

World Health Organization (WHO) (1984) Health Promotion: A Discussion Document on the Concept and Principles. World Health Organization, Regional Office for Europe, Copenhagen.

WHO (1986) Ottawa Charter for Health Promotion. World Health Organization, Health and Welfare Canada, Canadian Public Health Association. Ottawa Charter for Health Promotion, Ottawa, Ontario, Canada. 21 November 1986. (Available through: Copenhagen: World Health Organization, Regional Office for Europe.)

WHO (1991) The Budapest Declaration of Health Promoting Hospital. World Health Organization, Regional Office for Europe, Copenhagen.

WHO (1992) Twenty Steps for Developing a Healthy Cities Project. World Health Organization, Regional Office for Europe.

WHO (1994a) Investment for Health in the Valencia Region: Mid-Term Report. World Health Organization, Regional Office for Europe, Health Promotion and Investment Programme, Copenhagen.

WHO (1994b) National Healthy Cities Networks in Europe. World Health Organization, Regional Office for Europe, Copenhagen.

WHO (1994c) The European Charter on Environment and Health. World Health Organization, Regional Office for Europe, Copenhagen.

WHO (1995a) Health in Social Development (WHO Position Paper. World Summit for Social Development, Copenhagen, March 1995). WHO, Geneva.

WHO (1995b) Securing Investment for Health: Report of a Demonstration Project in the Provinces of Bolzano and Trento. World Health Organization, Regional Office for Europe, Health Promotion and Investment Programme, Copenhagen.

WHO (1996a) Investment for Health in Slovenia. World Health Organization (Intersectoral Health Development Unit, Health Promotion and Investment Programme), Copenhagen.

WHO (1996b) Networking the Networks. World Health Organization, Regional Office for Europe, Copenhagen.

WHO (1996c) The Ljubljana Charter on Reforming Health Care in Europe. World Health Organization, Copenhagen.

WHO (1996d) The Role of Health Promotion in Health Care Reforms. A Consensus Statement of the European Committee for Health Promotion Development. World Health Organization, Regional Office for Europe, Health Promotion and Investment Programme, Copenhagen.

WHO (1997) Investment for Health in Hungary. World Health Organization, Regional Office for Europe, Health Promotion and Investment Programme, Copenhagen.

WHO (1998a) The World Health Report. World Health Organization, Geneva.

WHO (1998b) Health 21—Leadership Guide to the Policy for Health for All in the European Region. World Health Organization, Copenhagen.

WHO (1998c) Health in Europe. Report on the Third Evaluation on Progress Towards Health for All in the European Region (1996–1997). World Health Organization, Regional Office for Europe, WHO Regional Publications, European Series No. 83, Copenhagen.

Who-European Commission-Council of Europe (1992) The European Network of Health Promoting Schools. World Health Organization, Regional Office for Europe, Copenhagen.

Who-European Commission-Council of Europe (1997) The European Network of Health Promoting Schools. (Updated Version). World Health Organization, Regional Office for Europe, Copenhagen.

Who-European Commission-Council of Europe (1998) The Health Promoting School—An Investment in Education, Health and Democracy. Conference Report. (First Conference of the European Network of Health Promoting Schools, Thessaloniki–Halkidiki, Greece, 1–5 May 1997.) World Health Organization, Regional Office for Europe, Copenhagen.

WHO–HEA (Health Education Authority, England) (1996) Health Promotion: European Countries—1996 Survey.

World Health Organization, Regional Office for Europe, Health Promotion and Investment Programme, Copenhagen.

WHO–HEA (1998) Health Promotion: European Countries—1998 Survey. World Health Organization, Regional Office for Europe, Health Promotion and Investment, Copenhagen.

Ziglio, E. (1993) European Macro Trends Affecting Health Promotion Strategies. WHO/EURO Working Paper. World Health Organization, Regional Office for Europe, Health Promotion and Investment Programme, Copenhagen.

Ziglio, E. (1998) Key issues for the new millennium. *Promoting Health: The Journal of Health Promotion for Northern Ireland,* **2**, 34–37.

Part II
And Bioethics

[5]

Public Health Ethics: Mapping the Terrain

James F. Childress, Ruth R. Faden, Ruth D. Gaare, Lawrence O. Gostin, Jeffrey Kahn, Richard J. Bonnie, Nancy E. Kass, Anna C. Mastroianni, Jonathan D. Moreno, and Phillip Nieburg

Public health ethics, like the field of public health it addresses, traditionally has focused more on practice and particular cases than on theory, with the result that some concepts, methods, and boundaries remain largely undefined. This paper attempts to provide a rough conceptual map of the terrain of public health ethics. We begin by briefly defining public health and identifying general features of the field that are particularly relevant for a discussion of public health ethics.

Public health is primarily concerned with the health of the entire population, rather than the health of individuals. Its features include an emphasis on the promotion of health and the prevention of disease and disability; the collection and use of epidemiological data, population surveillance, and other forms of empirical quantitative assessment; a recognition of the multidimensional nature of the determinants of health; and a focus on the complex interactions of many factors — biological, behavioral, social, and environmental — in developing effective interventions.

How can we distinguish public health from medicine? While medicine focuses on the treatment and cure of individual patients, public health aims to understand and ameliorate the causes of disease and disability in a population. In addition, whereas the physician-patient relationship is at the center of medicine, public health involves interactions and relationships among many professionals and members of the community as well as agencies of government in the development, implementation, and assessment of interventions. From this starting point, we can suggest that public health systems consist of all the people and actions, including laws, policies, practices, and activities, that have the primary purpose of protecting and improving the health of the public.[1] While we need not assume that public health systems are tightly structured or centrally directed, we recognize that they include a wide range of governmental, private and non-profit organizations, as well as professionals from many disciplines, all of which (alone and together) have a stake in and an effect on a community's health. Government has a unique role in public health because of its responsibility, grounded in its police powers, to protect the public's health and welfare, because it alone can undertake certain interventions, such as regulation, taxation, and the expenditure of public funds, and because many, perhaps most, public health programs are public goods that cannot be optimally provided if left to individuals or small groups.

The Institute of Medicine's landmark 1988 definition of public health provides additional insight: "Public health is what we, as a society, do collectively to assure the conditions in which people can be healthy."[2] The words "what we, as a society, do collectively" suggest the need for cooperative behavior and relationships built on overlapping values and trust. The words "to assure the conditions in which people can be healthy" suggest a far-reaching agenda for public health that focuses attention not only on the medical needs of individuals, but on fundamental social conditions that affect population levels of morbidity and mortality. From an ethical standpoint, public health activities are generally understood to be teleological (end-oriented) and consequentialist — the health of the public is the primary end that is sought and the primary outcome for measuring success.[3] Defining and measuring "health" is not easy, as we will emphasize below, but, in addition, "public" is a complex concept with at least three dimensions that are important for our discussion of ethics.

First, public can be used to mean the "numerical public," i.e., the target population. In view of public health's goal of producing net health benefits for the population, this meaning of public is very important. In measurement and analysis, the "numerical public" reflects the utilitarian view that each individual counts as one and only one. In this context, ethical analysis focuses on issues in measurement, many of which raise considerations of justice. For example, how should we define a population, how should we compare gains in life expectancy with gains in health-related quality of life, and whose values should be used in making those judgments?

Second, public is what we collectively do through government and public agency — we can call this "political public." Government provides much of the funding for a vast array of public health functions, and public health professionals in governmental roles are the focal point of much collective activity. In the United States, as Lawrence Gostin notes, government "is compelled by its role as the elected representative of the community to act affirmatively to promote the health of the people," even though it "cannot unduly invade individuals' rights in the name of the communal good."[4] The government is a central player in public health because of the collective responsibility it must assume and implement. The state's use of its police powers for public health raises important ethical questions, particularly about the justification and limits of governmental coercion and about its duty to treat all citizens equally in exercising these powers. In a liberal, pluralistic democracy, the justification of coercive policies, as well as other policies, must rest on moral reasons that the public in whose name the policies are carried out could reasonably be expected to accept.[5]

Third, public, defined as what we do collectively in a broad sense, includes all forms of social and community action affecting public health — we can call this "communal public." Ethical analysis on this level extends beyond the political public. People collectively, outside of government and with private funds, often have greater freedom to undertake public health interventions since they do not have to justify their actions to the political public. However, their actions are still subject to various moral requirements, including, for instance, respect for individual autonomy, liberty, privacy and confidentiality, and transparency in disclosure of conflicts of interest.

General Moral Considerations

In providing a map of the terrain of public health ethics, we do not suggest that there is a consensus about the methods and content of public health ethics.[6] Controversies persist about theory and method in other areas of applied or practical ethics, and it should not be surprising that variety also prevails in public health ethics.[7] The terrain of public health ethics includes a loose set of general moral considerations — clusters of moral concepts and norms that are variously called values, principles, or rules — that are arguably relevant to public health. Public health ethics, in part, involves ongoing efforts to specify and to assign weights to these general moral considerations in the context of particular policies, practices, and actions, in order to provide concrete moral guidance.

Recognizing general moral considerations in public health ethics does not entail a commitment to any particular theory or method. What we describe and propose is compatible with several approaches. To take one major example, casuistical reasoning (examining the relevant similarities and differences between cases) is not only compatible with, but indispensable to our conception of public health ethics. Not only do — or should — public health agents examine new situations they confront in light of general moral considerations, but they should also focus on a new situation's relevant similarities to and differences from paradigm or precedent cases — cases that have gained a relatively settled moral consensus. Whether a relatively settled moral consensus is articulated first in a general moral consideration or in precedent cases does not constitute a fundamental issue — both are relevant. Furthermore, some of the precedents may concern how general moral considerations are interpreted, specified, and balanced in some public health activity, especially where conflicts emerge.

Conceptions of morality usually recognize a formal requirement of universalizability in addition to a substantive requirement of attention to human welfare. Whatever language is used, this formal feature requires that we treat similar cases in a similar way. This requirement undergirds casuistical reasoning in morality as well as in law. In public health ethics, for example, any recommendations for an HIV screening policy must take into account both past precedents in screening for other infectious diseases and the precedents the new policy will create for, say, screening for genetic conditions. Much of the moral argument will hinge on which similarities and differences between cases are morally relevant, and that argument will often, though not always, appeal to general moral considerations.[8] We can establish the relevance of a set of these considerations in part by looking at the kinds of moral appeals that public health agents make in deliberating about and justifying their actions as well as at debates about moral issues in public health. The relevant general moral considerations include:

- producing benefits;
- avoiding, preventing, and removing harms;
- producing the maximal balance of benefits over harms and other costs (often called utility);
- distributing benefits and burdens fairly (distributive justice) and ensuring public participation,

Volume 30:2, Summer 2002

including the participation of affected parties (procedural justice);
- respecting autonomous choices and actions, including liberty of action;
- protecting privacy and confidentiality;
- keeping promises and commitments;
- disclosing information as well as speaking honestly and truthfully (often grouped under transparency); and
- building and maintaining trust.

Several of these general moral considerations — especially benefiting others, preventing and removing harms, and utility — provide a *prima facie* warrant for many activities in pursuit of the goal of public health. It is sufficient for our purposes to note that public health activities have their grounding in general moral considerations, and that public health identifies one major broad benefit that societies and governments ought to pursue. The relation of public health to the whole set of general moral considerations is complex. Some general moral considerations support this pursuit; institutionalizing several others may be a condition for or means to public health (we address this point later when we discuss human rights and public health); and yet, in particular cases, some of the same general moral considerations may limit or constrain what may be done in pursuit of public health. Hence, conflicts may occur among these general moral considerations.

The content of these various general moral considerations can be divided and arranged in several ways — for instance, some theories may locate one or more of these concepts under others. But, whatever theory one embraces, the whole set of general moral considerations roughly captures the moral content of public health ethics. It then becomes necessary to address several practical questions. First, how can we make these general moral considerations more specific and concrete in order to guide action? Second, how can we resolve conflicts among them? Some of the conflicts will concern how much weight and significance to assign to the ends and effects of protecting and promoting public health relative to the other considerations that limit and constrain ways to pursue such outcomes. While each general moral consideration may limit and constrain public health activities in some circumstances, for our purposes, justice or fairness, respect for autonomy and liberty, and privacy and confidentiality are particularly noteworthy in this regard.

Specifying and weighting general moral considerations

We do not present a universal public health ethic. Although arguably these general moral considerations find support in various societies and cultures, an analysis of the role of cultural context in public health ethics is beyond the scope of this paper. Instead, we focus here on public health ethics in the particular setting of the United States, with its traditions, practices, and legal and constitutional requirements, all of which set directions for and circumscribe public health ethics. (Below we will indicate how this conception of public health ethics relates to human rights.)

General moral considerations have two major dimensions. One is their meaning and range or scope; the other is their weight or strength. The first determines the extent of conflict among them — if their range or scope is interpreted in certain ways, conflicts may be increased or reduced. The second dimension determines when different considerations yield to others in cases of conflict.

Specifying the meaning and range or scope of general moral considerations — the first dimension — provides increasingly concrete guidance in public health ethics. A common example is specifying respect for autonomy by rules of voluntary, informed consent. However, it would be a mistake to suppose that respect for autonomy requires consent in all contexts of public health or to assume that consent alone sufficiently specifies the duty to respect autonomy in public health settings. Indeed, specifying the meaning and scope of general moral considerations entails difficult moral work. Nowhere is this more evident in public health ethics than with regard to considerations of justice. Explicating the demands of justice in allocating public health resources and in setting priorities for public health policies, or in determining whom they should target, remains among the most daunting challenges in public health ethics.

The various general moral considerations are not absolute. Each may conflict with another and each may have to yield in some circumstances. At most, then, these general moral considerations identify features of actions, practices, and policies that make them *prima facie* or presumptively right or wrong, i.e., right or wrong, all other things being equal. But since any particular action, practice, or policy for the public's health may also have features that infringe one or more of these general moral considerations, it will be necessary to determine which of them has priority. Some argue for a lexical or serial ordering, in which one general moral consideration, while not generally absolute, has priority over another. For instance, one theory might hold that protecting or promoting public health always has priority over privacy, while another might hold that individual liberty always has priority over protecting or promoting public health. Neither of these priority rules is plausible, and any priority rule that is plausible will probably involve tight or narrow specifications of the relevant general moral considerations to reduce conflicts. From our standpoint, it is better to recognize the need to balance general moral considerations in particular circumstances when conflicts arise. We cannot determine their weights in advance, only in particular contexts that may affect their weights — for instance, promises may not have the same moral weights in different contexts.

Resolving conflicts among general moral considerations

We do not believe it is possible to develop an algorithm to resolve all conflicts among general moral considerations. Such conflicts can arise in multiple ways. For example, it is common in public health practice and policy for conflicts to emerge between privacy and justice (for instance, the state collects and records private information in disease registries about individuals in order to allocate and provide access to resources for appropriate prevention and treatment services), or between different conceptions of justice (for instance, a government with a finite public health budget must decide whether to dedicate resources to vaccination or to treatment of conditions when they arise). In this paper, however, we focus on one particular permutation of conflicts among general moral considerations that has received the most attention in commentary and in law. This is the conflict between the general moral considerations that are generally taken to instantiate the goal of public health — producing benefits, preventing harms, and maximizing utility — and those that express other moral commitments. For conflicts that assume this structure, we propose five "justificatory conditions": effectiveness, proportionality, necessity, least infringement, and public justification. These conditions are intended to help determine whether promoting public health warrants overriding such values as individual liberty or justice in particular cases.

Effectiveness: It is essential to show that infringing one or more general moral considerations will probably protect public health. For instance, a policy that infringes one or more general moral considerations in the name of public health but has little chance of realizing its goal is ethically unjustified.

Proportionality: It is essential to show that the probable public health benefits outweigh the infringed general moral considerations — this condition is sometimes called proportionality. For instance, the policy may breach autonomy or privacy and have undesirable consequences. All of the positive features and benefits must be balanced against the negative features and effects.

Necessity: Not all effective and proportionate policies are necessary to realize the public health goal that is sought. The fact that a policy will infringe a general moral consideration provides a strong moral reason to seek an alternative strategy that is less morally troubling. This is the logic of a *prima facie* or presumptive general moral consideration. For instance, all other things being equal, a policy that provides incentives for persons with tuberculosis to complete their treatment until cured will have priority over a policy that forcibly detains such persons in order to ensure the completion of treatment. Proponents of the forcible strategy have the burden of moral proof. This means that the proponents must have a good faith belief, for which they can give supportable reasons, that a coercive approach is necessary. In many contexts, this condition does not require that proponents provide empirical evidence by actually trying the alternative measures and demonstrating their failure.[9]

Least infringement: Even when a proposed policy satisfies the first three justificatory conditions — that is, it is effective, proportionate, and essential in realizing the goal of public health — public health agents should seek to minimize the infringement of general moral considerations. For instance, when a policy infringes autonomy, public health agents should seek the least restrictive alternative; when it infringes privacy, they should seek the least intrusive alternative; and when it infringes confidentiality, they should disclose only the amount and kind of information needed, and only to those necessary, to realize the goal.[10] The justificatory condition of least infringement could plausibly be interpreted as a corollary of necessity — for instance, a proposed coercive measure must be necessary in degree as well as in kind.

Public justification: When public health agents believe that one of their actions, practices, or policies infringes one or more general moral considerations, they also have a responsibility, in our judgment, to explain and justify that infringement, whenever possible, to the relevant parties, including those affected by the infringement. In the context of what we called "political public," public health agents should offer public justification for policies in terms that fit the overall social contract in a liberal, pluralistic democracy. This transparency stems in part from the requirement to treat citizens as equals and with respect by offering moral reasons, which in principle they could find acceptable, for policies that infringe general moral considerations. Transparency is also essential to creating and maintaining public trust; and it is crucial to establishing accountability. (Below we elaborate a process-oriented approach to public accountability that goes beyond public justification to include, as an expression of justice and fairness, input from the relevant affected parties in the formulation of policy.)

Screening program example

An extended example may illustrate how these moral justificatory conditions function in public health ethics. Let us suppose that public health agents are considering whether to implement a screening program for HIV infection, tuberculosis, another infectious or contagious disease, or a genetic condition (see Figure 1 for some morally relevant features of screening programs).

The relevant justificatory conditions will require public health agents to consider whether any proposed program will be likely to realize the public health goal that is sought (effectiveness), whether its probable benefits will outweigh the infringed general moral considerations (proportionality), whether the policy is essential to realize the end (necessity), whether it involves the least infringement possible consistent with realizing the goal that is sought (least infringement), and whether it can be publicly justified. These conditions

Volume 30:2, Summer 2002

FIGURE 1. FEATURES OF PUBLIC HEALTH SCREENING PROGRAMS.

		Degree of Voluntariness	
		Voluntary	Mandatory
Extent of Screening	Universal		
	Selective		

will give priority to selective programs over universal ones if the selective programs will realize the goal (as we note below, questions may arise about universality within selected categories, such as pregnant women), and to voluntary programs over mandatory ones if the voluntary programs will realize the goal.[11]

Different screening programs may fail close scrutiny in light of one or more of these conditions. For instance, neither mandatory nor voluntary universal screening for HIV infection can meet these conditions in the society as a whole. Some voluntary and some mandatory selective screening programs for HIV infection can be justified, while others cannot. Mandatory screening of donated blood, organs, sperm, and ova is easily justified, and screening of individuals may also be justified in some settings where they can expose others to bodily fluids and potential victims cannot protect themselves. The question of whether and under what conditions screening of pregnant women for HIV infection should be instituted has been particularly controversial. Even before the advent of effective treatment for HIV infection and the identification of zidovudine (AZT) as effective in reducing the rate of perinatal transmission, there were calls for mandatory screening of pregnant women, especially in "high risk" communities. These calls were defeated by sound arguments that such policies entailed unjustifiable violations of autonomy, privacy, and justice.[12] In effect, the recommended policies failed to satisfy any of the justificatory conditions we have proposed here.

However, once it was established that zidovudine could interrupt maternal-fetal transmission of HIV, the weight of the argument shifted in the direction of instituting screening programs of some type. The focus of the debate became the tensions between the public health interests in utility and efficiency, which argued for mandatory, selective screening in high-risk communities, and considerations of liberty, privacy, and justice, which argued for voluntary, universal screening.[13]

In many situations, the most defensible public health policy for screening and testing *expresses* community rather than *imposes* it. Imposing community involves mandating or compelling testing through coercive measures. By contrast, expressing community involves taking steps to express solidarity with individuals, to protect their interests, and to gain their trust. Expressing community may include, for example, providing communal support, disclosing adequate information, protecting privacy and confidentiality, and encouraging certain choices. This approach seeks to make testing a reasonable, and perhaps moral, choice for individuals, especially by engendering public trust, rather than making it compulsory. Several diseases that might be subjected to screening for public health reasons involve stigma, and breaches of privacy and confidentiality may put individuals' employment and insurance at risk. Expressing community is often an appropriate strategy for public health, and, *ceteris paribus*, it has priority over imposing community through coercive policies.

PROCESSES OF PUBLIC ACCOUNTABILITY

Our discussion of the fifth justificatory condition — public justification — focused on providing public reasons for policies that infringe general moral considerations; this condition is particularly applicable in the political context. While public accountability includes public justification, it is broader — it is prospective as well as retrospective. It involves soliciting input from the relevant publics (the numerical, political, and communal publics) in the process of formulating public health policies, practices, and actions, as well as justifying to the relevant publics what is being undertaken. This is especially, but not only, important when one of the other *prima facie* general moral considerations is infringed, as with coercive protective measures to prevent epidemics. At a minimum, public accountability involves transparency in openly seeking information from those affected and in honestly disclosing relevant information to the public; it is indispensable for engendering and sustaining public trust, as well as for expressing justice.[14]

Public accountability regarding health promotion or priority-setting for public health funding additionally might involve a more developed fair process. Noting that in a pluralistic society we are likely to find disagreement about which principles should govern issues such as priority-setting in health care, Norman Daniels calls for a fair process that includes the following elements: transparency and publicity about the reasons for a decision; appeals to rationales and evidence that fair-minded parties would agree are relevant; and procedures for appealing and revising decisions in light of challenges by various stakeholders. He explains why this process can facilitate social learning: "Since we may not be able to construct principles that yield fair decisions ahead of time, we need a process that allows us to develop those reasons over time as we face real cases."[15]

Public accountability also involves acknowledging the more complex relationship between public health and the public, one that addresses fundamental issues such as those involving characterization of risk and scientific uncertainty. Because public health depends for its success on the satisfaction of deeply personal health goals of individuals and groups in the population, concepts such as "health" and "risk" cannot be understood or acted upon on the basis of *a priori*, formal definitions or scientific analysis. Public accountability recognizes that the fundamental conceptualization of these terms is a critical part of the basic formulation of public health goals and problems to be addressed. This means that the public, along with scientific experts, plays an important role in the *analysis* of public health issues, as well as in the development and assessment of appropriate *strategies* for addressing them.

Risk characterization provides a helpful example. A National Research Council report, *Understanding Risk: Informing Decisions in a Democratic Society*, concluded that risk characterization is not properly understood if defined only as a summary of scientific information; rather, it is the outcome of a complex analytic-deliberative process — "a decision-driven activity, directed toward informing choices and solving problems."[16] The report explains that scientific analysis, which uses rigorous, replicable methods, brings new information into the process, and that deliberation helps to frame analysis by posing new questions and new ways of formulating problems, with the result that risk characterization is the output of a recursive process, not a linear one, and is a decision-driven activity.

Assessment of the health risks of dioxin illustrates this process. While scientific analysis provides information about the dose-response relationship between dioxin exposure and possible human health effects, public health focuses on the placement of waste incinerators and community issues in which dioxin is only one of many hazardous chemicals involved and cancer only one of many outcomes of concern. The critical point is that good risk characterization results from a process that "not only gets the science right," but also "gets the right science."[17]

Public health accountability addresses the responsibility of public health agents to work with the public and scientific experts to identify, define, and understand at a fundamental level the threats to public health, and the risks and benefits of ways to address them. The appropriate level of public involvement in the analytic-deliberative process depends on the particular public health problem.

Public accountability requires an openness to public deliberation and imposes an obligation on decision-makers to provide honest information and justifications for their decisions. No ethical principle can eliminate the fact that individual interests must sometimes yield to collective needs. Public accountability, however, ensures that such trade-offs will be made openly, with an explicit acknowledgment that individuals' fundamental well-being and values are at stake and that reasons, grounded in ethics, will be provided to those affected by the decisions.[18] It provides a basis for public trust, even when policies infringe or appear to infringe some general moral considerations.

Public Health Interventions vs. Paternalistic Interventions

An important empirical, conceptual, and normative issue in public health ethics is the relationship between protecting and promoting the health of individuals and protecting and promoting public health. Although public health is directed to the health of populations, the indices of population health, of course, include an aggregation of the health of individuals. But suppose the primary reason for some restrictions on the liberties of individuals is to prevent harm to those whose actions are substantially voluntary and do not affect others adversely. The ethical question then is, when can paternalistic interventions (defined as interventions designed to protect or benefit individuals themselves against their express wishes) be ethically justified if they infringe general moral considerations such as respect for autonomy, including liberty of action?

Consider the chart in Figure 2: An individual's actions may be substantially voluntary (competent, adequately informed, and free of controlling influences) or non-voluntary (incompetent, inadequately informed, or subject to controlling influences). In addition, those actions may be self-regarding (the adverse effects of the actions fall primarily on the individual himself or herself) or other-regarding (the adverse effects of the actions fall primarily on others).

Paternalism in a morally interesting and problematic sense arises in the first quadrant (marked by the number "1" in Figure 2) — where the individual's actions are both voluntary and self-regarding. According to John Stuart Mill, whose *On Liberty* has inspired this chart, other-regarding conduct not only affects others adversely, but also affects them directly and without "their free, voluntary, and undeceived consent and participation."[19] If others, in the maturity of their faculties, consent to an agent's imposition of risk, then the agent's actions are not other-regarding in Mill's sense.

Whether an agent's other-regarding conduct is voluntary or non-voluntary, the society may justifiably intervene in various ways, including the use of coercion, to reduce or prevent the imposition of serious risk on others. Societal intervention in non-voluntary self-regarding conduct is considered weak (or soft) paternalism, if it is paternalistic at all, and it is easily justified. By contrast, societal interference in volun-

Volume 30:2, Summer 2002

FIGURE 1. TWO MODELS OF STIGMA.

		Adverse Effects of Individuals' Actions	
		Self-regarding	Other-regarding
Voluntariness of Individuals' Actions	Voluntary	1	2
	Non-voluntary	3	4

tary self-regarding conduct would be strong (or hard) paternalism. Coercive intervention in the name of strong paternalism would be insulting and disrespectful to individuals because it would override their voluntary actions for their own benefit, even though their actions do not harm others. Such interventions are thus very difficult to justify in a liberal, pluralistic democracy.

Because of this difficulty, proponents of public health sometimes contend that the first quadrant is really a small class of cases because individuals' risky actions are, in most cases, other-regarding or non-voluntary, or both. Thus, they insist, even if we assume that strong or hard paternalism cannot be ethically justified, the real question is whether most public health interventions in personal life plans and risk budgets are paternalistic at all, at least in the morally problematic sense.

To a great extent, the question is where we draw the boundaries of the self and its actions; that is, whether various influences on agents so determine their actions that they are not voluntary, and whether the adverse effects of those actions extend beyond the agents themselves. Such boundary drawing involves empirical, conceptual, and normative questions that demand attention in public health ethics. On the one hand, it is not sufficient to show that social-cultural factors influence an individual's actions; it is necessary to show that those influences render that individual's actions substantially non-voluntary and warrant societal interventions to protect him or her. Controversies about the strong influence of food marketing on diet and weight (and, as a result, on the risk of disease and death) illustrate the debates about this condition.

On the other hand, it is not sufficient to show that an individual's actions have some adverse effects on others; it is necessary to show that those adverse effects on others are significant enough to warrant overriding the individual's liberty. Controversies about whether the state should require motorcyclists to wear helmets illustrate the debates about this condition. These controversies also show how the inclusion of the financial costs to society and the emotional costs to, say, observers and rescue squads can appear to make virtually any intervention non-paternalistic. But even if these adverse financial and emotional effects on others are morally relevant as a matter of social utility, it would still be necessary to show that they are significant enough to justify the intervention.

Either kind of attempt to reduce the sphere of autonomous, self-regarding actions, in order to warrant interventions in the name of public health, or, more broadly, social utility, can sometimes be justified, but either attempt must be subjected to careful scrutiny. Sometimes both may represent rationalization and bad faith as public health agents seek to evade the stringent demands of the general moral consideration of respect for autonomy. Requiring consistency across an array of cases may provide a safeguard against rationalization and bad faith, particularly when motives for intervention may be mixed.

Much of this debate reflects different views about whether and when strong paternalistic interventions can be ethically justified. In view of the justificatory conditions identified earlier, relevant factors will include the nature of the intervention, the degree to which it infringes an individual's fundamental values, the magnitude of the risk to the individual apart from the intervention (either in terms of harm or lost benefit), and so forth. For example, even though the authors of this paper would disagree about some cases, we agree that strong paternalistic interventions that do not threaten individuals' core values and that will probably protect them against serious risks are more easily justifiable than strong paternalistic interventions that threaten individuals' core values and that will reduce only minor risks. Of course, evaluating actual and proposed policies that infringe general moral considerations becomes very complicated when both paternalistic and public health reasons exist for, and are intertwined in, those policies.

SOCIAL JUSTICE, HUMAN RIGHTS, AND HEALTH

We have noted potential and actual conflicts between promoting the good of public health and other general moral considerations. But it is important not to exaggerate these conflicts. Indeed, the societal institutionalization of other general moral considerations in legal rights and social-cultural practices generally contributes to public health. Social injustices expressed in poverty, racism, and sexism have long been implicated in conditions of poor health. In recent years, some evidence suggests that societies that embody more egalitarian conceptions of socioeconomic justice have higher levels of health than ones that do not.[20] Public health activity has traditionally encompassed much more than medicine and health care. Indeed, historically much of the focus of public health has been on the poor and on the impact of squalor and sanitation on health. The focus today on the social determinants of health is in keeping with this tradition. The data about social determinants are impressive even though not wholly uncontroversial. At any rate, they are strong enough to warrant close attention to the ways conditions of social justice contribute to the public's health.

Apart from social justice, some in public health argue that embodying several other general moral considerations, especially as articulated in human rights, is consistent with and may even contribute to public health. For example, Jonathan Mann contended that public health officials now have two fundamental responsibilities — protecting and promoting public health and protecting and promoting human rights. Sometimes public health programs burden human rights, but human rights violations "have adverse effects on physical, mental, and social well-being" and "promoting and protecting human rights is inextricably linked with promoting and protecting health."[21] Mann noted, and we concur, that, ultimately, "ethics and human rights derive from a set of quite similar, if not identical, core values," several of which we believe are captured in our loose set of general moral considerations.[22] Often, as we have suggested, the most effective ways to protect public health respect general moral considerations rather than violate them, employ voluntary measures rather than coercive ones, protect privacy and confidentiality, and, more generally, express rather than impose community. Recognizing that promoting health and respecting other general moral considerations or human rights may be mutually supportive can enable us to create policies that avoid or at least reduce conflicts.

While more often than not public health and human rights — or general moral considerations not expressed in human rights — do not conflict and may even be synergistic, conflicts do sometimes arise and require resolution.[23] Sometimes, in particular cases, a society cannot simultaneously realize its commitments to public health and to certain other general moral considerations, such as liberty, privacy, and confidentiality. We have tried to provide elements of a framework for thinking through and resolving such conflicts. This process needs to be transparent in order to engender and sustain public trust.

Acknowledgments

This work was supported by a grant from The Greenwall Foundation. Other project participants were John D. Arras and Paul A. Lombardo, both of the University of Virginia, and Donna T. Chen of the National Institute of Mental Health and Department of Bioethics, National Institutes of Health.

References

1. Our definition builds on the definition of health systems offered by the World Health Organization: Health systems include "all the activities whose primary purpose is to promote, restore, or maintain health." See *World Health Report 2000 Health Systems: Improving Performance* (Geneva: World Health Organization, 2000): at 5.

2. Committee for the Study of the Future of Public Health, Division of Health Care Services, Institute of Medicine, *The Future of Public Health* (Washington, D.C.: National Academy Press, 1988): at 1.

3. We recognize that there are different views about the ultimate moral justification for the social institution of public health. For example, some communitarians appear to support public health as an instrumental goal to achieve community. Others may take the view that the state has a duty to ensure the public's health as a matter of social justice. Although these different interpretations and others are very important for some purposes, they do not seriously affect the conception of public health ethics that we are developing, as long as public health agents identify and inform others of their various goals.

4. L.O. Gostin, *Public Health Law: Power, Duty, Restraint* (Berkeley: University of California Press; New York: The Milbank Memorial Fund, 2000): at 20.

5. T. Nagel, "Moral Epistemology," in R.E. Bulger, E.M. Bobby, and H.V. Fineberg, eds., Committee on the Social and Ethical Impacts of Developments in Biomedicine, Division of Health Sciences Policy, Institute of Medicine, *Society's Choices: Social and Ethical Decision Making in Biomedicine* (Washington, D.C.: National Academy Press, 1995): 201–14.

6. For some other approaches, see P. Nieburg, R. Gaare-Bernheim, and R. Bonnie, "Ethics and the Practice of Public Health," in R.A. Goodman et al., eds., *Law in Public Health Practice* (New York: Oxford University Press, in press), and N.E. Kass, "An Ethics Framework for Public Health," *American Journal of Public Health*, 91 (2001): 1776–82.

7. We do not explore here the overlaps among public health ethics, medical ethics, research ethics, and public policy ethics, although some areas of overlap and difference will be evident throughout the discussion. Further work is needed to address some public health activities that fall within overlapping areas — for instance, surveillance, outbreak investigations, and community-based interventions may sometimes raise issues in the ethics of research involving human subjects.

8. Recognizing universalizability by attending to past precedents and possible future precedents does not preclude a variety of experiments, for instance, to determine the best ways to protect the public's health. Thus, it is not inappropriate for different states, in our federalist system, to try different approaches, as long as each of them is morally acceptable.

9. This justificatory condition is probably the most controversial. Some of the authors of this paper believe that the language of "necessity" is too strong. Whatever language is used, the point is to avoid a purely utilitarian strategy that accepts only the first two conditions of effectiveness and proportionality and to ensure that the non-utilitarian general moral considerations set some *prima facie* limits and constraints and establish moral priorities, *ceteris paribus*.

10. For another version of these justificatory conditions, see T.L. Beauchamp and J.F. Childress, *Principles of Biomedical Ethics*, 5th ed. (New York: Oxford University Press, 2001): at 19–21. We observe that some of these justificatory conditions are quite similar to the justificatory conditions that must be met in U.S. constitutional law when there is strict scrutiny because, for in-

Volume 30:2, Summer 2002

stance, a fundamental liberty is at stake. In such cases, the government must demonstrate that it has a "compelling interest," that its methods are strictly necessary to achieve its objectives, and that it has adopted the "least restrictive alternative." See Gostin, *supra* note 4, at 80–81.

11. Of course, this chart is oversimplified, particularly in identifying only voluntary and mandatory options. For a fuller discussion, see R. Faden, M. Powers, and N. Kass, "Warrants for Screening Programs: Public Health, Legal and Ethical Frameworks," in R. Faden, G. Geller, and M. Powers, eds., *AIDS, Women and the Next Generation* (New York: Oxford University Press, 1991): 3–26.

12. Working Group on HIV Testing of Pregnant Women and Newborns, "HIV Infection, Pregnant Women, and Newborns," *Journal of the American Medical Association*, 264, no. 18 (1990): 2416–20.

13. See Faden, Geller, and Powers, *supra* note 11; Gostin, *supra* note 4, at 199–201.

14. In rare cases, it may be ethically justifiable to limit the disclosure of some information for a period of time (for example, when there are serious concerns about national security; about the interpretation, certainty, or reliability of public health data; or about the potential negative effects of disclosing the information, such as with suicide clusters).

15. N. Daniels, "Accountability for Reasonableness," *British Medical Journal*, 321 (2000): 1300–01, at 1301.

16. P.C. Stern and H.V. Fineberg, eds., Committee on Risk Characterization, Commission on Behavioral and Social Sciences and Education, National Research Council, *Understanding Risk: Informing Decisions in a Democratic Society* (Washington, D.C.: National Academy Press, 1996): at 155.

17. *Id.* at 16–17, 156.

18. See, for example, N. Daniels and J. Sabin, "Limits to Health Care: Fair Procedures, Democratic Deliberation, and the Legitimacy Problem for Insurers," *Philosophy and Public Affairs*, 26 (Fall 1997): 303–50, at 350.

19. J.S. Mill, *On Liberty*, ed. G. Himmelfarb (Harmondsworth, England: Penguin Books, 1976): at 71. For this chart, see J.F. Childress, *Who Should Decide? Paternalism in Health Care* (New York: Oxford University Press, 1982): at 193.

20. See, for example, the discussion in I. Kawachi, B.P. Kennedy, and R.G. Wilkinson, eds., *Income Inequality and Health*, vol. 1 of *The Society and Population Health Reader* (New York: The New Press, 2000).

21. J.M. Mann, "Medicine and Public Health, Ethics and Human Rights," *The Hastings Center Report*, 27 (May-June 1997): 6–13, at 11–12. Contrast Gostin, *supra* note 4, at 21. For a fuller analysis and assessment of Mann's work, see L.O. Gostin, "Public Health, Ethics, and Human Rights: A Tribute to the Late Jonathan Mann," S.P. Marks, "Jonathan Mann's Legacy to the 21st Century: The Human Rights Imperative for Public Health," and L.O. Gostin, "A Vision of Health and Human Rights for the 21st Century: A Continuing Discussion with Stephen P. Marks," *Journal of Law, Medicine, and Ethics*, 29, no. 2 (2001): 121–40.

22. Mann, *supra* note 21, at 10. Mann thought that the language of ethics could guide individual behavior, while the language of human rights could best guide societal-level analysis and response. See Mann, *supra* note 21, at 8; Marks, *supra* note 21, at 131–38. We disagree with this separation and instead note the overlap of ethics and human rights, but we endorse the essence of Mann's position on human rights.

23. See Gostin, *supra* note 4, at 21.

[6]

Ethics and Public Health: Forging a Strong Relationship

The field of bioethics arose in the late 1960s in response to the emerging ethical dilemmas of that era. The field for many years focused in general on the dilemmas generated by high-technology medicine rather than on issues of population health and the ethical problems of public health programs and regulations. The time has come to more fully integrate the ethical problems of public health into the field of public health and, at the same time, into the field of bioethics. Public health raises a number of moral problems that extend beyond the earlier boundaries of bioethics and require their own form of ethical analysis.

| Daniel Callahan, PhD, and Bruce Jennings, MD

WHEN THE FIELD OF BIOETHICS emerged in the late 1960s and early 1970s, it represented a significant broadening of medical ethics. It moved the subject beyond the doctor-patient relationship and medical professionalism into the new territory of, among other things, organ transplants, genetics, reproductive biology, and resource allocation. But little attention was paid by bioethics in its early years to the distinctive ethical problems inherent in public health. That is perhaps not surprising. Bioethics received its initial stimulus from the abuses of human subjects research, the emergence of the patients' rights movement, and the drama of high-technology medicine. That focus on technology has continued, as has a lack of thoroughgoing engagement with issues of social and economic inequality, which have been staples of attention in public health since the 19th century.

In early bioethics, the good of the individual, and particularly his or her autonomy, was the dominant theme, not population health. The bioethics movement, moreover, shadowed the rapid expansion of the biomedical research enterprise, first in the search for cures through better biological understanding and technological innovation and then in the ensuing struggle over issues of equitable access as the cost of health care steadily rose. Meanwhile, the field of public health—though sporadically brought to public attention by the polio epidemics of the 1950s, by the smoking and lung cancer reports, and by the AIDS pandemic—was moved to the shadows to some extent by the drama of advances in biomedicine.

But the times are changing, as they should, and some fresh winds are blowing. The last decade or so has produced a much-needed resurgence of public visibility for public health. There are at least 2 reasons for this. One is the unwelcome reminder that infectious disease has not, in fact, been conquered. The second is the recognition that the health of populations is a function more of good public health measures and socioeconomic conditions than of biomedical advances, even though it is true that public health needs biomedicine to do its work fully, especially through disease screening programs and the biomedical techniques they require. This has long been a commonplace within the public health community, but it has been a neglected truth by most outside the field.

As the concern of health policymakers turns toward health outcomes, cost-effectiveness, and preventive measures throughout the life cycle (primary, secondary, and tertiary prevention), the field of public health is gaining increased public and legislative attention. Research!America, a leading advocacy group long focused on biomedical research advocacy, is now working with a strong coalition to promote health and disease prevention research, and many private foundations are giving such research a more conspicuous position on their agendas.

Of course, the prominence of public health has not displaced that of biomedicine, which, during this same period, has had the Human Genome Project, among other things, to sustain it. Nonetheless, public health is once more a force to be reckoned with, and it is increasingly apparent that public health must contribute to the definition of the ends as well as the means of health policy. It is hard to overestimate the chastening effect that HIV/AIDS, multiple-drug-resistant tuberculosis, Lyme disease, and other serious infectious diseases have had on this development. Nor should we forget how much research in the field of public health has, since the 1960s, taught us about the looming challenges of health care in an aging society: chronic illness, high-risk health-related behavior, injuries, and the interaction between health and the environment.

As the field of public health becomes more prominent, so will the ethical issues associated with it.[1] As more teaching and research are done on ethics in public health, it is important to begin a focused conversation within the field and between the field and others. What are the basic ethical issues of public health? What ethical orientations are most helpful in the clarification and resolution of these issues? How are ethical principles and concepts incorporated into decision making in public health agencies and programs? How adequately are the ethical dimensions of public health policy identified and debated? What are the chances for a fruitful collaboration between public health and bioethics, and what factors would be conducive to its success?

For its part, bioethics has become restless for change, and it is particularly looking for a value orientation that may bring it into closer proximity with public health. There has always been an undercurrent of resistance to the individualistic, autonomy-driven mainstream orientation within bioethics, and that orientation has held sway. And why not? In keeping with the cultural trends of the 1970s and 1980s, it has often brought together the political left and the market-oriented right in a celebration of choice and freedom. But the obvious need for universal health care, the persistence of racial and ethnic disparities in health status, and the importance of background social and economic factors have caught the eye of many.[2] A shift of direction in the field of bioethics was called for, and it has already begun. By the mid-1990s, increased interest in population health had emerged, the ethical dilemmas faced by public health programs were attracting attention, and courses on ethics and public health had begun to appear with greater frequency in the curriculum of schools of public health.

Although interest in public health and ethics has been present in the field for many years—one thinks of the long-standing concern among epidemiologists—those in the field of public health seem to welcome the growing interest among their colleagues in bioethics. There is a small but growing cadre of ethicists writing and teaching within the field of public health itself. In the 1980s, the American Public Health Association established a special primary interest group on bioethics, the Forum on Bioethics (now called the Forum on Ethics), that certainly facilitated the discussions and networking of public health ethics scholars.

The importance of ethics was recognized again in 1997, when the Centers for Disease Control and Prevention (CDC) established an ethics subcommittee of the Director's Advisory Committee. Ethical guidelines have been developed by the American College of Epidemiology and the American Statistical Association. Most recently, a work group of the Public Health Leadership Society established a group to develop a code of ethics for the field, and the Association of Schools of Public Health (ASPH) initiated a curriculum development project designed to advance the teaching of ethics in public health.

The interest in ethics and public health is clearly there, and the question now is how to bring it to maturity so that it can make the most helpful contributions. The benefits can and should run in 2 directions, toward illuminating some important problems in public health and enriching and expanding bioethics. Still, it is fair to say that there are some significant obstacles to such a dialogue. We have already alluded to one such obstacle, namely, the difference between the individualistic orientation of bioethics and the population and societal focus of public health. This is not so much an intrinsic difference between the 2 fields as it is a difference between the perspectives of the public health and policy world, on the one hand, and the world of clinical medicine (in which bioethics has principally operated), on the other.

More difficult will be the tension produced by the predominant orientation in favor of civil liberties and individual autonomy that one finds in bioethics, as opposed to the utilitarian, paternalistic, and communitarian orientations that have marked the field of public health throughout its history.[3] The ethical and policy issues concerning, for example, HIV and multidrug-resistant tuberculosis already have thrust public health ethics into the thick of this clash of values. And, if the issue of paternalism (limiting the freedom of the individual for the sake of his or her own greater good or best interests) were not enough, the cognate clash between individualistic civil liberties and a communitarian orientation (limiting the freedom of the individual for the sake of the common good or public interest) will also provoke lively discussion.

Neither of these conflicts are intractable, however. Beginning with the civil libertarian concerns of the AIDS epidemic in the 1980s, a rights-based orientation has made a strong mark, occasioning some important struggles about the relationship between individual and society and seeking better ways to balance community health needs and individual rights. Moreover, the international human rights framework, which has been given serious consideration in public health by Jonathan Mann, Lawrence Gostin, Sophia Gruskin, and others, is one potential path of synthesis among these conflicting ethical perspectives, and other frameworks described later in this commentary, such as the analytic and critical ethical frameworks, may be able to come to the same resolution as well.[4]

THE SCOPE OF PUBLIC HEALTH ETHICS

Just as public health is broad in its scope, the range of ethical issues in the field is uncommonly wide, encompassing ethics *in* public health as well as the ethics *of* public health. If ethics is understood to be a search for those values, virtues, and principles necessary for people to live together in peace, mutual respect, and justice, then there are few issues in public health that do not admit of an ethical perspective. To begin to map the scope of this broad terrain, 4 general categories of such issues should be noted: health promotion and disease prevention, risk reduction, epidemiological and other forms of public health research, and structural and socioeconomic disparities in health status.

Health Promotion and Disease Prevention

Programs designed to promote health and prevent disease and injury raise questions about the responsibility of individuals to live healthy lives; about the government's role in creating an environment in which individuals are able to exercise their health-related responsibility; about the role of government in coercing or influencing health-related behavior or in developing educational programs; about the use of incentives, economic or otherwise, to promote good health; and about the relative importance for society of pursuing good health, particularly in a culture that prizes autonomy and does not always look fondly on government intervention.[5]

Risk Reduction

Risks to the health of the public are many, and many methods are used to reduce or eliminate them.[6] Almost all can pose one or more ethical problems. The concept of risk itself is seemingly impossible to define in value-neutral terms and is inherently controversial. Even more ethically charged is the question of what level or degree of risk is socially acceptable to individuals and communities. Who should decide about that, and how should exposure to risk be distributed across the affected population?[7] Researchers in epidemiology are often reluctant to draw broad general conclusions from their data, but pressure from policymakers on public health professionals is often intense to provide a definitive recommendation or answer.

A significant debate in public health ethics is whether and to what extent the so-called "precautionary principle" should be followed. In essence, this principle places the burden of proof on those who would initiate risk to demonstrate that the benefits will outweigh the dangers and that the risk is rationally worth taking. There is, however, often an inconsistency in that those who propose the removal of risk find that the burden is on them to prove that their cause is worth spending money on.

Routine public health practice entails a number of interventions and policies designed to prevent harm to individuals and to lower health risks within the population. These include various forms of screening and testing of different age groups, many of which are legally mandatory and paternalistic or are administered in a way that does not follow the requirements of informed consent. Epidemiologic practice, especially when mandated by state laws, may not always follow appropriate ethical protocols on the rights of human subjects, and the collection of health information may sometimes put the public health practitioner in a position of possessing information that certain individuals (e.g., employers, insurance providers) might have an interest in knowing. The responsibilities of the public health researcher regarding individual notification and protection of personal privacy and confidentiality are not yet clearly set out as a matter of consensus within the profession. The experience with HIV/AIDS in the past 2 decades has shown how problematic it can be when public health officials seek to employ fairly standard practices such as contact tracing and partner notification to curb the spread of sexually transmitted diseases.[8,9]

Epidemiological and Other Public Health Research

Research with human subjects has been a central ethical problem for biomedicine for at least 100 years, but particularly since World War II. Yet, is the biomedical model—focused on individual informed consent and tightly regulated research with those at risk of exploitation—an appropriate model for public health, one that may either pose no medical or other risks to individuals or make consent impractical to gain in research encompassing large communities? And should the research standards used in the United States be exactly the same for research in other countries, particularly developing countries?

Structural and Socioeconomic Disparities

It has been known for many years that socioeconomic disparities have a major impact on health status. Equitable access to decent health care and reductions in health status disparities have been long-sought goals in American society but have not always been dealt with in the context of socioeconomic disparities. What is the appropriate role for the public health community in seeking greater justice in health care, and how should it balance its fact-finding and educational role with its historically strong advocacy mission?

What is the appropriate role for the public health community in seeking greater justice in health care, and how should it balance its fact-finding and educational role with its historically strong advocacy mission?

To some, for example, it is surprising and disturbing that more attention has not been paid by the public health community and in the ethics literature to ethical issues of occupational health and safety and to the ethical problems that arise when considering the health implications of environmental policy. These are 2 major areas in which the following of lines of inquiry on ethical and social value issues is likely to expose the need for far more attention to empirical research than public health specialists have yet provided. Finally, to what extent, if any, should the field adopt a politically partisan posture, taking a public stand on important policy issues and legislative initiatives?

TYPES OF ETHICAL ANALYSIS

While the preceding classification of broad issues by no means exhausts the possible categories of topics, it is sufficient to make evident that no single method of ethical analysis can be used for all of them (or even for the great variety of subtopics involved with any of the particular issues). In our pluralistic society, numerous ethical perspectives coexist on matters of such widespread interest and importance as public health. Ethical analysis can be usefully divided into a number of different types, depending on the point of view and needs from which it originates. One or more of them might be appropriate for any specific ethical problem.

Professional Ethics

The study of professional ethics tends to seek out the values and standards that have been developed by the practitioners and leaders of a given profession over a long period of time and to identify those values that seem most salient and inherent in the profession itself. Applied to public health, this perspective entails identifying the central mission of the profession (e.g., protection and promotion of the health of all members of society) and building up a body of ethical principles and standards that would protect the trust and legitimacy the profession should maintain.

Applied Ethics

Another approach to public health ethics comes from the field that has emerged in recent years as applied or practical ethics. Bioethics is one area among others within this domain of ethics. The applied ethics perspective differs from the professional ethics perspective principally in that it adopts a point of view from outside the history and values of the profession. From this more general moral and social point of view, applied ethics seeks to devise general principles that can then be applied to real-world examples of professional conduct or decision making. These principles and their application are designed to give professionals guidance and to provide those individuals affected by professional behavior, as well as the general public, with standards to use in assessing the professions. Thus, in applied ethics, there is a tendency to reason abstractly and to draw from general ethical theories rather than from the folkways and knowledge base of the professions. The emphasis tends to be on professional conduct rather than on the virtues of professional character.

Advocacy Ethics

If there is a characteristic ethical orientation within the field of public health today, it is probably less theoretical or academic than either professional ethics or applied ethics. While on occasion it can pose difficulties for civil servants, the ethical persuasion most lively in the field is a stance of advocacy for those social goals and reforms that public health professionals believe will enhance general health and well-being, especially among those least well off in society. Such advocacy is in keeping with the natural priorities of those who devote their careers to public health. It has a strong orientation toward equality and social justice. Much of the research and expertise in public health throughout its history has shown how social deprivation, inequality, poverty, and powerlessness are directly linked to poor health and the burden of disease. In recent years, a growing international movement in support of human rights has exerted an important influence on public health as well.

Critical Ethics

Finally, we would distinguish yet another possible perspective on ethics that could be directed toward the distinctive issues and problems of public health. For want of a better term, we label it "critical ethics." In many ways, it attempts to combine the strengths of the other perspectives mentioned. Like professional ethics, it is historically informed and practically oriented toward the specific real-world and real-time problems of public health, but, like applied ethics, it brings larger social values and historical trends to bear in its understanding of the current situation of public health and the moral problems faced. These problems are not only the result of the behavior of certain disease organisms or particular individuals. They are also the result of institutional arrangements and prevailing structures of cultural attitudes and social power.

The perspective of critical ethics has much in common with the egalitarian and human rights–oriented discourse of advocacy ethics in public health. One possible advantage of critical ethics is its call for discussions of ethics and public health policy to be genuinely public or civic endeavors: not the advocacy of a well-intentioned elite on behalf of needy clients, but a search for forums and programs of meaningful participation, open deliberation, and civic problem solving and capacity building. Some of the best examples of public health practice, from this point of view, grow out of efforts to champion communities as places of mutual support, respect, and self-esteem, thereby reinforcing health-promoting behaviors among their individual members.

We submit that a rich discourse on ethics and public health cannot be advanced without relating it to the background values of the general society, and the particular communities, in which it will be carried out. Our Canadian neighbors in public health have much more consciously attempted to relate public health and the sociopolitical values of that country's society.[10] It is one thing to say that public health rests on a communitarian foundation and quite another to determine how best to relate that foundation to our individualist culture, particularly in that members of this culture have been historically hostile toward government. The conflict, long endemic in our society, between the right of individuals to be left alone and the needs of the larger public does not make it easy to develop population-based health strategies that must, on occasion, ignore the special needs of individuals.

AN ETHICAL CODE?

The work of the Public Health Leadership Society in initiating a process to establish a code of ethics for public health is important. Where does a code of ethics fit into a broader confrontation with ethical issues? Most professions have a code, and of course many professionals in public health belong to one or another of such professions. Considering this, is there any need for an additional code for public health? There are at least 3 reasons to have a code. One of them is to respond to scandals in a field, aiming to ensure better future conduct. Some business and governmental codes of ethics had that aim as their origin. Another is to help establish the moral credibility of a field and its professional status and to provide principles to deal with common dilemmas. Such was the 19th-century origin of the code of ethics of the American Medical Association. Still another purpose is to provide a profession with a moral compass and to set forth its ideals. Some professional codes, such as that of the American Bar Association, include a large number of concrete rules to deal with almost every kind of ethical problem.

This is not the place to discuss ethics codes in detail, but some general considerations are worth noting. Public health has rarely been attacked for a lack of professionalism or for scandals, and the field is unlikely to be attracted to a code similar to that of the American Bar Association. The greatest challenge in writing a code is to specify clearly the ideals of the field and then to specify some general guidelines that will be illuminating for the wide array of problems practitioners can encounter. Historically, many if not most professional codes have been written because of structural changes in a profession that have generated new ethical problems and made it necessary to shore up public confidence in the profession's integrity.

We believe that the integrity of the profession of public health is sound, but the changing situation of public health practice may be a good reason to more precisely specify the ethical obligations that those in the field take on when they become practitioners. Code developments and revisions, it might be noted, have often been most successful when they are accompanied by lengthy and strenuous debate engaging the entire professional community and not simply those with a special interest in ethics.

SCIENCE AND PUBLIC HEALTH ETHICS

Public health ethics and public health science are often connected. A good example is the ethics of public health decision making. Public health professionals recommend preventive interventions that presumably will—on balance—benefit the public's health. Existing scientific evidence and, especially, its interpretation play important roles in these decisions.

What makes the ethics of decision making so difficult is the presence of scientific complexity and scientific uncertainty. The evidence used in making claims about disease causation and about the efficacy of preventive interventions typically arises from several sources: biological (laboratory) science, epidemiological and clinical sciences, and the social and behavioral sciences. Furthermore, the methods used to summarize evidence are more qualitative than quantitative. Making valid and reliable claims under those circumstances is difficult.[11] Public health decisions carry with them varying levels of empirical uncertainty. The extent to which the public's health ultimately benefits or does not benefit in the face of such uncertainty is not well established.

There are other ethical concerns that emerge from public health's strong connection to science. Research ethics provides many examples, such as scientific misconduct.[12] The choice of research topics is another. The values that determine where and how public health research dollars are spent have important ethical implications.

LAW AND ETHICS

Public health is one of the few professions that has, in many matters, legal power—in particular, the police power of the state—behind it.[13] It can, through use of the law, coerce citizens into behaving in some approved, healthy way: for example, by forcing immunization on their children, by restricting their right to smoke in public places, or by quarantining them to stop the spread of infectious disease. Public health also has the distinction, along with a few others—such as city management, public administration, and law enforcement—of being a profession in which many practitioners are government employees and officials. It thus has an obligation both toward government, which controls it, and toward the public that it serves.

Because of its public and governmental roles, public health has ethical problems unlike those of most other professions. The relationship between ethics and law is a long and tangled one, but it is safe to say that most public health laws and regulations have behind them an explicitly moral purpose: that of promoting and protecting the lives of citizens. Because the police power of the state is involved, however, a number of moral conflicts are generated. The tension between individual health and rights, on the one hand, and government obligations and population health, on the other, is an obvious instance of this kind of conflict. The economic and social impact on communities of public health measures, requiring some form of cost-benefit analysis, is another.

The relationship between ethics and law is a tangled one, but most public health laws have behind them an explicitly moral purpose: that of promoting and protecting the lives of citizens.

Health is an important human need, and good health is highly valued. But health is not the only need or good health the only value. Laws must always find ways of balancing various goods, and the centrality of laws for the work of public health brings uncommon visibility to its actions and an uncommon need for public accountability.

POLITICS AND PUBLIC HEALTH

As public arguments over fluoridation or HIV disease amply demonstrate, public health measures can quickly become politicized. Political controversy is often treated as some kind of disaster for calm reflection and measured rationality. This is sometimes in fact the case, but given the governmental role of public health and its use of coercion for many purposes, politics is unavoidable and necessary. It is unavoidable because there is no way to stop the public from turning to legislatures or the courts to express their values and needs; nor should there be. Politics is a necessary component of public health, moreover, precisely in order to achieve public health policies and practices consistent with American traditions and values. Politics is the messy arena in which ultimate questions of the public good are worked out. Ethics, Aristotle wrote 2500 years ago, is a branch of politics—a shrewd insight—and it is surely true in this country that the most important moral struggles almost always end in the public arena.

Yet, there can be responsible and irresponsible politics. Public health can best serve the cause of responsible politics, even when it has a self-interested stake in the outcome, when it makes available good data, when it is sensitive to community sentiments, and when it makes clear by all of its actions that it is not (as the stereotype would have it) just one more self-serving, distant government bureaucracy. Public health receives its money from the public, gains its legal powers from the public, and must be judged by the effectiveness of its service to the public. As long as this is kept clearly in mind, public health can survive the imposition of politics on its work and can, in fact, flourish.

CURRICULUM DEVELOPMENT

One crucial question toward which the preceding discussion points is how to promote a greater awareness and a more sustained, sophisticated discussion of ethical issues among public health practitioners and researchers themselves, as well as among the broader public. In any professional field, ethical sensitivity and discernment exist, to the extent that they exist, only if they begin early in the educational and socialization processes of the field and only if ethics is a discipline that is taken seriously both by the academic wing of the profession in its writing and teaching and by the practice wing of the profession in its conduct. In these respects, we reluctantly observe, the field of public health has an important opportunity for advancement. Ethics education has a university-based ("preservice") component and a workplace-based or continuing education ("in-service") component. Both are essential, and the in-service setting is particularly crucial in public health because so many practitioners receive their academic training in cognate fields.

The Teaching of Public Health Ethics

An obvious and crucial step to take is to promote the teaching of ethics in all schools of public health in the United States. In the past decade, a handful of public health programs have integrated some ethics education into their course offerings, but not to the extent of their close neighbors, medical and nursing schools. Much more needs to be done if there is going to be serious study and discussion of the myriad ethical issues arising in public health comparable to the impressive body of work achieved by medical ethics and bioethics.

In the first place, the teaching of ethics in public health is still quite limited. In a 1999 study, 24 schools of public health were surveyed to assess their formal ethics instruction. Only 8 schools required course work in ethics, and only 1 school required it of all students. Fourteen more schools offered an elective course. Many schools had occasional ethics lectures and symposia.[14,15] This means that a significant percentage of each graduating class at the master's level has not been exposed to a systematic and sustained analysis of ethical issues in the field, led by a faculty member with sufficient training in ethics.

Moreover, a review of syllabi collected through an ASPH-conducted project revealed that most of the courses listed in the curricula of schools of public health are in fact primarily courses in medical ethics. While it is beneficial for members of the public health community to be aware of bioethical issues, it is even more important to isolate those practice and policy issues that are distinctive to public health or that set up a balance between the interests of health care consumers and the public health objectives of the society as a whole. In a number of cases, the teaching of ethics in public health is not, strictly speaking, public health ethics but rather some generic offering of bioethics with one or two public health topics salted in. Such courses will introduce students of public health to the rudiments of ethical reasoning but will do little to advance ethical solutions to dilemmas that arise in public health practice. Of course, there are prominent exceptions to this general observation, but their example has not been widely followed.

Why has more not been done? The fact is that the teaching of ethics in any professional school is controversial, intellectually difficult, institutionally challenging, and expensive. (The same is true for ethics education in in-service settings.) Nonetheless, there are good reasons why ethics in public health can and should be taught.

The teaching of ethics is controversial primarily because the dominant ethos of most professions is empiricist, quantitative, and oriented toward precise, definitive solutions to discrete problems. This often does not comport well with the intellectual characteristics of ethical analysis, which focus on the multifaceted nature of problems—the difficulty in finding definitive solutions to problems that take complex forms as analogies, narratives, or dilemmas—and on the qualitative and interpretative character of moral judgment in contrast to the quantitative knowledge that carries legitimacy in most professional fields. In public health there is an opening for the teaching of ethics in part because it has been so well accepted in medicine, which still exerts a powerful influence in the field of public health, and in part because public health is itself a multidisciplinary field. Although there are certainly strongly quantitative elements present in public health, there is also a substantial influence from history, law, and the social sciences, areas in which qualitative reasoning akin to ethics is well regarded.

Beyond these academic considerations, however, support for the teaching of ethics in many fields has come from students themselves, on the one side, and from practitioners, on the other. Students want to engage the value and social issues of their chosen profession and not merely its most technical aspects. For their part, practitioners well recognize the inevitability of the ethical quandaries in the world beyond graduate preparation. They need and expect young professionals to emerge from their training with more than technical information and intelligence. They want precisely the kinds of reasoning ability and capacity for judgment that ethics education, properly conducted, provides. There is no reason why the combined forces of student interest and the practice needs of the profession should not succeed in prompting the addition of ethics to the public health curriculum as well.

The teaching of ethics in schools of public health will be intellectually challenging for many of the reasons we have reviewed here. The field is not well unified and does not have a clear consciousness of itself as a profession. The conceptual and intellectual framework necessary to develop a public health ethics is not yet in place. In consequence, the academic qualifications appropriate for faculty in public health ethics and a solid body of written work for students to study are lacking. Rarely will existing faculty in schools of public health step forward to teach a course in ethics. Qualified people will have to be brought in from the outside or recruited from other faculties within the university. Those who have been teaching bioethics in medical school or at the undergraduate level will find that a substantially new and different course should be created for public health students.

Institutionally, any change in an already crowded and overtaxed curriculum is difficult. Qualified faculty must be put in place, and that costs money. Ethics faculty may not be able to bring in the kinds of research grants that scholars in other disciplines can generate. Moreover, if space is to be made for ethics, some other work may have to give way. The advance of biomedical science is unrelenting; arguably, subjects such as genetics need much more attention in the public health curriculum than they have had before. The same could be said for economics or health services research.

If a case is to be made for giving time to ethics in a crowded scientific curriculum, it must be made on the basis of a conception of the profession that is richer than the mastery of technical knowledge and skills. It also must be made on the basis of a conception of the qualities and abilities that a public health professional should possess if he or she is to be truly educated toward public service: sound judgment, ability to recognize and analyze ethical issues, tolerance for ambiguity, and capacity for a moral imagination with which seemingly isolated issues or events can be placed in a broader context of human experience and value. These are educational goals worthy of an attempt to overcome whatever institutional or financial challenges curriculum innovation in public health may require.

Continuing Ethics Education

Another step that can be taken to encourage better discussion of and sensitivity toward ethical issues in public health is to promote, insofar as is practical, continuing education materials and programs for public health practitioners in the field. Because the profession is so dispersed in its work—from employment in private managed care organizations and clinics to international nongovernmental organizations and federal, state, and local agencies—it is difficult to know where to begin with this in-service ethics education effort. Perhaps state departments of health would be as good a place as any to start. And university graduate schools of public health should do more to reach out to the practice community and support the development of in-service ethics programs.

There is no reason why the combined forces of student interest and the practice needs of the profession should not succeed in prompting the addition of ethics to the public health curriculum as well.

RECOMMENDATIONS

To promote the discussion and advancement of ethics in public health, we offer the following recommendations.

1. *Leaders in public health should support the development of conferences and symposia on the theme of ethics and public health.* Creating these forums will encourage both scholars and practitioners to turn their attention to original research and writing, will help to sharpen the issues, and

will attract the attention of scholars in other fields such as bioethics, history, sociology, and political science, encouraging them to undertake new work on topics relating to public health and public health ethics. The US Public Health Service, the surgeon general, and the CDC could take the lead in this effort. Such symposia could be sponsored and supported by federal and state agencies, schools of public health, the leading public health professional journals, and major foundations that have an abiding interest in the field of public health as a scientific and professional resource for the country.

2. *The editors of leading public health and bioethics journals should give high priority to accepting and soliciting rigorous work in public health ethics for publication.* This type of recognition will lead to the acceptance of work in public health ethics as valid scholarship within the field, and it will produce the reading materials that courses in public health ethics can use.

3. *Efforts should be undertaken to compile a set of case materials for ethics discussion and teaching.* These materials, in fact, have pedagogical uses that are not limited to ethics. They could be akin to the case studies developed by the Harvard Business School, and they should explore in detail the complexity of public health practice and the ethical issues that are embedded within it.

4. *The specific topic of ethical issues in public health research should be a focus.* This topic certainly deserves fresh attention, and it should be part of the current agenda for the various governmental and private bodies that oversee the human subjects research area. There is a tremendous resurgence of interest in research ethics in biomedicine across the board today, and epidemiological and public health research should be firmly included on that agenda as well.

5. *The accreditation process for schools of public health should involve an increase in ethics instruction requirements.* It may be premature to mandate that all students take required course work in ethics, but all schools of public health should give priority to ethics in their curriculum development planning. Ethics-related learning objectives could at least be incorporated into existing courses in the curriculum. This indirect approach should give way to more systematic instruction once the field has had time to develop the necessary faculty expertise and literature in ethics.

6. *As a profession, public health should develop continuing education requirements and make ethics prominent among them.* This type of initiative could start at the governmental level: anyone employed as a public health officer or professional should attend periodic programs designed to educate practitioners on ethical issues they face.

7. *Public health agency managers and supervisors at the federal, state, and local levels should be encouraged to provide the time and resources necessary for periodic in-service ethics sessions.* There is value in having in-service programs conducted at workplaces so that discussions can involve multidisciplinary and multilevel coworkers. With the right support and leadership, such sessions can create an atmosphere of trust and candor so that problems can be addressed and solutions sought. Those involved with similar programs in other professions have discovered that such sessions not only serve to provide education about ethics but also can improve working relations and morale.

8. *Scholars in the field of ethics should educate themselves about public health and develop a more sophisticated understanding of how ethical issues in public health might best be approached.* Throughout, all activities should run a strong and imaginative effort to better specify the nature and range of ethical issues and how they might best be analyzed. The field of public health ethics has great promise. Careful thought, blended with experience, will be necessary to fulfill that promise. Academics, practitioners, and ethicists within the field and those outside it should cooperate in this important endeavor. ■

About the Authors

The authors are with The Hastings Center, Garrison, NY. They are writing for members of the Hastings Center Project on Ethics and Public Health: Ronald Bayer, Columbia University School of Public Health; Allan Brandt, Harvard Medical School; Daniel Callahan, The Hastings Center, Ruth R. Faden, Johns Hopkins University; Lawrence O. Gostin, Georgetown University Law School and Johns Hopkins University; Bruce Jennings, The Hastings Center; Jeffrey Kahn, University of Minnesota; Jan Malcolm, Minnesota State Department of Health; Donald R. Mattison, March of Dimes; Thomas L. Milne, National Association of County and City Health Officials; Phillip Nieburg, Centers for Disease Control and Prevention; Margaret Pappaioanau, Centers for Disease Control and Prevention; Ann Robertson, University of Toronto; Dixie E. Snider, Centers for Disease Control and Prevention; Bonnie Steinbock, State University of New York at Albany; and Douglas L. Weed, National Cancer Institute.

Requests for reprints should be sent to Daniel Callahan, The Hastings Center, 21 Malcolm Gordon Dr, Garrison, NY 10524-555 (e-mail: callahan@thehastingscenter.org).

This commentary was accepted October 4, 2001.

Contributors

D. Callahan and B. Jennings both led the writing of this commentary.

Acknowledgment

We wish to acknowledge the generous support of the Robert Wood Johnson Foundation.

References

1. Beauchamp TE, Steinbock B, eds. *New Ethics for the Public's Health.* New York, NY: Oxford University Press Inc; 1999.

2. Faden R. Bioethics and public health in the 1980s: resource allocation and AIDS. *Annu Rev Public Health.* 1991;12:335–360.

3. Leichter H. *Free to Be Foolish.* Princeton, NJ: Princeton University Press; 1992.

4. Mann J, Gruskin S, Grodin MA, eds. *Health and Human Rights: A Reader.* New York, NY: Routledge; 1999.

5. Faden R. Ethical issues in government sponsored public health campaigns. *Health Educ Q.* 1987;14:27–37.

6. Leviton L, Needleman CE, Shapiro MA. *Confronting Public Health Risks: A Decision Maker's Guide.* Thousand Oaks, Calif: Sage Publications; 1998.

7. Stern PC, Fineberg HV, eds. *Understanding Risk: Informing Decisions in a Democratic Society.* Washington, DC: Academy Press; 1996.

8. Fox DM. From TB to AIDS: value conflicts in reporting disease. *Hastings Center Rep.* 1986;11:11–16.

9. Bayer R, Toomey KE. HIV prevention and the two faces of partner notification. *Am J Public Health.* 1995;85: 1569–1576.

10. Robertson A. Health promotion and the common good: reflection on the politics of need. In: Callahan D, ed. *Promoting Healthy Behavior: How Much Freedom? Whose Responsibility?* Washington, DC: Georgetown University Press; 2001:76–94.

11. Weed DL. Epistemology and virtue ethics. *Int J Epidemiol.* 1998;27:343–349.

12. Weed DL. Epistemology and ethics in epidemiology. In: Coughlin SS, Beauchamp TL, eds. *Ethics and Epidemiology.* New York, NY: Oxford University Press Inc; 1998:79–94.

13. Gostin LO. *Public Health Law: Power, Duty, Restraint.* Berkeley, Calif: University of California Press/Milbank Memorial Fund; 2000.

14. Coughlin SS, Katz WH, Mattison DR. Ethics instruction at schools of public health in the United States. *Am J Public Health.* 2000;90:768–770.

15. Coughlin SS. Model curricula in public health ethics. *Am J Prev Med.* 1996;12:247–251.

[7]

Broadening the Bioethics Agenda*

Dan W. Brock

ABSTRACT. Bioethics has focused principally on ethical issues arising in clinical medicine. When it has addressed justice or equity, it has focused on access to health care and on defending a general moral right to health care. This dual focus on establishing a right to health care and on health care rather than health has left bioethics largely silent on two issues of fundamental importance for a full account of justice and health. First, the focus on establishing a right to health care has contributed to a failure to address difficult issues in developing ethical standards for equitably prioritizing limited resources in health care. Second, the focus on inequalities in access to health care has ignored the much greater impact of social determinants of health, in particular socioeconomic class and inequality, on health and health inequalities. Bioethics must broaden its agenda.

I AM GOING TO BEGIN with some armchair history that helps explain why the bioethics agenda has failed to address seriously two areas of concern to me. Bioethics was born in the clinic, and as well in biomedical research, though I will not say more about the second birthplace (Jonsen 1998; Rothman 1991). In the late 1960s and 1970s, clinical medicine was undergoing profound changes that shaped the early concerns of bioethics. The older traditional paternalistic or authoritarian physician-patient relationship was challenged and, in this period of profound change in the expectations and responsibilities of patients and professionals, ethical problems and dilemmas proliferated in the day to day interactions among health care professionals and their patients and patients' families—prob-

* This paper was originally presented as the annual André Hellegers Memorial Lecture at the Kennedy Institute of Ethics, Georgetown University, in September 1999 and as a plenary lecture at the annual meeting of the American Society for Bioethics and Humanities in October 1999. My intent was to stimulate further interest and work in two relatively underdeveloped but important areas of bioethics, rather than to present my own more narrowly focused and detailed work on specific issues within those areas. I have left the paper in that form for publication with only very minor changes and references added.

lems about paternalism and autonomy, informed consent, forgoing life support, being truthful with patients, the limits of patient confidentiality, and how to use the never ending array of new technologies developed by medical researchers. These problems gained the increasing attention of clinicians and of early bioethicists. And because of how much is often at stake for patients in need of health care, the ethical problems and issues that arise in the clinical setting should always have an important place in bioethics.

To the extent that this early work in bioethics drew on more general work in moral philosophy, and specifically in normative ethical theory, it drew on the ethics of personal relations, often suitably interpreted to apply to the setting of professional ethics (Beauchamp and Childress 1979).

In the 1980s, as the extent of the shameful failure to provide access to health care for all Americans became better appreciated, and the number of uninsured individuals became clearer and continued to grow, a still relatively small minority of bioethicists turned their attention to issues of justice or equity in the distribution of health care (Daniels 1985; Churchill 1987; Menzel 1983). Important though this work was, and I believe it both was and still remains important, it had two significant shortcomings. First, it focused on health care to the exclusion of health, and, second, much of it was framed in terms of defending a moral right to health care. Though they were understandable, each of these features had unfortunate consequences.

I am going to argue that this dual focus on health care instead of health and then on establishing a general moral right to health care has contributed to bioethics' failure to confront two of the most important issues in an account of justice and health. First, the focus on establishing a right to health care has left bioethicists largely silent on the important and complex moral issues faced when limited health care resources must be prioritized by either public, government health care programs or private health insurers or providers. Second, the focus on health care rather than health fosters the assumption that differential access to health care is the principal inequity in the health sector in the United States, and elsewhere, and the principal cause of inequalities in health (Marchand, Wikler, and Landesman 1998). But in fact differences in access to health care account for only a very small proportion of the differences in health between different groups in society, as public health experts have long known and bioethicists should know. Other more important social determinants of health should be as much our concern as the differences arising from inequities in access to health care (Wilkinson 1996).

HEALTH CARE VERSUS HEALTH

Why has bioethics' work on distributive justice focused on health care instead of health? For one thing, it is possible to affect directly the distribution of health care by how one structures and organizes the health care system; that system is a social system within social control. The distribution of health, on the other hand, is not entirely within either individual or social control. Individuals' genetic inheritance, which is increasingly understood to have a major impact on health, is largely beyond anyone's control. So too are the effects of many of the vicissitudes of life—accidents, exposures to infectious disease, and the like. Philosophical theories of justice, as well as ordinary people, generally presuppose that justice concerns individual actions, social institutions, and outcomes that are within human control (Rawls 1971). So it was natural to assume that social justice in the health sector focuses fundamentally on the actions and institutions that determine the distribution of health care, not on the distribution of health. For similar reasons, moral rights in the health sector were framed as rights to health care, which could be secured for all, rather than to health, which cannot.

Framing such concerns about equity in access to health care in terms of a moral right to health care is the first narrowing of the bioethics agenda that I will address. There is no denying that the principal inequity in the U.S. health *care* system is the 44 million Americans currently without health insurance, and so without a regular and assured source of adequate health care. This fact is now a commonplace, and given this obvious and shameful inequity, it is understandable that bioethics work in the 1980s and 1990s would focus on showing that justice required closing that gap, and arguing for a general moral or human right to health care was a natural way to do so.[1] The question was often posed in terms of whether health care should be a right or, instead, a privilege and commodity like other commodities; recognizing it as a right was thought to provide the strongest moral basis for the claim that everyone should have access to needed health care. Rights and rights-based theories are prominent in moral and political philosophy, and rights have a natural and strong purchase in American moral and political discourse.

Failure to Address Health Care Priorities

It was widely recognized that it was both morally problematic and politically counterproductive to frame the right to health care as an unlimited right and claim on resources to meet every health care need at the highest possible level—the opportunity costs for other, nonhealth needs, such as education and housing, would be too great, and major new unlimited entitlement programs had little chance of political success. Different theorists recognized the necessary limitation of the right in different ways—some characterized it as a right to a decent minimum of health care (Buchanan 1984), the President's Commission (1983) to an adequate level of health care, and a few specified basic broad categories of services that should be included (Daniels 1985). But while all sought to make clear that they were not defending an unlimited right, not much was done to specify in detail what the right encompassed since the main moral and political task was to establish the right to health care of those presently without health insurance, not to determine what the limits of the health care guaranteed should be.

Moreover, specifying in detail what services the right encompassed, and in particular what services it did not encompass, smacked of and was easily attacked as rationing. Although most bioethicists recognized the unavoidability and even the desirability of rationing, few politicians did, at least openly, and in public and health policy debates one's views were often an easy target for discrediting if they could be tarred with the label of rationing. The general public, irresponsibly encouraged by many politicians and physicians, preferred to believe that in a rich country like ours with such an important good as health care, rationing was not necessary and did not in fact occur. Of course, this perspective overlooked the rationing imposed on the uninsured, as well as on others, but somehow this cognitive dissonance survived widely. And, given the pervasive belief that rationing did not occur, was not necessary, was politically dangerous, and would be morally wrong if it did occur, serious public discussion of it and of the limits to the right to health care was unlikely, and in fact rarely occurred. All this was quite remarkable during a period, which continues to this day, in which cost containment was the dominant issue of health policy, since the most obvious means of controlling health care costs is to deny some people some care, that is to ration care. But the preference was to believe that, by such means as cutting the "waste, fraud, and abuse" out of the health care system, costs could be adequately controlled without rationing.

The upshot of all this has been a general failure to address seriously how health care resources and programs should be prioritized, and in particular the moral standards for doing so. Yet I believe there are few issues more important for the nature of our health care system in coming years. And from a perspective that looks beyond our own borders, a perspective that American bioethics sorely needs, these problems are much more pressing, not just in poorer, less developed countries, but in other developed countries as well. Even the other developed countries, virtually all of which, unlike the United States, provide access to health care to all their citizens, spend substantially less than the U.S. per capita and as a proportion of their GDP on health care, and so face greater resource scarcity in the health sector and a more pressing need to prioritize health care services and programs. In fact many of the interesting and promising prioritization efforts as well as ethical analyses of rationing issues in recent years have been done overseas.

There are of course exceptions to the general picture that I have been painting. The most prominent public attempt in the United States to address setting health care priorities was Oregon's overhaul of its state Medicaid program, though no other state has followed its lead. Daniel Callahan (1987) has been a prominent proponent of recognizing that health care needs will always outrun available resources and of setting limits on care. And Norman Daniels (1985), Paul Menzel (1983, 1990), and Frances Kamm (1993), among others, have explored some "rationing problems" that arise when we face up to the need to prioritize resources, programs, and patients. But the fact remains that the issues and problems have only begun to be explored in a serious way.

Problems for Prioritization Efforts

In a common, though by no means universal, view in much public policy and health economics, the standard for prioritization is straightforward and clear, even if there are many complexities in applying it in practice. Since health resources are inevitably scarce, it seems obvious and even axiomatic to many that they should be used in whatever way will produce the most health benefits and thereby maximize the overall or aggregate health of the population being served. Cost-effectiveness (Gold et al. 1996) is the natural and standard analytic tool for pursuing this goal since it enables policymakers to determine how a given sum of money or other resources should be allocated to different health programs, interventions, or patients in order to produce the maximum health gains. Cost-effectiveness analysis is indifferent to the distribution of health benefits except in so far as it affects aggregate health benefits; it does not matter who receives how much health benefit so long as those benefits are maximized. This standard for distributing limited resources, of course, is a utilitarian or consequentialist moral standard, and its account of distributive justice is widely considered consequentialism's most unacceptable feature. It fails to give any direct attention to fairness and to various forms and degrees of inequality in different distributions (Brock 1998; Daniels 1998).

The commitment in many public health and health policy circles to *maximizing* population health is one reason that the shift being promoted by many today from a focus on meeting the needs of individual patients to promoting the health of populations, a shift that has much to recommend it, will not in itself focus attention on the issues of prioritization and allocation that need to be addressed. Population-based medicine that addresses the health of populations *need* not ignore issues such as the welfare of the less well-off, but doing so will require abandoning the common public health and health policy ethic of maximizing aggregate welfare, which is also the typical understanding that many managed care plans have of their responsibilities.

Space constraints do not permit me even to mention all of the resource prioritization issues that have not been adequately addressed in the bioethics literature (Menzel et al. 1999), much less to explore them in any detail, but I do want to highlight two to make clear the sort of issues I have in mind. The first was noted as an unsolved rationing problem by Norman Daniels (1993) some years ago, but he did not explore it in any detail, and there has been only limited progress on it since then.

It is a commonplace in general theories of justice that special concern is required for the worse-off members of society, and that the justice of a society can be judged by how it treats its least well-off members. Empirical work by such investigators as Erik Nord (1993) in Norway and Peter Ubel et al. (1996) in this country has indicated a willingness both by the general public and by health planners to sacrifice significant aggregate health benefits in order to ensure treatment for the sickest patients when health resources must be prioritized. However, complex and difficult questions are raised in applying the idea that justice requires a special concern for those who are worse off; questions that must be articulated in detail before alternative answers to them can even be developed, much less assessed. But before saying more about these questions, I shall give several brief practical examples in which the question of priority to individuals who are worse off arises so that it is clear that this is not merely an abstract, theoretical issue.

In an Institute of Medicine project on priorities for future vaccine development of which I was a member, we faced the question of what priority should be given to vaccines for patients who would be sickest if their disease was not prevented, for example a cryptosporidium vaccine for patients with AIDS whose quality of life will remain low because of their AIDS, as opposed to vaccines for generally less serious but more prevalent diseases like mumps or chicken pox that might produce overall greater benefits. Hospitals face this type of resource allocation issue when they must decide the relative priority of expanding an ICU for critically ill patients, many of whom will receive only limited benefits, versus expanding primary care or prenatal care clinics for less serious health problems, but which hold out the promise of greater aggregate health benefits from the much greater numbers served. Managed care plans face the issue when deciding about coverage for expensive, last chance therapies without well-established benefits, such as bone marrow transplants for patients with metastatic breast cancer, or for the extension of screening programs for potentially fatal diseases to populations for whom the risk and pick up rate are extremely low. In each case, these treatments or screening programs reach patients with, or at risk for, potentially fatal conditions, but provide less benefit than expanding presently inadequately funded treatment programs for nonfatal conditions such as substance abuse.

What then are the moral issues at play in deciding what priority to give the worse-off members of society? They include the questions: What *reasons* exist for giving priority to the worse off? *Who* are the worse off? *How much* priority should the worse off receive in health resource prioritization? These questions are interdependent since the answers given to each will often have implications for the others. Consider the first question—why should the worse off receive priority in health care allocation? One reason might be a commitment to equality in outcomes such as health states, so far as it can be achieved. However, that position is subject to what Derek Parfit (1991) has called the "leveling down" objection; for example, equality would be promoted by making the sighted blind even if doing so benefitted the blind in no way, but there would be nothing good in doing so. Alternatively, if inequalities are only morally objectionable when they are unjustly caused, there is no support for giving priority to worse-off persons whose worse health is not unjustly caused, such as people with severe genetically transmitted disabilities that are no one's fault. A commitment to equality of opportunity, as it is affected by disease and disability, will not help if it means maximizing the aggregate opportunity of *all* persons. What is needed is a justification for it being morally more important to benefit persons the worse off they are. One line of reasoning gives weight to the subjective point of view of each individual and appeals to the fact that the subjective importance of a health benefit to a person benefitted will be greater the worse off the person is because the proportional improvement from a benefit of a given size will be greater the worse off one is. A different line of reasoning appeals to the idea that the greater a person's undeserved deprivation, the greater the unfairness and the stronger his moral claim is to have it reduced or eliminated. Different possible reasons for giving priority to the worse off need to be elaborated and assessed.

If some justification for giving priority to the worse off succeeds, one then faces the issue of how to determine which individuals are the worse off. One issue for health resource allocation is whether justice requires priority for those with worse health or to those with worse overall well being. General theories of justice that address well being will most plausibly address individuals' overall well being, not just the limited domain of health. Alternatively, a "separate spheres" approach would restrict the considerations relevant to the distribution of health care to the limited domain of people's relative health and health needs (Kamm 1993; Walzer 1983). Even with the restriction of those who are worse off to those with worse health, additional issues remain. For example, are the worse off those with poorer overall levels of health or those who are sicker now and have the more serious disease in need of treatment. These categories can conflict, as when otherwise healthy persons have a more serious illness than others who have substantial background disabilities but a less serious illness. It is questionable whether a separate spheres approach, even, should ignore background levels of health in determining who are worse off with regard to health. And should one assess only who is sicker or has the worse level of health now, or also take account of individuals' past levels of health and how long they have suffered poor health?

Even after answering these and related questions, one faces the question of how much priority to give to the worse off. Giving the worse off absolute priority is not plausible because it leads to the bottomless pit problem. For example, if the worst off are individuals with very severe cognitive and physical impairments who have a very low health-related quality of life, there may be almost no end to the resources that might be devoted to them in the form of health care, medical research, and other supportive services that would provide them with only very small benefits but at very great cost. Giving absolute priority to the worse off would leave few resources for the health needs of most of the population. Some balance is required between giving special priority to the worse off and using limited resources to meet the needs of those who are better off. The extent to which there is a principled basis for this tradeoff is unclear, but we certainly have not yet developed it. At some point, we may have to turn to fair procedures, either political or within private health plans, to make these tradeoffs (Daniels and Sabin 1997). Or we might rely on empirical research that asks people, using various hypothetical choice scenarios, how much benefit to better off persons they are willing to sacrifice in order to treat the worse off. There is an important place in work on prioritization problems for empirical research of the sort done by Nord, Ubel, and others on the tradeoffs people make when confronted with various prioritization problems. But there is a danger that this research will yield only raw preferences, not reflective considered judgments. The empirical work must proceed hand in hand with the best philosophical or normative work, at least once more of it has been done, that articulates and critically evaluates alternative moral standards for these tradeoffs. We want to know how real people would make these tradeoffs after they have considered the best reasons and arguments bearing on them.

Finally, one must explore the different contexts in which prioritization and rationing decisions are made—at the bedside, in practice guidelines, in insurance plan coverage, in the funding and development of programs and facilities, in research priorities, and so forth. It is important to look both at the different forms the issues take in each setting and at when and how contextual factors should affect their resolution. It is an open question how far we can advance in developing determinate standards on giving priority to the worse off through moral argument, but there is no reason to believe that significant progress is beyond our grasp. Too little serious and systematic effort has been given to the task to warrant that conclusion.

This issue is just one example of a number of distributive constraints based in justice and fairness on maximizing health benefits with limited resources. There are other somewhat different, but also difficult and controversial, issues as well; one example is what costs and benefits should be considered when comparing and prioritizing different health programs. It is widely agreed that the direct health benefits for individuals of their medical treatment, such as improving renal function or reducing joint swelling should be counted; these are the intended health benefits of the treatments. On the cost side of the ledger, the direct costs of medical treatment such as the costs of health care professionals' time and of health care facilities, equipment, and supplies should also be counted.

But both medical and public health interventions often have large indirect benefits and costs. For example, advocates for increased funding for substance abuse treatment commonly appeal in support of their cause to the very great economic costs in lost work time of substance abuse, as well as to the economic, social, and psychological burdens on family members of substance abusers. And the indirect costs and benefits of many health problems and programs are so great as to swamp their direct costs and benefits. The question is when and to what extent the indirect economic and social burdens of disease and benefits of its treatment should be given weight in determining the priority to be given to different health programs?

These indirect costs and benefits are real costs of disease and real benefits of its treatment or prevention, even if not direct health benefits and direct treatment costs, and so there is at least a presumption that they should not be ignored when prioritizing scarce resources and programs in the health sector. But there are moral worries grounded in a conception of the moral equality of persons about using these indirect costs and benefits in health resource prioritization. Giving priority to the treatment of one group of patients over another because treating the first group would produce indirect benefits for others (for example, other family members who are dependent on these patients) or would reduce indirect economic costs to others (for example, the employers of these patients who incur less lost work time) could be argued to fail to give equal moral concern and weight to each person's health care needs. Instead, giving lower priority to those patients whose treatment is not a means to the indirect benefits or cost savings produced by treating the other patients gives the former patients and their health care needs lower priority simply because they are not a means to these indirect benefits or cost savings to others. Doing so would appear to violate the Kantian moral injunction against treating people solely as means for the benefit of others (Kamm 1993). This is an issue where who is making decisions in what context—for example, physicians at the bedside or health planners allocating resources to health programs—is likely to be morally important.

I have touched on only two of the moral issues that arise when we explicitly face the prioritization and rationing of health resources, or of patients in need of those resources, and I have explored the details of neither of them. Systematic exploration of moral standards for the full range of prioritization and rationing issues is the first broadening of the bioethics agenda with which I am concerned in this paper.

SOCIAL DETERMINANTS OF HEALTH

Now, let me turn briefly to the second broadening of focus that I believe bioethics needs. As I have already noted, when bioethics has taken a macro focus, its attention has been on health care and establishing a right to health care. Bioethicists seem typically to have assumed that the main causes of health inequities are the inequities in the health care system, in particular inequities in access to health care. But health care's impact on both health and health inequalities is quite limited; for example, medical care is estimated to account for only about one fifth of life expectancy gains in the twentieth century (Wilkinson 1996; Mann 1997). More important, *inequalities* in health among individuals and groups that are within human and social control are not primarily the result of inequalities in access to or use of health care. This is not to deny, of course, that medical care is often of great importance for the life and well-being of individual patients. But differences in access to and use of health care have only a negligible effect on health inequalities among social groups, in particular individuals of different socioeconomic classes. The crucial point is that differences in the *incidence* of illness and injury from social causes swamp the effects on health of differences in access to and use of medical care to *treat* that illness and injury (Wilkinson 1996). So if inequalities in access to health care are of moral concern because they result in inequalities in health, then focusing on health care will miss most of the action on the real matter of concern—health and health inequalities.

Some other important determinants of health are the familiar staple of preventive medicine and public health. I have in mind individual behaviors, such as high fat diets, smoking, substance abuse, and lack of exercise, that we know are risk factors for a variety of diseases. There are important issues of justice here as well since many of the most important behavioral risk factors for poor health are disproportionately concentrated in particular minorities and disadvantaged groups. However, behavioral risk factors, while important at the individual level, account at most for only about one quarter of the social gradient in health (Wilkinson 1996); furthermore, they have proved strongly resistant to change. Such risk factors are well known to bioethicists and are not my principal concern here.

Instead, I want to focus briefly on important *social* determinants of health that I believe are less widely appreciated by bioethicists, and so have received too little of our attention. My specific concern is with the effects on health of socioeconomic inequality. Here much of the data concerns mortality and life expectancy, so I shall focus on them, but the effects are largely replicated with morbidity and health as well. It is widely appreciated that severe poverty is associated with poor health and decreased life expectancy. The differences are most dramatic in the international context where life expectancy in some very poor under developed countries is little more than half that of many developed countries. The differences are less dramatic within the U.S. but persist here as well—extreme poverty is bad for your health. But the health effects of income differences between different countries tend to disappear when per capita income reaches around $5,000 and countries undergo the epidemiological transition from largely infectious to largely degenerative causes of death (Wilkinson 1996). Among the advanced industrial countries there is no significant correlation between per capita wealth and life expectancy. Beyond a per capita income well below that of the U.S. and the rest of the developed world, increases in a country's wealth do not produce better health. And other factors have strikingly large effects—among countries with comparable per capita incomes of around $5,000 or below there are differences in life expectancies of up to 20 years. Something beyond differences in wealth is at work. *Within* societies, however, differences in income beyond poverty levels do have substantial effects on the health of different socioeconomic classes. This social gradient in health suggests that *relative*, not absolute income levels are what impact health.

The most important social impact on health and life expectancy appears to be from socioeconomic inequality and class; education too is highly correlated with both health and socioeconomic class. Class differences in health and life expectancy exist at every level of the social hierarchy in developed and less developed countries, and cannot be explained by differences in social mobility, genetics, or lifestyle. As one moves up the socioeconomic scale, there is a consistent increase in life expectancy. The first major, and still classic, study demonstrating this effect—the Whitehall study—found that as one went up each grade in the British civil service there was a consistent increase in life expectancy, all in the absence of material deprivation at any grade (Townsend and Davidson 1983; Davey Smith, Shipley, and Rose 1990). Moreover, the differences in life expectancy were not small—between the highest and lowest grades it was 4.4 years, greater than the effect on mortality of all coronary disease (Wilkinson 1996; Marmot 1999). But it is not just where one stands in the socioeconomic hierarchy that affects health, but also the degree of socioeconomic inequality in the society. Higher societal income inequality adversely affects citizens' health and life expectancy; for example, infant mortality and death rates of the lowest social classes in Sweden, which has low inequality in income, are lower than those of the highest social classes in England and Wales, which have much less egalitarian income distributions (Wilkinson 1996). So there are at least two important social determinants of health at work, *where one stands* in the socioeconomic hierarchy affects one's health, and *the degree of income inequality* in a society affects the society's overall level of health and health inequality. If the effects of poverty and inequality are combined, even in a rich country like the United States, the size of the impact is striking. In the U.S. the difference in age-adjusted mortality between metropolitan areas with the combination of high inequality and low per capita income and those with low inequality and high per capita income is greater than the combined loss of life from lung cancer, diabetes, motor vehicle crashes, HIV infection, suicide, and homicide (Lynch et al. 1998).

How does socioeconomic inequality adversely affect health? This is not fully understood and the precise nature of the causal pathways are controversial, but there is considerable agreement about some major causal factors (Wilkinson 1996; Marmot 1999; Kawachi and Kennedy 1999). Because in developed countries it is one's relative rather than one's absolute income that is important, it appears to be the psychosocial rather than the material effects of income levels and inequality that are important. The social gradient in health is largely determined by relative deprivation. Socioeconomic status is correlated with the degree of social supports and participation in social networks outside the family, which have strong protective effects on health. Socioeconomic class strongly determines individuals' degree of control in the workplace and elsewhere, which also is strongly correlated with health, and in particular with levels of heart disease. More egalitarian societies exhibit stronger social cohesion and community life. In a variety of ways, the lower economic classes are subject to higher chronic psychological stress, which has a powerful effect on death and illness rates. Put generally, the quality of the social life in a society and the social capital of its members are two of the most powerful determinants of health, and they are very closely related to the degree of socioeconomic inequality and to the particular socioeconomic position of individual members of a society.

What are the implications of this social determination of health for bioethics? I confess that I am not at all confident about the answer, but I am convinced of the need to explore this question much more fully than bioethicists have in the past. The health inequalities in question are not inevitable ones about which we can do nothing. They are caused by social inequalities that are, at least largely, within social control, as demonstrated in international comparisons where differences in degrees of economic inequality result in differences in societal levels of health and health inequality. Moreover, and to reiterate, the impact of socioeconomic inequality on health inequality is clearly more important than that of the inequalities in access to health care, on which bioethics traditionally has focused its work on justice. The recent trends in the U.S. of widening economic inequality can be expected only to increase health inequalities, as well as to negatively affect overall levels of health. It may be tempting to throw up one's hands and say that, like the poor, economic inequality and so health inequality will always be with us. Especially in these conservative, market dominated times, there seems to be little political will to reduce economic inequality and certainly little that bioethicists can do to reduce it. But one could say the same about increasing access to health care—for long periods there has been limited political will to do that—which bioethicists nevertheless have taken to be a proper area of their concern. Despite the dominant clinical focus of bioethics, bioethicists have helped to increase public awareness of injustices in access to health care and to put and keep them on the public policy agenda. Our commitment to justice and to health has required such efforts, even when they had limited prospects of success, and it requires them in the area of socioeconomic inequalities and health as well. Moreover, there may be many practical policies that could reduce these health inequalities, as illustrated by the 39 policy recommendations of the recent Independent Inquiry into Inequalities in Health in Britain (Independent Inquiry 1999).

One issue for bioethics raised by the social determination of health inequality is what the proper account of health, as opposed to health care, equity is–i.e., which inequalities in health are unjust (Marchand, Wikler, and Landesman 1998)? What is the distributive goal at which justice in health should aim? The answer is a good deal less clear than it might seem, and I cannot explore the various possible answers here. One important complexity is that accounts of health equity and of social justice more generally are interdependent in ways that often are not fully appreciated. Most general theories of justice appear to assume that it is possible to determine which socioeconomic inequalities are unjust independent of their effects on health. For example, in Rawls's theory the Difference Principle permits economic inequalities to the extent that they improve the economic expectations of the least advantaged representative group (Rawls 1971). It is tempting to assume as well that an account of health equity will be independent of an account of economic justice, though it will of course be influenced by some background assumptions about justice more generally. But accounts of economic justice and health equity may conflict; for example, economic inequalities permitted by Rawls's Difference Principle may cause health inequalities that are condemned by the account of health equity. In effect, society would face a tradeoff of socioeconomic benefits and inequality with health and health inequality. How that tradeoff should be made is far from clear, but at least some otherwise justified economic inequalities might be, all things considered, unjust because of the health inequalities they cause. However, until we have a clear account of health equity it will not be possible to assess this tradeoff, and I think it plain that we do not have a clear account of health equity. An important implication for political philosophy is that it is a mistake to assume that the justice of socioeconomic inequalities can be assessed independent of their substantial effects on health.

Public health has been the discipline most concerned with the social determinants of health, but I think it lacks an adequate ethical framework for evaluating their ethical implications. Some have proposed human rights, which traditionally focus on the necessary social conditions for human well-being and dignity, as the most promising basis for developing that ethical framework (Mann 1997). Others have turned to the resources of political philosophy, beginning to explore how greater economic justice and the conditions for full democratic citizenship and participation would shape these social determinants (Daniels, Kennedy, and Kawachi 1999). What ultimately will best illuminate these issues is not yet clear. It is clear that the resources of personal and professional morality that bioethicists have so effectively utilized in developing a framework for the ethical issues that arise between patients and health care providers in clinical medicine will not be adequate to the task. We need now to forge links with public health comparable to those that we have forged with clinical medicine, to draw on the best work in social and political philosophy not just personal morality, and to use our expertise and training in ethical analysis to help develop an ethical framework adequate for addressing health inequalities and their social determinants.

NOTE

1. The most prominent exception to framing the issue in terms of a right to health care was Daniels (1979, 1985), who explicitly sought to ground his account in a general theory of justice. Nevertheless, his early work focused on why justice required guaranteeing access to health care to all.

REFERENCES

Beauchamp, Tom L., and Childress, James F. 1979. *Principles of Biomedical Ethics*. New York: Oxford University Press. (Fourth edition published in 1994.)

Brock, Dan W. 1998. Ethical Issues in the Construction of Summary Measures of Population Health. In *Summarizing Population Health: Directions for the Development and Application of Population Metrics*, ed. Marilyn J. Field and Marthe R. Gold, pp. 73-85. Washington, DC: Institute of Medicine.

Buchanan, Allen. 1984. The Right to a Decent Minimum of Health Care. *Philosophy & Public Affairs* 13: 55-78.

Callahan, Daniel. 1987. *Setting Limits: Medical Goals in an Aging Society*. New York: Simon & Schuster.

Churchill, Larry. 1987. *Rationing Health Care in America.*. Notre Dame, IN: Notre Dame University Press.

Daniels, Norman. 1979. Rights to Health Care: Programmatic Worries. *Journal of Medicine and Philosophy* 4: 175-91.

———. 1985. *Just Health Care*. Cambridge: Cambridge University Press.

———. 1998. Distributive Justice and the Use of Summary Measures of Population Health. In *Summarizing Population Health: Directions for the Development and Application of Population Metrics*, ed. Marilyn J. Field and Marthe R. Gold, pp. 58-71. Washington, DC: Institute of Medicine.

———. 1993. Rationing Fairly: Programmatic Considerations. *Bioethics* 7: 224-33.

——— and Sabin, James. 1997. Limits to Health Care: Fair Procedures, Democratic Deliberation, and the Legitimacy Problem for Insurers. *Philosophy & Public Affairs* 26: 303-50.

Daniels, Norman; Kennedy, Bruce P.; and Kawachi, Ichiro. 1999. Why Justice is Good for Our Health: The Social Determinants of Health Inequalities. *Daedalus* 128: 215-51.

Davey Smith, G.; Shipley, M. J.; Rose, G. 1990. Magnitude and Cause of Socioeconomic Differentials in Mortality: Further Evidence from the Whitehall Study. *Journal of Epidemiology and Community Health* 44: 265-70.

Gold, Marthe R.; Siegel, Joanna E.; Russell, Louise B.; and Weinstein, Milton C. 1996. *Cost- Effectiveness in Health and Medicine*. New York: Oxford University Press.

Independent Inquiry into Inequalities in Health Report. 1999. http://www.Official-documents.co.uk/document/doh/ih/ih.htm.

Jonsen, Albert. 1998. *The Birth of Bioethics*. New York: Oxford University Press.

Kamm, Frances M. 1993. *Morality, Mortality. Volume I: Death and Whom to Save From It*. Oxford: Oxford University Press.

Kawachi, Ichiro, and Kennedy, Bruce P. 1999. Income Inequality and Health: Pathways and Mechanisms. *Health Services Research* 34: 215-27.

Lynch, John W.; Kaplan, George A.; Pamuk, Elsie R.; et al. 1998. Income Inequality and Mortality in Metropolitan Areas of the United States. *American Journal of Public Health* 88: 1074-79.

Mann, Jonathan M. 1997. Medicine and Public Health, Ethics and Human Rights. *Hastings Center Report* 27 (3): 6-13.

Marchand, Sarah; Wikler, Daniel; and Landesman, Bruce. 1998. Class, Justice, and Health. *Milbank Quarterly* 76: 1-19.

Marmot, Michael. 1999. Social Causes of Social Inequalities in Health. *Harvard Center for Population and Development Studies. Working paper Series 99.01*.

Menzel, Paul T. 1983. *Medical Costs, Moral Choices*. New Haven: Yale University Press.

———. 1990. *Strong Medicine: The Ethical Rationing of Health Care*. New York: Oxford University Press.

———; Gold, Marthe R.; Nord, Erik; et al. 1999. Toward a Broader View of Values in Cost-Effectiveness Analysis of Health. *Hastings Center Report* 29 (3): 7-15.

Nord, Erik. 1993. The Trade-Off Between Severity of Illness and Treatment Effect in Cost-Value Analysis of Health Care. *Health Policy* 24: 227-38.

Parfit, Derek. 1991. *Equality or Priority?* Lawrence: University of Kansas Libraries.

President's Commission for the Study of Ethical Problems in Medicine. 1983. *Securing Access to Health Care*. Washington, DC: U.S. Government Printing Office.

Rawls, John. 1971. *A Theory of Justice*. Cambridge: Harvard University Press.

Rothman, David. 1991. *Strangers at the Bedside: A History of How Law and Bioethics Transformed Medical Decision Making*. New York: Basic Books.

Townsend, Peter, and Davidson, Nick. 1983. *Inequalities in Health: The Black Report*. London: Penguin.

Ubel, Peter; Scanlon, Dennis; Loewenstein, George; and Kamlet, Mark. 1996. Individual Utilities are Inconsistent with Rationing Choices: A Partial Explanation of Why Oregon's Cost-Effectiveness List Failed. *Medical Decision Making* 16: 108-19.

Walzer, Michael. 1983. *Spheres of Justice*. New York: Basic Books.

Wilkinson, Richard G. 1996. *Unhealthy Societies*. London: Routledge.

[8]

HOW INFECTIOUS DISEASES GOT LEFT OUT – AND WHAT THIS OMISSION MIGHT HAVE MEANT FOR BIOETHICS

LESLIE P. FRANCIS, MARGARET P. BATTIN, JAY A. JACOBSON, CHARLES B. SMITH, AND JEFFREY BOTKIN

ABSTRACT

In this article, we first document the virtually complete absence of infectious disease examples and concerns at the time bioethics emerged as a field. We then argue that this oversight was not benign by considering two central issues in the field, informed consent and distributive justice, and showing how they might have been framed differently had infectiousness been at the forefront of concern. The solution to this omission might be to apply standard approaches in liberal bioethics, such as autonomy and the harm principle, to infectious examples. We argue that this is insufficient, however. Taking infectious disease into account requires understanding the patient as victim and as vector. Infectiousness reminds us that as autonomous agents we are both embodied and vulnerable in our relationships with others. We conclude by applying this reunderstanding of agency to the examples of informed consent and distributive justice in health care.

At the time bioethics emerged as a field – the period of the late 1950s through the 1970s – infectious disease was largely thought to have been an area of medicine almost completely conquered. In 1972, as we are now often reminded, the United States Surgeon General opined, 'It is time to close the book on infectious disease.'[1] In this article, we explore how the absence – or oblique and

[1] This much-cited quotation apparently stems from a speech by William Stewart, the Surgeon General in 1967. William H. Stewart. 1967. A Mandate for State Action. Presented at the Association of State and Territorial Health Officers, Washington, DC, Dec. 4, 1967. See http://pages.pomona.edu/~nvh04747/Bio189L/intro.html#1 (accessed 15 May 2005); see also Margie

partial treatment – of infectious disease examples and cases and of the consideration of the characteristic features of infectious disease may affect the choice, framing, and discussion of ethical problems in health care. To this end, we begin by demonstrating that infectious disease was largely absent from the early texts in bioethics that were formative in the development of the field. Infectious disease, to put it in a word or two, simply got left out.

But this omission, we think, was not benign. We explore the significance of the absence of infectious disease by providing two examples of issues in the field, informed consent and distributive justice, where the very limited and oblique treatment of infectious disease examples may have shaped the discussion in important ways. The remedy for this unfortunate situation might be simply attending to the features of infectious disease in the discussion of central issues in bioethics, employing bioethics' familiar conceptual tools like notions of autonomy and the harm principle in more thoroughgoing ways. If so, infectious disease examples could enrich bioethics discussions without revamping fundamental theoretical paradigms. We end, however, by suggesting that things are not quite so simple, and that the absence of infectious disease in the formative period of bioethics has left bioethics with deeper conceptual problems about how to understand the patient suffering from communicable disease. These problems reach to the heart of how autonomy itself should be understood. The final section of this article sketches several concerns about how autonomy has been understood in bioethics, concerns that arise when the patient is both disease *victim* and disease *vector*.

I. INFECTIOUS DISEASE AND EARLY TEXTS IN BIOETHICS

The earliest texts in bioethics, as the field is currently understood, date from the late 1950s. We have reviewed nineteen texts published before the advent of HIV/AIDS – when infectious disease reappeared as a major health concern – to determine the extent and manner of their consideration of infectious disease. These include the texts most widely used in bioethics courses[2] and

Patlak. Book Reopened on Infectious Disease. In FDA Consumer Magazine (April 1996) available at http://www.fda.gov/fdac/features/396_infe.html (accessed 15 May 2005).

[2] See Tom L. Beauchamp & James F. Childress. 2001. *Principles of Biomedical Ethics (5th edition)*. New York. Oxford University Press; Tom L. Beauchamp & James F. Childress. 1979. *Principles of Biomedical Ethics (1st edition)*. New York. Oxford University Press; Samuel Gorovitz, Ruth Macklin, Andrew L. Jameton, John M. O'Connor & Susan Sherwin, eds. 1983. *Moral Problems in Medicine (2nd edition)*. Englewood Cliffs, N.J. Prentice-Hall; Samuel Gorovitz. 1982 (paperback ed. 1985). *Doctors' Dilemmas: Moral Conflict and Medical Care*. New York. Oxford University Press.

clinical teaching at the time.[3] Our finding (a detailed account of this finding will appear at a later date – Battin, Francis, Jacobson, Smith, Botkin, in progress) is that systematic discussion of infectious disease is manifestly absent from these early texts, and that even cases and examples involving infectious conditions are rare at best. Several texts reflect the view that infectious disease is a largely resolved problem.[4] No text devotes attention to the characteristics of infectious disease that might be ethically relevant, such as that the patient is both victim and vector; that infectious disease may present in a manner that is both acute and rapidly fatal; that infectious disease may strike anyone at any age, but is more prevalent among the poor and malnourished; and that treating infectious disease may be a matter of resolving an acute episode rather than managing a long-term chronic illness or dying process.[5]

Confidentiality is the principal issue where examples drawn from infectious disease are apparent. Several early texts consider the conflict between patient confidentiality and protection of others by using infectious disease examples.[6] Infectious disease examples also appear in discussions of the need to protect health care workers or the public.[7] But only one text[8] presents materials that consider ethical problems in public health in a sustained manner, including mention of the socio-economic impact of

[3] Albert R. Jonsen, Mark Siegler & William J. Winslade. 1982. *Clinical Ethics.* New York. Macmillan Publishing Co.

[4] Tom L. Beauchamp & LeRoy Walters, eds. 1978. *Contemporary Issues in Bioethics.* Encino Ca. Dickenson Publishing Co: 58; John W. Davis, Barry Hoffmaster & Sarah Shorten, eds. 1978. *Contemporary Issues in Biomedical Ethics.* Clifton, N.J. The HUMANA Press: vi.

[5] See, for example, Charles B. Smith, Margaret P. Battin, Jeffrey Botkin, Leslie P. Francis & Jay J. Jacobson. Are there Characteristics of Infectious Disease that Raise Special Ethical Issues? *Developing World Bioethics* 2004; 4(1): 1–16.

[6] Joseph Fletcher. 1954, 1979. *Morals and Medicine.* Princeton. Princeton University Press: 56–57; Albert R. Jonsen, Mark Siegler & William J. Winslade. 1982. *Clinical Ethics.* New York. Macmillan Publishing Co: 154; Thomas A. Mappes & Jane S. Zembaty. 1981. *Biomedical Ethics.* New York. McGraw-Hill: 117; Charles J. McFadden. 1956. *Medical Ethics (4th ed.)* Philadelphia. F.A. Davis Co: 435.

[7] Quarantine is mentioned in Robert Hunt & John Arras, eds. 1977. *Ethical Issues in Modern Medicine.* Palo Alto. Mayfield Publishing Company: 334; Jonsen, Siegler & Winslade, ibid. p.171; Charles J. McFadden. 1956. *Medical Ethics (4th ed.)* Philadelphia. F.A. Davis Co: 433; Wade L. Robison & Michael S. Pritchard, eds. 1979. *Medical Responsibility.* Clifton NJ. The HUMANA Press: 30.

[8] Stanley Joel Reiser, Arthur J. Dyck & William J. Curran, eds. 1977. *Ethics in Medicine: Historical Perspectives and Contemporary Concerns.* Cambridge. The MIT Press.

infectious conditions such as yellow fever. Only Hunt and Arras portray control of an infectious condition (viral hepatitis) as a 'foremost' problem in preventive medicine.[9]

As a comparison, we examined the first and fifth editions of a primary text in the field, Beauchamp and Childress's *Principles of Biomedical Ethics* (1979, 2001). Although infectious disease is slightly more prominent in the later edition, the difference is due largely to the advent of HIV/AIDS. The 1979 edition mentions infectious disease only twice.[10] The 2001 edition gives greater attention to infectious disease but principally in the context of HIV/AIDS. HIV/AIDS is viewed as a conflict between autonomy (of the patient) and beneficence (to others); as a potential conflict between the health care provider's obligation to treat the patient and the risks of transmission to the provider; as an example of the need for express consent to certain forms of testing; as an example of the role of uncertainty in treatment; as an example of how various proposals for screening threaten patient privacy; as an example of balancing patient privacy against public policy reasons that support mandatory screening or treatment, where HIV/AIDS is discussed with tuberculosis; and as an example of justified infringement of rules of confidentiality. These references to HIV/AIDS are the only additional references to infectious diseases in the 2001 edition.[11] Notably, the discussion of conflicts of fidelity and divided loyalties[12] does not reference infectious disease examples. Willowbrook remains the only infectious disease case presented in the appendix.[13] Outside of HIV/AIDS, drug-resistant tuberculosis, and Willowbrook, there is no mention of other infectious conditions in the 2001 edition.

Our more exhaustive review in preparation will document this history in greater detail. Nevertheless, it is clear that infectious disease was not at the forefront – and perhaps not even on the back burner – of early discussions in bioethics. HIV/AIDS has changed this picture somewhat, but apparently not in systematic ways, if Beauchamp and Childress are to be taken as an example. To be sure, discussions of ethics in public health have increased impressively, especially since 2001.[14] But until quite recently,

[9] Hunt & Arras, *op. cit.* note 7.

[10] Beauchamp & Childress, 1979, *op. cit.* note 2, pp. 219–220, 276–277.

[11] Beauchamp & Childress, 2001, *op. cit.* note 2, pp. 20, 43, 67, 201, 293, 297–300, 309–310.

[12] Ibid. pp. 312–319.

[13] Ibid. pp. 428–430.

[14] E.g. Dan E. Beauchamp & Bonnie Steinbock. 1999. *New Ethics For the Public's Health.* Oxford. Oxford University Press.

public health, ethics with its utilitarian and population-based bent, has remained a separate sphere of discussion from bioethics. *The Journal of Law, Medicine and Ethics* (2003) and *Bioethics* (2004) have each recently devoted special issues to ethics and public health. At the 2004 meeting of the IAB in Sydney, Australia, Wikler and Brock argued that this should change, calling for bioethicists to explore 'bird's eye', flying from above population-based approaches to issues in the field.[15] What they hint at is an entirely new paradigm for bioethics, one drawn from what they characterize as the population-basis of public health. In what follows, we begin within bioethics, sketching instead how attention to infectious disease examples might have altered how typical problems in the field, such as informed consent and distributive justice, were framed and analyzed. In the final section of this article, we raise several suggestions for how autonomy, a value core to bioethics as the field has developed, might be understood in light of the patient as both infected victim and contagious vector.

II. THE SIGNIFICANCE OF INFECTIOUSNESS FOR ISSUES IN BIOETHICS

With infectious disease, a patient may be both victim and vector. The patient has contracted the disease from somewhere – another person, perhaps an animal, perhaps a mosquito bite, or an exposure of another kind. When the condition is contagious, the patient is also a vector, capable of transmitting the disease to others. Infectious disease thus reminds us of our vulnerability to assaults from outside the person. And it places us in the position of putting others at risk, whether or not we want to be in this position. In this section, we illustrate how these and other features of infectious disease might affect discussion of selected issues in bioethics, one (informed consent) affecting the provider-patient relationship directly and the second (distributive justice) raising broader social issues.

Informed consent

The requirement of informed consent is seen as critical to respect for the agency of the individual patient. If patients are ill-informed, or if their consent is not sought at all, they are unable

[15] Daniel Wikler & Dan W. Brock. 2004. Ethical Issues in Population Health: Mapping a New Agenda. Sydney, Australia. IAB.

to exercise choice with respect to what will happen to their bodies. The standard template for informed consent thus includes that the patient must understand his/her condition, be informed about likely alternatives and their consequences (including the alternative of foregoing treatment), and be permitted to choose among these alternatives without coercion or pressure. The informed consent requirement applies only to competent patients, who are able to understand the information they are given, have a reasonable appreciation of their values, and can process the information to reach a decision in accord with those values.[16] Critical discussions of informed consent question the capacity of vulnerable patients to understand and deal calmly with information, or the wisdom of seeing health care decisions as a matter of the patient's individual choice rather than as a decision shared with the physician.[17] Discussions of competence raise questions such as whether there should be a heightened standard when the consequences are serious and irreversible.[18]

These discussions of informed consent focus myopically on the significance of the treatment decision for the individual patient. No general discussion of informed consent of which we are aware brings to the forefront information about the extent to which the patient's decision about treatment – or nontreatment – may affect the health status of others. Seriousness and irreversibility, for example, are seen as a matter of whether the patient is likely to die if treatment is refused.[19] The checklist of information to be provided to the patient – nature of the condition, alternatives, and likely results of each alternative – reference the patient's own condition and the likely effects of treatment on himself/herself – not what might happen to the patient's family, friends, or community if the patient remains untreated.

A similar pattern is apparent in the discussion of informed consent in research. No major policy statements or regulations about consent in research highlight the issues of possible effects on third parties when patients participate in research involving infectious conditions or agents. Recent research involving

[16] Allen Buchanan & Dan W. Brock. 1989. *Deciding for Others: the Ethics of Surrogate Decisionmaking*. Cambridge. Cambridge University Press.

[17] Ezekiel J. Emanuel & Linda L. Emanuel. Four Models of the Physician-Patient Relationship. *JAMA* 1992; 267(16): 2221–2226; Franz Ingelfinger. Arrogance. *NEJM* 1980; 303(26): 1507–1511.

[18] Buchanan & Brock, *op. cit.* note 16; James Drane. Competency to Give an Informed Consent: A Model for Making Clinical Assessments. *JAMA* 1984; 525(7): 925–927.

[19] E.g. Buchanan & Brock, *op. cit.* note 16.

xenografts or the use of viral vectors in gene therapy has raised the possibility of infectiousness to others, but this discussion has been localized to these modalities which are regarded as especially dangerous. The US federal regulations governing human subject research, for example, do not mandate information about effects on others as a regular part of the informed consent process – nor do they require IRBs to consider whether information about infectiousness should be provided to third parties at risk or whether such third parties should be involved in the consent process.[20]

Distributive justice

There are of course many different accounts of distributive justice in health care. These accounts typically consider either the process for achieving justice (Should we determine what is just through a democratic process? Is Rawls-style hypothetical consent the appropriate model?) or substantive requirements (Is health care a right or a privilege? Does justice in health care require a decent minimum for everyone? Is it compatible with allowing some to buy more if they are able?). Norman Daniels, for example, argues that persons behind a Rawlsian veil of ignorance, choosing health care for a society in which they would expect to lead their full lives, will opt to provide the health care people need to achieve the normal opportunity range over a species-typical life span. Daniels thus argues for an emphasis on preventive care and care that is likely to enable people to achieve a normal lifespan rather than an especially long life.[21]

But as Selgelid[22] has pointed out, this approach frames the problem of distributive justice within the contours of individual patients and societies. People are seen as deciding what the decent minimum should be for their society, without knowing their individual places in it with respect to health or to social status. On Daniels' analysis, people would consider their own normal opportunity range; there is no direct attention to whether certain care modalities might be preferred because they lower

[20] These claims are documented in Leslie Pickering Francis, Margaret P. Battin, Jeffrey Botkin, Jay A. Jacobson & Charles B. Smith. 2004. Research Ethics and Infectious Disease: the Moral Significance of Communicability. Sydney, Australia. IAB.

[21] Norman Daniels. 1985. *Just Health Care.* Cambridge. Cambridge University Press.

[22] Michael Selgelid. Ethics and Infectious Disease. *Bioethics* 2005; 19(3) (preprint): 283.

overall risks of disease transmission. Although this factor could certainly be taken into account in an analysis of justice in health care, its absence is telling. Even more so is the conceptualization of justice in health care as a domestic matter, to be resolved within individual societies. Infectious disease is no respecter of borders. One society can achieve a decent minimum of health care for its members, but prove suddenly vulnerable to a deadly epidemic from afar, as the potential for avian flu most currently reminds us. If we consider the patient's status as victim, or as vector, the emphasis might shift, from the health care that might be most desirable for the individual patient to broader social concerns and the worldwide distribution of care that might enable all to achieve opportunities over a reasonable life span, as Selgelid argues.[23]

Significance of infectious disease's absence

It might seem that in these and other issues, the absence of infectious disease is an oversight that can be corrected relatively easily. Consider informed consent. Patients, after all, are likely to recognize that others play important roles in their lives and to want information about how their treatment decisions may affect their loved ones. This is the typical justification for including information about the risks of transmitting HIV to sexual partners and the need to inform partners about HIV status in the counseling of HIV+ patients. Or, consider justice. If the goal of distributive justice is to ensure a basic minimum of health care for all, surely interactive effects need to be taken into account in the design of health care institutions that will reach this goal. Thus if a failure to treat one person might push another below the basic minimum, this would surely be of consequence to the design of just institutions. This point is central to the argument that it is as important to provide health insurance to the parents of impoverished children as to the children themselves, as well as to the point that justice must be considered on an international scale rather than merely between the citizens of an individual country.

But are things so simple? Behind this easy grafting of infectiousness onto the treatment of these and other issues in bioethics, we speculate, lurk deeper tensions. Consider again informed consent. If the patient is informed about his/her infectiousness, and still refuses treatment, what then? Is informed consent – and the autonomy it protects – simply to be ignored? Discussions of informed consent tend to falter here, indicating to physicians that

[23] Ibid.

this is a difficult choice, or that they should be relieved if the law steps in to require them to report infectious conditions, thus in some sense pre-empting their decision. In experimentation, does autonomy require that it be solely the individual patient's choice whether to enter a study where contagion is a possibility, or would it violate the patient's autonomy to inform third parties or, even more, to require third party consent?

Or, consider justice. What if there are trade-offs between achieving a decent minimum within a society, and the means needed to provide sufficient health care elsewhere to reduce the risk of reservoirs of infectious disease? Is there a conflict between the two, so that we must sacrifice justice to some to reduce risks to themselves or others?

Finally, consider the relationship between informed consent and justice. The standard litany of principles in bioethics owing to Beauchamp and Childress places autonomy first, followed by beneficence, nonmaleficence, and justice. Although the principles are not prioritized, discussions in bioethics often proceed as though this order reflects their importance. But there are surely tensions between autonomy and justice; a greater range of choices for some may well result in curtailed prospects for others.[24] The possibility that the patient is both victim and vector adds to this tension. As victim, the patient may see his/her plight as the responsibility of others, deserving care as a result. As vector, the patient may ignore his/her effects on others, thus worsening the problem of achieving a decent minimum of care for them by his/her individual choices.

One conclusion to draw here might be that these tensions are inevitable. Individual patient choice just may conflict with the choices or needs of others. Bioethics must simply live with these tensions, resolving them as best it can by trying to think through which value is more important in the solution of a given problem. Another conclusion might be that the traditional conceptual framework of bioethics would have been adequate if it had only been fully applied: that concepts like autonomy and the harm principle are adequate tools and that the understanding that autonomy can be overridden by principles like nonmaleficence and justice could have been more fully brought into play. Still another conclusion would appeal to the principles more frequently utilized in public health, which recognize the need for

[24] Kahn et al. explore the conflict between respecting autonomy and improving distributive justice in research. Jeffrey C. Kahn, Anna C. Mastroianni & Jeremy Sugarman. 1998. *Beyond Consent: Seeking Justice in Research.* Oxford. Oxford University Press.

state interference in individual autonomy in the face of infectious disease. In the following section, we suggest that these alternatives may give up too soon. The roots of this conflict may lie in how autonomy has been understood in bioethics. While we stop short of arguing for a different notion of autonomy, our goal is to point out that agency might have been seen somewhat differently had infectious disease examples been at the forefront of the framing of problems in bioethics. Understanding what it means for patients to be both victims and vectors may lead us to reframe our understanding of patients as individuals, and hence provide a different perspective on the tensions identified above.

III. AUTONOMOUS AGENCY AS RELATIONAL AND EMBODIED

What might infectious disease mean for how we understand the autonomous agent in bioethics? The traditional view of autonomous choice is that it is a matter of individual liberty. As Beauchamp and Childress wrote in 1979, 'autonomy is a form of personal liberty of action where the individual determines his or her course of action in accordance with a plan chosen by himself or herself'.[25] Risks to others, such as risks of contagion, set constraints on how it is ethically permissible to act. Quarantine, restricting liberty to move about in the world, is an extreme such constraint. But also constricting are restrictions on sexual activity or reproduction, on attending school, on keeping matters secret, or on refusing medical interventions, or on getting health care from one's chosen providers. These constraints are seen as arising externally from agency and are not connected to it in any deep sense. They are limits from the outside.

On this view, infectiousness is like other dangers people pose to each other. In many areas of the world, people are not permitted to walk around freely carrying concealed weapons; this constrains liberty of choice, as defenders of a particular interpretation of the Second Amendment to the United States Constitution are fond of pointing out. Quarantine is a more radical, but similarly structured constraint on choice. Like firearms, infectiousness poses a danger to others. As such, it may even legitimate legal or social interference with what we do.

Indeed, the standard account in liberal theory is that it is permissible to interfere with the actions of one person to protect others from harm. This is the 'harm principle' of John Stuart

[25] Beauchamp & Childress, 1979, *op. cit.* note 2, p. 56.

Mill's *On Liberty*: society is justified in intervening to prevent harm to others, but not to protect us from ourselves or to compel us to do what is morally right. Although Mill described the harm principle as 'one very simple' principle, it is famously complex. The complexity of relevance here concerns cases in which people are not acting intentionally to harm others, but nonetheless pose risks of harm to them. In the case of infectious disease, when the patient is a vector, s/he may not be acting at all, and may even be unaware of his/her potential vector status. The harm may be uncertain: we may not know the probability of the risk, its degree of severity, or its duration. The victims may be unknown as well; at the time decisions need to be made about whether to act, there may be no identified victims at all.

The suggestion we sketch here is that the standard picture drawn from liberal theory is simplistic, for reasons that are many and deep, and that the application of the harm principle as it is drawn from public health is also inadequate. It is not merely that the risks we pose to each other of transmitting disease perhaps provide a harm principle justification for social interference with what we do, interference that is imposed from outside and that constricts our liberty. Nor is it merely that the difficulties in understanding this justification consist mainly in understanding how to extend the harm principle justification to cases in which the harm is merely probabilistic or speculative. Nor is it simply that bioethics could have used the conceptual tools available to it in a more sophisticated way. Infectious disease is more than the risk of contagion, although that is surely one of its core features. In some cases, it is the risk of rapidly fatal, rapidly-moving, illness. Infection strikes young and old, well and sick, rich and poor alike. With some infectious diseases, people are literally well one day, gravely ill the next, and either dead or fully recovered the next – infections such as meningitis can move exactly this fast. This complex of features of infectious disease, we suggest, may give us reason to rethink the structure of autonomy as it has sometimes been understood in bioethics. To put the point summarily, infectious disease reminds us that we are related in our vulnerability, and this has implications for how we should think about standard accounts of autonomous decision making in bioethics.

Autonomy – the standard view

The standard paradigm of autonomy, as we used it in the discussion of informed consent above, goes roughly as follows.[26]

[26] See, for example, Buchanan & Brock, *op. cit.* note 16.

Autonomy means reasoned choice by a competent individual. Autonomous agents must have a relatively clear idea of their preferences and values. They must have a decent understanding of the alternatives available to them and their likely outcomes. Autonomous agents must also be able to fit the two together in a reasoned way; decision making that is merely capricious or inexplicable does not count as autonomous choice. On Buchanan and Brock's view, moreover, as decisions become more serious and irrevocable, more is required for autonomous agency. Thus with a deadly, fast-moving infectious condition, to count as an autonomous decision, an agent's choice should be especially well-informed, clear, and rooted in the agent's values and preferences. Even when much less is on the line, however, autonomy does not just mean choosing whatever an agent wants, or choice by an agent who is incapable of choosing – it requires reasonable decisions by a competent actor.

Risks to oneself or to others figure into this portrait of autonomous decision-making as part of an understanding of likely alternatives and outcomes. To take mundane examples first, if one is contagious and goes to work, one may infect others. By failing to get sufficient rest, one may remain sicker for a longer period of time and recover more slowly. These are costs that must be taken into account in the choice of whether or not to go to work. They do not require us to rethink preferences and values, change the kind of information that is considered in making a well reasoned choice, re-examine the standard reasoning structure of trying to select the alternative that will most realize preferences and values, or even reconsider the determination of who is a reasoning agent.

On this account of autonomy, the autonomous agent acts as an individual, in contingent relationships with others. Acting autonomously, the agent may or may not choose to take risks for him/herself, or to take risks that affect others. These choices by an agent are typically seen as voluntary. Core to what it is to be autonomous is to be able to choose how one relates to and affects other persons. Autonomous persons can choose whether or not to assault others, and whether or not to pose risks to them. They are responsible for the choices they make, but the choices are theirs nonetheless. To impose limits on these choices is to limit autonomy.

To be sure, aspects of infectious disease fit this understanding of the autonomous person. Individuals do have choices, and standard views about responsibility do apply, at least when individuals knowingly infect others or put them at risk. Deliberately sneezing on one's competitor, having sex when one is aware of the possibility of transmitting disease – these are (ir)responsible acts. Similar notions of responsibility, praise and blame apply to them, as to other reckless acts that put persons at risk: leaving toxic waste near a competitor's workplace, having sex without protection against pregnancy, and so on. And they also apply to more sinister acts involving infectious agents, such as bioterrorism. But with contagious, infectious disease, the situation of the individual agent in relation to others is sometimes quite different. Infectiousness is not always under voluntary control, either for victim or for vector. One may be unaware that one is infectious or even that one is ill or at risk of being ill, at the very point one is most likely to transmit disease to others. Whether one transmits disease or not may not even be the subject of agency; with respect to some infectious diseases, spread to susceptible hosts may occur despite our very best efforts at prevention.

In what follows, we explore whether it is adequate to understand infectious disease in this standard way suggested by traditional understandings of autonomy, as altering information about risks and alternatives. We will contend that infectious disease poses deeper challenges to our understanding of autonomous agency in bioethics, in at least two ways. First, when the patient is both victim and vector, s/he cannot be seen simply as an isolated reasonable agent, deliberating about what to do. His/her agency must be seen as embodied – hence vulnerable to infection – and related – hence at risk of transmitting infection to others. This picture requires rethinking our picture of agency as a matter of understanding the agent's preferences and values and attempting to achieve them in light of information about risks and alternatives. Second, respect for agency requires more than respect for the choices made by the agent seen as an isolated individual. At times, both the agent's vulnerability and the agent's status as vector may mean that his/her choices must be viewed in these terms. These are necessary features of agency, not contingent ones. Consideration of these factors thus should be brought within the understanding of what is involved in autonomous choice. Thus seen, choice is subject to moral limits, but these are limits based on the understanding of agency – not merely limits imposed from outside.

Alternative understandings of autonomy

Lest this view seem too strange, before we develop it further, let us mention two theoretical developments about autonomy that are in some respects similar to what we are suggesting. First, there have been accounts of relational autonomy, particularly in feminist works.[27] These views emphasize familial and caring relationships: partners, parents, caregivers and ones cared-for. What is different when the patient is victim and vector, however, is that the relationships may be personal and intimate or accidental and among strangers. Contagion may occur despite whether the victim knows the vector, and even despite whether the victim can even identify the vector or the time of contagion. The feminist emphasis on relationality, while it reminds us of our interconnectedness and even our sociality, does so in a more immediate and less universal way than infectious disease.

Another development in theorizing about autonomy reflects the idea of agency as embodied. We are finite, mortal. We are vulnerable.[28] Infectious disease, with its potential for rapid fatality, attacking the well and the sick alike, likewise reminds us of our immediate vulnerability. This vulnerability is not one we can always choose to avoid, by taking especial care for our own safety, even if in some conditions, like malaria or HIV, we are familiar with basic precautions. It is an ineluctable feature of our agency; no matter how we try, we cannot avoid the fact that we are at risk of infection from others – even others far distant from ourselves.

Infectious disease brings these two suggestions about autonomous agency – that it is relational and embodied – to the forefront. Contagious, infectious disease, moving quickly from individual to individual, reminds us that we do not exercise our agency as an island. We are – and this is not our choice – creatures that may infect and be infected by others. To make these points is by no means to embrace a holism that ignores the status of the individual; it is instead to say that the individual cannot be understood in isolation, with merely accidental connections to others. Our relationality and embodiment are part of what we are as individual agents.

Autonomy in the context of infectious disease

How, then, might autonomous agency be conceptualized in light of infectious disease? With contagious, infectious conditions we are vulnerable in relationship to each other. We can, even without

[27] Catriona Mackenzie & Natalie Stoljar. 2000. *Relational Autonomy: feminist perspectives on autonomy, agency, and the social self*. New York. Oxford University Press.

[28] See, for example, Susan Brison. 2002. *Aftermath: violence and the remaking of a self*. Princeton. Princeton University Press.

knowing it, be each other's victims and each other's vectors. The traditional bioethics literature, more often than not, ignores parts of this equation. The traditional understanding of autonomous agency ignores our vulnerability to disease and our potential for passing it on – it ignores our embodiment and relationality. To adopt the ideal of autonomy as just a matter of individual choice, we might say, is too centered on the individual, ignoring how we are both potential victims and potential vectors. On the other hand, discussions in public health typically overlook the other side of the equation, that we are nonetheless agents, despite being both victims and vectors. These discussions direct the focus away from the individual, rather than suggesting a reunderstanding of the nature of the individual agent.

Our suggestion here is that infectious disease may challenge us to rethink the significance of being both victim and vector for our understanding of agency. Instead of understanding autonomous decision making as a matter of analyzing the patient's own values, alternatives, and risks and benefits to the patient, we might want to think about how this calculation is affected by the patient's vulnerability. This vulnerability is internal to who the patient is – not imposed from outside as an external constraint on agency.

Seeing agency in this way, we suggest, can lead us to reframe many of the standard issues in bioethics. Consider again informed consent. The standard clinical view, treating this patient as the primary concern and the effects of the illness on others as secondary, is a perspective reinforced because the individual provider does not even know who those patients might be. But we cannot rely solely on this perspective. Contagious patients are not just ill by themselves; they are ill because of something that has come from others and could go to others. The information required for informed consent should take these facts into account. So might our understanding of the relative importance of informed consent itself. Is it a violation of agency, if the patient who has him/herself been a victim is required to consider how s/he might victimize others? Or if the ability of patients to enter clinical studies depends on both their own choices and the involvement of others to whom they might pose risks? Or consider justice, where providing a decent minimum of care world-wide may be critical to reducing everyone's vulnerability to disease.

All this is not to say that we should ignore individual agency in bioethics. We are not, for example, defending a perspective on which all that matters is aggregate health – or that public health is of primary and exclusive importance. Indeed, we would suggest the importance of individual agency is a critical caveat to the renewed attention to infectious disease in the light of bioterrorism threats. Individual agency reminds us that as we consider prevention and intervention in transmission, we are also obligated to take into account the circumstances and values of the potentially transmitting vector. Our suggestion is simply that *if* we understand human agents as vulnerable to disease transmission from others, as well as unwilling vectors to others, we may raise different concerns in the analysis of standard problems in bioethics, from the examples of informed consent and justice that we have given here, to problems as diverse as reproductive liberty (is the vertical transmission of infectious disease to be regarded as on a par with the vertical transmission of genetic disease?) and end of life care (how should infectiousness figure into the provision of life-sustaining therapy?).

These challenges raised by infectious disease are serious ones. They have been largely unnoticed in the development of bioethics as a field where infectious disease examples were notable by their absence. Our goal in this article has been to suggest that understanding the significance of the patient as victim and vector for agency is an important task for bioethics. It seems to us an even more urgent task in light of the possibility that agency might itself be marginalized in discussions of threats of bioterrorism and global pandemics.

Leslie P. Francis
Margaret P. Battin
Jay A. Jacobson
Charles B. Smith
Jeffrey Botkin
Division of Medical Ethics
Salt Lake City
Utah 84143
USA
francis1@law.utah.edu
battin@utah.edu
ldjacob@ihc.com
chuckandjudy@hotmail.com
jeffrey.botkin@hsc.utah.edu

Acknowledgements

We are grateful to Beverly Hawkins for assistance with the data from bioethics texts cited in part one, and to Linda Carr-Lee for research assistance.

[9]

Public Health Ethics: From Foundations and Frameworks to Justice and Global Public Health

Nancy E. Kass

Public health ethics in the future will be distinguished from public health ethics in the past by this new subfield being labeled as such, acknowledged, and called upon for service. Ethical dilemmas have been present throughout the history of public health. The question of whether to force Henning Jacobson to be immunized in 1905 in accordance with the 1902 Massachusetts smallpox vaccination law was one of ethics as well as law.[1] How Thomas Parran, Surgeon General in 1936, chose to respond to a raging syphilis epidemic in the United States in the early part of the 20th century raised considerable moral debate in determining the appropriate public health response for a government.[2] More recently, questions have arisen concerning the appropriate reach of government in controlling HIV, banning smoking, or promoting healthy lifestyles. Debates over government infringement, morality, and justice recur throughout the history of public health. What has changed, however, is that "public health ethics," articulated as such, has now begun in even small ways to be part of the academic and professional discourse. As such, recent conceptual work defining and mapping the terrain of public health ethics has been put forward and will be further refined. In the future, public health ethics not only will continue to be more widely recognized, but also will likely move into new areas that have been shortchanged, as a whole, by bioethics. In the next decade, there is likely to be considerable scholarly and practical attention devoted to questions of global justice and public health, environmental justice, and whether ethics requirements for public health research differ systematically from ethics requirements for other types of research with humans. This paper will begin a discussion of one of these emerging areas: global justice and public health.

Before examining the relationship between bioethics and public health, however, a brief background on public health is in order, as well as how this background might suggest that a subfield of public health ethics — distinguished in certain ways from bioethics as a whole — is warranted. Public health is the societal approach to protecting and promoting health. The goal in public health is to improve the health of *communities*, and, in general, public health uses societally-oriented strategies, rather than individually-oriented actions, to achieve this goal. By maintaining a safe water supply, immunizing school children, or engaging in epidemiologic research, public health seeks to ensure societal conditions under which people can lead healthier lives,[3] minimizing threats to our health "that can be averted or lessened only through collective actions aimed at the community."[4] The providers of public health interventions often are governments, rather than private practitioners. Indeed, the provision of health services, generally the domain of medicine, becomes the responsibility of public health departments when provided by public clinics or hospitals.

This paper is divided into three parts. The first part sketches a brief history of issues that animated ethics and public health since the "birth of bioethics," focusing predominantly on the 1970s through the 1990s. This was a period when considerable attention was devoted to the ethics of health promotion, resource allocation, and the civil liberties/public health debates raised by the HIV/AIDS epidemic. The second section of this paper describes the second "era" of public health ethics. The period of 2001 and 2002 was noteworthy in that, rather than discussing the ethics of a particular issue of public health ethics, several scholars attempted more broadly to label, define, categorize, and give practical application to public health ethics as a named subfield of bioethics. Finally, the last section of this paper is devoted to questions of ethics, justice, and *global* public health. Thus, the last section of this paper discusses what is meant by global justice and public health, why public health ethics, as a subfield of bioethics, is perfectly situated to contribute, and what future contributions might be most valuable. Taking on new areas of inquiry will allow the existing and nascent frameworks of public health ethics to be refined and improved such that they can be more useful to practitioners and scholars alike.

The Early Era: 1970s-1990s

Bioethics emerged as a new field in the 1960s and 1970s in order to examine the moral dilemmas facing health policy, research, and scientific discovery.[5] Given this broad, societal scope, the birth of bioethics might have been a natural time for discussions of bioethics and public health specifically to emerge, since public health also is oriented foundationally to social and public policy interests. The language of public health was rarely invoked among bioethicists of these earlier decades, however. Nonetheless, extraordinary contributions to public health ethics were made during this time, particularly in three areas of inquiry: the ethics of health promotion, resource allocation, and the civil liberties vs. public health questions precipitated by the HIV/AIDS epidemic.

Ethics and Health Promotion

Significant work was published in the 1970s and 1980s examining the appropriate ethical reach of health education, health promotion, and of government sponsored health campaigns.[6] Growing data demonstrated the significant behavioral contribution to many major public health problems. Health education, therefore, was added to the public health professional's toolbox, joining more traditional interventions like sanitation, disease reporting, and contact tracing. In 1975, the U.S. Government announced that lifestyle reform would be needed to further improve the public's health.[7] The degree to which governments should become involved in regulating personal behavior became a matter of heated debate, and several scholars began to address the *ethics* issues inherent to health promotion, government involvement, and public health.

Daniel Wikler suggested that one might interfere with health in order to further others' own well being. This paternalistic justification demands asking whether the behavior change being advocated or forced actually *will* lead to better health. Moreover, "it is not self-evident that this vision of a safe society, with its lack of immoderation, stress, and risk-taking, is to be favored over others whose constitutive elements have incidental adverse effects upon health."[8]

There may be economic justifications for health promotion. If person A prudently maintains her health, but person B does not, why should person A bear the costs of person B's negligence? Questioning such economic justifications, however, was growing literature in the late 1970's and 1980's suggesting that prevention, while laudable in many respects, often does not save money.[9] And even if it did, it is not a shared belief that money should be more highly valued than the ability to pursue one's own goals. Finally, health promotion might be justified in terms of shared economic and/or national security interests, which depend on a healthy populace. This raises how far the government can intrude for the sake of public well being.

Edmund Pellegrino described an ethics of prevention.[10] Preventive interventions, he suggested, fell along a spectrum of voluntariness from health education, to opinion manipulation through mass media, to tax and insurance incentives and disincentives, to legal prohibitions. Faden and Faden, similarly, described a spectrum of interventions from facilitation to persuasion to manipulation to coercion.[11] In determining a response, there should be proportionality: the burden should be low and the benefit high. Incentives should be favored over disincentives, true education should be favored over manipulative messages, and government intervention cannot occur unless the measure's effectiveness is unequivocal.

Scholars of this period agree that voluntary approaches are ethically preferable to compulsory ones. The Society of Public Health Educators' code of professional ethics goes further, however, calling voluntariness the *only* acceptable approach. According to the Code, health educators must "support change by choice, not by coercion."[12]

Purely voluntary interventions do not always work, however.[13] The operative question for ethics scholars, then, became whether or under what conditions more directive or controlling interventions could be implemented. Further, since it would be governments implementing stricter measures, how could one ensure that the agenda was related to public health rather than to politics?[14] Involuntary measures also assume "a benign, wise, and responsive government, something history finds singularly rare."[15]

Shifting in focus from what governments can impose on individuals was Dan Beauchamp. Beauchamp suggested that the legal authority of public health should be used to regulate the behavior of those who market and distribute harmful products rather than regulating the behavior of individuals.[16] If outside influences allow an individual unknowingly to alter his or her preferences, this diminishes the autonomy with which those choices are made.[17] Coercive measures may be needed to control the facilitation, persuasion, and manipulation of messages that run counter to the interests of public health.

Resource Allocation[18]

In the 1970's and 1980s, a significant body of literature emerged regarding the fair distribution of health care

Volume 32:2, Summer 2004

resources. Articles examined access to health care and whether there was a moral "right" to health care.[19] The President's Commission for the Study of Ethical Problems in Medicine and Biomedical and Behavioral Research commissioned papers on this topic,[20] and other scholars built on this work.

Since many political figures and advocates were calling for a right to health care, philosophical examinations of rights theory emerged during this period. A right to health care differs from health care being a privilege, or being provided out of charity.[21] Given that there is no legal right to health care in this country, scholars have examined whether morally there is the obligation to provide citizens with health care. During this period, contrasting views of justice were put forward,[22] yet all scholars agreed that health care access must be improved. Further, despite differences about how to achieve it, there was agreement that individuals should be guaranteed some minimum of health care services.

Inevitably, questions of increasing access to health care led to questions of how to most fairly allocate limited resources.[23] There were calls to recognize both the implicit rationing inherent in the American health care system and the need for a morally acceptable and explicit rationing policy. One of the more controversial proposals was to ration by age. Both Daniel Callahan and Norman Daniels wrote books suggesting it is morally defensible to use age in resource allocation decisions.[24] Pellegrino and Thomasma, by contrast, stated that most of the hard rationing decisions could be avoided if we shifted spending from less valuable goods, such as the $65 billion spent on cosmetics or the $30 billion spent on alcohol.[25]

While the allocation and rationing literature of this period did not explicitly discuss public health or invoke the language of public health ethics, scholars ultimately argued that preventive and primary care services should be privileged in resource allocation decisions. Mainstays of public health care delivery — prenatal care and immunizations — often were cited as among the least controversial services to be included in a basic, minimum package of services.[26]

HIV and Bioethics

Few public health challenges have brought as wide a range of ethical issues to bear as HIV/AIDS. Essentially all of the classic public health moral tensions emerged, from societal rights vs. individual liberties to justice and health care access. As policy makers contended with tough decisions, bioethics contributed significant literature, much in what might now be called public health ethics. Indeed, arguably, it was the HIV epidemic that introduced much of the bioethics world to the mainstream of public health, its priorities, tools, and responses.

In 1983, the Public Health Service recommended that gay men be discouraged from donating blood.[27] Ronald Bayer, among the founders of public health ethics, responded with one of the earliest pieces on ethics and HIV.[28] Two major U.S. public policy documents, *Confronting AIDS* from the quasi-public Institute of Medicine[29] and the *Report of the Presidential Commission on the Human Immunodeficiency Virus Epidemic*[30] included significant sections on the ethical issues raised by the epidemic. Fear and uncertainty precipitated calls for restrictive proposals, from tattooing infected persons to full quarantine. While there was almost uniform rejection from the bioethics and legal communities of isolation of this sort,[31] policy proposals continued that advocated for the exclusion of HIV-infected persons from specific opportunities, such as employment, housing, insurance, and school. The bathhouses of San Francisco and the case of Ryan White — a child with hemophilia and HIV, barred from his school — became symbols of the fear and discrimination that prompted questions about how to respond to the new public health crisis. Bioethics could not help but jump into the fray to help articulate an appropriate public health response.

Bridging clinical and public health ethics were examinations of the moral responsibilities of physicians to the wives of bisexual men, particularly HIV-infected bisexual men. Public health traditionally has protected unknowing contacts from risks of infection, while clinical medicine has enforced a tradition of patient confidentiality. Could bioethics help navigate the right response when these duties conflicted? Arguably, the area in which bioethics most engaged with the HIV epidemic and traditional public health was in debates about how best to design HIV screening programs. Screening is a mainstay of public health. Back in the 1920s criteria were established that needed to be satisfied before screening programs could be implemented.[32] In response to HIV, bioethicists, for the first time, put forward ethical requirements that must be in place before a public health screening program can be imposed.[33] What types of screening programs should be implemented was particularly vexing in the mid 1980s, a time when the screening tool had been licensed, but no treatments were yet available. Thus, those screened would not be helped, and they would be subject to discrimination. HIV screening was put forward so that infected persons might learn their status and, theoretically, would take precautions to prevent the spread to unknowing *others*. Little empirical evidence was available to demonstrate whether this assumption was true, however. Indeed, the limited research available provided somewhat contradictory findings.[34] One study found that, while HIV infected persons decrease their risky sexual practices once learning their status, *uninfected* persons engage in *riskier* behavior once they are told they are uninfected.[35] Such findings have tremendous implications given that, even in the highest prevalence communities, screening is likely to identify more uninfected persons than infected ones.

HIV also renewed interest in the ethics of other traditional tools of public health. Calls were made for mandatory reporting of HIV, contact tracing, and partner notification. Advocates of reporting suggested that more accurate understanding of the disease could be achieved with mandatory reporting and that education and potential treatments could be targeted to those found to be infected. Critics argued that education and potential treatments can be provided with or without reporting, while reporting was an unjustified invasion of privacy, particularly when strong anti-discrimination laws did not exist. As a result, they feared, at risk individuals would be driven from testing out of fear of the consequences. Not surprising, the momentum for mandatory reporting increased when treatments became available.

HIV also prompted ethics analysis regarding health education, duty to treat, resource allocation, access to care, and health care financing. Indeed, HIV stimulated public policy debate in almost every existing area of public health. As HIV gripped the United States, so did it grip the community of bioethicists, who became introduced to public health, why it exists, and how it operates. Through this more intimate knowledge of public health, bioethics began to ponder when, ethically, public health should use particular response tools, and what criteria must be satisfied before the more invasive tools of public health can be dispatched. The phrase "public health ethics," again, was not yet used, but the foundation of the field had been laid.

Stage II: The emergence of Frameworks, the language of Public Health Ethics

In the second era, there was growing recognition, at least in certain small circles, that public health ethics was in some ways distinct from other areas of bioethics and, as such, deserved its own scholarly and practical attention. While scholars who articulated principles for bioethics generally were clear to suggest that none of the major principles of bioethics — beneficence, respect for persons, and justice — ought to have moral superiority over any other,[36] the issues given significant attention in the early years of bioethics — such as patients' right to refuse care, and research subjects' right to voluntary and informed consent — were ones where the principle of respect for autonomy, perhaps given too little moral attention previously, was now given preeminent moral status.[37] Medical ethics codes were revised to give patients' right to non-interference higher priority, and new codes of research ethics made non-interference with study participants paramount. Thus, on the one hand, issues such as resource allocation, health promotion, the right to health care, and HIV were being given increasing attention in both public health and bioethics circles. On the other hand, the existing formal codes and frameworks of bioethics continued to give priority to autonomy and individuals' right of refusal, arguably a poor fit for public health practitioners seeking ethics guidance for their community-oriented work. Of note, we identified only two commentators plus one collection of cases that invoked either the language or the clear themes of a distinctive notion of "public health ethics" before 2000.

In the 1970s and 1980s Dan E. Beauchamp raised the point that social justice and communitarian traditions are and ought to be the driving forces behind public health practice and that these might define a somewhat separate "ethic."[38] While public health practitioners, as stated above, had recognized the relationship between social conditions and health, Beauchamp was striking in laying out for the first time within bioethics, that exclusive attention to individual interests, particularly through a notion of market justice, "plague attempts to protect the public's health...This new ethical paradigm will require thinking about and reacting to the problems of disability and premature death as primarily collective problems of the entire society."[39]

Further, Beauchamp arguably set the stage in suggesting that the work of public health is to further the interests of community. Community, Beauchamp asserts, does not mean simply that the government ensures that individuals' interests are not offended by the actions of others. Rather, community means that we have shared commitments to one another, and that through collective actions related to health and safety, for example, we share a commitment to the common life, "a central practice by which the body politic defines itself and affirms its values."[40] While Beauchamp did not literally use the words "public health ethics," his work is foundational in describing how public health has its own set of moral priorities, and that these are critical to the functioning of a civil society.

In 1986, Marc Lappe wrote an ethics chapter for the key textbook of public health, *Maxcy-Rosenau Public Health and Preventive Medicine.*[41] Lappe compared medical ethics to public health ethics. Medical ethics is more concerned with individual autonomy and the duties of single health professionals, whereas public health ethics focuses more on equity and efficiency in the distribution of health resources as well as on the community in having its health protected. Lappe suggested that individual rights can be compromised for the sake of community interests, but only when there is proportionality. That is, the benefit must be larger than the sacrifice, and the absolute level of infringement on individual rights must be minimal. Related, since many public health programs do not grant the right of refusal, there must be evidence that the programs will provide the good on which they are premised. At least as much as community good vs. individual rights being at stake, he suggested, there is an inevitable tension between utilitarianism and justice or, stated differently, between efficiency and equity. An ethic of public health captures

Volume 32:2, Summer 2004

the urgency for efficiency, while recognizing the special standing of those in greatest need of health protection and health services.

After the important work of Beauchamp and Lappe, there was somewhat of a hiatus in thinking about public health ethics, formally, for another 15 years.[42] Beginning in 2000, however, there was an explosion of interest in public health ethics, labeled and articulated as such. Several commentators offered frameworks, definitions, and analyses of public health ethics, claiming public health ethics to be its own subfield of bioethics, with its own priorities and approaches. In 2001 and 2002, four articles were published that defined public health ethics, its territory, and/or offered tools to use in its analysis,[43] and in 2002, for the first time, the American Public Health Association, and organization that had existed since 1832, published its first code of ethics.[44]

One article called for a framework of analysis for public health ethics that might differ from the existing frames for medical and research ethics.[45] Such a framework would give priority to certain public health interests while keeping in moral check the legally sanctioned police powers of public health. Another article sought to "map the terrain" of public health ethics and identified particular ethics considerations that arise predictably in public health, from maximizing utility to preventing harm to distributing benefits fairly.[46] Both of these contributions provide frameworks for analysis that include identifying program goals, determining effectiveness, minimizing burdens, proportionality, and procedural justice.

Callahan and Jennings pointed out that public health has been concerned with social and economic inequality since the 19th century, while bioethics, in its first decades, was more visibly concerned with the good of the individual. They identified four areas of public health that typically raise ethics issues: health promotion, risk reduction, epidemiologic research, and interventions to reduce structural and economic disparities. They then argue for a professional code of public health ethics and more training in public health ethics for both students and professionals.[47] Notably, they call for bioethics as a community to become more aware of the ethics issues that arise in public health.

Not coincidentally, all three of these articles also devote attention to social justice. Social justice is highly correlated with better health outcomes, and social justice is a recurring theme of public health. Indeed, as will be described subsequently, public health practitioners rarely go far in an epidemiologic investigation without finding correlations related to social class and social position. To what extent, then, do public health professionals have an affirmative obligation to better *social* rather than, narrowly, health-related, conditions, in the name of public health?

Stage II of public health ethics was a crucial one. The name of Public Health Ethics was claimed, defined, and beginning frameworks articulated. The earlier work was crucial in identifying distributional and public policy dilemmas in public health. This laid the foundation for the terrain to be mapped and frameworks to be created. While the dilemmas that animated the first decades of public health ethics will likely remain part of its landscape, we expect the field to take on three new areas that, arguably, have been neglected by the mainstream of the bioethics community: global justice, environmental ethics, and public health research.

The Future

As bioethics becomes only more deeply engaged with public health, scholarship in the field will expand in new directions. Already, there are several areas in which bioethics, arguably, has fallen behind. Three areas where new attention from public health ethics may be most pronounced are environmental justice; ethics and public health research; and justice and global public health. The remainder of this paper will be devoted to a discussion of global justice and public health ethics, and only brief descriptions of the other two issues will be provided.

The environmental justice movement is concerned with potential inequities in the distribution of risks and consequences of environmental exposures. According to the Institute of Medicine, certain communities are in "double jeopardy" in that they "(1) experience higher levels of exposure to environmental stressors in terms of both frequency and magnitude and (2) are less able to deal with these hazards as a result of limited knowledge of exposures and disenfranchisement from the political process."[48] Domestically, there has been a longstanding concern that toxic waste sites and other environmental risks are not distributed equitably across class or racial lines. Internationally, there is growing awareness that disparities in access to clean and safe resources are growing only wider.[49] While given little attention by public health ethics, environmental health is one of the five core areas of public health.[50] Given the enormity of the health risks associated with environmental health burdens, and given the attention that bioethics has devoted historically to questions of distributive justice, it is a glaring omission that bioethics, generally, and public health ethics, as a subfield, have devoted so little attention to questions of environmental justice to date.

Second, there likely will be new attention devoted to defining public health research and determining whether ethics requirements for public health research differ from those for other types of research. The last few years have seen articles published that attempt to distinguish public health research from public health practice.[51] Articles have examined whether research activities that procedurally resemble certain practice activities (such as quality assurance or public health surveillance) ought to be subject to different oversight mechanisms than those generally required under existing human subjects regulations. Missing from the literature, however, is discussion of whether public health research is conceptually different from other types of research with human subjects. Indeed, much "public health research" will resemble other research in that it is intended for generalizable knowledge and may involve more than minimal risk. Conceptually, however, public health research often considers a population to be the "public health patient."[52] While all investigators struggle with conflicting loyalties to the individual subject vs. the community at large,[53] how this conflict is resolved ultimately may differ in certain categories of public health research. If true, this would be analogous to how certain types of compromises to individuals' rights or even well-being can be made under limited circumstances in the context of public health practice. This is related, in part, to the notion that public health research is inextricably linked to broader public concerns.[54] As more studies are conducted to examine questions of traditional public health priority, such as attempts to reduce certain environmental hazards, or attempts to test the efficacy of preventive interventions, or attempts to test the safety of new vaccines against public health threats such as smallpox, the weight given to conflicting demands during ethics review may differ if the study is thought to be of high priority for public health *practice*. Future work likely will articulate these categories further, and will provide guidance to help navigate these challenges for those charged with reviewing and deciding about the acceptability of proposed research.

Having raised but not elaborated on two areas of future public health ethics attention, the remainder of this paper will be devoted to the third area where public health ethics likely will witness an explosion of new interest: global justice and public health. That the mainstream of public health ethics and, more broadly, bioethics, will move into scholarship related to global justice will mean two changes for the field: most dramatic is a shift toward *global* issues when considering what is central to public health ethics. Second will be involvement by bioethics in examinations of equity and health outcomes, a relationship long explored in public health, but given less attention historically in bioethics.

Public health practitioners have noted the relationship between health and social inequity for more than a century. Sir Edwin Chadwick demonstrated in the early 1800s that differences in social conditions led to a more than twofold difference in life expectancy between upper and lower classes in England.[55] Europe experienced increases in life expectancy during the 18th and 19th centuries despite few effective medical interventions.[56] A century later, in the 1960s, the Whitehall study demonstrated that inequities among 12,000 civil servants in England were highly correlated with differences in health outcomes, even in an affluent country. Indeed, if social class was further refined by including employment grade and car ownership, mortality could be predicted even more precisely.[57] The Whitehall data stimulated further public health interest in inequity and health, since all individuals studied were employed and had access to free health care through the National Health Service. The Multiple Risk Factor Intervention Trial (MRFIT) demonstrated that participants' incomes and death rates were so closely correlated "that it made no difference [in] eleven out of the twelve groupings whether they were ranked according to ascending income or descending health rates."[58] The field of social epidemiology emerged,[59] suggesting that what have been thought of as *individual* risk factors for disease cluster in one's social position.[60] Moreover, there are particular community attributes that are independent of the individual that further predict health status.[61]

Most of the bioethics literature examining justice and health, as stated earlier, has focused on the just access to health *services*. Less attention has been devoted to how one's social context relates to health status. This is beginning to change. Norman Daniels, who argued in the 1980s for certain minimal levels of health care, more recently advocated that justice requires focusing on underlying inequalities, as social conditions contribute more significantly to health status than health care access.[62] Richard Wilkinson writes that the differences in health status associated with income inequality represent the "scale of excess," or the degree of potentially preventable mortality that exists as a result of existing social constructs.[63] Stated differently, "equity in health can be defined as the absence of systematic disparities in health (or in the major social determinants of health) between social groups who have different levels of underlying social advantage/disadvantage — that is, different positions in a social hierarchy."[64] The dramatic health differences that result from inequities "challenge our sense of justice and provoke our scientific curiosity."[65]

The relationship between inequity and health is even more pronounced globally.[66] F.M. Mburu, of Kenya, has warned that increasing socioeconomic inequities, "measured in levels of income, and land ownership, social injustice, and inaccessibility to social services contribute not only to poverty but also to worsening health status."[67] He concludes that low health status among a significant segment of any population "is a sure sign that national wealth is inequitably distributed." Ilona Kickbush has suggested that the best means of improving global public health is to "address the larger issues of social justice, democracy, and law that are paramount to health in the context of globalization."[68] A recent analysis, based significantly on UNICEF and World Bank data, determined that targeting health interventions to poor people is not enough to improve child survival; equity itself must be a priority in designing interventions.[69]

Fabienne Peter and Timothy Evans provide one of the

Volume 32:2, Summer 2004

few analyses of global health equity and *ethics*[70] and charge bioethics with failing to address fairness in the social patterning of health. Inequity, they say, exists when populations have unequal access to effective public health interventions, such as adequate nutrition, antibiotics, vaccines, and universal education, and thus have unequal opportunity to reap the social and health benefits that result. Inequities are particularly troubling, they suggest, when they fall along racial, ethnic, or geographic lines and/or result from deliberate discrimination. Margaret Whitehead, similarly, concludes that some health outcome disparities are more unfair than others.[71] She suggests that unequal health outcomes that result from biological variation or individual informed choice are more likely to be fair, whereas those that result from work conditions, limited access to health care or other services, or limited choice in lifestyle are more likely to be the result of inequities. Barbara Starfield suggests that inequities, by definition, must be remediable and affect the health status of groups in a systematic way.[72] Unfortunately, and critical to this area of scholarship, few measures of equity exist. Indeed, this is one of the areas in which public health ethics must make contributions.[73]

Bioethics could and must contribute to discussions of global justice and public health. First, additional, convincing argument is needed concerning whether and why there is a moral imperative to reduce global injustice and to improve global public health. Important work from political philosophy exists addressing whether we have responsibilities for the global poor. Scholarship from bioethics must build on this work, informed by global epidemiologic data and framed in terms of public health outcomes. Second, bioethics can contribute by articulating and setting standards for what constitutes just structures, especially as relevant to public health. Bioethics, in general, has had longstanding commitments to fairness. Existing models and approaches to fairness, however, must be tested with public health in mind, and with real global communities and diverse cultural and political arrangements at play. Attempts to define equity in global public health generally have emerged from public health, rather that from bioethics. Normal Daniels again deserves credit for making one such attempt from bioethics. Daniels, Jack Bryant, and others have designed a policy tool to measure fairness in local public health structures of diverse global communities.[74] Third, public health ethics and bioethics can put forward arguments concerning whether the cause of global health disparities is relevant to the type of response to be mounted. While some scholars believe that inequities caused by others' neglect or abuse are due greater response than inequities that result from biological differences, others believe everyone experiencing misfortune is deserving of response.

Finally, bioethics must be a voice in discussions of strategy. How, by whom, and to whom, should interventions be targeted, and what are the moral implications of the various options? What ought to be the role of rich countries vs. poor countries in fashioning a response to inequities? What does it mean, morally, to have powerful countries attach strings to particular strategies, even when designed to reduce inequities or encourage more democratic political regimes? What does it mean for less powerful countries to have a stronger voice than they have, and what is the relevance of some of these countries still sporting political structures that exacerbate existing inequities? If, to inform the dialog, public health outcomes data must be collected, what does it mean to collect and publish data from nations with questionable records with regard to human rights?[75] Public health ethics is but one voice in answering these questions, but it is a failing of our field to ignore them.

Ultimately, the goal of public health ethics is to further local, national, and global public health through mechanisms that are respectful and just. That social conditions, arguably, are the greatest predictor of health outcomes has not yet entered the discourse of mainstream bioethics. How societies, political institutions, and economies are and ought to be constructed has more readily fallen instead in the domain of political science, developmental economics, and political philosophy. The lexicon of public health has long included discussion of the relationship between societal structures and health outcomes. That bioethics, for the most part, has been absent from these discussions, is unfortunate. Ironically, the public's health becomes most vulnerable in contexts where bioethics should be well situated to make meaningful contribution. Public health falters when there is injustice; analysis and scholarship on justice have been a mainstay of bioethics. Thoughtful contributions of what more just arrangements might look like, how far one should go in reducing inequities, and why societies ought to have an interest in a healthier populace all are ways in which bioethics could contribute to the furthering of public health planning and practice.

A significant bioethics literature already exists regarding distributive justice and putting forward alternative theories of justice.[76] More recently, two philosophers, Peter Singer and Thomas Pogge, have taken on questions of *global* justice specifically. Peter Singer, a utilitarian, argues that, while it would be good for the richer countries to care about the world's poor out of compassion, it will be more strategic, politically, to argue for reducing global disparities based on self-interest. Poverty and inequity provide fertile conditions for terrorism and violence. The more we neglect the world's poor, he reasons, and allow for inequity to flourish, the more likely we are to be subject to international terrorism of the sort that precipitated the September 11 attacks in the United States.[77]

Thomas Pogge takes a different approach, one that falls under the frame of compensatory justice.[78] Most people, he assumes, are against oppression, hunger, and extreme poverty. The disagreements arise when discussing responsibilities.

He claims that certain political and economic structures not only allow but perpetuate world poverty. Thus, "our economic policies and the global economic institutions we impose make us causally and morally responsible for the perpetuation — even aggravation — of world hunger."[79] The existing global order reflects the interests and priorities of the wealthy and powerful states and systematically compromises the interests of the global poor. To that end, he argues, we in the richer states have affirmative obligations, not out of charity, but out of cause, to ameliorate existing inequities.

While neither Singer nor Pogge situated their discussions in the context of public health, the conceptual thinking that has emerged from these scholars, and from earlier bioethics scholarship on distributive justice, form the foundation on which public health ethics must build when embarking into this new area. Public health ethics, ultimately, is a practical field. Building on the more theoretical disciplines, such as philosophy, political science, and economics, that lay critical groundwork related to politics, economics, and the justness of global structures, public health ethics must seek to design just structures in real time, with real constraints, and in real situations. Bioethics must contribute to both the theoretical and practical work. Practical guidance from public health ethics must evolve hand in hand with increasingly refined and responsive theory related to justice and global public health. The problems are vast, and responses must have the best scholarship behind them.

To become more concrete, public health ethics must tackle the most critical and practical questions with regard to global public health and global justice. For example, what do the data reveal about the relationship between alternative social and political arrangements and health outcomes, and what are the implications of these findings for the development of fair political and public health structures? What is known about the root and proximal causes of existing inequities, and how does this refine existing theory? What is the responsibility of a government toward its own people, and what are the responsibilities of richer countries toward the global poor? Are there incremental yet progressive changes in structure that can be identified and sustained, even in the context of repressive governments? Are some causes of diverging public health outcomes more unfair than others and, if so, do they warrant different responses? Which world bodies can be enlisted as actors and advocates to further global justice and to further global public health?

And ultimately, what exactly are our responsibilities to the global poor? How does one make headway in translating justice *scholarship* into practice, given the gross inequities that presently exist, and given that many of those with the power to change existing structures will have a strong interest in maintaining them? Scholarship must concentrate on how, practically, to further justice in an explicitly unjust world. What can be learned empirically from regions that have successfully decreased human rights abuses? What can be learned from societies boasting fewer inequities?

It is inevitable that public health ethics would turn to questions of global public health. Globalization has become a household word. Telecommunication, global trade agreements and satellite media make the global nature of daily life more apparent. Accompanying a greater awareness of a global community, however, is greater awareness of the growing global disparities in health, wealth, and social standing,[80] disparities that may be exacerbated by globalization itself.[81] The AIDS epidemic has been a further vehicle for increasing awareness of poverty and suffering across the world. The HIV/AIDS epidemic also fueled interest by bioethicists in international research ethics. The majority of international research ethics dilemmas, however, fundamentally stem from global injustices. Indeed, questions of appropriate standards of care or what is owed to participants post-trial become moot if the distribution of global resources were more equitable. Bioethics, which has tackled challenges of research ethics since the birth of the field, has thus begun to engage in questions of global justice without necessarily seeking to do so.

Public health ethics emerged as a subfield of bioethics organically, as the questions addressed by the larger field of bioethics fell more obviously in the domain of public health. The topics addressed by bioethics over its 30-40 year history now situate it naturally to take on questions of global justice and public health. Indeed, since its inception, bioethics has examined questions of justice in a variety of contexts, and bioethics has adapted theoretical constructs to navigate through practical challenges as a matter of course.

New for the mainstream of bioethics will be the examination of questions of global concern, but it is only fitting that such should occur at this stage of the evolution of the field. Bioethics emerged out of a need to confront problems close to home. The boundary between local issues and global issues is increasingly blurred in the current environment, however, with local economic and political structures increasingly playing a role in global concerns. To the extent that bioethics is sincerely committed to furthering public health, we cannot make substantial progress without attention to global public health. It is in the context of global public health where the most significant, most preventable, and thus, most tragic, of public health problems exist. As a global community, we have the power to eliminate the vast majority of public health burden that currently exists. Perhaps bioethics can be one of the voices working to set us on the path to justice, which will, in turn, be the path to improved global public health.

References

1. *Jacobson v. Massachusetts*, 197 U.S. 11 (1905).

2. A. Brandt, *No Magic Bullet: A Social History of Venereal Disease in the United States Since 1880* (New York: Oxford University Press, 1985).

3. Institute of Medicine, *The Future of Public Health* (Washington, D.C.: The National Academy Press, 1988).

4. *Id*, 20.

5. A. Jonsen, *The Birth of Bioethics* (New York: Oxford University Press, 1998); J. K. Walter and E. P. Klein, *The Story of Bioethics: From Seminal Works to Contemporary Exploration* (Washington, DC: Georgetown University Press, 2003).

6. R. R. Faden, "Ethical Issues in Government Sponsored Public Health Campaigns," *Health Education Quarterly* 14, no. 1 (1987): 27-37; E. D. Pellegrino, "Health Promotion as Public Policy: The Need for Moral Groundings," *Preventive Medicine* 10 (1981): 371-378; D. I. Wikler. "Coercive Measures in Health Promotion: Can They be Justified?" *Health Education Monographs* 6, no. 2 (1978): 223-241; R. R. Faden and A. I. Faden. "The Ethics of Health Education as Public Policy," *Health Education Monographs* 6, no. 2 (1978): 180-197.

7. D. I. Wikler, "Persuasion and Coercion for Health," *Milbank Memorial Fund Quarterly* 56 (1978): 303-333.

8. D. I. Wikler. "Coercive Measures in Health Promotion: Can They be Justified?" *Health Education Monographs* 6, no. 2 (1978): 223-241.

9. L. B. Russell, *Is Prevention Better than Cure?* (Washington DC: Brookings Institution, 1986).

10. E. D. Pellegrino. "Health Promotion as Public Policy: The Need for Moral Groundings," *Preventive Medicine* 10 (1981): 371-378.

11. R. R. Faden and A. I. Faden. "The Ethics of Health Education as Public Policy," *Health Education Monographs* 6, no. 2 (1978): 180-197.

12. Society for Public Health Education. "Code of Ethics for the Health Education Profession." Section 4 (1976) revised 1977, 1983, 1992, at <http://www.sophe.org/about/ethics.html> (last visited May 8, 2004).

13. K. Glanz, F.M. Lewis, B.K. Rimer (Eds.) *Health Behavior and Health Education: Theory, Research and Practice (2nd Ed.)* (San Francisco, CA: Jossey-Bass, 1997); D.L. Roter, J.A. Hall, R. Merisca, B. Ruehle, D. Cretin, and B. Svarstad, "Effectiveness of Interventions to Improve Patient Compliance: A Meta-Analysis," *Medical Care* 36 (1998): 1138-1161.

14. R. R. Faden, "Ethical Issues in Government Sponsored Public Health Campaigns," *Health Education Quarterly* 14, no. 1 (1987): 27-37.

15. E. D. Pellegrino, "Health Promotion as Public Policy: The Need for Moral Groundings," *Preventive Medicine* 10 (1981): 371-378.

16. D. E. Beauchamp, "Alcoholism as Blaming the Alcoholic," *International Journal of Addiction* 11 (1976): 41-52.

17. D. I. Wikler, "Persuasion and Coercion for Health," *Milbank Memorial Fund Quarterly/Health and Society* 56 (1978): 303-333.

18. Note that this section and the following section are drawn considerably from a previous work, *viz.*, R. R. Faden and N.E. Kass, "Bioethics and Public Health in the 1980s: Resource Allocation and AIDS," *Annual Reviews of Public Health* 12 (1991): 335-360.

19. N. Daniels, "Health-Care Needs and Distributive Justice." *Philosophy and Public Affairs* 10, no. 2 (1981): 146-79.; T. L. Beauchamp and R. R. Faden. "The Right to Health and the Right to Health Care." *Journal of Medicine and Philosophy* 4, no. 2 (1979): 118-131; C. Fried, "Equality and Rights in Medical Care," *Hastings Center Report* 6, no. 1 (1976): 29-34; C. Fried, "Rights in Health Care—Beyond Equity and Efficiency," *New England Journal of Medicine* 293, no. 5 (1975): 241-245; H. T. Engelhardt, "Rights to Health Care, Social Justice, and Fairness in Healthcare Allocations," in *Foundation of Bioethics* (New York: Oxford University Press, 1986); P.T. Menzel, *Medical Costs, Moral Choices: A Philosophy of Health Care Economics in America* (New Haven, Conn: Yale University Press, 1983).

20. President's Commission for the Study of Ethical Problems in Medicine and Biomedical and Behavioral Research, *Securing Access to Health Care: The Ethical Implications of Differences in the Availability of Health Services*, Vol. 1 (Washington, DC: Government Printing Office, 1983).

21. T. L. Beauchamp and R. R. Faden, "The Right to Health and the Right to Health Care," *The Journal of Medicine and Philosophy* 4, no. 2 (1979): 118-131.

22. R. M. Green, "The Priority of Health Care," *Journal of Medical Philosophy* 8, no. 4 (1983): 373-380; N. Daniels, *Just Health Care* (New York: Cambridge, 1985); A. Gibbard, "The Prospective Pareto Principle and Equity of Access to Health Care," *Milbank Memorial Fund Quarterly* 60, no. 3 (1982): 399-428; B. Brody, "Health Care for the Haves and Have Nots: Toward a Just Basis of Distribution," in E.E. Shelp, ed., *Justice and Health Care* (Boston: Reidel, 1981):151-159; A. E. Buchanan, "The Right to a Decent Minimum of Health Care," *Philosophy and Public Affairs* 13, no. 1 (1984): 55-78; M. Walzer, *Spheres of Justice* (New York: Basic Books, 1983).

23. R.H. Blank, *Rationing Medicine* (New York: Columbia University Press, 1988); D. Callahan, "Meeting Needs and Rationing Care," *Law, Medicine and Health Care* 16, no. 3-4 (1988): 261-66; L. Churchill, *Rationing Health Care in America* (Notre Dame, Ind: University of Notre Dame Press, 1987); E.D. Pellegrino, "Rationing Health Care: The Ethics of Medical Gatekeeping," in J.F. Monagle and D.C. Thomasma, ed., *Medical Ethics: A Guide for Health Professionals* (Rockville, MD: Aspen, 1988): 261-270; G.R. Winslow, "Rationing and Publicity," in: G.J. Agich and C.E. Begley, eds., *The Price of Health* (Boston: Reidel, 1986): 199-215.

24. D. Callahan. *Setting Limits: Medical Goals in an Aging Society* (New York: Touchstone Books, 1988); N. Daniels, *Am I My Parent's Keeper? An Essay on Justice Between the Young and Old* (New York: Oxford University Press, 1990).

25. E. C. Pellegrino and D. C. Thomasma, *For the Patient's Own Good* (New York: Oxford University Press, 1988).

26. President's Commission for the Study of Ethical Problems in Medicine and Biomedical Behavioral Research, *Securing Access to Health Care: The Ethical Implications of Differences in the Availability of Health Services*, Vol. 1 (Washington, DC: GPO, 1983); L. Churchill, *Rationing Health Care in America* (Notre Dame, Ind: University of Notre Dame Press, 1987).

27. Centers for Disease Control, "Current Trends Prevention of Acquired Immune Deficiency Syndrome: Report of Inter-Agency Recommendations," *Morbidity and Mortality Weekly Report* 32, no., 8 (1983):101-3.

28. R. Bayer, "Gays and the Stigma of Bad Blood," *Hastings Center Report* 13 (1983): 5-7.

29. Institute of Medicine, *Confronting AIDS: Directions for Public Health, Health Care, and Research* (Washington D.C.: National Academies Press, 1986).

30. Presidential Commission on the Human Immunodeficiency Virus Epidemic, *Final Report* (Washington DC: GPO, 1988).

31. L. Gostin and W.J. Curran, "The Limit of Compulsion on Controlling AIDS," *Hastings Center Report* 16 (Suppl.) (1986): 24-29; C.E. Koop, "Surgeon Generals report on Acquired Immune

Deficiency Syndrome," *Journal of the American Medical Association* 256 (1986): 278-89; R. Macklin, "Predicting Dangerousness and Public Health Response to AIDS," *Hastings Center Report* 16 (Suppl.) (1986): 16-23; D.F. Musto, "Quarantine and the Problem of AIDS," *Milbank Memorial Fund Quarterly* 64 (Suppl.) (1986): 113; R. Porter, "History Says No to the Policeman's Response to AIDS," *British Medical Journal* 293 (1986): 1589-90.

32. J.M.G. Wilson and F. Jungner, "Principles and Practice of Screening for Disease," *Public Health Papers* 34 (Geneva: WHO 1968); A.L .Cochrane and W.W. Holand, "Validation of Screening Procedures," *British Medical Bulletin* 27 (1971): 3-8; L.G. Whitby, "Screening for Disease: Definitions and Criteria," *Lancet* 7884 (1974): 819-822.

33. R. Bayer, "Ethical and Social Policy Issues Raised by HIV Screening: The Epidemic Evolves and So Do the Challenges," *AIDS* 3 (1989): 119-24; R. Bayer, C. Levine and S.M. Wolf, "HIV Antibody Screening: An Ethical Framework for Evaluating Proposed Programs," *Journal of the American Medical Association* 256 (1986): 1768-74; L. Gostin and W.J. Curran, "Legal Control Measures for AIDS: Reporting Requirements, Surveillance, Quarantine, and Regulation of Public Meeting Places," *American Journal of Public Health* 77 (1987): 214-218; L. Gostin, W.J. Curran, M.E. Clark, "The Case Against Compulsory Casefinding in Controlling AIDS—Testing, Screening and Reporting," *American Journal of Law and Medicine* 12 (1987): 7-53; N.D. Hunter, "AIDS Prevention and Civil Liberties: The False Security of Mandatory Testing," *AIDS Public Policy Journal* 2 (1987): 1-10; J.F. Childress, "An Ethical Framework for Assessing Policies to Screen for Antibodies for HIV," *AIDS Public Policy Journal* 2 (1987): 28-31.

34. T.J. Coates, R.D. Stall, S.M. Kegeles, B. Lo, S.F. Morin and L. McKusic "AIDS Antibody Testing," *American Psychology* 43 (1988): 859-64; L.S. Doll, W. Darrow, P. O'Malley, T. Bodecker, and H. Jaffe, "Self-reported Behavioral Change in Homosexual Men in the San Francisco City Clinic Cohort," Presented at International AIDS Conference, 3rd, Washington, DC.; J. McCusker, A.M. Stoddard, K.H. Mayer, J. Zapka, C. Morrison, S.P. Salzman, "Effects of HIV Antibody Test Knowledge on Subsequent Sexual Behaviors in a Cohort of Homosexually Active Men," *American Journal of Public Health* 78 (1988): 462-67; G.J.P. Van Griesven, E.M.M. De Vroome, R.A.P. Tielman, J. Goudsmit, J. Van Der Noordaa, et al. "Impact of HIV Antibody Testing on Changes in Sexual Behavior Among Homosexual Men in the Netherlands," *American Journal of Public Health* 79 (1988): 1575-77.

35. R. Fox, N.J. Odaka, R. Brookmeyer, B.F. Polk, "Effect of HIV Antibody Disclosure on Subsequent Sexual Activity in Homosexual Men," *AIDS* 1 (1987): 241-46.

36. T. L. Beauchamp and J. L. Childress, *Principles of Biomedical Ethics* (New York: Oxford University Press, 1979).

37. D. Callahan, "Autonomy: A Moral Good, Not a Moral Obsession," *The Hastings Center Report* 14, no. 5 (1984): 40-42; D. Steinbock, "Liberty, Responsibility, and the Common Good," *The Hastings Center Report* 26, no. 6 (1996): 45-47; E. Pellegrino and D. C. Thomasma, *For the Patient's Good: The Restoration of Beneficence in Health Care* (New York: Oxford University Press, 1988).

37. D. E. Beauchamp, "Public Health as Social Justice," *Inquiry* 13 (1976):1-14; D. E. Beauchamp, "Community: The Neglected Tradition of Public Health," *The Hastings Center Report* 15 (1985): 28-36.

38. *Id.*

39. D. Beauchamp, 1985 *supra* note 38.

40. M. Lappe, "Ethics and Public Health," in J.M. Last, ed., *Maxcy-Rosenau Public Health and Preventive Medicine,* Twelfth Ed. (Norwalk, Connecticut: Appleton-Century-Crofts, 1986): 1867-1877. Note that the 11th edition of the same text book (1980) had a chapter entitled "Legal and Ethical Issues in Public Health" by Sidney Shindell. The bulk of this chapter is devoted to legal issues in public health, however, rather than ethics issues, and thus is not discussed here.

41. During this period, there were numerous important contributions to ethics and epidemiology as well. These are not described in the main body of this work, however, as they relate to the large body of scholarship on research ethics than they do to defining an ethics of public health. Examples of such literature include L. Gordis, E. Gold, and R. Seltser, "Privacy Protection in Epidemiologic and Medical Research: A Challenge and A Responsibility," *American Journal of Epidemiology* 105 (1977): 163-168; D. L. Weed, "The Merger of Bioethics and Epidemiology," *Journal of Clinical Epidemiology* 44, Suppl. I (1991): 15S-22S.; T. L. Beauchamp, "Ethical Theory and Epidemiology," *Journal of Clinical Epidemiology* 44, Suppl. I (1991): 5S-8S.

42. N. E. Kass, "An Ethics Framework for Public Health," *American Journal of Public Health* 91 (2001):1776-1782; D. Callahan and B. Jennings. "Ethics and Public Health: Forging a Strong Relationship," *American Journal of Public Health* 92, no. 2 (2002):169-176; J. F. Childress, R. R. Faden, R. D. Gaare, L. O. Gostin, J. Kahn, R. J. Bonnie, N. E. Kass, A. C. Mastroianni, J. D. Moreno, and P. Nieburg, "Public Health Ethics: Mapping the Terrain," *Journal of Law, Medicine, and Ethics* 30 (2002):170-178.; M. J. Roberts and M. R. Reich, "Ethical Analysis in Public Health," *The Lancet* 359 (2002): 1055-1059.

43. <www.apha.org/codeofethics/> (last visited April 27, 2004).

44. N. E. Kass, "An Ethics Framework for Public Health," *American Journal of Public Health* 91 (2001): 1776-1782.

45. J. F. Childress, R. R. Faden, R. D. Gaare, L. O. Gostin, J. Kahn, R. J. Bonnie, N. E. Kass, A. C. Mastroianni, J. D. Moreno, and P. Nieburg, "Public Health Ethics: Mapping the Terrain," *Journal of Law, Medicine, and Ethics* 30 (2002): 170-178.

46. Roberts and Reich similarly suggested that public health professionals need more training in ethical analysis and applied philosophy. M.J. Roberts and M.R. Reich MR, "Ethical Analysis in Public Health," *Lancet* 359, no 9311 (2002): 1055-59.

47. Institute of Medicine, *Toward Environmental Justice: Research, Education, and Health Policy Needs* (Washington, DC: National Academy Press, 1999).

48. Working Group on Environmental Justice, Harvard University, <http://ecojustice.net/> (last visited April 27, 2004).

49. <http://www.asph.org/document.cfm?page=301> (last visited May 8, 2004).

50. Centers for Disease Control, *Guidelines for Defining Public Health Research and Public Health Non-Research* (Atlanta: CDC, 1999); D. Casarett, J.H.T. Karlawish, and J. Sugarman, "Determining When Quality Improvement Initiatives Should Be Considered Research: Proposed Criteria and Potential Implications," *Journal of the American Medical Association* 283, no. 17 (2000): 2275-2280; E. Bellin and N. Neveloff Dubler, "The Quality Improvement-Research Divide and the Need for External Oversight," *American Journal of Public Health* 91, no. 9 (2001): 1512-1517; P. Amoroso and J. Middaugh, "Research vs. Public Health Practice: When Does a Study Require IRB Review?" *Preventive Medicine* 36 (2003): 250-253.

51. Centers for Disease Control, *supra* note 51.

52. S. Hellman and D. Hellman. "Of Mice but not Men: Problems of the Randomized Clinical Trial," *New Eng. J. Med.* 324 (1991): 1585-9.

53. D. L. Weed and P. J. Mink, "Roles and Responsibilities of Epidemiologists," *Annals of Epidemiology,* 12, no. 2 (2002): 67-72.

54. E. Fee, "A History and Development of Public Health," in F. D. Scutchfield and C. W. Keck, eds., *Principles of Public Health Practice*(Boston: Delmar Publishers, 1977):10-30; also see <http://www.civeng.ucl.ac.uk/edwin.htm> (last visited April 29, 2004).

55. G. Bloom. "Equity in Health in Unequal Societies: Meeting Health needs in Contexts of Social Change," *Health Policy* 57 (2001): 205-224.

56. G. D. Smith, M. J. Shipley, G. Rose, "Magnitude and Causes of Socioeconomic Differentials in Mortality: Further Evidence from the Whitehall Study," *Journal of Epidemiology and Community Health* 44 (1990): 265-270

57. M. G. Marmot, M.J. Shipley, and G. Rose, "Inequalities in Death — Specific Explanations of a General Pattern," *Lancet* 8384 (1984): 1003-1006.

58. L. Berkman and I. Kawachi, (eds.), *Social Epidemiology* (New York: Oxford University Press, 2000

59. F. Diderichsen, T. Evans and M. Whitehead. "The Social Basis of Disparities in Health" in T. Evans, M. Whitehead, F. Diderichsen, A. Bhuiya, and M. Wirth, eds., *Challenging Inequities in Health: From Ethics to Action* (New York: Oxford University Press, 2001).

60. I. Kawachi and B.P. Kennedy, "Health and Social Cohesion: Why Care about Income Inequality?" BMJ 314, no 7086 (1997): 1037-40.

61. J. N. Daniels, "Justice, Health, and Healthcare," *American Journal of Bioethics* 1 (2001): 2-16, at 6 .

62. R. Wilkinson. *Unhealthy Societies: The Afflictions of Inequality* (New York: Routledge, 1996): 59.

63. P. Braveman and S. Gruskin, "Defining Equity in Health," *Journal of Epidemiology and Community Health* 57 (2003): 254-258.

64. F. Diderichsen, T. Evans, and M. Whitehead, "The Social Basis of Disparities in Health," in T. Evans, M. Whitehead, F. Diderichsen, A. Bhuiya, and M. Wirth, eds., *Challenging Inequities in Health: From Ethics to Action* (New York: Oxford University Press, 2001): 13-23, at 13.

65. J.A. Macinko and B. Starfield, "Annotated Bibliography on Equity and Health, 1980-2001," Internation Journal for Equity in Health 1 (2002): 1-42.

66. F.M. Mburu. "Health Systems as Defenses Against the Consequences of Poverty: Equity in Health as Social Justice," *Social Science and Medicine* 17 (2003): 1149-1157.

67. I. Kickbush. "Influence and Opportunity: Reflections on the U.S. Role in Global Public Health," *Health Affairs* 21 (2002): 131-141.

68. C. G. Victora, A. Wagstaff, J. A. Schellenberg, D. Gwatkin, M. Claeson, and J.P. Habicht. "Applying an Equity Lens to Child Health and Mortality: More of the Same is not Enough," *Lancet* 362 (2003): 233-41.

69. F. Peter and T. Evans, "Ethical Dimensions of Health Equity," in T. Evans, M. Whitehead, F. Diderichsen, A. Bhuiya, and M. Wirth, eds., *Challenging Inequities in Health: From Ethics to Action* (New York: Oxford University Press, 2001): 25-33.

70. M. Whitehead. "The Concepts and Principles of Equity and Health," *International Journal of Health Services* 22. no. 3 (1992): 429-445.

71. B. Starfield, "Improving Equity in Health: A Research Agenda," International Journal of Health Services 31, no. 3 (2001): 545-566.

72. *Id.*

73. N. Daniels, J. Bryant, R.A. Castano, O.G. Dantes, K.S. Khan, S. Pannarunothai, "Benchmarks of Fairness for Health Care Reform: A Policy Tool for Developing Countries," *Bulletin of the World Health Organization* 78, no. 6 (2000): 740-750.

74. C. Beyrer and N. Kass, "Human Rights, Politics, and Research Ethics Review," *Lancet* 360 (2002): 246-51.

75. J. Rawls, *A Theory of Justice* (Cambridge: Harvard University Press, 1971); R. Dworkin, "What is Equality?" *Philosophy and Public Affairs* 10 (1981): 283-345; A. Sen, "Equality of What?" in A. Sen, ed., *Choice, Welfare, and Measurement* (Cambridge: Cambridge University Press, 1982); J. Feinberg, "Justice and Personal Desert," *Doing and Deserving* (Princeton, NJ: Princeton University Press, 1970); D. Parfit, *Reasons and Persons* (Oxford: Oxford University Press, 1986).

76. P. Singer, *One World: The Ethics of Globalization* (New Haven: Yale University Press, 2002); By contrast, Ilona Kickbush notes that focusing arguments to reduce global poverty on self-interest may be strategic in the short run, but will not be as effective in the long run. It has been argued that the United States should commit funds to global public health in order to save the millions of dollars associated with global diseases increasingly affecting Americans, or the costs of global social unrest, terrorism, and violence borne out of poverty and poor health. Justifying aid this way, Kickbush suggests, has resulted in the United States moving out of multilateral public health and aid efforts and "reinforcing global unilateralism at a time when many of the health issues require a truly global response and the cooperation of many actors". I. Kickbush, "Influence and Opportunity: Reflections on the U.S. Role in Global Public Health," *Health Affairs* Nov./Dec. (2002): 131-141.

77. T. W. Pogge, "Relational Conceptions of Justice: Responsibilities for Health Outcomes," forthcoming in S. Anand, F. Peter, and A. Sen, eds., *Health, Ethics, and Equity* (Oxford: Clarendon Press, 2003); T W. Pogge, "Priorities of Global Justice," in T. Pogge, ed., *Global Justice* (Oxford: Blackwell Publishers, 2001): 6-23.

78. T. W. Pogge, "Priorities of Global Justice," in T. Pogge, ed., *Global Justice* (Oxford: Blackwell Publishers, 2001): 15.

79. World Health Organization, *World Health Report 2002: Reducing Risks, Promoting Healthy Life* (Geneva: WHO, 2002).

80. G. Pappas, A. A. Hyder, and M. Akhter, "Globalization: Toward a New Framework for Public Health," *Social Theory and Health* 1 (2003): 91-107.

[10]

ETHICS AND INFECTIOUS DISEASE[1]

MICHAEL J. SELGELID

ABSTRACT

Bioethics apparently suffers from a misdistribution of research resources analogous to the '10/90' divide in medical research. Though infectious disease should be recognized as a topic of primary importance for bioethics, the general topic of infectious disease has received relatively little attention from the discipline of bioethics in comparison with things like abortion, euthanasia, genetics, cloning, stem cell research, and so on. The fact that the historical and potential future consequences of infectious diseases are almost unrivalled is one reason that the topic of infectious disease warrants more attention from bioethicists. The 'Black Death' eliminated one third of the European population during the 14th Century; the 1918 flu killed between 20 and 100 million people; and, in the 20th Century smallpox killed perhaps three times more people than all the wars of that period. In the contemporary world, epidemics (of AIDS, multi-drug resistant tuberculosis, and newly emerging infectious diseases such as SARS) continue to have dramatic consequences. A second reason why the topic of infectious disease deserves further attention is that it raises difficult ethical questions of its own. While infected individuals can threaten the health of other individuals and society as a whole, for example, public health care measures such as surveillance, isolation, and quarantine can require the infringement of widely accepted basic human rights and liberties. An important and difficult ethical question asks how to strike a balance between the utilitarian aim of promoting public health, on the one hand, and libertarian aims of protecting privacy and freedom of movement, on the other, in contexts involving diseases that are – to varying degrees – contagious, deadly, or otherwise dangerous. Third, since their burden is most heavily shouldered by the poor (in developing countries), infectious diseases deeply involve issues of justice – which should be a central concern of ethics. I conclude by providing sociological and historical explanations

[1] A version of this paper was presented at the VI World Congress of Bioethics, Brasilia, Brazil, October 2002.

of why the topic of infectious disease has not already received more attention from bioethicists.

I. DISTRIBUTION OF RESEARCH RESOURCES

The '10/90 divide' is a phenomenon whereby 'less than 10 percent of [medical] research funds are spent on the diseases that account for 90% of the global burden of disease . . . [D]iseases affecting large proportions of humanity are given comparatively little attention.'[2] Because medical research so often aims at the promotion of profits rather than solutions to the world's most urgent medical problems, a majority of funds focus on the wants of a minority of the world's population – those who are relatively wealthy. As a result, health care is often unavailable to those who need it most.

A situation analogous to the 10/90 divide in medical research apparently holds true for research in bioethics. A quick flip through most bioethics texts and journals (or a visit to any number of websites) reveals attention on abortion, euthanasia, assisted reproduction, genetics, and doctor-patient relationships. To a large extent the issues examined one way or another involve advanced technologies or expensive interventions available primarily in wealthy developed nations. 'Distribution of resources' is a common topic; but discussion here often (at least implicitly) concerns domestic allocation rather than issues of *international* justice. Greatly lacking, in comparison, is discussion of ethical issues involving infectious disease and the (related) health care situation in the developing world. Infectious diseases (such as AIDS, tuberculosis, and a variety of other emerging and re-emerging pathogens) and the health care situation in developing countries pose some of the most serious problems of our times, but they have received relatively little attention from medical ethicists. In what follows I will (1) argue that the topic of infectious disease should be recognized as one of *the* most important topics for the discipline of bioethics, (2) briefly illustrate that it has received comparatively little attention from bioethicists,[3] and (3) attempt to explain why it has not received the attention it warrants.

[2] K. Lee, and A. Mills. Strengthening Governance for Global Health Research. *British Medical Journal* 2000; 321: 775–776, at http://www.bmj.com/cgi/content/full/321/7264/775.

[3] Although I shall not in this article discuss this point at great length, others who have worked in this area, such as Margaret Battin and Solomon Benatar,

II. THE ETHICAL IMPORTANCE OF INFECTIOUS DISEASE

The lack of bioethics discussion of infectious disease is both odd and unfortunate. Given that infectious disease was traditionally a – if not *the* – primary focus of medicine, for example, one would expect this to be obvious territory for a discipline concerned with 'medical ethics.'[4] More specific reasons why this should be recognized as one of the most relevant and important topics for bioethics are the following:

1. The historical and likely future consequences of infectious diseases are almost unrivalled,
2. Infectious diseases raise exceedingly difficult ethical questions of their own, and
3. The topic of infectious disease is closely connected to the topic of justice – which is a central concern of ethics.

1. Consequences

First, the paramount ethical importance of infectious diseases is illustrated by the fact that their consequences have been, and will likely continue to be, enormous. Epidemics have constituted some of the most catastrophic events in human history. The Black Death, for example, is famous for eliminating approximately one third of the European population between 1347 and 1350.[5] Another devastating epidemic occurred in 1918 when a nasty strain of influenza killed somewhere between 20 and 100 million people. According to the historian Alfred Crosby, the 1918 flu undoubtedly 'killed more humans than any other disease in a period of similar duration in the history of the world.'[6] Gina Kolata writes that the 1918 flu killed 'more Americans in a single year than died in battle in World War I, World War II, the Korean War, and the Vietnam War.'[7] (According to the *New York Times,* '[J]ust about everyone who has studied the disease says [that] a new pandemic is inevitable.')[8]

have agreed that it is quite correct. A similar point is made by (especially Chapter 8 of) P. Farmer. 2003. *Pathologies of Power: Health, Human Rights, and the New War on the Poor.* Los Angeles. University of California Press.

[4] I shall use the expressions 'bioethics', 'biomedical ethics', and 'medical ethics', interchangeably.

[5] P. Ziegler. 1969. *The Black Death.* London. Penguin.

[6] A.W. Crosby. 1989. *America's Forgotten Epidemic: The Influenza of 1918.* Cambridge, UK. Cambridge University Press: 203.

[7] G. Kolata. 1999. *Flu.* London. Pan Books: xii.

[8] B. Gewen. 'The Great Influenza' and 'Microbial Threats to Health': Virus Alert. *The New York Times* March 14, 2004, available at: http://www.nytimes.com/2004/03/14/books/review/14GEWENT.html.

A third major killer, which has received high-profile attention in American newspapers recently, is smallpox. Smallpox allegedly killed more people in history than any other infectious disease. In the 20th Century alone it killed somewhere between 300 and 540 million people – or 'more than all the wars and epidemics [of that century] combined.'[9] Michael Oldstone claims that smallpox killed three times more people during the 20th Century than were killed by all the wars of that period.[10] Although the disease was declared eradicated by the World Health Organization (WHO) in 1980, fears about smallpox have resurfaced. It has recently come to light that the Soviet Union, until its fall in the early 1990s, manufactured and froze tens of tons of smallpox for military purposes. Many are worried that stocks of the Soviet supply may have fallen into the hands of 'rogue nations' or terrorists. Experts claim that a smallpox bioterrorist attack could spark a catastrophic global epidemic now that the world population largely lacks immunity (because routine vaccination ended 20 or 30 years ago).[11] Modeling has shown that a smallpox attack could cause the devastation of (perhaps a series of) nuclear attack(s).

Smallpox aside, it is important to recognize that the enormous impact of infectious diseases is not just a matter of history. Infectious diseases are currently the world's largest 'killer[s] of children and young adults. They account for more than 13 million deaths a year – one in two deaths in developing countries.'[12] The rapidly growing HIV/AIDS epidemic perhaps provides the clearest illustration that infectious diseases continue to have the power of their past. AIDS is arguably 'the greatest health disaster in history.'[13] In 24 years, it has killed 20 million people[14] (whereas the Black Death killed only 9 to 11 million people in Europe

[9] J. Miller, S. Engelberg & W. Broad. 2001. *Germs: The Ultimate Weapon.* London. Simon and Schuster: 58.

[10] M.B.A. Oldstone. 1998. *Viruses, Plagues, and History.* New York. Oxford University Press: 3.

[11] For more on smallpox, see M.J. Selgelid. Smallpox Revisited? *American Journal of Bioethics* 2003; 3, 1, available at http://www.bioethics.net/journal/j_articles.php?aid=91, accessed 1 March 2005; and M.J. Selgelid. Bioterrorism and Smallpox Planning: Information and Voluntary Vaccination. *Journal of Medical Ethics* 2004; 30, 6: 558–560; available at http://jme.bmjjournals.com/cgi/reprint/30/6/558, accessed 1 March 2005.

[12] World Health Organization. 1999. Report on Infectious Diseases, Chapter 16, Removing Obstacles to Healthy Development, available at http://www.who.int/infectious-disease-report/pages/textonly.html, p. 2.

[13] C. Gilbert. AIDS Draws New Attention. *Milwaukee Journal Sentinel,* 15 April, 2002.

[14] See http://www.redribbon.co.za/.

between 1346 and 1350).[15] HIV prevalence rates commonly exceed 30% (of adults) in sub-Saharan Africa, and similar scenarios may follow in parts of Asia and the former Soviet Union. As of 1999, anyway, only 5% of those infected could afford life-extending antiretroviral therapy.[16] In 2004, 3 million people died from AIDS, and 5 million people were newly infected with HIV. At the end of 2004, an estimated 39 million people were living with HIV.[17]

A related, but less well publicized, scenario involves the re-emergent spread of tuberculosis. Previously thought to be controlled, or at least considered controllable, TB was declared a global health emergency by the World Health Organization in 1993 and currently kills more people than ever before. 'Each year, 2 to 3 million people die from tuberculosis . . . despite the fact that the disease in its most common form is entirely preventable and treatable.'[18] One third of the world's population is infected with the latent form of the disease; and, a tenth of these are expected to develop active illness. 'It is estimated that between 2000 and 2020, nearly one billion people will be newly infected, 200 million people will get sick, and 35 million will die from TB – if control is not further strengthened.'[19] Of particular concern is the rise and spread of multi-drug resistant TB, resulting from the improper use of medication (in Russian prisons, for example).

The recent emergence and spread of SARS (Severe Acute Respiratory Syndrome) is, of course, the latest indicator that the impact of infectious diseases will continue to be severe. According to studies, the 'death rate from SARS may be . . . up to 55 percent in people 60 and older, and up to 13.2 percent in younger people . . . unless the numbers fall drastically, SARS would be among the infectious diseases with the highest death rates . . . By contrast, the influenza pandemic of 1918 . . . had an estimated mortality rate, overall, of 1 percent or less.'[20] In the meanwhile,

[15] L. Garrett. 2000. *Betrayal of Trust: The Collapse of Global Public Health.* New York. Hyperion: 474.

[16] Ibid., p. 473.

[17] UNAIDS: AIDS Epidemic Update, 2004. Available at www.unaids.org.

[18] L.B. Reichman and J.H. Tanne. 2002. *Timebomb: The Global Epidemic of Multi-Drug-Resistant Tuberculosis.* New York. McGraw Hill: x–xi. See also P. Farmer. 1999. *Infections and Inequalities: The Modern Plagues.* Berkeley, CA. University of California Press.

[19] World Health Organization. Tuberculosis, Fact Sheet No. 104, revised April 2000, available at http://www.who.int/inf-fs/en/fact104.html, p. 1.

[20] L.K. Altman. Death Rate from SARS is Revised Upward. *International Herald Tribune* May 8, 2003.

there is no treatment, vaccine, or reliable diagnostic test for the SARS virus – which 'can survive on surfaces [such as doorknobs] for up to four days.'[21] Isolation, quarantine, travel advisories, travel restrictions, and related public health measures were put into effect; and the economic impact, alone, was staggering – '[j]ust a few weeks after SARS was identified, WHO [calculated] that the cost of the disease [was] already close to $30 billion.'[22]

It is now widely acknowledged that, in addition to posing global health and economic threats, AIDS and other infectious diseases threaten global security. Historical studies reveal that factors such as high infant mortality, low life expectancy, decreasing life expectancy, etc. – which are being severely affected in places like sub-Saharan Africa and the former Soviet Union – are among the most reliable indicators of major social upheaval. Given the serious historical and potential future consequences of infectious disease, it is no wonder that the CIA recently conducted (and published) a special investigation of '*The Global Infectious Disease Threat and Its Implications for the United States.*'[23] It is puzzling, on the other hand, that medical ethicists have not had more to say about infectious disease – compared to abortion, euthanasia, and genetics, for example, which have saturated the literature.

2. *Difficult ethical questions*

A second reason why infectious diseases warrant more of bioethics' attention is that they raise serious, difficult philosophical/ethical questions of their own. Obvious examples arise from the fact that infectious diseases can be contagious. Depending on the disease in question, infected individuals can threaten the health of other individuals or society as a whole. The public health measures required to protect other individuals and society from contagion (again, depending on the disease) might sometimes involve surveillance, mandatory testing, mandatory vaccination or treatment, notification of authorities or third parties, isolation (of individuals), quarantine (of entire regions), or travel restrictions. Because such public health care measures could infringe upon

[21] Ibid.

[22] I. Kickbusch. A Wake-Up Call for Global Health. *International Herald Tribune* April 29, 2003.

[23] Available at http://www.odci.gov/cia/publications/nie/report/nie99-17d.html. One conclusion of the report is that we should perhaps worry most about new infectious diseases – more dangerous than AIDS – likely to emerge in the future.

widely accepted basic human rights and liberties, we are here confronted with conflicting values.

An extremely difficult ethical question asks how, in situations of conflict, the utilitarian aim to promote the greater good in the way of public health should be balanced against libertarian aims to protect privacy and individual rights and liberties such as freedom of movement, and so on. Most philosophers, policy makers, and ordinary citizens would (upon reflection, I imagine) deny that *either* liberty or aggregate utility should *always* be given *absolute* priority over the other regardless of the degree (in terms of likelihood and severity) to which the other is threatened. So the challenge is to find a principled way of striking a balance between these presumably legitimate, but apparently conflicting, social aims in contexts involving diseases that are – to varying degrees[24] – contagious, deadly, or otherwise dangerous.[25] I will later say more about the difficulty of ethical issues raised by infectious disease.

3. Justice

Third, infectious disease should be recognized as a crucial topic for bioethics because the topic of infectious disease is closely connected to the topic of justice. Pathogens primarily prey upon the poor. Bad nutrition, dirty water, crowded living conditions, poor education, lack of access to basic medicines, disempowerment of women, and a complex host of other factors combine to make the populations of developing nations especially vulnerable to infectious diseases:

> Most deaths from infectious diseases occur in developing countries – the countries with the least money to spend on health care. In developing countries, about one third of the population – 1.3 billion people – live on incomes of less than $1 a day. Almost one in three children are malnourished. One in five

[24] I highlight variation in severity to suggest that there is likely no simple, obvious answer to this question. I should here point out the practical importance, in addition to theoretical difficulty, of this kind of question. It is now widely acknowledged, for example, that quarantine policy is outdated and in need of revision. Biodefense planning and the emergence of SARS provide the most recent illustrations of the immediate importance of this issue.

[25] This topic, of course, has not been altogether ignored. For discussion in the context of AIDS see U. Schuklenk. 1998. AIDS: Individual and 'Public' Interests, in *A Companion to Bioethics*, P. Singer & H. Kuhse. eds. Oxford, UK. Blackwell: 343–354. For recent discussion of quarantine policy in light of the smallpox bioterrorist threat, see G.J. Annas. Bioterrorism, Public Health, and Civil Liberties. *The New England Journal of Medicine* 2002; 346: 1337–1342.

> are not immunized by their first birthday. And over one third of the world's population lack access to essential drugs.[26]

Today it is widely acknowledged that ailments called 'tropical diseases' are often not peculiar to tropical regions at all. To a large extent 'tropical diseases' are those that afflict poor developing countries, rather than necessarily tropical ones.[27] Sanitation, hygiene, vaccination, antibiotics, other drugs, and general improvements in living conditions have, in recent decades anyway, left privileged populations relatively sheltered from the scourges of the developing world.

Relationships between poverty and disease are well illustrated by the AIDS pandemic and the health care situation in Africa at the beginning of the 21st Century. Of the (roughly) 40 million people estimated to be living with HIV/AIDS in 2002, 28 million – or 70% – lived in sub-Saharan Africa.[28]

> [A]nd 95% [in 2001] live[d] in developing nations. Most of the infected people who live in these countries have no access to new or existing drugs for HIV/AIDS. But the problem of access to medications goes far beyond the HIV/AIDS pandemic: people in developing nations also cannot afford medications used to treat or prevent malaria, tuberculosis, cholera, dysentery, meningitis, and typhoid fever. The affordability problem also extends beyond a lack of access to new drugs designed to treat devastating, infectious diseases: 50% of people in developing nations do not have access to even basic medications, such as antibiotics, analgesics, broncho-dilators, decongestants, anti-inflammatory agents, anti-coagulants, or diuretics.[29]

The fact that those who are already worse-off in virtue of their poverty thus have their misfortunes compounded – as they are more likely to fall victim to disease – will strike most of us as an injustice in itself.[30] It seems especially unjust when the ailments that cause the already unfortunate to suffer and die are – sometimes easily and inexpensively – treatable or preventable with existing medications (that have often been developed at least

[26] World Health Organization, *op. cit.* note 12.

[27] N.L. Stepan. 2001. *Picturing Tropical Nature.* Ithaca, NY. Cornell University Press; L. Garrett. 1994. *The Coming Plague: Newly Emerging Diseases in a World Out of Balance.* New York. Penguin.

[28] Gilbert, *op. cit.* note 13.

[29] D.B. Resnik. Developing Drugs for the Developing World: An Economic, Legal, Moral, and Political Dilemma. *Developing World Bioethics* 2001; 1: 11.

[30] Others, to the contrary, might claim that this situation is 'unfortunate' but not necessarily 'unfair' or 'unjust'.

partly through public funding). Egalitarians and utilitarians should agree on this point.

Poverty and (consequent) illness in many cases can also be attributed to what should be considered injustices even by staunch libertarians. As (one of) the wealthiest African nation(s), for example, South Africa should have been better able than its sub-Saharan neighbors to stave off AIDS. It has, however, famously failed to do so. This country has more HIV positive persons than any other country in the world; and, its (increasing) prevalence rate is estimated (from antenatal clinic data) to be almost 25% of adults.

> About 5 [million] South Africans are living with HIV and, at the current rate of infection, about half the country's teenagers under 15 can expect to contract it. By 2005 South Africa is likely to have about 1 [million] orphans.[31]

A recent Medical Research Council (MRC) report estimates that AIDS, which is already the leading cause of death in the country, will kill between four and seven million South Africans within a decade.[32]

This situation is not merely *unfortunate*. We here suffer social and political *injustice*. The facts that the current South African government (for mysterious reasons) consistently[33] but (apparently) illegitimately (1) challenged the causal link between HIV and AIDS (and perhaps even the very existence of HIV and AIDS), (2) challenged the safety and efficacy of antiretroviral therapy, (3) suppressed scientific research which cast doubt on its HIV/AIDS stance,[34] (4) failed to provide inexpensive (or, in some cases, free) antiretroviral treatment to reduce the risk of mother-to-child transmission of HIV, (5) refused to comply with court orders requiring it to do so, (6) forbid provision of prophylactic antiretroviral therapy to rape victims (some of which were *gang-raped babies*, less than a year old),[35] and (7) over-spent

[31] Fighting Back. *The Economist* May 11–17, 2002, 27.

[32] R. Dorrington, D. Bourne, D. Bradshaw, R. Laubscher & I.M. Timaeus. The Impact of HIV/AIDS on Adult Mortality in South Africa. Burden of Disease Research Unit, Medical Research Council of South Africa, available at: http://www.mrc.ac.za/bod/index.htm.

[33] At the time of this writing the South African Government appears to finally be changing its stance on HIV/AIDS.

[34] This seemed to occur with regard to the above-mentioned MRC Report, for example.

[35] Note that points (4)–(6), at least, appear to conflict with the South African constitution by failing to respect what are recognized as human rights here. The same thing may be said about the failure to provide antiretrovirals to HIV-positive South Africans more generally speaking.

on the military (in an apparently scandalous fashion) while under-spending on health care are only a part of what I have in mind.

The current state of AIDS in South Africa – and the government's failure to effectively deal with the situation – should also be attributed to wrongs with longer histories. The etiology of the AIDS epidemic is extremely complex; its present state is the result of a wide variety of social, political, economic, and historical factors. The new South African government's failure to ameliorate the situation is at least partly forgivable – or, in any case, explainable – by virtue of the fact that it had so many other enormous tasks to accomplish in the aftermath of apartheid. In addition to overhauling the political apparatus of the country, provision of decent education, housing, sanitation, and water to those who were victims of systematic racial oppression for decades – i.e. the vast majority of the population – posed monumental challenges for the new South African government. The shambles in which apartheid left this country is thus at least partly to blame for the health care *status quo*.[36] The fact that urbanization, overcrowded living conditions, migrant working conditions, poor education, fatalistic behavior, prostitution, and other ravishes of poverty (including poor nutrition, widespread infection with worms, and lack of treatment for other STDS[37]) each contribute to the AIDS epidemic – and are each (at least partly) the result of exploitative racist colonial oppressive practices – corroborates the point that the South African AIDS epidemic should largely be blamed on social injustice.

Similar things can be said about other developing nations where health care is compromised because of impoverishment resulting from colonialization, oppression, exploitation, protectionist trade policies, domestic corruption, failure of democracy, and so on. According to Solomon R. Benatar, for example, the poverty and consequent poor health of many in the developing world should be attributed to (militarization and) exploitative global economic activities involving irresponsible business practices of multi-national corporations in particular. The result is a

[36] See D. Webb. 1997. *HIV and AIDS in Africa.* London. Pluto Press; A. Whiteside & C. Sunter. 2000. *AIDS: The Challenge for South* Africa. Cape Town. Human & Rousseau; & H. Marais. 2000. *To the Edge: AIDS Review 2000.* Pretoria, South Africa. University of Pretoria, Centre for the Study of AIDS.

[37] Increased risk of HIV infection results, for example, in the presence of other untreated STDs or when immune systems are weakened from poor nutrition or infection with worms.

widening of the gap – in terms of both wealth and human rights protection – between the haves and have-nots.[38]

Pulitzer Prize-winning journalist Laurie Garrett provides an extreme example of the link between disease and injustice. In her recent book *Betrayal of Trust: The Collapse of Global Public Health*, she blames the famous 1995 Ebola (hemorrhagic fever) epidemic in Zaire (now the Democratic Republic of the Congo) on the corruption of the leader Mobutu who stole billions of dollars from public coffers, leaving public hospitals (which were primary *sources* of infection) in complete disarray and lacking the most basic supplies.

> Two things are clear: Ebola spread in Kikwit because the most basic, essential elements of public health were nonexistent. And those exigencies were lacking in Kikwit – indeed, throughout Zaire – because Mobutu Sese Seko and his cronies had for three decades looted the national treasuries. Ebola haunted Zaire because of corruption and political repression . . . [Ebola's] emergence into human populations required the special assistance of humanity's greatest vices: greed, corruption, arrogance, tyranny, and callousness. What unfolded in Zaire in 1995 was not so much the rain forest terror widely depicted then in popular media worldwide as an inevitable outcome of disgraceful disconcern – even disdain – for the health of the Zairois public.[39]

Garrett implicates American meddling in the affair, insofar as the U.S. government backed Mobutu and propped him into power. She insinuates CIA involvement with the murder of his predecessor Patrice Lumumba, unfavored because of supposedly socialist sympathies. In her earlier book *The Coming Plague: Newly Emerging Diseases in a World Out of Balance*, Garrett suggests that the AIDS epidemic in Africa was at least partly fueled by the fact that underequipped hospitals in places like Congo sometimes had no choice but to use the same unsterilized syringes over and over and over again.

III. WHY THE NEGLECT?

Based on what I have said so far, one would expect that infectious disease would already be a typical topic of dedicated discussion in a discipline called 'medical ethics.' One would expect that

[38] S.R. Benatar. Global Disparities in Health and Human Rights: A Critical Commentary. *American Journal of Public Health* 1998; 88: 295–300.

[39] Garrett, *op. cit.* note 15, p. 59.

there would be books on ethics and infectious disease and that articles and sections specifically devoted to ethical aspects of infectious diseases would be regular fare in bioethics journals and anthologies. In reality, however, 'infectious disease' is hardly found even in indexes of standard bioethics texts; and I have never seen a book on this general topic. An October 2002 *Google* (internet) search of the phrase 'ethics and infectious disease' yielded only 11 entries.[40] Six of these referred to a single project (of Margaret Battin), and some of the others were false positives. In March 2005 a similar search yielded 35 entries[41] – while a search of 'ethics and genetics' led to 5,100 entries.

1. High tech medicine

Why, then, has the topic been neglected by bioethics? It is likely that part of the explanation relates to the origins of the discipline of medical ethics itself. Although the roots of bioethics extend twenty-five hundred years back to the world of Hippocrates, bioethics' birth as an autonomous discipline is a relatively recent phenomenon. Medical ethics really came into its own during the last four or five decades, largely as a result of advancements in biological science and technology. With revolutionary developments in medical technology came unprecedented moral and policy dilemmas, and hence an academic discipline was born.[42] If

[40] Search conducted on October 30, 2002 at www.google.com.

[41] Many of these referred to a more recent work of Ronald Bayer. There have of course been books and anthology sections on ethical issues associated with AIDS in particular. And Internet searches of 'Ethics and AIDS', as was pointed out by Peter Singer in discussion, will yield more results – i.e. 408 results on 1 March 2005. The fact remains, however, that discussion of infectious diseases in general (which would likely inform discussion of particular diseases such as AIDS) is lacking. In my opinion even AIDS – with the exception of doctor-patient relationship issues (especially the 'duty to treat') and AIDS-related international research ethics (especially the debate over 'standards of care') – has not received adequate attention in mainstream bioethics literature, given the magnitude of the problem. On 1 March 2005, in any case, a Google search of 'ethics and tuberculosis' yielded only 42 results (though tuberculosis kills two or three million persons per year) and 'ethics and malaria' yielded zero (though malaria kills one million per year). On the same date, 'ethics and stem cells' yielded 440 results – despite the newness of stem cell research (in comparison with AIDS).

[42] The development of elaborate life-sustaining technologies made the question of euthanasia, for example, more urgent. I should note that – in addition to technological advance – the birth of bioethics was also importantly related to the civil rights movement of the 1960s. See H. Kuhse and P. Singer. 1998. What is Bioethics? A Historical Introduction, in *A Companion to Bioethics*, P. Singer and H. Kuhse eds. Oxford, UK. Blackwell: 3–11.

this rough sketch of the birth of bioethics captures much truth, then there should be less surprise that there has been a high-tech, wealthy-world slant to discussion within the discipline.

2. Optimism in medicine

A second probable reason why infectious disease has not received more attention of medical ethicists similarly relates to the timing of the birth of the discipline. The rise of bioethics coincided with a period of tremendous optimism in medicine. The development of antibiotics in the 1940's and the hugely successful Salk Polio vaccination program in the 1950's, and other developments such as the discovery of DDT, led the medical community to believe that infectious disease would soon be defeated through medical progress.[43] As early as

> 1948 U.S. Secretary of State George C. Marshall declared at the Washington, D.C., gathering of the Fourth International Congress on Tropical Medicine and Malaria that the conquest of all infectious diseases was imminent. Through a combination of enhanced crop yields to provide adequate food for humanity and scientific breakthroughs in microbe control, Marshall predicted, all the earth's microscopic scourges would be eliminated.[44]

In 1955 the World Health Organization decided to 'eliminate all malaria on the planet' via the eradication of mosquitoes with DDT. 'Few doubted that such a lofty goal was possible: nobody at the time could imagine a trend of worsening disease conditions; the arrow of history always pointed towards progress.'[45] 'By 1965, more than 25,000 different antibiotic products had been developed; physicians and scientists felt that bacterial diseases, and the microbes responsible, were no longer of great concern or of research interest.'[46] In 1967 U.S. Surgeon General William H. Stewart was so convinced of success that he told a White House gathering of health officers 'that it was time to close the book on

[43] See Garrett, *op. cit.* note 27, pp. 30–52, esp. pp. 30–31.

[44] Ibid., pp. 30–31.

[45] Ibid., p. 31. Not only did it fail, but this program was somewhat counterproductive. DDT-resistant mosquitoes returned in higher numbers than before; and misuse of medication promoted drug-resistant strains of malaria. By '1975 the worldwide incidence of malaria was about 2.5 times what it had been in 1961 . . . A new global iatrogenic form of malaria was emerging – "iatrogenic" meaning created as a result of medical treatment. In its well-meaning zeal to treat the world's malaria scourge, humanity had created a new epidemic' (p. 52).

[46] Ibid., p. 36.

infectious diseases and shift all national attention (and dollars) to what he termed "the New Dimensions" of health: chronic diseases.'[47] 'In 1972, the Nobel laureate Macfarlane Burnet concluded that "the most likely forecast about the future of infectious disease is that it will be very dull." '[48] Fields such as bacteriology and parasitology appeared less important and subsequently fell out of vogue in the medical scientific community. The rise of medical ethics thus occurred at a time when it was popular – though perhaps hubristic – to think that infectious disease would no longer be a central concern of medicine. This presumably explains at least part of the neglect on the part of those concerned with medical ethics.

3. 'The other'

AIDS, of course, has been on the scene for more than twenty years already – and thus overlaps with roughly half the lifespan of bioethics proper. And it has been clear for quite some time that malaria, TB, and other infectious diseases would not just disappear as planned. To the contrary, plenty of pathogens have developed more dangerous drug-resistant strains. And many morbid microbes – such as SARS and Ebola – have newly emerged during the last few decades.

A third reason why infectious diseases receive sparse discussion by academic ethicists is that they have likely been relegated as problems of 'the other.'[49] AIDS, for example, for a long time was, and perhaps still is, considered a problem for homosexuals, IV drug users, and poor black people in Africa. AIDS and other infectious diseases are, as has already been said, by far more prevalent in the developing world. Given that the vast majority of professional medical ethicists are straight, non-drug-injecting, relatively well-to-do whites who reside and work in wealthy developed nations, it should not be entirely unexpected that they have focused most on matters of more obvious central domestic concern, rather than problems of 'strangers' on the fringe of society and foreigners in faraway places. This third explanation involves both psychological and practical elements. Regarding the latter, (relatively conservative) university employers (and research funders) likely expect academic ethicists to focus most on

[47] Ibid., p. 33.
[48] Gewen, *op. cit.* note 8.
[49] See H. Joffe. 1999. *Risk and the Other*. Cambridge, U.K. Cambridge University Press; & N.L. Stepan, *op. cit.* note. 27, for discussions of how AIDS and tropical diseases, respectively, are regularly understood and portrayed as problems of others.

pressing local issues rather than (radically) concentrating on international justice.[50] This has *explanatory* power, but I doubt it makes the failure of medical ethicists to further discuss one of world's most consequential topics *excusable*. Ethics and morality essentially involve elements of impartiality; and, *tenured* professors, in any case, have substantial freedom to choose their topics.

4. Complexity

A fourth explanation of neglect by bioethicists relates to the complexity of the issues in question.[51] Traditional topics in medical ethics already require difficult interdisciplinary study. Expertise in both ethics and science are required to do bioethics well. Though many scholars have expertise in the discipline of ethics and many scholars expertise in scientific and technological aspects of biology and medicine, it is rare to find both kinds of expertise embodied in single individuals. One result is the relatively weak reputation of medical ethics within philosophical circles. Philosophers commonly complain about a 'low level' of discussion in medical ethics. This is attributed to the fact that (1) contributors with philosophical mastery in ethics often fail to get the science right and are thus unrealistic while (2) contributors with scientific backgrounds too often lack sufficient training in rigorous philosophical argumentation to get the ethics right, and (3) too few contributors are skilled enough in both areas to generate a consistently high level of discussion.

I have been discussing the challenging nature of the interdisciplinarity of medical ethics scholarship because I believe this difficulty is greatly exacerbated with discussion of infectious disease and the health care situation in the developing world. In addition to grounding in ethics and science/medicine (the latter of which is itself complicated by entry into the realm of epidemiology and drug-resistant pathogen emergence), we here need a greater grip on complex social, political, historic, and economic dynamics in order to *explain* – and thus comment upon the justice of – the current global healthcare situation.[52] A similarly

[50] Udo Schuklenk suggested this point in conversation.

[51] This was (independently) suggested by Mary Tjiattas. Peter Singer concurred in conversation.

[52] I do not mean to imply that other issues in bioethics do not require appreciation of social, political, historical, and economic phenomena. My point is one of degree: assessment of the health care situation in the developing world *often* requires substantially *more* contact with these other disciplines. Others who have worked in this area will agree.

broadened understanding is needed to realistically assess – and base moral/policy prescriptions upon – *predictions of impact*. Exploring the issues I have in mind requires more *empirical* work than most (medical) ethicists are likely to be trained for or accustomed to.[53] With regard to distribution of resource questions, confrontation with issues of international (rather than merely domestic) justice is an additional obvious way in which *theoretical* discussion is complicated.[54] The fact that infectious diseases do not respect international borders is just one of the ways in which the topic is inherently international. My fourth explanation, thus, is that questions concerning infectious disease and the healthcare situation in the developing world have been neglected by biomedical ethicists at least partly because of the *difficulty* of working on them.

5. Apparent ease

My fifth explanation, ironically, is that this area has been ignored because of a *misperception* that the questions raised are all-too-easy. The injustice of the situation, which has received substantial *media* attention at least, whereby AIDS medications are unavailable because they are unaffordable – at least partly because of prices set by profit-driven pharmaceutical companies – to populations in sub-Saharan Africa where they are by far needed most will strike many as a clear and blatant injustice. 'Of course this is wrong. Of course more should be done to make medication available to AIDS victims in Africa,' many might say, 'and you don't need to be a philosopher – or priest – to figure that out.' Questions about the justice of the health care situation in the developing world, where the innocent poor are sick and suffering, at first glance anyway, *appear* to lack the deep philosophical significance of questions upon which medical ethicists usually focus their attention.[55] Topics such as euthanasia and abortion, for example, raise what might look like deeper and more intellectually challenging issues: When is it morally permissible to kill another human being? What is a person? Upon what is the moral status of human beings based? What does quality of life consist in? Notice that emerging bioethical debates surrounding genetics and embryo/stem cell

[53] For further illustration of what I here have in mind see M.J. Selgelid. Ethics, Economics, and AIDS in Africa. *Developing World Bioethics* 2004; 4, 1: 96–105.

[54] See D. Moellendorf. 2002. *Cosmopolitan Justice*. Boulder, Colorado. Westview Press.

[55] This objection was (independently) raised by Julian Savulescu in discussion.

research often revolve around these same sorts of questions. In comparison with these more theoretical (or perhaps *metaphysical*) questions, the injustice of a situation where tens of millions of (relatively innocent) people will soon suffer and die because they are too poor to buy medications might look like a no-brainer.

6. Religious hijacking

My final explanation of why infectious disease has not received more attention from bioethicists refers to the fact that bioethicists have been kept so occupied by discussion of *religious objections* to things like abortion, euthanasia, cloning, stem cell research, and so on. Contrary to Paul Farmer,[56] my own belief is that most bioethicists *are* (at heart, anyway) genuinely concerned about issues of justice. Liberal-minded bioethicists presumably would have focused much more attention on the topic of infectious disease and the injustice of the health care situation in the developing world if they hadn't been kept so busy battling the illiberal policy agenda (regarding abortion, euthanasia, cloning, stem cell research, etc.) advocated by the church.[57] Debate in bioethics has thus, to a large extent, been hijacked by religion.

CONCLUSION

I have offered six explanations of why ethical issues associated with infectious disease (and the related health care situation in the developing world) have not been more prominent in medical ethics literature. I have suggested that this is the case roughly because (1) bioethics was born (as an autonomous discipline) with advances in medical technology and thus has largely focused on these, (2) bioethics' birth and initial development (as an autonomous discipline) came at a time when it was believed that infectious disease would be conquered by medicine, (3) infectious diseases are often seen as problems of others, (4) bioethical research on infectious disease in the developing world is especially difficult because so empirical and interdisciplinary, (5) ethical questions about infectious disease (in the developing world) might not *appear* to pose the kinds of deep philosophical questions that academic ethicists are interested in, and (6) bioethics debate has been hijacked by the church. These are just

[56] In discussion.

[57] James William Ley, philosophy Ph.D. student at the University of Sydney, encouraged explicit inclusion of this point.

suggestions; and this list is not meant to be exhaustive. Rather than choosing between these alternative explanations, I believe that they each likely capture *parts* of the story we are after. In any case, as argued above, it would be entirely wrong to explain the lack of discussion of infectious diseases by denying their central importance and/or relevance to the discipline of bioethics.

Michael J. Selgelid, Ph.D.
Sesqui Lecturer in Bioethics
Centre for Values, Ethics and the Law in Medicine; and
Unit for History and Philosophy of Science
University of Sydney
selgelid@med.usyd.edu.au

Part III
The Historical Debate

[11]

The Importance of Social Intervention in Britain's Mortality Decline *c*.1850–1914: a Re-interpretation of the Role of Public Health.[1]

By SIMON SZRETER*

SUMMARY. It continues to be generally accepted that the iconoclastic research work of Professor Thomas McKeown and associates conclusively demonstrated that the medical establishment—including all the efforts of the public health movement—played only a minor role in the grand historical and demographic drama of the period, the secular decline in national mortality levels. According to McKeown's apparently authoritative analysis and interpretation of the available epidemiological statistics, the mortality decline in England and Wales can be primarily accounted for by the benevolent 'invisible hand' of gradually rising living standards, particularly in the form of increases in per capita nutritional consumption. The coherence of this view is brought into question by a critical re-examination of the supporting evidence and arguments presented by McKeown *et al*. It is anticipated that for many of those not closely acquainted with the 'McKeown thesis', the fragility of the case may come as something of a surprise. An alternative interpretation of the same epidemiological evidence then forms the basis for a revisionist account which directs attention to the leading role played by the public health movement and its locally administered preventive health measures in combating the urban congestion created by industrialization.

KEYWORDS: Britain, living standards, local government, mortality decline, nutrition, public health, social intervention.

I. *Introduction*

Dr John Tatham of the General Register Office, looking back in 1905 over more than half a century's achievements by the public health movement since the passing of the first Public Health Act of 1848, found it necessary deprecatingly to remind his readers that 'it will be well to utter a caution at this stage against the prevalent tendency to attribute to the results of sanitary administration alone the whole of the life-saving which has taken place . . .'.[2] As most undergraduates today in medicine or modern history will know, it is now widely considered that this confidently expressed belief, that directed

[1] This is a revised and expanded version of Discussion Paper No. 121, in the series issued by the Centre for Economic Policy Research (CEPR). I am grateful to the editors and the anonymous referees of this journal for their helpful suggestions, and also to Sir George Godber for much valuable comment and stimulation. The terms 'Britain' and 'British' are frequently employed instead of the tiresome use of 'England and Wales', with apologies to the Scots since most of the evidence discussed relates only to the area south of the Tweed.

[2] *Supplement to 65th Annual Report of the Registrar-General* (PP, 1905, XVIII), p. xii. John Francis Walkingame Tatham (1844–1924), FRCP, a former Medical Officer of Health for Salford (1873–88) and Manchester (1888–93), was William Farr's second successor, after William Ogle (1827–1912), at the General Register Officer (GRO), holding the key post of Superintendent of Statistics 1893–1908.

* *Gonville and Caius College, Cambridge CB2 1TA.*

human agency informed by medical and sanitary science was the principal source of improvement in the nation's health, has been apparently conclusively deflated and debunked by the historical epidemiological research project of Professor Thomas McKeown and associates.

The strong currency which McKeown's new orthodoxy continues to enjoy was illustrated recently by a leading article in the *British Medical Journal* which concluded that improving nutrition—the essence of the 'McKeown thesis'—is still the best explanation we have for the historical fall in mortality in Britain.[3] The main purpose of this article will be to argue that McKeown's analysis of the empirical data has been misleading and to show that closer attention to the crucial elements of his own quantitative evidence in fact confirms the essential spirit of Tatham's contemporary assessment. It will be urged that the public health movement working through local government, rather than nutritional improvements through rising living standards, should be seen as the true moving force behind the decline of mortality in this period.

Professor Thomas McKeown's *The Modern Rise of Population* was published in 1976 as an accessible summary of over two decades of painstaking empirical work, applying the insights of current medical and epidemiological knowledge to a historical analysis of Britain's detailed national series of death records.[4] This work achieved something of a conceptual revolution in the disciplines of history and medicine, overturning a long-standing general orthodoxy regarding the importance of medical science and the medical profession in bringing about the decline in mortality which accompanied industrialization in Britain.[5] It effectively demonstrated that those advances in the science of medicine which form the basis of today's conventional clinical and hospital teaching and practice, in particular the immuno- and chemo-therapies, played only a very minor role in accounting for the historic decline in mortality levels. McKeown simply and conclusively showed that many of the most important diseases involved had already all but disappeared in England and Wales before the earliest date at which the relevant scientific medical innovations occurred.

It should be stressed at the outset that this achievement of McKeown's work,

[3] S. C. Farrow, 'McKeown Reassessed', *BMJ* 294, (1987), 1631–2. It was somewhat surprising to see repeated in Farrow's review certain critical assumptions of the 'McKeown thesis' which have now been rendered obsolete by the important findings of historical demographic work: E. A. Wrigley and R. S. Schofield, *The Population History of England 1541–1871, A Reconstruction* (London, 1981). In particular, the statement early on in the review that 'The rise [in population] is generally agreed to have been caused by a fall in mortality rather than an increase in birth rates' is precisely the opposite of our new understanding of these matters since 1981.

[4] The major earlier reports of this research were: T. McKeown and R. G. Brown, 'Medical Evidence Related to English Population Changes in the Eighteenth Century', *Pop. Studies*, ix (1955), 119–41; T. McKeown and R. G. Record, 'Reasons for the Decline of Mortality in England and Wales during the Nineteenth Century'; ibid., xvi (1962), 94–122; T. McKeown, R. G. Record, and R. D. Turner, 'An Interpretation of the Decline of Mortality in England and Wales during the Twentieth Century', ibid., xxix (1975), 391–422.

[5] This previous orthodoxy derived principally from historical documentation in two works, both published in 1926: G. T. Griffith, *Population Problems of the Age of Malthus* (Cambridge, 1926); M. C. Buer, *Health, Wealth and Population in the Early Days of the Industrial Revolution* (London, 1926).

in deflating the historical claims of one particular section of the medical profession and its 'high tech' invasive and biochemical medicine, remains unaffected by the arguments set out below. McKeown's unanswerable point is precisely that this modern kind of applied medical science virtually did not exist during the period addressed here. However, in addition to this *negative* finding that the forward march of modern 'scientific medicine' cannot be given the credit for the historical fall in mortality, McKeown also propounded a *positive* explanatory thesis. He claimed that his analysis of the epidemiological evidence showed that the major factor responsible was 'a rising standard of living, of which the most significant feature was improved diet'.[6] It is this distinct positive thesis, regarding the overwhelming importance of nutritional improvements derived from a rising standard of living in driving mortality decline, which is the subject of criticism in what follows.

As a result of this strong nutritional thesis, combined with the impact of McKeown's devastating case against the pretensions of the 'technocratic' section of the post-war medical profession, the notion seems to have spread like a contagion that all medicine, the medical profession and, in fact, organized human agency in general had remarkably little to do with the historical decline of mortality in Britain until the inter-war period at the earliest. Although 'municipal sanitation' and 'hygiene improvements'—in other words, the public health movement addressed by this article—were identified by McKeown as positive influences, their impact and effects were deemed to be very much of a secondary and merely reinforcing kind. McKeown believed that his empirical work on the nineteenth-century evidence had conclusively established this in two ways. First, that part of the mortality decline supposedly attributable exclusively to increased nutrition was claimed to have occurred earliest, whereas public health measures came along relatively late in the day, when the momentum of declining mortality was already established. Secondly, that on etiological grounds, according to the available epidemiological records tracking changes in the incidence of different causes of death, sanitary measures could only have had at the maximum the potential to eliminate roughly a quarter of all deaths, whereas rising nutritional standards had probably been responsible for about twice that proportion.[7] Thus, nutritional improvements were unequivocally presented as the prime moving and primary sustaining forces in accounting for the Victorian mortality decline. However, it is shown below that neither of these arguments can be sustained on a careful re-examination of the historical evidence.

Britain's history in this respect has been seen as something of an exception by development economists and demographers, since the wider, cross-national comparative work of Samuel Preston has demonstrated that for almost all other countries it has been upward shifts in the level of medical technology and services available and the successful introduction of public health measures

[6] McKeown and Record, 'Reasons for the Decline', p. 120.

[7] McKeown, *The Modern Rise of Population* (London, 1976), chap. 9 'Conclusions'. See McKeown and Record, 'Reasons for the Decline', pp. 118–22 for the original statements.

which have been markedly more significant than rising per capita incomes (a gross proxy for rises in the general standard of living) in accounting for their falling levels of mortality.[8] But social and economic historians have never found it conceptually difficult to treat the experience of the first industrial nation as a special case. In this respect, the supposedly predominant importance of the airborne disease, respiratory tuberculosis (TB, 'consumption', and phthisis are its common synonyms), has always been emphasized by McKeown as the key to Britain's unique mortality decline.

Thus, although the most recent collection of essays to be published on the British mortality decline contained a welcome examination of several public health aspects, its editors still found it necessary to concede that Britain in particular 'differs from the norm because of the high incidence of respiratory tuberculosis', and that rising living standards may therefore have been important here 'without the relationship being both a necessary and a universal one'.[9] McKeown's authority is generally endorsed, even by those engaged in research on various aspects of public health in Britain. It is agreed that, 'In terms . . . of aggregate and cause-specific mortality and the environmental determinants of the reduction in deaths from infectious diseases during the nineteenth century, the work of Thomas McKeown is central'.[10] It is broadly assumed, after McKeown, that, whatever their research might indicate regarding occasional local or episodal advances, the public health movement *in the aggregate* was not particularly instrumentally effective in achieving its aims, whatever the fond delusions of those who devoted their lives to this work, such as John Tatham.

But is the British case, indeed, the exception? How strong is either the evidence that respiratory TB was the dominant component leading national mortality trends, or the argument that this component was driven primarily by changing nutritional inputs? Are there alternative interpretations consistent with the data analysed and presented by McKeown? What might the existence

[8] See, in particular, S. H. Preston, 'The Changing Relation between Mortality and Level of Economic Development', *Pop. Studies*, xxix (1975), 231–48; S. H. Preston, *Mortality Patterns in National Populations* (New York, 1976). Another early report of this comparative work was: S. H. Preston and V. E. Nelson, 'Structure and Change in Causes of Death: an International Summary', *Pop. Studies*, xxviii (1974), 19–51; S. H. Preston and E. van de Walle, 'Urban French Mortality in the Nineteenth Century', ibid., xxxii (1978), 275–97 was also an important pioneering comparative local study illustrating the impact of differing public health measures on mortality rates in three French cities.

[9] R. I. Woods and J. Woodward (eds.), *Urban Disease and Mortality in Nineteenth Century England* (London, 1984), p. 32. See also, for instance, the useful introductory essay to the subject by J. M. Winter, 'The Decline of Mortality in Britain 1870–1950' in T. Barker and M. Drake (eds.), *Population and Society in Britain 1850–1980* (London, 1982), pp. 101–20. This provides a particularly judicious introduction to the field, observing many flaws in the 'McKeown thesis' and yet still coming down firmly in favour of living standards and nutrition as the driving-force behind mortality decline. But note that in Woods's most recent work there has been a decided shift away from any sympathy with the 'McKeown thesis'. See below, n. 75, and also R. Woods and R. Hinde, 'Mortality in Victorian England: Models and Patterns', *Jnl. Interdisc. History*, xviii (1987), 27–54.

[10] B. Luckin, *Pollution and Control. A Social History of the Thames in the Nineteenth Century* (Bristol, 1986), p. 2.

of such an alternative imply for our social and medical history of modern Britain? These are the questions which it is intended to address here.

This paper has, therefore, three sequential aims. First, to identify and delineate the essential argument and evidence presented by McKeown in favour of nutrition. Secondly, to subject this to critical scrutiny. Thirdly, to offer the outline of an alternative revisionist interpretation of the onset of Britain's modern mortality decline. This will suggest that human agency, in the form of a gradually negotiated expansion of preventive public health provisions and services at the local level, rather than the impersonal 'invisible hand' of inexorably rising nutritional and living standards, should be reinstated at the centre of our attempts to explain the modern mortality decline in Britain. There is, therefore, much more scope in this field of modern British history than has perhaps been previously appreciated for fruitful exchange between, on the one hand, social historians of medicine, public health, and local government and, on the other hand, demographic and economic historians of large-scale social change.

II. *The 'McKeown Thesis'*

In its fully developed form, McKeown originally presented a grandiose all-encompassing thesis accounting for Britain's demographic growth since the early eighteenth century and the subsequent rise in world population as a whole. It was decreases in mortality, rather than any significant increase in fertility which was claimed to have been mainly responsible and this, in turn, was primarily due to an increasing per capita nutritional intake.[11] However, this ambitious general explanation was based on a number of purely speculative premises regarding the characteristics of the pre-industrial demographic regime. These have since been radically undermined as a result of the revolutionary empirical findings that have emerged from the recent work of demographic historians, utilizing the quantitative information contained in Britain's parish registers, dating back to the mid-sixteenth century.[12]

It has, for instance, been shown first that the rapid population growth associated with initial industrialization in Britain was principally due to rising fertility (mainly as a result of earlier marriage), rather than to falling mortality.[13]

[11] McKeown tends to refer rather imprecisely to expansions in the 'food supply'. However, it is clearly acknowledged in at least one place in the 1976 text that the essential meaning intended is that of increases in per capita nutritional consumption: 'Whether the population was *better* fed in the eighteenth and nineteenth centuries is . . . central . . . in this context . . . whether nutrition improved during the period' (emphasis added), *Modern Rise*, p. 130.

[12] The work of the ESRC Cambridge Group for the History of Population and Social Structure, systematically exploiting a 4% sample of the 10,000 parochial registers of baptisms, burials, and marriages in England and Wales, has put our understanding of the changing demography and economy of British society in the period before the first census, 1541–1801, at an entirely new level of sophistication. The major publication to date has been: Wrigley and Schofield, *Population History*.

[13] Ibid., chaps. 7 and 10; see also J. A. Goldstone, 'The Demographic Revolution in England: a Re-examination', *Pop. Studies*, xl (1986), 5–34, for an important further refinement of this interpretation.

Secondly, although there was indeed a fall in mortality in the course of the eighteenth century, it was of a scale quite within the bounds of previous pre-industrial fluctuations in the sixteenth and seventeenth centuries. The relatively low level of mortality attained by the 1820s after a century of improvement was the same as that previously experienced in the late sixteenth century. Thereafter, overall mortality ceased to fall for almost half a century throughout the central decades of the mid-nineteenth century.[14] Thus, the notion which underpinned McKeown's grand thesis, that there had been a single movement of continuous and uninterrupted mortality decline across the last three centuries, can no longer be considered valid. Nevertheless, despite the obsolescence of this grand version of the McKeown thesis, the substantial empirical work of analysis which he and his team performed on the national death registration data for the subsequent period from 1837 onwards seems to have ensured that McKeown's nutritional thesis has continued to enjoy an authoritative status at least with respect to that part of the improvement in the nation's health which is known to have occurred during the Victorian and Edwardian periods. Attention is, therefore, confined here to a detailed reassessment of this remaining aspect of the 'McKeown thesis': his interpretation of the civil registration data.

The analysis of death-rates in nineteenth- and twentieth-century Britain which was presented by McKeown *et al.* is based on a uniquely detailed historical source material. These are the returns of deaths classified by age and certified cause of death which are available for the entire population of Britain, excluding Scotland, from July 1837 onwards.[15] Details about the numbers dying from each disease by age and sex was combined with comparable information regarding the total population alive at each of the national censuses taken every ten years to produce a series of age-specific, cause-specific death-rates, published decennially by the Registrar-General in a special supplement.[16]

The summary results of McKeown's analysis of this data were presented in a series of tables in chapter 3 of *Modern Rise*. The accompanying table, (page 8), is directly derived from this information, based on age-standardized death-rates for the most important individual diseases which can be identified. It shows how much the changing incidence of each disease has contributed to the overall fall in recorded mortality that has occurred between approximately 1851 and 1971, dividing up that overall amount of change into the percentage which occurred before and after 1901.

[14] Wrigley and Schofield, *Population History*, chaps. 7 and 10.

[15] The GRO was established by parliamentary statute in 1836 for the express purpose of administering a nationwide compulsory system of vital registration in England and Wales. Acts for Scotland and for Ireland followed in 1854 and 1863, respectively. For further details on the system's development, see in particular D. V. Glass, *Numbering the People* (Farnborough, 1973).

[16] McKeown's summary analysis commences with the years 1848–54 because of certifying and recording inadequacies in the early years. Of course nosological practices have changed dramatically over the last 150 years. A good example of this is typhus, a disease spread by the body louse, and typhoid fever, which is due to a water-borne microbe. In this case their similar names reflect the fact that they were at one time indistinguishable to medical science; they were not separated in the R.-G.'s reports until 1869: McKeown, *Modern Rise*, p. 50.

McKeown grouped the individual diseases into four broad etiological categories, according to what modern medical science understands to be the main pathways of transmission involved in the spread of each particular disease. Three of McKeown's four categories relate to diseases which are due to the invasion of the human host by a micro-organism, meaning usually bacteria or a virus. First, there is the airborne category of diseases, where the microbes in question can simply float about in suspension in the air usually associated with tiny droplets of water vapour or saliva spray from the exhalations of infected victims or carriers. Secondly, there are the diseases caused by water- and food-borne microbes. Thirdly, there is a small residual category of other diseases also attributable to micro-organisms, where the vector of transmission is neither air- nor food- nor water-borne. These include strictly contagious diseases, that is, those passed by direct contact between animals and humans (e.g. plague, typhus) or just between humans (e.g. sexually transmitted diseases). Finally, there is the category of afflictions which are not microbiotically caused, such as congenital defects and the degenerative diseases which are associated with the normal processes of ageing (subject, of course, to modification by lifestyle, diet, and overall environment). These include cancers and coronary heart diseases as the most significant examples. As can be seen from the table below, the first two categories are by far the most important in the earlier stages of the mortality decline with which we are here concerned.

With this simple but very useful classification system established, McKeown went on to argue that any observed fall in the incidence of a disease must be due to one of the following five causes:

(i) an autonomous decline in the virulence of the micro-organism itself;
(ii) an improvement in the overall environment so as to reduce the chances of initial exposure to potentially harmful organisms. This could either be:
  (*a*) as a result of scientific advances in immunization techniques;
  (*b*) through a public health policy designed to sanitize the urban environment—McKeown calls this 'municipal sanitation' or 'hygiene improvements';
(iii) an improvement in the human victims' defensive resources *after* initial exposure to hostile organisms. This could occur either:
  (*a*) through the development of effective scientific methods of treating symptoms;
  (*b*) via an increase in the level and quality of the exposed population's average nutritional intake, that is better and more abundant food, thereby improving the individual's own natural defences.

McKeown's strategy in presenting his argument was to assess each of these five candidate 'causes' of mortality decline in turn, regarding their possible proportionate contributions to the overall observed fall in mortality levels.

First, he dealt with (i) the possibility that there might have been a spontaneous change in the virulence of some of the infective micro-organisms (chapter 4 of *Modern Rise*). In fact the discussion of this issue was far from conclusive for

England and Wales. Standardized Death Rates/million:

Rate/million for all causes: 1848/54: 21,856	1901: 16,958	1971: 5,384
Of total reduction 1848/54–1971:	% occurring 1848/54–1901	% occurring 1901–1971
Airborne micro-organisms:		
Respiratory tuberculosis	9·0	8·5
Scarlet fever; diphtheria*	4·0	2·0
Smallpox	1·5	—
Other	1·0	5·5
Bronchitis, pneumonia, influenza	+3·0	10·0
Water/Food-borne micro-organisms:		
Cholera; diarrhoea	3·5	7·5
Typhoid; typhus**	5·0	1·0
Other	1·0	3·5
Other micro-organisms: (principally 'convulsions' before 1901)	4·5	8·0
Other conditions: (not micro-organisms)	2·5	23·0
Total (all causes)	30·0	70·0

Source: adapted from T. McKeown, *The Modern Rise of Population*, chap. 3. All figures rounded to nearest 0·5 per cent and, therefore, do not sum exactly to 100 per cent.

* These two diseases were not separately distinguished until 1855. All of the reduction before 1901 was due to declining incidence of scarlet fever, as diphtheria did not begin to fall until the turn of the century, when antitoxin treatment began (McKeown, *Modern Rise*, pp. 56 and 98).

** Typhus should be in the 'Other micro-organisms' category, but was not distinguished from typhoid before 1869. However, much the greatest part of the reduction before 1901 is attributable to typhoid alone, occurring from the 1870s onwards. See *45th Annual Report of the Registrar-General, Supplement* (PP, 1884–5, XVII), p. xiii.

the simple reason that in some very important cases there is no current scientific consensus whilst in others the historical evidence is inadequate for a clear assessment to be made.[17] When in 1962 McKeown and Record had originally presented their analysis of the data for 1851–1901, they had cautiously concluded that this aspect 'may have been responsible for not less than one-fifth of the total improvement and—as a very rough estimate—for not more than one-third'.[18] Following this, in his 1976 text McKeown was willing to allow that two of the airborne diseases, scarlet fever and influenza, probably declined

[17] To take an important example, Sir Robert Philip concluded that natural immunity to respiratory tuberculosis can be inherited to some extent across generations. G. Clayson, 'Sir Robert Philip and the Conquest of Tuberculosis', *BMJ*, ii (1957), 1505. See also McKeown, *Modern Rise*, pp. 83–5. However, since we do not know what the prior pattern of incidence was before the mid-nineteenth century, there is no way of assessing the dimensions of this effect on the subsequent patterns: those that we are observing in the R.-G.'s data series from 1848 to 1854 onwards.

[18] McKeown and Record, 'Reasons for the Decline', p. 119.

spontaneously in this manner.[19] However, in his 1976 conclusion the impression was given, by taking a wider sweeping perspective including the eighteenth and twentieth centuries as well, that this factor was relatively insignificant and could be more or less ruled out as a significant component of the mortality decline.[20]

Next, chapter 5 dealt with what was called the medical contribution, by which was meant first, scientific advances in protective immunization and secondly, scientific advances in chemotherapy and hospitalized treatment of sufferers, that is, (ii)(*a*) and (iii)(*a*), respectively. Hospitals were dismissed outright, referring back to an article published in 1955, which had concluded that at least until the hospital reforms in the last third of the nineteenth century prompted by Florence Nightingale's highly critical revelations in her *Notes on Hospitals*, 'on balance the effects of hospital work in this period were probably harmful'.[21] The chapter then proceeded to demonstrate for each of the major diseases in turn that, with the exception of smallpox and diphtheria, the dates at which either effective immunization procedures or scientific medical treatments first became available were often far too late in time to be able to account for all but the last few percentage points of the overall decline of the disease. This was certainly true of respiratory tuberculosis, measles, and scarlet fever; and broadly true for whooping cough and the bronchitis, pneumonia, and influenza group. All had been declining very considerably in incidence long before effective chemotherapy or other scientific techniques had become available.

Having eliminated in this fashion both aspects of advances in medical science, McKeown was now left with just two possible causal factors out of the original five, to account between them for the lion's share of the decline in mortality. In trying to adjudicate between them the grouping of individual diseases into etiological categories now played a crucial role in the apparent demonstration that nutritional improvement was much more significant than sanitary and hygienic measures. The argument presented was as follows.[22] It can only have been the water- and food-borne diseases which could have been controlled by municipal sanitation and similar preventive public health measures in the nineteenth and early twentieth centuries. Airborne diseases by contrast could not be prevented in this way from spreading or from occurring. It was admitted that isolation of individuals with symptoms might have some net effect, but then the efficacy of the hospitals had already been roundly dismissed, whilst it

[19] McKeown, *Modern Rise*, pp. 82–3, 89.

[20] cf. ibid., chap. 9 'Conclusions', points 4 and 6 on p. 153, with references cited in previous two footnotes.

[21] Ibid., p. 150 referring to p. 119 of McKeown and Brown, 'Medical Evidence'. It is to be noted that this harsh judgement is not one that has been entirely endorsed by more recent research. See, for instance, S. Cherry, 'The Hospitals and Population Growth: the Voluntary General Hospitals, Mortality and Local Populations in the English Provinces in the Eighteenth and Nineteenth Centuries', Parts 1 and 2, *Pop. Studies*, xxxiv (1980), 59–75 and 251–66.

[22] The overall strategy in the presentation of the argument in *Modern Rise* is not explicitly set out in the manner summarized here. However, it can be discerned by consulting the following pages: 53, 73–4, 91–2, 110–17, 126–7, 128, 152–4, 159.

was pointed out that many airborne diseases could be carried and spread by persons not even manifesting symptoms. McKeown argued, therefore, that any real decline in the incidence of mortality from the airborne category of diseases could *only* be the result of improvements in the potential victim's resistance to the disease by virtue of an improved nutritional and dietary status, since the chances of initial exposure to the disease could not be affected by public health preventive measures, whilst all other possibilities had now been excluded. Therefore, it followed that if the historical evidence showed a greater decline in the airborne diseases category then this indicated a greater role for nutritional improvement, whilst the larger the fall in the water- and food-borne category of diseases the more significant the role of public health and hygiene measures.

Using this a priori argument, McKeown's data apparently showed that the airborne category of diseases was responsible for about twice the percentage share of the total reduction in death-rates in both periods, before and after 1901. Accordingly, this constituted irrefutable evidence that above all else it has been improvements in nutritional intake brought about by rising living standards, rather than any other factor—including public health measures—which has been the most important cause of the decline in mortality in Britain. And, of course, McKeown felt it legitimate to extrapolate this finding backwards into the eighteenth century, too, on the assumption that the mortality decline was a unitary process across all three centuries.

III. *Critique of McKeown's Interpretation*

First, as has been pointed out by many others, the weight of presumption in favour of improvements in nutrition as the primary causal factor in the registered mortality decline emerged merely by default, as a result of the sceptical devaluation of other factors including medical intervention, rather than because of any convincing positive evidence in its favour. Indeed, whenever such positive evidence has been examined either for the eighteenth or nineteenth centuries, it has failed to provide any convincing support for McKeown's hypothesis.[23] The presumption was in fact achieved by a rhetorical sleight of hand using the logic of the argument by exclusion—the (in)famous analogy with the eliminatory detective method of Sherlock Holmes.[24] Of the five 'suspect' causal factors which McKeown cross-examined, the 'culprit'—nutritional improvement through a rising standard of living—was left to last. As a result, the evidence for or against it was never subjected to the same highly critical appraisal which each of the other four candidate factors received. It therefore benefited accordingly in the estimation of its relative importance,

[23] P. E. Razzell, 'An Interpretation of the Modern Rise of Population in Europe: A Critique', *Pop. Studies*, xxviii (1974), 5–17, D. J. Oddy, 'Working Class Diets in Late Nineteenth Century Britain', *Ec.H.R.*, xxiii (1970), 314–23.

[24] McKeown and Record, 'Reasons for the Decline', p. 94; McKeown, *Modern Rise*, p. 128.

since what the others lost through sceptical downgrading, it inevitably gained by the zero-sum rules of the argument by exclusion.[25]

Secondly, and related to this, the argument by exclusion is only legitimate if *all* the suspects have been correctly identified and are separately examined. But here 'the standard of living' acts very much as a conceptual, residual catch-all, simply subsuming by fiat a variety of other possible factors, which are, therefore, not explicitly addressed in the analysis. Thus, Caldwell has recently complained that McKeown:

> identified potential change in health inputs with medical discoveries and attempted to show that these were of little consequence . . . He implicitly included everything else . . . under material progress. Similarly, he did not consider the expansion of the health infrastructure, although admittedly there was probably little in the way of additional medical technology to import and no political thought of creating a universal free health service.[26]

Although a simplification, Caldwell's main thrust is sound: the form and economistic terminology of McKeown's argument by exclusion has resulted in the suppression of any explicit consideration of the *independent* role of those socio-political developments which were responsible for such hard-won improvements as those in working conditions, housing, education, and various health services. One might at least have expected in a study coming out so strongly in favour of nutrition as the major factor that there would at the very least have been some detailed consideration given to the history of food adulteration and the battle for its regulation and control. But all this is blandly subsumed under the economistic term, 'standard of living'. McKeown's interpretation of the epidemiological evidence has, therefore, been crucially misleading in suggesting that these social, cultural, and political dimensions can quite properly be conceived merely as the automatic corollary of changes in a country's per capita real income. However, as will be demonstrated below, even without altering McKeown's own analytical categories, reappraisal of the same detailed epidemiological evidence in fact leads to quite the opposite conclusions.

In his interpretation of the data, McKeown was particularly impressed with the importance of the overall long-run decline of the single airborne disease, respiratory tuberculosis (TB). In 1848–54 this had been the most lethal single cause of death, accounting for 13·3 per cent of all deaths occurring at that time. Furthermore, McKeown claimed that TB was in fact already in a process of decline at the date when the Registrar-General's (R.-G.) data series began.[27] When taken in combination with the fact that all the other airborne diseases contributed importantly to the overall reduction in mortality, taking the period 1848 to 1971 as a whole, and also with the apparent demonstration that neither

[25] See Woods and Woodward (eds.), *Urban Disease*, chap. 1, for a helpful graphical illustration of this point.

[26] J. C. Caldwell, 'Routes to Low Mortality in Poor Countries', *Population and Development Review*, xii (1986), p. 205.

[27] McKeown, *Modern Rise*, p. 68.

clinical medicine nor municipal sanitation could account for the decline in such airborne diseases, these observations led McKeown to stress strongly the part played by nutritional improvement in the overall modern mortality decline, as we have seen. However, if attention is concentrated more closely on the nineteenth century, McKeown's own evidence provides far from unequivocal support either for the contention that a fall in airborne disease is the leading epidemiological feature of the period, or for the derivative conclusion that this could *only* be primarily the reflection of general improvement in dietary standards and nutritional levels.

According to McKeown's analysis the annual standardized death-rate per million living in England and Wales fell from about 22,000 in the mid-nineteenth century to about 5,400 by 1971, with 30 per cent of this overall reduction occurring before 1901. On referring to the above table and the notes at the foot (see p. 8), we can see that the initial stages of the fall, before 1901, were mainly the result of the reduced incidence of five individual causes of death. First, respiratory tuberculosis appears to have been responsible for about two-sevenths of the nineteenth-century decline. Secondly, typhoid (sometimes referred to as 'enteric fever') accounted for a further one-seventh of the fall as a result of dramatic decline from the 1870s. Thirdly, scarlet fever virtually vanished and so accounted for an almost similar fraction of the decline. Fourthly, the elimination of cholera alongside a considerable fall in diarrhoeal diseases also accounted for almost a one-seventh part of the reduction. Finally, a somewhat problematic cause of death, 'convulsions', contributed again about one-seventh part. It is likely that much of the apparent fall in this latter category represented more accurate classification of infant deaths to other causes, notably diarrhoea, to which category, therefore, some part of this reduction should be re-allocated.[28]

Apart from respiratory TB, therefore, there were two other airborne diseases which declined very significantly in the nineteenth century, scarlet fever and smallpox. However, neither of these can be used to support the nutrition hypothesis, although they are within the airborne category. It has long been recognized that human intervention, in the form of inoculation starting in the eighteenth century and then vaccination, quarantining, and isolation procedures in the nineteenth century, must be granted the major role in the case of smallpox.[29] As for scarlet fever, McKeown is prepared to acknowledge that the epidemiological evidence strongly suggests that this was in all probability a disease which burned itself out spontaneously.[30] But most disconcerting of

[28] Ibid., p. 61; Luckin, *Pollution and Control*, p. 103.

[29] P. E. Razzell, 'Population Change in Eighteenth Century England: a Re-appraisal', *Ec.H.R.*, xviii (1965), 312–32. Id., *The Conquest of Smallpox* (Firle, 1977). See also A. Hardy, 'Smallpox in London: Factors in the Decline of the Disease in the Nineteenth Century'; *Med. History*, xxvii (1983), 111–38. Hardy emphasizes the *continuing* importance throughout the nineteenth century of public health officials' vigilance in finally eradicating the disease in the face of relative public apathy.

[30] McKeown, *Modern Rise*, pp. 82–3. There was a probable shift in the immunological complexion of the population which did not suit the streptococcal bacteria involved (*Strep. pyogenes*).

all for McKeown's general interpretation, is the behaviour of the composite airborne category, 'bronchitis, pneumonia and influenza', which has so far been omitted from the discussion. This was the second most important cause of death in 1848–54, accounting for 10·25 per cent of all deaths. It actually registered a very considerable *absolute increase* in mortality of well over 20 per cent down to 1901. By the turn of the century this category was clearly the most important single killer, contributing over 16 per cent of all deaths, a greater proportion of the total than respiratory TB had represented in the mid-nineteenth century.

Thus, McKeown would have us treat the airborne diseases as a single unitary group, which between them accounted for about half of the decline in mortality before 1901 and would have us believe that nutritional improvements, made possible by a rising standard of living, can alone be considered responsible for the large-scale reduction of the group as a whole. Yet, on closer examination, we find that this completely ignores the important contrary trend exhibited by one of the two most lethal disease categories in the group. Furthermore, we find that the nutrition argument applies almost exclusively to only one of the several diseases within the group, respiratory TB.

But how strong is McKeown's case that even this one disease's reduction was due to rising living standards and food consumption *alone*? First, contrary to McKeown's sweeping assertion, it should be pointed out that overall exposure of the population to airborne diseases would have been affected by the general level of crowding and ventilation in domestic or working environments. Droplet-transmitted airborne diseases will spread most effectively where humans are in close and unventilated proximity with the exhalations of victims or carriers. It is most probable that overcrowded conditions of living, sleeping, and working became more prevalent as industrialization and urbanization intensified. The reversal of this trend was not simply the by-product of rising real wages but more the result of a complicated history of struggle and pressure for relevant clauses in Factories and Workshops Acts, Housing, and Crowding Acts, and the enforcement of building regulations and by-laws (see below). Thus incidence of airborne diseases probably was influenced by certain public health and preventive measures. Secondly, the etiology of respiratory TB is a highly complex one, which is far from completely understood.[31] Although it is probable that absence of malnutrition in a population is a necessary condition for the elimination of tuberculosis mortality altogether, it is equally probable that danger is decreased if other risk factors are reduced: particularly, frequency of incidence of other infectious diseases; but also overcrowding, lack of sunlight, air ventilation, and various occupational hazards.[32] Thus, G. Cronjé has found adult male rates of TB mortality consistently above female rates in urban registration counties 1871–1900, yet

[31] See, for example, A. R. Rich, *The Pathogenesis of Tuberculosis* (2nd edn. Oxford, 1951). A new general historical study by L. Bryder of TB in Britain in the twentieth century is to appear shortly.

[32] H. D. Chalke, 'Some Historical Aspects of Tuberculosis', *Public Health*, lxxiv (1959), 93.

the reverse situation in rural counties, where rates were generally a little lower.[33] Such anomalous sex differentials seem to suggest that general nutritional factors were less important than certain sex-specific activities in determining the relative incidence of TB.[34] Cronjé notes that urban men were on average much more exposed to the uncontrolled atmospheres of overcrowded factories and workshops than either their womenfolk or the rural men; whilst rural women were on average more subjected to childbearing than their urban counterparts during this period of urban fertility decline.[35] It would certainly seem presumptuous, therefore, to attribute a long-term reduction in TB mortality to one single factor, such as improving nutritional standards.

What, then, were McKeown's grounds for this bold assertion? The critical factor was the apparent empirical finding that respiratory TB was already declining from the late 1830s and 1840s, before any other major disease had begun to fall (apart from smallpox which had probably been on the wane since the latter part of the eighteenth century). This chronological priority in TB's decline was vitally important for McKeown's interpretation. First, it effectively ruled out the possible influence of urban environmental improvements, since these cannot be seriously claimed for the 1830s and 1840s. However, it is of even greater importance in establishing the plausibility of a strong 'nutritional determinism' thesis for the following reason. Tuberculosis often takes a lethal hold where an individual has already been weakened by attack from a previous infection by another category of disease, notoriously so with whooping cough. Thus, any general decrease in the incidence of *other* diseases would probably have a secondary 'knock-on' effect in reducing the number of temporarily weakened individuals available to fall victim to TB. It is also generally true, vice versa, that the presence of TB impedes an individual's capacity to resist attack from other diseases, so that a prior decline in TB could also be claimed to exert a secondary influence, facilitating the decline of other diseases. Therefore, the apparent discovery that TB led in the general decline of disease incidence means that in addition to the primary influence that rising standard of living had in reducing this airborne disease through enhanced nutritional defences, it can be claimed that in all probability there was an additional knock-on effect on other diseases.

As so often in matters of causation, precise chronology, therefore, becomes extremely important. How robust is this all-important empirical finding regarding TB's chronological priority? McKeown's 1976 text merely offers it

[33] G. Cronjé, 'Tuberculosis and Mortality Decline in England and Wales 1851–1910', pp. 79–101 in Woods and Woodward (eds.), *Urban Disease*. See pp. 93–4 and 99–100.

[34] Indeed, the available evidence suggests that working-class wives tended to sacrifice their own dietary requirements to maintain their husbands' health and morale, as the family's main breadwinner. See, for example, Oddy, 'Working Class Diets', pp. 320–1; J. Burnett, *Plenty and Want* (rev. edn., London, 1983), pp. 161, 185; M. Pember Reeves, *Round About a Pound a Week* (London 1913), chap. 10.

[35] Of course, this should not be taken to mean that repeated child-bearing alone can cause greater susceptibility to TB. However, in combination with the generally unsatisfactory environment in which the majority of the labouring population continued to live, it may well have been a significant factor.

as an assertion that 'The number of deaths from tuberculosis fell rapidly from 1838, and this disease was associated with nearly half of the total decrease of the death rate during the second half of the nineteenth century'.[36] The evidence and primary research, upon which this view was based, is contained in the earlier article of 1962. An examination of the evidence originally adduced there by McKeown and Record to demonstrate the early decline of TB is, in fact, far from convincing.

Their detailed analysis of 'this treacherous evidence' (their own words),[37] provided by the cause-specific vital registration data of deaths for the individual years 1838–50, cautioned that reliable and robust conclusions regarding TB trends could only be made on the basis of a joint consideration of the movements in both the phthisis (respiratory TB) and bronchitis figures aggregated together. This was specifically because of the inadequacy of distinction between the two causes of death by contemporary certifying authorities.[38] Particularly damaging to the validity of any inference in favour of a trend decline in TB was the possibility of 'changes in certification (especially from tuberculosis to bronchitis)'.[39] From such a consideration the authors concluded that although the direction of change during the period 1838–46 was entirely uncertain, it could confidently be asserted that there was a definite fall in TB mortality in the years 1847–50 because both diseases were falling together during this brief period.[40] However, on the basis of this microscopic examination it was then unjustifiably asserted that the fall across these 4 years was the commencement of a general and sustained drop in TB mortality continuing for the rest of the century. The authors omitted to mention at this point in the analysis that their own graph, entitled 'Secular trend in mortality from consumption or phthisis' and printed five pages earlier, showed a strong resurgence of mortality from respiratory TB over the ensuing 5 years after 1850 and thereafter no clear trend decline until after 1866–7.[41] In other words, 1847–50 was merely a short-term fluctuation and not a major turning-point in the trends. So, there is, in fact, no good evidence for TB's chronological priority in the mortality decline. And in any case, there had always been the claim of the much earlier, medically induced decline in smallpox, the quantitative importance of which McKeown failed to acknowledge. Although smallpox did not appear to be a predominant factor in the civil registration returns which McKeown analysed, this was precisely because it had already been beaten back considerably by the 1830s.

[36] McKeown, *Modern Rise*, p. 68. There is a similar assertion on p. 56.

[37] McKeown and Record, 'Reasons for the Decline', p. 113.

[38] As late as 1860 possibly as many as 20 per cent of all deaths were still being registered without any certificate from a medical practitioner. This situation was formally remedied by the 1874 Registration Act. See J. M. Eyler, *Victorian Social Medicine: The Ideas and Methods of William Farr* (Baltimore, 1979), p. 62; Glass, *Numbering the People*, p. 188.

[39] McKeown and Record, 'Reasons for the Decline', p. 113.

[40] Ibid., p. 112.

[41] Ibid., Fig. 9 on p. 108. Great care should be taken when inspecting this graph, as the authors have included a suppositional pecked line for the period 1838–47, despite their own warnings against placing any reliance on that information. It is this invalid pecked line which gives the impression of an apparently obvious fall in train before 1866–7.

All the evidence of medical testimony in the eighteenth and early nineteenth centuries suggest that it had been a major scourge, especially of childhood.[42]

Finally, there still remains to be taken into account the strong counter-trend, already remarked upon, which the increasingly lethal bronchitis group of airborne respiratory diseases exhibited throughout the rest of the nineteenth century. This constitutes the most awkward and serious general caveat on the validity of McKeown's airborne/'nutritional determinism' interpretation, however it is explained. Either this anomalous 20–25 per cent increase in the incidence of bronchitis group fatalities has to be simply accepted as genuine, in which case it constitutes a direct contradiction of the view that a general fall in airborne diseases is the principal epidemiological feature of the nineteenth century and so the whole case falls to the ground. Or else it could perhaps be argued, in view of McKeown's own warnings regarding imprecision of certification and the likelihood of transfers between the two categories, that this rise was not real and should be offset against the apparent decrease in reported TB death-rates.[43]

However, even this expedient would be no less damning for the 'McKeown thesis'. According to the above table, the remaining drop in pulmonary (respiratory) TB, after subtraction of the increase in bronchitis fatalities, would only be 6 per cent of the total fall, or one-fifth of the 30 per cent reduction which occurred before 1901. This would then be only of the same order of absolute magnitude as either the typhoid/typhus reduction (5 per cent) or the cholera/diarrhoea reduction, if the latter's figure of 3½ per cent were to be inflated by, say, one-third part of the fall attributed to 'convulsions'.[44] Thus, with the anomalous rise in bronchitis group fatalities properly acknowledged, the classic sanitation diseases come to the fore in quantitative terms. These two water/food-borne categories would between them be responsible for at least 8½ per cent and perhaps 10 per cent of the overall mortality decline. That is one-third part of the nineteenth-century reduction, or over half as much again as that attributable to the airborne combination of TB and the bronchitis group. Furthermore, the much later date suggested here for onset of phthisis decline (after 1866–7 at the earliest, or perhaps even later once the effect of adding back in the bronchitis group has been properly taken into account), implies that the fall in respiratory TB itself may have been a secondary and derivative effect of earlier, or at least concomitant, falls in the sanitation diseases, rather than vice versa.

Improvement in respiratory TB would, then, no longer appear to have been either the chronologically prior or the quantitatively predominant feature of the nineteenth-century mortality decline in England and Wales. According to

[42] Razzel, *The Conquest of Smallpox.*

[43] Such an interpretation would also satisfy an independent reason for treating the two diseases together, supplied by informed contemporary medical opinion: Dr John Hogg specifically pointed out, in his work of 1860, that whilst bronchitis was often recorded as the actual cause of death, in many cases active tuberculosis was the crucial predisposing factor. J. Hogg, *Observations on the Prevention of Consumption* (London, 1860), p. 41.

[44] See discussion in text at n. 28.

the logic of McKeown's own arguments, the foregoing would indicate a primary role for sanitary reform and public health measures, rather than rising nutritional levels or living standards. The changing incidence of mortality from respiratory TB in Victorian Britain, rather than being cast in the role of a leading and determining influence, can be seen as a dependent function of the general intensity and frequency of *other* debilitating diseases. Many of these were themselves killers but only of a certain proportion of their infected victims, leaving the remainder weakened and prey to late breakdown disease from a previous primary TB infection.[45] This conceptualization of mortality from TB, as essentially a secondary effect of the aggregate incidence of other infectious and sanitation diseases, is strongly suggested by William Farr's early analyses of the rural–urban differentials in cause-specific mortality patterns. Although respiratory TB was the largest single cause of death at that time, Farr observed that wherever the overall death-rate was relatively high, as in most urban and industrial registration districts, this was not primarily because of enhanced risks of respiratory TB, which was only about 20–25 per cent more lethal in the towns as against the countryside.[46] By contrast certain other major killers were about 200 per cent more lethal, and it was these which reflected the primary risks of city life. They included notably 'convulsions' ('a frequent intercurrent symptom in diarrhoea' noted Farr),[47] hydrocephalus, teething, gastro-enteritis, diarrhoea, 'typhus' (i.e. both typhus and typhoid), smallpox, measles, and the bronchitis group of respiratory diseases.[48] Farr specifically pointed out that the latter's high incidence was a result of the common *sequelae* of frequent measles and influenza epidemics in the cities.[49] According to this analysis, therefore, the peculiarly pernicious disease pattern of the urban districts in the late 1830s was not so much due to differentially excessive respiratory TB, but to problems caused by absence of sanitation and hygiene, taking a particularly high toll at birth and in early infancy, and compounded by certain frequently epidemic infectious diseases.

[45] I am grateful to Sir George Godber for pointing out to me that this would be in accord with clinical experience of the nature of respiratory TB gained in the course of the twentieth century. For instance, a London survey of 1930 cited by Cronjé ('Tuberculosis and Mortality Decline', p. 81) found TB still present in 82 per cent of 14- to 15-year-olds. This suggests that most urban adolescents and adults in the nineteenth century would have already suffered and survived a primary infection in early childhood. Actual death from TB, which was especially high in the age groups 15 to 35 in the nineteenth century, would usually, therefore, have been the result of subsequent breakdown disease, rather than a first contact, and would be triggered by a weakening in the body's normal equilibrium as a result of the strains imposed by other non-lethal disease episodes. It is certainly interesting to note that the two recorded phthisis peaks of 1853–5 and 1866 both coincided with cholera epidemics, although this was apparently not true of the largest cholera crisis of all, that of 1848–9.

[46] *1st Annual Report of the Registrar-General* (hereafter *ARRG*), (PP, 1839, XVI), pp. 108–18; *5th ARRG* (PP, 1843, XXI), p. 408.

[47] *1st ARRG*, p. 110.

[48] Ibid., see especially Tables C and D, pp. 148–51; *5th ARRG*, pp. 403–5.

[49] *1st ARRG*, p. 111.

IV. *An Alternative Interpretation: Urban Congestion Remedied by Social Intervention*

Thus, according to the reinterpretation of McKeown's epidemiological evidence proposed above, it is no longer the decline of airborne diseases as a unitary category which appears to be the predominant and leading characteristic of changing mortality patterns in nineteenth-century England and Wales, but rather the behaviour of the classic sanitation and hygiene diseases. There can be little doubt that the first two-thirds of the nineteenth century witnessed an increasing incidence of such diseases, which was directly attributable to the unplanned proliferation of overcrowded cities and towns lacking even the most basic sanitary facilities such as proper water supply and waste disposal systems.[50] Conversely, the ensuing disappearance of water-borne diseases in the last third of the century was due to the eventual provision of adequate sanitary facilities, long delayed but finally implemented. McKeown himself noted of the nineteenth century:

> . . . the appearance of cholera, possibly for the first time, leaves little doubt that . . . hygienic conditions deteriorated. The rapid movement of population from country to towns must have led to deterioration of hygiene and increased exposure to diseases spread by water and food.

so that,

> Mortality from these infections . . . did not begin to decline until there were improvements in water supplies and sewage disposal, in England and Wales from the seventh decade . . . [of the nineteenth century].[51]

Between 1801 and 1871 the rate of urban growth in Britain was quite unprecedented, both in the provinces and the metropolis. At the commencement of the nineteenth century no provincial town contained as many as 100,000 inhabitants. By 1871 there were seventeen cities over this size on mainland Britain, apart from London. Glasgow and Liverpool each numbered around half a million, whilst the capital had tripled to over three million.

National aggregate mortality patterns only indirectly reflect the full impact of this period of intensive but chaotic and disorganized urban expansion on the nation's health. According to the best single summary measure currently available, Wrigley and Schofield's series for the expectation of life at birth (e_0), an upward secular trend dating from either the 1680s or 1730s (depending on how one chooses to interpret the behaviour of the index across that period), whereby average life expectancy at birth rose from around 30 years to about 40 years, then slowed to a halt at the end of the first quarter of the nineteenth century. For about half a century, from the 1820s until the 1870s, there was virtually no perceptible further improvement. Thereafter, a gradual rise to about 47–8 years by the end of the century, followed by a somewhat faster

[50] Even as late as 1851, Birmingham (population 233,000) still had only 8 miles of mains sewers. By comparison, the square mile of the City of London, with only about half the population, had already constructed about 45 miles of sewers by this time. R. J. Lambert, *Sir John Simon and English Social Administration 1816–1904* (London, 1963), pp. 81–2.

[51] McKeown, *Modern Rise*, pp. 68–9.

rise, to just over 60 years by 1931.[52] Paradoxically—for McKeown's thesis—it had been almost exactly at this same point in time, when the long eighteenth-century rise in life expectancy had stalled to a halt, that a concomitant eighteenth-century *fall* (or at best stagnation) in national aggregate real wages was reversed and there had begun a trend of continual, although not continuous, improvements in average real wages throughout the rest of the nineteenth century.[53]

McKeown entirely discounted the possibility of any chronological discontinuity of this sort, assuming instead a reasonably direct long-term correlation between uninterrupted upward trends in economic growth, food supply, rising living standards, and improving mortality levels (his own mortality data did not extend back beyond 1838 and the course of demographic movements over the previous couple of centuries was largely a matter of conjecture in the 'pre Wrigley-and-Schofield' era).[54] The explanation of the inverse relationship is not, however, difficult if it is simply accepted that the relative state of insalubrity in the expanding urban environments, rather than improvements in average real wages or the food supply, must have been the more predominant factor influencing national mortality trends in the nineteenth century. The historical process of industrialization was able to generate massive productivity gains as a result of innovations in the technology of production, most of which entailed a geographically more intensive demand for labour than had hitherto existed. It is no paradox, therefore, but simply two sides of the same coin that this process could simultaneously engender higher wage-rates for the industrial workers and their families congregating at the places where these new enterprises were emerging, yet also simultaneously exert a negative influence on their average life expectancy because of the crowded and chaotic living conditions prevalent in the mushrooming towns and cities created by the rapidly expanding employment opportunities.

The stationary national figure for expectation of life at birth across the second and third quarters of the nineteenth century merely summarizes the nation's average mortality experience, urban and rural populations aggregated together. This quite certainly belies wide geographical divergences in experience. Those remaining in the countryside were very probably continuing to experience the

[52] Wrigley and Schofield, *Population History*, chap. 6. The protracted nineteenth-century discontinuity was not known to McKeown in 1976, who assumed that there was a linear trend of continuous fall in mortality down to the present day beginning at some point in the mid-eighteenth century. For twentieth-century figures, see Table 1 of Winter, 'Decline of Mortality'.

[53] Real wage trends form the best available single index for historical changes in 'the standard of living' in McKeown's sense, since they aim to measure changes in average money wage-rates deflated by a cost-of-living factor, in which subsistence food prices play a predominant role (especially the price of wheat, as bread was the main staple at this time). M. W. Flinn, 'Trends in Real Wages 1750–1850', *Ec.H.R.*, xxvii (1974), 395–413, first identified the second decade of the nineteenth century as a turning point, due primarily to falls in food prices. Recent econometric work has substantially confirmed this chronology: P. H. Lindert and J. G. Williamson, 'English Workers Living Standards', *Ec.H.R.* xxxvi (1983), 1–25; 88–92 (comment by Flinn). Of course, regional variations are also very important: see, for example, E. W. Hunt and F. W. Botham, 'Wages in Britain during the Industrial Revolution', *Ec.H.R.*, xl (1987), 380–99.

[54] See McKeown, *Modern Rise*, pp. 64–5 for his own conjectures on the subject.

trajectory of slow but steady improvement which had characterized the second half of the eighteenth century. By contrast those who migrated to the expanding towns and cities to bring up their families—a rapidly growing proportion of the national aggregate throughout this period—must have experienced a real fall in life expectancy on so doing.[55] Such a divergence in rural and urban experiences during the first half of the nineteenth century was clearly indicated in the results of William Farr's famous pioneering construction of comparative life-tables for Liverpool, London, and rural Surrey. Average expectations of life at birth in *c.*1841 were found to be a respectable 45·1 in Surrey, a worrying 36·7 in London, and an appalling 25·7 in Liverpool, a city that had already more than tripled in size since the first census of 1801.[56]

Whilst increasingly huge populations continued to concentrate ever more intensively in townships growing into cities but lacking the appropriate social overhead capital to preserve—let alone promote—health, then morbidity and mortality risks inevitably proliferated. Equally inevitably, these multiplying and compounding health hazards could only be alleviated through the appropriate social and political responses: the technical development of, and proper deployment of, precisely that infrastructure which was previously largely unnecessary. For instance, despite its rapid growth and the unhealthy overcrowded conditions which this implied, a mains sewer system for London as a whole, which dumped the waste securely downstream of its population, was not completed until 1865—the first such large-scale integrated system in the country. This followed a long period of extremely harmful, highly localized initiatives by the property-owning classes. They were the first to install their own water-flushing closets in large numbers from the 1770s onwards; but in the absence of a mains sewage system, these were simply allowed to empty

[55] Note that this point stands regardless of whether or not there was an *absolute* deterioration in urban conditions during this period, which is a matter of dispute. It is perfectly possible arithmetically to show that although the national average figure for life expectancy ceased to rise across these decades, nevertheless, each registration district around the country *could* have recorded continual improvement throughout. This simple paradox can occur if the different districts all start with somewhat varying figures and it happens to be the case that those with the lowest life-expectancy figures experience disproportionate growth in their population sizes over time, whilst those with higher figures correspondingly shrink (at least relatively) in population size. This is broadly what happened at this time as a result of migration from the countryside to the towns. The figure for the overall national average expectation of life is weighted by the relative population sizes of each district and is, therefore, strongly influenced by such an underlying shift in overall population composition towards residence in relatively high mortality districts. R. I. Woods has produced some estimates, which illustrate precisely this possibility during the period 1801–61: see Table 3 of 'The Effects of Population Redistribution on the Level of Mortality in Nineteenth-Century England and Wales', *Jnl. Ec. History*, xlv (1985), 645–51. However, it must be stressed that Woods's table offers only hypothetical estimates of *possibilities* for this earlier period, since unfortunately the censuses before 1851 are not reliable sources for detailed trends in individual districts. Furthermore, and against the implications of Woods's exercise, must be set the evidence of probably the only town for which adequate data is agreed to be available (as a result of the private initiative of the local physician, John Heysham). This in fact shows a significant increase in mortality across the period: W. A. Armstrong, 'The Trend of Mortality in Carlisle Between the 1780s and the 1840s: A Demographic Contribution to the Standard of Living Debate', *Ec.H.R.*, xxxiv (1981), 94–114.

[56] *5th ARRG* (PP 1843, XXI), pp. 33–7.

into the nearest culvert or river, from which much of the town's population in turn took their drinking water.[57] Unfortunately, this development was to be repeated in other cities and towns around the country in the course of the nineteenth century.[58] The lethal lesson was only slowly learned that selective sanitation for the upper classes alone was not a sufficient panacea in the prevention of water-borne disease.

Sewering alone, without commensurate attention to the purity of the water supply, could prove a downright liability, as was tragically demonstrated by London's final cholera epidemic of 1866–7, immediately following the completion of London's sewers system. This was the last such epidemic and it was the famous occasion on which William Farr was able, using a method pioneered at the previous outbreak of 1853/4, to trace precisely the culprit. By dividing London into districts according to the different companies supplying water, the problem was narrowed down to the East London Waterworks Co., who were illegally supplying water from the Old Ford reservoir in Bethnal Green, which was contaminated by the recently completed West Ham sewage system.[59] This is a perfect example of the kind of medical science in the public health field, which was vital in stimulating what McKeown loosely calls 'municipal sanitation' or 'hygiene'. The narrow definition of medical intervention, as either scientific discovery or the effects of clinical and hospital practices only, misleadingly understates the importance of medical men, and human agency in general, in bringing about the nineteenth-century decline in mortality. Sanitarians contributed by convincing public opinion of the need for strategic measures to improve the urban environment (the particular contribution of the GRO), by demonstrating the practical worth and feasibility of such schemes, and then by administering their operation.

The period from the late 1830s to 1875 has come to be seen as encompassing a 'heroic age' of pioneering advances in public health activism and legislation. The era began with probing investigations by medical men such as William Farr at the GRO, Drs Arnott, Kay, and Southwood Smith, stimulating the formulation by Edwin Chadwick of his ambitious programme, 'The Sanitary Idea', which eventually issued in the first Public Health Act of 1848. Despite the notorious reaction which this provoked amongst those jealous to protect their local influence and power against the apparent encroaching intentions of a Chadwickian centralizing state and despite Chadwick's fall from office, energetic central direction of public health affairs by Sir John Simon still continued.[60] Royston Lambert long ago showed that the check to central

[57] L. B. Wood, *The Restoration of the Tidal Thames* (London 1982), p. 19.

[58] See, for example, F. B. Smith, *The People's Health* (London, 1979), p. 227.

[59] See Eyler, *Victorian Social Medicine*, pp. 118–19. Luckin, *Pollution and Control*, pp. 88–95, has provided the most detailed recent account of this incident and the water company's successful subsequent evasion of legal retribution.

[60] Sir John Simon was London's first Medical Officer of Health (1848–58) and then Chief Medical Officer to the Privy Council (1858–71) and finally, the first Chief Medical Officer to the Local Government Board from its statutory inception in 1871. The superb, if somewhat partisan, biography by Royston Lambert is the standard work: Lambert, *Sir John Simon*.

government activism supposedly represented by the 1858 Local Government Act was only relative and not absolute, more in spirit than fact.[61]

It has generally been considered that this dynamic phase petered out with the creation of the Local Government Board in 1871 resulting in the subordination within that institution of expansionary and interventionist public health interests to the reactionary, conservative instincts of an upper administrative staff drawn mainly from the Poor Law Board. After 4 years of increasing frustration at the restrictions being imposed on his medical staff, John Simon resigned in 1875, marking the formal end of this 'heroic' period.[62] Although important scientific developments in preventive medicine and epidemiology of course continued, the period from 1875 to the end of the century has tended to be seen as a contrasting and less dynamic period, during which Gladstonian budgetary control and Treasury retrenchment stifled the initiatives of those medical men and their sympathizers in government, who were the progressive advocates of the public health movement.[63] Thus, on the assumption that it was the three middle decades of the nineteenth century when most progress was occurring in the field of public health, the lack of any obvious chronological fit between public health advances and the general fall in mortality from infectious and sanitary diseases, which did not occur until the last third of the century, has perhaps discouraged historians from assigning any particular significance to the expansion of preventive public health measures as the major influence on mortality patterns.

However, an entirely different chronology emerges if we shift the focus of attention away from the central government departments and the nationally famous figures who led the public health crusade, and instead look to the provinces and the municipalities. Although a comprehensive coverage of the history of municipal sanitation in every growing town and city throughout Britain is quite beyond us as yet, there are clear signs that this will prove a very profitable line of enquiry. Anthony Wohl's *Endangered Lives* (1983) has certainly presented enough evidence in an accessible form to show that despite the slowing down in *central* government activity and the relative quiescence of sanitarians in and around Westminster and Whitehall, it was in fact the last 30 years of the nineteenth century when most of the significant improvements and works of construction and concrete applications of preventive health measures went forward and were actually occurring on the ground throughout the provincial cities and towns of Britain.

[61] R. J. Lambert, 'Central and Local Relations in Mid-Victorian England: The Local Government Act Office 1858–71', *Victorian Studies*, vi (1962–3), 121–49.

[62] R. M. Macleod designated 1860–75 as encompassing 'the heroic age' of State Medicine. R. M. Macleod, 'The Anatomy of State Medicine: Concept and Application' in F. N. L. Poynter (ed.), *Medicine and Science in the 1860s* (London, 1968), pp. 226–7.

[63] This view was first put forward by Simon himself, in his influential *English Sanitary Institutions, Reviewed in Their Course of Development, and in Some of their Political and Social Relations* (London, 1890). Until very recently, there has continued to be a broad consensus of agreement on this, founded on such major studies as S. E. Finer, *The Life and Times of Sir Edwin Chadwick* (London, 1952); Lambert, *Sir John Simon*; R. M. Macleod, *Treasury Control and Social Administration* (London, 1968); also R. M. Macleod, 'The Frustration of State Medicine', *Medical History*, xi (1967), 15–40.

With the rise in the 1860s of a genuine ethos of local civic pride in their muncipalities, the long-standing strategy of the GRO had added effect. This was the deliberate fostering of an atmosphere of rivalry and competition between local authorities by publishing comparative information on local death-rates as regularly as possible and with graphic comparisons in terms of numbers of lives needlessly lost in the 'Black Spots', relative to the more salubrious 'Healthy Districts'. The optimal health conditions were thereby insidiously established by this clever propaganda manœuvre as an objective to which all responsible local authorities aspired. Commerce and business was believed to be attracted to those cities with the lowest death-rates, a macabre inversion of today's logic of commercial location which seeks out those authorities with the lowest local fiscal-rates![64]

The broad-based 1850s backlash against Chadwick's centralizing Poor Law and Health Boards had clearly demonstrated to all in government and administration that formal adherence to the principal of local autonomy was a non-negotiable political necessity. Sanitary progress within these political rules was, nevertheless, perfectly possible once proponents of public health had adjusted their programme appropriately so as to work through and with local authorities, rather than attempting to override them, as Chadwick initially had. However, whilst this adjustment in thinking was occurring, Victorian public health remained hamstrung at the local level by the twin problems of a multiplicity of overlapping authorities and the non-compulsory, merely permissive nature of most of their statutory duties. Steps to improve the urban environment often clashed with the pecuniary interests of factory and workshop owners, landlords, and shopkeepers.[65] In these circumstances the ambiguity, or positive obstructionism of economizing ratepayers could all too easily prevail over public health arguments for expensive local facilities and services. By the mid-1860s, however, sanitarians were focusing their attentions forcefully on precisely these local political and administrative obstacles blocking their path. Having reluctantly accepted localism in public health, the solution was to compel local government to be effective, as the reforming barrister Edward Jenkins perceived, writing in 1866: 'To a sanitary reformer there is no greater bugbear than a permissive enactment. A system which involves expense to persons interested in that expense is sure, in nine cases out of ten, to be unheeded.'[66]

[64] From the mid-1850s the GRO produced a list of quarterly returns of the general mortality rates for all the large cities, which was published and discussed in the press; J. M. Eyler, 'Mortality Statistics and Victorian Health Policy: Program and Criticism', *Bulletin of the History of Medicine*, l (1976), 342. More generally, on the important role of the GRO in the public health movement, see the forthcoming publication, edited by S. R. S. Szreter, based on papers presented to a symposium held at the Wellcome Institute for the History of Medicine on 27 November 1987: 'The General Register Office in the Nineteenth Century: a Comparative Perspective.'

[65] E. P. Hennock, *Fit and Proper Persons: Ideal and Reality in Nineteenth Century Urban Government* (London, 1973).

[66] E. Jenkins, 'The Legal Aspects of Sanitary Reform' in A. P. Stewart and E. Jenkins (eds.) (reprint ed. M. Flinn), *The Medical and Legal Aspects of Sanitary Reform* (Leicester, 1969), p. 93.

The basis for a programme of increasingly effective pursuit of the nation's health within the framework of local government and administration was provided by the three Acts in the 1870s which followed the recommendations of the report of the famous Royal Sanitary Commission of 1869–71. The Commission was itself the Government's response to a public health debate, instigated by those sanitarians, such as Jenkins among many others, who were galvanized by the tantalizing failure of the path-breaking 1866 Sanitary Act: its defective drafting had confounded the novel system of compulsory local sanitary duties subject to central inspectorial supervision which it was intended to establish. It was the 1871 Local Government Act which finally produced a unified department of state to deal with most aspects of local government with a Minister responsible for implementation, the President of the newly created Local Government Board; the 1872 Public Health Act established the corresponding national network of literally hundreds of local sanitary authorities, each with a now obligatory Medical Officer of Health; and it was the great consolidating Public Health Act of 1875 which clearly laid down most of the public health functions and statutory duties of these local authorities and their staff, remaining in force until the subsequent Act of 1936.

Thus, while it is true that a centralized system of 'state medicine' of the sort which had been ambitiously envisaged by H. W. Rumsey was not adopted,[67] historians of the central departments and national figures have perhaps dwelled too much and somewhat Whiggishly on this aspect of the 'sanitary revival' of these years: the non-emergence of a prototype centralist Ministry of Health. In so doing there has been a failure to give due credit to the political realism of what was actually achieved through the relatively successful harnessing of local and provincial energies and administrative structures to the subsequent promotion of the nation's public health.

With the essential machinery of unambiguous local accountability in place, effective take-up of public health measures began to gather pace. Alongside this was a continual process of modification and diversification in local authorities' powers and duties, as the practical experiences of their officials in attempting to fulfil statutory duties revealed new administrative, technical, and financial obstacles and requirements. For instance, the 1872 Public Health Act obliged local authorities as one of their statutory duties to ensure a pure water supply. In turn, this led to pressure for the 1878 Public Health (Water) Act whereby municipal purchase of private waterworks was made truly financially feasible. Whereas in 1879 only 415 urban local authorities were in charge of their water supplies, by 1905 over two-thirds of the 1,138 urban sanitary authorities then in existence were running the local waterworks, so that the health of the populace was decreasingly left in the hands of the likes of the East London Waterworks Co.[68] Another example is that of the increasingly close regulation of the quality of the urban food supply, which duly resulted from the attention

[67] H. W. Rumsey, *Essays on State Medicine* (London, 1856).

[68] A. S. Wohl, *Endangered Lives. Public Health in Victorian Britain* (London, 1983), p. 111; *Report on Public Health and Social Conditions* (PP 1909, CII), p. 81.

which Medical Officers in the 1860s had begun to pay to adulterated and defective foodstuffs, particularly meat and milk, as a source of disease.[69] The Adulteration of Foods Acts followed in the 1870s, leading to the appointment of professional inspectors and public analysts by most local authorities in the 1880s; also Weights and Measures Acts in 1878 and 1889 and a final consolidating Sale of Food & Drugs Act 1899. The last third of the century was the classic period in which all the hectic activity of the Public Health political and administrative pioneers finally began to bear fruit and to take concrete effect. Of course, all this was only achieved as a result of innumerable unsung local skirmishes between frequently underpaid health officials, often lacking security of tenure, and their local allies—other sanitary officials, the district registrars of births and deaths, perhaps the town's press and occasionally some members of the local councils themselves—as against the parsimonious representatives of the majority of ratepayers. It is precisely the importance and *necessity* of this slow dogged campaign of a million Minutes, fought out in town-halls and the local forums of debate all over the country over the last quarter of the nineteenth century which has been missing in our previous accounts of the mortality decline.[70]

A. S. Wohl has noted that Sir John Simon himself always regarded the extent of public works loans contracted by local authorities from the central government funds as the true barometer of sanitary progress and real local activity.[71] This was the system whereby local authorities were enabled to borrow long-term loans of cash at lower than market interest rates for provision of sanitary facilities and services. Between 1858 and 1870 only £11 million in such loans were requested, whereas between 1871 and 1897 £84 million was borrowed, £65 million of it by urban authorities.[72] In addition, in the town-hall building age of the civic gospel of municipal progress symbolized by Joseph Chamberlain's go-ahead Mayorship of Birmingham, 1873–5, there began the deliberate development of municipal trading activities in gas, electricity, and transport in order to generate funds and revenue for municipal social services and facilities independent of the various strings attached both to central government sources of finance and to the local rates. Charles Feinstein's

[69] Smith, *The People's Health*, pp. 203–15. Burnett, *Plenty and Want*, pp. 99–120.

[70] Some idea of the kinds of problems faced, and often eventually surmounted, by MOHs, assisted by the LGB and by other local proponents of public health, can be gained from R. K. F. J. Young, 'Sanitary Administration under the L.G.B. 1871–88' (University of Oxford B.Litt. Thesis, 1964). Unfortunately, this is not included in Wohl's otherwise very helpful list of relevant theses, in the bibliography of *Endangered Lives*. Two other highly informative unpublished D.Phil. and Ph.D. theses, too recent for inclusion by Wohl are: Anne Wilkinson (now known as Anne Hardy), 'The Beginnings of Disease Control in London: the Work of the Medical Officers in Three Parishes 1856–1900' (University of Oxford, 1980); Dorothy E. Watkins (now known as Dorothy Porter), 'The English Revolution in Social Medicine', (University of London, 1984). Two other useful unpublished archive surveys are A. B. Cooper, 'Local Reports on Public Health by Government Medical Inspectors 1869–1908' (Loughborough University M.Lib. Studies dissertation, 1981); C. A. Bellamy, 'Central–Local Relations 1871–1919 (LGB)' SSRC End of Grant Report HR7579 (1982).

[71] Wohl, *Endangered Lives*, p. 112.

[72] Ibid., pp. 113 and 162–3.

figures for gross domestic fixed capital formation show that whereas local authorities were only spending about £5 million per annum on such enterprises in the period 1856–71, this rose to an average of £12–14 million per annum for the period 1874–94, and by the Edwardian period had reached an annual expenditure of about £30 million per annum.[73] Furthermore, and despite the expanding revenues of municipal trading, by 1890 subventions from the Imperial exchequer to local authorities represented 6·7 per cent of total national revenue and by 1913 this figure had risen to 11·6 per cent, by which date local government spending represented virtually one-half of total government expenditure.[74]

I would argue, therefore, that there is a sound prima facie case to be answered that the decline in mortality, which began to be noticeable in the national aggregate statistics in the 1870s, was due more to the eventual successes of the politically and ideologically negotiated movement for public health than to any other positively identifiable factor. The resulting implementation of preventive measures of municipal sanitation and regulation of the urban environment and food market actually arrived on the ground in the many new cities throughout the country during the last third of the nineteenth century and the first decade of the twentieth.[75]

The all but complete eradication by the end of the century of typhoid, cholera, and smallpox each testify in different ways to the importance and effectiveness of various aspects of the large-scale strategic public health measures which were introduced during this period. Provision of a sufficiently clean local water supply was essential in the cases of both typhoid and cholera. Due to their epidemic nature, elimination of cholera and smallpox additionally required a properly functioning national system of surveillance to identify and snuff out local outbreaks which could otherwise quickly become major incidents. Port sanitary authorities established by the 1872 Public Health Act, alongside the initiative of the GRO in establishing regular communications with foreign authorities so as to gain advance warning of any outbreaks abroad, helped to ensure—in the absence of an entirely secure national water supply—that Britain successfully evaded all three subsequent European visitations of

[73] C. H. Feinstein, *National Income, Expenditure and Output of the U.K. 1855–1965* (2 vols., Cambridge, 1972, 1976), Table 39.

[74] P. J. Waller, *Town, City and Nation. England 1800–1950* (Oxford, 1983), p. 264. Throughout the period 1879–1914 it was always the cost of works for water supply, drainage, and purification which constituted between half and two-thirds of the aggregate capital indebtedness on utilities of all municipalities, despite the not inconsiderable capital costs associated with gas, transport, and electricity utilities, especially in the Edwardian period. See the Table in ibid., p. 307, which shows water accounting for 19 out of 28·5 millions of such indebtedness in 1879–80 rising to 132 out of 224 millions by 1914–15.

[75] The illustrative estimates recently prepared by Woods (see n. 55) are founded on a much firmer empirical basis for 1861 and for 1911 than for the earlier period. These clearly show that it was the big cities which experienced the greatest falls in mortality across this later period. Woods has therefore concluded that 'The importance of that set of administrative advances usually labelled the "Sanitary Revolution" appears to be re-emphasized by these estimates of rural and urban life expectations.' Woods, 'The Effects of Population Redistribution', p. 651.

Asiatic cholera in 1873, 1884–6, and 1892–3[76] Smallpox continued to appear despite its preventability because of the unfortunate involvement of the unpopular Poor Law as the official agency of compulsory vaccination. As a result vaccination was far from universal, especially amongst the Metropolitan poor where a particularly virulent form was in evidence at this time. The final eradication of smallpox, therefore, was in fact further testament to the efficiency of the Metropolitan Medical Officers of Health: their effective operation of the Notification of Infectious Diseases Act of 1889 allied to the provision by the Metropolitan Asylums Board of isolation facilities on hospital ships in the Thames.[77]

By contrast, the apparent rise in the bronchitis group of airborne respiratory diseases may well be evidence that in those areas of the urban and industrial environment where preventive legislation and action was *not* forthcoming, serious consequences followed. Clean air was one obvious omission from the late nineteenth-century sanitary reform arsenal and one need look no further than the appalling urban smogs to explain such anomalously high levels of respiratory disease in the Victorian period. Although there was a Metropolitan Smoke Nuisance Abatement Act as early as 1853 and relevant sections in many other towns' Improvement Acts, these often unenforced clauses applied only to commercial premises. However, it was not factories so much as coal-burning domestic fires which caused the smogs, hence London's were reputedly the worst, rather than those of the northern industrial towns. The Great Fog of 1886 sent the Metropolitan death rate up to almost equal that of the worst years of cholera epidemics, as over 11,000 inhabitants in the capital were recorded as dying of bronchitis alone that year.[78] Futhermore, in many northern and midland industrial towns an entirely separate and also continuing source of respiratory disease (including TB: see Cronjé's work, noted above) was the unregulated factory atmospheres of textile, pottery, and especially metal-grinding industries, demonstrated in the differential occupational death-rates of those employed in these industries. For instance, male textile workers in the 1890s, a numerically large segment of the factory working class, had a two-and-a-half times higher death-rate from respiratory diseases than agricultural labourers, despite their considerably higher pay and better access to a varied diet—the main factors stressed by McKeown in accounting for secular falls in the incidence of airborne diseases.[79]

It is a well-rehearsed observation that the slower improvement in average expectation of life in the three decades before 1901, by comparison with the

[76] Smith, *The People's Health*, p. 233.

[77] Hardy, 'Smallpox in London', pp. 131–8.

[78] Wohl, *Endangered Lives*, p. 213. For comparison: the final cholera epidemic of 1866 had accounted for 15,000 deaths spread over the whole country. Only the worst cholera outbreak of 1848–9 had accounted for more than 11,000 deaths in the capital (when a total of 62,000 had perished throughout the country as a whole). See Smith, *The People's Health*, pp. 230–1. The last killer fog in London before effective controls were finally introduced was as recently as 1952, when, yet again, over 10,000 perished.

[79] *Supplement to 55th ARRG*, Pt. II (PP 1897, Cmd. 8503), Table on p. xcvi.

three following, was because improvement was confined primarily to the age-groups 2 to 34 for males and 2 to 54 for females. Infant mortality (i.e. age 0 to 1) remained stubbornly high at about 150 per thousand throughout England and Wales in the later nineteenth century. However, almost exactly at the turn of the century the nation's infant mortality rate suddenly plummetted, already reaching 110 per thousand by 1910–12 and then 80 per thousand by 1920–2 despite the intervention of the First World War, and thereafter continuously declining at a somewhat slower rate down to the present minimal level, reaching 18 per thousand in 1970–2.[80] How, then, does this fit into the general interpretation being presented here? As McKeown himself noted, it was the water- rather than food-borne diseases which had declined first, in the period before 1901: 'It is worth underlining the fact that the rate of decline of mortality before the turn of the century was much greater for the enteric [intestinal] diseases, then spread mainly by water, than for the diarrhoeal diseases spread mainly by food.'[81] This reflects the limits of what was possible through the 'municipal sanitation' movement alone. Although improvement of the urban environment at the strategic level by providing pure water, paved streets, refuse collection, and a proper mains sewage system could eradicate the water-borne diseases which thrived where collective sanitary facilities were defective, such measures could not alter the shortcomings of living conditions and especially food preparation in the overcrowded, working-class domestic environment of the back-to-back. Nor could they educate a populace into more hygienic habits of food preparation for weaning infants, hence McKeown's observation that before the twentieth century there was relatively little decline in food-borne diarrhoeal diseases.

However, several relevant developments affecting the working-class home environment were beginning to take noticeable effect by the first decade of the twentieth century. First, and most importantly, the problems of housing quantity and quality were gradually being alleviated. There was an ever stricter enforcement of minimal standards of design and especially insistence on the provision of basic sanitary and hygiene facilities in the new homes being built or improved during the long boom in house-building 1897–1907.[82] For instance, whereas in London the Metropolitan Management Act as long ago as 1855 had in theory empowered vestries to compel landlords and builders to connect houses to mains drains (a provision extended to the whole country by the flawed 1866 Sanitary Act), one of the few local studies that has been completed found that in Camberwell such regulations were consistently hood-winked until by-laws in 1889 brought in official on-site inspections before

[80] On the nation's health during the First World War, see J. M. Winter, *The Great War and the British People* (London, 1985); D. Dwork, *War is Good for Babies and Other Young Children: A History of the Infant Welfare Movement in England, 1898–1918* (London, 1986).

[81] McKeown, *Modern Rise*, p. 61.

[82] An average of about 130,000 houses per year were built across these years, as against only about 80,000 per annum over the previous 17 years. B. R. Mitchell and P. Deane, *Abstract of British Historical Statistics* (Cambridge, 1962), p. 239.

drains were covered over by builders.[83] A further significant step forward in Metropolitan housing standards came 2 years later with the Public Health Act (London), which stipulated that every single new and rebuilt house should have its own 'proper and sufficient water supply'.[84] Following the 1890 Housing Act, expansion in the provision of municipal housing itself was at last made financially feasible, incorporating minimum crowding and sanitary standards following earlier private philanthropic initiatives (such as the Peabody estates and Rothschild buildings).[85] Between 1895 and 1907, for instance, the number of occupants municipally housed rose by a factor of 5 in Manchester, to 3,500; by a factor of 7 in Liverpool to 7,500; by a factor of 14 in London to 36,000.[86] These were admittedly as yet small numbers. However, there are also the ambitious philanthropic and municipal town-planning initiatives to be included, such as Bournville or New Earswick, and Hampstead or Letchworth Garden Cities, respectively. If it is reasonable to assume that the very worst houses and slums tended to be the first to be knocked down and, in effect, replaced by these schemes and by the private building boom, then overall the average quality of the housing stock available, especially in terms of provision of basic utilities for effective domestic hygiene, may have been improving substantially from the 1890s onwards as a net result of all these various factors.[87] For instance, P. J. Waller cites an inter-war survey of a sample of northern and midland industrial towns, which estimated that between 1894 and 1914, the proportion of homes with a fitted bath multiplied fourfold from 5 per cent to 20 per cent.[88]

Secondly, there was the expansion of local health and maternity services. As I. H. Buchanan's highly effective study of eight mining communities has shown, although actual clinics were rare before the First World War, the health-visiting system, whilst by no means universal, was well established throughout

[83] Wilkinson, thesis, pp. 270–1.

[84] A. Hardy, 'Water and the Search for Public Health in London in the Eighteenth and Nineteenth Centuries', *Medical History*, xxviii (1984), 274.

[85] The 1875 Artizans' and Labourers' Dwellings Improvement Act (Cross Act) had similarly stimulated the earlier 'five per cent' philanthropic dwelling companies and had also been followed by a short house-building boom, with about 120,000 built per annum 1875–8. Wohl, *Endangered Lives*, p. 320. Mitchell and Deane, *Abstract*, p. 239. J. N. Tarn, *Five Per Cent Philanthropy* (London, 1974); J. White, *Rothschild Buildings* (London, 1980).

[86] *Report on Public Health and Social Conditions* (PP, 1909, CII), Table on p. 22.

[87] However, it must be acknowledged that a contraction in the lowest-rent housing stock through slum demolition may not necessarily have had a net beneficial effect in the short term on the welfare of lowest-income sections of the population, given the higher rents which may have been demanded for better quality housing. State enforced rent control of some sort might well be a necessary adjunct. This is what subsequently happened during the First World War. For similar reasons, the growing practice of family limitations among various groups of the working population may not necessarily have helped alleviate overcrowding since there is no reason why smaller families might not simply be pushed into smaller, perhaps subdivided, tenements if left to market forces in the context of a relatively fixed housing stock. See D. Englander, *Landlord and Tenant in Urban Britain 1838–1918* (London, 1983). Also, more generally, M. J. Daunton, *House and Home in the Victorian City* (London, 1983); A. S. Wohl, *The Eternal Slum* (London, 1977).

[88] Waller, *Town, City and Nation*, p. 303.

much of the country and could have a considerable educational effect.[89] This activity had a long pre-history in certain towns, such as London, Brighton, Newcastle, and Manchester.[90] But it was not until the 1890s and 1900s that Lady Health Visitors, alongside midwives, became a more professionalized occupation and began to form an integrated component of a growing network of health services organized by local authorities. By 1909 the official committee reporting on the working of the Midwives Act of 1902, was able to note that a formal division of responsibilities had become a practical norm in many places, with midwives involved for the first 10 days after a birth and health visitors thereafter.[91] Services were co-ordinated in the larger authorities under the direction of the local county or borough Medical Officers of Health, whose coverage of the local community was increasingly comprehensive once adoption of the 1907 Notification of Birth Acts enabled them quickly to locate and follow up all births (this Act became compulsory for all local authorities in 1913).

Another possibly important contemporaneous development, stressed by McKeown himself, was the regulation of the urban milk supply. This was facilitated greatly after the Dairies, Cowsheds and Milkshop Order of the Local Government Board in 1899. However, this development in isolation probably should not be accorded any particular significance. Despite the very considerable attention given to the issue of artificial feeding by the contemporary middle classes, it seems probable that breast-feeding was still the norm for the vast majority of the working-class population, although reliable information is unusually hard to find on this subject.[92] Furthermore, Dwork has recently pointed out that although purity of the milk supply at source was a necessary step, it was not sufficient in itself, as it was no remedy for the absence of domestic hygiene surrounding the subsequent preparation of infant feeds from

[89] I. H. Buchanan, 'Infant Mortality in British Coal Mining Communities, 1880–1911' (unpublished Ph.D. thesis, University of London, 1983), pp. 278–84.

[90] Missionary Biblewomen were in effect the first paid social workers acting as 'Sanitary Missionaries' under the aegis of the Ladies Sanitary Association, founded with Royal patronage in 1857 for 'the diffusion of sanitary knowledge and the promotion of physical education'. W. C. Dowling, 'The Ladies Sanitary Association and the Origins of the Health Visiting Service' (unpublished MA thesis, University of London, 1963), p. 82.

[91] Buchanan, thesis, p. 278.

[92] Dwork, *War is Good for Babies*, p. 117, cites a rare study, made by the Salford Health Committee in 1905, where only 9·8 per cent of 1,595 infants were found to be bottle-fed. If this low rate was general, then it seems quite plausible to suggest that contemporary middle-class animation over this issue derived primarily from the symbolic importance of breast-feeding at a time when the rigid sex-roles established by Victorian bourgeois culture were under cultural and political threat. However, I do not believe that gender conflicts in the middle classes can supply a satisfactory general interpretation of the history of the infant and maternal health movement at this time. For a balanced and stimulating general study of developments in infant and maternal health services, see Dwork, *War is Good for Babies*, which offers a somewhat different overall interpretation to that of three other well-known recent studies: J. Lewis, *The Politics of Motherhood* (London, 1980); A. Davin, 'Imperialism and Motherhood', *History Workshop Journal*, 5 (1978), 9–65; C. Dyhouse, 'Working Class Mothers and Infant Mortality in England 1895–1914', *Jnl Social History*, xii (1978), 248–67.

that milk.[93] A safe milk supply had to be combined with new practices of more hygienic preparation of feeds for infants, before any benefits in terms of lives saved might reasonably be expected to follow. This, then, leads us back to the fundamental importance of the two factors already mentioned: housing and instruction in hygiene. Although breast-feeding would certainly confer some protection in the first months before weaning, the root of the general problem of infants' vulnerability lay in the fundamentally unhygienic conditions and associated practices of the urban working-class home, virtually inevitable in small overcrowded households lacking their own water supply and water-closet.

Until it began to be improved from the 1890s onwards, such an environment was continuously introducing infants to bacterial organisms (in particular some strains of *Escherichia coli*) which, although not harmful to the more developed digestive system of elder children and adults, could produce fatal diarrhoea attacks in infants.[94] This was a particularly unfortunate problem since it was commonsense practice among working people that food which was safe for adults was safe for infants. It would seem helpful to point out here the significance of making a conceptual distinction between under-nutrition and malnutrition (food-poisoning) as two separable causes of what is normally referred to simply as 'malnutrition', meaning lack of adequate nourishment, without distinguishing the cause. The implication of the distinction in this context is that in order to explain high infant mortality and its subsequent improvement in Britain, it is not enough to consider, as McKeown did, only issues of per capita nutritional intake (the issue of under-nutrition) because a greater intake of food is counterproductive for the preservation of infant life, when that food is inappropriate and crawling with pathogens (the issue of malnutrition, or chronic food-poisoning).

This general interpretation receives further support from one or two local studies which have been reported recently. For instance, Parton has given an account of Huddersfield's famous 'Special Scheme Against Infantile Mortality' established by its energetic mayor, P. Broadbent, through a local Act of Parliament in 1905.[95] It was to become a model for the future operation of the Notification of Births Act 1907. A combination of volunteer Lady Health Visitors worked in partnership with local government officials under the direction of the Medical Officer of Health, Dr S. G. H. Moore, with payments to parents sanctioned for notification of births within 48 hours (but a projected milk depot was not established nor a day nursery). Huddersfield's infant mortality rate (IMR per thousand) was already much better than many large towns even before these initiatives, standing at 134 per thousand in 1900–2 (Broadbent had been Chairman of the town's Health Committee since 1893:

[93] D. Dwork, 'The Milk Option: an Aspect of the History of the Infant Welfare Movement in England 1898–1918', *Medical History*, xxxi (1987), 151–69.

[94] McKeown, *Modern Rise*, p. 122.

[95] C. Parton, 'The Infant Welfare Movement in Early Twentieth Century Huddersfield', *Jnl Regional and Local Studies*, iii, Pt. 2 (1983), 69–77.

the IMR had been a little over 150 per thousand until the latter 1890s).[96] However, apart from the notoriously bad year of 1911 (a nationwide problem due to a severe winter followed by a long hot summer), Huddersfield succeeded in continually improving on this after 1906, recording rates between 95 per thousand and 111 per thousand each year between 1907 and 1915, and thereafter even lower.[97] In another study, G. M. Nolan has found that in Derby the most important identifiable factors responsible for a drop after 1900 in the infant mortality rate were: the better feeding practices promoted by health visitors and, to a lesser extent, urban improvements.[98] Other factors addressed, such as changes in levels of earnings, in the birth-rates, or in the quality of the milk supply alone, were found to have less influence. The infant mortality rate fell dramatically from 154 per thousand in 1900–2 to 91 per thousand in 1912–14, although, unlike Huddersfield, there was then no further improvement in infant mortality in Derby until after the First World War.

Thus, whereas the reduction in the mortality of elder children and younger adults througout the last third of the nineteenth century reflected improvement of the urban environment at the strategic level outside the home, that of infants had to await the more probing and detailed regulations and the expansion of skeletal social services, which had only just begun by the turn of the twentieth century to penetrate into and improve the conditions existing in the infant's 'environment': the working-class domestic household itself.

That this should have been 'the last frontier' for the public health movement will perhaps come as no surprise, when we recall that this is the culture where 'an Englishman's home is his castle'. A strong libertarian respect for domestic privacy was the twin to the ideological position that took it as a matter of patriotic duty to resist despotic 'Bonapartist' centralizing government officials, as Chadwick had found to his cost. It seems probable, then, that part of an explanation for the popularity of the anticontagionist etiology of miasmata, dominant in mid-Victorian England, was its convenient policy implication that it was the public environment of the streets and courts, and not the domestic space, that required regulation and control. However, once contagionism had eventually gained general acceptance during the 1880s and 1890s, as a result of the publicization of the microscopic findings of bacteriological science, the castle's drawbridge was hauled down. But the portcullis might yet remain lowered by the occupants inside. To be truly effective any increased intervention by 'middle-class' agents of local authorities inside the 'working-class' home would have needed a reciprocal positive attitude from the recipients of this attention: active learning on their part in response to the teaching of their social superiors. It seems quite possible that there was indeed some kind of

[96] Ibid., 70–3.

[97] All post-1900 IMRs cited here for towns derived from: J. M. Winter, 'The Impact of the First World War on Infant Mortality in Britain', Final Report to SSRC on grant HR 5091 (1979), Table 4.

[98] G. M. Nolan, 'Infant Mortality as an Indicator of Environmental and Social Change, 1890–1939, with Special Reference to Derby' (unpublished Ph.D. thesis, University of Nottingham, 1982).

sea-change in the relevant aspects of class relations in the wake of the turbulent 1880s; but this must remain only a speculative inference, as there seems to have been little research done as yet on working-class attitudes to the preventive health services or to local authorities in general during this period.[99]

V. *Conclusions*

As the Professor of Social Medicine at Birmingham University, only the second such department to be established in the country, McKeown was one of the leading members of a post-war generation who rose high and fast into this new discipline, whilst academic enthusiasm for public health waned.[100] For them 'public health' symbolized an obsolete approach to looking after the nation's health, whereby a disparate collection of local government departments were charged with various duties aimed at preventing known pathogens from entering the environment. The institutional and administrative character of public health was formed during the difficult Victorian adolescence of public preventive medicine in Britain, when it had had to come to terms with the awkward political constraints of the prevailing ideology of *laissez-faire* and local autonomy, as discussed above. Social medicine provided an altogether grander vision of positive health enhancement for the populace through deployment of the resources and organization of the State, guided by the requirements and recommendations of modern medical science. McKeown's professional and political battle was primarily directed against those who argued for ever greater diversion of the new National Health Service resources into curative technical medicine—invasive surgery and biochemical 'treatments'—at the expense of preventive, humanist medicine—efforts to understand and modify the health implications of the environment in its widest sense, including lifestyle, behaviour, and diet.[101] McKeown's exploration of the historical record was fantastically effective in these professional, political terms, thoroughly puncturing the inflated claims to importance, on the grounds of a supposed long history of life-saving achievements, of the medical 'technocrats'.

However, in the course of this most brilliant attack on the historical claims of his main target, 'scientific medicine', McKeown's detailed historical research work led him to produce an ambitious general interpretation of the causes of mortality decline, which minimalized the role of directed human agency in

[99] See Smith, *People's Health*, p. 229 for fragmentary evidence on this. For working-class attitudes to education, see J. S. Hurt, *Elementary Schooling and the Working Classes 1860–1918* (London, 1979); there are also some stimulating general insights of relevance in G. Stedman Jones, 'Working Class Culture and Working Class Politics in London, 1870–1900: Notes on the Remaking of a Working Class', in his *Languages of Class* (London, 1983), pp. 179–238.

[100] C. Webster, 'The Origins of Social Medicine in Britain', *Society for Social History of Medicine Bulletin*, xxxviii (1986), 52–5.

[101] The most complete statement of this position by McKeown is *The Role of Medicine* (Oxford, 1979). Probably the most important seminal document endorsing this approach has been *A New Perspective on the Health of Canadians* (Ottawa, 1974), by Marc Lalonde, in his capacity as Minister of National Health and Welfare in the Canadian government.

general, not just that which could be identified as the precursor of modern hospital and clinical practice. Ironically, the innocent passenger-seat victim of McKeown's reckless driving was itself the historical ancestor of that kind of preventive and humanist medicine, which McKeown was himself advocating from the 1940s onwards. Perhaps because of his lack of a formal background in the public health tradition itself, McKeown seems to have been particularly opaque to the existence and significance of a long historical record of professional and political struggle to implement a programme of health reforms informed by a similarly environmentalist, humanist, and legislative approach to health and medical services to his own, albeit constrained by a different political and ideological climate.[102] Paradoxically as a result, his account, whilst motivated by the promotion of the best interests of social and preventive forms of medicine in the present, attains the historical aspect of a parricide!

It has been argued here that the historical epidemiological evidence presented by McKeown *et al.* does not in fact offer the conclusive and exclusive support, which it has long been assumed to do, for the contention that rising living standards and associated nutritional improvements have been the predominant source of mortality decline in Victorian and Edwardian Britain. It has been shown that a completely alternative interpretation of the same evidence is much more plausible, even within the same analytical terms of reference set by McKeown. This revisionist interpretation departs from a significant redefinition of the timing and character of the mortality decline itself, to take into account first, our new knowledge, now extended well back into the pre-industrial past, of long-term movements in the average expectation of life and, secondly, the simple point that urban and rural experiences differed, indeed diverged, during the nineteenth century. The revised account indicates a primary role for those public health measures which combated the early nineteenth-century upsurge of diseases directly resulting from the defective and insanitary urban and domestic environments created in the course of industrialization.

If the broad outlines of this reappraisal of the quantitative epidemiological evidence are accepted, then it directly follows that the true motivating 'causes' of the modern mortality decline lie in those agencies which brought about the implementation of these preventive health measures throughout the length and breadth of the country. This, therefore, entails a radically alternative concept of the nature of the causation involved. The 'invisible hand' of rising living standards, conceived as an impersonal and ultimately inevitable by-product of

[102] Thomas McKeown was born in 1912 and came to England from Canada as a postgraduate on a Rhodes Scholarship, completing an Oxford D.Phil. in the Department of Human Anatomy in 1939. He then underwent formal medical training, acquiring an MB in the University of London in 1942. Apparently, he was offered the Chair in the new discipline of Social Medicine at Birmingham in 1944 because he had so impressed the interviewing panel when he unsuccessfully applied for the Chair of Anatomy the previous year (which went to Solly Zuckerman). Hence his academic and medical background was somewhat independent of the British public health tradition, where most of those involved had had extensive practical experience as Medical Officers of Health. I am indebted to Sir George Godber for his recollections of conversations in 1943 with Sir Leonard Parsons, then Dean of the Birmingham Medical School (pers. comm., 23 July 1987).

general economic growth, no longer takes the leading role as historical guarantor of the nation's mortality decline. Indeed, economic growth in itself, even with rising real wages, seems just as likely to harm as to benefit the nation's health, witness the urban experience of the first two-thirds of the last century. It seems, then, that it all depended on how the fruits of that growth were deployed. This, in turn, depended on the cumulative net outcome of a rich history of political, ideological, scientific, and legal conflicts and battles at both national and local levels throughout the period under review.[103] Fallible, blundering, but purposive human agency is returned to centre stage in this account of the mortality decline.

Furthermore, support for such an interpretation does not derive solely from scrutiny of the nationally aggregated epidemiological evidence. There has been a prevalent tendency among the generation of post-war historians who were McKeown's contemporaries to undervalue the expansion of public health activity at the local level in the latter part of the nineteenth century, giving pride of place in their accounts instead to an earlier 'heroic age' in which the intellectual origins of the grand administrative approach to national health could be discerned. In a sense this can be seen as the direct historiographical effect of the rapid post-war decline in academic enthusiasm for 'public health' due to the competing attractions of 'social medicine'. However, the fourth section of the article has shown that once the focus of attention is shifted away from the central government departments and out to the provinces, then there is already considerable evidence, even from the modest amount of research that has so far been completed by a new generation of historians of public health, to demonstrate the importance of increasingly effective public health activity administered through local government. This was gathering momentum throughout the last half of Victoria's reign and on into the new century *pari passu* with the now-revised chronology of urban-dominated mortality decline. Thus, the proliferating density of local government functions in this period may well have played a much more important and instrumentally effective role in shaping the course of our recent history than has perhaps been previously appreciated, even with respect to such a large-scale phenomenon as the mortality decline.

Although national enabling and compulsory legislation occurred at specific points in time, its effective adoption was a locally mediated matter and varied greatly from one local authority to another—some even implemented measures

[103] One extremely rich vein of recent work and debate concerns issues in the complex history of biomedical science and its changing theory across this period. The seminal English-language contribution here was E. H. Ackernecht's Garrison Lecture of 1948, 'Anticontagionism Between 1821 and 1867', *Bull. of the History of Medicine*, xxii (1948), 562–93; and a major revisionist contribution was M. Pelling, *Cholera, Fever and English Medicine 1825–65* (London, 1978). Luckin, *Pollution and Control*, provides the most recent extended discussion of various relevant aspects of this historiography. The issues involved are too important and complex for a merely superficial treatment, which is all that space would allow here, and so I hope at some point to be able to offer a separate treatment of the significance of these matters with respect to the expansion of public and preventive health measures.

in advance of such parliamentary legislation.[104] These complications of local political and administrative history will confound any attempt to test rigorously the interpretation being offered here through analysis of aggregate national- or even county-level statistics, alone. Properly researched local studies are required, where there is the chance of refining our detailed understanding of the nature of the relationship between the deployment of specific preventive services and facilities and the changing local social and epidemiological patterns.[105] However, these are still all too rare and are unlikely to be perceived as attractive research projects until there has been a conceptual emancipation from the orthodox assumptions regarding the primacy of a 'nutritional determinism'.

It has been the principal aim of this article to encourage the exploration of such a new approach, which examines agency not process. In order to re-open the question of causation, it has been necessary to expose to the full the limitations and inadequacies of the established orthodoxy. In view of the sustained nature of the attack mounted here on the conventional wisdom, it should be emphasized that the argument is not that improving nutrition and living standards were entirely unimportant in accounting for the mortality decline, but that the role of a battling public health ideology, politics, and medicine operating of necessity through local government, is more correctly seen as the principal causal agency involved. It is necessary to rescue those who gave their lives to the struggle for the nation's health from 'the enormous condescension of posterity', to borrow a famous historiographical clarion call.

Finally, a comment on the wider context of the subject-matter. As mentioned in the introduction, the McKeown thesis continues to animate debate beyond the bounds of British historiography, amongst economists, demographers, and policy scientists generally. Britain's experience of industrialization continues to be a particularly influential model, not just because it was the first industrial nation but because its history in these respects is considered to be established on an unusually firm and extensive empirical basis. The quantitative data available are particularly rich and of high quality, perfectly exemplified in the detailed epidemiological evidence analysed by McKeown. Much of this was

[104] Another example of this, apart from the Huddersfield scheme mentioned in the text above, would be the famous 'Leicester System' of notification and isolation of infectious diseases pioneered in the mid-nineteenth century by Sir James Simpson. See Hardy, 'Smallpox in London', pp. 122–3. More generally on the varied histories of local governments' politics and administrations in the nineteenth century, see, for example, Hennock, *Fit and Proper Persons*, D. Fraser, *Urban Politics in Victorian England* (Leicester, 1976), and A. Offer, *Property and Politics 1870–1914* (Cambridge, 1981).

[105] The Ph.D. thesis by Buchanan (see n. 89) is an exemplary study of this sort, which any prospective research student would benefit from reading. This involved a comparison of eight communities including two from Scotland. An important novel finding, which could only emerge as a result of the local perspective adopted there, was that at least until 1911–12 the relative incidence of infantile diarrhoea seems to have been strongly influenced not simply by general 'urban insanitation', but more specifically by the relative prevalence and behaviour of house-flies, as a disease vector, and that this, in turn, was determined by the local authority's attitude and policy with respect to the proximity of rubbish tips to residential housing.

generated by all the government-sponsored surveillance and inquiry that was undertaken throughout the nineteenth century by a host of departments and agencies,[106] which is a nice irony since Britain is supposedly a leading and extreme example of successful economic and demographic growth achieved mainly through the operation of free market forces and with a minimum of effective state intervention.[107]

Indeed, McKeown's work on Britain continues to provide the only thoroughly researched empirical support for the extreme *laissez-faire* position that health and welfare gains may be generated most effectively merely as a by-product of economic growth and that government policies should, therefore, simply be directed at maximizing economic growth alone (which for the liberal economic purist means minimizing government in general, and all forms of market intervention). If it should emerge, however, that, to the contrary, even in this historical case, per capita national income growth and associated real wage gains were no guarantee of higher life expectancies and that it was, after all, social and medical intervention, albeit unevenly implemented and only weakly centralized, that was the principal source of the nation's health improvements before the First World War, then clearly the authenticity and 'realism' of the case against interventionist social welfare and health policies must suffer some loss of intellectual credibility.

If the British historical case has any direct lessons to offer, it would seem to be that a significant life-saving 'expansion in the health infrastructure' of a country does not *necessarily* require advanced 'medical technology' nor necessarily require, at least initially, the political act of 'creating a universal free health service'.[108] Of course, the latter must certainly remain an ultimate and highly desirable goal, at least for any society which actively seeks the positive promotion of its citizens' health, not normally a politically contentious aim. It may well also be crucial for achievement of the quickest route to low mortality. However, there may be other *effective*, albeit slower, paths available, especially in circumstances where either economics or politics are against the speedier but more expensive and centralized route, as was the case in Victorian Britain. Here, the history of mortality decline shows that committed local government, or its analogous parochial institutions, can have quite considerable potential and scope as an agency to promote health improvements and general social change, if led by appropriately exhortatory but flexible central direction.

[106] Such as the vast web of over 2,000 paid district registrars who, from July 1837 onwards, relayed quarterly the detailed mortality information collected from their locality to the central office of the R.-G., forming the database discussed in this article.

[107] A recent example, from two relatively well-informed authors: 'Thus, McKeown may be correct in arguing that national public health measures were not very important in the reduction of mortality in England and Wales during the nineteenth century'; S. R. Johansson and C. Mosk, 'Exposure, Resistance and Life Expectancy: Disease and Death during the Economic Development of Japan, 1900–1960', *Pop. Studies*, xli (1987), 218.

[108] Caldwell, 'Routes to Low Mortality', p. 205; and see fuller quotation cited above, at n. 26.

[12]

The rise of surveillance medicine

David Armstrong

Guy's and St. Thomas's Medical and Dental School, University of London.

Abstract Despite the obvious triumph of a medical theory and practice grounded in the hospital, a new medicine based on the surveillance of normal populations can be identified as emerging in the twentieth century. This new Surveillance Medicine involves a fundamental remapping of the spaces of illness. This includes the problematisation of normality, the redrawing of the relationship between symptom, sign and illness, and the localisation of illness outside the corporal space of the body. It is argued that this new medicine has important implications for the constitution of identity in the late twentieth century.

Introduction

Perhaps the most important contribution for understanding the advent of modern medicine has been the work of the medical historian Ackerknecht (1967), who described the emergence of a number of distinct medical perspectives during the early and late eighteenth century. In brief, he identified an earlier phase of Library Medicine in which the classical learning of the physician seemed more important than any specific knowledge of illness. This gave way to Bedside Medicine when physicians began to address the problems of the practical management of illness, particularly in terms of the classification of the patient's symptoms. In its turn Bedside Medicine was replaced by Hospital Medicine with the advent of hospitals in Paris at the end of the eighteenth century.

Hospital Medicine was clearly an important revolution in medical thinking. Also known as the Clinic, pathological medicine, Western medicine and biomedicine, it has survived and extended itself over the last two centuries to become the dominant model of medicine in the modern world. Even so, a significant alternative model of medicine can be discerned as materialising during the twentieth century around the observation of seemingly healthy populations.

Medical spaces

The commanding medical framework of Hospital Medicine first emerged at the turn of the eighteenth century with the appearance of the now familiar medical procedures of the clinical examination, the post-mortem, and hospitalisation. Foucault (1973) has described these changes in terms of a new 'spatialisation' of illness.

Primary spatialisation referred to the cognitive mapping of the different elements of illness. In the early eighteenth century, under a regime of Bedside Medicine, illness was coterminous with the symptoms that patients experienced and reported. A headache or abdominal pain was the illness. This two-dimensional model of illness in which symptoms were classified as in a table, was replaced by Hospital Medicine in which the relationship of symptoms and illness was reconfigured into a three-dimensional framework involving symptom, sign and pathology. In this new arrangement, the symptom, as of old, was a marker of illness as experienced by the patient, but to this indicator was added the sign – an intimation of disease as elicited by the attentive physician through the clinical examination. For example, the patient's symptom of abdominal pain might be linked to the sign of abdominal tenderness that the physician could discover; but neither symptom nor sign in itself constituted illness: both pointed to an underlying lesion that was the disease. In contrast to the previous regime of Bedside Medicine in which the overt symptom was the illness, the 'clinical picture' as drawn by both symptom and sign enabled the pathology that existed beneath experience to be inferred. This 'clinico-pathological correlation' marked a new relationship between surface and depth. Accordingly, the subtle characteristics of an abdominal pain which in an earlier time would have comprised the illness were now linked with the findings of the clinical examination (the signs), to indicate the presence of a hidden pathological lesion.

Secondary spatialisation referred to the location of the lesion in relation to the body of the patient. The clinician's task under Bedside Medicine was to identify and classify illness through the distinctiveness of clusters of symptoms. Thus, the mobility of illness through the body could be captured by closely monitoring the sequencing of symptoms. In Hospital Medicine, on the other hand, the physician had to infer from symptoms and signs the underlying pathological lesion within the patient's body. In consequence, for the first time, the patient's body as a three-dimensional object became the focus of medical attention. This in turn led to the invention of the classical techniques of the clinical examination – inspection, percussion, palpation and auscultation – that allowed the volume of the human body to be mapped, and to the spread of the postmortem as a procedure to identify incontrovertibly the exact nature of the hidden lesion.

Finally, tertiary spatialisation referred to the locus of illness in the context of health care activity. Under Bedside Medicine, illness was best identified in the natural space of the patient's own home; in Hospital Medicine it required the 'neutral' space of the hospital so that the indicators of the underlying lesion might by properly identified without the contaminants of extraneous 'noise'. This facet of the new medicine was marked by the subsequent dominance of the clinic as the prime centre for health care provision as hospitals were rapidly built throughout Europe.

The novel spatialisation of illness that marked the new pathological alignment of Hospital Medicine came to dominate the nineteenth century and has succeeded in maintaining its ascendancy in the twentieth. To be sure, the techniques for identifying the hidden lesions of the body have grown more sophisticated. Indeed, Jewson (1976) has argued that the addition of laboratory investigations to the repertoire of clinical indicators of disease towards the end of the nineteenth century marked yet another medical model that he called Laboratory Medicine, not least because the body of the patient became even more objectified and the identity of the 'sick man' further lost. But, while clinical investigations in the form of X-rays, pathology reports, blood analyses, etc, marked an extension of the technical apparatus of medical procedures it did not challenge the underlying spatialisation of illness nor the logic of clinical practice: experience and illness were still linked through surface and depth, inference of the true nature of the lesion still dominated medical thinking, and the hospital still – indeed even more so – remained the centre of health care activity.

Despite the clear hegemony of Hospital Medicine over the last two centuries, it is the contention of this paper that a new medicine based on the surveillance of normal populations can be identified as beginning to emerge early in the twentieth century. This new Surveillance Medicine involves a fundamental remapping of the spaces of illness. Not only is the relationship between symptom, sign and illness redrawn but the very nature of illness is reconstrued. And illness begins to leave the three-dimensional confine of the volume of the human body to inhabit a novel extracorporal space.

Problematisation of the normal

Hospital Medicine was only concerned with the ill patient in whom a lesion might be identified, but a cardinal feature of Surveillance Medicine is its targeting of everyone. Surveillance Medicine requires the dissolution of the distinct clinical categories of healthy and ill as it attempts to bring everyone within its network of visibility. Therefore one of the earliest expressions of Surveillance Medicine – and a vital precondition for its continuing proliferation – was the problematisation of the normal.

No doubt there were nineteenth century manifestations of the idea that a person – or more frequently, a population – hung precariously between health and illness (such as the attempts to control the health of prostitutes near military establishments with the Contagious Diseases Acts), but it was the child in the twentieth century that became the first target of the full deployment of the concept. The significance of the child was that it underwent growth and development: there was therefore a constant threat that proper stages might not be negotiated that in its turn justified close medical observation. The establishment and wide provision of antenatal care, birth notification, baby clinics, milk depots, infant welfare clinics, day nurseries, health visiting and nursery schools ensured that the early years of child development could be closely monitored (Armstrong 1983). For example, the School Medical (later Health) Service not only provided a traditional 'treatment' clinic, but also provided an 'inspection' clinic that screened all school children at varying times for both incipient and manifest disease, and enabled visits to children's homes by the school nurse to report on conditions and monitor progress (HMSO 1975).

In parallel with the intensive surveillance of the body of the infant during the early twentieth century, the new medical gaze also turned to focus on the unformed mind of the child. As with physical development, psychological growth was construed as inherently problematic, precariously normal. The initial solution was for psychological well-being to be monitored and its abnormal forms identified. (The contemporary work of Freud that located adult psychopathology in early childhood experience can be seen as part of this approach.) The nervous child, the delicate child, the eneuretic child, the neuropathic child, the maladjusted child, the difficult child, the neurotic child, the over-sensitive child, the unstable child and the solitary child, all emerged as a new way of seeing a potentially hazardous normal childhood (Armstrong 1983, Rose 1985, 1990).

If there is one image that captures the nature of the machinery of observation that surrounded the child in those early decades of the twentieth century, it might well be the height and weight growth chart. Such charts contain a series of gently curving lines, each one representing the growth trajectory of a population of children. Each line marked the 'normal' experience of a child who started his or her development at the beginning of the line. Thus, every child could be assigned a place on the chart and, with successive plots, given a personal trajectory. But the individual trajectory only existed in a context of general population trajectories: the child was unique yet uniqueness could only be read from a composition which summed the unique features of all children. A test of normal growth assumed the possibility of abnormal growth, yet how, from knowledge of other children's growth, could the boundaries of normality be identified? When was a single point on the growth and weight chart, to which the sick child was reduced, to be interpreted as abnormal? Abnormality was a relative phenomenon. A child was abnormal with reference to other children, and even then only by degrees. In effect, the growth charts were significant for distributing the body of the child in a field delineated not by the absolute categories of physiology and pathology, but by the characteristics of the normal population.

The socio-medical survey, first introduced during World War II to assess the perceived health status of the population, represented the recruitment to medicine of an efficient technical tool that both measured and reaffirmed the extensiveness of morbidity. The survey revealed the ubiquity of illness, that health was simply a precarious state. The post-war fascination with the weakening person-patient interface – such as in the notion of the clinical iceberg which revealed that most illness lay outside of health care provision (Last 1963), or of illness behaviour which showed that people experience symptoms most days of their lives yet very few were taken to the doctor (Mechanic and Volkart 1960) – was evidence that the patient was inseparable from the person because all persons were becoming patients.

The survey also demanded alternative ways of measuring illness that would encompass nuances of variation from some community-based idea of the normal. Hence the development of health profile questionnaires, subjective health measures, and other survey instruments with which to identify the proto-illness and its sub-clinical manifestations, and latterly the increasing importance of qualitative methodologies that best capture illness as an experience rather than as a lesion (Fitzpatrick *et al.* 1984).

The results of the socio-medical survey threw into relief the important distinction between the biomedical model's binary separation of health and disease, and the survey's continuous distribution of variables throughout the population. The survey classified bodies on a continuum: there were no inherent distinctions between a body at one end and one at the other, their only differences were the spaces that separated them. (Perhaps the celebrated debate between Pickering and Platt on whether blood pressure was bimodally or continuously distributed in the population was another manifestation of this disharmony between alternative ways of reading the nature of illness (Pickering 1962)). The referent external to the population under study, which had for almost two centuries governed the analysis of bodies, was replaced by the relative positions of all bodies. Surveillance Medicine fixed on these gaps between people to establish that everyone was normal yet no-one was truly healthy.

For a long time, in the past, death came in the shape of a black-cloaked figure to mark the end of life: such deaths were natural in as much as it was nature that came to reclaim her own. The advent of Hospital Medicine two hundred years ago transformed the natural death into the pathological one (Foucault 1973). Death did not come from outside life, but was contained within life from the moment of birth – or, more correctly, conception – as physiological and pathological processes battled for supremacy. (Though it took biomedicine nearly a century to abolish the designation of death from 'natural causes' (Smith 1979).) Since the 1960s, the analysis of death has again shifted. Medical professionals are now encouraged to persuade the dying to speak the truth about their death to the listening ear (Armstrong 1987). The surveillance machinery is trained to hear the anxieties of the dying and through reflection normalise them: the natural death, the pathological death, and now the normal death.

Dissemination of intervention

The blurring of the distinction between health and illness, between the normal and the pathological, meant that health care intervention could no longer focus almost exclusively on the body of the patient in the hospital bed. Medical surveillance would have to leave the hospital and penetrate into the wider population.

The new 'social' diseases of the early twentieth century – tuberculosis, venereal disease, problems of childhood, the neuroses, etc – were the initial targets for novel forms of health care, but the main expansion in the techniques of monitoring occurred after World War II when an emphasis on comprehensive health care, and primary and community care, underpinned the deployment of explicit surveillance services such as screening and health promotion. But these later radiations out into the community were prefigured by two important inter-war experiments in Britain and the United States that demonstrated the practicality of monitoring precarious normality in a whole population.

The British innovation was the Pioneer Health Centre at Peckham in south London (Pearse and Crocker 1943). The Centre offered ambulatory health care to local families that chose to register – but the care placed special emphasis on continuous observation. From the design of its buildings that permitted clear lines of sight to its social club that facilitated silent observation of patients' spontaneous activity, every development within the Peckham Centre was a conscious attempt to make visible the web of human relations. Perhaps the Peckham key summarises the dream of this new surveillance apparatus. The key and its accompanying locks were designed (though never fully installed) to give access to the building and its facilities for each individual of every enrolled family. But as well as giving freedom of access, the key enabled a precise record of all movement within the building. 'Suppose the scientist should wish to know what individuals are using the swimming bath or consuming milk, the records made by the use of the key give him this information' (Pearse and Crocker 1943:76–7).

Only 7 per cent of those attending the Peckham Centre were found to be truly healthy; and if everyone had pathology then everyone would need observing. An important mechanism for operationalising this insight was the introduction of extensive screening programmes in the decades following World War II. However, screening, whether individual, population, multi-phasic, or opportunistic, represented a bid by Hospital Medicine to reach out beyond its confines – with all its accompanying limitations. First, it was too focused on the body. It meant that screening still confronted the localised lesion (or, more commonly, proto-lesion) within the body and ignored the newly emerging mobile threats that were insinuated throughout the community, constantly reforming into new dangers. Second, techniques to screen the population have always had to confront points of resistance, particularly the unwillingness of many to participate in these new procedures. The solution to these difficulties had already begun to emerge earlier in the twentieth century with the development of a strategy that involved giving responsibility for surveillance to patients themselves. A strategy of health promotion could potentially circumvent the problems inherent in illness screening.

The process through which the older techniques of hygiene were transformed into the newer strategy of health promotion occurred over several decades during the twentieth century. But perhaps one of the earliest experiments that attempted the transition was the collaborative venture between the city of Fargo in North Dakota and the Commonwealth Fund in 1923. The nominal objective of the project was the incorporation of child health services into the permanent programme of the health department and public school system (Brown 1929) and an essential component of this plan was the introduction of health education in Fargo's schools, supervised by Maud Brown. Brown's campaign was, she wrote, 'an attempt to secure the instant adoption by every child of a completely adequate program of health behaviour'. (Brown, 1929:19)

Prior to 1923 the state had required that elements of personal hygiene he taught in Fargo's schools 'but there was no other deliberately planned link between the study of physical well-being and the realization of physical well-being'. The Commonwealth Fund project was a two pronged strategy. While the classroom was the focus for a systematic campaign of health behaviour, a periodic medical and dental examination both justified and monitored the educational intervention. In effect 'health teaching, health supervision and their effective coordination' were linked together. In Fargo 'health teaching departed from the hygiene textbook, and after a vitalizing change, found its way back to the textbook'. (Brown 1929:19) From its insistence on four hours of physical exercises a day – two of them outdoors – to its concern with the mental maturation of the child, Fargo represented the realisation of a new public health dream of surveillance in which everyone is brought into the vision of the benevolent eye of medicine through the medicalisation of everyday life.

After World War II this approach began to be deployed with more vigour in terms of a strategy of health promotion. Concerns with diet, exercise, stress, sex, etc, become the vehicles for encouraging the community to survey itself. The ultimate triumph of Surveillance Medicine would be its internalisation by all the population.

The tactics of Hospital Medicine have been those of exile and enclosure. The lesion marked out those who were different in a great binary system of illness and health, and processed them (in the hospital) in an attempt to rejoin them to the healthy. The tactics of the new Surveillance Medicine, on the other hand, have been pathologisation and vigilance. The techniques of health promotion recognise that health no longer exists in a strict binary relationship to illness, rather health and illness belong to an ordinal scale in which the healthy can become healthier, and health can co-exist with illness; there is now nothing incongruous in having cancer yet believing oneself to be essentially healthy (Kagawa-Singer 1993). But such a trajectory towards the healthy state can only be achieved if the whole population comes within the purview of surveillance: a world in which everything is normal and at the same time precariously abnormal, and in which a future that can be transformed remains a constant possibility.

Spatialisation of risk factors

The extension of a medical eye over all the population is the outward manifestation of the new framework of Surveillance Medicine. But more fundamentally there is a concomitant shift in the primary spatialisation of illness as the relationship between symptom, sign and illness are reconfigured. From a linkage based on surface and depth, all become components in a more general arrangement of predictive factors.

A symptom or sign for Hospital Medicine was produced by the lesion and consequently could be used to infer the existence and exact nature of the disease. Surveillance Medicine takes these discrete elements of symptom, sign and disease and subsumes them under a more general category of 'factor' that points to, though does not necessarily produce, some future illness. Such inherent contingency is embraced by the novel and pivotal medical concept of *risk*. It is no longer the symptom or sign pointing tantalisingly at the hidden pathological truth of disease, but the risk factor opening up a space of future illness potential.

Symptoms and signs are only important for Surveillance Medicine to the extent that they can be re-read as risk factors. Equally, the illness in the form of the disease or lesion that had been the end-point of clinical inference under Hospital Medicine is also deciphered as a risk factor in as much as one illness becomes a risk factor for another. Symptom, sign, investigation and disease thereby become conflated into an infinite chain of risks. A headache may be a risk factor for high blood pressure (hypertension), but high blood pressure is simply a risk factor for another illness (stroke). And whereas symptoms, signs and diseases were located in the body, the risk factor encompasses any state or event from which a probability of illness can be calculated. This means that Surveillance Medicine turns increasingly to an extracorporal space – often represented by the notion of 'lifestyle' – to identify the precursors of future illness. Lack of exercise and a high fat diet therefore can be joined with angina, high blood cholesterol and diabetes as risk factors for heart disease. Symptoms, signs, illnesses, and health behaviours simply become indicators for yet other symptoms, signs, illnesses and health behaviours. Each illness of Hospital Medicine existed as the discrete endpoint in the chain of clinical discovery: in Surveillance Medicine each illness is simply a nodal point in a network of health status monitoring. The problem is less illness *per se* but the semi-pathological pre-illness at-risk state.

Under Hospital Medicine the symptom indicated the underlying lesion in a static relationship; true, the 'silent' lesion could exist without indicating its presence but eventually the symptomatic manifestations erupted into clinical consciousness. The risk factor, however, has no fixed nor necessary relationship with future illness, it simply opens up a space of possibility. Moreover, the risk factor exists in a mobile relationship with other risks, appearing and disappearing, aggregating and disaggregating, crossing spaces within and without the corporal body.

In terms of secondary spatialisation Hospital Medicine operated within the three-dimensional corporal volume of the sick patient. In contrast, the risk factor network of Surveillance Medicine is read across an extracorporal and temporal space. In part, the new space of illness is the community. Community space incorporates the physical agglomeration of buildings and homes and their concomitant risks to health, though risks from the physical environment reflect more on nineteenth century concerns with sanitation and hygiene (Armstrong 1993). Twentieth century surveillance begins to focus more on the grid of interactions between people in the community. This multifaceted population space encompasses the physical gap between bodies that needs constant monitoring to guard against transmission of contagious diseases, such as tuberculosis, venereal disease and childhood infections. But the space between bodies is also, from the early twentieth century, a psycho-social space which is marked by the shift in the psychiatric/medical gaze from the binary problem of insanity/sanity to the generalised population problems of the neuroses (which affect everyone) (Armstrong 1979), and the crystallisation of individual attitudes, beliefs, cognitions and behaviours, limits to self-efficacy, ecological concerns, and aspects of lifestyle that have become such a preoccupation of progressive health care tactics.

A further important feature of the new population space of illness is its emphasis on a temporal axis. Hospital Medicine contained temporal elements but relied essentially on a cross-sectional nosographic technique: patients had to be classified according to the nature of their internal lesion so that appropriate therapy could be introduced. Diseases, of course, had antecedent causes and they had resulting consequences, but these aspects of illness were analysed from the point of the present: what caused the lesion that presented (better to guide therapy) and what was the future prognosis for the patient? The new medical discourse of the late twentieth century opens up this static model so as to place illness in a wider temporal context. Perhaps this analysis is particularly evident in twentieth century concerns with the problem of development, especially in its relation to children (and recently 'ageing'), but temporal concerns can also clearly be seen in the mid-twentieth century identification of the category of 'chronic illness' as a major medical problem; and it can be identified in the temporal space in which risk factors materialised. Risk factors, above all else, are pointers to a potential, yet unformed, eventuality. For example, the abnormal cells discovered in cervical cytology screening do not in themselves signify the existence of disease, but only indicate its future possibility. The techniques of Surveillance Medicine – screening, surveys, and public health campaigns – would all address this problem in terms of searching for temporal regularities, offering anticipatory care, and attempting to transform the future by changing the health attitudes and health behaviours of the present.

Illness therefore comes to inhabit a temporal space. Illness has a life history: from a series of minor perturbations that indicated its early presence to its 'pre-' forms, from its subtle indicators of being to its overt clinical manifestations, from its first appearance to the medical attempts to alter its natural history. The sub-division of prevention into primary, secondary and tertiary forms summarises the points at which medicine can intervene in the great new cycle of illness. The clinical techniques of the hospital had invested the three-dimensional body of the patient; surveillance analyses a four-dimensional space in which a temporal axis is joined to the living density of corporal volume. Pathology in Hospital Medicine had been a concrete lesion; in Surveillance Medicine illness becomes a point of perpetual becoming.

Reconfiguration of identity

The advent of Hospital Medicine not only signified a new way of thinking about and dealing with illness, it also marked out the three-dimensional outline of the familiar passive and analysable human body. From the primary spatialisation of illness that linked surface and depth, through the techniques of clinical method that celebrated the volume of that body, to its unencumbered observation in the hospital ward, the medicine of the Clinic defined and redefined a discrete corporal space (Foucault 1973). In effect, an identity was forged in the practical anatomy of clinical work.

The integrity of the corporal body co-existed with a form of medicine that kept illness and health separated by a conceptual and practical gesture; the dissolution of the boundary between health and illness under a regime of Surveillance Medicine implies a loss of that anatomical detachment. Identity then begins to crystallise in a novel temporal and multidimensional space whose main axes are the population – within which risk is located and from which risk is calculated – and a temporal space of possibility. The implication is that self and community begin to lose their separateness.

Thus, Surveillance Medicine maps a different form of identity as its monitoring gaze sweeps across innovative spaces of illness potential. The new dimensionality of identity is to be found in the shift from a three-dimensional body as the locus of illness to the four-dimensional space of the time-community. Its boundaries are the permeable lines that separate a precarious normality from a threat of illness. Its experiences are inscribed in the progressive realignments implied by emphases on symptoms in the eighteenth century, signs in the nineteenth and early twentieth, and risk factors in the late twentieth century. Its calculability is given in the never-ending computation of multiple and interrelated risks. Its subject and object is the 'risky self' (Ogden 1995).

The rise of a major new form of medicine during the twentieth century that offers a fundamental reformulation of the epistemological, cognitive and physical map of illness – and, it might be added, its very close alliance with social sciences – merits recognition. But its real significance lies in the way in which a surveillance machinery deployed throughout a population to monitor precarious normality delineates a new temporalised risk identity.

Address for correspondence: Dr David Armstrong, Department of General Practice UMDS, Guy's Hospital, London. SE1 9RT.

Acknowledgements

I am grateful to Jane Ogden for helpful comments on earlier drafts of this paper.

References

Ackerknecht, E. (1967) *Medicine at the Paris Hospital 1774–1848*. Baltimore: Johns Hopkins.

Armstrong, D. (1979) Madness and coping, *Sociology of Health and Illness*, 2, 293–316.

Armstrong, D. (1983) *Political Anatomy of the Body: Medical Knowledge in Britain the Twentieth Century*. Cambridge: Cambridge University Press.

Armstrong, D. (1987) Silence and truth in death and dying, *Social Science and Medicine*, 24, 651–7.

Armstrong, D. (1993) Public health spaces and the fabrication of identity, *Sociology*, 27, 393–410.
Brown, M. A. (1929) *Teaching Health in Fargo*. New York: Commonwealth Fund.
Fitzpatrick, R. Hinton, J., Newman, S., Scambler, G. and Thompson, J. *The Experience of Illness*. London: Tavistock.
Foucault, M. (1973) *The Birth of the Clinic: An Archaeology of Medical Perception*. London: Tavistock.
Jewson, N. (1976) The disappearance of the sick-man from medical cosmologies: 1770–1870, *Sociology*, 10, 225–44.
Kagawa-Singer, M. (1993) Redefining health: living with cancer, *Social Science and Medicine*, 37, 295–304.
Last, J. M. (1963) The clinical iceberg, *Lancet*, 2, 28–30.
Mechanic, D. and Volkart, E. H. (1960) Illness behaviour and medical diagnoses, *Journal of Health and Human Behaviour*, 1, 86–90.
Ogden, J. (1995) Psychosocial theory and the creation of the risky self, *Social Science and Medicine*, 40, 3, 409–15.
Pearse, I. H. and Crocker, L. H. (1943) *The Peckham Experiment: A Study in the Living Structure of Society*. London: George Allen and Unwin.
Pickering, G. (1962) Logic and hypertension, *Lancet*, 2, 149.
Rose, N. (1985) *The Psychological Complex*. London: Routledge and Kegan Paul.
Rose, N. (1990) *Governing the Soul: The Shaping of the Private Self*. London: Routledge.
Smith, F. B. (1979) *The People's Health: 1830–1910*. London: Croom Helm.
The School Health Service: *1908–74*. London: HMSO (1975).

Part IV
Research Issues

[13]

Ethical Principles for the Conduct of Human Subject Research: Population-Based Research and Ethics

Larry Gostin

Ethical principles for the protection of human subjects in clinical research are now well recognized,[1] and rooted in the inherent worth and dignity of the individual.

Respect for persons recognizes people as autonomous agents and requires that their choices be observed. For persons who are not fully autonomous, the principle of respect for persons requires that they are protected from risks and adverse consequences of research, even sometimes excluded from research.

Beneficence (do good) and *non-maleficence* (do no harm) are complementary ethical principles that impose affirmative duties on researchers to maximize any benefits for subjects and minimize any risks. Thus, researchers must go beyond mere respect for a person's choices. The researcher must be vigilant to ensure that the subject receives all possible benefits and avoids all possible harms from participating in the research.

Justice requires that human beings be treated equally unless there is a strong ethical justification for treating them differently. Thus, the distribution of benefits and burdens in research should be equitable. In thinking about justice toward subjects, researchers need to consider equitable selection so that individuals are chosen on the basis of factors clearly relevant to the problems being studied. Researchers also need to consider equitable distribution of advantages to research subjects and others who could benefit from the knowledge gained by the research.

These ethical principles have found expression in international guidelines for the conduct of clinical research[2], and have been codified in national statutes and regulations, particularly in the developed world.[3]

Ethical principles help support autonomy and self-determination, protect the vulnerable, and promote the welfare and equality of human beings. But traditional ethics focuses primarily on individual rights and duties, and does not always see individuals as part of wider social orders and communities. A person dominated medical ethic is insufficient for the task of setting moral and human rights boundaries around the conduct of research on populations.

This paper provides a halting first step in organizing a set of ethical guidelines for the conduct of population-based research, surveillance and practice. These principles are not distinct from, but an expansion of, traditional ethics. Research ethics, which matured significantly from the Nuremberg Code through to the Helsinki IV and the CIOMS guidelines, nourished the individual human spirit. Ethical principles should have a similarly profound impact in the development of science and the protection of human populations in the 1990s and beyond.

The application of ethical principles to populations

Ethical principles applied to larger groups of people or populations are designed to protect the human dignity, integrity, self-determination, confidentiality, rights, and health of populations and the people comprising them. The kinds of social groupings encompassed in this definition include communities, cultures, social orders, and populations of various description including racial, ethnic, religious, cultural, and other minorities. Ethical principles also establish positive moral responsibilities of persons and authorities which sponsor, conduct, or oversee research on populations. This includes governments, funders, and investigators in the country which embarks on the research as well as the country which hosts the research.

The importance of group identity, and of treating social communities with dignity and respect, is increasingly well recognized. Human beings gain security, happiness, and enjoyment by forming networks based upon their special national or sub-national characteristics.[4] Respect and beneficence for populations requires researchers to observe choices made by local communities, and to avoid any activity which stigmatizes, demeans, harms, or disintegrates human populations, intentionally or inadvertently.

The term "population-based research" is broadly defined to include all research and practice performed on, or which affects, groups of people or populations. This includes epidemiologic research and surveillance, and intervention epidemiology, including field trials for drugs or vaccines.

Population based research, surveillance, and practice can have extraordinary benefits and risks. The potential for human good, measured in improvement of health and decreased morbidity and mortality from population-based research and practice represents one of the great triumphs of science in the 20th century. But, the potential to cause harm to human beings and the groups they comprise is also much greater.

Population-based research and practice affect not only individual research subjects but integrated groups of people, sometimes of considerable size. This can entail large scale collection, storage, transfer, and use of sensitive health care, demographic, social, and behavioral data. Modern field trials can also actively intervene in the behaviors, lifestyles, social and family interactions, or environments, of communities. Levine provides illustrations of risks to societies such as introduction of a new microorganism, spread of infection to persons outside the trial, and premature or inappropriate dissemination of findings or opinions of researchers which may result in harmful changes in behavior, false hopes for cures, or lowered self-image.[5]

Foundational principles must also be developed to protect the dignity and integrity of all populations including vulnerable populations which are non-dominant, poor, disenfranchised, compromised, persecuted, or restricted. This paper enunciates five such principles: (i) the overriding imperative to protect the health and well-being of populations, (ii) respect for populations and their right to self-determination, (iii) protection of vulnerable populations and the need for special justifications for research, (iv) protecting the privacy, integrity, and self-esteem of populations, and (v) the equitable distribution of benefits to populations and the importance of building infra-structure.

First do no harm

The Geneva Declaration does not specifically cover human subject research, but restates the first principle of medicine enunciated in the Hippocratic oath—a doctor's first duty is to his or her patient.[6] In the context of population-based research the investigator has a dual responsibility to individual subjects and to the populations they are part of. The first principle in this area of ethics is not to harm the subject population.

The duty not to harm is grounded in the principles of beneficent treatment of, and respect for, populations. Application of the principle of beneficence toward individuals in biomedical research often is measured by a favorable benefit to harm ratio. The potential benefits of a new pharmaceutical or vaccine must be well understood from laboratory models, the risks must be reasonable, and the adverse effects must be carefully monitored and controlled.

Beneficence toward populations certainly requires a favorable balance of potential benefits and harms. But, the concern is not merely with the physical health of the human subject, but also with the potential benefits and harms to the group or culture that is being studied. Human subjects, for example, may be medically protected, but the research may be of little value to, or reflect poorly on, the group to be studied.

A prerequisite of ethical research is that it is based upon a sound objective recognized as a priority in the country to be studied. The research, therefore, should be clearly relevant to the public health problems in the local community. Is it ethically justified to conduct research in a host country for the overwhelming benefit of another country? Research of intrinsic scientific value or a value established in one country may not be valid if conducted in another country which has little interest in, or need for, that scientific information. Research to address a pressing public health problem in developed countries (e.g. coronary heart disease) may be irrelevant in developing countries which may be more concerned with diarrheal disease and maternal-child health. If the preponderant benefits of a study are in the source, rather than in the host country, a strong justification would have to be made to initiate the research.[7]

The ethical question is not only whether the research is needed in the host country, but also whether it is wanted. Respect for populations suggests that representatives who can legitimately speak for the people ought to have control over whether, and how, research is conducted, and how the outcomes of research are distributed and used to benefit the population.

Good science is always an overarching requirement of ethical research. The quality of research is established where the scientific protocol is reviewed in both countries using processes that are developed in culturally and legally appropriate ways in each country. Good scientific research, wanted and reviewed by all relevant parties, ultimately provides the best protection for human populations.

Respect for people and populations: Individual consent, permission and community consensus

The focus on individualism in traditional ethics is most clear when the principle of respect for persons is examined. The primary way to respect individuals is to abide by their choices, whether or not others believe their choices are wise or beneficial. "To show lack of respect for an autonomous agent is to repudiate that person's considered judgments, to deny an individual the freedom to act on those considered judgments, or to withhold information necessary to make a considered judgment."[8] Autonomy and self-determination are illuminated by the antagonistic principle of paternalism, where decisions are made for, not by, individuals because others know better what is in that person's interests.

Since the Nuremberg Code, international human rights declarations have focused on autonomy rather than paternalism. International law perceives individuals as capable of exercising the power of choice. People must be free to decide whether to participate in research or to withdraw their participation without any influence of coercion, fraud, deceit, or constraint.[9] Helsinki IV[10] and the CIOMS Proposed Biomedical Research Guidelines[11] focus on the need for advance information on research methods, objectives, benefits, and risks to allow an informed choice.

Autonomy and individual consent are invaluable principles which allow competent persons to keep control over health and research decisions. Ethical research always places the desires and needs of the subject over those of the investigator.[12] The principle of consent thus helps prevent abuse by overzealous governments or researchers who are sometimes under great pressure to conduct expeditious and successful research into the overwhelming health problems facing both developed and developing countries.

The limits of consent as a method of preserving human dignity and health, however, are increasingly well understood. As a safeguard against abuse consent is, at best, an imperfect instrument. Informed consent, even in developed countries which originated the doctrine, is an ideal which does not always work in practice.[13] The inequality of expertise and influence between researcher and subject can be so great as to undermine the real authority of subjects to withhold or withdraw consent. Innumerable problems can interfere with a truly informed and voluntary relationship between clinician/investigator and patient/subject: the fine line between therapeutic practice and scientific research; the lack of access to innovative treatments outside of established clinical trials; the payment of money or other inducements to enter and remain in research; the differences in linguistic and cultural understandings between researchers and human subjects; and the sheer complexity of written informed consent forms often thought necessary or expedient for the purposes of the legal system.

Thus, even in well developed countries where the legal system and culture foster the concept of informed consent, practical realities may impede voluntariness and effective communication between researcher and subject. This is particularly true when research is undertaken in urban ghettos or poor rural areas where problems of illiteracy, and mistrust based upon race, culture, or social class may undermine the researcher/subject relationship.

The practical obstacles to obtaining voluntary and informed consent in international collaborative research are even more evident: the marked inequality of power and resources; the vast differences in law and culture; and the pressing problems of disease, hunger, illiteracy, and poverty.[14]

Law and regulation in technologically developed countries may require detailed written informed consent for participation in research even if it is conducted in another country with different laws and customs.[15] Regulators in parts of the developed world sometimes forget that written documentation is merely evidence of the consent, not the consent itself, and that documentation is an alien concept in many cultures. Requiring a person who may be illiterate and whose first language may be different to comply with Northern/Western conceptions of written informed consent is unrealistic.

In some communities the very concept of respect for persons as individuals may be at variance "with more relational definitions of the person found in other societies...which stress the embeddedness of the individual within society and define a person by his or her relations to others."[16] In some cultures there is little perception of conflict between self and society, except perhaps if the society is someone else's.[17] For example, in the Indian subcontinent and West Africa great deference may be given to clinicians/healers/elders.[18] Decisions are characteristically made in consultation with leaders in the setting of village meetings.[19] If permission has already been given by a community or family representative, the idea of an informed refusal by the individual may not even arise. Henderson *et al.* found that obedience to tribal leaders is a strong factor influencing participation in research in West Africa.[20] Where indigenous cultural beliefs exist the research may take on a wholly different meaning in the local country than the Northern scientist understands.[21] Ajayi illustrates this point with the socio/cultural/religious beliefs in West Africa regarding blood letting, biopsy, and post-mortem examinations.

Giving impoverished people in the developing world money, drugs, and food in exchange for their agreement to enter and remain in clinical trials may make it inconceivable that they would say no.[22] Yet, providing reasonable compensation to impoverished subjects who may have to take time from life sustaining work is entirely justified.

Despite the real problems of importing a Northern/Western concept of informed consent in Third World countries, some culturally appropriate agreement to participate in research is essential. "While consent procedures must be adapted to accommodate cultural mores, there must always be a requirement for consent from the individual prospective subject."[23] It is false to equate illiteracy or cultural differences with the inability to make decisions. Information should be presented to subjects in a manner which is comprehensible and consistent with local language, custom and culture. It is equally incorrect to assume that an individual's strong relationship with family and society are inconsistent with informed consent. The fact that individuals, in deciding whether to give consent, give deference to the views of family and community leaders, and carefully consider the benefits to society, does not negate their consent.

The CIOMS Proposed Guidelines on Biomedical Research[24] recommend that, if a person cannot give adequate informed consent, it is desirable to obtain proxy consent through the intermediary of a trusted community leader.[25] While it may be important to recognize the cultural importance of community or family leaders, it is unwise to refer to this process as a consent. It is more accurately labeled as "permission." The leader may represent the interests of the community more than the individual and may him or herself be susceptible to inducements which undermine the purpose of consent.

Large scale research raises a further issue as to how consent is given on behalf of the population. Specifically, can a legitimate representative of the community give consent on behalf of each of its members? Clearly, community leaders cannot realistically give consent on behalf of the entire population, for they have no way of knowing what decision each person would make. "Consent" is the wrong concept because each of the traditional elements is lacking: specific information on benefits and risks, voluntariness, and competency. A better conception is to say that leaders ought to be consulted to obtain a "community consensus" on population-based research.

In many situations it may be difficult to ascertain who is the legitimate representative of the community. Governments or public health agencies may, or may not, be elected by the people and have their rights and best interests at heart. Some leaders have no formal or recognized legal authority to speak for the population, but may be widely looked to as religious, cultural or social representative of the people. In seeking community consensus for large scale research, investigators must be knowledgeable of, and sensitive to, local perceptions of those who are in true leadership positions.

It would be antithetical to all understanding of human rights to suggest that a leader could give "permission" for an individual or provide "consensus agreement" for the community, as a substitute for individual consent. Rather, researchers have an ethical obligation to seek consent from the individual, as well as permission or consensus, when culturally appropriate. Thus, the inter-related concepts of individual consent, permission, and consensus should be regarded as additive ethical obligations which are to be examined within the context both of international human rights norms and local cultural and ethical beliefs.

An effective model of consent, permission and consensus has been reported by Hall in Gambia. Individual agreement is sought through a hierarchical chain beginning with the government, then moving to the chief of the district, and to the head of the village. Village meetings are held to explain the study, and each individual is asked if he or she agrees to the study in his or her household.[26]

Protection of vulnerable people and populations

Not every human being can give a competent and voluntary consent to research. Some people have diminished autonomy due, for example, to young age, mental illness or mental retardation. Others, such as prisoners, or, in some countries, the military, are so impeded in their freedoms and so subject to authority, that their consent is not entirely voluntary. For some individuals such as pregnant women, there can be increased risks associated with research; the woman herself may be subjected to heightened risk due to her condition, and the fetus may be unnecessarily exposed to harm. Respect for people with diminished capacity, those who are not entirely free to choose, or those with a heightened risk may require protection from potential harms of research. People may be so vulnerable that strict criteria must apply before they can even participate in a clinical trial.

Traditional micro-ethical principles, therefore, require a special justification before research is conducted on vulnerable individuals. In general, vulnerable subjects are selected only if the research is directly relevant to the person or class of persons—e.g., the very issue to be studied is prevalent in, or unique to, the group.[27]

Ethical principles would similarly require a special justification for research on vulnerable populations. Vulnerable populations could be defined as a class of individuals or groups who are non-dominant, subservient, or subject to restrictions in the culture where they live. It could include a minority race, religion, ethnic group, indigenous people, or aliens. These groups may have retained social, cultural, economic and political characteristics which are distinct from those of other segments of national populations.[28] Examples of epidemiologic research on non-dominant social groups include studies of prostitutes for sexually transmitted infections, drug users for needle-borne infections, women and children for vertical transmission of disease, and gays or hemophiliacs as risk groups for HIV infection. Vulnerable populations might also include persecuted non-minorities such as women in cultures where they are wholly subservient to their spouses.

Non-dominant populations should be regarded as vulnerable for much the same reasons that apply to individuals. Non-dominant populations are inherently likely to be exploited. Poverty makes a population more susceptible to financial or other inducements; their culturally or politically insular position may undermine their autonomy and ability to resist the suggestion of authorities that they participate in research; their illiteracy and lack of adequate communication networks makes it difficult to disseminate comprehensive and comprehensible information; their hunger and poor health may heighten the risks and burdens of research. Under such circumstances, the principles of respect and beneficence toward populations militates against imposing burdens without a special justification.

Special circumstances justifying research on vulnerable groups

What are the special circumstances that might justify research on vulnerable groups? A particularly favorable benefit to burden ratio would be one prime factor. If it could be established that the health advantages to the population clearly outweigh the minimal risks or burdens, this would help protect the population.

Second, the problem to be studied should be clearly relevant to the unique or special health problems of the population. A study of tropical disease, for example, in an endemic area may be completely justified, even though the population is highly vulnerable. The principle of justice, of course, would require that the vulnerable population has access to the present and future benefits of the research.

Third, every effort should be made to maximize the rights of the population to self-direction and protection from harm. The voices of vulnerable populations should be heard and respected not only on issues of subject selection, but also on the ethical conduct and outcomes of the research. Thus, genuine representatives of the population (as well as the individuals who comprise the population) must agree to participate, must have the right to withdraw at any time, and must be consulted in the use of the information generated from the study. If the study may cast aspersions on, or in some way disintegrates, the community, this must be discussed as part of the process of consent, permission, and consensus.

The relevant criteria, then, are whether there is a favorable benefit to burden ratio, whether the problem is relevant to the special health problems of the population, and whether the population chooses the research. To many, however, research may be justified when it provides a potential for overwhelming benefit for humankind, even if the benefit to the research population is in doubt. Consider the real ethical quandary over HIV anti-viral or vaccine research in Africa, particularly if undertaken on especially vulnerable groups such as prostitutes. Field trials may be accomplished more expeditiously in endemic areas because of the greater incidence of infection. The scientific advantages are that reliable results could be obtained more quickly and at less expense. The local population, however, may never see the benefit of a safe and efficacious drug or vaccine due to the prohibitive cost, and an expensive anti-viral might be low on the health care priorities of the host country. Similarly, in a vaccine trial for HIV, beneficent treatment of persons would require that subjects were counselled to avoid high risk behavior. This would undoubtedly result in a relatively smaller measured influence, requiring a larger sample size to demonstrate the efficacy of the vaccine.

Cost and expediency alone are seldom sufficient ethical justifications for subject selection. The key questions are how much benefit and harm might accrue to the population? Are there adequate laboratory or animal models to predict efficacy and risk? What are the reasons that other, less vulnerable, subjects cannot be used, and can they be used in parallel?

First World research in Third World countries

In international collaborative research First World investigators conduct research in poorer Third World countries. Because of the inherent inequality in economic and political power, these local communities may also be thought of as vulnerable populations and subjected to ethical rules that are similar to those applied to vulnerable individuals and groups within the same country. It is a legitimate ethical inquiry to ask why investigators choose to do their research abroad rather than at home. First, and most cynically, governments, sponsors and investigators may be prepared to impose risks and burdens on Third World populations which they are reluctant to impose on their own populations. A particularly risky, intrusive, or politically controversial piece of research may be perceived to be easier to conduct thousands of miles from home. A key international principle for research on human beings is that "a nation should not allow or support, in other countries, research which does not conform to ethics review standards at least equivalent to those in force within the nation."[29] Clearly, if research could be conducted as effectively on home populations, there should be special justifications before carrying it out on poorer populations abroad. Indeed, similar reasoning would prohibit research on the poor, illiterate, and unhealthy dweller of the ghetto if the research could just as effectively be carried out in an affluent suburb.

Second, researchers might choose poorer populations for their research because of financial, management, and administrative reasons. A Third World population may be regarded as more available, manageable, and less expensive than in a developed country. Naked financial or administrative considerations are rarely sufficient justifications for imposing risks and burdens on poorer populations. However, if appropriate subjects in the dominant populations have been saturated, some believe it is appropriate to utilize more vulnerable populations. Whether a recruitment problem itself provides a sufficient justification for research on non-dominant populations depends upon the context.

Third, the conditions in Third World populations may result in higher seroprevalence and greater incidence of transmission of disease. Clearly a study conducted under such conditions might be completed more quickly and more reliably, providing some justification for the decision. But, if populations at home have similar characteristics, they would be more appropriate subjects for research.

The overriding justification for research in Third World countries is that the disease studied is either rare or non-existent in the country of origin. This justification is as rigorous as that used for research on vulnerable individuals and groups within a country. The ideal circumstances for international collaborative research are when the scientific inquiry is focused on a genuine health problem of the local population, there is a low risk and a good prospect of benefit to the research subjects, and the outcome of the research will be available to promote the health of Third World populations.

Can exclusion of vulnerable populations from beneficial research be unethical?

Ethical principles requiring special justifications for research on vulnerable individuals were based upon an assumption that is not entirely true today. In the past it was presumed that all research subjects bear risks and burdens, making it a sacrifice to be selected. But, special benefits (sometimes of considerable worth) may be afforded to research subjects, which may make vulnerable persons and populations particularly eager to be selected. A fine line can be drawn between pure research and innovative treatment. For some poor groups, the only access to innovative therapies is by participation in research. To exclude vulnerable populations from participation in research may be to deny them their only realistic hope and promise of effective treatment and services.

A drug or vaccine that has not been tested on poorer, more vulnerable populations may also prove more risky or less beneficial to them in future. The generalizability of research to vulnerable populations may require that those populations be involved in clinical trials. A decision to exclude vulnerable populations from research impedes scientific understanding about their health problems and the most promising interventions to meet their health needs.

Over-protection of vulnerable populations, therefore, may be paternalistic and ultimately harmful. A balance needs to be struck between protecting vulnerable people and providing them the benefit of therapeutic innovation. Overly strict ethical and legal limits placed on vulnerable persons to enter research can impede humanitarian investigation of problems relevant to their medical needs.

Protecting the privacy of people and populations

The concept of privacy is as complicated as human affect itself. Research subjects may claim a right to privacy on three levels: the right to have space in the physical, personal, or social sense (e.g., the absence of intrusive surveillance or questioning); a right to control the disclosure of information about their health, behavior or life circumstances (e.g. sexual or drug use history); and the right to maintain intimacy and confidences in their personal, family or social relationships (e.g. their interactions with sexual partners, spouses, and professional counselors).

If sensitive information is linked to an individual it can cause him or her harm both of a tangible and intangible kind. It can result in the person being subjected to discrimination by employees, educators, landlords, or insurers (tangible harms);[30], or it can result in a sense of personal violation, shame, or hurt (a wrong).[31]

The ethical foundation for privacy is respect for the person. Respecting human beings means giving them the right to choose who has access to confidential information and under what circumstances.[32] It means recognizing the legitimacy of personal secrets and allowing the individual to define what is secret and to control how secrets are used.[33]

The importance of privacy is underscored by the promises that researchers make, implicitly or explicitly, to keep information confidential. Research subjects come to think about investigators partly as clinicians, and they reasonably anticipate that their confidences will not be unreasonably disclosed. Each culture has its own mores about confidential information and relationships. It is incumbent upon researchers from other countries to learn about and be sensitive to local customs, and religious and personal beliefs about the sanctity of confidential information.

From a researcher's perspective, maintaining confidentiality has a utilitarian value. Recruiting and keeping human subjects will become much more difficult if researchers cannot ensure that information obtained as a consequence of the study will not be disclosed outside of the research team.

There are, of course, constant pressures to disclose the confidences of research subjects. Researchers may choose to disclose information in furtherance of their scientific purpose; they may be required to report the information to government agencies or sponsors; or they may receive a court order or subpoena to divulge the information for the administration of justice.

A breach of confidentiality does not occur if a competent adult gives informed consent, specifying the information that may be disclosed and to whom. Clear rules, however, are needed to govern effectively when disclosure can ethically occur in the absence of consent.

Three kinds of justification can be offered for divulging confidences obtained in the course of research. First, disclosure may be thought necessary to present a more credible or authoritative scientific report. A case study which does not disclose certain identifying characteristics may omit scientifically relevant information. In epidemiology, often the very object of the research is to obtain demographic, health or behavior related data. Restrictions on publication or other dissemination may defeat the very purpose of the research. A prior understanding about dissemination of information between the investigator and the individual and/or population can overcome confidentiality problems.

Second, disclosure may be thought necessary to protect the health and safety of others. The United States *Tarasoff* case[34] created a legal duty on psychiatrists to disclose to a third party if a psychiatric patient poses an immediate and grave danger. The "duty to warn" may extend to third parties or populations who face a serious and imminent health risk—such as a sexual or needle sharing partner of a person infected with HIV, an environmental risk from hazardous waste, or the risk of disease from food or water contamination. Knowledge gained in epidemiologic research, then, may be necessary to curtail a serious health risk to a population. Requirements to report instances of child abuse or communicable diseases to public health authorities also illustrate the need for disclosure for the protection of others. It is important in evaluating a "duty to warn" whether the health risk is serious and probable, or whether it is based upon a low probability of harm or even irrational fear or prejudice.

Finally, researchers may believe that disclosure is in the best interests of the research subject, such as when the subject needs medical treatment. One controversial issue is whether a mature minor deserves confidentiality when she seeks an abortion without informing the father or her family. Ordinarily, the principle of respect for persons requires the researcher to follow a competent person's own judgment about where his or her best interests lie.

Ethical principles of privacy and confidentiality are applicable to individual invasions, but need strengthening to safeguard adequately the privacy of populations. The potential for violating privacy rights is formidable where there is wide scale collection, transfer and use of information. Systematic gathering, reporting, and sharing of information about a group can be highly detrimental to the group and its members. The use of sophisticated computer technology to store and use personal data among countless sources only heightens the concern over privacy, stigmatization, and discrimination within populations. Capron emphasizes that information can be obtained from, and transferred to, government agencies (such as census, vital statistics, revenue collection, health, social services, and defense), schools, health care services and police.[35]

Data suggesting that particular groups are more likely to be infected with, and hence, capable of transmitting communicable or sexually transmitted diseases can reinforce prejudice and irrational fear of members of that group. Data which create or reinforce negative cultural stereotypes can be extremely hurtful. Examples of such data include research purporting to demonstrate that HIV originated in Africa,[36] that homosexuals, drug abusers, and prostitutes spread sexual and blood borne disease, that mentally ill people are dangerous, or that certain races have less intelligence. Derogatory information associated with a group can result in real harms such as discrimination against members of the group in employment, housing, or insurance. Derogatory information can also cause intangible hurt to groups such as lowering their self-esteem and racial or cultural pride. Derogatory information about a sub-population can stigmatize and wound its people as much as breaches of confidentiality can affect an individual. The information collected from groups, just as the information about individuals, need not be blatant or intentional to cause harm or hurt. Even the best intentioned and careful research can trigger concerns about privacy.

Consider, for example, the widespread practice in the United States and elsewhere of reporting HIV seroprevalence data broken down by race and ethnicity. Although the data are collected for a valuable purpose and do not identify individuals, the method of reporting emphasizes the disproportionate impact on African Americans and Hispanics. A valid reason may, in fact, exist for so publicly characterizing race and ethnicity as risk markers (but not risk factors) for HIV, rather than using more neutral classifications such as socio-economic status or geographic area. The practice is so well entrenched, however, that no one asks whether the public health justification is significant enough to outweigh the potential impact on the dignity and self-esteem of the populations affected.

Even publicly available information, which the microethical principle of confidentiality often does not safeguard, takes on a new meaning when it is joined with information from a variety of sources. Some information, while technically "public" in the sense that it is theoretically available by, say, a freedom of information request or a national census, may hurt a person or a group by its public disclosure. Isolated facts by themselves may be innocuous, but when analyzed together with a chain of information, may reveal personal or group secrets. Thus, even if people agree to the release of particular information as an isolated event, they have not given meaningful consent unless they are aware of the totality of the collection and use of the information.

The ethical principle of privacy of populations, then, would view an entire pattern of collection and use of information, and not merely be concerned with unauthorized disclosure of an individual's research record.

Could individuals in a study each give consent to disclosure of information, and yet the study would violate the right of the collective to privacy? The answer is yes if one believes that populations have a right to defend their reputation and dignity as much as individuals do. It is conceivable, even where the information revealed about each member of the group is non-consequential or is not personally identifiable, that the group can be harmed. Blind seroprevalence studies, for example, raise few concerns about individual confidentiality because the name of the person is not identifiable. But the very purpose of the study is to obtain information about the population. To be sure, much of the information collected in good epidemiologic surveillance is potentially beneficial to the health of the community. Still, the power (whether intentional or inadvertent) to use the information in ways which undermine the dignity of the culture is always present. The right of populations to have some say in the collection and spread of data that they believe reflect badly on their identity is an important ethical principle.

Distributive justice in international collaborative research

The concept of justice is hardly foreign to the framework of ethics. "Justice" is an often used but seldom clearly defined term. It is frequently taken to mean that the benefits and burdens of research should be fairly distributed. This definition begs the question, for it does not explain what is fair or appropriate in allocating benefits and burdens. The legal concept of equal protection, more precisely, states that similarly situated individuals or classes of individuals should be treated equally, unless there is a relevant and compelling reason to treat them differently.[37]

This section suggests an entitlement to benefits, services, and resources which some traditional ethical thinkers may feel goes too far. Those who initiate, sponsor, and conduct research (including governments, funders, industry, and investigators) have an obligation to share the benefits of research not only with subjects while they are participating in a clinical trial, but with those subjects after the trial, as well as their communities.

Consider a case where researchers from the First World are undertaking a large field trial for a candidate vaccine or drug in the Third World. What responsibilities do they have to the subjects and the wider community during the trial, and what responsibilities do they have once the trial is over? Traditional ethical principles would certainly require protection of subjects while they are in the clinical trial, at least from any harms that may arise directly from their participation. This would mean that qualified clinicians would carefully observe any adverse effects of the research on subjects and provide immediate treatment. Once the drug or vaccine is shown to be efficacious, the study should cease so that those in the control group could be beneficially treated.

Taking ethical obligations further, do researchers have an obligation to confer benefits on research subjects which are not strictly relevant to the study? Many Northern/Western researchers working in technologically developing countries provide prevention and health care services for the local community.

Investigators have a duty not merely to prevent harm to subjects, but to affirmatively protect their health and well-being by providing, within reasonable limits, prevention and health services. Research subjects should not be viewed as mere tools for the purposes of the research, but as whole persons with diverse health needs. In accordance with the principle of distributive justice, a primary ethical justification for selecting vulnerable populations for study is that benefits are conferred in exchange for their participation. This can include the direct benefits of the drug or vaccine provided in the study design, as well as risk reduction and health care services. Persons on the margins of survival give up productive time to contribute to the scientific endeavors of the research team. They can reasonably expect minimal services in return.

Once a person enters a research project, particularly if he or she is poor and lacks adequate access to medical care, the investigator assumes some duty of care to safeguard that person's health and welfare. Doctors involved in a trial cannot turn their backs on obvious illness and health care needs of trial participants.

From a utilitarian perspective, researchers have an interest in maintaining the health and welfare of subjects. Subjects who are healthy and satisfied are far more likely to be cooperative and reliable partners in research.

In addition to the arguments based upon equity and utility, it can also be argued that researchers should adhere to explicit or implicit promises. Unless the research team makes it otherwise clear, subjects expect that their basic health care needs will be met by health care professionals involved in the study. Subjects may not perceive the fine distinctions made by researchers between treating direct adverse effects of the drugs provided in the study design, and more general health care needs.

Ethical duties may extend after the study is complete. Is it ethical to summarily withdraw all health care services that the community has benefited from and come to expect, once the study is over? Some ongoing responsibility for subjects and communities extends beyond the temporal limits of the study. If research is viewed from the subjects', rather than solely from the investigators', perspective, a sense of loss and unmet expectations naturally occur the day after the research is completed and services are withdrawn. Sponsors and researchers who leave behind some continuing capacity to meet needs, even if at a reduced level, will help ensure receptivity to future research ideas and longer term health research planning.

Let us assume the results of the field trial are positive and the drug or vaccine is shown to be safe and effective. What is the responsibility of the research team to make the drug or vaccine available to the local population? A strong ethical responsibility exists to provide the efficacious agent to the subjects of the research. This requires that the agent is available as long as it is clinically appropriate. The World Health Organization consultation on candidate HIV vaccines said that justice requires that the "population in which the vaccine is tested is entitled to first priority in receiving the vaccine after its safety and efficacy have been established."[38] One might argue that it also includes the ancillary medical support and supervision necessary to monitor the adverse effects and toxicity of the agent.

Do other people in the local community have an ethical claim to the drug or vaccine? The choice of one subject over another in the community is often random and certainly unrelated to any morally rational choice. It would be inequitable if certain members of the population were to receive a benefit from which others were excluded. If Third World populations are to be used to create a health benefit for humankind, careful consideration should be given to making that benefit available to those who cannot afford it.

Why, it may be asked, are there affirmative ethical duties owed to local populations? The agreement required for international collaborative research is entered into not merely with subjects but with entire communities. Government and community leaders in host countries are consulted and provide permission for research. The understanding between collaborators may be that the community receives improved health services, as well as bearing any fruits that the research provides. By agreeing to become involved, research subjects and their communities anticipate that any knowledge, therapeutic agent, or vaccine that is advanced in the study will be used to improve their health.

Persons who sponsor and conduct research in Third World communities obtain a substantial benefit from the research. Investigators gain access to otherwise unavailable populations for research. Those populations bear the risks and burdens of research, the fruits of which will go to benefit many others. Industry may benefit financially from government subsidies in the development of a product. In some countries, industry is also permitted to set the price at whatever level it wishes. The commercial developers of new drugs or vaccines stand to make substantial profits in the marketplace. Arguments for making the product available more widely to the local population, then, are based upon the mutual exchange of benefits, and the equities of access to essential health improvements irrespective of the ability to pay.

Research conducted in the Third World sometimes can be inequitable in its allocation of benefits and burdens. All areas of the world benefit, for example, from the development of an efficacious vaccine or pharmaceutical. But a significant burden of experimentation rests on poorer Third World countries. At the same time, economic poverty and underdeveloped medical services realistically prevent Third World countries from buying and distributing beneficial preventive or therapeutic agents.[39] It would be unjust if the populations which bear significant burdens of research were to reap the fewest rewards.

Developing sound and enduring infra-structures

Developing infra-structures in the host countries is an important objective of international collaborative research. Host countries can richly contribute both to local public health needs and to research objectives if their scientists and health care professionals are provided the resources and capacity to function as equal partners. Infra-structure building requires the development of high quality training and education, laboratory and other vital equipment, and prevention, health care, and hospital services.

The development of infra-structures provides stability for meeting ongoing public health and scientific needs. This is advantageous not only to host investigators and their institutions, but also to their collaborating partners in the North/West who will gain from ongoing relationships. A sound infra-structure that can endure through lengthy studies and enable future research to flourish emerges as an essential component of international public health planning and research.

Ethical imperialism and ethical relativism

"Ethical imperialism appears to be the imposition on one society of solutions culturally appropriate to another society, on the pretext that they represent ethical absolutes."[40] Certainly, no single country has the right to set universal standards to which other countries must comply. But, the foundation of international human rights from Nuremberg to Helsinki and beyond is the conviction that there is an irreducible set of international ethical standards common to all societies, which local law, politics, or custom cannot bend.[41]

Foundational principles for population-based research include: (1) the overriding imperative to protect the health and well-being of populations; (2) the right of populations to self-determination, including the right to refuse participation; (3) protection of vulnerable populations and the need for special justifications for research; (4) protecting the privacy, integrity, and self-esteem of populations; and (5) the equitable distribution of benefits and burdens of research. How these principles operate in practice requires an understanding of the mores of other people and places.[42]

The purpose of this paper is to define a set of ethical principles which extend beyond the person dominated ethics of Helsinki to a view of ethics based upon the integrity of populations. In so doing, a deeper respect for, and toleration of, cultures steeped in the tradition of social relationships can be nurtured.

References

The author would like to thank the researchers and ethical thinkers on the WHO/CIOMS steering committee who assisted in the formulation of this paper, particularly Zbigniew Bankowski, Jay Bryant, Bernard Dickens, David Heymann, John Last, and Robert Levine.

1. National Commission for the Protection of Human Subjects of Biomedical and Behavioral Research. *The Belmont Report: Ethical principles and guidelines for the protection of human subjects of research.* Office of Protection from Research Risks, U.S. Public Health Service: Bethesda, Md., April 18, 1979; R.J. Levine, *Ethics and Regulation of Clinical Research.* Yale University Press: New Haven, 2d ed. 1988.

2. Nuremberg Code 1947, printed in Trials of War Criminals Before the Nuremberg Military Tribunals Under Control Council Law No.10, vol. II (Washington, DC: U.S. Government Printing Office, 1949, at 181–182); World Medical Association Declaration of Helsinki: Recommendations Guiding Medical Doctors in Biomedical Research Involving Human Subjects, adopted by the 18th World Medical Assembly, Helsinki, Finland, 1964, revised by the 29th WHA, Tokyo, Japan, 1975, and the 35th WHA in Venice, Italy, 1983. Reprinted in Medical Ethics Declarations. *World Medical Journal.* 1984; 31:4; World Health Organization and Council for International Organizations of Medical Sciences. Proposed International Guidelines for Biomedical Research Involving Human Subjects. Geneva, 1982.

3. Law Reform Commission of Canada. Biomedical Experimentation Involving Human Subjects: Working Paper 61. Ottawa, 1989; U.S. Department of Health and Human Services Rules and Regulations, 45 CFR 46C (Revised as of March 8,1983); French Consel d'Etat. De l'ethique au droit. Paris 1988.

4. L. Gostin,"Collective and Individual Rights: Towards Resolving the Conflict." In: L. Gostin (ed), *Civil Liberties in Conflict*, Routledge: London and New York, 1988.

5. R.J. Levine, supra note 1 at 52.

6. Geneva Declaration 1948, amended 1968, reprinted in Medical Ethics Declarations. World Medical Journal 1984;31:3.

7. O.O. Ajayi, "Taboos and Clinical Research in West Africa," *J. Med. Ethics* 1980;6061–63.

8. *The Belmont Report*, supra note 1.

9. Nuremberg Code, supra note 1, first principle.

10. Declaration of Helsinki, supra note 2, article I,9.

11. WHO/CIOMS, supra note 2, at 23–24.

12. Council of Europe. Recommendation No. R(90)3 Concerning Medical Research on Human Beings (6 Feb. 1990).

13. G.J. Hill, "Research on humans published in *JAMA*" (letter). *J. Amer. Med. Assn.* 1987; 258:1604.

14. E.O. Ekunwe and R. Kessel, "Informed Consent in the Developing World," *Hastings Cen. Rep.* 1984; 14:23–24.

15. U.S. Department of Health and Human Services, Rules and Regulations, 45 CFR 46, para. 46.116 (Revised as of March 8, 1983). Yet, some highly developed countries expressly reject the concept of informed consent. Sidaway v. Bethlehem Royal Hospital Governors [1985] A.C. 871.

16. N.A. Christakis, "The Ethical Design of an AIDS Vaccine Trial in Africa." *Hastings Center Rpt.* 1988;18:31–37.

17. O.O. Ajayi, supra note 7; D. Adityanjee, "Informed Consent: Issues Involved for Developing Countries." *Med. Sci. & Law* 1986; 26: 305–307; WHO/CIOMS, supra note 2; R.J. Levine, "Validity of Consent Procedures in Technologically Developing Countries. In: *Human Experimentation and Medical Ethics*," Z. Bankowski, N. Howard-Jones, eds. Geneva: CIOMS, 1982, pp.16–30.

18. Indian Council of Medical Research. Policy statement on ethical considerations involved in research on human subjects 1980; New Delhi, ICMR.

19. A.J. Hall, "Public Health Trials in West Africa: Logistics and Ethics." *IRB* 1989; 11:8–10.

20. Henderson et al., "Assessment of Vaccination Coverage, Vaccination Scar Rates and Small Pox Scarring in Five Areas of West Africa." *Bull. WHO* 1973;84:183–194.

21. O.O. Ajayi, supra note 7.

22. D. Adityanjee, supra note 17; O.O. Ajayi, supra note 7.

23. World Health Organization. Criteria for international testing of candidate HIV vaccines, 27 February – 2 March, 1989.

24. WHO/CIOMS, supra note 2.

25. WHO/CIOMS, supra note 2, paras. 14–15.

26. A.J. Hall, supra note 19.

27. R.J. Levine, supra note 5.

28. Centre for Human Rights, United Nations. *The Rights of Indigenous Peoples.* U.N.: Geneva, 1990.

29. J. Miller, "Towards an International Ethic for Research with Human Beings." *IRB* 1988; 10:9–11.

30. L. Gostin, "The AIDS Litigation Project: A National Review of Court and Human Rights Commission Decisions, Part II: Discrimination." *J. Am. Med. Assn.* 1990;263:2086–2093; PANOS Institute. *The Third Epidemic: Repercussions of the fear of AIDS.* 1990, PANOS, London.

31. T.L. Beauchamp, J. Childress, *Principles of Biomedical Ethics.* Oxford University Press, New York. 2nd ed. 1983.

32. R.J. Levine, supra note 5; H.C. Kelman, "Privacy and Research with Human Beings." *J. Soc. Issues* 1977; 33:169–195.

33. S. Bok, "The Limits of Confidentiality." *Hastings Ctr. Rpt.* 1983;13:24–31.

34. Tarasoff v. Board of Regents of California (1976) 17 Cal.3d 452 (Tarasoff II), *vacating* 13 Cal.3d 117 (Tarasoff I).

35. A. Capron, "Protection of Research Subjects: Do Special Rules Apply in Epidemiology." Paper presented at the IEF Conference on Ethics in Epidemiology, June 12–13, 1989, Birmingham, Alabama.

36. E. Tabor, R.J. Gerety, J. Cairns, A.C. Bayley, "Did HIV and HTLV Originate in Africa?" (letter). *JAMA* 1990; 264: 691–692.

37. L. Gostin, "The Future of Public Health Law." *Amer. J. Law & Med.* 1987;12:461–490.

38. WHO, supra note 2.

39. N.A. Christakis, "Responding to a Pandemic: Interna-

tional Interests in AIDS Control." *Daedalus* 1989; 118:113–134.

40. F. Gilks and J.B.O. Were, "Ethical Imperialism" (letter) *N. Engl. J. Med.* 1990; 322:200

41. M. Angell, "Ethical Imperialism? Ethics in International Collaborative Clinical Research." *N. Engl. J. Med.* 1990; 319:1081–1083.

42. M. Barry, "Ethical Considerations of Human Investigation in Developing Countries: The AIDS Dilemma." *N.Engl. J. Med.* 199; 319:1083–1086.

[14]

PROTECTION OF RESEARCH SUBJECTS: DO SPECIAL RULES APPLY IN EPIDEMIOLOGY?

A. M. Capron

Law Center and School of Medicine, University of Southern California, Los Angeles, CA 90089-0071, U.S.A.

Abstract—Epidemiological studies raise somewhat different ethical issues than those that usually confront IRBs in their review of biomedical research. Although epidemiologic research seldom risks direct harm to subjects, it may still wrong them if it invades their interests (such as privacy) or treats them merely as means. Review by an IRB is thus justified if it improves the benefit–risk ratio; even more important, in most circumstances, informed consent should be obtained in advance from subjects, to promote subjects' autonomy, to improve the quality of research, to regularize the relationship of investigators and potential subjects, and to protect subjects' privacy. Nonetheless, in certain circumstances—illustrated here by considering three hypothetical studies—alternatives to the usual consent rules are acceptable.

Compensation Debriefing Deontology Ethics Harm to subjects Informed consent Peer consultants Privacy Self-determination Wrongs to subjects

INTRODUCTION

Imagine, if you will, a place where health, hospitalization, education, military, employment, law enforcement, housing, tax and financial records, as well as disease registries and the data sources for the census, vital statistics, and all aspects of people's private activities, are meticulously kept, fully linked together, and easily accessible to qualified researchers. What is that place? Epidemiologists' heaven.

Of course, formidable problems face epidemiologists trying to reach heaven. The data sources on many aspects of our lives are incomplete and the means of linking them are typically non-existent or partial at best. But even if the data all existed, there would be a further "catch": epidemiologists would probably find themselves facing great obstacles in gaining access to the data.

Epidemiologists sometimes think of "ethics" as the source of those obstacles, which are believed to be embodied in the federal rules for the protection of research subjects—colloquially called 45 *CFR* Part 46—especially as they are interpreted by some institutional review boards (IRBs). It has even been suggested by Dr Rothman that review procedures and consent requirements could render epidemiology impossible [1]. This seems a strange result, not the least because many of the concerns that justify prior scrutiny of research protocols by IRBs are simply absent for most epidemiological research. Thus, not surprisingly, epidemiologists cry foul when they find—as two Harvard investigators did a few years ago—their research being burdened by the requirement that they obtain written informed consent from subjects who would merely be asked to answer a few questions in an interview [2–4]. I suspect that a major cause for confusion—despite provisions in the federal regulations intended to avoid (or the very least, to speed up) inappropriate or unnecessary reviews—is that most IRBs, being used to reviewing clinical research, may impose expectations that are poorly suited to epidemiological research.

Yet before we dismiss ethics as nothing more than a cause of confusion and needless worry, I think we need to take a careful look at epidemiologists' ethical obligations to research subjects. In doing so, we should pay particular attention to three points: first, the difference between harming someone and wronging them; second, the role of informed consent in protecting against such wrongs; and third, the steps that can be taken to avoid or minimize particular harms associated with breaches of privacy and confidentiality.

THE ETHICAL TENSION

The aspect of epidemiology addressed in this essay is that involving research on the association of a population's health status with particular genetic and environmental factors, rather than studies involving prospective, manipulative interventions, such as clinical trials of drugs or devices, on the one hand, or officially authorized or mandated surveillance for public health purposes, on the other hand. Yet an adequate description of epidemiological research must locate it within moral—not merely factual—terrain because it rests on competing ethical orientations about research involving human beings, roughly involving the competition between deontology and utilitarianism.

A good exposition of a conservative deontological tradition can be found in the writings of philosopher Hans Jonas [5]. He argues that research is usually warranted only when those who are exposed to risk have knowingly agreed to bear that risk; otherwise, the prospect of improving the social condition does not justify imposing a sacrifice on anyone. In his words, "progress is an optional goal, not an unconditional commitment" [5, p. 255]. Since such sacrifices fall outside the social contract, only activities necessary for the continued existence of society can command something from us beyond what we choose to give.

Such a deontological view would strictly limit researchers, including epidemiologists. At the opposite pole is the position that investigators have not merely a duty but also a right to advance human knowledge [6–8]. Rather than either extreme, I think society accepts the more modest notion that scientists have an obligation which extends beyond non-maleficence (not harming others) to beneficience (the positive duty to remove existing harms and produce social benefits when that is within their powers).

The prospect of providing much needed benefits exists for epidemiology today as never before. Beyond its past role in studying the incidence of infectious disease—a role that remains vital in the area of AIDS—the field has much to contribute to our understanding of environmental and occupational risks, of the relative effectiveness of health care interventions, and of the role genetics plays in both human illness and human capabilities [9]. Therefore, while never doubting that the present discussion turns on a conflict of values, I would submit that this conflict does not admit of absolute resolution. That is, we will be required to weigh the value of knowledge (both for its own sake and as a means for improving life) against many other values, prime among them autonomy, beneficence and justice.

THE DIFFERENCE BETWEEN HARMS AND WRONGS

Traditional concerns in biomedical research

At the heart of the protection of research subjects—through the federal regulations and the institutional review process—is concern for the physical well-being of the human beings who become involved in research projects. While everyday biomedical research, conducted by responsible investigators in approved projects, seems to be at least as safe as medical care itself, the history of research has been marked by some horrific examples of harm to subjects. (In this discussion, I am referring to what is often termed "harms to interests" rather than "moral harm," which "is inflicted on someone when some course of action produces in that person a greater propensity to commit wrongs" [10, p. 178].) Most of these harms have involved injury to, or even loss of, health and life. Beyond physical harm have been instances of psychological harm, especially among subjects who were deceived about the purpose of a study or the nature of their participation in it. Finally, in some instances, the requirements of research design—such as the use of a control group that receives a placebo—involves a reverse risk to subjects, viz. that they will find themselves in the less beneficial arm of the protocol. Hence the need for protection, both through IRB approval of the benefit/harm ratio and through the requirement of informed consent from research subjects.

Risks created by epidemiological research

Epidemiologic research can also involve the risk of harm, but it is typically of a different sort. Since, in most cases, investigators do not intervene physically with the subject and may not even have direct contact of any sort, physical and psychological injuries are unlikely. Yet other sorts of harm may occur. First, if data dealing with sensitive matters—either raw data or final results—can be linked to subjects, they may suffer social harm, such as ostracism or loss of employment. Second, even when individuals cannot be linked to information that is embarrassing (or worse), findings that paint an adverse picture of an entire population may eventuate in harm to that group, either directly or as a result of the adoption of laws or policies that have a negative impact on the welfare of group members.

Despite these risks, the harms entailed in epidemiological research seem less grave, seldom touching on matters of physical or even emotional well-being; moreover, their avoidance either seems simpler (e.g. merely taking care to disguise any facts that could be linked to a particular subject) or may, in fact, seem inappropriate where group harms are involved, since a group can hardly claim any right to a preferential social policy rather than one based on an accurate understanding of the true facts.

Wrongs beyond harms

The argued unfairness of binding epidemiology to the same Procrustean bed as biomedical research rests largely on this perception of different, and markedly less significant, risks. This argument is fine as far as it goes, but it fails to note another, less tangible but no less significant, concern: people may have been wronged even when they have not suffered harm. Some things are both harms and wrongs, while others amount to harming another's interest (as, for example, when one seller takes business away from another) without committing a wrong (as when no duty exists to avoid the harm) [10, p. 177]. My concern in this essay is with situations in which the consequence of an epidemiological study might be characterized as a wrong even though subjects' interests (material as well as physical) have not been harmed.

Consider the following example: suppose that I enter your house (through an unlocked back door) while you were away. Suppose that I not only leave everything undisturbed but also that I do not even know your identity. Have you suffered a harm? Not in the usual sense—as you would if I took something from the house or if you come home while I was still there and I surprised or, even worse, injured you. But I have wronged you. And that wrong is not overcome if I happen to be a scientist studying dustballs in their native habitat (viz. under sofas) rather than a mere Nosey Parker. The wrong is the invasion of your privacy without your consent, what is known in the law as trespass.

Wrongs of this type may clearly be implicated in epidemiological research. If I have allowed information to be gathered about me—e.g. by my personal physician, in the course of being evaluated and treated by the physician—and a researcher goes through that information, a wrong has been done even if I do not know about the intrusion. Information about me is an aspect of myself, just as is a physical space that I occupy, and someone looking through it has intruded on me as surely as if he or she had entered my home. The gravity of the wrong will depend on several factors. How personal is the information—data on one's sex life is not the same as height and weight—and to what extent would a person have a reasonable expectation that the information would not be known to people beyond those rendering care?

Wrongs may occur in other ways besides trespasses. Treating people solely as means to an end not chosen by them wrongs them even when it does not harm them. It is a wrong because it treats them as an instrument not as a person [11]. For an epidemiologist to commit a wrong against a person would thus violate two ethical principles: respect for autonomy (i.e. respecting persons and allowing them to make choices about their lives rather than having choices imposed upon them) and non-maleficience (i.e. the duty to avoid injuring a person). Accordingly, the risk that epidemiological studies could wrong people explains why one ought not simply to dismiss ethical guidelines as irrelevant, even if one believes that the risk of direct harm to subjects is negligible.

THE BASIC ROLE OF INFORMED CONSENT

Consent as a means of minimizing harm

How, then, have the law and ethics dealt with the risk of subjects being harmed? Primarily through two requirements: first, research must undergo review by a properly constituted body—usually called an IRB—which is supposed to foreclose studies that entail an unfavourable benefit–risk ratio, that are unfair in the distribution of risk in the population, or that do not provide for an adequate consent process.

The second means of protecting against harm is through requiring that investigators obtain the informed and voluntary consent of subjects before studying them. Since everyone has his or her own particular sense of what constitutes harm, the agreement of each subject to participate in a study—based upon disclosure of all information material to an informed choice—is necessary if the harm caused by the study is to be minimized. Simply put, if I tried to decide for you whether participation was acceptable and my sense of what constitutes a harm and how grave it is differs markedly from yours, the presumed maximization of benefit-to-risk from the research could be very erroneous.

The same principle applies to studies that involve potential wrongs to subjects rather than harms; indeed, a wrong is entailed in a study that would make use of some aspect of a person without consent. The question then is whether the potential of wronging subjects erects an absolute barrier to a study, or whether there are circumstances when research may proceed without subjects' consent nonetheless, perhaps because of other benefits expected to be derived from the research.

SEVERAL ADDITIONAL FUNCTIONS OF INFORMED CONSENT

To answer this question requires a closer—albeit still brief—look at the functions that informed consent serves in research. Four stand out: promoting autonomy and self-determination, improving research, regularizing relationships between investigators and subjects, and protecting privacy [12]. If these purposes can be met without individual subjects giving informed consent, then the omission of consent may be more ethically acceptable.

Promoting autonomy and self-determination

In the brief sketch of informed consent offered above, I viewed consent primarily in pragmatic terms: that respect for self-determination is necessary in order that the harm generated by research be minimized, since potential subjects are the best judges of the gravity of any prospective harm. The first purpose I want to argue for now expands on that, viz. that the requirement of informed consent manifests the human desire "to be conscious of [oneself] as a thinking, willing, active being, responsible for his choices and able to explain them by reference to his own ideas and purposes," as Sir Isaiah Berlin put in [13]. In other words, the requirement of informed consent protects the human status of research subjects by reminding everyone involved in a research project of the Kantian imperative against using human beings merely as means. A subject who has truly consented to participate has thereby become a collaborator with the investigators by effectively adopting the study's ends as his or her own.

Of course, to reach this goal, informed consent must be a reality, embodying both the autonomous authorization described by Faden and Beauchamp [14] (viz. a competent subject who substantially understands the circumstances and who, in the absence of significant control by others, authorizes the researcher to proceed) and the dialogic process between investigator and subject urged by Jay Katz as well as the President's Commission [15, 16] (viz. a discussion in terms understandable to both parties in which both exchange information and both agree to proceed).

Improving research

A second purpose served by informed consent relates to good research design and education. In preparing to explain a project to prospective subjects, investigators should be provoked to scrutinize it with additional care; further, the obligation of informed consent may have a beneficial "reflexive effect," as Paul Freund put it, "on the management of the experiment itself" [17]. Besides the benefits of greater thoughtfulness on the investigators' part, in some kinds of ongoing studies, the active collaboration of informed subjects may increase the accuracy and pertinence of the data collected. Finally, by educating people about both the methods and purposes of scientific investigation, the informed consent process can improve the public climate in which research is conducted and supported.

Regularizing relationships

Third, requiring consent allows the relationship of subjects and investigators to be brought within the norms of more typical social interactions. Especially in research that involves the observation of people, or collection of disparate pieces of information about them, the investigators "have changed the normal relationship of equality between freely associating individuals in society into one which they have usurped power over aspects of their subjects' lives and personalities" [12].

Protecting privacy

This leads into the fourth function of informed consent that I want to mention, safeguarding people from unwanted invasions of their privacy. The term privacy is today a rich and multifaceted one in ethics and the law. In addition to referring to the protection of private space, it connotes guarantees against the public disclosure of facts that falls short of defamation. "Privacy is not simply an absence of information about us in the minds of others," as Charles Fried has written, "rather it is the control we have over information about ourselves" [18].

THREE HYPOTHETICAL STUDIES

Having in mind these varied functions of informed consent, imagine three hypothetical research projects in which an epidemiologist might argue that obtaining informed consent is undesirable (for reasons of research design), impractical, or even impossible.*

PROJECT SMOKE intends to discover whether the peer-pressure methods of reducing cigarette smoking employed among seventh graders by school officials in District 1 were more effective than the didactic techniques used in District 2 junior highs. The researchers plan to question 17-year-olds in the two school districts to determine whether they smoke, 5 years after their exposure to the programs. The researchers wish to pass out anonymous questionnaires that ask a number of questions about personal habits and health status, but they do not want to explain the purpose of the study (for fear of biasing the answers) nor to obtain explicit consent in advance (for fear of lowering the participation rate and thereby biasing the results).

PROJECT FAMILY is an inquiry into the effects on juvenile delinquency of various judicial and social service interventions with families in which child abuse has occurred. The researchers would use public records to follow the course, from the official response to a report of child abuse to later juvenile court dispositions involving any child in the family. These results would be compared with the prior judicial and social service involvement with the families of juvenile offenders whose families were never found to be abusive. Since there will be no direct contact with any of the families or juveniles, the researchers argue that they should not face the burden of obtaining their consent to review and link the records involved.

The third hypothetical is PROJECT HIV in which the investigators are interested in the natural history of HIV injection in a group of individuals who have been discharged from the armed services after having been identified as HIV-positive through HIV screening, which is mandatory for service personnel. In addition to linking service records with the National Death Index, VA hospitalization and death records, and CDC's AIDS registry, the investigators want to ask the HIV-positive individuals to release their post-service medical records, to fill out a questionnaire, and to submit to a clinical examination. The researchers will need access to the individuals' service records before they obtain consent from them to participate in the research.

The justifications for not seeking consent differ in these three hypotheticals, as do the risks—both of harming subjects (PROJECT FAMILY and PROJECT HIV, for example, involve information about subjects that could pose social and economic harms if known widely) and of wronging them. Let us turn, then, to consider the alternatives to informed consent that might be available to an IRB called upon to decide whether to permit these projects.

Alternatives to prospective, indivdiual consent

One approach is to see whether a project falls outside the federal government's regulatory requirements in 45 *CFR* Part 46. Section 46.101 (b) (5) exempts

> "Research involving the collection or study of existing data, documents, records, pathological specimens, or diagnostic specimens, if these sources are publicly available or if the information is recorded by the investigator in such a manner that subjects cannot be identified, directly or through identifiers linked to the subjects."

In effect, this rule—which might apply to PROJECT SMOKE and PROJECT FAMILY

*These hypotheticals were without reference to any studies that might actually be—or have been—undertaken. While any resemblance to actual studies may enhance the hypotheticals' credibility and even their usefulness in analyses, it is purely accidental, and the comments in this essay should not be taken as judgments about any actual study.

—seems to be premised on the notion that subjects are not wronged when public records or anonymous data are used by researchers. I believe that the goals of good research design and minimization of harm would still be best served were such research to be reviewed by and IRB—so as to overcome the blind-spots that researchers have about their own studies—but I would agree that consent is not always the only means to serve these goals. What about the other purposes of consent we discussed earlier, such as promoting autonomy and self-determination, regularizing relationships, and protecting privacy? One's answer to the question depends upon whether one thinks that the subjects in a study using public records differ in their relationship to the investigator from that of other people and whether reasonable expectations of privacy are violated in these circumstances. It is my own view that, except in situations involving records that are truly public, there is something unique here that requires either consent or some reasonble substitute therefore.

What might such alternatives be? To place this question in context: section 46.116 (d) of the regulations provides that an IRB may approve an alternative to the usual consent procedures (including a complete waiver) when the research, which may "involve no more than minimal risk to the subjects," could not otherwise be carried out and when the "waiver or alteration will not adversely affect the rights and welfare of the subjects." We may take from this, again, that the harm-prevention goal of informed consent is met by the IRB reveiw process, but this does not, I would argue, necessarily respond to the other purposes of informed consent that we have discussed.

One alternative to individual consent might be to convene what Diana Baumrind has termed "peer consultants," selected from the study population [19]. This would symbolize the investigator's respect for the human beings involved in the study as rational agents worthy of consideration; the peers would take the place of the subjects as collaborators in the design of the research, thereby approximating "self-determination"; and the information given to peers could serve the same function as informed consent in educating and reassuring the public. Of course, for this strategy to be successful, it must be approached conscientiously and with ingenuity, making sure that those asked to serve as the peer consultants accurately represent the study population and are positioned so as to make the sort of choices one would want a proxy to make on one's behalf. This would appear to be applicable to all three hypotheticals. Peer consultants might also be used for more than proxy consent; a medical anthropological approach could provide richly detailed case studies, which might serve both to illustrate the statistical findings for eventual readers of the study and, perhaps more important, to give a human face to the nameless research subjects, thereby deepening the empathy of the epidemiologists and perhaps increasing their ability truly to understand the meaning and significance of their data.*

A related—but distinct—strategy is to obtain permission for the use of records from their custodians. In the case of PROJECT FAMILY, for example, the cooperation of officials in the judicial and social service offices would doubtless be essential. I think it is, however, misleading to say that subjects have given implied consent to the researcher's use of data about them when officials give their permission in such circumstances; rather, one could say that the goal of regularizing relationships has been fulfilled because the subjects' relationship to the researchers resembles their relationship to the judicial and social service process, since in both cases they are involuntarily entangled in a process intended to benefit society. The same cannot be said about PROJECT HIV, in which the subjects' relationship to the researchers is "irregular" compared with their relationship with the treating physicians who are the source of the initial information used by the researchers to identify and contact the HIV-infected individuals.

Another alternative to prospective informed consent is to employ after-the-fact debriefing and informed veto. This gives subjects an opportunity to exercise self-determination as to at least part of the study, it symbolizes the researchers' respect for subjects' autonomy, and it removes the implication of coercion that inheres in non-voluntary participation in research. For example, in PROJECT SMOKE, questionnaires could bear identifying numbers and each respondent could be given an envelope with a form bearing the matching number. After the questionnaires are turned in, respondents could be provided with an explanation of the true purposes of the research, and any who wished to have his or her questionnaire removed

*I am indebted to Kathleen M. West, MPH, for this point.

from the data set could check off on the form. This alternative is probably not feasible for PROJECT FAMILY, however, because of the difficulty of contacting all involved family members and asking for their permission. In PROJECT HIV, a veto is effectively given to subjects when they are contacted by the researchers to ask for their cooperation, provided that the researchers—at the risk of biasing the results—delete any information about non-cooperating subjects from the data set. (We shall return to this issue in the final section.)

Finally, provisions could be made to compensate subjects for any injury they suffer as a result of being studied without their advance consent. Since this entire exception is limited to situations involving negligible risk, the need for compensation for harm should be small, but providing compensation can still serve some purposes of consent, such as encouraging self-scrutiny by the investigator and providing a further incentive to choose among reasonable research designs in order to maximize subjects' welfare. We should recognize, however, that it will be much easier to measure the extent to which compensation is owed for harms to a person than for wrongs, which typically involve injury to a dignitary interest that is not easily monetizable.

The special problem of groups

Obviously, this brief list does not exhaust all alternatives to consent that might be argued to be legitimate to the extent they fulfill some of the same purposes as consent. One additional purpose is sometimes attributed to the requirement of obtaining subjects' consent, viz. that it permits members of a group to prevent a study from being conducted of which they disapprove. Thus stated, the effect is descriptively accurate and normatively true, as an aspect of self-determination. But if the idea is that informed consent protects groups against studies that will reveal information that is, from some viewpoint, harmful to the group, then I believe too much is claimed for informed consent. As an ethical matter, I do not believe—outside of situations in which a group can be taken to speak as whole through duly constituted leaders—that the notion of a group veto has anything to do with informed consent; and, as a practical matter, so long as *some* members of a group are willing to participate in a study, the group as a whole has no guarantee against being affected by the results of the study.

MINIMIZING BREACHES OF PRIVACY AND CONFIDENTIALITY

The discussion of the harms and wrongs intended to be avoided by the requirement of advance informed consent should already have made apparent that personal privacy is one of the major concerns in the protection of research subjects. Related to this is the notion of confidentiality, which requires those to whom private information has been conveyed for a professional purpose not to disclose that information outside the bounds drawn by that purpose. The courts have recognized that the protection of personally identifiable information is important to the success of epidemiology and hence serves a public good that may outweigh other social goods, such as full disclosure of information in the judicial process [20, 21]. Regrettably, in the medical world today, confidentiality is often honored in the breach, which is especially ironic when one considers that medical records today probably contain more information about people than ever, thanks in large measure to the electronics revolution and to the ever-increasing demands for more data for various reimbursement and other management purposes.

When a researcher uses data collected for other purposes, it is important for the researcher—and then the IRB—to consider the privacy and confidentiality expectations that attached to the data when the subjects provided it. Especially when direct consent for the use of data is not sought from the subjects, the researchers should realize that they are, in effect, being brought into the circle of confidentiality that attaches to the data, and they are governed by the same strictures against unauthorized release that attach to the persons who originally gathered the data. Indeed, to the extent that new information has effectively been generated by the researchers having linked together data from several sources, they are under a greater obligation than that applicable to the original sources, so far as protecting their files from public disclosure.

Public disclosure is usually associated with one form or another of psychological or social (including financial) harm. But even when confidentiality is not breached by the investigator, the mere fact that the investigator has gained access to private information may constitute a wrong to the subject. In PROJECT FAMILY, for example, if the researcher has access to files maintained by social workers who dealt with the abusing families—files that are not usually thought of as part of the *public* record—then merely reading those files (even with identifiers removed) is in some sense to intrude on the privacy of the people involved. (One can be sure that the social workers would feel that *their* privacy had been invaded were the files reviewed without their advance approval [22–24].)

It would, therefore, usually be appropriate to have the contact with the potential subject come initially from someone who is inside the circle of confidentiality before any disclosure is made to a researcher. Thus, in PROJECT HIV it would seem advisable for the treating physician, rather than the researcher, to contact the potential subject, so as to have permission for enlarging the circle before any information is disclosed. There is a risk, however, that the potential subject's agreement to participate may not be truly voluntary because the request to participate in research comes from a person on whom the subject is dependent in some sense [25]. This should be less of a problem in situations like PROJECT HIV, when the physician–patient relationship is not current; in any event, it is important always to make explicit to the subject that further services are not conditioned upon an agreement to participate and to be alert to the need to re-enforce this message, which subjects may have a hard time accepting or believing, perhaps for unconscious reasons. (In the context of treatment, Laurence Tancredi has noted that "the physician's predisposition will influence the way the information is presented and bias the patient toward (or away from) particular . . . options" [26].)

None of the strategies discussed previously are fully responsive to the concerns about privacy, although after-the-fact debriefing and veto rights comes closest if it means that any data involving an objecting subject will be removed from the researcher's files. Nonetheless, the use of peer consultants might at least serve to alert investigators to situations in which people in the subject population take the veiw that certain aspects of their lives are particularly private matters, onto which the researchers should be especially reluctant to intrude. If a small modification of study design would provide a means of steering clear of such problems, the use of proxies could avoid wronging the actual subjects in a significant fashion.

REFERENCES

1. Rothman KJ. The rise and fall of epidemiology, 1950–2000 A.D. **N Engl J Med** 1981; 304: 600–602.
2. Chann CI, Rothman KJ. IRBs and epidemiologic research: how inappropriate restrictions hamper studies. **IRB: A Journal of Human Subjects Research** 1984; 6(4): 5–7.
3. Hershey N. IRB jurisdiction and limits in IRB actions. **IRB: A Journal of Human Subjects Research** 1985; 7(2): 7–9.
4. Cann CI, Rothman KJ. Reply: overcoming hurdles to epidemiologic research. **IRB: A Journal of Human Subjects Research** 1985; 7(2): 9.
5. Jonas H. Philosophical Reflections on Experimenting with Human Subjects. **Daedalus** 1969; 98: 219–245.
6. de Sola Pool I. The New Censorship of Social Research. **Public Interest** 1980; 59: 56–88.
7. Patullo EL. Who risks what in social research. **IRB: A Journal of Human Subjects Reearch** 1980; 2(3): 1–3, 12.
8. Robertson J. The scientist's right to research: a constitutional analysis. **So Cal L Rev** 1979; 51: 1203–1281.
9. Gibbs RA, Caskey CT. The application of recombinant DNA technology for genetic probing in epidemiology. **Ann Rev Public Health** 1989; 10: 27–48.
10. MacIntyre A. Risk, harm, and benfit assessments as instruments of moral evaluation. In: Beauchamp T, Faden R, Wallace R, Walters L, Eds. **Ethical Issues in Social Science Research. Baltimore,** Md: Johns Hopkins University Press; 1982: 175.
11. Dworkin G. Must subjects be objects? In: Beauchamp T, Faden R, Wallace R, Walters L, Eds. **Ethical Issues in Social Science Research.** Baltimore, Md: Johns Hopkins University Press; 1982: 246, 247–248.
12. Capron AM. Is consent always necessary in social science research. In: Beauchamp T, Faden R, Wallace R, Walters L, Eds. **Ethical Issues in Social Science Research.** Baltimore, Md: Johns Hopkins University Press; 1982: 215, 220–229.
13. Berlin I. **Two Concepts of Liberty.** Oxford: Clarendon Press; 1958: 16.
14. Faden RR, Beauchamp TL. **A History and Theory of Informed Consent.** New York: Oxford University Press; 1986.
15. Katz J. **The Silent World of Doctor and Patient.** New Haven: Yale University Press; 1983.
16. President's Commission for the Study of Ethical Problems in Medicine and Biomedical and Behavioral Research. **Making Health Care Decisions.** Washington, D.C.: Government Printing Office; 1982.
17. Freund P. Legal frameworks for human experimentation. **Daedalus** 1969; 98: 323.
18. Fried C. Privacy. **Yale L J** 1968; 77: 482.
19. Baumrind D. Nature and Definition of Informed Consent in Research Involving Deception. In: National Commission for the Protection of Human Subjects of Biomedical and Behavioral Research. **The Belmont Report: Ethical Principles and Guidelines for the Protection of Human Subjects of Research,** DHEW Publication No. (OS) 78-0014. Washington, D.C.: Government Printing Office; 1978: Appendix, Vol. 2. 23–42.
20. Farnsworth v. Procter and Gamble Co.; 758 F.2d 1545 (11th Cir. 1985).
21. Curran WJ. Protecting Confidentiality in Epidemiologic Investigations by the Centers for Disease Control. **N Engl J Med** 1986; 314: 1027–1028.
22. Hughes EC. Who studies whom? **Hum Organ** 1974; 33: 327–334 (threats inhere in studying people in institutions).
23. Geller JL, Lidz CW. When the subjects are hospital staff, is it ethical (or possible) to get informed consent? **IRB: A Journal of Human Subjects Research** 1987; 9(5): 4–5 (problems with obtaining informed consent from employees).

24. Pattullo EL. Exemption from review, not informed consent. **IRB: A Journal of Human Subjects Research** 1987; 9(5): 6–8 (consent to observe employees' work can be given by employer).
25. Capron AM. The law of genetic therapy. In: Hamilton M, Ed. **The New Genetics and the Future of Man.** Grand Rapids, Mich.: Eerdmans Publishing Co.; 1972: 133, 150–152.
26. Tancredi L. The new technology of psychiatry: ethics, epidemilogy and technology assessment. In: Tancredi L, Ed. **Ethical Issues in Epidemiologic Research.** New Brunswick, N.J.: Rutgers University Press; 1986: 1, 16.

[15]

Children in HIV/AIDS Clinical Trials: Still Vulnerable after All These Years

Carol Levine

"All things considered, I chose what was best for my children, or what I thought was best..." confessed Jean-Jacques Rousseau in 1782. What more can one expect from a parent or a professional entrusted with decisions about children? What Rousseau thought was "best" for each of his five infants, however, was to dispatch them to foundling homes in Paris, without even keeping a record of their birthdates, thus leaving them to an unknown but probably dismal fate. [1]

Acting from moral and often legal obligations to protect vulnerable persons from harm and to enhance their welfare, adults daily make decisions about and for children. Professionals and policy makers fulfill their social responsibilities by creating and implementing policies and practices that enable children's caregivers to fulfill these same goals. While instances of adult self-interest overriding children's interests are seldom as blatant as Rousseau's (even he later regretted his actions), it is not always easy to decide what is truly in a particular child's best interests or what will benefit children as members of a group (for example, a family, school class, or an abstract collective). It is even more difficult to determine, when justifiable goals conflict, which should prevail.

The conflicts have been particularly sharply drawn in the area of human subjects research. Even in the 19th century, when Pasteur inoculated nine-year-old Jacob Meister with a rabies vaccine, some of his colleagues protested that he had not yet established the efficacy of his treatment in animals. This in fact had been Pasteur's own rationale for refusing to inoculate other children bitten by rabid dogs.[2] In the 1950s, researchers at the Willowbrook State Home in Staten Island, New York, infected institutionalized mentally retarded children with hepatitis as part of an experimental study.[3] The study was justified on the grounds that the children would be exposed to hepatitis in the institution anyway and criticized for both its methods and its recruitment procedures, which offered inducements to parents to consent. In the 1960s and 1970s there was a prolonged debate between those, like Paul Ramsey, who opposed "unconsented touching" on the basis of a strict interpretation of the principle of respect for persons, and Richard McCormick, who stressed children's status as members of society and their obligations to contribute to the general welfare when no risk is involved. In the federal regulations, Ramsey's extreme position was rejected in favor of a strong protectionist stance, including the development of special regulations for research involving children.[4] As a consequence, some potential benefits to children have been foregone. The HIV/AIDS epidemic among children is challenging the status quo.

The ethical imperative to do pediatric HIV/AIDS research

Nearly all drugs approved for marketing by the Food and Drug Administration (FDA) carry a label warning that "this drug is not to be used in children..." or "is not recommended for use in infants and young children, since few studies have been carried out in this group...." Pediatricians are forced to extrapolate and estimate dosages and indications for their young patients. As long ago as 1968 H.C. Shirkey coined the term "therapeutic orphans" to refer to infants and children, who take prescription drugs that have been tested only in adults.[5] (The term now applies to drugs with a potential market under 200,000 patients; the Orphan Drug Act of 1983 was created to give pharmaceutical sponsors economic incentives to bring them to market.[6])

In evaluating the overall risk-benefit ratio, Robert J. Levine concludes that "If we consider the availability of drugs proved safe and effective through the devices of modern clinical pharmacology a benefit, then it is unjust to deprive classes of persons, e.g., children and pregnant women, of this benefit." Furthermore, he points out, "We have a tendency to distribute unsystematically the unknown risks of drugs in children and pregnant women, thus maximizing the frequency of their occurrence and minimizing the probability of their detection."[7]

Against this background, consider the catastrophic impact of the new disease of HIV/AIDS on the world's children. The World Health Organization (WHO) estimates that during the 1980s 200,000 HIV-infected infants were born worldwide, mostly as a result of perinatal transmission. By 1992, in Africa alone, 250,000 are likely to have been born. In some African and Caribbean countries, 10 percent of the AIDS cases are in children under the age of five.[8] In the United States, as of June 1991, 3,140 cases of AIDS among children 13 years or younger had been reported.[9] AIDS is expected to move into the five leading causes of death in children in the next few years.[10] AIDS in children, as in adults, is still ultimately fatal.

Given the threat of HIV/AIDS to the world's children, there is a powerful ethical imperative to do research involving children. The motivations are several and not always easily distinguishable: to understand and describe this new childhood disease; to prolong the lives of already sick children and to improve the quality of their existence; to develop effective treatments and vaccines for future generations; to test drugs in a population that is more easily controlled and compliant than adults and that has a shorter life span than adults so that reductions in mortality can be demonstrated more quickly.

In the past few years there have been significant advances in pediatric research: notably studies on AZT, ddI, and ddC. The National Institute of Allergy and Infectious Diseases (NIAID) now has 15 pediatric AIDS Clinical Treatment Units (ACTUs) within the AIDS Clinical Treatment Group (ACTG). The National Institute of Child Health and Development (NICHD) also has a clinical trials network, and several other NIH institutes, such as the National Cancer Institute (NCI) are also involved in pediatric research. But much of this effort has been criticized as too little, too late, too uncoordinated.

Asserting that research aimed at the adult disease "will inevitably fail to respond adequately to the emerging epidemic in the pediatric population," in 1988 the Secretary's Work Group on Pediatric HIV Infection and Disease from the Department of Health and Human Services (HHS) called for "substantial increases in funding for all aspects of pediatric and maternal HIV disease research....targeted to specific issues (e.g., early diagnosis, surveillance to quantify the number of infected newborns, and timing of HIV transmission...."[11]

In 1991 the Institute of Medicine's Committee to Study the AIDS Research Program of the National Institutes of Health recommended that NIH "increase participation of currently underrepresented populations (i.e., minorities, current and former users of intravenous drugs, women, and children)." This goal can be accomplished, the IOM stated, by making entry criteria for clinical trials less stringent, where appropriate, and by improving outreach and the provision of ancillary services. The IOM report also recommended methods for better coordination and oversight.[12]

A working group convened to develop a consensus document on ethical principles and policies for clinical research on HIV/AIDS concluded:

> No group should be categorically excluded, on the basis of age, gender, mental status, place of residence or incarceration, or other social or economic characteristic from access to clinical trials or other mechanisms of access to experimental therapies.[13]

These conclusions are based on clinical and ethical arguments. There is, in addition, a compelling emotional incentive to do research. Kathleen Nolan describes the "special pathos" of HIV infection and AIDS in children:

> From infancy to adolescence, children hold our hopes for the future. They are given into our care to nurture and protect. As daunting additions to the long litany of modern hazards threatening pediatric well-being, HIV infection and AIDS thus force us to confront vulnerability and dependence, not as totally unique issues but with a starkness and urgency imposed both by the nature of the disease and by its social context.[14]

After years of powerlessness, pediatric AIDS specialists see the beginning of a new era, in which they can offer their young patients something of value. "Pediatrics always lags behind adult medicine in funding and clinical trials," says James Oleske. "So the medical profession has got to really get in there and fight for these kids."[15]

The limits of the ethical imperative

Protocols involving sick children present particularly difficult choices for investigators, Institutional Review Boards (IRBs), primary care physicians, and parents. The locus of ethical justification is shifting, however, in significant ways. Investigators typically present information to IRBs to justify the participation of children. Given the ethical imperative to do research on HIV/AIDS, an IRB will be hard pressed to justify any delays or significant revisions in a pediatric protocol.

The current federal regulations establish the basic framework for evaluating pediatric protocols. The familiar problems of consent, harm-benefit ratios, and selection of subjects have become even more important in a fatal disease that affects primarily children from poor minority families.

Consent

According to Robert Levine, the central problem presented by proposals to do research involving children is that "children, as a class of persons, lack the legal capacity to consent" and that many, especially young children, "are incapable of sufficient comprehension to meet the high standards of consent to research developed in such documents as the Nuremberg Code."[16]

Because children lack the legal and mental capacity to consent to participation in research, parents are their traditional advocates and decision makers. Middle-class parents, in consultation with their child's doctor, may become "experts" in a childhood disease, searching for specialists, research protocols and the most advanced investigational drugs. Even so, the decision to enter their child in a clinical trial is a weighty one. The parents of children with HIV/AIDS—the majority of them with few resources and many problems, not the least of which may be their own HIV illness—may not fit this model. While they, no less than other parents, want the best for their child, they may not have access to the information, independent evaluation, and social supports that are often necessary to participate in a research project. They are typically dependent on the public health care delivery system with all its problems of access, underfunding, and poor coordination. They may be distrustful of researchers and unwilling to enroll their child in anything as uncertain as an "experiment." Moreover, many poor parents feel alienated from their child's care by health care workers who fail to include them in discussions and to inform them fully about options. Their consent may be legally valid but less than fully informed.

Many potential subjects are in the care of foster parents or relatives who lack the legal right to consent to research. Judith M. Martin and Henry S. Sacks surveyed state agencies to determine their policies concerning participation of foster children in clinical trials.[17] Only seven states—Connecticut, Georgia, Illinois, Massachusetts, New Jersey, Texas, and Wyoming_reported having formal policies. Five states—California, Maryland, New York, North Carolina, and Pennsylvania—reported having a mechanism making it possible to enroll foster children in trials. In four of the twelve states with policies or mechanisms—Illinois, New York, Pennsylvania, and Wyoming—foster children cannot be enrolled in trials unless their biological parents consent.

When the natural parent is unavailable or unable to consent, alternative methods have been created: increased efforts to communicate with the parent and assistance to the pediatric investigator (Pennsylvania); case-by-case determinations (North Carolina, California, New Jersey, Texas); medical guardianship for the foster parent (Maryland); a central review board to approve protocols and enrollment of individual children on a case-by-case basis (Georgia, Massachusetts, and proposed in Connecticut).

More than 331,000 children are currently in foster care (defined as any out-of-home placement); of these, the agencies reported, 785 were known to be HIV-infected, and only 15 were enrolled in clinical trials. Martin and Sacks also surveyed 51 pediatric investigators currently conducting NIH-funded clinical trials. The respondents reported that 432 children were enrolled in trials, and that 69 (16 percent) were in foster care. They also reported knowing of a total of 181 foster children who were eligible for their trials but could not be enrolled because a valid consent was not available.

In New York City, which has the nation's greatest concentration of pediatric AIDS cases, a process for expediting consent for children in foster care while still protecting individual children's rights and interests is still being worked out. In 1990 the Child Welfare Administration (CWA), a division of the City's Human Resources Administration (HRA), created a review system for requests to enroll foster children. Under that system, the investigator requested HRA, which has custody of the child, to consent to enrollment in a particular trial. A medical panel advised CWA of the risks and benefits of proposed trials. The investigator then presented his or her case to a meeting with three or four representatives of the panel, together with HRA staff. The medical panel then reported in writing on the results of their deliberations and their recommendation as to whether foster children could be enrolled. The final decision was made by the HRA Commissioner in consultation with legal staff. If a study was approved, HRA entered an agreement with the participating hospital concerning the treatment of children in the study and with NIH concerning the confidentiality of information.

Responding to criticisms that this system was "cumbersome, needlessly time consuming and posing a barrier to care in some instances," the present HRA Commissioner, Barbara Sabol, has streamlined the process. Protocols will be reviewed as soon as they become available, rather than after a particular hospital decides to participate. The medical panel will meet regularly to discuss protocols. Standardized agreements will be drawn up for the enrollment of HIV-infected foster children in clinical studies. When HRA determines that a particular trial is appropriate for foster children, the agency will notify AIDS specialized medical facilities of its approval and will issue a proposed agreement. Once the hospital and HRA have completed the agreement, HRA's part in the process is over. It is then up to the foster care agency to communicate with the natural parent, including visiting the parent's last known address at least once and sending a mailgram stating the need for the parent's consent. If these efforts fail, the foster care agency has to certify its "diligent search." At that point, the physicians can enroll the child and simply inform CWA's Pediatric AIDS Unit.[18]

This proposal is a conscientious attempt to remove the bureaucratic barriers that have impeded the enrollment of HIV-infected children in research studies. It reflects the desire of those responsible for the well-being of foster children to enhance their opportunities for access to promising new drugs. In relying so heavily on medical judgments, however, the proposal does not give full weight to the other factors that influence a decision to participate in a trial. A determination that a protocol is acceptable for foster children is not the same as a determination that a protocol is the best option for a particular foster child. The child's medical history, psychological and social development, and prior association with the medical team and the foster family all may influence a decision. One child may be well enough adjusted to participate in a protocol that involves many trips to a clinic and additional venipunctures or other research procedures; another child who is also eligible on medical grounds may be traumatized by the process. The final decision should not rest with the investigator; an independent evaluation should be conducted. The child's primary care physician, if there is one, should play an important role in the process. Formal advocates for children are not required by federal regulations; nevertheless, advocates can assist in ensuring that the consent process is appropriate (for example, that natural parents, when contacted, are given full information and options) and that a particular child's best interests are served, whether that means rapid enrollment in a clinical trial or a decision not to participate.[19]

Harm-benefit ratios

Several questions concern harm-benefit ratios. First, at what point should children be enrolled in Phase I clinical trials? (Phase I trials are designed to study safety and drug activity, and do not offer any benefit to participants.) To speed up the process of drug testing in children and to take account of the different manifestations of HIV in children, the Secretary's Work Group recommended that "selected Pediatric AIDS Centers should also carry out early testing of promising agents in infants, children, and adolescents *simultaneously with their Phase I testing in adults* [emphasis in original]." [20] Another argument in favor of parallel phase I testing in children and adults, according to Nolan, is that "children may in some cases have fewer adverse reactions to a particular agent than might have been predicted by adult studies, and possibly useful agent may therefore never be evaluated in the very population for which they would be most likely to be safe and effective."[21] This recommendation has not been adopted, however.

As Terrence Ackerman points out, the goal of expediting pediatric research to enhance the welfare of HIV-infected children as a group in this instance may "compromise the welfare of individual child-subjects." Ackerman gives several reasons:

> First, children recruited for phase I trials will be in the later stages of their illness, since they are usually not eligible until phase II or III drugs have proven ineffective or unacceptably toxic in their treatment. As a result, they will have incurred a substantial burden of prior suffering and may be significantly debilitated. Second, many subjects in phase I trials do not receive potentially therapeutic doses of the drugs being studied, because the increments in dosing for consecutive groups of subjects usually begin with a very conservative low dose. Third, exposure to unexpected toxicities and additional monitoring procedures may compound the suffering...Further, many drugs that enter phase I testing do not yield evidence of potential efficacy....Finally, the harm/benefit ratio of participating in a phase I trial must be compared to the alternative management strategy of using only measures that enhance the comfort of the patient.[22]

The work group on clinical research ethics proposed a compromise between parallel Phase I testing in adults and children and long delays awaiting completion of trials in adults:

> Drugs or procedures intended to be used in all age groups should be tested in children only after Phase I/II studies have demonstrated safety and drug activity in adults. Phase II/III trials involving children should be conducted in parallel with Phase II/III trials in adults.

A second research design issue concerns the inclusion in studies of asymptomatic, HIV-positive infants whose true infection status cannot be reliably determined. All children born to HIV-positive mothers carry maternal HIV antibodies; the rate of transmission of HIV from mother to child is now estimated at between 20 and 30 percent. That is, at least two-thirds of babies who test HIV-positive at birth are not truly infected. They cannot benefit and may be harmed by the administration of toxic drugs for a condition they do not have. On the other hand, early intervention for truly infected infants may offer considerable benefits, both in prolonging life and in preventing developmental delays and opportunistic infections.

In this instance the interests of sick children (both current and future) in receiving potentially beneficial drugs is in conflict with the interests of well children in not receiving them. This situation is not unique to HIV, according to Nolan.[23] The 1950s Salk polio vaccine trials included thousands of children who were not truly "at risk" for developing polio. At the time it was not known whether the vaccine was effective or not. The analogy would be more compelling if it compared potential HIV vaccine trials with the Salk trials. Vaccines are designed to prevent illness, not to treat it. (The Salk HIV vaccine trials in already infected individuals are more properly called immunotherapy.) The inclusion of healthy infants in drug trials, especially ones that involve serious risks and burdens, calls for much more stringent justification. Only if other markers besides HIV seropositivity are present (age-adjusted decreases in CD4 T-lymphocyte counts, HIV culture, or p24 antigen assay, for instance[24]) can the inclusion of asymptomatic infants in research be justified.

Third, can placebo-controlled trials be justified? In general, with an ultimately fatal disease like AIDS, it is difficult but not impossible to justify the inclusion of a placebo arm in a trial where the endpoints are death or permanent disability.[25] Placebo controls, always problematic in pediatric protocols,[26] become even more so in HIV/AIDS studies because of the short lifespan of the child-subjects and the additional burdens that may be imposed. Active controls, where available, are preferable.

One of the first major trials involving children was criticized precisely because it had a placebo arm. This trial was designed to answer an important and hotly debated question: whether intravenous immune globulin is effective in preventing secondary bacterial infections in children at various stages of HIV illness. The trial enrolled 372 children, over three quarters of whom were under five years of age, with clinical or immunological evidence of HIV disease. They were randomly assigned to receive either intravenous immune globulin or intravenous placebo. Each group received infusions every 28 days for two years. The results of the trial showed a significantly increased time free from serious infection for the group of treated children with CD4+ lymphocyte counts of 200 per cubic millimeter or more at entry. After 24 months 67 percent of the children receiving immune globulin had not had a serious infection, compared to 48 percent of those in the placebo group. No such benefits were seen in sicker children, i.e., those with CD4+ lymphocyte counts below 200 at entry. There was no difference in survival between the treatment and the placebo group.[27]

Was this placebo necessary? The value of immune globulin therapy in HIV-infected children was a legitimate question for scientific inquiry; it was in a state of "clinical equipoise."[28] That is, there was a dispute among clinicians about the efficacy of this treatment. The ethical question was not the withholding of treatment to those in the placebo group, but the method of administration. Beyond the relatively minor physical risks (and attendant discomforts) associated with the placement and maintenance of an intravenous line, there were psychological risks that accompany repeated trips to clinics for the lengthy procedures. The authors of the study reported only minor adverse effects associated with the infusion procedure, but did not comment on the social or psychological effects.

This study was approved by the IRBs at the 28 cooperating clinical centers and all the subjects were entered with the written consent of a parent or legal guardian. Were there no qualms about subjecting some very sick and even dying children to intravenous infusions of placebo?

Traditionally, blinded trials are justified on the basis that they eliminate investigator bias. (They may also reduce investigator discomfort at having to administer a known placebo to a sick child.) Since the endpoints in this trial were death or the laboratory-confirmed or clinically diagnosed occurrence of one or more serious bacterial infections—neither of which is a subjective determination—the trial might have been designed with a treatment arm and a matched control group of untreated children.

In trial design, the working group on clinical research ethics asserted,

> In addition to scientific validity, the ethical values of respect for persons, individual beneficence, and justice must be considered....[29]

Implementing this guideline will require creative, thoughtful, and non-reflexive approaches.

Adolescents as research subjects

In drug development generally, the eldest group of "therapeutic orphans" is adolescents—too old for pediatric protocols (which generally include children up to age 13) and too young for adult protocols (which often set a minimum age of 18). Yet there are many questions specific to teenagers. For example, in 1990 the Food and Drug Administration (FDA) approved the use of Norplant, an implantable birth control method. Iris Litt points out that this agent has the potential of delaying pregnancy until the highest-risk adolescent years have passed. There are no data, however, about efficacy and side effects of the hormonal implant in this population, and no information about costs, acceptance, and access for teenagers. Moreover, there has been no consideration of the potential impact on sexually transmitted diseases and HIV of introducing a non-barrier method of birth control.[30]

Even where protocols may allow adolescents to participate, there may be formidable legal barriers.[31] The economic barriers to medical care are even more daunting. Nationally a third of poor adolescents have no health insurance. Virtually all adolescents who are privately insured receive their health care under their parents' plans. As a result parents control access to care. One of the primary reasons parental consent is required is to establish financial liability. Even in a state with liberal eligibility requirements for Medicaid, such as New York, there are serious problems for teenagers seeking to enter the system.[32] Limited access to medical care becomes even more limited access to clinical research.

To address some of the problems, the working group

on clinical research ethics in HIV/AIDS recommended that

> States must establish clear rules to enable mature and emancipated minors [such as those who have demonstrated an independent life pattern or who have borne a child or entered the armed services] to provide legally adequate consent for counselling, testing, treatment, and research.[33]

But the group also recognized that adolescents have special developmental characteristics. Their autonomy can be enhanced by the advice of a knowledgeable, sympathetic adult—a family member, or an independent counselor-advocate.

International research

HIV affects children around the world; but will the world's children share in the burdens and benefits of research? In poor countries where children do not receive basic immunizations and primary health care, or even adequate nutrition, the question of whether there will be access to newly developed HIV/AIDS drugs seems frivolous. Yet such populations might be considered as potential research targets, especially for vaccine research.

Collaborative international studies can provide much useful information on the natural history, epidemiology, and treatment of HIV/AIDS in different areas of the world. To meet the standards of justice, however, subjects who contribute to the research effort should be intended beneficiaries.

The continuing need for special protections for children and other vulnerable subjects has become even more apparent in the international arena. Two examples will suffice. First, in October 1990, WHO recommended that the Romanian government ban the use of FLV 23-A, an unlicensed drug, in experiments on 83 orphaned children with AIDS in a Bucharest hospital. The drug had been developed by a British oil engineer without any medical training; a Tulane University pediatrician was involved as a "private observer." The British Foreign Office had earlier urged the Romanian Health Ministry to stop the trials because they believed the drug to be useless, and the National Cancer Institute found samples of the drug to be "totally inactive" against HIV in the laboratory.[34] The Romanian government was reported to have agreed to the testing in return for shipments of medical supplies.

Second, in 1986, Daniel Zagury initiated an AIDS vaccine program in Zaire, using a recombinant vaccinia virus originally supplied to him by an NIH scientist. Zagury first immunized himself; the next subjects were 10 healthy, HIV-seronegative children between the ages of two and nine, and eight healthy, HIV-seronegative children between the ages of 10 and 18. According to Zagury, the mothers, who had AIDS, urged him to let their children participate in this project and he agreed on a "humanitarian" basis. Results from 12 of these 19 these subjects were reported in *Nature* (March 19, 1987 and April 21, 1988) with no indication that apart from Zagury all the subjects were children. Zagury claims that all the immunized children remain healthy, but this has not been independently verified.[35]

As a result of its investigation of the collaboration of NIH scientists in these and other studies, OPRR has required NIH to develop appropriate oversight mechanisms in future collaborative research and has placed restrictions on Robert Gallo's research activities with investigators outside the U.S. since he participated in several different aspects of Zagury's work. Furthermore, no research activities involving Zagury will be permitted without OPRR's prior written approval.

Administrative oversight aside, this example indicates how easily ethical considerations can be swept aside under the rubric of "humanitarianism" or "compassion." These children had escaped perinatal transmission; they were not at risk through casual contact with their mothers. There could be no possible benefit to them and there was potentially serious harm.

The Romanian and Zairian examples stand as cautions against allowing the current wave of optimism and enthusiasm for redressing the prior injustice of failing to consider the needs of pediatric HIV/AIDS patients to swamp the need to protect these vulnerable children. As Geison remarks, "It was in one sense an act of immense courage and humanitarianism for Pasteur to undertake the treatment of Meister....Nonetheless, it is also a form of courage and humanitarianism to *refuse* to use a potentially beneficial procedure in the face of resolvable uncertainty."[36] In HIV/AIDS, both kinds of courage are needed as well as the wisdom to distinguish between them.

References

1. Jean-Jacques Rousseau, *Confessions* (Paris, 1964 [1782]). Quoted in John Boswell, *The Kindness of Strangers* (New York: Vintage Books, 1990), pp. 1, 20–21 (fn 42).
2. Gerald L. Geison, "Pasteur's Work on Rabies: Re-examining the Ethical Issues," *Hastings Center Report*, April 1978, pp. 26–33.
3. Jay Katz, *Experimentation with Human Subjects* (New York: Russell Sage Foundation, 1972), pp. 633, 1010–17).
4. Department of Health and Human Services Rules and Regulations, 45 CFR 46: Subpart D-Additional Protections for Children Involved as Subjects in Research (March 8, 1983).
5. H. C. Shirkey, "Therapeutic Orphans," *Journal of Pediatrics*, Vol. 72 (1968): 119–20.
6. Public Law No. 97–414, 96 Stat. 2049 (1983).
7. Robert J. Levine, *Ethics and Regulation of Clinical Research*, 2nd edition (New Haven: Yale University Press, 1988), p. 240.
8. Unicef, "Children and AIDS: An Impending Calamity" (New York: 1990), pp. 4–5.

9. Centers for Disease Control, "HIV/AIDS Surveillance," July 1991, p. 5.

10. Department of Health and Human Services, Secretary's Work Group on Pediatric HIV Infection and Disease, "Final Report" (Washington: 1988), p. 7.

11. Secretary's Work Group on Pediatric HIV Infection and Disease, pp. 16, 18.

12. Institute of Medicine, *The AIDS Research Program of the National Institutes of Health: Report of a Study* (Washington, DC: 1991), p. 12.

13. Carol Levine, Nancy Neveloff Dubler, and Robert J. Levine, "Building a New Consensus: Ethical Principles and Policies for Clinical Research on HIV/AIDS," *IRB: A Review of Human Subjects Research*, Vol. 13, Nos. 1–2 (January–April 1991), p. 14.

14. Kathleen Nolan, "AIDS and Pediatric Research," *Evaluation Review*, Vol. 14, No. 4 (October 1990), 465.

15. Quoted in Sari Staver, "Apply Adult HIV Drug Studies to Kids' Care, Experts Urge," *American Medical News*, September 22/29, 1989, p. 40.

16. Levine, R.J., p. 236.

17. Judith M. Martin and Henry S. Sacks, "Do HIV-Infected Children in Foster Care Have Access to Clinical Trials of New Treatments?" *AIDS & Public Policy Journal*, Vol. 5, No. 1 (1990), 3–8.

18. Barbara J. Sabol, letter to Sarmistha Hauger, M.D., Assistant Medical Director, New York State AIDS Institute, May 28, 1991.

19. See Levine, Dubler, and Levine, p. 15 for a further discussion of the role of a child advocate.

20. Secretary's Work Group, p. 21.

21. Nolan, pp. 471–72.

22. Terrence Ackerman, "Protectionism and the New Research Imperative in Pediatric AIDS," *IRB: A Review of Human Subjects Research*, Vol. 12, No. 5 (September/October 1990), p.2.

23. Nolan, p. 474, citing Charles Fried, *Medical Experimentation: Personal Integrity and Social Policy* (New York: Elsevier, 1974).

24. Andrea Kovacs, Toni Frederick, Joseph Church, Andrea Eller, Margaret Oxtoby, and Laurence Mascola, "CD4 T-Lymphocyte Counts and *Pneumocystis carinii* Pneumonia in Pediatric HIV Infection," *JAMA*, Vol. 265, No. 13 (April 3, 1991), 1702.

25. Levine, Dubler, and Levine, p. 8.

26. See, for example, Ernest D. Prentice, Dean L. Antonson, Andrew Jameton, Benjamin Graver, and Thomas Sears, "Case Study: Can Children Be Enrolled in a Placebo-Controlled Trial of Synthetic Growth Hormone?" *IRB: A Review of Human Subjects Research*, Vol. 11, No. 1 (January/February 1989), pp. 6–10.

27. National Institute of Child Health and Human Development Intravenous Immunoglobulin Study Group, "Intravenous Immune Globulin for the Prevention of Bacterial Infections in Children with Symptomatic Human Immunodeficiency Virus Infection," *New England Journal of Medicine*, Vol. 325, No. 2 (July 11, 1991), 73–80.

28. Benjamin Freedman, "Equipoise and the Ethics of Clinical Research," *New England Journal of Medicine*, Vol. 317, No. 3 (1987), 141–45.

29. Levine, Dubler, and Levine, p. 6.

30. Iris Litt, "Adolescent Medicine," *JAMA*, Vol. 265, No. 23 (June 19, 1991), 3100.

31. See, e.g., Gary Melton, "Ethical and Legal Issues in Research and Intervention," *Journal of Adolescent Health Care*, Vol. 10 (1989), 36S–44S.

32. Ad Hoc Committee on Adolescents and HIV, New York State AIDS Advisory Council, "Illusions of Immortality: The Confrontation of Adolescence and AIDS," New York, n.d. [1991], pp. 29–33.

33. Levine, Dubler, and Levine, p. 15.

34. "Romanian Halts AIDS Drug Test," *New York Times*, October 30, 1990.

35. Office of Protection from Research Risks, Division of Human Subject Protections, "Findings and Required Actions Regarding Investigation of Noncompliance with HHS Regulations for the Protection of Human Subjects Involving the National Institutes of Health Intramural Research Program," July 3, 1991. The author was a member of a panel of special consultants to OPRR during this investigation; the information presented here is drawn solely from OPRR's "Interim Report."

36. Geison, p. 32.

[16]

Protecting Communities in Research: Philosophical and Pragmatic Challenges

CHARLES WEIJER

The Need to Protect the Community in Research

The issue of the protection of communities in clinical research first arose 10 years ago in studies conducted in technologically developing countries by scientists from technologically developed nations. The question was, which ethical standards ought to apply, those of the Western investigators or local standards?

Proponents of Western practices, including the requirement for written informed consent, argued that so-called Western ethical requirements for the conduct of research are truly international. They are articulated not only in American regulations, but also in a variety of international statements, including the International Covenant on Civil and Political Rights[1] and World Medical Association's Declaration of Helsinki.[2–4] Failing to recognize the force of these international documents would, they warned, be cultural relativism.

Those arguing for local standards pointed out that the ethics of research is largely a Western construction and its heavy reliance on the rights of the individual is not shared by all.[5,6] Imposing Western values on distant communities reflects a lack of respect for other cultures, they cautioned, and amounts to cultural imperialism. Given the intractability of the debate in philosophy over ethical universalism versus relativism, it is not surprising that the issue of appropriate standards for research on communities in technologically developing countries remains controversial to this day.[7,8]

Recently, a new issue has arisen with regard to communities in research. It involves the standards for the protection of communities within North America that are involved in research studies. The applicability of Western standards for the conduct of research, including those set out in the federal Common Rule, is not at stake in this case (and thus the debate of ethical universalism versus relativism is sidestepped). Rather, the issue is: Are additional measures, above and beyond those currently afforded individual research participants, required to protect communities in research?

The concerns expressed by some communities are perhaps seen most immediately through the lens of risk. While risks to individual research participants

This paper was commissioned by the U.S. National Bioethics Advisory Commission. Prof. Weijer's work is supported by the Department of Clinical Bioethics, Warren G. Magneson Clinical Center, National Institutes of Health, a Scholar Award and Operating Grant from the Medical Research Council of Canada, and a Clinical Scholar Award from Dalhousie University.

This paper is dedicated to the memory of my friend and mentor, Benjamin Freedman, Ph.D., Professor of Medicine and Philosophy, McGill University. I am grateful to Gary Goldsand, M.A., doctoral student in religious studies and bioethics at the University of Toronto, who assisted me in preparing the background research for this paper.

are all too familiar, risks to communities are rarely considered. How might a study place a community at risk? Two recent research projects on the genetics of cancer in Ashkenazic Jews illustrate the problem well:

- Streuwing and colleagues reported work on the frequency in Ashkenazic Jews of one particular mutation (185delAG) in the BRCA1 gene associated with a high risk of developing breast and ovarian cancer.[9] Samples for the project were collected from databanks established for Tay-Sachs disease and cystic fibrosis screening. Since identifying information was removed from all samples, the NIH Office of Human Subjects Review did not require individual informed consent.[10] The investigators found that 0.9% of Ashkenazic Jews carry the mutation, a much higher rate than in the general population.
- Laken and colleagues also used anonymized samples from a Tay-Sachs data bank in their search for the frequency in Ashkenazic Jews of a particular mutation in a gene predisposing to colon cancer (I1307K in the APC gene).[11] They found that the mutation was present in 6.1% of the Jews in the sample and none of the non-Jews. The authors noted with understandable excitement that this is the commonest cancer-associated mutation in a specific population yet described.

Since identifying information was removed from the DNA samples in both of these research projects, there are no risks of study participation for any of the individuals whose DNA was analyzed. But what of the community? The results of these studies may have a substantial impact on the community of Ashkenazic Jews. These two research reports may give further credence to the suggestion that Jews are more susceptible to malignancies such as breast cancer,[12,13] and this in turn may engender discrimination. A recent report in *Nature* expressed precisely this concern:

> Such findings, which have already led to Jewish groups being targeted as a potential market for commercial genetic tests, could create the perceptions that Jewish people are unusually susceptible to disease.... As a result ... anyone with a Jewish-sounding name could face discrimination in insurance and employment as companies struggle to keep down health-care costs.[14]

Reacting to the specter of discrimination, U.S. Jewish leaders have asked the National Human Genome Research Institute to discuss the possibility for developing guidelines for the conduct of genetic research on Ashkenazi Jews.[15]

Before considering what such guidelines might mandate, we must first establish that they are required. What is the current framework for ethical issues in clinical research? Does it capture adequately concerns arising from communities in research?

The Current Ethical Framework and Its Critics

The U.S. National Commission for the Protection of Human Subjects of Biomedical and Behavioral Research (National Commission) was charged, inter alia, with the task of defining a set of ethical principles that could serve to guide the conduct of research involving human subjects.[16] The objective was to "provide an analytical framework that will guide the resolution of ethical problems arising from research involving human subjects."[17] In their final publication, the *Belmont Report*, the members of the National Commission laid out three such principles: respect for persons, beneficence, and justice. Each of the principles is "generally accepted" and stems from "our cultural tradition."[18] The principle of respect for persons requires that individual autonomy be acknowledged and that persons with diminished autonomy be protected. The principle of beneficence requires that persons not only be protected from harm, but also that steps be taken to ensure their well-being. Justice, as conceived by the members of the National Commission, refers to the fair distribution of goods; in the context of research, it refers to the equitable distribution of the risks and potential benefits of research participation.

The ethical framework articulated in the *Belmont Report* focuses primarily on individual research subjects (and groups insofar as they might be wrongfully included in or excluded from research). When research involves communities, for example aboriginal communities, new issues arise.[19] Autonomous communities have their own politics, beliefs, and values and research may affect any of these elements. In a community that makes decisions collectively, merely seeking informed consent from individuals may harm the political structure. Providing information on disease treatment may negatively affect beliefs regarding traditional healing. Taking samples for genetic testing may offend the community that subscribes to a principle of natural harmony. It is hard to see how these concerns for the community in research fit within the *Belmont* framework. Indeed, the word *community* does not appear once in the document.

Robert J. Levine notes that the work of the National Commission has come under attack for overemphasizing individual rights and failing to talk about the community.

> In each of its publications, it [the National Commission] seems to embrace an atomistic view of the person. The person is seen as a highly individualistic bearer of duties and rights; among his or her rights, some of the most important are to be left alone, not to be harmed, and to be treated with fairness. Except, perhaps, in its report on research involving children, there is little or no reference to persons in relationship to others or as members of communities.[20]

Levine goes on to point out that the emphasis on individual rights was purposeful. The fight against physician paternalism peaked at the time of the National Commission's deliberations and patient autonomy was the main rallying cry in this struggle. Larger societal forces undoubtedly also influenced the document. The consumerism movement swept America in the early 1970s and concern for individual rights was very much a part of the zeitgeist. The failure of the *Belmont Report* to deal adequately with families and communities does not, Levine argues, render it useless: "Having said this, I do not think the Commission's recommendations are obsolete. . . . [I]t is usually quite appropriate to view investigator-subject relationships as relationships between strangers. Thus, in general an individualistic ethics is appropriate."[21]

The general approach of analyzing ethical problems via principles ("principlism") has attracted fire from many camps. Beauchamp and Childress originated this approach to medical ethics in their classic work *Principles of Biomedical*

Ethics.[22] The authors of this book contributed to the work of the National Commission: Beauchamp was on the commission's staff and Childress provided a contract paper. The critics of principlism are many. Impartial rule theorists have argued that without an overarching ethical theory principles are mere placeholders for utterances like, "consider justice."[23] Casuists suggest that principles themselves are too abstract to be of any use.[24] Moral reasoning involves, they claim, appeals to well-accepted cases that illustrate one principle or another. Virtue theorists point out that principles in and of themselves are unlikely to lead to the satisfactory resolution of a moral problem.[25,26] The moral agent must embody character traits such as honesty and integrity. Feminist thinkers have challenged the lack of attention to human relationships, to the "relational nature of human life."[27,28] Emanating from this critique, important implications for our understanding of justice have been traced[29] and a proposal to incorporate an "ethics of care" into research ethics has been put forward.[30]

The line of criticism most relevant to the problem of protecting communities in research, though, comes from communitarian philosophers. They argue that self-determination presupposes the existence of a community from which an individual receives many of his or her values. Miller summarizes the arguments as follows:

> First, the socialization process determines, or shapes, the values and preferences of individuals, hence, the idea of autonomously chosen values is factually incorrect. Second, an individual's actions, desires, and objectives are comprehensible only within the context of social conventions and institutions. . . . Third, the view that an autonomous individuals chooses his or her own values, preferences, and desires presupposes a self that does the choosing. This self will have to have a core of values with which to choose, in which case either there are values not autonomously chosen, or it is inexplicable how individuals come to have a set of values.[31]

In short, the communitarians argue that the principle of respect for persons must take account of the fact that an individual is situated within a particular community. It is further suggested that members of a community ought to have certain virtues, perhaps including compassion and love, and that "they should recognize a commitment to maintain social practices and institutions that establish and promote these obligations and virtues."[32]

A New Ethical Principle for Research?

The ethical framework articulated in the *Belmont Report* does not capture the moral issues stemming from community involvement in research. This leads us to a particularly difficult question: Do we need a new ethical principle in order to capture these concerns adequately? The communitarian critique raises the possibility that we do not. Perhaps all that is needed is enrichment of the existing principles: situating the individual in a particular community. Indeed, one of the authors of *Principles*, Childress, acknowledges that a reinterpretation of the view of the person inherent in the principles is necessary:

> Any serviceable account of biomedical ethics in a liberal society requires a central place for the principle of respect for autonomy. However, its

> demands are often unclear because of the complexity of personal actions and values, and because it is not the only source of moral guidance. In fact, the richest resolutions of debates in bioethics presuppose attention to the claims of other ethical principles as well as a fuller interpretation of selves in time and community.[33]

The communitarian has been successful in establishing two claims. First, that self-determination is impossible unless we presuppose an individual located within a community (otherwise choice can never "get off the ground"). Second, that the interests of the individual may include the continuation of certain communal practices. The two claims are sufficient for us to conclude (with Childress) that the view of person in the principles needs to be enriched. Having acknowledged this, I believe nonetheless that a new principle is required to capture fully the issue of communities in research.

Although the authors of the *Belmont Report* intended the three principles to be comprehensive, others have suggested additional principles, including principles of validity and value,[34] honesty and accuracy,[35] and respect for communities.[36] Levine (1982) made the first call for a principle of "respect for cultures":

> Perhaps we should not attempt to develop universally valid standards for informed consent. Perhaps instead we should recognize the validity of certain forms of cultural relativism and have each culture decide how it should show respect for its own persons. If the guiding principle must have a name, I suggest that it might be "respect for cultures."[37]

More recently, McCarthy made a similar call, one that captures the cases in which we are interested more clearly:

> The principles have achieved notoriety in countries that stress individual liberty and place less emphasis on the rights and dignity of the community. However, many third world countries have much to teach developed nations about community values. For this reason I believe that the principles of justice, beneficence and respect for persons should be supplemented by a fourth principle, dealing with respect for the family and the community of the research subjects.[38]

Unfortunately, in both cases, little argumentation is presented as to why a new moral principle is needed.

I believe a fourth ethical principle must be added to those found in the *Belmont Report:* the principle of "respect for communities." At least three arguments can be summoned in support of this position. First, even if the continuation of some communal practices is in the interest of the individual, community interests are separable from individual interests. Indeed, individual and community interests may even conflict. The separable nature of these interests is illustrated by the studies on cancer genetics in Ashkenazic Jews mentioned above. In both cases the fact that individual identifiers were removed meant that there were no risks to individual research participants. Since the community to which these individuals belong was identified, the community was placed at risk. One can also imagine circumstances in which individual and community interests may conflict. Gostin provides an interesting example:

> Could individuals in a study each give consent to disclosure of information, and yet the study would violate the right of the collective to

> privacy? The answer is yes if one believes that populations have a right to defend their reputation and dignity as much as individuals do. It is conceivable, even where the information revealed about each member of the group is non-consequential or is not personally identifiable, that the group can be harmed. . . . The right of populations to have some say in the collection and spread of data that they believe reflect badly on their identity is an important ethical principle.[39]

Conflict may also occur if during the conduct of a study, and after informed consent has been obtained from individual study participants, the community decides to withdraw from the study. If individual participants are still willing, or even anxious, to continue study participation, their wishes are in direct opposition to those of the community. A new ethical principle will allow us to capture the fact that the community has interests that are, at times at least, separate from those of individual community members.

Second, an ethical principle does not merely serve the purpose of capturing existing moral debate; in other words, principles are not merely descriptive. Ethical principles also serve to acknowledge the moral status of players. The principle of respect for persons makes clear that the individual has moral status and that the wishes and interests of the individual must be taken seriously in moral analysis. A new ethical principle, respect for communities, would similarly accord moral status to the community and require that the wishes and interests of the community be taken seriously.

Third, the principle of respect for communities can be justified as other ethical principles have been. The sorts of justification required to establish a new principle depend on just what one thinks ethical principles are. Justification is simplest for the impartial rule theorist, for she believes principles are more or less meaningless anyway. Concerns about the community in research, and ultimately moral rules regarding the proper treatment of the community, may be loosely collected under the placeholder "Be sure and think about the community"—the principle of respect for communities.

The view of the impartial rule theorist is problematic for many reasons outlined elsewhere and gives principles too little credit.[40] The principles are best understood as prima facie duties[41] and hence the principle of respect for communities confers upon the researcher an obligation to respect the values of the community in research and, wherever possible, to protect the community from harm. As a prima facie duty, as opposed to an absolute duty, this obligation may be set aside if a sufficiently compelling justification to do so exists. Ethical principles in bioethics are not justified by appeal to moral theory, but rather by appeals to tradition and reflective equilibrium (principles informing cases; cases informing principles). The duty to respect communities is best described as an emerging tradition. The protection of the community in research is coming to be acknowledged as an important moral consideration. Reflective equilibrium suggests that the current principles do not capture adequately this concern and hence a new principle of respect for communities is needed.

Implementing the Principle

If a new ethical principle of respect for communities is required, how ought it to be implemented? Little guidance is currently available for researchers working in communities. The only provision in U.S. Department of Health and Human Services regulations pertains to standards for international research. Research in foreign countries may follow procedures in those countries provided the department or agency head determines that those procedures are "at least equivalent to those provided in this [DHHS] policy."[42] Research carried out under the auspices of the U.S. Food and Drug Administration is not eligible for this exemption. The *IRB Guidebook* notes that the "at least equivalent" requirement is a high standard and is unlikely to be met by broad policy outlines, including the Nuremberg Code or the Declaration of Helsinki, alone.[43] Dickens, Gostin, and Levine believe that the guidelines articulated by the Council for International Organizations of Medical Sciences (described below) likely meet the required standard.[44]

The Council for International Organizations of Medical Sciences (CIOMS) has two sets of international guidelines governing research. One document refers to clinical research in general; the other is specific to epidemiological research. Some direction for research involving communities is found in both documents. The former document, *International Ethical Guidelines for Biomedical Research Involving Human Subjects*, takes the stand that underdeveloped communities are potentially vulnerable and hence research involving such communities may only be carried out if the following conditions are met: (1) the research could not reasonably be done in a developed community; (2) it meets the health needs and priorities of the community; (3) informed consent is obtained from individual participants; and (4) the project has been approved by an ethics review committee knowledgeable about the community.[45]

The CIOMS guidelines for epidemiologists, *International Guidelines for Ethical Review of Epidemiological Studies*, provide more detailed requirements for research involving communities. These guidelines for conduct include the following: (1) "Investigators must respect the ethical standards of their own countries and the cultural expectations of the societies in which epidemiological studies are undertaken"; (2) when individual informed consent cannot be obtained, consent may be sought from a community representative; (3) if the study is objectionable to the community, individual informed consent "may not be sufficient to render a study ethical"; (4) wherever possible, investigators should not expose groups to harm, including the harm of disruption of social mores; (5) healthcare may be provided to the community as a benefit; (6) when possible, investigators should train local health workers; and (7) the community should be represented in the ethics review process.[46]

The clearest guidance is available for researchers working within their own countries with aboriginal communities. Since 1986 guidelines for research in first nations communities have appeared in Australia,[47] Canada,[48–50] and the United States.[51] The Australia National Health and Medical Research Council (NHMRC) document is the first document of its sort and remains one of the most comprehensive.[52] The need for detailed direction for research involving aboriginals in Australia was identified at a national conference, "Research Priorities in Aboriginal Health," held in Alice Springs in December 1986. The first draft of the document was written the following year at a meeting in Camden, New South Wales (August 1987) attended by thirty aboriginal community representatives and two NHMRC observers. The finalized document sets out a wide array of additional responsibilities for Australian researchers working with aboriginal communities.

The NHMRC document envisions the relationship between the community and the researcher as a partnership; that is, both parties are accorded equal moral status. Accordingly, the community is involved throughout the life of the research project, from its genesis to publication of findings. The community must be consulted in the preparation of the research proposal, and the study must be potentially useful to the community and conducted with sensitivity to the community's culture and politics. After the community as a whole has been informed about the study through face-to-face meetings with the researcher and given adequate time to reflect upon this information, the written informed consent of the community must be obtained before individual subjects are approached for consent. The community will be involved in the actual conduct of the study, including offering community members the opportunity to assist in the research, and the community will be reimbursed for any community resources made use of. The disposition of data and biological samples is a sensitive issue: who shall possess them at the end of the study must be negotiated, and any further use for other projects requires the consent of the community. Before the data are published, the community must be presented with a copy of the findings, and the published research may not identify the community without permission and will give proper acknowledgment to individuals and communities who took part in the research. Researchers should seek the consent of the community before providing comments about the study to the media.

Stepping into a Language Trap

Standards for research involving first nations communities are well established and deserve to be both respected and enforced. Given the existence of these guidelines, it is perhaps natural to assume that they may be applied to research involving other sorts of communities, for example, Ashkenazic Jews. The only document of which I am aware that has taken this stance is the 1996 draft *Code of Conduct for Research Involving Humans* issued by Canada's Tri-Council Working Group on Ethics. In this document, the members of the Tri-Council Working Group set out a wide range of additional requirements derived from aboriginal research guidelines for researchers working with all sorts of communities.[53] Even though the authors of the code of conduct partly revised this position in a later draft[54] and ultimately abandoned it in the final *Tri-Council Policy Statement*,[55] important lessons may be distilled from this early attempt to protect nonaboriginal communities in research

The 1996 Code of Conduct defines community—"collectivity" in the parlance of the document—very broadly:

> Collectivities are "population groups with social structures, common customs, and acknowledged leadership." Collectivities include nations, cultural groups, small indigenous communities and some neighborhood groups. The definition is also explicitly intended to include families.[56]

Clearly, a wide variety of groups fall into this definition of community and the document explicitly includes persons with HIV/AIDS and Ashkenazic Jews as potentially falling within the scope of the definition. As such, researchers working with communities are subject to a number of requirements above and beyond the protections afforded to individual research subjects.

It is clear from the document that requirements for research on communities were taken directly from guidelines for first nations communities. The Tri-Council document, a sparsely referenced work overall, cites in the section on communities American, Canadian, and Australian aboriginal guidelines. Its reliance on these documents is at times substantial. For example, the entire list of aspects of the study to be disclosed to the community was taken from the document authored by the American Indian Law Center.[57] Additional requirements for researchers set out in the code of conduct are very similar to those found in the Australia National Health and Medical Research Council document: (1) permission to conduct the research must be sought from the community; (2) research ought to meet the needs of the community and in order to ensure this, the community should participate in the design of the study; (3) community members ought to be given opportunities for research training; (4) the community must have a chance to comment on a draft of the findings; and (5) credit must be given to the community or its members where due.

Although these requirements make perfect sense for a first nations community, they seem potentially problematic when research is conducted in other communities. Imagine these guidelines being applied to one of the above-described cancer genetic studies in Ashkenazic Jews. Numerous difficult, if not impossible, questions arise immediately: Who is empowered to give permission on behalf of Ashkenazic Jews (and who ought to be informed of the risks and benefits of the study)? What are the needs of the community and who will participate in the design of the study to ensure these needs are met? Which community members should be given an opportunity for research training? How can the draft research findings be distributed to Ashkenazic Jews for comment? Which members of the community should be credited (should the community as a whole receive credit too?)?

Some of the proposed requirements cannot possibly be applied to Ashkenazic Jews. Take, for example, the issue of community permission or consent. Community consent presupposes that the community has a legitimate political structure. That is, if consent is to be obtained from the community, there must be community leaders who are empowered to give such consent. As for many sorts of community, there is no such legitimate political structure for Ashkenazic Jews. Thus it is an error to apply guidelines originally written for first nations communities to Ashkenazic Jews.

As it turns out, this is a very interesting type of error. The authors of the code of conduct have fallen into a language trap.[58] Wittgenstein describes the trap as "[a] picture [that] has held us captive. And we could not get outside it, for it lay in our language and language seemed to repeat it to us inexorably."[59] The members of the Canada Tri-Council Working Group on Ethics acted as if all communities were more or less the same as first nations communities and this is a mistake. In other words, the "picture" of one sort of community held them captive. In fact, we use the word *community* to describe a wide variety of human associations: ethnic, cultural, political, religious, geographical, municipal, professional, artistic, sexual, and even disease "communities"—an incomplete list. As if this weren't enough, we continue to invent new uses for the word. A recent editorial in *Science* referred to persons connected by the Internet as "virtual communities."[60] The same word is used to name essentially different things. This is what Wittgenstein means when he says, "language seemed to repeat it [the error] to us inexorably."[61]

What is the solution? The first step is to recognize the error. We must acknowledge that it is an error to blindly apply guidelines written for one community to another community. If meaningful guidelines for research on other sorts of communities are to be written, we must get clear about our use of language. Others might suggest that a clear definition of community is needed to restrict, in a sense, the proper use of the word. I do not agree. As Wittgenstein says, "[p]hilosophy may in no way interfere with the actual use of language; it can in the end only describe it."[62] He is suggesting that the road to a solution is to get clear about how we use the word *community* in day-to-day life. We need to "command a clear view of the use of our words"[63] by cataloguing carefully the differing ways that we use the word *community:*

- What sorts of community are there (and by this I mean how do we use the word *community*)?
- What properties do each of the communities have?
- Do they have legitimate political authority?
- Do they have communally defined needs and priorities?
- Is there a way of communicating with the entire community? And so on.

Once this cataloguing is complete, we will be in a better position to say what sorts of guidelines (e.g., community consent, community comment on draft findings) can be applied to a particular community. We will also be able to decide whether a set of guidelines written for one community is, either in whole or in part, potentially applicable to another community.

Conclusions and Recommendations for Future Work

In this paper I have considered the question, Are additional measures, above and beyond those currently afforded individual research participants, required to protect communities in research? The major conclusions and recommendations for further work are as follows:

1) A community in North America may by placed at risk when members of that community participate in a research study designed to produce information about the community as a whole.
2) The ethical issues raised by communities in research are not adequately captured by the current ethical framework for human subjects research as articulated in the *Belmont Report.*
3) While the atomistic view of person contained within the *Belmont Report* does need to be enriched (to situate the person within a particular community), even this change does not adequately capture the ethical issues at hand. A new principle of respect for communities should be added to the three principles found in the *Belmont Report.*
4) Clear guidelines exist for research involving first nations communities and the guidelines must be respected and ought to be enforced.
5) Difficult challenges lay in the way of developing guidelines for research on other sorts of communities.

6) Further work is required to catalogue the differing ways we use the word *community* in language.
7) Further work must also enumerate the properties of these communities with reference to possible guidelines (i.e., does community x possess property y which is required if guideline z is to be implemented in that community?).

Notes

1. General Assembly of the United Nations. International covenant on civil and political rights [1958]. In: Reich WT, ed. *Encyclopedia of Bioethics*, Rev ed. New York: Simon & Schuster MacMillan, 1995:2765.
2. World Medical Association. Declaration of Helsinki, [1964, rev 1975, 1983, 1989]. In: Reich WT, ed. *Encyclopedia of Bioethics*, Rev ed. New York: Simon & Schuster MacMillan, 1995:2765–7.
3. Angell M. Ethical imperialism? Ethics in international collaborative clinical research. *New England Journal of Medicine* 1988;319:1081–3.
4. Ijsselmuiden CB, Faden R. Research and informed consent in Africa—another look. *New England Journal of Medicine* 1992;326:830–4.
5. Christakis NA. The ethical design of an AIDS vaccine trial in Africa. *Hastings Center Report* 1988;18(4):31–7.
6. Levine RJ. Informed consent: some challenges to the universal validity of the Western model. *Journal of Law, Medicine & Health Care* 1991;19:207–13.
7. Lurie P, Wolfe SM. Unethical trials of interventions to reduce perinatal transmission of the human immunodeficiency virus in developing countries. *New England Journal of Medicine* 1997; 337:853–6.
8. Angell M. The ethics of clinical research in the third world. *New England Journal of Medicine* 1997;337:847–9.
9. Streuwing JP, Abeliovich D, Peretz T, Avishai N, Kaback MM, Collins FS, et al. The carrier frequency of the BRCA1 185delAG mutation is approximately 1 percent in Ashkenazi Jewish individuals. *Nature Genetics* 1995;11:198–200.
10. 45 CFR 46.101(b)4.
11. Laken SJ, Peterson GM, Gruber SB, Oddoux C, Ostrer H, Giardiella FM, et al. Familial colorectal cancer in Ashkenazim due to a hypermutable tract in APC. *Nature Genetics* 1997;17:79–83.
12. Kelsey JL, et al. Exogenous estrogens and other factors in the epidemiology of breast cancer. *Journal of the National Cancer Institute* 1981;67:327–33.
13. Westin JB, Richter E. The Israeli breast-cancer anomaly. *Annals of the New York Academy of Sciences* 1990;609:269–79.
14. Lehrman S. Jewish leaders seek genetic guidelines. *Nature* 1997;389:322.
15. See note 14, Lehrman 1997.
16. National Commission for the Protection of Human Subjects of Biomedical and Behavioral Research. The Belmont Report: ethical principles and guidelines for the protection of human subjects of research. *OPRR Reports* 1979;April 18:1–8.
17. See note 16, National Commission 1979:3.
18. See note 16, National Commission 1979:4.
19. Glass KC, Weijer C, Lemmens T, Palmour RM, Shapiro SH. Structuring the review of human genetics protocols part II: diagnostic and screening studies. *IRB: A Review of Human Subjects Research* 1997;19(3,4):1–11,13.
20. Levine RJ. *Ethics and Regulation of Clinical Research*, 2nd ed. New Haven: Yale University Press, 1988:13.
21. See note 20, Levine 1988:13–14.
22. Beauchamp TL, Childress JF. *Principles of Biomedical Ethics*, 4th ed. New York: Oxford University Press, 1994.
23. Clouser KD, Gert B. A critique of principlism. *Journal of Medicine and Philosophy* 1990;15:219–36.
24. Jonsen A, Toulin S. *The Abuse of Casuistry*. Berkeley: University of California Press, 1988.
25. MacIntyre A. *After Virtue*. Notre Dame: University of Notre Dame Press, 1981.
26. Pelligrino ED, Thomasma DC. *For the Patient's Good: The Restoration of Beneficence in Health Care*. New York: Oxford University Press, 1988.

27. Lebacqz K. Feminism. In: Reich WT, ed. *Encyclopedia of Bioethics*, Rev. ed. New York: Simon & Schuster MacMillan, 1995:808–18.
28. Keller J. Autonomy, relationality and feminist ethics. *Hypatia* 1997;12:152–64.
29. Sherwin S. *No Longer Patient: Feminist Ethics and Health Care*. Philadelphia: Temple University Press, 1992:158–75.
30. Fisher CB. A relational perspective on ethics-in-science decisionmaking for research with vulnerable populations. *IRB: A Review of Human Subjects Research* 1997;19(5):1–4.
31. Miller B. Autonomy. In: Reich WT, ed. *Encyclopedia of Bioethics*, Rev. ed. New York: Simon & Schuster MacMillan, 1995:215–20.
32. See note 31, Miller 1995.
33. Childress JF, Fletcher JC. Respect for autonomy. *Hastings Center Report* 1994;24(3):34–5.
34. Freedman B. Scientific value and validity as ethical requirements for research: a proposed explication. *IRB: A Review of Human Subjects Research* 1987;9(6):7–10.
35. Weijer C, Shapiro S, Fuks A, Glass KC, Skrutkowska M. Monitoring clinical research: an obligation unfulfilled. *Canadian Medical Association Journal* 1995;152:1973–80.
36. Weijer C. Research methods and policies. In: Chadwick R, ed. *Encyclopedia of Applied Ethics*. New York: Academic Press, 1998:853–60.
37. Levine RJ. Validity of consent procedures in technologically developing countries. In: Bankowski Z, Howard-Jones N, eds. *Human Experimentation and Medical Ethics: Proceedings of the XV CIOMS Round Table Conference*. Geneva: Council for International Organizations of Medical Sciences, 1982:16–30.
38. McCarthy C. A North American perspective. In: Bankowski Z, Levine RJ, eds. *Ethics and Research on Human Subjects: International Guidelines*. Geneva: Council for International Organizations of Medical Sciences, 1993:208–11.
39. Gostin L. Ethical principles for the conduct of human subject research: population-based research and ethics. *Journal of Law, Medicine & Health Care* 1991;19:191–201.
40. Degrazia D. Moving forward in bioethical theory: theories cases, and specified principlism. *Journal of Medicine and Philosophy* 1992;17:511–39.
41. Ross WD. *The Right and the Good*. Oxford: Clarendon Press, 1930.
42. 45 CFR 46.101(h).
43. Office for Protection from Research Risks. *Protecting Human Research Subjects: Institutional Review Board Guidebook*. Washington, D.C.: U.S. Government Printing Office, 1993:6.56.
44. Dickens BM, Gostin G, Levine RJ. Research on human populations: national and international ethical guidelines. *Journal of Law, Medicine & Health Care* 1991;19:157–61.
45. Council for International Organizations of Medical Sciences (CIOMS). *International Ethical Guidelines for Biomedical Research Involving Human Subjects*. Geneva: CIOMS, 1993.
46. Council for International Organizations of Medical Sciences (CIOMS). *International Guidelines for Ethical Review of Epidemiological Studies*. Geneva: CIOMS, 1991.
47. Australia National Health and Medical Research Council. *Guidelines on Ethical Matters in Aboriginal and Torres Strait Islander Research*. Canberra: NHMRC, 1991. (Publication no. E13).
48. Canada Royal Commission on Aboriginal Peoples. *Ethical Principles for Research*. N.d.
49. Association of Canadian Universities for Northern Studies. *Ethical Principles for the Conduct of Research in the North*. Ottawa: ACUNS, 1982.
50. Inuit Circumpolar Conference. Principles and elements on northern scientific research. In: *Principles and Elements for a Comprehensive Arctic Policy*. Montreal: Centre for Northern Studies and Research, 1992:142–6.
51. American Indian Law Center. *Model Tribal Research Code: With Materials for Tribal Regulation and Checklist for Indian Health Boards*. Albuquerque, New Mexico: American Indian Law Center, 1994.
52. Maddocks I. Ethics in Aboriginal research: a model for minorities or for all? *Medical Journal of Australia* 1992;157:553–5.
53. Canada Tri-Council Working Group on Ethics. *Code of Conduct for Research Involving Humans* [draft]. Ottawa: Minister of Supply and Services, 1996.
54. Tri-Council Working Group on Ethics. *Code of Conduct for Research Involving Humans* [final version]. Ottawa: Minister of Supply and Services, 1997.
55. Medical Research Council of Canada, Natural Sciences and Engineering Research Council of Canada, Social Sciences and Humanities Research Council of Canada. *Tri-Council Policy Statement: Ethical Conduct for Research Involving Humans*. Public Works and Government Services Canada, 1998.
56. See note 53, Canada Tri-Council Working Group on Ethics 1996:article 13.1
57. See note 51, American Indian Law Center 1994.

58. Hacker PMS. *Insight and Illusion: Wittgenstein on Philosophy and the Metaphysics of Experience.* Oxford: Clarendon Press, 1972:128–35.
59. Wittgenstein L. *Philosophical Investigations.* Trans. Anscombe GEM. Oxford: Basil Blackwell, 1991:s.115.
60. Etzioni A, Etzioni O. Communities: virtual vs. real. *Science* 1997;277:295.
61. See note 59, Wittgenstein 1991:s.115.
62. See note 59, Wittgenstein 1991:s.124.
63. See note 59, Wittgenstein 1991:s.122.

[17]

REITERATION

Sick individuals and sick populations

Geoffrey Rose

Rose G (Department of Epidemiology, London School of Hygiene and Tropical Medicine, Keppel Street, London WC1E 7HT, UK). Sick individuals and sick populations. *International Journal of Epidemiology* 1985;**14**:32–38.

Aetiology confronts two distinct issues: the determinants of individual cases, and the determinants of incidence rate. If exposure to a necessary agent is homogeneous within a population, then case/control and cohort methods will fail to detect it: they will only identify markers of susceptibility. The corresponding strategies in control are the 'high-risk' approach, which seeks to protect susceptible individuals, and the population approach, which seeks to control the causes of incidence. The two approaches are not usually in competition, but the prior concern should always be to discover and control the causes of incidence.

The Determinants of Individual Cases

In teaching epidemiology to medical students, I have often encouraged them to consider a question which I first heard enunciated by Roy Acheson: 'Why did *this* patient get *this* disease at *this* time?'. It is an excellent starting-point, because students and doctors feel a natural concern for the problems of the individual. Indeed, the central ethos of medicine is seen as an acceptance of responsibility for sick individuals.

It is an integral part of good doctoring to ask not only, 'What is the diagnosis, and what is the treatment?' but also, 'Why did this happen, and could it have been prevented?'. Such thinking shapes the approach to nearly all clinical and laboratory research into the causes and mechanisms of illness. Hypertension research, for example, is almost wholly pre-occupied with the characteristics which distinguish individuals at the hypertensive and normotensive ends of the blood pressure distribution. Research into diabetes looks for genetic, nutritional and metabolic reasons to explain why some people get diabetes and others do not. The constant aim in such work is to answer Acheson's question, 'Why did *this* patient get this disease at this time?'.

The same concern has continued to shape the thinking of all of us who came to epidemiology from a background in clinical practice. The whole basis of the case-control method is to discover how sick and healthy individuals differ. Equally the basis of many cohort studies is the search for 'risk factors', which identify certain individuals as being more susceptible to disease; and from this we proceed to test whether these risk factors are also causes, capable of explaining why some individuals get sick while others remain healthy, and applicable as a guide to prevention.

Department of Epidemiology, London School of Hygiene and Tropical Medicine, Keppel Street, London WC1E 7HT, UK.

Based on a lecture to the Xth Scientific Meeting of the International Epidemiological Association, 27 August 1984, Vancouver, Canada.

To confine attention in this way to within-population comparisons has caused much confusion (particularly in the clinical world) in the definition of normality. Laboratory 'ranges of normal' are based on what is common within the local population. Individuals with 'normal blood pressure' are those who do not stand out from their local contemporaries; and so on. What is common is all right, we presume.

Applied to aetiology, the individual-centred approach leads to the use of relative risk as the basic representation of aetiological force: that is, 'the risk in exposed individuals relative to risk in non-exposed individuals'. Indeed, the concept of relative risk has almost excluded any other approach to quantifying causal importance. It may generally be the best measure of aetiological force, but it is no measure at all of aetiological outcome or of public health importance.

Unfortunately this approach to the search for causes, and the measuring of their potency, has to assume a heterogeneity of exposure within the study population. If everyone smoked 20 cigarettes a day, then clinical, case-control and cohort studies alike would lead us to conclude that lung cancer was a genetic disease; and in one sense that would be true, since if everyone is exposed to the necessary agent, then the distribution of cases is wholly determined by individual susceptibility.

Within Scotland and other mountainous parts of Britain (Figure 1, left section)[1] there is no discernible relation between local cardiovascular death rates and the softness of the public water supply. The reason is apparent if one extends the enquiry to the whole of the UK. In Scotland, everyone's water is soft; and the possibly adverse effect becomes recognizable only when study is extended to other regions which have a much wider range of exposure ($r = -0.67$). Even more clearly, a case-control study of this question within Scotland would have been futile. Everyone is exposed, and other factors operate to determine the varying risk.

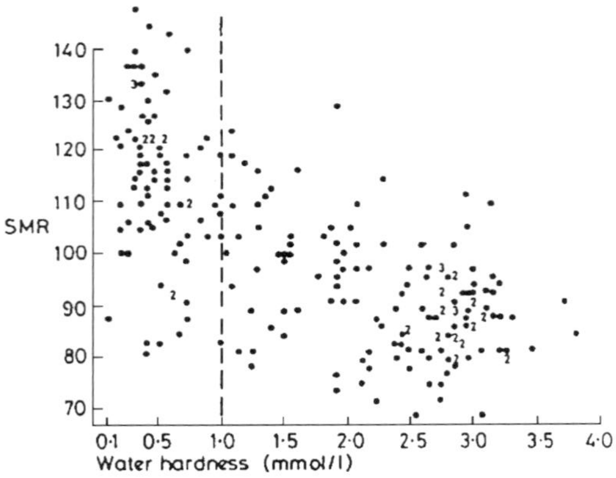

Figure 1 Relation between water quality and cardiovascular mortality in towns of the UK[1]

Epidemiology is often defined in terms of study of the determinants of the distribution of the disease; but we should not forget that the more widespread is a particular cause, the less it explains the distribution of cases. The hardest cause to identify is the one that is universally present, for then it has no influence on the distribution of disease.

The Determinants of Population Incidence Rate

I find it increasingly helpful to distinguish two kinds of aetiological question. The first seeks the causes of cases, and the second seeks the causes of incidence. 'Why do some individuals have hypertension?' is a quite different question from 'Why do some populations have much hypertension, whilst in others it is rare?'. The questions require different kinds of study, and they have different answers.

Figure 2 shows the systolic blood pressure distributions of middle-aged men in two populations—Kenyan nomads[2] and London civil servants.[3] The familiar question, 'Why do some individuals have higher blood pressure than others?' could be equally well asked in either of these settings, since in each the individual blood pressures vary (proportionately) to about the same extent; and the answers might well be much the same in each instance (that is, mainly genetic variation, with a lesser component from environmental and behavioural differences). We might achieve a complete understanding of why individuals vary, and yet quite miss the most important public health question, namely, 'Why is hypertension absent in the Kenyans and common in London?'. The answer to that question has to do with the determinants of the population mean; for what distinguishes the two groups is nothing to do with the characteristics of individuals, it is rather a shift of the whole distribution —a mass influence acting on the population as a whole. To find the determinants of prevalence and incidence rates, we need to study characteristics of populations, not characteristics of individuals.

A more extreme example is provided by the population distributions of serum cholesterol levels[4] in East Finland, where coronary heart disease is very common, and Japan, where the

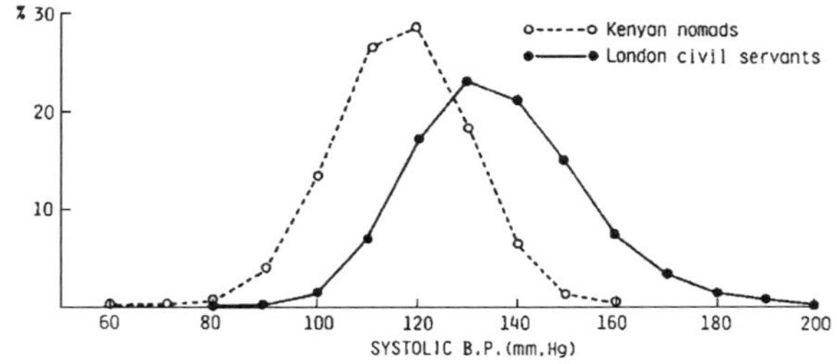

Figure 2 Distributions of systolic blood pressure in middle-aged men in two populations[2,3]

incidence rate is low: the two distributions barely overlap. Each country has men with relative hypercholesterolaemia (although their definitions of the range of 'normal' would no doubt disagree), and one could research into the genetic and other causes of these unusual individuals; but if we want to discover why Finland has such a high incidence of coronary heart disease we need to look for those characteristics of the national diet which have so elevated the whole cholesterol distribution. Within populations it has proved almost impossible to demonstrate any relation between an individual's diet and his serum cholesterol level; and the same applies to the relation of individual diet to blood pressure and to overweight. But at the level of populations it is a different story: it has proved easy to show strong associations between population mean values for saturated fat intake *versus* serum cholesterol level and coronary heart disease incidence, sodium intake *versus* blood pressure, or energy intake *versus* overweight. The determinants of incidence are not necessarily the same as the causes of cases.

How do the Causes of Cases Relate to the Causes of Incidence?

This is largely a matter of whether exposure varies similarly within a population and between populations (or over a period of time within the same population). Softness of water supply may be a determinant of cardiovascular mortality, but it is unlikely to be identifiable as a risk factor for individuals, because exposure tends to be locally uniform. Dietary fat is, I believe, the main determinant of a population's incidence rate for coronary heart disease; but it quite fails to identify high-risk individuals.

In the case of cigarettes and lung cancer it so happened that the study populations contained about equal numbers of smokers and non-smokers, and in such a situation case/control and cohort studies were able to identify what was also the main determinant of population differences and time trends.

There is a broad tendency for genetic factors to dominate individual susceptibility, but to explain rather little of population differences in incidence. Genetic heterogeneity, it seems, is mostly much greater within than between populations. This is the contrary situation to that seen for environmental factors. Thus migrants, whatever the colour of their skin, tend to acquire the disease rates of their country of adoption.

Most non-infectious diseases are still of largely unknown cause. If you take a textbook of medicine and look at the list of contents you will still find, despite all our aetiological research, that most are still of basically unknown aetiology. We know quite a lot about the personal characteristics of individuals who are susceptible to them; but for a remarkably large number of our major non-infectious diseases we still do not know the determinants of the incidence rate.

Over a period of time we find that most diseases are in a state of flux. For example, duodenal ulcer in Britain at the turn of the century was an uncommon condition affecting mainly young women. During the first half of the century the incidence rate rose steadily and it became very common, but now the disease seems to be disappearing; and yet we have no clues to the determinants of these striking changes in incidence rates. One could repeat that story for many conditions.

There is hardly a disease whose incidence rate does not vary widely, either over time or between populations at the same time. This means that these causes of incidence rate, unknown though they are, are not inevitable. It is possible to live without them, and if we knew what they were it might be possible to control them. But to identify the causal agent by the traditional case-control and cohort methods will be unsuccessful if there are not sufficient differences in exposure within the study population at the time of the study. In those circumstances all that these traditional methods do is to find markers of individual susceptibility. The clues must be sought from differences between populations or from changes within populations over time.

Prevention

These two approaches to aetiology—the individual and the population-based—have their counterparts in prevention. In the first, preventive strategy seeks to identify high-risk susceptible individuals and to offer them some individual protection. In contrast, the 'population strategy' seeks to control the determinants of incidence in the population as a whole.

The 'High-Risk' Strategy

This is the traditional and natural medical approach to prevention. If a doctor accepts that he is responsible for an individual who is sick today, then it is a short step to accept responsibility also for the individual who may well be sick tomorrow. Thus screening is used to detect certain individuals who hitherto thought they were well but who must now understand that they are in effect patients. This is the process, for example, in the detection and treatment of symptomless hypertension, the transition from healthy subject to patient being ratified by the giving and receiving of tablets. (Anyone who takes medicines is by definition a patient.)

What the 'high-risk' strategy seeks to achieve is something like a truncation of the risk distribution. This general concept applies to all special preventive action in high-risk individuals—in at-risk pregnancies, in small babies, or in any other particularly susceptible group. It is a strategy with some clear and important advantages (Table 1).

Table 1 Prevention by the 'high-risk strategy': advantages

1. Intervention appropriate to individual
2. Subject motivation
3. Physician motivation
4. Cost-effective use of resources
5. Benefit: risk ratio favourable

Its first advantage is that it leads to intervention which is appropriate to the individual. A smoker who has a cough or who is found to have impaired ventilatory function has a special reason for stopping smoking. The doctor will see it as making sense to advise salt restriction in the hypertensive. In such instances the intervention makes sense because that individual already has a problem which that particular measure may possibly ameliorate. If we consider screening a population to discover those with high serum cholesterol levels and advising them on dietary change, then that intervention is appropriate to those people in particular: they have a diet-related metabolic problem.

The 'high-risk' strategy produces interventions that are appropriate to the particular individuals advised to take them. Consequently it has the advantage of enhanced subject motivation. In our randomized controlled trial of smoking cessation in London civil servants we first screened some 20 000 men and from them selected about 1500 who were smokers with, in addition, markers of specially high risk for cardio-respiratory disease. They were recalled and a random half received anti-smoking counselling. The results, in terms of smoking cessation, were excellent because those men knew they had a special reason to stop. They had been picked out from others in their offices because, although everyone knows that smoking is a bad thing, they had a special reason why it was particularly unwise for them.

There is, of course, another and less reputable reason why screening enhances subject motivation, and that is the mystique of a scientific investigation. A ventilatory function test is a powerful enhancer of motivation to stop smoking: an instrument which the subject does not quite understand, that looks rather impressive, has produced evidence that he is a special person with a special problem. The electrocardiogram is an even more powerful motivator, if you are unscrupulous enough to use it in prevention. A man may feel entirely well, but if those little squiggles on the paper tell the doctor that he has got trouble, then he must accept that he has now become a patient. That is a powerful persuader. (I suspect it is also a powerful cause of lying awake in the night and thinking about it.)

For rather similar reasons the 'high-risk' approach also motivates physicians. Doctors, quite rightly, are uncomfortable about intervening in a situation where their help was not asked for. Before imposing advice on somebody who was getting on all right without them, they like to feel that there is a proper and special justification in that particular case.

The 'high-risk' approach offers a more cost-effective use of limited resources. One of the things we have learned in health education at the individual level is that once-only advice is a waste of time. To get results we may need a considerable investment of counselling time and follow-up. It is costly in use of time and effort and resources, and therefore it is more effective to concentrate limited medical services and time where the need—and therefore also the benefit—is likely to be greatest.

A final advantage of the 'high-risk' approach is that it offers a more favourable ratio of benefits to risks. If intervention must carry some adverse effects or costs, and if the risk and cost are much the same for everybody, then the ratio of the costs to the benefits will be more favourable where the benefits are larger.

Unfortunately the 'high-risk' strategy of prevention also has some serious disadvantages and limitations (Table 2).

The first centres around the difficulties and costs of screening. Supposing that we were to embark, as some had advocated, on a policy of screening for high cholesterol levels and giving dietary advice to those individuals at special risk. The disease process we are trying to prevent (atherosclerosis and its complications) begins early in life, so we should have to initiate screening perhaps at the age of ten. However, the abnormality we seek to detect is not a stable lifetime characteristic, so we must advocate repeated screening at suitable intervals.

Table 2 Prevention by the 'high-risk strategy': disadvantages

1.	Difficulties and costs of screening
2.	Palliative and temporary—not radical
3.	Limited potential for (a) individual (b) population
4.	Behaviourally inappropriate

In all screening one meets problems with uptake, and the tendency for the response to be greater amongst those sections of the population who are often least at risk of the disease. Often there is an even greater problem: screening detects certain individuals who will receive special advice, but at the same time it cannot help also discovering much larger numbers of 'borderliners', that is, people whose results mark them as at increased risk but for whom we do not have an appropriate treatment to reduce their risk.

The second disadvantage of the 'high-risk' strategy is that it is palliative and temporary, not radical. It does not seek to alter the underlying causes of the disease but to identify individuals who are particularly susceptible to those causes. Presumably in every generation there will be such susceptibles; and if prevention and control efforts were confined to these high-risk individuals, then that approach would need to be sustained year after year and generation after generation. It does not deal with the root of the problem, but seeks to protect those who are vulnerable to it; and they will always be around.

The potential for this approach is limited—sometimes more than we could have expected—both for the individual and for the population. There are two reasons for this. The first is that our power to predict future disease is usually very weak. Most individuals with risk factors will remain well, at least for some years; contrariwise, unexpected illness may happen to someone who has just received an 'all clear' report from a screening examination. One of the limitations of the relative risk statistic is that it gives no idea of the absolute level of danger. Thus the Framingham Study has impressed us all with its powerful discrimination between high and low risk groups, but when we see (Figure 3)[5] the degree of overlap in serum cholesterol level between future cases and those who remained healthy, it is not surprising that an individual's future is so often misassessed.

Often the best predictor of future major disease is the presence of existing minor disease. A low ventilatory function today is the best predictor of its future rate of decline. A high blood pressure today is the best predictor of its future rate of rise. Early coronary heart disease is better than all the conventional risk factors as a predictor of future fatal disease. However, even if screening includes such tests for early disease, our experience in the Heart Disease Prevention Project (Table 3)[6] still points to a very weak ability to predict the future of any particular individual.

This point came home to me only recently. I have long congratulated myself on my low levels of coronary risk factors, and I joked to my friends that if I were to die suddenly, I should be very surprised. I even speculated on what other disease—perhaps colon cancer—would be the commonest cause of death for a man in the lowest group of cardiovascular risk. The painful truth is that for such an individual in a Western population the commonest cause of death—by far—is coronary heart disease! Everyone, in fact, is a high-risk individual for this uniquely mass disease.

There is another, related reason why the predictive basis of the 'high-risk' strategy of prevention is weak. It is well illustrated

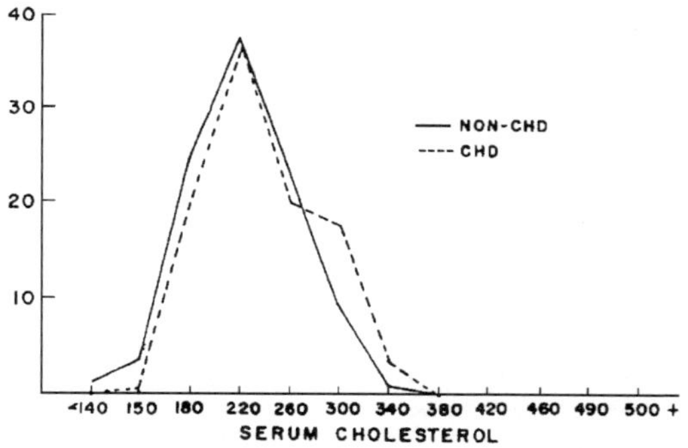

Figure 3 Percentage distribution of serum cholesterol levels (mg/dl) in men aged 50–62 who did or did not subsequently develop coronary heart disease (Framingham Study[5])

Table 3 Five-year incidence of myocardial infarction in the UK Heart Disease Prevention Project

Entry characteristic	% of men	% of MI cases	MI incidence rate %
Risk factors alone	15	32	7
'Ischaemia'	16	41	11
'Ischaemia' + risk factors	2	12	22
All men	100	100	4

Table 4 Incidence of Down's syndrome according to maternal age[7]

Maternal age (years)	Risk of Down's syndrome per 1000 births	Total births in age group (as % of all ages)	% of total Down's syndrome occurring in age group
<30	0.7	78	51
30–34	1.3	16	20
35–39	3.7	5	16
40–44	13.1	0.95	11
⩾45	34.6	0.05	2
All ages	1.5	100	100

by some data from Alberman[7] which relate the occurrence of Down's syndrome births to maternal age (Table 4). Mothers under 30 years are individually at minimal risk; but because they are so numerous, they generate half the cases. High-risk individuals aged 40 and above generate only 13% of the cases.

The lesson from this example is that *a large number of people at a small risk may give rise to more cases of disease than the small number who are at a high risk.* This situation seems to be common, and it limits the utility of the 'high-risk' approach to prevention.

A further disadvantage of the 'high-risk' strategy is that it is behaviourally inappropriate. Eating, smoking, exercise and all our other life-style characteristics are constrained by social norms. If we try to eat differently from our friends it will not only be inconvenient, but we risk being regarded as cranks or hypochondriacs. If a man's work environment encourages heavy drinking, then advice that he is damaging his liver is unlikely to have any effect. No-one who has attempted any sort of health education effort in individuals needs to be told that it is difficult for such people to step out of line with their peers. This is what the 'high-risk' preventive strategy requires them to do.

Table 5 Prevention by the 'population strategy': advantages

1.	Radical
2.	Large potential for population
3.	Behaviourally appropriate

The Population Strategy

This is the attempt to control the determinants of incidence, to lower the mean level of risk factors, to shift the whole distribution of exposure in a favourable direction. In its traditional 'public health' form it has involved mass environmental control methods; in its modern form it is attempting (less successfully) to alter some of society's norms of behaviour.

The advantages are powerful (Table 5). The first is that it is radical. It attempts to remove the underlying causes that make the disease common. It has a large potential—often larger than one would have expected—for the population as a whole. From Framingham data one can compute that a 10 mm Hg lowering of the blood pressure distribution as a whole would correspond to about a 30% reduction in the total attributable mortality.

The approach is behaviourally appropriate. If non-smoking eventually becomes 'normal', then it will be much less necessary to keep on persuading individuals. Once a social norm of behaviour has become accepted and (as in the case of diet) once the supply industries have adapted themselves to the new pattern, then the maintenance of that situation no longer requires effort from individuals. The health education phase aimed at changing individuals is, we hope, a temporary necessity, pending changes in the norms of what is socially acceptable.

Table 6 Prevention by the 'population strategy': disadvantages

1. Small benefit to individual ('Prevention Paradox')
2. Poor motivation of subject
3. Poor motivation of physician
4. Benefit: risk ratio worrisome

Unfortunately the population strategy of prevention has also some weighty drawbacks (Table 6). It offers only a small benefit to each individual, since most of them were going to be all right anyway, at least for many years. This leads to the *Prevention Paradox*:[8] 'A preventive measure which brings much benefit to the population offers little to each participating individual'. This has been the history of public health—of immunization, the wearing of seat belts and now the attempt to change various life-style characteristics. Of enormous potential importance to the population as a whole, these measures offer very little—particularly in the short term—to each individual; and thus there is poor motivation of the subject. We should not be surprised that health education tends to be relatively ineffective for individuals and in the short term. Mostly people act for substantial and immediate rewards, and the medical motivation for health education is inherently weak. Their health next year is not likely to be much better if they accept our advice or if they reject it. Much more powerful as motivators for health education are the social rewards of enhanced self-esteem and social approval.

There is also in the population approach only poor motivation of physicians. Many medical practitioners who embarked with enthusiasm on anti-smoking education have become disheartened because their success rate was no more than 5 or 10%: in clinical practice one's expectation of results is higher. Grateful patients are few in preventive medicine, where success is marked by a non-event. The skills of behavioural advice are different and unfamiliar, and professional esteem is lowered by a lack of skill. Harder to overcome than any of these, however, is the enormous difficulty for medical personnel to see health as a population issue and not merely as a problem for individuals.

In mass prevention each individual has usually only a small expectation of benefit, and this small benefit can easily be outweighed by a small risk.[8] This happened in the World Health Organization clofibrate trial,[9] where a cholesterol-lowering drug seems to have killed more than it saved, even though the fatal complication rate was only about 1/1000/year. Such low-order risks, which can be vitally important to the balance sheet of mass preventive plans, may be hard or impossible to detect. This makes it important to distinguish two approaches. The first is the restoration of biological normality by the removal of an abnormal exposure (e.g. stopping smoking, controlling air pollution, moderating some of our recently-acquired dietary deviations); here there can be some presumption of safety. This is not true for the other kind of preventive approach, which leaves intact the underlying causes of incidence and seeks instead to interpose some new, supposedly protective intervention (e.g. immunization, drugs, jogging). Here the onus is on the activists to produce adequate evidence of safety.

Conclusions

Case-centred epidemiology identifies individual susceptibility, but it may fail to identify the underlying causes of incidence. The 'high-risk' strategy of prevention is an interim expedient, needed in order to protect susceptible individuals, but only for so long as the underlying causes of incidence remain unknown or uncontrollable; if causes can be removed, susceptibility ceases to matter.

Realistically, many diseases will long continue to call for both approaches, and fortunately competition between them is usually unnecessary. Nevertheless, the priority of concern should always be the discovery and control of the causes of incidence.

References

1 Pocock SJ, Shaper AG, Cook DG *et al.* British Regional Heart Study: geographic variations in cardiovascular mortality and the role of water quality. *Br Med J* 1980;**283:**1243–9.

2 Shaper AG. Blood pressure studies in East Africa. In: The Epidemiology of Hypertension. J Stamler, R Stamler, TN Pullman (eds). New York, Grune and Stratten, 1967. pp. 139–45.

3 Reid DD, Brett GZ, Hamilton PJS *et al.* Cardiorespiratory disease and diabetes among middle-aged male civil servants. *Lancet* 1974;**1:** 469–73.

4 Keys A. Coronary heart disease in seven countries. American Heart Association Monograph Number 29. American Heart Association, New York, 1970.

5 Kannel WB, Garcia MJ, McNamara PM *et al.* Serum lipid precursors of coronary heart disease. *Human Pathol* 1971;**2:**129–51.

6 Heller RF, Chinn S, Tunstall Pedoe HD *et al.* How well can we predict coronary heart disease? Findings in the United Kingdom Heart Disease Prevention Project. *Br Med J* 1984;**288:**1409–11.

7 Alberman E, Berry C. Prenatal diagnosis and the specialist in community medicine. *Community Med* 1979;**1:**89–96.

8 Rose G. Strategy of prevention: lessons from cardiovascular disease. *Br Med J* 1981;**282:**1847–51.

9 Committee of Principal Investigators. A co-operative trial in the primary prevention of ischaemic heart disease. *Br Heart J* 1978;**40:** 1069–118.

Part V
Public Health and Autonomy

[18]

Symposium on ethics and public health

Should public health respect autonomy?

Spencer A Hall *New Mexico, USA*

Author's abstract

This paper suggests that public health, due to its community orientation, may be ignoring certain ethical principles – namely the rights of individuals and communities to self-determination. The expectation of individual rights as a member of a community is reviewed and the additional right of a community for self-determination is proposed. The influences on ethical evaluations by the legal and economic environments are suggested, using US examples. The conclusion argues that as the focus of health-care delivery changes, it will become more important to consider these questions of group ethics.

Public health is aimed at improving the health of communities. The ways in which this is attempted vary, but are often aimed at improving individuals' health in the community, thus giving the entire community a net benefit. Very few of these changes may be accomplished without addressing individual behaviours. Any potential interference with individuals raises certain ethical considerations – considerations which are not routinely addressed by public health, a fact which has recently provoked both comment and criticism (1).

An explanation for this lies in the different training and focus of public health practitioners. They are trained to promote the aggregate health of a population group, rather than deal with individuals and their diseases (2). By concentrating on groups, it is easy to ignore rights of individuals. Of course, the focus of public health practitioners should be the health of the community, but they should take into account other factors such as ethics when they plan public health interventions. It is only recently, as individual rights are being recognised more commonly, that the question of public health practitioners' respect for individual rights should be raised and the logical extension of analogous rights to the community be recognised.

In considering the moral questions involved in any public health intervention, there are two primary areas which must be recognised. The first is what the nature of a given community implies as to the rights of its members. The second is what rights, if any, the community has on its own. Each of these has a unique status with regard to public health actions. The individual rights of each member of a community should be respected in accordance with the norms of that community. The community itself should be granted self-determination.

Key words

Autonomy; community; ethics; public health.

Individuals' rights in a community

There are a couple of conceptualisations of community which imply different degrees of rights for their members (3). Communities all exist based on some degree of an underlying social contract – without agreement, a fundamental notion of obligation and organisation, there cannot be a community. Where communities differ is in the nature of these obligations. One view (4) holds that communities are merely groups of individuals held together by the duty of refraining from harm to others. In this type of society, known as a minimalist community, personal freedoms are of the highest importance and, with the exception of harming others, non-regulated. In this type of community, it would be difficult for public health to justify many interventions that are now commonplace. Many diseases are of little direct harm to others, therefore they should be only of personal, rather than community, concern. A minimalist community lacks moral power to dictate behaviours which are matters of personal concern (5). This view of community is in the minority, and its entire philosophy has been criticised as leading to moral chaos (6).

A more common definition of community holds that communities are more complex than outlined above. In addition to duties of not harming others, elements of personal freedom may be given in exchange for other goods; by purchasing elements such as caring and beneficence, individuals strengthen the ties that form their community. These communities are more likely to strive to meet basic human needs such as food and housing, as well as having the moral inclination, and experience, to act and to ask their individuals to act for the increased benefit of the group as a whole. This inclination is not absolute however; although certain aspects of personal autonomy may have been yielded to the group (7), many elements of self-determination remain. Thus, any intervention for the good of the community must still be weighed against a possible insult to personal autonomy. Individuals may still retain the right to refuse to act in accord with public health demands.

In some instances, it seems that individuals make health-care decisions which are 'unwise' when viewed impartially. In these cases, it seems that it would be appropriate for the community to dictate the actions/choices of its members. After all, it could only benefit the community to help its individual members. The behaviour of the group in dictating the actions of its members is commonly called paternalism – 'The interference with a person's liberty of action justified by reasons referring exclusively to the welfare, good, happiness, needs, interests or values of the person being coerced' (8). Paternalistic interventions, not limited to public health measures, are an area of hot debate in modern ethics. There are those who believe that any affirmation of paternalism would 'justify the imposition of a Spartan-like regime requiring rigorous physical exercise and abstention from smoking, drinking, and hazardous pastimes' (9). Additionally, paternalism is unique in being absolutely prohibited in the philosophy of J S Mill (10), unlike his mere conditional prohibitions against lying and other behaviours. A less strict approach holds that paternalistic influence may be justified under certain conditions. Some believe this is because there is tacit prior consent to this type of intervention by anyone who is a member of the society (11), indeed, allowing this interference may be a price of membership. Others hold that interventions are justified only if the rational subject would consent after the intervention proved to be beneficial (12). Both of these views are ultimately based on respect for autonomy, however, because the very notion of consent implies that the individual's wishes are considered. True paternalism, in the nature of a parent caring for the best interests of a child or the State for an incompetent, does not rely on consent. It is based in beneficence and must rest on moral justification of the action (13). This justification is based on finding that the intervention is necessary to prevent a grave danger to the individual by the means least burdensome to that individual's autonomy.

Thus, regardless of our conceptualisation of community or paternalism, individual autonomy remains to some degree. The degree will depend on the community. For example, members of the military usually give up much more of their autonomy than do students in a college. This remaining right to self-determination should be addressed when any public health intervention which impinges on personal freedoms is considered. There is no evidence that this is now being done by public health planners, even though there is increasing respect for personal autonomy by doctors caring for individual patients (14) and US federal legislation mandating hospitals to do so (15). Granted, it is easier to consider the personal autonomy of a single patient than many simultaneously, but mere difficulty should not be used as an excuse for depriving individuals of their rights.

There is one strong argument which is sometimes used against community respect for autonomy – the notion that an individual's right to respect is abrogated by virtue of that individual's responsibility for causing the problem in the first place (16). In other words, he or she may be punished for 'bad' behaviour, such as a self-inflicted illness, by loss of certain rights such as autonomy. Cigarette-smoking provides many examples of this sort of debate. The problem with this reasoning is that a person is not always solely responsible for his/her own behaviour:

'To assert that individuals have had a part, even a good part, in causing their illness and deriving from this a loss of communal responsibility to come to their aid are two different things ... genetic predisposition, social circumstances, early conditioning, educational focus, environmental pressures, and many more, play a vital role not only in determining what habits we shall assume, but likewise condition the way we look at (and at times, the way we resist or fail to resist) those habits' (17).

Since much of what people are depends on the community in which they are raised, then the community cannot divorce itself from subsequent responsibility for persons' disabilities. The community, rather than stripping individuals' autonomy rights, should owe them at least this level of consideration.

Community rights

In addition to individual autonomy, there is another area of rights to be considered. This is that of respect for the community. One might also deem this autonomy of a sort; autonomous actions are those actions made with intention, knowledge and understanding, and free from controlling influences (18). There is no clear precedent for 'community autonomy', but the right of a group of individuals collectively to determine their group's actions is arguably an appropriate extension of personal rights. Communities as well as individuals may wish to make choices about their behaviours that outsiders deem unwise. Individuals have this right, whether communities presently do, is less clear.

Consideration of the rights of the affected community makes pragmatic as well as moral sense. Conflict with community autonomy is likely to occur where identification of a public health 'problem' is made outside the community and attempts to rectify the problem are also directed from outside. Without input and agreement from the target community, it is not surprising that these types of interventions often fail (19).

A possible foreshadowing of respect for community autonomy is seen in the blossoming of community-health-decision organisations which are trying to move some health care concerns from being individualistic to more communitarian (20), though what has been seen to date is prompted more by pragmatic and economic concerns than respect for autonomy. In fact, some have gone so far as proposing 'a move from individual consent to what some have called "informed community consent" by granting local communities the ethical and political authority to articulate and to enact their own conception of the good' (21). There is no question that in order to do this community autonomy must be recognised; the very notion of informed consent requires full autonomy for the actor giving consent (22).

Legal environment

Unfortunately, perhaps, moral arguments are not able to be separated from the legal environment in which they may apply. Communities all have a structure of formal rules which may dictate behaviour, regardless of the ethical impact. A brief discussion of the United States legal philosophy with regard to the issues discussed above will demonstrate this point. The legal outlook is similar in the other common law countries; the Public Health (Disease Control) Act of 1984 in Great Britain espouses a similar approach towards public health problems to that outlined initially below.

The current US legal position on public health stems from a 1904 case in which the Supreme Court ruled that a State could fine individuals who did not comply with a vaccination order (23). Although this is an old case, it is very much alive, because it is the only case clearly to set forth a discussion of what limits may be put on public health interventions. It is still widely cited in this context. This case has been used over the years to justify governmental intrusion upon personal autonomy when there is a 'compelling interest' (24). The question of when a public health intervention reaches the level of a compelling interest is open to debate, but it would likely do so when legislation is required to correct some serious health threat. Quaratine laws are a good example of this sort of legislation.

It is interesting however, that this landmark-case reflects an early awareness of the tension between paternalism and individual rights:

'There are manifold restraints to which every person is necessarily subject for the common good. On any other basis, organised society could not exist without safety to its members' (25).

is contrasted with

'There is, of course, a sphere within which the individual may assert the supremacy of his own will, and rightfully dispute the authority of any human government, – especially of any true government existing under a written constitution, – to interfere with the exercise of that will' (26).

This may have been prophetic. In the US, the recent legal trend has increasingly emphasised the importance of personal decisions in health care. This has extended as far as decriminalising suicide and allowing terminally-ill patients to order the withdrawal of their life-support (27). The right to refuse medical treatments easily extends to those modalities used commonly in public health interventions, for example screening tests.

The current AIDS epidemic is demonstrating a continued turnaround in legal philosophy. Many States in the US have enacted laws granting confidentiality to individuals who are infected with AIDS. This runs directly contrary to established epidemic treatment which depends on identification of disease-carriers and explicitly recognises the empowerment of individual rights to the detriment of public health.

Economic environment

In addition to the legal environment, economic factors may increasingly influence health care decisions by raising issues of distribution and access in a time of limited resources. The economic pressures on all health care decisions will only increase in the future.

'It is now almost universally believed that the resources available to meet the demands for health care are limited .... We as a nation [US], will have to think very carefully about how to allocate the resources we are willing to make available for health care' (28).

Again, a couple of brief examples drawn from the US may clarify this reasoning.

The treatment of hypertension (HTN) was not found to pay for itself in savings from heart attack or stroke (29). Additionally, the cost of from $10,000 to $20,000 per quality-year-of-life for treatment was questioned as a reasonable price to pay. Similarly, it does not seem appropriate to screen individuals for colon cancer (30), although this is one of the most frequent neoplasms. These conclusions raise serious ethical questions that directly impact public health practitioners (31). Now it would seem that another factor the practitioner must weigh in the decision to undertake a public health intervention is a cost-effectiveness determination. It could be argued that it would be unethical to waste limited resources by doing low-yield interventions.

Public health interventions, especially in the areas of health promotion and disease prevention, are usually more cost-effective in the long run than individual patient-care advances. It is likely that we will be seeing more of them in the future. If they are to succeed in an environment of increasing awareness of autonomy, both personal and community, even efficient interventions must deal with their ethical impact.

Conclusion

Many medical practitioners deal with ethical questions

routinely. This is not the case with public health practitioners, but the situation is likely to change. There will be two main causes for this.

The first is that the continuing increase in respect for individual autonomy will force public health practitioners to become more aware of the impact any of their interventions will have on individuals, and to allow individuals more freedom in anticipation. An increased awareness of personal autonomy may translate to an increase in interest among individuals in their own health care, of which public health is an important part.

This increase in personal freedoms is not without bounds. Both the legal and economic environment will apply pressure on the individual to conform in behaviours which may threaten others in the community. For example, individuals still have the right to smoke, but this occurs at the cost of increased insurance rates, and, most significantly, increased chance of illness or death. Additionally, investigating what responsibilities an individual may have towards his or her community by accepting his or her role as a citizen may represent a new way of balancing individual autonomy and social responsibility (32).

The second factor forcing an awareness of self-determination on public health will be the increasing presence of communities as actors in health care delivery. Formerly, communities were merely targets for public health interventions, but in the future they will be more active consumers. The situation is foreseen by a leading US bioethicist, Daniel Callahan, co-founder of the Hastings Center, who writes:

'We will not, I believe, be able to work out the problems of our health care system unless we shift our priorities and bias from an individual-centered to a community-centered view of health and human welfare. We cannot, and ought not to give up a respect for individual needs and dignity, but we can place them within a social perspective and allow that to color our understanding ... . At present we ordinarily begin by asking just what it is that individuals need for their good health; if there are communal concerns, they are put in a subordinate position. I want to reverse that priority – to begin with the communal needs and to put individual needs, rights, and interests in the subordinate position. It is the latter that must act as restraint upon the former, not the other way around as at present' (33).

If communities will be taking the primary role in future health care, then they should be granted autonomy as a recognition of the implications of this role.

Public health has an enviable history. Disease prevention strategies have done more to promote health than any treatment regimen yet discovered. As times change however, it is appropriate to ask if public health is currently recognising the rights of self-determination possessed by the individuals and communities on which its actions impact.

Perhaps an early recognition of the importance of these issues is reflected in a numerical model developed to prioritise public health problems in times of limited resources (34). This model incorporates community and individual acceptance of the proposed intervention into the ranking in a way that will cancel any and all other considerations supporting the intervention if it is merely not wanted.

Let us hope that this awareness of the importance of self-determination by public health practitioners will continue and increase.

Spencer A Hall, MD, JD, is engaged in the practice of emergency medicine and consults on legal issues related to health, in Lincoln, New Mexico, USA. He is licensed to practise both law and medicine.

References and notes

(1) Skrabanek P. Why is preventative medicine exempted from ethical constraints? *Journal of medical ethics* 1990; 16: 187–190.
(2) McBeath W H. Executive director of the American Public Health Association; testimony before the subcommittee on health and the environment of the Committee on Energy and Commerce of the US House of Representatives, 1981 Jul 29.
(3) Loewy E H. Communities, self-causation and the natural lottery. *Social sciences and medicine* 1988; 26: 1133–1139.
(4) Engelhardt H T. *The foundations of bioethics*. New York: Oxford University Press, 1986.
(5) The indirect cost to the minimalist community for support of chronic-disease patients is not an issue, as the connection of harm to others is vague and the community owes no duty of care to individual members.
(6) Callahan D. Minimalist ethics. *Hastings Center report* 1981; Oct 11, 5: 19–25.
(7) Childress J F. The place of autonomy in bioethics. *Hastings Center report* 1990; Jan/Feb, 20 (1): 12–13.
(8) Dworkin G. Paternalism. *The monist* 1972; 56: 65.
(9) Harris R. Private consensual/adult behavior: the requirement of harm to others in the enforcement of morality. *UCLA law review* 1967; 14: 585n.
(10) See reference (8): 70.
(11) See reference (8): 64–84.
(12) Carter R. Justifying paternalism. *Canadian journal of philosophy* 1977; 7: 133–145.
(13) Beauchamp T L, Childress J F. *Principles of biomedical ethics*. New York: Oxford University Press, 1989.
(14) This interest has been highlighted in recent years by increasing court recognition of autonomy rights, and is evidenced, for example, by patients' bills of rights.
(15) The Patient Self-Determination Act (PSDA) of 1990, included in the Omnibus Budget Reconciliation Act (OBRA) of 1990.
(16) Dworkin G. Taking risks, assessing responsibility. *Hastings Center report* 1981; Oct 11, 5: 26–31.
(17) See reference (3): 1138.
(18) See reference (13): 69.
(19) Geiger H J. Community control – or community conflict. *National Tuberculosis and Respiratory Disease Association bulletin* 1969; 55: 4–11.
(20) Jennings B, ed. Grassroots bioethics revisited: health care priorities and community values (a collection of

summary articles). *Hastings Center report* 1990; Sept/Oct 20, 5: 16–23.
(21) Emanuel E J. A community view of care for incompetent patients. *Hastings Center report* 1987; Oct/Nov 17, 5: 15–20.
(22) See reference (13): 74–85.
(23) Jacobson v Massachusetts 197 US 11, 1904.
(24) See, for example: Thornburgh v American College of Obstetrics and Gynecology 476 US 747, 808–809, 1985.
(25) 197 US 11, 26.
(26) 197 US 11, 29.
(27) See, for example: Quinlan 355 A2d 647 and subsequent cases.
(28) Weinstein M C, Stason W B. Allocating resources: the case of hypertension. *Hastings Center report* 1977; Oct 7, 5: 24–29.
(29) Weinstein M C, Stason W B. Foundations of cost-effectiveness analysis for health and medical practices. *New England journal of medicine* 1977; 296: 716–721.
(30) Ransohoff D F, Lang C. Screening for colorectal cancer. *New England journal of medicine* 1991; 325: 37–41.
(31) Stason W B, Weinstein M C. Public health rounds at the Harvard School of Public Health: allocation of resources to manage hypertension. *New England journal of medicine* 1977; 296: 732–739.
(32) Danis M, Churchill L R. Autonomy and the common weal. *Hastings Center report* 1991; Jan/Feb 21, 1: 25–31.
(33) Callahan D. *What kind of life: the limits of medical progress*. New York: Simon and Schuster 1990: 28.
(34) Vilnius D, Dandoy S. A priority rating system for public health programs. *Public health reports* 1990; 105: 463–470.

[19]

OBLIGATORY PRECAUTIONS AGAINST INFECTION

MARCEL VERWEIJ

ABSTRACT

If we have a duty not to infect others, how far does it go? This question is often discussed with respect to HIV transmission, but reflection on other diseases like influenza raises a number of interesting theoretical issues. I argue that a duty to avoid infection not only yields requirements for persons who know they carry a disease, but also for persons who know they are at increased risk, and even for those who definitely know they are completely healthy. Given the numerous ways in which human interaction facilitates the spread of communicable diseases, a maximum level of precaution would be very demanding – possibly unreasonably demanding. The 'over-demandingness problem' is mostly invoked as a criticism of utilitarianism, as this theory requires moral agents to always maximise general welfare, even at significant cost for themselves. However, I argue that, with respect to precautions against infectious diseases like influenza, utilitarianism is able to avoid the over-demandingness problem. A contractualist account, on the other hand, whilst able to explain how one's obligations to avoid infection can be limited, given that other persons have opportunities and responsibilities to protect themselves, in the end requires precautions that raise the over-demandingness problem.

I. INTRODUCTION

Public health ethics and concerns about infectious diseases have shifted attention in bioethics from issues of personal and professional moral responsibility to practical problems on a political level. The most salient forms of public health interventions are quarantine, isolation, and mandatory treatment of infected persons. Such interventions raise conflicts between citizens' liberties and public health interests. Notwithstanding the importance of these political issues, questions of personal obligation should not be overlooked. To what extent do individuals have a moral obligation to avoid spreading a disease? Though this issue is primarily relevant on the level of personal morality, it will have implications for public health policies. For example, if citizens have a moral duty to accept vaccination because in this way they will protect others (e.g. the elderly and chronically ill) for whom influenza poses a serious risk, this will give support to a general vaccination policy.

The question whether we have a moral obligation to avoid infecting others was taken up by John Harris and Søren Holm in a short paper, several years ago.[1] Harris and Holm argued that people who know they carry a communicable disease have a strong *prima facie* obligation to prevent further spread of the disease. To fail to act on this obligation is deliberately to harm others. Moral responsibility (and even criminalisation) for forgoing precautions against spreading a disease is mostly discussed with respect to safe sex and HIV prevention. Harris and Holm argued that the mode of transmission is morally neutral, and, moreover, that 'more trivial' diseases can be harmful as well. Hence, the duty not to infect others also applies to diseases such as the flu, pertussis, or even the common cold. Persons who carry a communicable disease should avoid infecting others, and this may imply, for example, that they temporarily avoid contact with other persons. On the other hand, it can be argued that these requirements should not be unreasonably demanding: 'The reasonableness of expecting people to live up to this obligation, however, depends on society reciprocating the obligation in the form of providing protection and compensation.'[2] For example, unless there is reasonable financial compensation, such as illness allowance, one cannot expect a sick person to stay at home for the sake of her colleagues.

In this paper I explore the foundation and scope of duties not to infect others. I argue that such duties are very broad in scope, and that they might be very demanding of moral agents – maybe unreasonably demanding. Yet the 'over-demandingness problem' arises where one would not expect it in the first place. The problem is mostly raised as critique of utilitarianism. I will argue however that, in the context of infectious disease prevention, utilitarianism can largely avoid the over-demandingness critique. On the other hand, while I think that a contractualist moral

[1] J. Harris & S. Holm. Is there a duty not to infect others? *BMJ* 1995; 311: 1215–1217.

[2] Ibid. p. 1215.

theory provides a more plausible ground for our obligations to avoid infection, such a theory, contrary to expectation, might yield moral requirements that are very demanding.

II. THE BROAD SCOPE OF A DUTY TO AVOID INFECTION

Harris and Holm focus on duties of persons who know they carry a communicable disease, notably their duty to isolate themselves and avoid contact with others. Yet, *if* there is a *prima facie* duty to avoid spreading a communicable disease, the implications go far beyond that. Let us focus, for the moment, on influenza. Influenza is a serious disease that can have fatal complications in the elderly and the chronically ill. Influenza viruses are spread primarily by aerosols of virus-laden respiratory secretions that are easily expelled into the air by infected persons during coughing, sneezing, or talking.[3] During average epidemics, approximately 10 to 20 percent of all persons in a community are infected. The attack rate in susceptible populations such as schoolchildren or nursing home residents can be up to 40 or 50 percent. Global pandemics occur when major genetic mutations in the virus lead to a new influenza strain. The morbidity and mortality of such a pandemic are devastating. The upper estimate of the death toll of the 1918 pandemic is that the virus may have killed 8 to 10 percent of all young adults world-wide at the time.[4]

If there is an obligation to avoid infecting others, then the most obvious precaution for persons with influenza symptoms is indeed to avoid contact with others. Harris and Holm emphasise the working place as a place to avoid, but obviously, infected persons have strong moral reasons to avoid all (indoor) places where many people meet. Moreover, precautions should not be confined to persons with influenza symptoms. Infected persons spread the virus as long as the virus is replicating, which occurs from one day prior to the onset of symptoms until five days after the onset.[5] So, at least to some extent, the same obligations to avoid contact might apply for persons who do not (yet) experience symptoms, yet know they have contacted other persons with influenza and might have been infected themselves.

Finally, effective precautions are neither limited to these specific groups, nor are they confined to avoiding contact. Unless

[3] N.J. Cox & K. Subbarao. Global Epidemiology of Influenza: Past and Present. *Annual Review of Medicine* 2000; 51: 407–421.

[4] J.M. Barry. 2004. *The Great Influenza*. New York. Viking.

[5] Centers for Disease Control. 2004. *Key Facts About the Flu*. http://www.cdc.gov/flu/keyfacts.htm (accessed 12 January 2005).

there is a major antigenic shift in the virus, the most effective prevention against influenza is vaccination. Vaccination protects the person who is immunised, but also prevents that person spreading the virus. For example, vaccination of nursing home staff helps prevent outbreaks within the nursing home, and this supports the claim that health professionals *ought* to accept vaccination in order to avoid harming their patients.[6] Moreover, given that all non-vaccinated persons can serve as a vehicle for the virus, a general obligation not to infect others might imply that *all* persons ought to accept influenza vaccination.

So, a duty to avoid infection will apply to persons who know they carry the influenza virus, and to persons who are at increased risk, and even to those who definitely know they are completely healthy. Another clear example concerns HIV transmission. From a public health perspective, it makes little sense to solely emphasise morally responsible sex practices for persons who know they are seropositive. If the latter ought to practise safe sex as a precaution against infecting others, arguably the same requirement holds for persons who know that they are at significantly increased risk but did not (yet) test positive for HIV. Moreover, one could even argue that *anyone*, either gay or straight, with either many or only few sexual contacts, should practise safe sex in order to prevent further spreading of the virus.

Are all proposed implications of a duty to avoid infection warranted? If we are morally responsible for all avoidable cases of infection, morality would, in Charles Fried's terms, paralyse us or make us obsessed with all possible (even remote risks of) harm.[7] This seems highly unreasonable. Without limits to our obligations to take precautions against harming others, morality would be over-demanding. Let us call this the *problem of excessive precautions*. In the remainder of this paper I will discuss a utilitarian and a contractualist account of obligatory precautions, and see if these can adequately deal with the problem. First however, I will briefly discuss one reply to the problem of excessive precautions that seems attractive at first sight, but, upon reflection, will be of little help.

[6] Nursing home staff have specific moral reasons for accepting vaccination, especially if they promote high vaccination among residents; this goal might be difficult to attain if they neglect the importance of vaccinating themselves. See M.A. van den Hoven and M.F. Verweij. Should we promote influenza vaccination of health care workers in nursing homes? *Age & Ageing* 2003; 32: 487–489.

[7] C. Fried. 1978. *Right and Wrong*. Cambridge. Harvard University Press.

III. THE DISTINCTION BETWEEN DOING AND ALLOWING

One response to the problem of excessive precautions is to deny that all types of precautions are required by one general moral principle. Some forms of preventive care can be considered as instances of non-maleficence, for example an HIV-seropositive person's decision not to engage in unprotected sex. Other forms might be seen as instances of beneficence, for example a person who seeks vaccination in order to protect the frail elderly against the flu. Beneficence is often conceived as a principle that is less stringent than non-maleficence,[8] and moreover, it covers supererogatory acts as well as imperfect duties. This might help us to see some precautions against infection as strict duties, and others as moral demands that are not strictly obligatory (though they might be morally advisable and praiseworthy). One can also distinguish cases of *doing* harm, such as intentionally infecting others, from cases of *allowing* harm to occur, for example forgoing vaccination that would possibly contribute to herd immunity.

These distinctions however do not provide us with a rationale for distinguishing obligatory from non-obligatory precautions. The common sense distinction between doing harm and allowing harm to occur is contested by many authors, but let us assume for the moment that a viable justification is available.[9] Authors who defend the doctrine of doing and allowing normally argue that doing harm is worse than allowing harm. Yet no one holds that this distinction draws a boundary between what is obligatory (refraining from harm) and what is optional (preventing harm from occurring). Obviously, many cases of allowing harm to occur are simply morally wrong. We often have a duty to intervene and help persons who are in pain or at risk of being harmed. Hence, neither the doctrine of doing and allowing, nor a distinction between non-maleficence and beneficence will clarify which precautions against infection are obligatory, and which are not.[10] Such clarification requires a normative theory that offers a coherent and plausible justification of our duties to avoid infection.

[8] W.D. Ross. 1930. *The Right and the Good.* Oxford. Clarendon Press: 21–22.

[9] Cf. W.S. Quin. Actions, intentions, and consequences: the doctrine of doing and allowing. *The Philosophical Review* 1989; 18: 287–312.

[10] Neither would it be of help to specify a concept of harm (e.g. Feinberg's concept of harm as wrongful setback to interests given a specific baseline) in order to see which actions or omissions leading to infection count as harm, and which do not. Such analysis is however relevant for justifying state interventions that *force* people to take precautions against infection. Cf. T. Dare. Mass Immunization programmes: some philosophical issues. *Bioethics* 1998; 125–149.

I will discuss two important candidates: utilitarianism and contractualism.

IV. UTILITARIANISM

The doctrine of doing and allowing is rejected by consequentialists. Consequentialism holds that moral agents should always *promote* intrinsic values such as friendship, health, or welfare, and this implies that whether an action is right or wrong depends on the amount of good and evil, for example, health and illness, that are present in the consequences. Deliberately infecting someone else is not *as such* morally different from deciding not to protect someone else against this disease. The most prominent consequentialist theory is utilitarianism. Now utilitarianism, given the aggregative nature of utility, is very well able to account for health effects on a population level, and therefore this theory is quite attractive in public health ethics. On the other hand, utilitarianism is vulnerable to the critique that its implications are too demanding for moral agents.[11] The principle of utility combines aggregation with maximization, requiring individuals to *always* do the best they can for the common good. Given the importance of health as a condition for welfare, utilitarianism might require anyone to take far-reaching precautions against spreading infectious diseases. Hence, the *problem of excessive precautions* seems to emerge in a utilitarian framework. Is this true or can utilitarianism make sense of a reasonable duty to avoid infection? I will argue that, with respect to infectious diseases control, utilitarianism's moral demands might not be excessive. However, I do have reservations about the plausibility of a utilitarian justification for our duty to prevent infection.

Utilitarianism gives a very clear account of how far our obligations concerning avoiding infection go. The theory extrapolates from how a rational individual assesses the necessity to take precautions against specific risks for herself.[12] In choosing how to act in the face of risk, a rational agent would assess different courses of action (taking the risk, taking limited precautions, avoiding all risks) and seek to maximise her benefits and minimise the costs. Obviously, benefits (avoided harms) and costs need to be multiplied by the probabilities that they will occur. In this way, it is

[11] M. Timmons. 2002. *Moral Theory*. Lanham. Rowman & Littlefield: 134–136; S. Scheffler. 1994. *The Rejection of Consequentialism (Revised Edition)* Oxford. Clarendon: 7–13.

[12] K.W. Simons. Negligence. *Social Philosophy and Policy* 1999; 16(2): 52–93. See pages 66–70.

rational to forgo costly precautions against a fatal infection like smallpox if the chance of acquiring the disease is extremely small. Other precautions, such as influenza vaccination for vulnerable persons, are highly rational, especially if the costs of such precautions are low. Utilitarianism, as a *moral* theory, requires one to aggregate the risks for *all* persons, and to weigh these against the expected costs of one's precautions. If specific precautions will maximise general welfare, then one ought to take them, even if such precautions involve forgoing important benefits. Precautions that are very simple and not demanding are likely to count as obligatory.

We noted above that obligations to avoid infection will apply to infected persons as well as non-infected persons. Moreover, even remote risks are relevant. What is troubling is that this implies that everyone should always be aware of possibilities to prevent transmission of viruses or potentially dangerous microbes, and that individuals should take excessive precautions against contributing to infection. Doesn't this lead to obligations of precaution that are unreasonably demanding for moral agents? In two important respects I think it does not.

The critique that utilitarianism is over-demanding has several grounds. One is that, if an individual is always to promote general welfare, this will be unreasonably costly for her. A strong interpretation of this critique is given by Liam Murphy.[13] Murphy argues that utilitarianism's demands are *unfair* in a non-ideal world. Utilitarianism commits individuals to maximising welfare even if others do not contribute. Arguably, if all persons and institutions in developed countries gave aid in response to world famine – if all would aim to maximise welfare in this respect – then this would not be too costly for any one individual. Yet given that many do not do their share, the demands of welfare maximisation will increase upon those who do comply. In short, utilitarianism requires me to do more if you choose to do less, and that is unfair.

Now interestingly, this problem applies to the issue of giving aid, but it works completely the other way around for obligations to prevent the spread of infectious diseases. For example, if most persons forgo vaccination against influenza, the effects on public health of my choice for vaccination will become negligible. If most persons who feel ill do not stay at home, my choice to isolate myself will become futile. In both cases, many others will get infected anyway, given common neglect of preventive measures.

[13] L. Murphy. 2000. *Moral Demands in Non-Ideal Theory*. Oxford. Oxford University Press: 88–93.

And this affects the consequences of my precautions: these will be relatively useless and arguably will not maximise welfare. Hence, if non-compliance is common, my obligation to contribute to prevention will weaken or even fade away. In this case, utilitarianism's demands are not excessively costly to members of the general public. Things are different for individuals who carry a dangerous and contagious disease that is not endemic or epidemic within a population: their preventative efforts will make a huge difference to public health, hence their obligations to avoid further spread of disease might go very far. For example, a person who believes she has just had close contact with a person with SARS has a strong obligation to isolate herself and avoid contacting others, even if there are no public health restrictions in place yet. The fact that others do not (yet) protect themselves only reinforces this specific person's obligation. Such a conclusion is however neither unfair nor unreasonable.

There is also a second ground for the critique that utilitarianism is over-demanding.[14] Even if due precautions against infection are not excessively costly for individuals, everyone is still morally required to be aware of the risks of transmission, and to take action if necessary. Now if one is required to look after the possible risks for well being of others all the time, this might strongly delimit one's possibilities to live a life of one's own. Utilitarianism is *pervasive*, that is, all facets of life, all one's possibilities for action become morally relevant. This pervasiveness is reinforced by the easy spread of a number of contagious diseases, such as influenza, the common cold, or pertussis. If we have to take all risks into account all the time, this will preoccupy our deliberation, and this would be paralysing for moral agents. The utilitarian can however rebut this critique by pointing out that calculating risks for public health all the time will not maximise general welfare. If excessive account of risks leads to paralysis, then evidently, this will promote neither public health nor general welfare. Hence, our obligation to take account of risks of

[14] There is also one specific case where utilitarianism might be extremely demanding to specific individuals – not because precautions involve severe burdens, but because they go against a person's religious convictions. In some Dutch orthodox protestant communities people refuse vaccination for religious reasons. As a result, vaccination rates in these regions are relatively low, which has led to three polio outbreaks during the last decades. By refusing vaccination these persons accept increased risks for themselves, and for others. Given these facts one might argue that, from a utilitarian point of view, vaccination is morally obligatory. Such obligation would require these persons to violate their religious principles, which is extremely demanding from their point of view. Discussion of this very specific case goes beyond the scope of this paper.

infection is necessarily limited. Those limits are directly justified by appeal to the principle that welfare is to be maximised.[15]

The belief that one does not have to care about all possible risks fits to some extent with how people actually live. We commonly accept or even ignore various risks in normal life. Accepting risk is part of what life is about, otherwise people could not ride bicycles, have sex, reproduce, or visit their hospitalised relatives. But is not the fact that some risks are *accepted* by others much more relevant than the utilitarian suggests? If others consent to risky actions, or if they deliberately accept risks that I might be able to prevent, this is reason for me to think I am not obliged to avoid or take away those risks. Take the example of safe sex. Two persons can agree to have unprotected sex and accept the very small chance that one infects the other with a disease like HIV or herpes genitalis. Arguably, utilitarianism would deem such unprotected sex morally wrong. Not only can they, by using condoms, simply avoid the risk of infecting one another; by doing so they also avoid further risks to future sexual contacts. Now the problem is that, in this way, future sexual contacts are solely considered in their capacity as moral patients, not as responsible persons who can and possibly should take care of their own health. If one takes other persons' responsibilities seriously, and given that *they* can choose safe sex, one has good reason to consider one's own responsibility for their health to be limited (which is not to say that one should be indifferent).[16] This thought however does not fit within a strictly utilitarian approach. From a utilitarian point of view, the salient issue is that one can promote health by opting for safe sex; whether or not others accept the risks of unprotected sex is relatively unimportant. In this way the scope of a person's responsibility for the health of others will be very broad indeed. But will such responsibilities be excessively demanding? The practical implication is that, apart from 'safe' monogamous relationships, people should always practise safe sex. Though many persons might consider this inconvenient, calling the requirement excessively demanding would be a gross exaggeration.

The analysis of utilitarianism leads to a remarkable result. Contrary to what one would expect, a utilitarian explanation of our duties to prevent infection does not directly yield moral requirements that are excessively demanding. The main reason why a

[15] Cf. Ph. Pettit. 1991. Consequentialism. In *A Companion to Ethics*. P. Singer, ed. Malden. Blackwell: 230–240.

[16] Obviously, this presupposes that others will be well-informed about risks and preventive measures and this is cannot always be taken for granted.

strict utilitarian account is unsatisfactory is not that it is clearly over-demanding, but that it gives insufficient credit to the idea that other persons are moral agents with responsibility for their own lives.

V. CONTRACTUALISM

The latter problem is reason to explore a different theoretical basis for our obligations with respect to avoiding infection. It is not that one should always take precautions that are necessary for maximising the aggregate good; one should be able to justify the level of precaution one takes *to any person who will bear the risks.* This idea is best accounted for in Thomas Scanlon's contractualist theory.[17] Scanlon argues that morality involves the justification of our actions to other persons. Treating others as rational beings involves treating them in ways they cannot reasonably reject. There are no a priori principles that specify which acts are morally justified and which are not. Scanlon's idea is that we can, as it were, construct or find such principles if we reflect on what we owe to each other. Suppose that we both aim to find moral principles that regulate our interaction and that can be accepted by both of us. If you then propose a principle that imposes many risks on me, but none for you, then it would be reasonable if I were to reject it (especially if there are alternative principles that would yield much lower risks). The rejection of the first principle is not just reasonable because I have a complaint about it. The rejection is reasonable because my reasons are not idiosyncratic: if you were in my position, you would have the same reasons. Moreover, given that we both aim at finding a principle that is acceptable to each of us, it makes sense to compare my reasons for rejecting principle A, with your reasons for rejecting a different principle B. In this way, we have reasons to find the principle that would yield the least strong complaint for any of us.

Now, in this contractualist framework, an act is wrong just in case any principle that permitted it would be one that *someone* could reasonably reject. A principle that allows any of us to forgo whatever precaution against infection would obviously be rejected by many others, notably those who face the risk and will be harmed. Yet, in the example of sexually transmitted disease, the complaints of other persons become much weaker if they are aware of the risks of unprotected sex, and have sufficient possibilities to protect themselves. Hence, my future sexual contacts

[17] T.M. Scanlon. 1998. *What We Owe To Each Other.* Cambridge. Belknap Press.

cannot simply reject any principle that allows my current partner and me to have unprotected sex today. Naturally, I do have certain obligations towards my sexual partner, but these depend on her evaluation of the risks of infection. If we both accept the risk, we can justify to one another our choice to have unprotected sex. If I can reasonably know that the other person might underestimate the risk (for example, she probably thinks I do not lead an overly risky sexual life, while in fact I do) then I should either disclose the risks, or opt for protected sex. This latter principle is one, I think, no one can reasonably reject.

It is however difficult to generalise this principle to other communicable diseases, such as influenza, pertussis, or even SARS, where infection occurs more easily and through less intimate human interaction. Such diseases are transmitted in situations where persons are unaware of risk, hence a principle that emphasises personal risk assessment, consent, and responsibility, will not be very helpful. Apparently then, different contexts, including spread of risk and modes of transmission, require different principles concerning the level of precaution that persons should take.

Now a fundamental problem is that, for diseases that are easily spread throughout the population, contractualism requires a level of precaution that is extremely demanding.[18] Take the example of influenza again. Persons most vulnerable to the disease do not respond optimally to vaccination themselves and therefore they will be much better protected if *everyone* were vaccinated, the old and young, the ill and the healthy.

This would create a level of herd protection that, arguably, prevents a number of deaths within high-risk groups. Therefore people at high risk could reasonably reject any moral principle that allows healthy persons to forgo vaccination. Moreover, they might reject any principle that allows healthy persons to forgo any effective precaution (because it leaves them at greater risk). This implies that everyone *ought* to accept vaccination and that, if there is an outbreak, everyone should take protective measures, for example wearing masks that cover mouth and nose, and certainly refraining from visiting hospitals and nursing homes – even if most residents and family members would be very unhappy if they could not see each other for a couple of weeks. This obviously imposes inconveniences and small burdens upon a very large population, but the complaints by any member of the large

[18] This argument is worked out in detail by Elisabeth Ashford in The demandingness of Scanlon's contractualism. *Ethics* 2003; 113: 273–302, p. 294ff.

population would be outweighed by the much stronger claim by any of the few persons for whom a less stringent precautionary practice will mean that they will catch an infection that might be fatal. The fact that one cannot know in advance for whom the less stringent policy will be fatal, is no reason for disregarding that particular point of view. On the other hand, the fact that the inconveniences and burdens are borne by almost everyone, hence would yield a significant negative utility if all burdens are taken together, is not important from a contractualist perspective. Moral principles must be justifiable to any *individual*, and therefore, if one individual has very strong reasons against a principle, these cannot be outweighed by less strong objections held by more (even many) persons. Scanlon's contractualism bans interpersonal aggregation, and this is one of the central features where his theory is distinguished from utilitarianism.

Now obviously, most people do not take precautions that go that far. For the utilitarian this fact is very relevant, because it deems futile the efforts of individuals who do comply. In this way, the utilitarian can avoid the problem of excessive precautions. I do not think this way of argument is open for the contractualist. Scanlon's contractualist deliberation does not focus on the consequences of individual acts, but on general principles that regulate how persons ought to act. The fact that others do not comply with a general moral principle of precaution will not help me to justify my non-compliance to persons who will be harmed. In this way, contractualism requires us to take precautions that seem to be excessive. They certainly go far beyond the precautions that are required by utilitarianism. This is not yet a decisive argument against the theory as a whole – after all, it might be that morality simply is extremely demanding in a world like ours.[19] Hence, the problem requires further analysis. Yet I hope to have made clear that the contractualist's ban on aggregation is appropriate in some cases in public health ethics, but raises problems in others.

VI. CONCLUSION

If people have a duty not to infect others, this will not only apply to persons who know they carry a communicable disease, but also to persons who know they might have been infected, and even to those who know they are completely healthy. This reinforces the need to reflect on the ground and scope of such duties: given the

[19] Cf. Ashford, ibid. p. 302; Murphy. *op. cit.* note 13, pp. 34–62.

manifold possibilities of prevention, obligatory precautions might be excessively demanding. I have argued that both a utilitarian and a contractualist understanding of our duties to take precautions face important theoretical problems. Neither theory is completely satisfactory, but the discussion leads to a somewhat unexpected result. Where one would expect that a maximising principle of utility would lead to a far reaching obligation to prevent spread of infectious diseases, it appears that, at least in some contexts, the requirements of contractualism are much more demanding. This especially holds for infectious diseases where transmission occurs easily throughout daily life, like influenza. On the other hand, the unsatisfactory elements of utilitarianism especially come to the fore in the context of safe sex precautions and sexually transmitted diseases. By focusing on aggregation of health and welfare the utilitarian disregards that other persons are moral agents, who can be aware of risks, who sometimes accept risk, and therefore have a responsibility for their own health as well. The latter claim is good reason for seeing my responsibility for their health as not unlimited.

Marcel Verweij
Ethics Institute
Utrecht University
P.O. Box 80103
NL-3508 TC Utrecht
The Netherlands
m.f.verweij@ethics.uu.nl

Part VI
Questions of Governance

[20]

GOVERNANCE, MICROGOVERNANCE AND HEALTH

Scott Burris[*]

Who can say what the optimal *level* of health is for the world's population? The best health achieved by the healthiest person on the globe may not be the best the human species can do. Even if we take health to be a characteristic of populations rather than of individuals, we do not know that a nation high on the list of accepted indicators – life expectancy, infant mortality – has reached the peak. We can much more clearly observe problems with the *distribution* of health: we see inequalities in health within countries and between countries across the globe. Significantly, these inequalities are not explained by absolute levels of deprivation or exposure or stress: both at the country and the individual level, health is distributed along a gradient, improving as socioeconomic status rises.[1] Moreover, we have powerful insights from theory and data as to why these inequalities occur. Simply put, ecological or eco-social theories of health and its determinants posit that lower status people are exposed to more stressors and have poorer access to resources (such as education and political power) that allow them to reduce or cope with their exposures.[2]

Following this theory of what causes health inequalities comes the question

---

* James E. Beasley Professor of Law, Temple University Beasley School of Law. I am grateful to Annemarie Bridy, Patricia Case, Zita Lazzarini, and the participants at the symposium on SARS and the Global Governance of Public Health for their helpful comments on this paper.

1. *See generally* SOCIAL DETERMINANTS OF HEALTH (Michael Marmot & Richard G. Wilkinson eds., 1999) (outlining scientific justification for links between socioeconomic status and health); Ichiro Kawachi, *Income Inequality and Health, in* SOCIAL EPIDEMIOLOGY 76 (Lisa F. Berkman & Ichiro Kawachi eds., 2000) (discussing links between income inequality and life expectancy).

2. *See generally* Eric Brunner & Michael Marmot, *Social Organization, Stress, and Health, in* SOCIAL DETERMINANTS OF HEALTH, *supra* note 2, at 17, 40-41 (describing how psychosocial factors contribute to stress and poor health along socioeconomic lines); Kawachi, *supra* note 1, at 174, 184-86 (identifying mechanisms that link social capital to health outcomes); Nancy Krieger, *Discrimination and Health, in* SOCIAL EPIDEMIOLOGY, *supra* note 2, at 36, 63-67 (discussing ways in which discrimination can harm health); Nancy Krieger, *Theories for Social Epidemiology in the 21st Century: An Ecosocial Perspective*, 30 INT'L J. EPIDEMIOLOGY 668, 673 (2001) (stating that eco-social perspective considers social determinants in order to explore link between society and biology); Bruce G. Link & Jo Phelan, *Social Conditions as Fundamental Causes of Disease*, 35 HEALTH & SOC. BEHAV. 80, 82 (1995) (arguing that greater consideration should be given to social conditions as a cause of illness); Juliana Maantay, *Zoning, Equity, and Public Health*, 91 AM. J. PUB. HEALTH 1033, 1038-39 (2001) (examining equity issues in zoning and potential impact of zoning on public health); Johannes Siegrist & Michael Marmot, *Health Inequalities and the Psychosocial Environment—Two Scientific Challenges*, 58 SOC. SCI. & MED. 1463, 1466 (2004) (noting links between an adverse psychological environment and lower levels of overall health). The proposition that inequality is itself a determinant of health at the population level – i.e., that *population* health outcomes are directly caused by inequalities – continues to be debated. *See generally* John Lynch et al., *Is Income Inequality a Determinant of Population Health? Part 1. A Systematic Review*, 82 MILBANK Q. 5, 5 (2004) (reviewing studies examining connection between income inequality and health).

of what to do about them. The more one recognizes that ultimate health outcomes reflect fundamental characteristics of social organization, and that health inequalities are durable characteristics of systems produced along many pathways, the less sense it makes to focus only (or even primarily) on particular diseases and proximate risk factors. Health being a product of a complex interaction of human beings, social systems, and environments over time, it is necessary to pursue with vigor the question of how to change the fundamental determinants or the broad mechanisms through which these determinants sort people for health. Under this view, the whole set of global and national legal systems, policies, and institutions are on the table, along with many other things, as potential targets for change. People concerned with health policy may well talk not just about the International Health Regulations and the structure of the World Health Organization, but the World Trade Organization, the United Nations, and the whole web of international institutions and agreements that govern global social and economic behavior. And so they should.[3] There is much that a commitment to reducing inequality can teach policy, and in some countries the reduction of health inequality has been to some degree built into the policymaking process.[4]

Governance, by which I mean the management of the course of events in a system, is obviously an overarching issue of concern to health from an ecological point of view.[5] Governance consists largely in the policing of social relations, environmental conditions, and the allocation of resources essential to well-being. Who decides, and how they decide, are key drivers of substantive policy. Moreover, there is at least some epidemiological evidence that the ability of people to participate in the governance of their communities is in itself significant for health.[6] Not that moving the health policy focus to governance is a panacea. The empirical reality of governance on the globe has outpaced our analytic frameworks, making it all that much more difficult to diagnose or treat the ways in which governance is failing. Even where our theoretical tools allow us a relatively clear view of various "problems," structures reflecting and embodying the power of entrenched interests are hard to change by peaceful (and even more difficult by violent) means. And I have another concern: I agree with social thinkers like Friedrich Hayek that it is enormously difficult to figure

3. *See generally* Wolfgang Hein, *Global Health Governance and National Health Policies in Developing Countries: Conflicts and Cooperation at the Interfaces, in* GLOBALISATION, GLOBAL HEALTH GOVERNANCE AND NATIONAL HEALTH POLICIES IN DEVELOPING COUNTRIES: AN EXPLORATION INTO THE DYNAMICS OF INTERFACES 33 (Wolfgang Hein & Lars Kohlmorgan eds., 2003) (analyzing interfaces between national governance and various international agreements including trade agreements and NGO's).

4. *See* Johan Mackenbach et al., *Strategies to Reduce Socioeconomic Inequalities, in* REDUCING INEQUALITIES IN HEALTH: A EUROPEAN PERSPECTIVE 25 (Johan Mackenbach & Martijntje Bakker eds., 2002) (noting adoption by WHO member nations of goals of Health For All, including equality target).

5. For other definitions, see, e.g., Hein, *supra* note 3, at 35-37 (noting international scholar James Rosenau's definition of governance as "all the structures necessary to maintaining a modicum of public order and movement toward the realization of collective goals. . . .").

6. Kawachi, *supra* note 2, at 90.

out *how* to manage a complex system towards specific ends,[7] which must instill a certain humility in the proponent of even the most apparently sensible reform.

A certain humility, but not enough to forestall the pursuit of "democratic experimentalism."[8] An effective take on the governance of health will come from the interplay of action and theory, and in this paper I will report on some efforts in both domains. An emerging theory of "nodal governance" is offered to describe the management of events in social systems. The use of this theory in mapping, assessing, and then productively "destabilizing" these systems is discussed, with particular attention to the extent to which promoting "microgovernance" institutions is a plausible strategy for improving population health. Nodal governance focuses attention on how governance happens–how power is wielded–at specific points within a system, and thus raises essential normative questions about democratic decision-making. But the theory, with its obvious intellectual debts to network theory, systems theory, and the work of Hayek, also seems to imply a challenge to the sort of thinking about regulation and law often encapsulated in the idea of the "risk society."[9] In the final section of the paper I conclude with some speculations about new, constitutive paradigms for social governance.

THE BREAKDOWN OF RECEIVED EXPLANATIONS

Conventional conceptions of governance are under stress in many fields. The Westphalian paradigm at the heart of traditional thinking about international governance is a good example, striking all the notes on the classic Hobbesian scale. (See Figure 1.) At the apex of action is the state–provider of public goods, accountable for events, representing the citizens in the affairs of the world. Governance within states is organized hierarchically, with the idea of the state itself and its functions and limitations tied to a distinction between public and private spheres. Governance is the prerogative of government, and is a top-down affair. States are places, and place–borders, distances–matters in both definitional and practical ways in governance. Individuals have a link of citizenship to one country; as citizens, they have claims to certain rights, while abandoning or accepting limits on others as consideration for the social contract; they do not have responsibility for providing social goods, nor do they "govern" others.

It would take a book to catalogue the problems that have been observed in this album of governance snapshots. In real life, states vary. Some have "failed," existing only as constitutional formalities or optimistic city-states. A few more or less totalitarian states persist in the effort to monopolize governance, but throughout the world we have also seen the rise of an ideology

7. *See, e.g.*, FRIEDRICH A. HAYEK, LAW, LEGISLATION AND LIBERTY 13 (1973) (noting overwhelming ignorance of most particular facts that determine the processes of society must be kept in mind whenever analyzing the theories of better managing that society).

8. ROBERTO MANGABEIRA UNGER, WHAT SHOULD LEGAL ANALYSIS BECOME 6-8 (1996).

9. The leading description is ULRICH BECK, RISK SOCIETY: TOWARDS A NEW MODERNITY (1992).

and a practice of transferring traditional state functions to non-state actors. Although the extent to which the state has been "hollowed out" is subject to dispute,[10] the "regulatory state" that steers but leaves the rowing to private actors offers many instances in which both state governance and hierarchical control are attenuated. Scholars have documented the increasing privatization of even essential services such as security, and discussed how this phenomenon raises basic questions about who is accountable for public goods and how responsibility can be conceptualized and enforced.[11] Some have referred to this new model as "Post-Westphalian" governance.[12] (See Figure 2.)

The shifting of traditional government functions from state to non-state actors obviously attenuates the public-private distinction. So, too, does the related use of ideas of private property to reconfigure the relationship of individuals to their surroundings. Shopping malls and gated communities are two prime examples of how the device of private property can be used to convert streets and markets from places of public assembly and activity to private spheres where speech and conduct are subject to the regulation of the owner. Such tracts of "mass private property" and the outsourcing of state activities create zones in which access to governance is determined primarily by economic criteria, creating a governance or democracy deficit on the balance sheet of traditional citizenship.[13]

Contracting out of government functions and privatizing formerly public spaces are just two ways in which governance in practice looks different from the old model. From any empirical perspective, the notion of top-down governance is flawed. The vast literature on legal implementation repeatedly demonstrates the limits of hierarchy and the potency of "bottom-up" factors in determining the shape of actual governance.[14] Scholars working from the "governmentality" perspective take it as an axiom that "'the state' is neither the only force engaged in the government of conduct nor the hidden hand orchestrating the strategies

10. See Michael Moran, *Review Article: Understanding the Regulatory State*, 32 BRIT. J. POL. SCI. 391, 391 (2002) for a review of the literature on the regulatory state.

11. *See, e.g.*, David H. Bayley & Clifford D. Shearing, *The Future of Policing*, 30 LAW & SOC'Y REV. 585, 587, 596 (1996) (noting that in western nations, private security outnumbers public police and that private security is only accountable to the client and not society as a whole); John Braithwaite, *The New Regulatory State and the Transformation of Criminology*, 40 BRIT. J. CRIMINOLOGY 222, 226 (2000) (analyzing trend towards privatization of policing in developed economies).

12. *See, e.g.*, David Fidler, *Constitutional Outlines of Public Health's "New World Order,"* 77 TEMP. L. REV. 247, 260 (2004) (citing preamble to WHO Constitution as embodiment of Post-Westphalian governance principles).

13. *See* Alfred C. Aman, Jr., *Globalization, Democracy, and the Need for a New Administrative Law*, 10 IND. J. GLOBAL LEGAL STUD. 125, 125-26 (2003) (noting that emerging forms of administration combine to reflect democracy deficit); Clifford Shearing & Jennifer Wood, *Nodal Governance, Democracy, and the New "Denizens,"* 30 J.L. & SOC'Y 400, 412 (2003).

14. *See* EUGENE BARDACH, IMPLEMENTATION GAME: WHAT HAPPENS AFTER A BILL BECOMES LAW 36-38 (1977) (enumerating elements that must be assembled before successfully implementing a program); JEFFREY L. PRESSMAN & AARON WILDAVSKY, IMPLEMENTATION: HOW GREAT EXPECTATIONS IN WASHINGTON ARE DASHED IN OAKLAND 90-91 (1973) (noting complexity inherent in local administration of federal programs and potential for conflict between participants).

and techniques of doctors, lawyers, churches, community organizations, pressure groups, and the myriad of other social actors seeking to shape events to certain ends."[15] Indeed, non-state actors have taken on the role of governing, not just other private entities but the state itself.[16] Greenpeace through public relations, the American Civil Liberties Union through litigation, and the Microsoft Corporation through all the means that money can buy, all regulate governments.[17] Even within state bureaucracies, governance no longer fits the Westphalian model. In what Anne-Marie Slaughter has referred to as the "Real New World Order," government agencies bind with each other formally and informally in "transgovernmental networks" of regulation.[18] And the mode of influence goes far beyond command and control. To take a close example, we saw during the SARS outbreak that the notoriously "weak" World Health Organization ("WHO") was able to exercise considerable control over states simply by issuing press releases: lacking formal power to compel the cooperation of affected states, WHO was able to use its ability to issue travel warnings to mobilize the considerable influence of travelers and those who decide where to place factory orders.

Within the classic model of state governance, all is hardly well in terms of rights and democracy: an attention to the formal rules (treaties, constitutions) seems to come at the expense of addressing how well public goods like human rights are delivered.[19] Where ultimate state responsibility has been eliminated by a property rule, or ambiguated by a contract, the responsibility for the production of public goods and the protection of human rights is less certain. The state is not necessarily either the chief guarantor or the chief threat. In practice, it is the private party who governs key goods, yet against the fellow private citizen the individual has little recourse; accountability and transparency do not run with the contract or the land. And for millions of people, the government on which they may make claims as citizens is not the government that matters to them: the mass movement of people in search of economic opportunity and in flight from various forms of violence and disorder makes citizenship a troublesome criterion and creates a new class of long term residents

15. Nikolas Rose, *Government and Control*, 40 BRIT. J. CRIMINOLOGY 321, 323 (2000). *See also* H.K. Colebatch, *Government and Governmentality: Using Multiple Approaches to the Analysis of Government*, 37 AUSTRALIAN J. POL. SCI. 417, 429 (2002) (describing the "governmentality" perspective).

16. For a review, see Colin Scott, *Private Regulation of the Public Sector: A Neglected Facet of Contemporary Governance*, 29 J.L. & SOC'Y 56, 57 (2002) (indicating continuing oversight of public institutions by private actors).

17. As Braithwaite puts it, "the corporatization of the world during the twentieth century . . . meant that the greatest regulatory capabilities lay with corporations rather than states." Braithwaite, *supra* note 12, at 229. He adds that "[b]y the mid-90s for the first time, a majority of the largest "economies" in the world were transnational corporations rather than states." *Id.*

18. Anne-Marie Slaughter, *The Accountability of Government Networks*, 8 IND. J. GLOBAL LEGAL STUD. 347, 347 n.1, 355 (2001).

19. *See* Oona A. Hathaway, *Do Human Rights Treaties Make a Difference?*, 111 YALE L.J. 1935, 2013 (2002) (noting that rewarding ratification of treaties rather than compliance can reduce pressure to actually improve human rights practices).

with whose needs and desires conventional models cannot cope.[20] A revolution in transport and information technology renders distance and borders ever more unimportant for governance purposes. This has been a long-term process, marked in health by the steady march of plagues from point A to B, but we have perhaps reached a new level in a geometric increase in intercommunication and mobility.[21]

That ways of being and ways of thinking might diverge is not unexpected in an adaptive system, yet scholarship on governance and regulation rarely considers how even the best-designed form of rule is affected by the passage of time and the strategic improvisations of the governed. Institutions develop and rules are made in response to current conditions in order to promote certain new behaviors and ends; even if successful at the time, over time the governed learn to game that system, evade the rules, or govern the governors. The meaning of essential concepts is transformed within or distributed across institutions within the system.[22] The result over time is that no matter how formally stable the system may be, in action it has transformed into something different altogether.

At a certain point, the usual descriptions obscure as much as they reveal, yet what Roberto Mangabeira Unger aptly calls "institutional fetishism" exerts an enormous intellectual gravity: despite the failure of current arrangements to deliver the goods whose delivery justified their formation, and the failure of conventional theory to illuminate the reasons why, we cling tenaciously to the belief that the contemporary array of institutions is the only one capable of producing a salubrious, prosperous, and democratic environment.[23] Change must therefore begin with different ways of seeing the present.

---

20. See Shearing & Wood, *supra* note 13, at 408 (describing a new type of civil person they call a "denizen"). Lant Pritchett writes:

> The ideas that support monarchy, colonialism, slavery in their day seem solid, impregnable, and yet, even a few decades later people wonder how otherwise rational and well meaning people could have been held in the thrall of such patently ludicrous, not to mention obviously morally despicable, notions. It is not inevitable, or perhaps even possible, but it is at least plausible that two key notions of the twentieth century—"nationalism" and that it is acceptable that restrictions on the movement of persons should hold human beings cruelly hostage to the place of their birth—will be seen in the twenty-first century as hopelessly wrong-headed.

Lant Pritchett, The Future of Migration: Irresistible Forces Meet Immovable Ideas, *at* http://ksghome.harvard.edu/~lpritch/research.htm (October 10, 2003) (paper presented to The Future of Globalization: Explorations in Light of the Recent Turbulence, Yale University, Center for the Study of Globalization).

21. *See* David G. Post & David R. Johnson, *"Chaos Prevailing on Every Continent": Towards a New Theory of Decentralized Decision-Making in Complex Systems*, 73 CHI.-KENT L. REV. 1055, 1058 (1998) (noting that location and boundaries are no longer controlling in human interaction).

22. *See* John Braithwaite, *Rules and Principles: A Theory of Legal Certainty*, 27 AUSTRALIAN J. LEGAL PHIL. 47, at 5 (2002) (noting wealthy participants in legal systems move the law not towards individual outcomes, but towards rules that benefit their interests), *available at*, http://papers.srn.com/sol3/Delivery.cfm/SSRN_ID329400_code020916560.pdf?abstractid=329400&mirid=2 (last accessed Sept. 6, 2004).

23. *See* UNGER, *supra* note 8, at 6-8 (analyzing impact of pervasive assumption that abstract concepts have single and necessary institutional expressions).

A THEORY OF NODAL GOVERNANCE

Peter Drahos, Clifford Shearing and I have recently set out a theory of "nodal governance."[24] In this theory, governance is a social adaptation accomplished in significant part through the creation and operation of "nodes." (See Figure 3.) Nodes, as the name suggests, are commonly points on a network, so that nodes can be understood as participating in the type of information-based governance described by Manuel Castells.[25] In Castells' work, social systems are seen as comprised of networks that govern through control of information, capital, production, and other basic functions and resources. Governing entities like states and firms are understood to be networks themselves, comprised of many subsidiary nodes, rather than as monolithic entities.[26]

The theory of nodal governance is intended to enrich network theory by focusing attention on and bringing more clarity to the internal characteristics of nodes and thus to the analysis of how power is actually created and exercised within a social system. While power is transmitted across networks, the actual point where knowledge and capacity are mobilized for transmission is the node. Given networks, nodal governance asks how local participation is organized and effectuated.

A node, according to the theory, is a site of governance exhibiting four essential characteristics:

- Ways of thinking (*mentalities*) about the matters that the node has emerged to govern;
- Methods (*technologies*) for exerting influence over the course of events at issue;
- *Resources* to support the operation of the node and the exertion of influence; and
- An *institutional structure*.[27]

To be a governing node as this theory defines it, a node must have some institutional form. It need not be a formally constituted or legally recognized entity, but it must have sufficient stability and structure to enable the mobilization of resources, mentalities, and technologies over time. A street gang

---

24. Scott Burris, Peter Drahos & Clifford Shearing, *Nodal Governance as an Approach to Regulation* (forthcoming).

25. Manuel Castells, *Materials for an Exploratory Theory of the Network Society*, 51 BRIT. J. SOC. 5, 10-11 (2000).

26. *Id.* at 11, 14.

27. *E.g.*, LES JOHNSTON & CLIFFORD D. SHEARING, GOVERNING SECURITY: EXPLORATIONS IN POLICING AND JUSTICE 13 (2003). The theory has emerged from practice, from efforts to understand the workings of governing systems in order to improve them. The four elements are heuristic rather than hermetic analytic categories. A technology of governance can be understood for some purposes as a resource of a node; many technologies of governance are essentially ways of thinking; much institutional structure is, as it were, in the mind. Likewise, the theory is meant not to supplant but facilitate the illuminating application of more general social theory, such as Bourdieu's or Foucault's. *See, e.g.*, Benoit Dupont, *Security in the Age of Networks*, 14 POLICING AND SOC'Y 77, 85 (2004) (analyzing the security network in terms of the actor's mobilization of distinct forms of resources to improve its position in the network).

can be a node, as can a police station, or even a particular shift at a firehouse. A node like this may be primarily part of an integrated network, like a department in a firm; it may be linked to other nodes in multiple networks without having a primary network affiliation, like a small lobbying firm; or it may be what we call a "superstructural node," which brings together representatives of different nodal organizations to concentrate the members' resources and technologies for a common purpose but without integrating the various networks–a trade association, for example.

"Mentality" refers to the culture of the node, its way thinking about itself and the world around it. A mentality operates to bring coherence and thus enable longevity and collective action within the node. Such a culture is not a blueprint for specific action, but a narrative of the world that guides the ongoing process of adaptive improvisation in a node.[28] A constellation of nodes in the same primary network, like a firm, may share a common organizational mentality, but each node may differentiate itself in part by having its own distinct culture as well. Agencies, bureaus, and offices across the many networks that constitute the federal government likely share some broad mentality of federal public service (at the very least they understand themselves all to be part of a hierarchical federal bureaucracy) but specific nodes within that system are as different in their missions and culture as, well, the Centers for Disease Control and the Federal Bureau of Investigation. Understanding the mentality of a node or nodal constellation is essential to understanding its behavior, and the mentality is also a fulcrum of change. Indeed, for some scholars, the mentality is the decisive characteristic of a node with respect to controlling behavior: changing the constitution of the target entity is the best, if not the only way, to bring about compliance with the desired norms.[29]

The technologies a node uses are also important to observe. Some of these are rather straightforward. Police departments use technologies of control like violence, the threat of punishment, and patrol. Lawyers use laws, lawsuits, and contracts. Lobbyists use money and information. The concept also draws upon more sophisticated ideas about the technologies of government that encompass the strategies through which problems are defined in ways that point to and legitimate certain solutions or problem solvers.[30] The Westphalian paradigm, for example, defines governance as a problem for governments to solve, and so operates to privilege states to exercise jurisdiction (and to exclude non-state actors). The paradigm is complementary to, but distinct from, other technologies, like armies and foreign aid.

28. *E.g.*, Clifford Shearing & Richard Ericson, *Culture as Figurative Action*, 42 BRIT. J. SOC. 482, 491 (1991).

29. *E.g.*, Gunther Teubner, *Juridification: Concepts, Aspects, Limits, Solutions*, *in* JURIDIFICATION OF SOCIAL SPHERES: A COMPARATIVE ANALYSIS IN THE AREAS OF LABOR, CORPORATE, ANTITRUST AND SOCIAL WELFARE LAW 38-39 (Gunther Teubner ed., 1987) (discussing need to pursue regulatory strategies that change internal culture of regulated entities).

30. These ideas, arising from Foucault's thoughts on governmentality, have been extensively elaborated by others. *See, e.g.*, Rose & Miller, *supra* note 16, at 183 (detailing technologies that facilitate regulation).

Resources take many forms. The object, number, and strength of network connections are important resources of a node. Nodes with many and strong connections, or connections to particularly strong nodes, are more significant regulators than those with fewer such resources. Money, armies, and information can all be resources that a node deploys to manage the course of events. The mentalities and technologies, measured in terms of apparent effectiveness, can be measured as resources of a node in comparing one to another. The ability to wield ideas like sovereignty, legitimacy, hierarchy, and a distinction between the private and the public is not evenly distributed in a nodal system: some nodes have it, others do not.[31] The public-private distinction is thus not a major element of nodal governance. WHO, for example, is a constellation of bureaus, regional, and country offices sharing to some extent the same mentalities and technologies, but also exhibiting some differences in these characteristics, some independence, and some degree of competition for resources. The network of nodes we call WHO has the mission of improving health around the world and, like other organizations, also doubtless many other missions like advancing the nodes' own welfare. It uses legal powers, public health science, public relations, and other tools to influence the course of events around the globe as they relate to health and the status of the WHO. Health GAP,[32] a group comprised of activists from a number of non-governmental organizations working to increase access of the poor to essential medicines, is a superstructural node. It has relatively few economic resources, but can use information gathered by its constituent members, demonstrations and its access to media networks to influence governments, drug companies and other

---

31. On a nodal governance view (and following the governmentality literature), concepts like hierarchy do not describe structural components of a governing system, but resources that some nodes possess and others do not. The management node of a firm can expect subsidiary nodes on the shop floor or the personnel office to obey its commands in part because of the mutual acceptance of the idea that the central office is "above" the lesser ones on the management chart and therefore must obey. If the "lower-downs" do not obey, the management node can fire the members of the subsidiary node; it can mobilize personnel staff to escort the offenders from the premises, cut off their salary payments, and so on. It is, again, not able to do this because it is structurally "above" the personnel office, but because management is accepted by the personnel office as being able to command. If everyone at the firm refused to obey, the management could go to court for state assistance in ejecting the rebels; once again, if it prevailed it would not be because it is structurally above the offenders but merely because the law and the court accept the claim that the management is in charge.

32. "GAP" stands for "Global Access Project." The group's website describes the group this way:

> We are an organization of U.S.-based AIDS and human rights activists, hippies, people living with HIV/AIDS, public health experts, fair trade advocates and concerned individuals who campaign against policies of neglect and avarice that deny treatment to millions and fuel the spread of HIV. We are dedicated to eliminating barriers to global access to affordable life-sustaining medicines for people living with HIV/AIDS as key to a comprehensive strategy to confront and ultimately stop the AIDS pandemic. We believe that the human right to life and to health must prevail over the pharmaceutical industry's excessive profits and expanding patent rights.

GAP, ABOUT HEALTH GAP, at http://www.healthgap.org/hgap/about.html (last modified Feb. 10, 2003).

powerful nodes influencing pharmaceutical access. WHO is a public international institution with powers based in treaties; Health GAP is an informal coalition without any official governance authority. In the theory of nodal governance, however, they are both governing nodes. They both manage the course of events of the systems they inhabit by getting other nodes to which they are linked to act or refrain from action. Where they differ are in mentalities, resources, and technologies.

If government nodes are themselves governed in important ways by non-governmental nodes, it is useful to see "governmentness" as an internal characteristic of some nodes–a resource–rather than as a category of node. In a world where traditionally "public" goods and services (like public health or security) are delivered by or their availability is set by "private" nodes, the public-private distinction hides more than it reveals. The theory of nodal governance invites consideration of how democracy looks different if sources of private governance are treated in their functional equivalence to public forms. A "company town," in which real authority is exercised by a corporation, for example, is not democratic merely because a weak mayor and council are elected.

APPLYING NODAL GOVERNANCE IN THE CAUSE OF DEMOCRACY AND HEALTH

Nodal governance is first a description of how resources are mobilized and power exercised in social systems. There is nothing essentially democratic about nodal or network governance. Individual nodes can be undemocratic, and of course, there are enormous power imbalances across nodal systems. Nodes able to mobilize greater resources, and which are perhaps historically located at many points of intersection having greater connective resources, can dominate.[33] In the following discussion, I use the theory of nodal governance normatively, to illuminate a path towards a more equitable distribution of resources necessary to health, including resources of governance that allow everyone to participate meaningfully in managing the course of events in their immediate surroundings and to have a voice in management of larger social systems.[34] The value of a nodal view to the pursuit of health equity arises mainly in the degree to which it can be used, as Les Johnston and Clifford Shearing put it, to transform relationships in ways that advance democracy.[35] In this section, I suggest two general ways in which this might occur. First, a nodal conception of governance could be useful in finding innovative institutional arrangements for the delivery of key social goods; nodal mapping of system governance could, that is, be a first step in a process of democratic experimentalism in which inhabitants of a system

33. *See* Dupont, *supra* note 27, at 85 (describing unequal distribution of different resources between agents in security network and the competition to monopolize capitals recognized as legitimate by all members of the network).

34. I do not mean to suggest that my conception of the good is an essential product or premise of nodal governance, or that it will necessarily be shared by participants in any of the activities I describe hereafter.

35. JOHNSTON & SHEARING, *supra* note 27, at 160.

find new forms of governance suitable to promoting their conceptions of the good. Second, I propose that nodal governance theory can guide efforts to create institutions of microgovernance for those without access to an effective governing node, turning diffuse knowledge and resources into collective efficacy.

Mapping Governance in a System

Nodal governance is potentially a useful tool for providing more accurate maps of governing networks in any given system, whether a neighborhood or the General Agreement on Tariffs and Trade ("GATT"). Nodal governance as a description of how management is organized in a system is a useful tool for seeing who has power, how power flows through a system, and how power in a system can be reconfigured. In any system, it is possible to identify the governing nodes, and to map their network connections. We can map not just for network position and the number and strength of connections, but also for the quality and performance of the internal elements of the node that are crucial to its governing potency: how do the people in the node understand their environments and their goals, what technologies do they deploy and how well do they work, what other resources do they possess? Such a map is equally important for its capacity to show who is *not* present in the governance system, for identifying people who do not have access to a node or whose nodes are weak and poorly connected. Certainly as a heuristic approach, and ultimately as an empirical one, nodal governance first provides a description of who is managing the course of events.

Such a map offers both normative and practical insights, a way of thinking about democracy in functional rather than formal or institutional terms. Consider the Agreement on Trade-Related Aspects of Intellectual Property Rights ("TRIPS agreement"). While it appears to fit neatly into the Westphalian model as a compact among states, its genesis, as described by Susan Sell and others, tells a different story.[36] In essence, the TRIPS agreement was a product of the regulation of states by corporate nodes. In the United States, pharmaceutical companies were able to link to government nodes through membership on a key advisory committee and through lobbyists. The use of campaign contributions, public relations, and direct advocacy led the United States to adopt an intellectual property agreement as a key goal of its GATT strategy, and the mobilization of similar corporate networks in other nations was instrumental in securing support from other governments.

This account of TRIPS emphasizes the ability of non-government nodes to govern the government. The potency of direct links to powerful government nodes, of the ability to bring money and propaganda to bear, is clear. The power of law as a technology of governance is seen in the success of intellectual property owners in using it to enhance the value of their holdings.[37] Using the

36. SUSAN K. SELL, PRIVATE POWER, PUBLIC LAW: THE GLOBALIZATION OF INTELLECTUAL PROPERTY RIGHTS 7-10 (2003) (describing the history and origin of TRIPS). *See generally* Burris, Drahos and Shearing, *supra* note 24.

37. *See generally* PETER DRAHOS & JOHN BRAITHWAITE, INFORMATION FEUDALISM: WHO

tool of an international treaty, certain actors in the system were able to encompass things they produce or control within a definition of property, and to invoke state power to protect and promote their interests in that property. Other interests, such as access of millions or billions of people to necessary medications, were effectively subordinated. Of course, the success of the effort was not just a function of the technology, but of the network architecture. Advocates of pharmaceutical access did not have a direct connection to the United States Trade Representative. They lacked the resources to mobilize sufficient opposition to stop TRIPS (though have since been instrumental in building a network aimed at limiting its effects).

The fact that the TRIPS agreement was advanced by a democratically elected state government through diplomats accountable to elected officials tells us very little about what actually happened in terms of respect for norms of human rights and democracy. If in fact Pfizer and a few other companies are to a considerable extent dictating the global availability of essential medicine, the description invites consideration of basic ideas such as the view that human rights obligations are directly binding only on states, or that the state is primarily responsible for ensuring the provision of a basic public good like disease control.[38] We can put concepts of democratic governance to more relevant tests than asking simply whether officials were duly elected. We may ask not whether voters or other stakeholders had some formal (or even actual) ability to generally influence the process within state nodes, but whether they had actual and meaningful opportunity to participate. We can compare the resources of the various stakeholder nodes, and their technologies and mentalities, and see quite practical differences in their capacity to assess and influence the course of events. We may consider how the architecture of governing networks and the internal characteristics of governing nodes influence how issues are framed and what considerations count. We can evaluate a health policymaking process in terms of the extent to which health considerations–and mentalities and technologies of health–were in any way brought to bear in the decision making process. We might, that is, define democracy and democratic decision-making about health in terms of access to decision-making nodes and a meaningful capacity to influence them.[39]

OWNS THE KNOWLEDGE ECONOMY? (2002). The TRIPS story is also one of forum or regime shifting. *See* JOHN BRAITHWAITE & PETER DRAHOS, GLOBAL BUSINESS REGULATION 66 (2000) (describing United States efforts to avoid forums where one-state-one-vote rules would dilute their power); Laurence R. Helfer, *Regime Shifting: The TRIPS Agreement and New Dynamics of International Intellectual Property Lawmaking*, 29 YALE J. INT'L L. 1, 20 (2004) (stating that the idea of an intellectual property treaty under the GATT system emerged from the dissatisfaction of its proponents with their ability to win the protection they wanted from the World Intellectual Property Organization).

38. *See* Fidler, *supra* note 12, at 249 (observing that national interests in health are integrated vertically among non-state actors).

39. Such mapping may also be useful in local as well as transnational systems. Zita Lazzarini, Patricia Case and I are using the theory to ground action research whose goal is to identify and support community efforts to change law enforcement practices that increase the spread of HIV in three cities in Eastern Europe and the former Soviet Union. The project is an elaboration of the

Such a map supports at least four strategies for change in the system dynamics relating to health:

- identifying opportunities for change in the internal characteristics of nodes whose governance behavior is important for health purposes but which are not currently addressing health issues;
- identifying weaknesses in the technologies, mentalities, or resources of existing health-promoting nodes that could be remedied to increase governing capacity;
- finding and patching "missing links"–places in the network where new connections could be advantageously developed between nodes; and
- finding "missing nodes"–clumps of local capacity and knowledge that are not currently mobilized to govern–and creating nodes to fill the gap.

None of these are radically new approaches in themselves. The potential value of a nodal governance perspective is that it facilitates the more ready recognition of pressure points within a system where change is possible and potentially useful. In the HIV context, for example, research has repeatedly shown that law enforcement practices have significant influence on the risk of infection faced by injection drug users and their sex partners. Changing the underlying criminalization of drug use is unlikely in the near future, but in a few places, systems have responded to the problem by creating new links between public health and law enforcement nodes, and by introducing the mentality of harm reduction into policing nodes.[40]

Microgovernance Strategies for Health and Systems Change

Nodes emerge in systems as a means of mobilizing disseminated knowledge and capacity. Nodes are crucial because they provide the means through which capacity is organized and made the stuff of actual governance. Any mapping is likely to show a deficit not only in the power of various nodes but of access to nodes at all. Some of those who have a stake, and have knowledge and capacity that could be useful to the system in terms of adjusting it towards more optimal

---

World Health Organization's Rapid Assessment and Response model. *See* Chris Fitch & Gerry Stimson, RAR-Review: An International Review of Rapid Assessments Conducted on Drug Use (2003); World Health Organization, *Rapid Assessment and Response Technical Guide*, *available at* http://www.who.int/docstore/hiv/core/index.html (last visited July 17, 2004). Investigators and community participants in several cities will organize qualitative data collection around the theory in order to understand how drug use and sex work are regulated. Within nodes, like local police stations, we will be seeking to understand how actors understand their work and mission, what tools they use, what their resources are, and where they come from. At the network level, we will seek to document how power is distributed and exercised in the local system, without recourse to the usual formal hierarchies of public-private divisions.

40. *See* Scott Burris et al., *Addressing the "Risk Environment" for Injection Drug Users: The Mysterious Case of the Missing Cop*, 82 MILBANK Q. 125, 139-140 (2004) (reporting that Australia and most Western European countries have incorporated harm reduction and disease prevention into their national drug policies).

states,[41] may have no mode of entry into the system's governance structure. Facilitating access for those who do not have it by opening up existing new nodes or, as I will discuss, creating new ones, can thus be thought to have potential effects in two directions. It may destabilize the system, bringing about a more optimal allocation of resources and governing power, spurring change in existing nodes and making the system as a whole more responsive to local needs;[42] and it may have a positive effect on the individuals whose capacity and knowledge are mobilized.

The theory of nodal governance, and the idea that microgovernance may be a health intervention, has been heavily influenced by work that Shearing and his colleagues have done (and in which I have played a minor part) in South Africa. This work is beginning to be described in the literature.[43] The Zwelethemba Model of local capacity governance creates a simple institution called a Peace Committee, which offers a community dispute resolution service and gathers members of the community to assess and solve underlying community problems. Anyone in a community can join or start a Peace Committee. The only limit on entry is the willingness to accept a simple Code of Good Practice. Peace Committee members are paid for each dispute they mediate, or community gathering they organize, and an equal payment is made to a fund controlled by the committee as a whole and earmarked for projects aimed at addressing community problems.

This work aims to change local conditions, and possibly influence larger social systems, by fostering institutions of microgovernance that mobilize the knowledge and capacity of poor people. Individuals in a community who have various resources such as good interpersonal skills, understanding of neighborhood social dynamics, organizational ability, and so on, find in the Peace Committee an institution where their ability and knowledge can be joined with that of others. The Code of Good Practice and simple mediation and community assessment technologies foster a forward looking, cooperative mentality, which in turn is supported by tangible rewards to individuals (in the form of payment) and the group (in the form of the ability to direct new resources to solving community problems). The stable institutional structure allows group learning and a longer time frame. Each Peace Committee thus

---

41. *See* Post & Johnson, *supra* note 21, at 1060 (explaining the inherent difficulty in determining the optimal structure of a complex system).

42. As Thomas Pogge has observed, when the operation of established institutions promotes or perpetuates health inequalities, it is fair to assume that the constituents of those institutions prefer their own welfare to that of the disadvantaged. Thomas W. Pogge, *Responsibilities for Poverty-Related Ill Health*, 16 ETHICS & INT'L AFF. 71, 72 (2002). Making it possible for the disadvantaged to effectuate their own self-interest is thus an obvious way to address such a state of affairs.

43. *E. g.*, Sevgi Aral et al., *Health and the Governance of Security: A Tale of Two Systems*, 30 J.L. MED. & ETHICS 632, 637-38 (2002) (explaining how Zwelethemba governance model gives poor communities ability to implement local capacity governance); Declan Roche, *Restorative Justice and the Regulatory State in South African Townships*, 42 BRIT. J. CRIMINOLOGY 514, 515 (2002) (outlining community-based conflict resolution process implemented by Clifford Shearing in South Africa); Shearing & Wood, *supra* note 13, at 416 (describing Zwelethemba governance model implemented by several South African communities).

constitutes a governmental node that operates to mobilize the residents to govern the communal spaces common to them.[44]

The project has been working successfully for over five years, and now has twenty-four committees in operation, conducting an average of about twenty-eight dispute resolution sessions per month. Committees are initially paid by philanthropic funders, but once operating successfully, committees have sought and received public funding. In the past two years, police agencies and committees in a number of sites have worked together to refashion the governance of security in mutually advantageous ways. In several communities, police stations have been turned into police-funded Peace Centers, cooperatively staffed by police and Peace Committees. Peace Committees can handle local problems more sensitively and more cheaply than police, who can put their resources into dealing with more serious crime. The police budget becomes the policing budget, shared between the police and other providers of security (Peace Committees); the job of security is realigned, with local people getting real control over how crime and disputes are handled, without sacrificing the ability to call on the police when needed.

The Zwelethemba Model experience (like, for example, the micro-lending movement of the Grameen Bank model) illustrates the extent to which even very poor people in marginal spaces have resources of knowledge and ability that are for one reason or other not mobilized for governance purposes. It illustrates the potential for creating local institutions that mobilize existing knowledge and capacity and thus enable collective efficacy that was latent in the system. The South African experience shows that creating such nodes is feasible, and that new nodes can destabilize even a fairly hide-bound system. The police in South Africa face many challenges, one of the greatest of which is expanding services to previously neglected (or oppressed) communities in an atmosphere of budget austerity. The emergence of Peace Committees has in some communities allowed the development of a new security network, in which police agencies hand over responsibility for "small" disputes to a node better suited to governing them, ceding real money and real control to their partners. There seem to be a number of possible modes of change: one is competition, in which the new node spurs older nodes to improve services or lower cost; another is collaboration, where a new node assists the existing nodes in the governance task; a third is reorganization of jobs or jurisdiction, in which some topic or area of governance is rethought and reconfigured. There is a little of all three going on in the South African story.

For health purposes, the creation of new nodes is also worth considering as a health intervention in and of itself. Research in health has long shown a relationship between neighborhood and health, but the precise mechanisms are

44. *See* Shearing & Wood, *supra* note 13, at 410-11 (describing emergence of communal spaces from mass private property and the governing of these spaces by local communities). There are other examples of new nodes or superstructural nodes having a powerful impact on health governance, including ACT-UP and South Africa's Treatment Action Campaign.

complex.[45] One lesson that can be taken from the body of eco-social epidemiology is that communities suffer relatively poor health (and other problems, like crime) when they cannot effectively manage the course of events in their place and time. This is, interestingly, the diagnosis of Robert Sampson and his colleagues from their large scale study of poor Chicago neighborhoods, and it leads axiomatically to one of their basic insights into how to address the problem: promote institutions that enable collective efficacy.[46] Under this view, governance *is* health, and interventions that promote new forms of "microgovernance" are a potentially important tool for dealing with the health problems of poor communities.

There are clearly some challenges ahead to microgovernance interventions for health. One is demonstrating that the theory is correct and that enabling collective efficacy through microgovernance does any good in health terms. A few specific, reasonably short term outcomes of at least certain kinds of microgovernance interventions may be postulated: the Zwelethemba Model, for example, may succeed in reducing violence related to unresolved disputes, as well as injuries and other negative consequences of coercive law enforcement interventions.[47] Microgovernance institutions may offer specific health programs; in the Zwelethemba Model, Peace Committees have launched nutrition and HIV education initiatives which could be conventionally evaluated.[48] Taking another

45. *See* KATHRYN PETTIT ET AL., URBAN INSTITUTE, NEIGHBORHOODS AND HEALTH: BUILDING EVIDENCE FOR LOCAL POLICY (MAY 30, 2003) (analyzing variables affecting health trends in several cities), *available at* http://www.urban.org/url.cfm?ID=410819.

46. Robert J. Sampson, *Transcending Tradition: New Directions in Community Research, Chicago Style*, 40 CRIMINOLOGY 213, 222 (2002); Jeffrey D. Morenoff et al., *Neighborhood Inequality, Collective Efficacy, and the Spatial Dynamics of Urban Violence*, 39 CRIMINOLOGY 517, 550-53 (2001); Robert J. Sampson & Stephen W. Raudenbush, *Systematic Social Observation of Public Spaces: A New Look at Disorder in Urban Neighborhoods*, 105 AM. J. SOC. 603 (1999).

47. Aral et al., *supra* note 43, at 633.

48. Syringe exchange programs ("SEP"s) are an example of new nodes that directly address health by providing health services, and also of the way a new node can change a system. The first SEP was introduced in Amsterdam in 1984. Initiated by a drug user organization, it was soon adopted by the Municipal Health Department of Amsterdam, where it became a fundamental component of HIV prevention activities among IDUs. In the late 1980's, SEPs were introduced in the United Kingdom, Australia, Canada and several other European countries, and has since expanded around the world. As of December 2000, there were at least 46 regions, countries and territories that reported having at least one SEP. Scott Burris et al., *Lethal Injections: The Law, Science and Politics of Syringe Access for Injection Drug Users*, 37 U.S.F. L. REV. 813, 817 (2003). The SEP is an institution that deploys a simple public health technology – exchanging new sterile syringes for used ones, delivering basic health information and services – within a mentality of harm reduction. They are relatively inexpensive to operate, and can do so without public funding or even clear legal recognition, yet they have managed to spread throughout the world and to influence public health policy, legislation, and the spread of blood-borne disease. *See, e.g.*, E. Drucker et al., *Measuring Harm Reduction: The Effects of Needle and Syringe Exchange Programs and Methadone Maintenance on the Ecology of HIV*, 12 Suppl A AIDS S217 (1998); Don C. Des Jarlais, *Structural Interventions to Reduce HIV Transmission among Injecting Drug Users*, 14 Suppl 1 AIDS S41, S44 (2000) (noting that most syringe exchange programs have functioned effectively, keeping rate of HIV infections low); A. R. Moss, *Epidemiology and the Politics of Needle Exchange*, 90 AM. J. PUB. HEALTH 1385, 1386 (2000) (arguing that more research is needed to measure effectiveness of syringe exchange programs); Steffanie A. Strathdee &

tack, one might measure intermediate outcomes theoretically associated with better population health, such as social capital or social cohesion or collective efficacy.[49] Some data from the Zwelethemba project are suggestive: repeated baseline surveys of the first peace committee site have found a steady increase in the number of community members who believe that people in their community are able to solve problems without calling the police.[50] Evaluation by specific disease outcomes may be difficult, confounded by many ecological and scale factors; moreover, the search for specific health outcomes (reduced HIV, or sexually transmitted diseases) is in tension with the underlying eco-social theory of health, in which specific diseases are simply the proximate causes of outcomes that are actually determined by more fundamental social determinants.[51]

Microgovernance has the advantage of addressing fundamental social determinants of health at the local level where they are embodied in actual lives, practices, and environments. But this is also a serious potential weakness. Two related objections in particular have been raised in early discussions of the approach: that it does not seriously address the underlying problem of poverty, and that it may weaken rather than enhance efforts to change the larger social system that determines the level and distribution of resources. Lurking behind both is a potential problem of scale.

As it has operated so far, microgovernance as represented in the Zwelethemba Model cannot be considered an antipoverty intervention. It does inject new money into the community, but only for Peace Committee members and those who are part of committee-funded problem solving programs. Yet there is more to poverty than lack of money: neighborhoods of similar socioeconomic level can vary considerably in their quality of life. Quite apart from the debate about the importance of institutions to economic development[52]

David Vlahov, *The Effectiveness of Needle Exchange Programs: A Review of the Science and Policy*, 1 AIDScience, (Dec. 13, 2001) (examining history, politics, and science surrounding needle exchange programs), *available at* http://www.aidscience.org/Articles/aidscience013.pdf; Phillip O. Coffin, *Marketing Harm Reduction: A Historical Narrative of the International Harm Reduction Development Program*, 13 INT'L J. DRUG POL'Y 209, 215 (2002) (noting that primary goal of SEPs is AIDS prevention but that the widespread dissemination of clean needles this required was often at odds with other publicly stated goals of SEPs such as facilitating treatment and getting dirty needles off the streets); AUSTRALIAN GOVERNMENT DEPARTMENT OF HEALTH AND AGEING, RETURN ON INVESTMENT ON NEEDLE AND SYRINGE PROGRAMS IN AUSTRALIA (2002) (studying economic effectiveness of needle and syringe exchange programs in Australia), *available at* http://www.health.gov.au/pubhlth/publicat/document/metadata/roireport.htm (last visited Aug. 26, 2004); Don C. Des Jarlais et al., *Public Funding of U.S. Syringe Exchange Programs*, 81 J. URB. HEALTH 118, 119 (2004) (surveying level of state and local government funding for SEPs).

49.. *See, e.g.*, Ichiro Kawachi et al., *Social Capital and Self-Rated Health: A Contextual Analysis*, 89 AM. J. PUB. HEALTH 1187, 1187 (1999); Kawachi, *supra* note 1, at 174 (stating that societal health cannot be measured by the health of the individual); *The Social Capital Community Benchmark Survey*, *at* http://www.cfsv.org/communitysurvey/index.html (last visited Aug. 12, 2004).

50. Aral et al., *supra* note 43, at 639.

51. *See, e.g.*, Link & Phelan, *supra* note 2, at 81 (stating that medical sociologists and social epidemiologists have made progress documenting the connection between social factors and disease).

52. *See* Jeffrey D. Sachs, *Institutions Matter, but Not for Everything: The Role of Geography and Resource Endowments in Development Shouldn't Be Underestimated*, FIN. & DEV., June 2003, at 38, 38

is the question of the contribution of institutions to health and quality of life. Effective local institutions make communities marginally better places to live, and the margin may be significant to the wellbeing of residents. If collective efficacy has an importance that is independent of socioeconomic conditions, then there is no reason not to invest in low-cost efficacy interventions as a complementary strategy to top-down antipoverty initiatives, and no reason for treating reduction of poverty as the only meaningful outcome. Microgovernance, like other approaches to enhancing collective efficacy, can thus be seen as a "misery intervention" that does deal with an important element of the poverty problem.

The other objection may be harder to answer. Arguably, interventions like this conform to a neo-liberal model of self-help, purporting to extend self-determination but in fact extending government control (through its funding of the local intervention) while shifting the burden of responsibility for change onto the shoulders of the dispossessed themselves.[53] At a certain level of abstraction, this argument is logically correct, and at any level it poses an important challenge to proponents of "misery" interventions. One response is simply to promote and operate microgovernance within a broader framework that also recognizes the need for substantial change in the world outside the community. Increasing local efficacy will improve the ability of people within a community to deflect or cope with stressors from the outside (from environmental insult to economic marginalization), but it is only a small step towards reducing those factors. Coupling continuing efforts at major change in local and global in equalities with serious efforts to mobilize local capacity and knowledge through microgovernance can be seen as an instance of what Paul Farmer called "pragmatic solidarity."[54]

(concluding that institutions are but one factor influencing economic life).

53. *See, e.g.*, Katharine N. Rankin, *Governing Development: Neoliberalism, Microcredit, and Rational Economic Woman*, 30 ECON. & SOC'Y 18, 20 (2001) (describing microcredit as a government controlled policy that makes individuals responsible for their own wellbeing). Rankin's study of microlending in Nepal also finds that even as the focus of the Grameen model on women raises possibilities of greater autonomy and control, implementation can occur in ways that perpetuate existing inequalities. Mobilizing capacity in a way that reconfigures local patterns of injustice is a second major challenge to microgovernance. This sort of work can be done through the design of the node, particularly in the mentality and the technology, though this is no easy task. It is nonetheless noteworthy that the Zwelethemba Model appears to be supporting the participation and leadership of women and young people.

54. Paul Farmer & Nicole Gastineau, *Rethinking Health and Human Rights: Time for a Paradigm Shift*, 30 J.L. MED. & ETHICS 655, 656-57 (2002). Recognizing that efforts at significant social or economic change often fail, Farmer writes:

> That we have failed to meet high goals does not imply that the next step is to lower our sights, although this has been the default logic in many instances. The next step is to try new approaches and to hedge our bets with indisputably effective interventions. Providing pragmatic services to the afflicted is one obvious form of intervention. In other words, social and economic rights cannot be excluded from the campaign for health and human rights. But the spirit in which these services are delivered makes all the difference. Service delivery can be just that, or it can be pragmatic solidarity, linked to the broader goals of equality and justice for the poor.

There is also the matter of scale. Microgovernance has the advantage of its concrete manifestation in the community. Like micro-lending, it is small and local. But can it become widespread enough that the knowledge and capacity thus mobilized begins to have an effect within the larger system? And what are the characteristics of a system (e.g., sufficient norms and structures of democracy to provide space for participation by such nodes) in which these nodes not only can be created but thrive and regulate? A major challenge for the next few years is to promote the diffusion of microgovernance.

SYSTEMS, DISPOSITIONS, AND THE PROBLEM OF PROBLEMS

The strategies emerging from a theory of nodal governance, and indeed a focus on governance itself, reflect the difficulties of getting social systems to produce or to stop producing particular outcomes. In the "risk society" mentality that currently prevails in most discussions of governance, activity is organized around the goals of identifying threats and mobilizing governing power to prevent them from occurring.[55] The same lens of risk is the one through which public health is viewed. This approach has at least two key premises. One is that the causes of specific outcomes can be identified. The other is that these causes of risk are sufficiently exogenous from the system producing them that undesirable outcomes can be prevented without substantially changing the system itself. That is, the bad things that happen in the world are "mistakes," like a lemon rolling off the Ford assembly line, and so meaningfully different in their genesis from the "good" outcomes the system ordinarily produces. Empirical analysis can find out why the defective outcome was produced and the system can be fine-tuned to eliminate any repetition. The implication is that the system is fundamentally sound, or the only viable way of arranging matters, and the job for governance (among other sectors) is to move the system towards its eventual perfection.[56]

A different view begins with the premise that social systems (from neighborhoods to nations) are complex outcome generating machines that constantly produce states of the world that in turn influence the further development of the system over time.[57] We inhabitants of outcome generating systems strive mightily to understand how they work and "how they are doing"–what outcomes they are producing–and forms of governance arise as adaptations in the course of this project of comprehension and management, but both understanding and managing the system are frightfully difficult. For a variety of reasons rooted in our perceptual apparatus and the fecundity of systems in the production of outcomes we fall prey to all sorts of errors. Science and social

---

Id. at 659.

55. As Braithwaite observes, this is related to but importantly independent from "the imperative to respond to certain risks that are extreme (and extremely difficult to manage)" like terrorism. Braithwaite, *supra* note 11, at 228.

56. *See* UNGER, *supra* note 7, at 26-29 (explaining the history and limitations of contemporary law and legal thought).

57. *See generally* Burris, Drahos & Shearing, *supra* note 24.

science are of some considerable help in describing the system, but also have limits.

This problem of complexity, with both epistemic and practical dimensions, has been stated before. It was powerfully set out in many of the writings of Hayek. The project of democratic experimentalism embodied in nodal governance theory represents an effort to take system complexity and perceptual fallibility seriously. Nodal governance does this in two ways. The first, which may be clear by now, is that as an approach to change it works by mobilizing diffused knowledge and capacity that has been excluded from governance rather than by prescribing a set of outcomes. The instigators of the Zwelethemba Model did not figure out how to solve the problems of the community, or even define precisely what the problems were, but put resources and technologies into the hands of Peace Committee members to manage the system according to their own lights. In this, microgovernance is analogous to the market mechanisms so prized by Hayek, but at the same time demonstrates that markets are not the only means through which such governance may be accomplished.

The second way in which nodal governance takes complexity seriously, which I will outline now, is to begin to think about the job of governance in a constitutive, prospective, and nonspecific way rather than a regulatory, retrospective, and problem-oriented way.[58] As Moran notes, more than one line of contemporary regulatory theory has converged on the idea that complexity requires strategies that in some way change, or at least thickly engage, the internal constitutions of the regulated entities, i.e., to mobilize and facilitate the resources of systems rather than simply seek to control and restrain them.[59] Gunther Teubner has been a strong proponent of this view.[60] A theory of nodal governance facilitates such strategies by offering insights into how nodes are governed and how they govern other nodes, but there is more here than simply the addition of another regulatory resource to an existing arsenal of possible strategies and devices of governance. The deployment of a theory of nodal governance invites a new approach to the occasion for and the object of governance: the recognition of the epistemic limits observed by Hayek—which I will describe here as "the problem of problems"—and a shift in orientation from solving problems to influencing the generative dispositions of a system.

The Problem of Problems

Following Michel Foucault, Nikolas Rose and Peter Miller observed that much of the business of governing is done in the definition of problems, an observation with which any effective politician or lawyer would likely agree.[61] In addition to its role in mobilizing collective action, the "problem" is a sort of shorthand for a larger amount of information. Problems carry a theory of their

58. For another effort at the same problem, see Post & Johnson, *supra* note 21, at 1064 (determining individual rules that will create maximum well-being for a group).

59. Moran, *supra* note 10, 411-412.

60. Teubner, *supra* note 29, at 39.

61. Rose & Miller, *supra* note 15, at 181.

causation; the definition of a problem and its causal antecedents leads to the generation of a response. The response may be aimed directly at the problem itself, without particular concern for the cause, or it may be directed at preventing the occurrence of the problem by addressing some link in the putative causal chain. Problems, then, are tools for collecting information and generating new courses of action.

For many unpleasant things produced by a system, a problem-driven approach works pretty well, particularly in the individual realm and in the short term. Thus antibiotics are great for dealing with individuals' bacterial infections, speed limits do a good job regulating the mean velocity of vehicles on the road, and an effective airplane safety program reduces crashes. This common approach to managing the course of events becomes increasingly strained as the size and complexity of the system producing the problems increases. There are several types of limits associated with governance understood as problem-solving.

Some are epistemic. "Problems" often contain poor information, and, like other heuristics, they work in part by excluding alternative theories of causation and options for response. The problem may be atypical, a rare product of the system, as, for example, a low risk event that is highly unacceptable. A "problem" may also make for regulatory difficulties when it is typical of the kinds of things produced by the system, but fungible. The outcome-generating capacity of a system is not just complex but flexible: a crucial observation from social epidemiology has been that preventing or curing one particular disease will not necessarily affect the level and distribution of health in a population, because the underlying factor determining health can express themselves through some other pathology.[62] Thus we can make considerable objective headway in reducing specific diseases without improving longevity or eliminating population health inequalities. The very idea of a problem as in some way an accidental, avoidable, or unnecessary event can obscure a view of the problematic event or condition as a characteristic of the system itself.[63]

A set of "mechanical" problems also beset problem-driven governance. It can take a long time to develop and implement a solution to a major problem, in which time the world being governed can change (and may change as people within the system adapt to get around the developing solution). Problems are also a means and a product of the distribution of governance jurisdiction. Artificial, if not arbitrary, lines of responsibility lead to duplicative, incomplete, and counterproductive interventions, and sometimes to strange allocational results as resources are deployed within rationalities bounded by jurisdictional lines.[64]

62. Link & Phelan, *supra* note 2, at 84.

63. *See* Niklas Luhmann, *Globalization or World Society: How to Conceive of Modern Society*, 7 INT'L REV. SOC. 67, 73 (1997) (comparing assumptions of a single global society with the assumptions of a global system of regional societies).

64. *See* Teubner, *supra* note 29, at 25 (stating that modern politics allows for the buildup of power by select groups without regard for the greater societal good).

Dispositions

If governance is social engineering, then governance based on problem-solving can be described as reverse engineering. The "problem" is the starting point of an inferential reconstruction of the system that produced it. The hazard is that the reverse-engineered system will be theoretically capable of producing the problem, but will bear little or no resemblance to the system that actually did so, and that continues to produce goods and bads in ways not addressed by the reverse-engineered solution. The interesting opportunity presented by nodal governance (and theories of constitutive regulation generally) is to practice governance as forward engineering, to influence the structure and operation of the system in order to turn problem-generating systems into goodness-generating systems.[65] To make this shift, it is necessary to abandon the idea that the "problem" (i.e., a particular outcome) is a reliable indicator of a system itself, or that a system could or should be designed to produce specific outcomes. Instead the focus shifts to understanding the constitution of the system of interest, and the durable relations between the ways various systems are constituted, and the range of outcomes they tend to produce. These durable relations may be called dispositions.

Take the system called "Sweden" for instance. Over time, it is possible to see many important things about Sweden: it has low infant mortality and murder rates; it imprisons a very small proportion of its people; the cuisine is rather bland; taxes are high; there is a high rate of political participation; recycling is common, and so on. We can say that there is something about this system that tends to produce these sorts of results instead of others. We may say that Sweden has certain dispositions in relation to various outcomes of interest. By this I do not mean to suggest any sort of intent or psychological state, but rather to assign to Sweden a "dummy variable" representing the apparent probabilities of various sorts of outcomes emanating from it.

Although we cannot figure out how, precisely, Sweden produces the outcomes it tends to produce, the identification of dispositions is nonetheless an important activity. If we take the system as the unit of analysis, we can begin to ask questions like "Why does Sweden, apart from the weather and the food perhaps, seem like a more salubrious place to live than the United States?"[66] We can begin to catalogue characteristics of systems and relate them to a range of outcomes. This is what Hayek engaged in, in his arguments about markets. This

65. It must be stated here that I am in no way suggesting that a theory of nodal governance or the sort of governance approach suggested here itself produces an account of the good, or suggests in any way that social agreement on the proper goals of governance is easy to achieve. The argument from complexity rests on the view that people and groups do form desires and seek to manage the system to achieve them, but not that these desires reflect a fully-informed, rational, or generally shared agenda. I have my ideas of what a good system looks like, which includes characteristics like a high level and an even distribution of health, and in this portion of the paper I talk about a systems-oriented approach to attaining such goodness by way of example, without presuming that my views are shared by others.

66. This line of questioning is associated in epidemiology with the thinking of Geoffrey Rose. Geoffrey Rose, *Sick Individuals and Sick Populations*, 14 INT'L J. EPIDEMIOLOGY 32, 32 (1985).

is what social epidemiologists and criminologists do now in trying to link health or crime rates to social capital, social cohesion, or other system characteristics.[67] It is important to recognize that while Hayek, Sampson, and Kawachi all have theories as to exactly how the structures they are identifying are converted into outcomes, it is not necessary to actually test those theories in order to take action based on the prior finding. If, for example, social cohesion in some way increases the tendency of a system towards good health outcomes and lower crime, then we can try to increase social cohesion even though we have only some theories as to why they might work. Indeed, Hayek's epistemic limit suggests that a project to explain exactly how a given condition of social capital produces a given distribution of health or crime outcomes must ultimately fail. The essence of the approach suggested by nodal governance is to regard the governance of dispositions as a primary goal rather a means of preventing specific problems. Problems are less important than the dispositions that produce them.

"Problems" are important as a means of social and political mobilization because they reflect a common way of thinking about events. The challenge to an alternative approach, then, is not just to be right but also salient. Managing dispositions to foster a greater likelihood of good results represents a quite familiar species of thinking, in which good conduct is rewarded with happy results. This approach is continuous with an enduring strain of political thought: that how a society is governed is an important determinant of how well the society thrives. The *Federalist Papers* are as good an example as one will find of the analysis between structure and practice, examined with the goal of creating a system disposed to produce liberty. What a theory of nodal governance does, though, is to create the possibility of far better specifying the governance conditions that matter.

CONCLUSION

Modes of governance structure health in the world. Access to effective participation in governance, even just the governance of one's immediate environment, may be good for health, and offers one way to destabilize suboptimal system states by mobilizing previously excluded knowledge and capacity. A theory of nodal governance offers both descriptive and normative insights into governance systems and the means of their transformation.

A systems-based view of governance is in some tension with the prevailing orientation of the "risk society" to organizing regulation around the identification and prevention of "problems." Complex systems (and even small social systems tend to be complex) have an enormous capacity to produce outcomes through a huge variety of means, many of which we are not capable of readily identifying or understanding. Problems, then, are a poor window on

67. *See, e.g.*, Kawachi, *supra* note 1, at 178 (comparing social cohesion with crime and suicide rates); Morenoff et al., *supra* note 46, at 550-51 (analyzing spatial embeddedness, internal structural characteristics, and social organizational processes to understand neighborhood-level rates of violence in Chicago).

what systems are doing and a poor guide to managing the system towards better outcomes, in health as in other domains. I suggest the need to develop a different, practically complementary approach, rooted in an attempt to understand the generative dispositions of various system configurations.

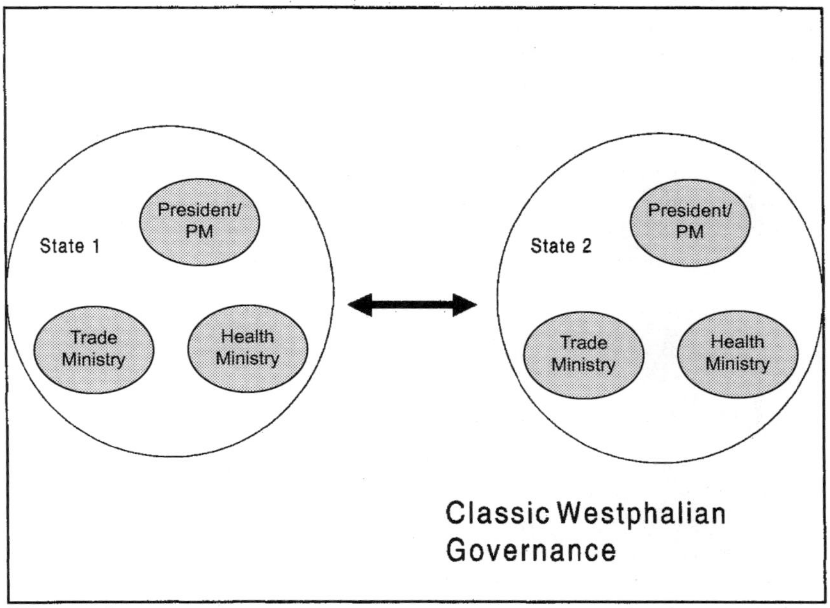
President/
PM
State 1
Trade
Ministry
Health
Ministry
President/
PM
State 2
Trade
Ministry
Health
Ministry
Classic Westphalian
Governance

Figure 1

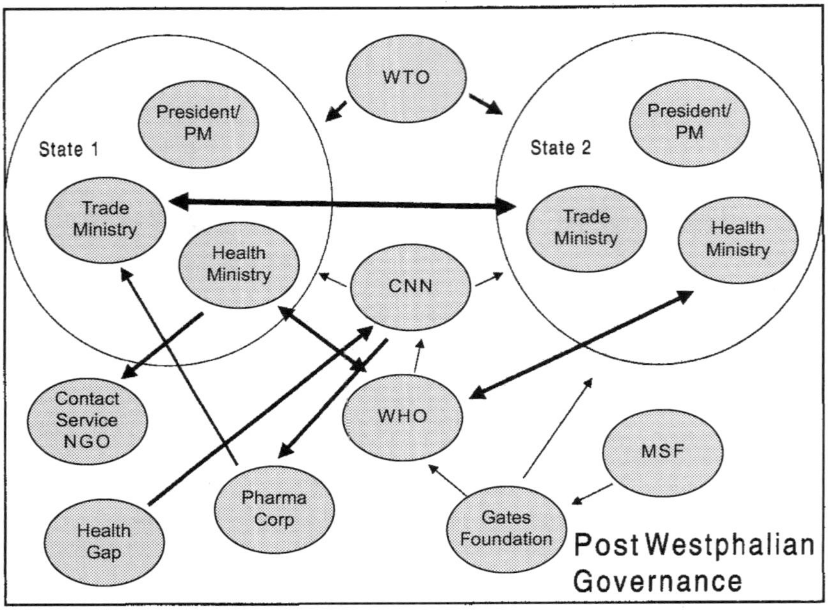
WTO
President/ PM
State 1
Trade Ministry
Health Ministry
CNN
State 2
President/ PM
Trade Ministry
Health Ministry
Contact Service NGO
WHO
MSF
Pharma Corp
Health Gap
Gates Foundation
Post Westphalian Governance

Figure 2

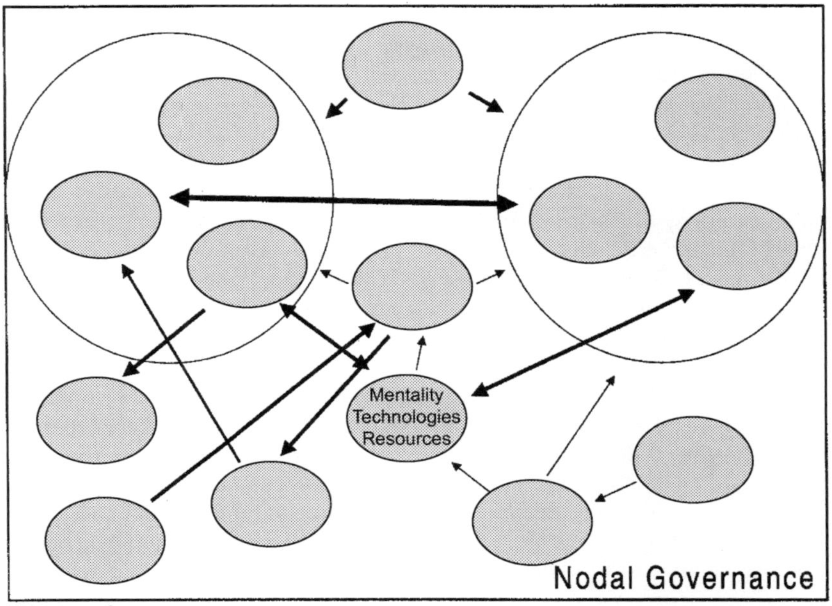

Figure 3

[21]

Globalization and Cholera: Implications for Global Governance

Kelley Lee and Richard Dodgson

Plague and pestilence have become an increasingly popular theme since the end of the Cold War among policymakers, journalists, fiction writers, and film directors searching for new threats to personal and national security. Ill health and, in particular, infectious diseases have generated a spate of popular, and often alarmist, literature.[1] This has been accompanied by growing high-level concern within governments and the medical community with global health issues that threaten national interests.[2] The emphasis in many of these discussions has been on emerging health threats that are perceived to pose potentially sudden and serious dangers to public health.

We begin this essay with the premise that the process of globalization has particular impacts on health and that there is a clear need to better understand and more effectively respond to these impacts. However, without underplaying the dangers posed by health emergencies caused, for example, by the genetic mutation of viral agents or epidemics of emerging infectious diseases, we seek to develop a broader understanding of the historical and structural factors behind the health challenges posed by globalization. As we discuss later, globalization can be defined as a process that is changing the nature of human interaction within a range of social spheres. Globalization's impact on health can be seen as part of a longer historical process firmly located in social change over decades, and perhaps centuries, rather than recent years.

From this perspective, an understanding of global health issues at the turn of the twenty-first century could benefit substantially from the voluminous literature on globalization from international relations, including the subfields of social and political theory and international political economy. This is a rich and highly relevant literature. It documents what structural changes are occurring toward a global political economy, how power relationships are embedded within this process of change, what varying impacts this may have on individuals and groups, and to what extent global governance could effectively mediate this process. These issues counterbalance the strong focus in the health literature on biomedical research, information systems, and other technical solutions. Although health is a classic transborder issue, it continues to receive limited attention in international relations.

We seek to bring together the international relations and health fields for two purposes. First, knowledge of the globalization process can be used to better understand the nature of health issues and the development of effective responses to them. To explore this link, we analyze cholera from the nineteenth century to the present, with particular attention to the seventh pandemic (1961–present). We argue that the particular form that globalization takes has created social conditions that have influenced the transmission, incidence, and vulnerability of different individuals and groups to the disease. Thus, we compare epidemiological patterns of the disease alongside changing patterns of human migration, transportation, and trade.

Second, knowledge of health and disease can be used to better understand the nature of globalization, because globalization is a highly contested concept, infused with embedded interests and having both positive and negative consequences.[3] Cholera has mirrored this process, highlighting the contradictions of globalization in its present form. A significant and often overlooked threat to human health, therefore, is the particular form globalization took in the late twentieth century. Thriving in the midst of increased poverty, widening inequalities within and across countries, pressures to shrink the public sector, and global environmental change, cholera can be seen as a reflection of the ills of globalization itself.

From analysis of this dual relationship between globalization and cholera, we conclude by considering the implications for existing mechanisms of international health cooperation. Following a brief review of measures for the transborder prevention, control, and treatment of infectious diseases, we explore the need for a system of global governance. We propose a definition of global governance for health and discuss key functions and characteristics that may be needed to protect human health on a global scale.

Globalization and Health: A Conceptual Framework

An understanding of the linkages between globalization and health depends foremost on one's definition of globalization and precise dating of the process. In this essay, we define globalization as a process that is changing the nature of human interaction across a range of social spheres, including the economic, political, social, technological, and environmental. This process is globalizing in the sense that many boundaries hitherto separating human interaction are being increasingly eroded. These boundaries—spatial, temporal, and cognitive—can be described as the dimensions of globalization.[4]

The *spatial dimension* concerns change to how we experience and perceive physical space. Roland Robertson writes of "a sense of the world as a single place" because of increased travel, communication, and other shared experiences.[5] Conversely, this "death of distance"[6] has also led to more localized, nationalized, or regionalized feelings of spatial identity. As such, globalization can be seen as a reterritorializing rather than deterritorializing process. Second, the *temporal dimension* concerns change to the actual and perceived time in which human activity occurs, generally toward accelerated time frames. A good example is currency trading of U.S.$1.7 trillion worldwide each day, two-thirds of this amount retraded after less than seven days. The speed of communication (e.g., facsimile, e-mail) and transportation (e.g., high-speed train, Concorde jet) has also accelerated social interaction. Third, globalization has a *cognitive dimension* that affects the creation and exchange of knowledge, ideas, beliefs, values, cultural identities, and other thought processes. Change has been facilitated by communication and transportation technologies that have enabled people to interact more intensely with others around the world. The production of knowledge has also become more globalized through research and development, mass media, education, and management practices. Contrasting forces are at play that, on the one hand, homogenize cognitive processes for better or worse (e.g., global teenager) and, on the other hand, encourage greater heterogeneity (e.g., religious fundamentalism).

In addition to the precise nature of globalization, the timing of the process has been subject to dispute. Some believe that it is a relatively recent phenomenon defined foremost by the activities of multinational corporations and their striving for global economies of scale.[7] While others agree that social relations have become more intense during the past ten to twenty years, they argue that such relations are not fundamentally new. Anthony Giddens and Robertson, for example, argue that globalization has historical roots from the fifteenth century.[8] Giddens asserts that, since the fifteenth century, globalization has developed with modernity. Robertson, however, disputes the view that globalization has followed a single *telos* or that its emergence can be linked to a single force such as modernity. Instead, he argues that there are a number of historical stages to globalization (Table 1), each characterized by what are currently regarded as features of a modern society and global system. These include, for instance, human migration, a system of global trade, urbanization, and the growth of international governance.

It is this conceptualization of globalization occurring across multiple spheres and dimensions and a time frame of centuries that we adopt in this essay as a useful framework for understanding its complex impacts on health. Briefly, the geographical spread of disease can be closely correlated with the migration of the human species across the globe. Robert Clark writes, "In becoming global, humans, plants, animals, and diseases

Table 1 Robertson's Historical Stages of Globalization

Stage	Time Scale	Spatial Center	Characteristics
Germinal	Circa 1500–1850s	Europe	Growth of national community, accentuation of the concept of the individual, spread of Gregorian calendar
Incipient	Circa 1850–1870s	Mainly Europe	Shift toward homogeneous unity of the state, formalized international relations
Takeoff	Circa 1870–1920s	Increasingly global	Inclusion of non-European states into international society, World War I, League of Nations
Struggle for hegemony	Circa 1920–1965	Global	Wars or disputes about the shape of the globalization process, atomic bomb, UN
Uncertainty	Circa 1965–present	Global	Inclusion of Third World, moon landing, end of Cold War, environment, HIV/AIDS

Source: Roland Robertson, *Globalization: Social Theory and Global Culture* (London: Sage, 1992).

have coevolved; i.e., evolved together as a package of interdependent life systems."[9] With the spread of human populations came changes to social organization into larger communities with different lifestyles, notably from hunting and gathering to agricultural and animal husbandry, to sustain such communities. Changes to disease patterns followed—increased zoonosis (e.g., tuberculosis, rabies, salmonella, helminths), nutritional ills, and dental decay. The establishment of permanent communities, accompanied by systems of irrigation and often ineffective sanitation and water supplies, led to increased diseases such as malaria and schistosomiasis.[10]

As J. N. Hays points out, human settlements on different continents remained relatively isolated until the late fifteenth century when the age of exploration brought Europe into contact with the Americas. Coinciding with a greater concentration of human populations into larger communities, the impact of the spatial dimension of globalization on health became increasingly evident. Periodically, epidemics could now become pandemics through intercontinental trade, migration, and imperialism. During this period, diseases such as plague and influenza traveled the silk route from Asia into Europe, or by ship to ports throughout the old and new worlds. Similarly, typhus from Asia and syphilis from the Americas were brought to Europe, while Europeans introduced measles, smallpox, typhus, plague, and other diseases to the new world, thus precipitating "the greatest demographic disaster in history."[11]

The greater frequency and intensity of human interaction across continents eventually made the temporal dimension of globalization more prominent. From the seventeenth century, industrialization, rapid urbanization, military conflict, and imperialism brought increased vulnerability to many populations. Coupled with inequalities in living standards and a lack of basic medical knowledge, many communicable diseases (e.g., syphilis, typhus, tuberculosis, and influenza) spread more rapidly than ever before. Another disease, the infamous "potato blight," was also able to travel quickly from the northeast of North America in 1840 to Europe by ship in 1845, eventually causing widespread starvation, notably in Ireland.[12]

By the late eighteenth century, these changes to the spatial and temporal dimensions of health risks and determinants led to greater efforts to develop public health knowledge and practice to respond to them. The nineteenth century brought the initiation of bilateral and regional health agreements, giving way from 1851 to periodic International Sanitary Conferences to promote intergovernmental cooperation on infectious disease control. This was accompanied by major advances in medical knowledge, including vaccination and microbiology, which were increasingly shared at international scientific meetings. This process of knowledge creation and application across countries signaled the cognitive dimension of globalization in health, which gained further momentum with the professionalization of the health field, creation of research and training institutions worldwide, and growth of scientific publications. Yet, as we show later, how health and ill health within and across societies were understood cannot be separated from prevailing beliefs and values characterizing these later stages of globalization. The creation of the World Health Organization (WHO) in 1948 was fueled by the postwar faith in scientific and technical solutions to defeat ill health, a belief that would be seriously shaken by the uncertainty of this phase of globalization in the late twentieth century.

Cholera in the Time of Globalization: The First Six Pandemics

We argue that an analysis of cholera from the nineteenth century can offer important insights into the nature of globalization and the specific challenges it poses for human health. Cholera is caused by the ingestion of an infectious dose of a particular serogroup of the *Vibrio cholerae* bacterium.[13] The bacterium is usually taken into the body through contaminated water or food, then attaches itself to the lining of the human bowel and produces a poison (enterotoxin). The infection is often mild or without symptoms, but approximately one in twenty cases is severe. In severe cases, cholera is an acute illness characterized by repeated vomiting and profuse watery diarrhea, resulting in rapid loss of body fluids and salts.

During this stage, the disease is highly infectious through further contamination of local water, soil, and food. Without treatment, this can lead to severe dehydration, circulatory collapse, and death within hours.[14]

Medical historians have long recognized that the epidemiology of cholera has been intimately linked to social, economic, and political change. Cholera had been confined for centuries to the riverine areas of the Indian subcontinent with occasional appearances along China's coast introduced by trading ships and in the Middle East transported by pilgrims traveling to Mecca. The pattern of the disease changed dramatically, however, in the early nineteenth century with the first of six pandemics over the next hundred years (Table 2). The intensification of human interaction during this period through imperialism, trade, military conflict, and migration (e.g., slave trade) was a significant factor. The first pandemic occurred between 1817 and 1823, with cholera suddenly moving far beyond its historical boundaries. A number of changes contributed to its spread in that period: the movement of British troops and camp followers throughout the region, construction of irrigation canals without sufficient drainage ditches to raise cash crops, building of a national railway system, impoverishment of rural people by land reforms and taxation, and mass migration as a result of economic hardship. For the first time, cholera became endemic throughout South Asia, from which it was then transported to the Far and Middle East via burgeoning trade links (e.g., tea, opium), religious pilgrimage, and notably military expansionism.

The geographical pattern of cholera during the next five pandemics continued to mirror human activity, spreading from country to neighboring country. Corresponding with the intensification of links between Asia, Europe, and the Americas, cholera became a worldwide disease in 1826. From India, the disease moved beyond Asia to Europe, the Americas, and to a lesser extent Africa; it traveled via immigration, troop movements during times of war and peace (e.g., Crimean War), and the slave trade. A particularly important factor was immigration from Europe to North America. Cholera first arrived in New York in June 1832 via immigrants from Dublin who, in turn, traveled inland via wagon train. This extended the second pandemic across North America and then south to the Caribbean and South America. Immigrants then became a repeated source of reinfection, facilitated by the building of the intercontinental railway.[15]

This close link between epidemiology and mode of transport can be observed throughout the history of the first six cholera pandemics. As well as extending the geographical incidence of the disease, the speed at which it spread also corresponded with prevailing technology. Until the twentieth century, cholera was limited to travel by land and sea. Compared to the seventh pandemic, which we discuss later, the rate of spread was relatively slow. For example, it took the disease three months to cross the sea via trade routes from Hamburg (where it arrived in August 1831) to Sunderland in the

Table 2 First Six Cholera Pandemics, 1817–1923

Date	Geographical Pattern of Spread
1817–1823 (6 years)	India (1817) Ceylon, Burma, Siam, Malacca, Singapore (1818–1820) Java, Batavia, China, Persia (1821) Egypt, Astrakhan, Caspian Sea, Syria (1823)
1826–1838 (12 years)	India (1826) Persia, Southern Russia (1829) Northern Russia, Bulgaria (1830) Poland, Germany, Austria, England, Mecca, Turkey, Egypt (1831) Sweden, France, Scotland, Ireland, Canada, United States (1832) Spain, Portugal, Mexico, Cuba, Caribbean, Latin America (1833) Italy (1835)
1839–1855 (16 years)	India, Afghanistan (1839) China (1840) Persia, Central Asia (1844–1845) Arabian Coast, Caspian and Black Seas, Turkey, Greece (1846–1847) Arabia, Poland, Sweden, Germany, Holland, England, Scotland, United States, Canada, Mexico, Caribbean, Latin America (1848) France, Spain, Portugal, Italy, North Africa (1850)
1863–1874 (11 years)	India (1863) Mecca, Turkey, Mediterranean (1865) Northern Europe, North America, South America (1866–1867) West Africa (1868)—limited
1881–1896 (15 years)	India (1881) Egypt (1883) North Africa, Southern Mediterranean, Russia China, Japan United States, Latin America (1887)—limited Germany (1892)
1899–1923 (24 years)	India (1899) Near and Far East Egypt, Russia, Balkan Peninsula Southern Europe, Hungary China, Japan, Korea, Philippines

Sources: Compiled from K. Kiple, ed., *The Cambridge World History of Human Disease* (Cambridge: Cambridge University Press, 1993), pp. 642–649; D. Barua, "The Global Epidemiology of Cholera in Recent Years," *Proceedings of the Royal Society of Medicine* 65 (1972): 423–432.

Note: Accurate historical data on the epidemiology of specific infectious diseases is notoriously incomplete, given the absence of standard reporting systems (e.g., lists of notifiable diseases), incompleteness of demographic data, and differences in disease nomenclature. This table draws on the limited data available to illustrate the general geographic pattern of early cholera pandemics. The spread of the disease by year and country cannot always be provided comprehensively.

northeast of England (where it arrived in October 1831). During later pandemics, the introduction of the steamship led to cholera spreading more quickly across major bodies of water. Hence, in 1848 cholera advanced from Poland to New Orleans in just over seven months. This more rapid move also coincided with the approximate doubling of railway lines and tonnage of steamships in operation,[16] correlating with the rapid spread of the disease throughout the Americas. By the time of the third and fourth pandemics, the spread of cholera into South America was hastened by the opening of the Panama Canal. A similar pattern can be observed in the Middle East with the opening of the Suez Canal.

Another feature during this period was cholera's close association with prevailing social conditions that enabled the disease to spread so widely and repeatedly, in the process becoming endemic in many parts of the world. In India, the cumulative effect of profound changes to local societies and ecology was, as Sheldon Watts writes, the transformation of a merely local disease, endemic in Bengal, into a chronic India-wide problem by 1817 and soon afterward an epidemic disease of worldwide proportions.[17] As cholera spread, it found fertile conditions for epidemic transmission in nineteenth-century industrialization. Poor sanitation, poverty, malnutrition, overcrowding, ignorance, and a lack of basic health services allowed cholera to flourish in the new urban centers of Europe and North America. Such was the link between cholera and social inequality during this period that the disease added impetus to fermenting unrest. In Russia, an uprising by revolutionaries known as the "cholerics" in the 1830s was because of the belief that the disease was actually a plot to kill off the poor. Although Czar Nicholas I quelled the movement, cholera continued to inflame class conflict across Europe.

By the middle of the nineteenth century, health policies to control epidemic diseases began to be adopted. But the link between disease and the squalid conditions of the poor had not yet been made officially. The experiences of Florence Nightingale with cholera during the Crimean War led the British Army to establish sanitary engineering as a new branch.[18] The first U.K. Public Health Act was adopted in 1848, followed by the creation of a General Board of Health, although cholera continued to be blamed on immorality and a lack of "proper habits."[19] Despite John Snow's historic gesture in 1854,[20] it was not until the discovery by Robert Koch in 1883 of the bacillus *Vibrio cholerae* as the causative agent of cholera that the relative inertia of government bodies toward the lack of safe drinking water and sanitation for poor people finally ended. This was gradually followed by the establishment of a public health infrastructure, eventually supported by a system of regulation and social welfare.

Internationally, governments complemented national efforts with meetings to promote cooperation and improve public sanitation. Between 1851 and 1911, twelve International Sanitary Conferences were held, which led to the formation of international public unions, such as the International Association of Public Baths and Cleanliness. In 1907, the Office International d'Hygiène Publique (OIHP) was created to standardize surveillance and reporting of selected communicable diseases, including cholera. Following establishment of the League of Nations, the work of these international public unions continued under the auspices of the League's Health Commission. In particular, the commission "established new procedures for combating epidemics and initiated studies in child welfare, public health training and many other subjects."[21] All of these efforts proved to be the forerunners of increasingly organized international health cooperation, leading to the eventual creation of the World Health Organization in 1948.

In summary, the first six pandemics of cholera can be understood in close relation to the prevailing socioeconomic and political structures of the period. From a local disease, cholera became one of the most widespread and deadly diseases of the nineteenth century, killing estimated tens of millions of people.[22] Not coincidentally, cholera traveled the same routes around the globe as European imperialism. The disease, in this sense, was an integral part of this stage of the globalization process, affected by changing spatial, temporal, and cognitive dimensions of human interaction but, in turn, also influencing the articulation or particular form that globalization has taken. It is within this historical context that the seventh pandemic can be understood.

Globalization and the Seventh Pandemic: Mirror, Mirror on the Wall

The seventh cholera pandemic began in 1961 in Sulawesi, Indonesia, after a gap of thirty-eight years. The disease remained endemic in a number of regions, including South and Southeast Asia, and cases were reported regularly until the 1960s. Nonetheless, there was a declining incidence overall, and worldwide transmission did not occur. The primary reasons were improvements in basic sanitation and water supplies in many countries, backed by international health cooperation. Until 1961, it was thought that cholera was disappearing.

But in 1961, cholera presented a new and unexpected challenge (Table 3). Unlike previous pandemics, which are believed to have been the result of the classical biotype, the cause of this new pandemic was discovered to be a different biotype of *Vibrio cholerae,* known as El Tor.[23] Although less virulent, this new strain has proven more difficult to eradicate. El Tor cholera causes a higher proportion of asymptomatic infections, allowing carriers to spread the disease through contamination of food or water. It survives longer in the environment and shows greater resistance to antibiotics and chlorine. It can also live in association with certain aquatic plants and animals, making water an important reservoir for infection.[24]

From Indonesia, El Tor cholera moved west to reach India and the Middle East by 1966. In 1970, it reached southern Europe (Russia) and

Table 3 Seventh and Eighth Cholera Pandemics, 1961–Present

Pandemic, Date, Type[a]	Countries
Seventh pandemic, 1961–present, El Tor biotype	Indonesia (1961)
	Indo-Pakistan Subcontinent (1963–1964)
	West Pakistan (Bangladesh), Afghanistan, Iran, Uzbekistan, Thailand (1965)
	Iraq (1966)
	Laos, South Korea, Hong Kong, Macao, Nepal, Malaysia, Burma, East Pakistan (1969)
	Russia (Astrakhan, Odessa/Kersh), Turkey, Czechoslovakia, France, U.K.,[b] Lebanon, Israel, Syria, Jordan, Libya, Tunisia, Dubai, Kuwait,[b] Saudi Arabia, Somalia, Ethiopia, Guinea, Sierra Leone, Liberia, Ghana, Côte d'Ivoire, Mali, Togo, Dahomey, Upper Volta, Nigeria, Niger, Japan[b] (1970)
	Muscat, Oman, Yemen, Morocco, Algeria, Cameroon, Chad, Mauritania, Senegal, Kenya, Uganda, Madagascar,[b] Spain, Portugal, France,[b] Sweden,[b] West Germany[b] (1971)
	United States (1973)
	Peru, Colombia, Chile, Bolivia, Brazil, Ecuador, Guatemala, Honduras, Mexico, Nicaragua, Panama, Venezuela (1991)
	Argentina, Belize, Costa Rica, El Salvador, French Guyana, Guyana, Surinam (1992)
	Paraguay (1993)
	Zaire, Ukraine (1994)
Eighth pandemic, 1993–present, 0139 Bengal serogroup	India, Bangladesh (1993)
	Pakistan, Thailand (1994)
	10 Southeast Asian countries, United States[b] (1995)

Sources: D. Barua, "The Global Epidemiology of Cholera in Recent Years," *Proceedings of the Royal Society of Medicine* 65 (1972): 423–432; Paul Epstein, "Emerging Diseases and Ecosystem Instability: New Threats to Public Health," *American Journal of Public Health* 85, no. 2 (February 1995): 168–172.

Notes: a. Many serogroups of *Vibrio cholerae* have been identified. During the first to seventh pandemics, only the 01 serogroup (of which two biotypes exist) caused cholera. Its classic biotype caused the first six pandemics and its El Tor biotype caused the seventh pandemic. A different serogroup—0139 Bengal—caused the eighth pandemic, and it is the first non 01 serogroup to have caused cholera.

b. Shows imported cases.

north, east, and west Africa. By 1971, outbreaks had been reported in thirty-one countries, one-third of them experiencing the disease for the first time. In that year, 150,000 cases were reported, including some 50,000 cases in West Bengal refugee camps. In most newly affected countries, the disease caused severe outbreaks with mortality rates of 40 percent or higher.[25] A year later, it reached the southeastern Mediterranean and eastern Europe. M. Narkevich and others describe the pandemic up to the 1990s as falling into three periods: 1961–1969, 1970–1977, and 1978–1989. The peak of the pandemic was during periods 1 and 2 (1967–1974), after which morbidity declined until 1985. Then, from 1985 to 1989, the pandemic seemed to accelerate once again, with 52,000 cases reported in thirty-six countries. In total, between 1961 and 1989, approximately 1.72

million cases of cholera were reported to WHO from 117 countries (see Table 4).[26]

Explanations for the origins of the pandemic were similar to previous ones, namely transmission around the world from an endemic country via travel. As Leonard Bruce-Chwatt observed, the impairment of sanitation on many Indonesian islands because of overpopulation of urban peripheries, military operations, and other disturbances, combined with certain cultural habits (e.g., use of night soil), allowed cholera to reach epidemic proportions.[27] However, the epidemiology of this pandemic has proven different in two fundamental ways: it has been more geographically widespread (spatial dimension) and has lasted longer (temporal dimension). First, the seventh pandemic has encompassed a large number of countries that have either never experienced cholera before, not done so for many decades, or never to such an intensity. In many parts of Africa, in particular, public health officials have experienced difficulty controlling the disease largely because of a lack of adequate surveillance, treatment, or prevention measures. As D. Barua wrote, "All the factors favoring endemicity of cholera exist in present-day Africa, particularly in the populous coastal and riverine areas, where there is little possibility of improving water supply, waste disposal and personal hygiene in the near future. In all probability, cholera is going to become, if it is not already, entrenched in this continent at least temporarily."[28] Barua's predictions have proven correct, and cholera has now become endemic throughout west, east, and southern Africa for the first time.[29]

This unprecedented geographical spread is also observable in the Americas, where the majority of cases have occurred in the 1990s. After disappearing from the Western Hemisphere for almost a century, El Tor cholera was simultaneously reported in two cities in Peru in January 1991. By mid-February, there were 12,000 confirmed cases. WHO described how the epidemic moved with "unexpected speed and intensity," traveling quickly 2,000 kilometers along the coast to Ecuador. By March–April, it had reached Colombia and Chile. By the end of the year, the epidemic had reached a new country every month, resulting in nearly 400,000 cases

Table 4 First Three Periods of the Seventh Cholera Pandemic, 1961–1989

Date	Reported Cases	Countries Reporting
1961–1969	419,968	24, mainly in Asia
1970–1977	706,261	73 (27 Asia, 32 Africa, 12 Europe, 2 Americas)
1978–1989	586,828	83

Source: Adapted from M. Narkevich et al., "The Seventh Pandemic of Cholera in the USSR, 1961–89," *Bulletin of the World Health Organization* 71, no. 2 (1993): 189–196.

and more than 4,000 deaths. This was more than the total number of reported cases worldwide for the previous five years. The epidemic continued into 1992, with more than 300,000 cases and 2,000 deaths in twenty countries.[30]

The second difference of the seventh pandemic has been its duration so far—thirty-nine years. This has been by far the longest pandemic, and it shows few signs of having run its course. As we discussed earlier, cholera took several months to spread from country to neighboring country during the nineteenth century, transported by land or sea. El Tor cholera has also traveled readily by land and sea. It is believed, for example, that the disease was imported into Turkey and Lebanon in the early 1970s by workers coming from neighboring affected countries. Similarly, severe outbreaks in Mali, Ghana, Niger, Nigeria, and Chad were traced to the arrival of individuals from infected areas. In India, an outbreak in 1971 was primarily among refugees from the former East Pakistan.[31] Perhaps most dramatically, it is thought that the epidemic in Latin America began after a ship from China emptied its ballast tanks in Peruvian waters. The vibrio then infected local seafood eaten by local people. El Tor is also thought to have arrived on the U.S. Gulf Coast in the hulls of ships from Latin America.[32]

Since the 1960s, however, the reduced cost of transportation and the addition of faster technologies (e.g., high-speed rail, ocean liners, and air travel) have brought unprecedented movement of human populations to and from endemic areas. Since the 1960s, mass travel (growth of 7.5–10 percent per annum) has been growing at a rate faster than global population growth (growth of 1.5–2.5 percent per annum).[33] This intensification of human mobility has posed new problems for public health officials, including their capacity to contain serious outbreaks of infectious disease. K. F. Kaferstein, Y. Motarjemi, and Douglas Bettcher note that "over the last two hundred years, the average distance travelled and speed of travel have increased one thousand times, while incubation periods of disease have not."[34] As the average journey time of an airliner or a bulk carrier is much shorter than the incubation period of a disease, these different forms of transportation are believed responsible for the increased spread of disease from one location to another.[35] Air travel, for instance, brings large numbers of people into close contact with each other within an enclosed space. In relation to cholera, the disease has been spread via contaminated food served on airplanes[36] and through global trade in food products (e.g., shellfish, frozen coconut milk).

Furthermore, the epidemiology of the disease has been geographically unpredictable. Whereas in the past cholera could be monitored from country to neighboring country, more recently it has "jumped" continents. In 1973, for instance, forty passengers traveling from London to Australia were infected with cholera from contaminated food taken on board in

Bahrain.[37] Similarly, thirty-one passengers were found to have cholera on a flight bound to Los Angeles from Buenos Aires, Argentina, in 1992.[38] At least seventy-five people contracted cholera by eating cold seafood salad loaded on a flight at Lima, Peru, bound for California.[39] It is estimated that, for air travelers from the United States to India, the reported rate of cholera cases is 3.7 cases per 100,000 travelers.[40] It is this "hypermobility" of the causative agent via worldwide transportation networks that has been a key factor in the continuation of the pandemic.

Technological change, however, does not tell the entire story of cholera in the late twentieth century. Indeed, like previous pandemics, socioeconomic and political structures have also been central. The 1920s to 1960s were perhaps a "boom" period for public health systems. Many countries created national health systems. And the aid to the health sector grew through bilateral aid agencies, multilateral organizations (e.g., WHO, UNICEF), charitable foundations (e.g., Rockefeller Foundation), and other nongovernmental organizations (e.g., Save the Children Fund, Oxfam). Although it was clear that not all benefited equally from this intense period of health development, facilitated by advances in medical knowledge, there was a feeling that progress against many traditional scourges of humankind was being achieved. Eradication campaigns against malaria and (more successfully) smallpox were reflections of this belief in the triumph of science over disease.

The seventh pandemic has been a reminder, however, of the persistent and, in many cases, growing inequalities that remain within and across countries. Life expectancy ranges from forty-three years in the poorest countries to an average of seventy-eight years in higher-income countries. Three-fifths of people in the developing world lack access to safe sanitation, one-third to clean water, and one-fifth to modern health services of any kind.[41] The initial outbreak of cholera in the early 1960s took advantage of these conditions to spread among the have-nots in many different societies. By the early 1970s, the pandemic seemed to peak, and cases gradually decreased over the next decade.

By the 1980s, however, cholera began to benefit from fundamental changes in many public health systems around the world. Despite the launch of the primary health care movement in 1978 by WHO and UNICEF, the 1980s saw a pulling back of the state from the financing and provision of health care. Detailed analysis of this period of health sector reform can be found elsewhere.[42] Briefly, as part of the World Bank's structural adjustment program, many lower-income countries were encouraged to reduce public expenditure on health throughout the 1980s and 1990s.[43] Globally, health sector reform in higher- and lower-income countries included policies to encourage market forces to play a greater role in health systems.[44] There was growing evidence in the late 1990s that these policies have impacted adversely on public health capacity in many countries,[45] and the growing awareness of globalizing forces has led to efforts to redefine public health functions in countries around the world.[46]

It was in this context that cholera opportunistically spread in the early 1990s. In Latin America, the adverse impacts of globalization on health systems have included increased national debt, rapid urbanization, environmental degradation, inequitable access to health services, and reduced public expenditure on public health infrastructure.[47] Cholera then arrived in 1991, spreading rapidly across the continent in an epidemic of 1.4 million cases and more than 10,000 deaths in nineteen countries.[48] This scenario has not, however, been confined to Latin America. In October 1994, El Tor cholera was reported in the former Soviet Union amid economic instability, deteriorating health services, drought, and poor hygiene. The most serious outbreak occurred in ten cities in the Ukraine and threatened a population of 50 million people.[49] As the head of the Ukrainian parliament stated at the time, "The spread of cholera and other infectious diseases is the calling card of an economy in trouble."[50]

Another contributory feature of the global political economy to the seventh pandemic has been the mass migration of people. In the early 1990s, it was estimated that 500 million people crossed international borders on commercial airlines annually. There are 100 million migrants in the world today, with an estimated 70 million people, mostly from low-income countries, working legally or illegally in other countries. In addition, a large proportion (30 million) of total migrants do so involuntarily, including 20 million refugees.[51] Enforced migration has become a particular feature of Africa, where 16 million people have been internally displaced.[52] In many cases, such migration has been a cause and effect of "complex emergencies," which have "a singular ability to erode or destroy the cultural, political, and economic integrity of established societies."[53] Given large numbers of displaced people, resulting in overcrowded living conditions, poor sanitation, unclean water supplies, and malnutrition, cholera has become a familiar feature. For example, the mass population movements as a result of the Pakistani-Indian war in 1971 led to thousands of deaths from cholera and further spread of the disease.[54] Between 1987 and 1991, cholera was diagnosed in Mozambican refugees as they migrated from their home villages to camps in Malawi.[55] In August 1994, El Tor cholera broke out in relief camps in Goma, Zaire, among Rwandan refugees. Within twenty-four hours, 800 people had died; the epidemic eventually caused 70,000 cases and 12,000 deaths.[56]

Finally, globalization in its present form is believed to be contributing to changes in the natural environment that enable infectious diseases such as cholera to thrive.[57] Like the British-built irrigation canals in India, which increased the incidence of malaria and cholera, rapid urbanization and industrialization without sufficient attention to sustainable economic development have led to contamination of drinking water. Historically, the

Ganges River has symbolized purification for Hindus, who believe drinking and bathing in its waters will lead to salvation. Today twenty-nine cities, seventy towns, and countless villages deposit about 345 million gallons of raw sewage a day directly into the river. Factories add another 70 million gallons of industrial waste and farmers another 6 million tons of chemical fertilizers and 9,000 tons of pesticides.[58] Perhaps more worrisome still, it is believed that widespread changes in coastal ecology are generating "hot systems" in which mutations of the cholera organism are being selected and amplified under new environmental pressures and then transferred to human populations through the food chain. This is the explanation for the appearance of *Vibrio cholerae* 0139 Bengal in 1992, a new strain of cholera and the first non 01 strain capable of causing epidemics, signaling the beginning of the eighth pandemic.[59]

In summary, the seventh pandemic is a reflection of the contradictions of globalization in the late twentieth century. As in previous pandemics, cholera and deprivation remain closely linked. Development of national health systems worldwide led to the reduction and to what was hitherto believed to be the eradication of cholera in many parts of the world. The global spread of cholera since the early 1960s, however, has revealed persistence and growing inequalities within and across countries. Other features of globalization, notably mass migration, social instability, and environmental degradation, present the disease with the opportunity to establish itself in new areas of the world. Cholera, in short, is a mirror for understanding the nature of globalization.

At the same time, an understanding of globalization is needed to explain the distinct epidemiological profile of El Tor cholera. Through changes in human interaction spatially, temporally, and cognitively, cholera has become more geographically widespread and persistent over time. That the disease can "jump" across continents within hours, for example, poses new challenges for national health systems. Indeed, the globalization of cholera may require new responses that more closely integrate different levels and types of governance.

Global Governance for Health: Learning Lessons Once Again from Cholera

The emergence of global governance as a central concept in international relations responds to a perceived change in the nature of world politics. In contrast to international governance, the defining feature of global governance is its comprehensiveness. Global governance views the globe as a single place within which the boundaries of the interstate system and nation-state have been eroded. Although the nation-state remains an important actor, processes and mechanisms of global governance are growing to encompass the structures of international governance that manage the system of nation-states. The emerging processes and mechanisms of global governance can be seen as forms of supraterritorial authority.[60]

The processes and mechanisms of global governance are diverse, as are the actors and structures that participate within them. In addition to nation-states, these actors include international institutions, governmental organizations, various nonstate actors, regimes, values, and rules.[61] These different actors compete with each other to shape the nature of global order, the establishment of which is the main purpose of global governance. Global governance may be used to stabilize and expand market capitalism on a global scale, as sought by the International Monetary Fund (IMF) and World Bank, or to establish an order based on greater social justice and redistribution of global resources.[62]

Although scholars, practitioners, and policymakers in the health field may not explicitly recognize or widely use the term *global governance,* there is growing recognition of the need to establish more effective mechanisms for addressing a range of global health issues. Such issues are wide-ranging and are reviewed elsewhere.[63] Developing responses to them lead to questions concerning scope of activity, distribution of authority, decisionmaking process, institutional structure, and resource mobilization and allocation.

The development of an effective system for the prevention, control, and treatment of infectious diseases is perhaps the classic transborder health issue. It has long been recognized that diseases do not recognize national borders and that states acting alone are unable to prevent their spread. In recent years, this message has been stated with renewed vigor in relation to emerging and reemerging diseases and globalization. As a U.S. report warns, "The modern world is a very small place, where any city in the world is only a plane ride away from any other. Infectious microbes can easily travel across borders with their human and animal hosts. . . . [And] diseases that arise in other parts of the world are repeatedly introduced into the United States, where they may threaten our national health and security."[64] Similarly, Paul Farmer writes that "EIDs [emerging infectious diseases] have often ignored political boundaries, even though their presence may cause a certain degree of turbulence at national borders. The dynamics of emerging infections will not be captured in national analyses, any more than the diseases are contained by national boundaries."[65]

A brief review of the existing institutional framework for international cooperation on infectious diseases shows a strong emphasis on biomedical understanding of human disease and state-based health systems. Since its founding in 1948, WHO has carried out surveillance and monitoring of various infectious diseases. Diseases deemed to pose a particular international threat, however, have been governed since 1951 under the International Health Regulations (IHR), a consolidation of various International

Sanitary Conventions adopted from the nineteenth century onward. Over the years, the IHR have been periodically updated to take account of changing health needs (e.g., removal of smallpox from the list of notifiable diseases after eradication). In their present form, the IHR set out procedures for limiting the transmission of infectious disease via shipping, aircraft, and other modes of transport. The regulations do not control the movement of international traffic directly but concentrate on controlling the spread of disease where transborder conveyance may occur. The IHR also call on states to "report to WHO, within specific periods, cases of these three diseases [i.e., cholera, plague, and yellow fever] within their territories. Second, to facilitate reporting and deter unnecessary interference with international travel and trade, members must limit their responsive health measures (applied to international traffic for the protection of their territories against these diseases) to maximum measures permitted by these regulations."[66]

Responsibility for the IHR and other infectious disease–related activities falls on WHO's Cluster on Communicable Diseases (CDS), formerly the Division of Emerging and Other Communicable Disease Surveillance and Control (EMC) (now referred to as Communicable Disease Surveillance and Response).

Other international agreements concerned with infectious diseases are the WHO and Food and Agriculture Organization's Codex Alimentarius, the World Trade Organization's Agreement on the Application of Sanitary and Phytosanitary Measures, and the International Civil Aviation Organization's Facilitation to the Convention on International Civil Aviation. Supporting international cooperation, in principle, is a network of national health systems led by ministries of health in each member state and extending to national health services, research institutions, public health laboratories, and monitoring and surveillance systems. Together, it is assumed that WHO coordinates top-down guidance and information, provided from the bottom up by national health systems.

In practice, there are gaps at both the international and national levels. Internationally, the IHR cover only three diseases, and WHO does not have the means to enforce compliance with even these limited stipulations. International surveillance and monitoring relies on the goodwill of governments, but fears of adverse effects on trade or tourism can lead to underreporting. India lost an estimated U.S.$1,700 million in exports, tourism, and transportation services because of the outbreak of plague in 1996.[67] Exports of shellfish by Latin American countries were similarly affected by reports of cholera in the region. Although efforts are in play to revise the IHR to stipulate reporting of "syndromes" rather than diseases, the question of authority remains.

Another difficulty lies in the limited resources available to mount rapid responses to major transborder outbreaks. Given the limits of WHO resources, the U.S. Centers for Disease Control (CDC) at times has stepped in more quickly in health emergencies (e.g., the outbreak of Ebola in northern Zaire in 1976 and the refugee camps in Goma, Zaire). At the national level, variation in health capacity is even more acute. Many lower-income countries have less than U.S.$4 per capita to spend on health care annually.[68] Structural adjustment programs place further pressure on public health expenditure, and the World Bank continues to attribute problems, such as the reemergence of cholera, on the failure to privatize rather than on a crisis in resources. As one World Bank study concludes,

> The return of cholera in 1991 to Latin America and [the] Caribbean region was only a symptom of the deep-seated problems and the fragility and inadequacy of publicly operated water supply and sanitation systems. Consequently, the agencies that operate these systems are entering a crucial phase of deciding whether they can greatly improve their operations while remaining in the public sector or whether they should seek increasing private sector financing and participation in both operations.[69]

To address these deficiencies, international efforts have focused on improving surveillance, monitoring, and reporting systems. WHO is now working to create a Global Surveillance Network using electronic links for rapid exchange of information.[70] In 1994, the Program for Monitoring Emerging Diseases (ProMED) was created with the impetus of sixty prominent experts in human, animal, and plant health. Accessed via the Internet, ProMED is intended to be a global system of early detection and timely response to disease outbreaks. Similarly, the Global Health Network was established to monitor the spread of emerging infectious diseases through links with public health organizations, multilateral organizations, NGOs, and independent research centers. Although such technology is clearly a vital feature of a global system of disease control, this emphasis on technical issues highlights two further flaws in the present system of international health governance.

First, underlying these initiatives is a rational model of policymaking, which assumes that lack of information is the key factor in the globalization of infectious disease. However, as we argue in this essay, the seventh cholera pandemic has been shaped by the structural features of the global political economy that have contributed to the vulnerability of certain populations and environments within and across countries. Second, globalization in its present course has created transborder externalities in the form of health risks that increasingly defy state-centric approaches of the past. Although national epidemiological data remain significant, there is also a need for disaggregated data that allow comparisons and analysis within and across countries and regions. Furthermore, focusing on control measures at the national level amid intensified human interaction has so far reinforced a fortress mentality among many governments.[71] Yet effective control of all infectious diseases at national borders is neither practicable nor ethical. Many diseases remain asymptomatic or have long periods of incubation.

It is here that the existing literature on global governance may offer ideas for creating new forms of authority and institutional linkages to address the challenges of global health. To begin with, the global governance literature highlights the need to be more comprehensive in our approach to global health. Needed, for instance, is a greater appreciation of the link between health and the environment. Douglas Bettcher and Derek Yach point out that public health issues are central components of sustainable development programs and should be incorporated into the system of global governance that has emerged from the United Nations Conference on the Environment and Development (1992) around sustainable development.[72] Piggybacking on strategies for global sustainable development may boost the chances of a system of global health governance being established. Similar linkages between health and changing governance of other sectors, such as agriculture, transportation, communications, and trade and finance, need far greater exploration.

Another central theme of the global governance literature is the need to ensure that the processes and mechanisms of global governance have the support of those governed. Various proponents of global governance agree that there is a need to reform the UN's core institutions so that they are more democratic and representative of the global population. WHO, for example, is an organization often described as governed by a "medical mafia" and influenced by the extrabudgetary funding of a small number of donor governments.[73] At the national and subnational levels, as well, there have long been calls for going beyond the traditional focus on ministries of health and government institutions. Civil society, in particular, is identified as requiring a greater role in policymaking at many levels. For example, the influence of certain global social movements, such as the women's health movement, has been recognized as positively contributing to the democratization of certain policy issues (i.e., population policy).

The nation-state and existing institutions of international health governance (e.g., the WHO and IHR) will remain central to any future system of global health governance. The challenge for scholars and policymakers is how to construct processes and mechanisms of global health governance that recognize the interests of nation-states and civil society. This is a massive challenge, yet recent developments in global health governance suggest some optimism about the ability to meet it. For example, plans for a Framework Convention on Tobacco Control bring together shared interests across nation-states, civil society, and the business community (e.g., the pharmaceutical sector) for a more comprehensive effort to control the production and consumption of tobacco. WHO's policy document "Health for All in the 21st Century" adopts a similar approach to deal with persistent inequalities in health within and across countries.[74] These initiatives are directly concerned with strengthening global health governance, proposed by an intergovernmental organization (i.e., WHO) and supported by an amalgam of member states, civil society groups, and individuals.

Finally, there is a need for critical analysis of health determinants that conceptualize social change in the context of long-term and fundamental socioeconomic structures, rather than shorter-term, technically specific change. Such an approach leads to a recognition of the structure-agent links that exist between globalization and health, including the possibility that present forms of globalization are, in fact, incompatible with human health. Importantly, critical theorists see globalization as a historical process constructed not by rationality but by embedded power relations and consequences. Locating cholera and other global health issues within this reflexive starting point therefore seeks to address, and ultimately redress, the underlying causal factors behind ill health.

Conclusion

In summary, we have analyzed cholera from the nineteenth century as a case study of the links between globalization and health. How human populations have lived—population size and distribution, social structure, cultural practices, distribution of resources—has historically been linked to patterns of health and disease. We have also sought to show how globalization is changing the nature of human societies across the world and, consequently, the health of populations. At the same time, cholera has been reflective of particular features of globalization from its earlier stages to the present.

Globalization has shaped the pattern of the disease, the vulnerability of certain populations, and the ability of public health systems to respond effectively. The contributing features of globalization to the epidemiologically distinct seventh pandemic have included socioeconomic instability, intensified human interaction and mobility, environmental degradation, and inequalities within and across countries.

As public health systems have struggled to control the seventh pandemic, reports of an eighth pandemic came in 1993. As we described earlier, the new pandemic involves a new strain of *Vibrio cholerae*, believed hardier than El Tor cholera in terms of environmental adaptation. Its emergence is thought to have resulted from changes to coastal ecologies in South Asia. By 1995, the pandemic spread to Calcutta, India, with 15,000 cases and 230 deaths, and then moved rapidly to Dhaka, Bangladesh, where 600 cases were reported daily. Severe flooding in Bangladesh in 1998 worsened conditions significantly. Reaching 100,000 cases by 1996, the disease has since spread to Pakistan, Thailand, and ten other Southeast

Asian countries. Travel-associated cases have been reported in the United States, Europe, and Japan.[75] Cholera is poised, it seems, to offer yet another opportunity to learn hard lessons.

Notes

Kelley Lee is senior lecturer in International Health Policy at the London School of Hygiene and Tropical Medicine. She is author of *Historical Dictionary of the World Health Organization* (1998) and chairs the WHO External Advisory Group on Globalization and Health. Richard Dodgson received his doctorate from the University of Newcastle upon Tyne, England. He has taught at the University of Newcastle upon Tyne, the University of Durham, and Sunderland University.

1. Richard Preston, *The Hot Zone* (New York: Corgi, 1994); Leslie Garrett, *The Coming Plague: Newly Emerging Diseases in a World Out of Balance* (New York: Farrar, Straus & Giroux, 1994); Frank Ryan, *Virus X: Understanding the Real Threat of the New Pandemic Plagues* (London: HarperCollins, 1996).

2. Institute of Medicine, *Emerging Infections: Microbial Threats to Health in the United States* (Washington, D.C.: National Academy Press, 1992); U.S. Committee on International Science, Engineering, and Technology Policy (CISET), *Global Microbial Threats in the 1990s* (Washington, D.C.: Working Group on Emerging and Re-emerging Infectious Diseases, 1995); Institute of Medicine, *America's Vital Interest in Global Health* (Washington, D.C.: National Academy Press, 1997).

3. Louise Amoore, Richard Dodgson, Barry Gills, Paul Langley, Don Marshall, and Iain Watson, "Overturning Globalisation: Resisting the Teleological, Reclaiming the Political," *New Political Economy* 2, no. 1 (1997): 179–195.

4. Kelley Lee, "Globalisation and Health Policy: A Review of the Literature and Proposed Research and Policy Agenda," in Pan American Health Organization, *Health and Human Development in the New Global Economy* (Washington, D.C.: Pan American Health Organization, 2000).

5. Roland Robertson, *Globalization: Social Theory and Global Culture* (London: Sage, 1992).

6. F. Cairncross, *The Death of Distance* (Cambridge: Harvard Business School Press, 1997).

7. Alan Rugman and Michael Gestrin, "New Rules for Multilateral Investment," *International Executive* 39, no. 1 (1997): 21–33.

8. Anthony Giddens, *The Consequences of Modernity* (London: Polity Press, 1990); Robertson, *Globalization*.

9. Robert Clark, "Global Life Systems: Biological Dimensions of Globalisation," *Global Society* 11, no. 3 (1997): 280.

10. Mark Nathan Cohen, "The History of Infectious Disease," in Mark Nathan Cohen, *Health and the Rise of Civilization* (New Haven: Yale University Press, 1989); Arno Karlen, *Man and Microbes, Disease and Plagues in History and Modern Times* (New York: Simon & Schuster, 1995).

11. J. N. Hays, "New Diseases and Transatlantic Exchanges," in J. N. Hays, *The Burdens of Disease, Epidemics and Human Response in Western History* (New Brunswick, N.J.: Rutgers University Press, 1998), pp. 62–77, quotation from p. 72.

12. Cohen, "The History of Infectious Disease."

13. There are more than sixty serogroups of *Vibrio cholerae,* but only serogroup 01 causes cholera. Serogroup 01 has two biotypes (classical and El Tor), and each biotype has two serotypes (Ogawa and Inaba).

14. World Health Organization, *Guidelines for Cholera Control* (Geneva: WHO, 1993).

15. R. S. Speck, "Cholera," in K. F. Kiple, ed., *The Cambridge World History of Human Diseases* (Cambridge: Cambridge University Press, 1993), p. 647.

16. Eric Hobsbawm, *The Age of Capital: 1848–1875* (London: Weidenfield & Nicolson, 1975), p. 310.

17. Sheldon Watts, "Cholera and Civilization: Great Britain and India, 1817 to 1920," in Sheldon Watts, *Epidemics and History, Disease, Power and Imperialism* (New Haven: Yale University Press, 1997), pp. 167–212.

18. R. S. Bray, *Armies of Pestilence: The Effects of Pandemics on History* (Cambridge: Lutterworth Press, 1996), pp. 180–183.

19. Watts, "Cholera and Civilization," p. 194.

20. Amid a severe cholera outbreak in London, John Snow found a concentration of cases around a pump in Broad Street. Hoping to prove his theory that cholera is a waterborne disease, he removed the pump handle in front of public officials; and the outbreak was contained.

21. David Armstrong, *The Rise of International Organisation: A Short History* (London: Macmillan, 1982), p. 43.

22. Bray, *Armies of Pestilence.*

23. The causative agent is named after the El Tor quarantine camp on the Sinai Peninsula, where it was first isolated in 1905 from the intestines of pilgrims returning from Mecca.

24. World Health Organization, *Guidelines for Cholera Control.*

25. Leonard Bruce-Chwatt, "Global Problems of Imported Disease," *Advances in Parasitology* 11 (1973): 86.

26. M. Narkevich et al., "The Seventh Pandemic of Cholera in the USSR, 1961–89," *Bulletin of the World Health Organization* 71, no. 2 (1993): 189–196.

27. Bruce-Chwatt, "Global Problems of Imported Disease."

28. D. Barua, "The Global Epidemiology of Cholera in Recent Years," *Proceedings of the Royal Society of Medicine* 65 (1972): 423–432.

29. J. van Bergen, "Epidemiology and Health Policy—A World of Difference? A Case-Study of a Cholera Outbreak in Kaputa Distict, Zambia," *Social Science and Medicine* 43, no. 1 (1996): 93–99.

30. Richard Guerrant, "Twelve Messages from Enteric Infections for Science and Society," *American Journal of Tropical Medicine and Hygiene* 51, no. 1 (1994): 27.

31. Barua, "The Global Epidemiology of Cholera in Recent Years," pp. 426–448.

32. S. McCarthy, R. McPhearson, A. Guarino, and J. Gaines, "Toxigenic Vibrio Cholerae 01 and Cargo Ships Entering Gulf of Mexico," *Lancet* 339 (1992): 624–625.

33. Andrew Cliff and Peter Haggett, "Disease Implications of Global Change," in R. J. Johnston, P. J. Taylor, and M. J. Watts, eds., *Geographies of Global Change: Remapping the World in the Late 20th Century* (Oxford, England: Blackwell, 1995), p. 209.

34. K. F. Kaferstein, Y. Motarjemi, and Douglas Bettcher, "Foodborne Disease Control: A Transnational Challenge," *Emerging Infectious Diseases* 3, no. 4 (1997): 8.

35. Bruce Jay Plotkin and Ann Marie Kimball, "Designing an International Policy and Legal Framework for the Control of Emerging Infectious Diseases: First Steps," *Emerging Infectious Diseases* 3, no. 1 (1997): 1–9.

36. David L. Heymann and Guenael R. Rodier, "Global Surveillance of Communicable Diseases," *Emerging Infectious Diseases* 4, no. 3 (1998): 1–5.

37. Bruce-Chwatt, "Global Problems of Imported Disease," p. 87.

38. William Booth, "Cholera's Mysterious Journey North," *Washington Post,* 26 August 1991.

39. Robert Tauxe, Eric Mintz, and Robert Quick, "Epidemic Cholera in the New World: Translating Field Epidemiology into New Prevention Strategies," *Emerging Infectious Diseases* 1, no. 4 (1995): 141–146.

40. J. Todd Weber, William C. Levine, David P. Hopkins, and Robert V. Tauxe, "Cholera in the United States, 1965–1991," *Archives of Internal Medicine* 154 (14 March 1994): 551–556.

41. Barbara Crossette, "Kofi Annan's Astonishing Facts," *New York Times,* 27 September 1998, p. WK16; United Nations Development Programme, *Human Development Report* (New York: UNDP, 1998).

42. Antonio Ugalde and J. Jackson, "The World Bank and International Health Policy: A Critical Review," *Journal of International Development* 7, no. 3 (1995): 525–542.

43. World Bank, *Financing Health Services in Developing Countries: An Agenda for Reform* (Washington, D.C.: IBRD, 1987); World Bank, *World Development Report: Investing in Health* (Washington, D.C.: IBRD, 1993).

44. Mary Ruggie, *Realignments in the Welfare State: Health Policy in the United States, Britain, and Canada* (New York: Columbia University Press, 1996).

45. Ankie Hoogvelt, *Globalisation and the Postcolonial World: The New Political Economy of Development* (London: Macmillan, 1997); Robert Beaglehole and Ruth Bonita, *Public Health at the Crossroads, Achievements and Prospects* (London: Cambridge University Press, 1997).

46. Douglas Bettcher, Steve Sapirie, and Eric Goon, "Essential Public Health Functions: Results of the International Delphi Study," *World Health Statistics Quarterly* 51 (1998): 44–54.

47. Alberto Cardelle, "Health Care in the Time of Reform: Emerging Policies for Private-Public Sector Collaboration in Health, *North-South Issues* 6, no. 1 (1997): 1–8.

48. Jose Sanchez and David Taylor, "Cholera," *Lancet* 349 (21 June 1997): 1825–1830.

49. World Health Organization, *The World Health Report 1996: Fighting Disease, Fostering Development* (Geneva: WHO, 1996).

50. Alexander Moroz, quoted in Ryan, *Virus X,* p. 108.

51. Mary Wilson, "Travel and the Emergence of Infectious Diseases," *Emerging Infectious Diseases* 1, no. 2 (1995): 39–46.

52. "Migration: The Facts," *New Internationalist*, no. 305 (1998): 18.

53. Mark Duffield, "Complex Emergencies and the Crisis of Developmentalism," *IDS Bulletin* 25, no. 4 (1994): 38. Duffield defines complex emergencies as "protracted political crises resulting from sectarian or predatory indigenous responses to socioeconomic stress and marginalisation."

54. A. Zwi, "Cholera in South Africa," *South African Outlook* 11 (1981): 172–177.

55. Susan Cookson et al., "Immigrant and Refugee Health," *Emerging Infectious Diseases* 4, no. 3 (1998): 1–2.

56. Sanchez and Taylor, "Cholera"; Heymann and Rodier, "Global Surveillance of Communicable Diseases," p. 2.

57. A. J. McMichael, B. Bolin, R. Costanza, G. Daily, C. Folke, K. Lindahl-Kiessling, E. Lindgren, and B. Niklasson, "Globalization and the Sustainability of Human Health: An Ecological Perspective," *BioScience* 49, no. 3 (1999): 205–210.

58. Crossette, "Kofi Annan's Astonishing Facts."

59. Paul Epstein, "Emerging Diseases and Ecosystem Instability: New Threats to Public Health," *American Journal of Public Health* 85, no. 2 (February 1995): 168–172.

60. Jan Aart Scholte, "The Globalization of World Politics," in John Baylis and Steve Smith, eds., *The Globalization of World Politics: An Introduction to International Relations* (Oxford: Oxford University Press, 1997), pp. 13–30.

61. James Rosenau, "Governance in the Twenty-first Century," *Global Governance* 1, no. 1 (January–April 1995): 13–43.

62. André C. Drainville, "The Fetishism of Global Civil Society," in M. P. Smith and L. E. Guarnizo, eds., *Transnationalism from Below* (London: Transaction Publishers, 1998), p. 37; Richard Falk, *On Humane Governance: Toward a New Global Politics* (Cambridge, England: Polity Press, 1995).

63. Lee, "Globalisation and Health Policy."

64. U.S. Committee on International Science, Engineering, and Technology Policy, *Global Microbial Threats in the 1990s.*

65. Paul Farmer, "Social Inequalities and Emerging Infectious Diseases," *Emerging Infectious Diseases* 2, no. 4 (1996): 259–266.

66. Quoted in Plotkin and Kimball, "Designing an International Policy and Legal Framework," p. 3.

67. Collette Kinnon, "Globalization, World Trade: Bringing Health into the Picture," *World Health Forum* 19 (1998): 397–406.

68. World Health Organization, *The World Health Report, 1995: Bridging the Gaps* (Geneva: WHO, 1995).

69. Emanuel Idelovitch and Klas Ringskog, *Private Sector Participation in Water Supply and Sanitation in Latin America* (Washington, D.C.: World Bank, Directions in Development Series, 1995).

70. World Health Organization, *Global Cholera Update* (Geneva: WHO, 1998).

71. Institute of Medicine, *America's Vital Interest in Global Health.*

72. Douglas Bettcher and Derek Yach, "The Globalisation of Public Health Ethics?" *Millennium: Journal of International Studies* 27, no. 3 (1998): 495.

73. D. Pitt, "Power in the UN Superbureaucracy: A New Byzantium?" in D. Pitt and T. Weiss, *The Nature of United Nations Bureaucracies* (London: Croom Helm, 1992), chap. 2; P. Vaughan, S. Mogedal, S. E. Kruse, K. Lee, G. Walt, and K. de Wilde, *Co-operation for Health Development: Extrabudgetary Funds and the World Health Organisation* (Oslo: Governments of Australia, Norway, and the United Kingdom, 1995).

74. World Health Organization, "Health for All: Policy for the 21st Century," WHO Doc. WHA51/5, May 1998.

75. Sanchez and Taylor, "Cholera."

[22]

Beyond Communicable Disease Control: Health in the Age of Globalization

Dyna Arhin-Tenkorang and Pedro Conceição

Health concerns have triggered systematic international cooperation for more than 150 years. Disease control was also the core concern of the first formal international organizations. After World War II this tradition of international cooperation was strengthened with the creation of the World Health Organization and expanded with the establishment of official development assistance. During the 1950s medical science and technology progressed, and ambitious initiatives for the eradication of communicable diseases were launched, creating great optimism that such diseases would be eliminated. Today, however, communicable diseases remain a challenge. Old diseases have reemerged, and new infectious diseases—especially HIV/AIDS—are causing living and health standards to regress in many developing countries. Why has this happened, and what is being done about it? Moreover, how can current responses be improved? These questions propel this chapter's analysis.

The chapter starts by summarizing international efforts to fight communicable diseases in the 19th century and the first half of the 20th century. It then describes the results of international cooperation on public health since the 1950s. To help understand why some communicable diseases have been tamed while others remain a problem, the chapter analyzes three health challenges. The main finding is that problems tend to persist when the publicness of the response is limited. Here publicness refers to three inputs crucial for controlling disease: available and accessible medical knowledge, a national public health infrastructure, and private household spending on complementary goods and services. The chapter's analysis focuses on the first two inputs. It then explains why health concerns have returned to the top of the international agenda and characterizes current actions to address international health challenges as efforts to enhance the publicness of responses. The chapter concludes by suggesting steps to consolidate and improve these responses.

A BRIEF HISTORY OF COMMUNICABLE DISEASE CONTROL

For the purposes of the analysis in this chapter, international efforts to control communicable diseases can be divided into two periods: responses before the 1950s and those since.

Focusing on "at the border" controls: responses until the 1950s

Past epidemics have led to an increasingly coordinated, centralized approach to communicable disease control. Desai (in this volume) describes how care for sick people evolved beyond the realm of the family and the church into the hands of public authorities—first local governments, then central governments.

As human activity expanded geographically, so did the spread of communicable diseases. Technological developments in transportation throughout the 19th century (the steam engine, railroads) made the global spread of communicable diseases easier than ever before. For example, in the early 19th century a cholera epidemic took eight years to spread globally: it broke out in India in 1826, reached eastern Russia in 1827, moved to Germany, Hungary, and Austria through 1831, and hit Paris, London, and New York in 1832, the U.S. Pacific coast in 1833, and Mexico City in 1834, where it apparently stopped (Cooper 1989, pp. 107–08).

The public policy response to global epidemics started by imposing strict quarantines at ports (Cooper 1989, pp. 103–07). But with each country fending for itself, quarantine requirements were often redundant, imposing a great burden on commerce and travel. As a result in 1834 the French government issued the first call for international cooperation to prevent the spread of diseases. But it took another global epidemic of cholera, in 1848–49, for the first international sanitary conference to be held, in 1851 (Lyons 1963, p. 240). Three more conferences followed—in 1859, 1866, and 1874.

Across the Atlantic yellow fever (of little worry in Europe) was as much a concern as cholera. Endemic to West Africa, yellow fever reached the Americas in the 17th century, becoming "the disease that sparked the greatest fear, claimed enormous numbers of lives, and ignited public health policies for decades to come" (Garrett 2000, p. 281). After a continentwide epidemic in the 1870s, and because the European-led sanitary conferences had failed to address yellow fever, a fifth international conference, called by North and South American states, was held in 1881 in Washington, D.C. (PAHO 1992).

None of these conferences resulted in binding agreements between countries. The main obstacle was a lack of understanding of diseases and of how communicable diseases were transmitted. Only as science and practical knowledge progressed was it possible to reach consensus. In 1892 countries finally adopted an International Sanitary Convention, agreeing on steps to fight the cross-country transmission of cholera (Cooper 1989, p. 210). Although the measures adopted continued to focus on quarantine, there was an effort to rationalize quarantine requirements and to improve the reporting and communication of the health condition of travelers. Thus international coordination focused on "at the border" controls, but countries were also starting to build national public health systems.

In 1902 North and South American nations went further, establishing the International Sanitary Bureau—the precursor to the Pan-American Health Organization (PAHO), the first formal international organization for public health (PAHO 1992). In Europe a second international organization dealing with international health issues was created in 1907: the International Office of Public Hygiene, based in Paris. The Health Organization of the League of Nations, created after World War I, became the third entity devoted to international public health. All three organizations became engaged in monitoring diseases and in sharing epidemiological and other scientific information (Zacher 1999). Still, their focus remained on at-the-border controls (especially quarantine regulations)—so much so that because influenza could not be quarantined and smallpox was considered a universal disease, neither was among the diseases addressed by these international organizations (Cooper 1989, p. 228).

International cooperation in health was not limited to governments and formal intergovernmental organizations. Volunteers and nongovernmental organizations have always played important roles, contributing to the diffusion of ideas and to the development of actions to mitigate ill health in the context of social, religious, and humanitarian movements (Loughlin and Berridge 2002, p. 9). For example, the International Committee of the Red Cross (created in 1863) contributed to the establishment of the Geneva Convention on the treatment of combatants, setting ethical standards and safeguards that were a precursor to later international health regimes (Dodgson, Lee, and Drager 2002). In 1913 the Rockefeller Foundation became active in the international promotion of public health, including by financing the Health Organization of the League of Nations.

Under these initial international arrangements for communicable disease control, action tended to follow crises. The first responses came at the local or national level, but as the ineffectiveness and difficulties of these uncoordinated actions became clear, calls for international cooperation emerged. International cooperation focused on limiting the international spread of diseases, especially by harmonizing border controls. The second half of the 20th century saw a new era of international cooperation in health: meeting diseases at their sources.

Meeting diseases at their sources: the creation of the World Health Organization and the emergence of aid

After its creation in 1948, the World Health Organization (WHO) became the locus of international cooperation on health. The WHO absorbed the International Office of Public Hygiene and the Health Organization of the League of Nations. The International Sanitary Bureau was renamed PAHO and became the WHO's regional office for the Americas (PAHO 1992, p. 42). In a period of great vitality in the scientific understanding of infectious diseases and of progress in medical technology—in vaccines for prevention and drugs for treatment—the WHO added eliminating communicable diseases at their sources to its mandate of containing their spread through its more traditional functions of coordinating international health regulations and serving as an information clearinghouse.

Addressing diseases at their sources required a new type of interaction between governments and the WHO. National health authorities provide most of the control of diseases at their sources. But for developing countries without the capacity or resources to control communicable diseases, the WHO helped do so—a move made possible by the recent creation of official development assistance, funded by industrial countries. The WHO's expanded mandate, coupled with official development assistance, also made possible systematic attempts to eradicate diseases, which require international coordination beyond the capacity of any one country.

Policy responses and achievements: limited publicness

So what have been the results of this new international framework for addressing communicable diseases? Some impressive achievements have been made. For example, the Onchocerciasis Control Programme was created in 1968 to control river blindness in 11 West African countries—and is ending in 2002 having achieved its goal. The program has also established national capacity so that countries can continue to control the disease.

In addition, smallpox has been eradicated. In 1967, when the eradication effort was intensified, smallpox infected 15 million people and caused 2 million deaths. Had smallpox not been eradicated, between 1967 and 1998 there would have been 350 million infections and more than 40 million deaths (http://www.who.int/archives/who50/en/smallpox.htm). Smallpox eradication cost nearly $300 million, with industrial (donor) countries paying for about one-third. It is estimated that the United States recoups the costs it incurred once every 26 days—every 26 days the benefits accruing from not having to deal with smallpox are equal to the total U.S. eradication cost (http://www.unfoundation.org/campaigns/polio/challenge.asp).

Other eradication efforts were less successful. In the mid- to late 1950s initiatives were launched to eradicate malaria. Although malaria was eliminated in some parts of the world (Southern Europe, Jamaica), in others (India, Sri Lanka) it recurred after eradication efforts stopped. The strategy for eradicating malaria presumed that its vector—certain mosquitoes—could be eliminated using the chemical DDT. But mosquitoes' ability to develop resistance to DDT was underestimated, and subsequent concerns about DDT's environmental effects made this strategy impossible to pursue. Aylward, Hennessey, and others (2000) find that successful eradication depends on a number of conditions: biological (no non-human reservoir for the infectious agent), technical (availability of an effective vaccine or treatment), economic (with benefits exceeding costs), political (political commitment), and social (social support). Malaria eradication was impeded by imperfect understanding of its biological feasibility and dwindling support for its strategy.

Today we know that the optimism of the mid-20th century was premature: communicable disease control is an enduring challenge. Communicable diseases account for one-third of the global disease burden (WHO 2001b, table 3) and in 1998 were the leading cause of premature death, causing nearly half of all deaths before age 45 (WHO 2000, p. 1). Old "killer diseases" have resurged: in 2000 malaria caused more than 1 million deaths, childhood infectious diseases caused 1.4 million deaths, and tuberculosis killed more than 1.5 million people (WHO 2001b, table 2). In 1999 there were 8.5 million new tuberculosis infections (WHO 2001b, table 10). And new diseases, especially HIV/AIDS (see below), are killing several million people a year. All of this is happening in a context where resistance to treatments for communicable diseases is limiting the available options for disease control.

To understand the challenges of communicable disease control, the analysis below focuses on three health challenges, chosen for the intriguingly different policy responses to them: poliomyelitis (polio), acquired immunodeficiency syndrome (AIDS) caused by the human immunodeficiency virus (HIV), and infections with antimicrobial-resistant agents. (Later in the chapter a noncommunicable condition, sickle cell disease, is also considered.) These three cases are of worldwide reach, and resolving any of them constitutes a condition-specific global public good: eradicating polio, controlling HIV/AIDS, and containing antimicrobial-resistant infections (table 1). Protecting a single individual from

TABLE 1

Characteristics of and responses to the four cases

Case	Criterion for adequate provision	Global reach?	Global awareness?	Inputs developed?	Global access to inputs?
Polio	Eradication	Yes	Yes	Yes	Yes
HIV/AIDS	Control	Yes	Yes	Yes, partially	Limited
Infections with antimicrobial-resistant agents	Containment	Yes	Yes	Minimally	Limited
Sickle cell disease	Control	Yes	No	Minimally	Very limited

infection has positive externalities because it constrains the spread of communicable diseases ("herd immunity"). Thus eradicating (when possible) or controlling communicable diseases that can spread globally is a global public good (Sandler and Arce M. 2002).

The difference among the first three cases in table 1 lies in the extent to which inputs to control them have been developed and deployed. Thus the analysis of the cases focuses on the three types of inputs that communicable disease control (or containment of antimicrobial-resistant agents) typically requires:

- Type 1: available medical knowledge (implying the generation of scientific knowledge and production of medical technologies) and access to pharmaceutical and other medical technologies (including their affordability in developing countries).
- Type 2: a functioning public health care system to detect disease outbreaks, channel interventions, and monitor and report progress on communicable disease control.
- Type 3: private spending—even if the previous two inputs are available and affordable, individuals and households need to have the means to make complementary expenditures.

In this analysis a disease is considered to have been met with a fully public response if all three types of inputs are developed and made available. Most of the analysis focuses on the first two. The first, medical knowledge and drugs for treatment or vaccines for prevention, can be considered global public goods for health (Sandler and Arce M. 2002; Mills 2001). These global public goods are often necessary (though insufficient) for communicable disease control. Knowledge about how a disease is transmitted can be used to control it. For example, the strategy for dracunculiasis (guinea worm) eradication is based largely on the knowledge that infection occurs after drinking contaminated water. Infection can be prevented through measures as simple as using water filter cloths. Because dracunculiasis control was associated with safe water, guinea worm eradication was one of the objectives for the International Water Supply and Sanitation Decade (the 1990s). The number of infections dropped from 3.6 million in 1986 to 75,000 in 2000, mostly as a result of providing access to filtered drinking water (http://www.who.int/ctd/dracun/progress.htm).

In other cases, as discussed below, effective control intervention requires developing and deploying medical technologies, including drugs for treatment and vaccines for prevention. Underprovision of or limited access to these global public goods reflects a limited publicness in the policy response. In many cases access is limited because the needed medicines are unaffordable in developing countries, even if there are no formal restrictions on access. However, the publicness of the response—and thus its success—also depends on the other two types of inputs, especially the public health care system.

Policy response to polio: public, determined, and inclusive

Polio is caused by three strains of polioviruses that destroy nerve cells, causing paralysis. Historically, polioviruses infected almost all infants, paralyzing and permanently disabling about 0.5 percent of all children (Aylward, Hull, and others 2000). Of those, 4–10 percent died. Before its accelerated control through vaccination, polio had global reach, affecting both industrial and developing countries—and within countries, both rich and poor people (Woodward, Smith, and others 2001).

The response to polio was spearheaded in the United States in the 1930s, driven by public concern accentuated by the fact that the disease affected public figures and mobilizing a strong response from civil society.[1] In the early 1950s polio figured in public opinion polls as the second most important concern of Americans, right after the threat of a nuclear confrontation (Seavey, Smith, and Wagner 1998). The National Foundation for Infantile Paralysis (known as the March of Dimes) funded treatment and vaccine research, leading to the development of the first polio vaccine in the mid-1950s by Jonas Salk. The March of Dimes also funded initial clinical tests for and mass delivery of the vaccine in the United States. The research outcomes funded by the March of Dimes were not allowed to be patented: they were made public by design.[2] Thus access to the vaccine was not impeded by a patent—so medical knowledge and technology (type 1 inputs) were widely available.

Mass vaccination reduced the number of polio cases in industrial countries by 86 percent between 1955 and 1957, but developing countries were excluded from the response. Polio had not been immediately recognized as a threat in developing countries. As a result, even in 1988, 350,000 cases of polio were detected in 125 countries. Making the formulation of the vaccine public was a crucial step toward controlling polio in industrial countries but was not sufficient in developing countries. Most of the costs of polio vaccination stem from support staff, vehicles, storage facilities, and other equipment—not from the vaccine—so successful vaccination initiatives depend on local health facilities and the ability to buy private goods (type 2 and 3 inputs). Lack of access to these inputs excluded many developing countries from benefiting from the polio vaccine.

In 1988 a combination of national self-interest and commitments from international organizations (WHO, United Nations Children's Fund) and philanthropic foundations (Rotary International) led to the Polio Eradication Initiative.[3] The initiative, still under way, mobilizes resources to deliver the vaccine even where public health facilities are inadequate. Between 1988 and 2000 the incidence of polio around the world was reduced by 99.9 percent (from the 350,000 cases in 1988 to less than 500 in 2001; WHO 2002, p. 100; http://www.polioeradication.org/all/news/_files/pdf/PN15-05-02.pdf). Almost half a century had passed since a similar response had been provided in industrial countries.

Action on eradication was driven by the technical feasibility of the endeavor (made possible by past investments in technology and a track record of success associated with the response to the disease in industrial countries) and by its significant health and economic benefits (prospects of future, and permanent, health and financial gains). Looking at polio eradication as a disease-specific global public good helps in understanding the evolving structure of incentives that led to the eradication effort. After the initial vaccination effort in industrial countries, incentives for eradication became different for industrial and developing countries. Successfully controlling polio in industrial countries amounted to national elimination of the disease. National elimination is a national public good. Once a country is disease-free, its incentives to invest in global eradication are limited—and in fact diminished if only health benefits are considered (see Barrett in this volume and Philipson 1999).

Because polio-free countries had fewer health-related incentives, the effort to eradicate polio at the global level moved toward an "international effort." International organizations and foundations assumed a leadership role in eradicating polio, in conjunction with countries not yet free of it.[4] Does that mean that global eradication has no benefits for countries already free of polio? There are benefits, but less of a health nature, since polio does not represent a direct health threat to polio-free countries. Whether global eradication is achieved or not, polio-free countries will not have the disease. But without global eradication, they will still have to pay a price: they have to continue to vaccinate. Providing the national public good of national elimination is costly to a country as long as the disease exists elsewhere. At the global level, polio eradication provides two types of benefits: financial, to countries that are polio free (which have to pay for this national public good), and health, to countries that still have the disease.

As the vaccination effort encompasses more countries, the cumulative global cost of defending against polio increases but the global disease threat becomes limited to fewer people. As the cost increases, the financial benefits of eradication become more appealing, since eradication would render vaccination needless, eliminating the costs. And as vaccination expands, what is required to achieve eradication, in light of past investments, becomes less demanding. Thus the incentive structure is eventually tipped to make the prospect of eradication attractive. The benefits of stopping all control measures once polio eradication has been achieved are estimated at $1.5 billion a year (Aylward, Hennessey, and others 2000).[5]

Figure 1 illustrates this coevolution of the global disease burden from polio and the global financial effort for polio prevention. As the world moves toward the right along the horizontal axis (that is, as it advances in time), fewer and fewer countries have polio but more and more need to vaccinate. Thus as the cumulative global threat of polio decreases, the financial effort of vaccination increases. The financial payoff occurs only when all control measures are stopped.[6]

FIGURE 1
Global disease burden from polio and financial effort for prevention as polio eradication progresses

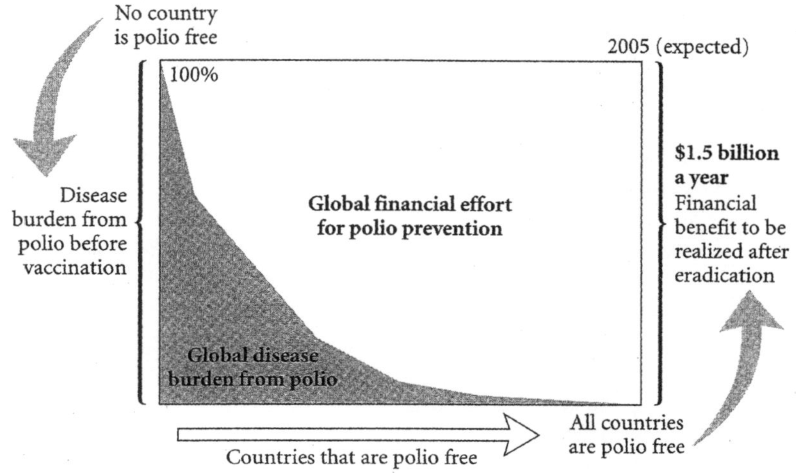

So, the case of polio shows how a fully public response developed, with the creation and deployment on a global scale of all the needed inputs for communicable disease control. Concern about polio in industrial countries led to investments in understanding the disease and in creating a vaccine (type 1 inputs). The vaccine was rapidly deployed in industrial countries, which had well-functioning public health systems. When the feasibility of eradication became clear and recognition of the health and financial benefits generated enough support, the global eradication campaign was launched, providing type 2 and 3 inputs to the developing countries that lacked them.

Policy response to HIV/AIDS: determined but partial

HIV attacks the immune system, exposing it to opportunistic infections and eventually causing AIDS. HIV has five major genetic subtypes. HIV-1B is the prevailing subtype in Europe and the United States. HIV-1C is the most common in Sub-Saharan Africa. Epidemiological studies suggest that HIV-1C is transmitted faster than the others because it is more transmissible through heterosexual intercourse and is inherently more pathogenic (Arhin-Tenkorang 2001). HIV/AIDS was initially regarded as a national public health problem. In Europe and the United States HIV/AIDS was made visible by politically active groups of homosexuals and intravenous drug users. These groups also influenced the design of control approaches and advocated for research and development on the disease.

As with polio, awareness increased as famous people became infected with the disease. Indeed, the pattern of the initial response to HIV/AIDS in the United States resembles that of the response to polio: acute public concern that mobilized society to respond to the threat.

As the epidemiology of HIV/AIDS became known, early responses in Europe and the United States focused on prevention. With the 1987 global AIDS program, the WHO took these responses to the international level. But by the early 1990s it was clear that prevention alone was not enough. A "risk and vulnerability" paradigm emerged, based on the idea that, beyond prevention, there would need to be measures to care for vulnerable populations so that they would have the economic and social capabilities to function. The resources mobilized for prevention and care in developing countries were never sufficient, but the limited publicness of the response has worsened because in recent years industrial countries have benefited from treatment. Antiretroviral therapy has added years of healthy, productive life for those infected with HIV. Lichtenberg (2001) estimates that each new HIV drug approved in the United States saves about 34,000 lives there. Developing countries have been largely excluded from this new dimension of the response to AIDS: type 1 inputs (though treatment drugs have been developed, their availability has been limited).

The reasons for the exclusion of developing countries result from the evolution of the response. New HIV/AIDS drugs are often protected by patents; in industrial countries concern about HIV/AIDS created markets for pharmaceuticals. In addition, most developing countries lack the infrastructure and human capacity needed for safe and effective antiretroviral therapy (type 2 inputs), though recent studies suggest that community-based alternatives can overcome a lack of fully functioning health systems as long as there is an uninterrupted supply of high-quality drugs (Farmer and others 2001). This suggests that community-based delivery can work, at least in the short run, overcoming the obstacles imposed by the lack of type 2 inputs.

The international community's focus on HIV prevention is being reconsidered. Scientific and empirical arguments for combining treatment with prevention have mounted. Antiretroviral therapy not only benefits those infected but also aids prevention (UNAIDS, International AIDS Society, and Bill and Melinda Gates Foundation Expert Group 2001). Reduced viral loads have been achieved in patients receiving antiretroviral treatment, lowering the probability of sexual transmission. The effectiveness of treatment in controlling the spread of HIV is reflected in the strategies recommended by the U.S. Centers for Disease Control and Prevention (USCDC 2001). Various scientific groups, including a team from Harvard University, have outlined modalities for the introduction of treatment that would minimize the risk of generating drug-resistant strains of HIV (Harvard University, Individual Members of the Faculty 2001).

The limited publicness of the response to HIV/AIDS, reflected in the lack of access to some key medical technologies, is impeding its control. By the end of 2001, 40 million people worldwide were infected with HIV/AIDS, up from 36.1 million in 2000. Since 1981 HIV/AIDS has been responsible for 24.8 million deaths. There were 5.3 million new infections in 2000 and another 5.0 million in 2001. In 2001 about three-quarters of AIDS deaths occurred in Sub-Saharan Africa (all figures from UNAIDS 2000, 2001). The incidence of HIV/AIDS is highly asymmetric, imposing an exceedingly high burden especially in Sub-Saharan countries. In Botswana, for example, life expectancy without HIV/AIDS would be 70 years; it is now 36. In Lesotho, Namibia, South Africa, Zambia, and Zimbabwe life expectancy without HIV/AIDS would be close to (in some cases more than) 20 years longer (UNDESA 2001, p. 59). It is now also recognized that the world may be witnessing the early stages of the global HIV/AIDS epidemic and that its long-term evolution is far from clear, with a high likelihood of explosive growth within the next few years (UNAIDS 2002).

In addition, medical technologies specific to the strain of HIV that most affects Sub-Saharan countries have not been developed. The scale and breadth of the efforts to treat HIV/AIDS in industrial countries often lead to results that, by chance, are also beneficial to developing countries. For example, antiretroviral drugs developed in industrial countries contribute to controlling the epidemic in Africa. But these spillovers are not always there. If vaccines are developed for the HIV strains prevalent in industrial countries, they are unlikely to work for the African strains.

Thus for HIV/AIDS the limited publicness of the response goes beyond restrictions on access to existing technologies: not even the incentives to invest in developing vaccines specific to African countries are in place. The limited publicness of the response to HIV/AIDS starts with lack of access to type 1 inputs (in the case of drugs in developing countries) and lack of availability of type 1 inputs (in the case of vaccines, not yet developed). Moreover, the lack of type 2 inputs (functioning public health care systems) adds even more to the exclusion, since it is used as a justification not to deploy existing interventions. After a long period of nationally centered responses (Tarantola 2001), HIV/AIDS is only now starting to receive an international response (Piot and Seck 2001).

Policy response to antimicrobial resistance: neglect

Antimicrobial resistance (AMR) is a natural biological process. Microorganisms evolve to develop resistance to the effects of antimicrobials. Resistant strains coexist with strains sensitive to antimicrobials, but over time the share of resistant microorganisms can reach 90 percent—rendering the antimicrobials ineffective. AMR has worsened recently as a result of the growing use and misuse of antimicrobials. About 10–15 years ago the share of resistant strains of *Staphylococcus aureus* (the most common cause of blood infection and postsurgical infection) was close to 0 percent, but today it ranges from 28 percent in the United States to 70 percent in Japan and the Republic of Korea (Smith and Coast 2001). The costs of AMR-related infections are mounting: in the United States treating resistant infections cost more than $4 billion in 1995, more than $7 billion in 1997, and more than $10 billion in 2001 (Woodward, Smith, and others 2001).

AMR is neither new nor surprising. But the depth and burden of the problem have increased substantially in recent years. In industrial countries excessive prescription and use of antimicrobials contribute to AMR, while in developing countries underconsumption of antimicrobials contributes to AMR (Smith 1999). Underconsumption in developing countries is due to high prices, low incomes, limited access to quality health care, and minimal regulatory capacity. Since it is easier to constrain and regulate excessive supply than to ease the budget constraints of households and governments in developing countries, the problem may be tackled more easily in industrial countries (Woodward, Smith, and others 2001).

Findings from a recent study illustrate the scale of the problem in developing countries. In Tanzania 91 percent of antibiotics are prescribed with incorrect dosages. In India 90 percent of prescriptions did not have dosage specifications. Inappropriate prescriptions of antibiotics were reported for viral respiratory tract infections in 97 percent of cases in China and 81 percent in Ghana (Holloway 2000). Irregular supplies, unofficial supplies, and incorrect prescriptions result in infections that are more drug resistant in developing countries.

In addition, there has been a marked decline in antimicrobial research (Kettler 2000; WHO 2000). Pharmaceutical companies see higher rewards in developing drugs for the chronic diseases of the affluent that require long (even lifelong) treatment than in doing so for the infections that overwhelmingly affect the poor and require treatment only until the infection has been controlled. Moreover, new drugs are often reserved for "last line" interventions, precisely to contain AMR, further limiting the scope of the market. The end result is a lack of sorely needed pharmaceuticals, often for "old" diseases—such as malaria and tuberculosis—that are acquiring fierce multidrug resistance.

Awareness of AMR is increasing, with some industrial countries presenting strategies for its containment. The increase in awareness has resulted from the role played by the scientific community, which has often sounded the alarm on important public health issues. But AMR containment is a case where national action alone will be ineffective. The WHO (2001a) has taken steps toward a coordinated international effort, formulating international policy advice and guidelines. But the response has been timid and lacking in the development of new medical knowledge and technologies—once again, limited in publicness, since not even type 1 inputs are being developed.

New international concern about health: enhancing the publicness of the policy response

Health is a major concern of the international community. An abundance of recent policy statements have expressed this concern and called for urgent, forceful action.[7] What explains the renewed interest in health? Why do past strategies apparently no longer work? This section addresses these questions and examines recent policy responses to global health concerns.

Why is health back at the top of the international agenda?
Two main forces are raising awareness and driving the renewed concern about health. The first is the crushing burden of disease (including noncommunicable diseases) in developing countries. The second is associated with new global risks generated by this excessive burden.

The crushing, unsustainable disease burden in developing countries. The asymmetry in the burden of disease between industrial and developing countries has increased (Evans and others 2001; Farmer 2001). Moreover, it is safe to assume that if communicable diseases receive only a partial policy response, the response to noncommunicable diseases is even more limited. Although the burden of communicable diseases is much larger in Africa than in other regions, the burden of noncommunicable diseases is about the same in all regions (figure 2).

In some cases the burden of noncommunicable diseases results from the "diffusion of behaviors," leading to the global spread of health conditions that lack the epidemiological characteristics of communicable diseases. Chen, Evans, and Cash (1999) show that international trade and the globalization of advertising campaigns have contributed to the spread of health conditions associated with smoking. In addition, genetic disorders—which spread slowly and only when children inherit them from their parents—have become less geographically circumscribed.

Consider sickle cell disease, a genetic disorder that spreads slowly and silently (see table 1). The disease is characterized by unusual red blood cells that are shaped like sickles and destroyed rapidly, causing a number of health conditions, including recurrent acute infections. Sickle cell disease was once confined to parts of Sub-Saharan Africa, northern Greece, southern Italy, southern Turkey, eastern Saudi Arabia, and central and southern India (Serjeant 1994). The slave trade introduced sickle cell disease to North and South America, but increased migration and interethnic relations have facilitated its global spread. An estimated 10 percent of the U.S. population is at risk for sickle cell disease (Arhin-Tenkorang 2001).

Poor people's large burden of communicable and noncommunicable diseases means that today's health challenges require more than monitoring and taking preventive action against infectious diseases. There is an important moral and

FIGURE 2

Burden of disease per capita by cause and region, 2000

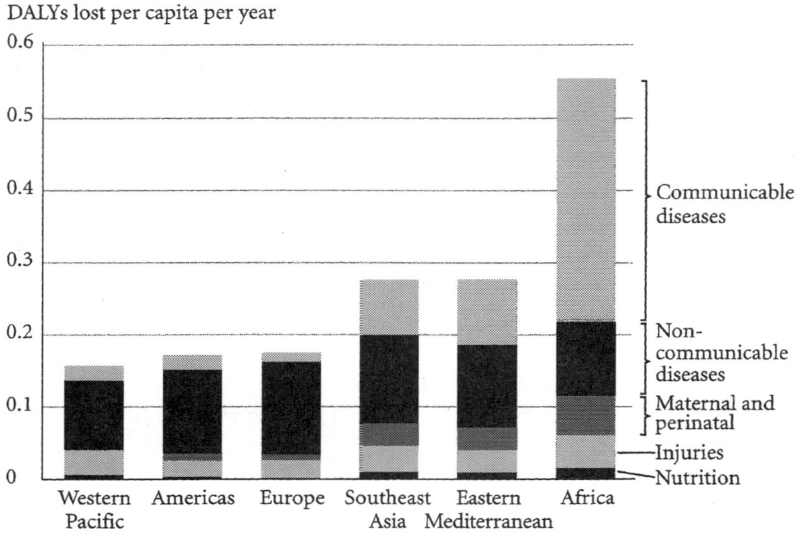

Note: The burden per capita is measured by dividing the disability-adjusted life years (DALYs) lost per year in each region by its population.
Source: WHO 2001b, pp.148–50.

ethical challenge: too many people are suffering from avoidable illness and premature death. And as discussed in the next section, this burden is becoming unsustainable, because it generates serious cross-border spillovers and growing global risks.

New global risks from the disease burden in developing countries. The excessive disease burden in developing countries has adverse effects on countries other than those suffering the direct consequences of high rates of illness and premature death. These adverse effects create new forms of negative global externalities:

- *Infections spread to industrial countries from developing countries with large disease burdens.* One example is the possible increased prevalence in industrial countries of Africa's HIV strain. New HIV infections in Switzerland have characteristics similar to those fueling the epidemic in Africa: a predominance of heterosexual transmission and a high frequency of the African strain of the virus (Böni and others 1999). Another example is the increased share of tuberculosis cases among foreign-born residents; in the United States this share rose from 30 percent in 1992 to 46 percent in 2000. Tuberculosis is seven times as common among foreign-born as among U.S.-born residents. While the proportion of tuberculosis cases exhibiting multidrug resistance fell from 3 percent in 1992 to 1 percent in 2000, the share of those cases occurring in foreign-born residents increased from 31 percent to 72 percent (USCDC 2002).

- *Large disease burdens harm economic growth and increase poverty.* Several studies have found a correlation between good health and other human development indicators, such as education, employment, and income.[8] The exceedingly large burden of disease in developing countries is crushing past development achievements and curtailing future development prospects. The disease burden exacerbates poverty, hinders economic performance, and augments population growth (Commission on Macroeconomics and Health 2001)—undermining the future of the countries affected as well as the international objective of global poverty reduction. These effects also limit investment and trade opportunities for firms in industrial countries. (About 42 percent of U.S. exports go to developing countries; Kassalow 2001.)
- *Large burdens of disease also threaten political stability and foster social unrest,* with possible global consequences. High infant mortality is strongly correlated with state collapse.[9] Indicators of disease-induced death are negatively correlated with state capacity (Price-Smith 2002). In industrial countries the rationale for public funding to control communicable diseases in developing countries is often associated with national and international peace and security (CIA 1999). Failure to control communicable diseases can heighten the perception of some countries' exclusion from growing economic integration, or at least exclusion from its benefits (UN Security Council 2000). Conceição (in this volume) presents preliminary estimates of the costs of the excessive disease burden.
- *Globalization risks losing its legitimacy,* because disease-stricken people in developing countries are likely to feel disenfranchised and abandoned. Directly or through their advocates, they may question why the asymmetries in addressing health challenges are so dramatic, especially now that politics and technology are bringing the world closer together.[10]

Recent policy responses: enhancing the publicness of the response

To address global health challenges, new responses are being designed and implemented that aim at moving toward "health for all," called for by the WHO in 1978 (WHO 1978). Achieving this goal requires acting to control communicable and noncommunicable diseases alike. The new responses are more public in the sense defined above: an effort is being made to develop and deploy all the inputs needed to improve the health conditions of all. Three main strategies are evident, with the first and second oriented toward the first type of disease control inputs and the third toward the second type:

- *Making health-related knowledge more public by design.* Lack of medical knowledge and technologies (drugs, vaccines) constrains the response to health challenges. As a result a number of initiatives, often taking the form of public-private partnerships (see appendix), have been established to conduct and support targeted research and development to create needed medical technologies. One example is the International AIDS Vaccine Initiative (http://www.iavi.org). The initiative has a dual objective: accelerating the development of HIV vaccines while ensuring that vaccines that receive support from the initiative will be made accessible worldwide. The Malaria Vaccine Initiative (http://www.malariavaccine.org) focuses on the same goals for malaria vaccines, while the Medicines for Malaria Venture (http://www.mmv.org) supports research and development for malaria drugs (see also http://www.emvi.org and http://www.amvtn.org). The Global Alliance for TB Drug Development (http://www.tballiance.org), similar to the Medicines for Malaria Venture, focuses on developing tuberculosis drugs that are more effective and easier to deploy.

- *Making medicines more affordable.* The response to diseases is often hindered not by the nonexistence of drugs and vaccines but by their cost. Protected by patents and priced according to the purchasing power of industrial countries, existing interventions may be beyond the reach of developing countries (Abbott 2002). Thus, at the urging of several developing countries[11] and civil society organizations,[12] the international community has reexamined rules for protecting intellectual property rights, notably the World Trade Organization (WTO) agreement on Trade-Related Aspects of Intellectual Property Rights (TRIPS). Oxfam's "cut the cost" campaign insistently urged the WTO to revise its intellectual property rules to make medicines more affordable (http://www.oxfam.org.uk/cutthecost), and the rules have been discussed in UN debates on human rights (UN Economic and Social Council 2000). At the 2001 WTO ministerial conference in Doha, Qatar, a declaration on TRIPS and public health recognized the scope and urgency of the public health problems posed by diseases such as HIV/AIDS, malaria, and tuberculosis. The declaration also recognized that the TRIPS agreement should not impede countries from declaring and dealing with public health emergencies, and acknowledged the possibility of allowing compulsory licensing. Correa (in this volume) explores mechanisms being considered to improve developing countries' access to medicines, including differential pricing, differential patenting, compulsory licensing, and parallel imports.
- *Strengthening capacity in developing countries.* Providing developing countries with needed interventions requires more than affordable medicines; it also requires type 2 inputs, that is, a national health infrastructure capable of delivering vaccines, administering treatments, and monitoring sickness and death. Some recent responses are trying to develop such infrastructure. For example, the Global Alliance for Vaccines and Immunization (http://www.vaccinealliance.org) is a public-private partnership that purchases and delivers vaccines in developing countries. The Global Fund to Fight AIDS, Tuberculosis, and Malaria (http://www.globalfundatm.org), created on the recommendation of the

UN Secretary-General (UN 2001), helps deliver interventions to control the three diseases. Both efforts work on the same principle of funding credible (externally and independently evaluated) country-based proposals. The aim is not only to deliver the urgently needed interventions, but also to build national health care capacity.[13]

Possible next steps

This chapter has interpreted the health challenges facing the international community as resulting from the limited publicness of responses to communicable diseases and other health concerns. The ensuing—and exceedingly large—disease burden in developing countries is not only dashing their hopes for development; it is also generating negative externalities that affect, or will likely soon affect, industrial and developing countries alike.

The international community has started to address these challenges by enhancing the publicness of the responses: making medical knowledge more public by design and more affordable and accessible (type 1 inputs) and implementing programs to deliver existing interventions within countries (type 2 inputs). Although some recent responses to global health concerns have been more public, additional steps may be required to consolidate and strengthen the publicness of such efforts.

Recognizing mutual benefits and tapping new sources of funding

Developing countries receive considerable direct benefits when their disease burden is reduced, but other benefits are shared around the world. Beyond moral and ethical considerations, further easing the burden would attenuate or eliminate the global spillovers described above. Because the benefits are shared by all, the costs of global health interventions should also be shared by all.

This could mean, for example, that health programs in developing countries would be financed not just by those countries' domestic resources and aid allocations. Additional sources could include the health budgets of industrial countries. Resources could also come from industrial country tax credits or from defense or national security budgets.[14] In addition, international pooling of resources, as in the Global Alliance for Vaccines and Immunization and the Global Fund to Fight AIDS, Tuberculosis, and Malaria, is becoming an important instrument.

Current resources are insufficient, and there has been reluctance to commit long-term financing on the scale required. The Commission on Macroeconomics and Health (2001) estimates that substantially reducing the disease burden of developing countries—including controlling major diseases such as HIV/AIDS, malaria, and tuberculosis—would require about $27 billion a year from industrial countries by 2007. About $8 billion of this should be devoted to the Global Fund to Fight AIDS, Tuberculosis, and Malaria. In early 2002 the fund had

$700–800 million available for disbursements, but by March 2002 it had received 316 proposals requiring $1.15 billion (http://www.globalfundatm.org). Increasing resources is crucial, and aid alone may not be sufficient.[15]

Some new financing could come at no additional net cost—for example, from a domestic tax on cigarette sales. Such a tax would reduce tobacco consumption and generate revenues that could pay for interventions and for administration and enforcement of the tax. Public policy incentives should be reviewed to identify the scope for possible budget restructuring.

Increasing incentives for global health research

Without knowledge about health conditions and without technologies to prevent and treat them (type 1 inputs), little can be done to fight disease. Research and development to improve basic knowledge about diseases and to deliver products to fight them have long been encouraged and conducted by both the public and the private sector. Beyond biomedical research, knowledge about health conditions also requires better understanding of the social and economic determinants of health—which calls for investments in research on social behavior, economics, and health systems (Kettler 2002).

During the first half of the 20th century developing and industrial countries had similar priorities in drug and vaccine development. Finding vaccines and cures for diseases ranging from yellow fever to smallpox, from polio to tuberculosis, was in the interest of both groups of countries. But priorities in developing medical technologies have since diverged. Private industry has little incentive to address poor people's diseases. And basic research, supported largely by public entities in industrial countries, only incidentally relates to the health problems of poor people.

At the international level, incentives to develop medical technologies produce a gap in the generation of much-needed medical knowledge and create large asymmetries in the ability to use existing technologies. According to the Global Forum for Health Research (http://www.globalforumhealth.org), only 10 percent of world spending on health research and development is related to the health conditions that account for 90 percent of the global burden of ill health (the 10/90 gap). Of 1,223 new medicines commercialized between 1975 and 1997, only 13 were specifically oriented toward tropical diseases, with 2 resulting from military research and 5 from veterinary research. Only 4 (0.3 percent) resulted from purposeful research on tropical diseases (Pécoul and others 1999). Efforts are being made to correct this imbalance (see appendix), but even these fail to address some of the most neglected diseases affecting developing countries (Trouiller and others 2002). Much more needs to be done.

Michael Kremer suggests that the response may require both "pull" incentives (creating markets for drugs where they are absent) and "push" incentives (providing incentives to conduct research and development). Kremer indicates that a particularly effective and efficient pull mechanism to encourage vaccine development would be the establishment by governments or private foundations of legally binding commitments to purchase needed vaccines if and when they are developed (box 1).

According to estimates by the Commission on Macroeconomics and Health (2001), about $3 billion a year would be required by 2007 to support research and development oriented toward neglected diseases. Of this, half should go to a new global health research fund devoted to supporting basic research and half to supporting targeted research and development for drugs, vaccines, diagnostics, and other medical technologies, through the support of existing initiatives such as those described in box 1. In addition, there should be a clear understanding that if specified products were developed in the future, part of this $1.5 billion in annual spending could be used to purchase them, as discussed in box 1.

BOX 1

A PURCHASE COMMITMENT FOR VACCINES

BY MICHAEL KREMER

Vaccines provide the best hope for a long-run sustainable solution for AIDS and the other infectious diseases devastating poor countries: they are typically easier to deliver than drugs, since they require no diagnosis and physicians are not needed to administer them. But because pharmaceutical firms see little chance of recouping their risk-adjusted research and development costs, little private research is being conducted on vaccines for malaria, tuberculosis, and African strains of HIV.

An extremely cost-effective way for international organizations, industrial nations, or private foundations to stimulate research on such vaccines is to commit to purchasing effective vaccines once they have been developed. Such a purchase commitment not only would provide the incentive for vaccine development, but also would ensure that price is not a barrier to people using the vaccines.

Efforts to encourage vaccine development can be divided into two broad categories: "push" programs subsidize research inputs—for example, through research and development tax credits or grants to researchers—while "pull" programs reward the development of a vaccine. Both approaches have important roles, but current policy underutilizes pull programs.

Push programs are well suited for financing basic research, while pull programs (such as a purchase commitment) have several attractive features for encouraging more applied work, such as the later stages of vaccine development. Importantly, the public pays nothing unless a viable vaccine emerges. Pull programs encourage researchers to select projects with a reasonable chance of yielding a viable product rather than overselling their research prospects to research

BOX 1 CONTINUED

administrators and the public. They allow politicians and the public to be confident that they are paying for an actual product rather than supporting a development effort that might not be scientifically warranted. Pull programs also provide strong financial incentives for researchers to focus on developing a marketable product rather than pursuing other goals, such as publishing journal articles.

Finally, appropriately designed pull programs can help ensure that if new products are developed, they will reach those who need them. For example, industrial countries or private foundations could commit to purchasing a malaria vaccine for $5 per immunized person and making it available to developing countries for free or in return for a modest copayment.

For such pull programs to be effective, potential developers must believe that sponsors will not renege on their purchase commitments. In fact, courts have held that similar public commitments to reward contest winners or to purchase specified goods constitute legally binding contracts and that decisions made by independent parties to adjudicate such programs are binding. Clear eligibility and pricing rules can enhance a program's credibility. For example, it could be stipulated that candidate products must be cleared by a regulatory agency such as the U.S. Food and Drug Administration or European Medicines Evaluation Agency. This would ensure that funds are spent on bona fide vaccines.

A candidate product could also be subjected to a market test: nations wishing to purchase the product would need to provide a modest copayment in proportion to their per capita income. Such copayments would give countries an incentive to carefully investigate whether candidate products are appropriate for local conditions and provide a useful test of countries' commitment to a program. If a country is willing to pay, it is also more likely to be prepared to take the steps necessary to ensure that the vaccine is delivered to the people who need it.

The market promised by a program should be large enough to induce substantial effort by vaccine developers, but less than the social value of the vaccine. Several researchers have concluded that a real annual market of $250–500 million would be needed to motivate substantial research. Over 10 years a commitment at this level could save about 1.9 billion discounted disability-adjusted life years—equivalent to saving the lives of 63 million 30-year-olds. The average cost per year of life saved would be $4.

Any of several organizations—including national governments, the World Bank, and private foundations—have the ability to create a credible purchase commitment to stimulate vaccine research. If a commitment to purchase new vaccines fails to induce their development, it will have cost nothing. If it succeeds, it will save millions of lives at a few dollars each.

Note: For more information, see Kremer (2001a, 2001b).

The governance of health research has been debated for more than a decade (see Global Forum for Health Research 2002, especially chapter 3). One option to manage the new global research fund would be through a system of governance akin to the one used by the U.S. National Institutes of Health or the U.K. Medical Research Council (as also proposed by Kaul and Faust 2001), in which funding to research is based on a scientific peer-review process. An important objective of the fund would be to help build long-term scientific capacity in developing countries. So, funding could be made available for research groups in developing countries, which would submit proposals individually or together with other research groups from industrial or developing countries.

Another initiative that could enhance global incentives for research and development would be extending national orphan drug legislation to global diseases, a measure also proposed by the Commission on Macroeconomics and Health (2001). Orphan drug legislation provides pull and push incentives (for example, by easing terms for regulatory approval and providing public funds for research and development) to develop drugs for diseases that, in the current national context, affect a small number of people (and so a limited market) and thus fail to elicit a response from the private sector. Extending the scope to the international market could generate interest in neglected diseases.

Deploying rapid response task forces

Though important and relevant, the above suggestions are oriented toward long-term results. The current global health situation is a crisis—especially in the case of HIV/AIDS—calling for immediate action. Solutions are needed that allow more rapid action than is often possible with the slow pace of international health cooperation. Ill health means that people's security is at risk. Just as efforts are being made to upgrade the international community's capacity to respond to international military crises, consideration should be given to developing capacity for rapid responses to health emergencies. This could involve, for example, dispatching international health teams to help countries control spreading diseases as quickly as possible. Building national capacity is the only sustainable solution, but doing so is a long-term effort. Disease-stricken countries cannot wait for new vaccines and drugs to be developed or for national capacity to mature. The current crisis calls for an emergency response that supports the enhanced publicness of the other responses.

Appendix. Biomedical research and development to treat poor people's diseases

Around the world about $70 billion a year is spent on biomedical research and development, but very little is devoted to the diseases of poor people. The oldest international initiative addressing the diseases of poor people is the Special

Programme for Research and Training in Tropical Diseases, a collaborative effort between the United Nations Development Programme (UNDP), World Health Organization (WHO), and World Bank. For more than 25 years this program has focused on orphan diseases. Malaria has long been among the diseases addressed by the program; tuberculosis was recently added.

The Global Forum for Health Research, a private foundation, was created in 1998 to help correct the 10/90 gap—the fact that just 10 percent of world spending on health research addresses 90 percent of the world's health problems. The forum works as a network of networks and as a catalyst to narrow the 10/90 gap.

An important new organizational arrangement has been the establishment of public-private partnerships. Such partnerships have been created in part because global health problems are so complex that no single agent (firm, government, or nonprofit) is likely to tackle them successfully. Some public-private partnerships are devoted to comprehensive responses to a disease, such as the Roll Back Malaria global partnership. But many have been created to support and conduct research and development for neglected diseases (see table).

The international initiatives listed in table have approximately $100 million in total annual funds, considerably less than the requirements suggested by the Commission on Macroeconomics and Health. But this amount excludes private and national spending on neglected diseases. While private spending is difficult to estimate, it is thought to be rather low. In terms of national spending, the U.S. National Institutes of Health is a particularly strong player. Its annual budget for AIDS research is about $2.5 billion (with proposed funding for 2002 of $357 million for research on an AIDS vaccine), while that for tuberculosis research is more than $80 million and for malaria research about $70 million (http://www.nih.gov).

Selected international initiatives supporting biomedical research and development for neglected diseases

Initiative	Funding year	Funding amount (millions of U.S. dollars)	Funders	Focus
Special Programme for Research and Training in Tropical Diseases A global program of scientific collaboration established in 1975 to coordinate, support, and influence global efforts to combat a portfolio of major diseases of the poor and disadvantaged. Supports R&D, training, and capacity building.	2002–03	95	UNDP, WHO, World Bank, private foundations, country contributions	Malaria (42%); TB (21%; added in 2000); others (each less than 6%); R&D, training, and capacity building
Global Forum for Health Research A private foundation that monitors the 10/90 gap, develops priority setting methodologies, and acts as a catalyst and as a "network of networks." Supports initiatives oriented toward reducing the gap, often providing seed money and administrative support.	2000 Endowment	2.3 1	Rockefeller Foundation, WHO, country contributions	Initiatives to reduce the 10/90 gap
International AIDS Vaccine Initiative A nonprofit scientific and charitable organization founded in 1996 to ensure the development of safe, effective, accessible HIV vaccines. Focuses on accelerating scientific progress, mobilizing public support through issue advocacy and education, encouraging industrial involvement in AIDS vaccine development, and working to ensure global access to a vaccine.	1999 2000 2001	3.9 11.5[a] 19.4[a]	Bill and Melinda Gates Foundation, Sloan Foundation, World Bank, country contributions, pharmaceutical industry	Development of an AIDS vaccine through support of R&D and enlargement of the number and scope of actors engaged in the effort

Medicines for Malaria Venture A public-private partnership established in late 1999 to address the market failure reflected in the lack of incentives to develop medicines for malaria. Supports R&D projects with varying degrees of risk.	2001 2002	4.2 15[a]	Private foundations, country contributions, World Bank, WHO, Global Forum for Health Research, pharmaceutical industry	R&D on malaria medicines (6 R&D projects in 2001; 14 expected in 2002)
Malaria Vaccine Initiative A public-private partnership created in 1999 to accelerate the development of a malaria vaccine. Works with national and international agencies and organizations, supporting laboratories, the coordination and management of pilot production, and the release of products for clinical trials.	1999	50[b]	William H. Gates Foundation	Vaccine for malaria
Multilateral Initiative on Malaria Created in 1997 to strengthen and sustain, through collaborative research and training, the capacity of malaria-endemic countries in Africa to carry out research required to develop and improve tools for malaria control.	No data available		Country contributions, U.S. National Institutes of Health, Wellcome Trust and other foundations, pharmaceutical industry	Coordination and mobilization of resources for cooperative malaria research
Global Alliance for TB Drug Development A public-private partnership created in 2000 with the aim of accelerating the discovery and development of cost-effective drugs, by outsourcing drug R&D projects, and moving drug compounds along the development line to regulatory approval and the market at affordable prices for countries with the highest burden from TB.	2001–05	150[a]	Rockefeller Foundation, Bill and Melinda Gates Foundation, country contributions, pharmaceutical industry	TB drug development, from research to regulatory approval and market placement at affordable prices

Selected international initiatives supporting biomedical research and development for neglected diseases

Initiative	Funding year	Funding amount (millions of U.S. dollars)	Funders	Focus
Action TB An international coordinated research program set up by GlaxoSmithKline in 1993 with the aim of finding new targets for TB therapies, identifying novel vaccine candidates, and identifying surrogate markers for use in clinical trials. Involves more than 20 academic research groups in Canada, South Africa, the United Kingdom, and the United States and supports the work of more than 40 researchers.	1993–2003	30	GlaxoSmithKline	TB drug development

a. Projected or expected funding.
b. One-time grant.
Source: Authors compilation from relevant documentation.

NOTES

1. Franklin D. Roosevelt, the U.S. president from the early 1930s through most of World War II, was a victim of polio.

2. Salk also thought that the vaccine should be made available to all. When asked who would control the new vaccine, Salk replied, "I'd say it belongs to everyone. I mean, could you patent the sun?" (Seavey, Smith, and Wagner 1998, p. 175).

3. To accelerate the eradication effort, in 1999 the Bill and Melinda Gates Foundation (http://www.gatesfoundation.org) provided $50 million and the UN Foundation (http://www.unfoundation.org) provided $28 million. The U.S. Centers for Disease Control and Prevention provides technical support, including genetic fingerprinting to identify the strains of poliovirus in an outbreak.

4. Although the continuing support of the U.S. Centers for Disease Control and Prevention to the eradication effort, as mentioned above, should not be understated.

5. It is not yet clear when and how immunization efforts would stop once the world is declared free of polioviruses. For an analysis of possible risks, see Dowdle and others (2002).

6. According to Cornes and Sandler (1986), eradication of diseases that spread indiscriminately around the world such as polio is a weakest link global public good: eradication cannot be achieved if one country stays out, so the global public good is provided only when the last country with the disease is certified as being free of it.

7. See UN (2000, 2001); the G-8 Okinawa Summit Declaration, 23 July 2000; and the Abuja Declaration and Framework for Action for the fight against HIV/AIDS, tuberculosis, and other infectious diseases in Africa, 27 April 2001 (http://www.oau-oua.org/afrsummit/docs.htm). U.S. public health policy is increasingly concerned with global health (Bunyavanich and Walkup 2001; http://www.globalhealth.gov); the United Kingdom has also shown concern for global health (UKPIU 2001).

8. Preston (1975) notes a negative relationship between per capita income and mortality. Abel-Smith and Leiserson (1978) examine health and economic development. Fogel (1994) shows the relationship between improvements in health and improvements in living standards for Europeans and North Americans. Strauss and Thomas (1998) provide an overview centered on developing countries.

9. Esty and others (1998, p. vii), analyzing the characteristics of states more likely to collapse, find that among hundreds of variables, high infant mortality is one of only three that consistently separate states that fail from others. In a critical assessment of this work, King and Zeng (2001, p. 650) question the validity of these conclusions—except in the case of infant mortality: "The infant mortality result is fairly striking: only states with governments that are sufficiently competent to keep infant mortality below the global median have comparatively low probabilities of state failure; other countries, even when they are alike in all other measured respects to the G7, have substantial probabilities of failure (as high as 0.25)."

10. For the multiple relationships between globalization and health, see Garrett (2000) and Lee, Buse, and Fustukian (2002). See also Dollar (2001), Cornia (2001),

and Woodward, Drager, and others (2001). Differing views on globalization and health are offered in Feachem (2001) and Lee (2002). Lee and Collin (2001) comprehensively summarize empirical research on globalization and health.

11. Notably South Africa, where a march organized by the Treatment Action Campaign (http://www.tac.org.za) contributed to the Global Treatment Access Campaign (http://www.globaltreatmentaccess.org/).

12. For example, the campaign for access to essential medicines by Médecins Sans Frontières (http://www.accessmed-msf.org/index.asp).

13. In the case of HIV/AIDS the response to the pandemic may have to be multifaceted, going beyond strengthening the health sector (UNDP 2002).

14. The tax credits could include credits for research performed in industrial countries on diseases affecting mainly developing countries and credits on sales to developing countries. See Attaran and others (2000) on the second proposal. See also *Vaccines for the New Millennium Act* of 2001 (U.S. Senate bill 895; U.S. House of Representatives bill 895) and UKPIU (2001), aimed at encouraging research to prevent and treat diseases primarily affecting developing countries.

15. There is also an indirect argument for increasing health spending in developing countries: national health systems become more efficient after a threshold level of health spending per capita has been achieved (Evans and others 2001). Thus increasing health spending in developing countries could help achieve this threshold, which would mean that further resources would be used more effectively.

References

Abbott, Frederick M. 2002. "WTO TRIPS Agreement and Its Implications for Access to Medicines in Developing Countries." Study Paper 2a. Commission on Intellectual Property Rights, London.

Abel-Smith, Brian, and Alcira Leiserson. 1978. *Poverty, Development and Health Policy*. Geneva: World Health Organization.

Acharya, Arnab, Sarah England, Mary Agocs, Jennifer Linkins, and Bruce Aylward. 2001. "Producing a Global Public Good: Polio Eradication." Paper presented at the International Development Research Center Workshop on Global Public Goods for Health, 4–6 June, Ottawa, Canada.

Arhin-Tenkorang, Dyna. 2001. "The GPG Dimensions of Enhanced Health Care of the Poor: A Case Study of Sickle Cell Disease and HIV/AIDS." United Nations Development Programme, Office of Development Studies, New York, N.Y.

Attaran, Amir, Michael Kremer, Jeffrey Sachs, and Sara Sievers. 2000. *A Tax Credit for Sales of HIV, Tuberculosis, and Malaria Vaccines*. Cambridge, Mass.: Harvard University, Center for International Development.

Aylward, R. Bruce, Karen A. Hennessey, Nevio Zagaria, Jean-Marc Olivé, and Stephen L. Cochi. 2000. "When Is a Disease Eradicable? 100 Years of Lessons Learned." *American Journal of Public Health* 90 (10): 1515–20.

Aylward, R. Bruce, Harry F. Hull, Stephen L. Cochi, Roland W. Sutter, Jean-Marc Olivé, and Bjorn Melgaard. 2000. "Disease Eradication as a Public Health Strategy: A Case Study of Poliomyelitis Eradication." *Bulletin of the World Health Organization* 78 (3): 285–97.

Böni, Jürg, Halina Pyra, Martin Gebhardt, Luc Perrin, Philippe Bürgisser, Lukas Matter, Walter Fierz, Peter Erb, Jean-Claude Piffaretti, Elisabeth Minder, Peter Grob, Johann J. Burckhardt, Marcel Zwahlen, and Jörg Schüpbach. 1999. "High Frequency of Non-B Subtypes in Newly Diagnosed HIV-1 Infections in Switzerland." *Journal of Acquired Immune Deficiency Syndromes* 22 (2): 174–79.

Bunyavanich, Supinda, and Ruth B. Walkup. 2001. "US Public Health Leaders Shift toward a New Paradigm of 'Global Health'." *American Journal of Public Health* 91: 1556–58.

Chen, Lincoln C., Tim G. Evans, and Richard A. Cash. 1999. "Health as a Global Public Good." In Inge Kaul, Isabelle Grunberg, and Marc A. Stern, eds., *Global Public Goods: International Cooperation in the 21st Century.* New York: Oxford University Press.

CIA (U.S. Central Intelligence Agency). 1999. "The Global Infectious Disease Threat and Its Implications for the United States." [http://www.odci.gov/cia/publications/nie/report/nie99-17d.html]. January 2002.

Commission on Macroeconomics and Health. 2001. *Macroeconomics and Health: Investing in Health for Economic Development.* Geneva: World Health Organization.

Cooper, Richard N. 1989. "International Cooperation in Public Health as a Prologue to Macroeconomic Cooperation." In Richard N. Cooper, Barry Eichengreen, C. Randall Henning, Gerald Holtham, and Robert D. Putnam, eds., *Can Nations Agree? Issues in International Economic Cooperation.* Washington, D.C.: Brookings Institution.

Cornes, Richard, and Todd Sandler. 1986. *The Theory of Externalities, Public Goods and Club Goods.* Cambridge and New York: Cambridge University Press.

Cornia, Giovanni Andrea. 2001. "Globalization and Health: Results and Options." *Bulletin of the World Health Organization* 79 (9): 834–41.

Dodgson, Richard, Kelley Lee, and Nick Drager. 2002. "Global Health Governance: A Conceptual Review." Global Health Governance Discussion Paper 1. London School of Hygiene and Tropical Medicine, Center on Global Change and Health.

Dollar, David. 2001. "Is Globalization Good for Your Health?" *Bulletin of the World Health Organization* 79 (9): 827–33.

Dowdle, Walter R., Howard E. Gary, Raymond Sanders, and Anton M. van Loon. 2002. "Can Post-Eradication Laboratory Containment of Wild Polioviruses Be Achieved?" *Bulletin of the World Health Organization* 80 (4): 311–16.

Esty, Daniel C., Jack A. Goldstone, Ted Robert Gurr, Barbara Harff, Marc Levy, Geoffrey D. Dabelko, Pamela T. Surko, and Alan N. Unger. 1998. "State Failure

Task Force Report: Phase II Findings." Science Applications International Corporation, McLean, Va.

Evans, David B., Ajay Tandon, Christopher J. L. Murray, and Jeremy A. Lauer. 2001. "Comparative Efficiency of National Health Systems: Cross-National Econometric Analysis." *British Medical Journal* 323: 307–10.

Farmer, Paul. 2001. *Infections and Inequalities: The Modern Plagues.* Berkeley: University of California Press.

Farmer, Paul, Fernet Léandre, Joia Mukherjee, Rajesh Gupta, Laura Tarter, and Jim Young Kim. 2001. "Community-Based Treatment of Advanced HIV Disease: Introducing DOT-HAART (Directly Observed Therapy with Highly Active Antiretroviral Therapy)." *Bulletin of the World Health Organization* 79 (12): 1145–51.

Feachem, Richard A. G. 2001. "Globalisation Is Good for Your Health, Mostly." *British Medical Journal* 323: 504–06.

Fogel, Robert. 1994. "Economic Growth, Population Health and Physiology: The Bearing of Long-Term Prospects on the Making of Economic Policy." *American Economic Review* 84 (3): 369–95.

Garrett, Laurie. 2000. *Betrayal of Trust: The Collapse of Global Public Health.* New York: Hyperion.

Global Forum for Health Research. 2002. *The 10/90 Report on Health Research 2001–2002.* Geneva: Global Forum for Health Research.

Harvard University, Individual Members of the Faculty. 2001. "Consensus Statement on Antiretroviral Treatment for AIDS in Poor Countries." [http://www.cid.harvard.edu/cidinthenews/pr/consensus_aids_therapy.pdf]. June 2001.

Holloway, Kathleen. 2000. "Who Contributes to Misuse of Antimicrobials?" *Essential Drugs Monitor* 28/29: 9.

Kassalow, Jordan S. 2001. *Why Health Is Important to U.S. Foreign Policy.* New York: Council on Foreign Relations.

Kaul, Inge, and Michael Faust. 2001. "Global Public Goods and Health: Taking the Agenda Forward." *Bulletin of the World Health Organization* 79 (9): 869–74.

Kettler, Hannah E. 2000. *Narrowing the Gap between Provision and Need for Medicines in Developing Countries.* London: Office of Health Economics.

———. 2002. "Using Innovative Action to Meet Global Health Needs through Existing Intellectual Property Regimes." Study Paper 2b. Commission on Intellectual Property Rights, London.

King, Gary, and Langche Zeng. 2001. "Improving Forecasts of State Failure." *World Politics* 53 (July): 623–58.

Kremer, Michael. 2001a. "Creating Markets for New Vaccines: Part I—Rationale." In Adam B. Jaffe, Josh Lerner, and Scott Stern, eds., *Innovation Policy and the Economy.* Cambridge, Mass.: MIT Press.

———. 2001b. "Creating Markets for New Vaccines: Part II—Design Issues." In Adam B. Jaffe, Josh Lerner, and Scott Stern, eds., *Innovation Policy and the Economy*. Cambridge, Mass.: MIT Press.

Lee, Kelley. 2002. "Informed and Open Debate on Globalisation and Health Is Needed." *British Medical Journal* 324: 44.

Lee, Kelley, and Jeff Collin. 2001. "A Review of Existing Empirical Research on Globalization and Health." Background paper for the Annual Meeting of the World Health Organization–HSD Scientific Resource Group on Globalization and Health. London School of Hygiene and Tropical Medicine.

Lee, Kelley, Kent Buse, and Suzanne Fustukian. 2002. Health Policy in a Globalizing World. Cambridge and New York: Cambridge University Press.

Lichtenberg, Frank. 2001. "The Effect of New Drugs on Mortality from Rare Diseases and HIV." NBER Working Paper 8677. National Bureau for Economic Research, Cambridge, Mass.

Loughlin, Kelly, and Virginia Berridge. 2002. "Historical Dimensions of Global Health Governance." Global Health Governance Discussion Paper 2. London School of Hygiene and Tropical Medicine, Center on Global Change and Health.

Lyons, F. S. L. 1963. *Internationalism in Europe 1815–1914*. Leyden: A. W. Sythoff.

Mills, Anne. 2001. "Technology and Science as Global Public Goods: Tackling Priority Diseases of Poor Countries." Paper presented at the Annual Bank Conference on Development Economics–Europe, Paris, June 25–26.

PAHO (Pan-American Health Organization). 1992. *Pro Salute Novi Mundi: A History of the Pan American Health Organization*. Washington, D.C.

Pécoul, Benard, Pierre Chirac, Patrice Trouiller, and Jacques Pinel. 1999. "Access to Essential Drugs in Poor Countries: A Lost Battle?" *Journal of the American Medical Association* 281 (4): 361–67.

Philipson, Thomas. 1999. "Economic Epidemiology and Infectious Diseases." NBER Working Paper 7037. National Bureau for Economic Research, Cambridge, Mass.

Piot, Peter, and Awa Marie Coll Seck. 2001. "International Response to the HIV/AIDS Epidemic: Planning for Success." *Bulletin of the World Health Organization* 79 (12): 1106–12.

Preston, Samuel H. 1975. "The Changing Relation between Mortality and Level of Economic Development." *Population Studies* 29: 231–48.

Price-Smith, Andrew T. 2002. *The Health of Nations: Infectious Disease, Environmental Changes, and Their Effects on National Security and Development*. Cambridge, Mass.: MIT Press.

Sandler, Todd, and Daniel G. Arce M.. 2002. "A Conceptual Framework for Understanding Global and Transnational Goods for Health." *Fiscal Studies* 23(2): 195–222.

Seavey, Nina Gilden, Jane S. Smith, and Paul Wagner. 1998. *A Paralyzing Fear: The Triumph over Polio in America.* New York: TV Books.

Serjeant, Graham R. 1994. *Sickle Cell Disease.* 2nd ed. Oxford: Oxford Medical Publications.

Smith, Richard D. 1999. "Antimicrobial Resistance: The Importance of Developing Long-Term Policy." *Bulletin of the World Health Organization* 77 (10): 862.

Smith, Richard D., and Joanna Coast. 2001. "Global Resistance to the Growing Threat of Antimicrobial Resistance." CMH Working Paper WG2: 17. World Health Organization, Commission on Macroeconomics and Health, Geneva.

Steckel, Richard H. 2001. "Health and Nutrition in the Pre-Industrial Era." NBER Working Paper 8542. National Bureau for Economic Research, Cambridge, Mass.

Strauss, John, and Duncan Thomas. 1998. "Health, Nutrition and Economic Development." *Journal of Economic Literature* 36 (2): 766–817.

Tarantola, Daniel. 2001. "Facing the Reality of AIDS—A 15-Year Process?" *Bulletin of the World Health Organization* 79 (12): 1095.

Trouiller, Patrice, Piero Olliaro, Els Torreele, James Orbinski, Richard Laing and Nathan Ford. 2002. "Drug Development for Neglected Diseases: a Deficient Market and a Public-health Policy Failure." *The Lancet.* 359, June 22: 2188–94.

UKPIU (U.K. Performance and Innovation Unit). 2001. T*ackling the Diseases of Poverty.* London: Cabinet Office.

UN (United Nations). 2000. "Millennium Declaration." General Assembly Resolution 55/2. New York.

———. 2001. "Declaration of Commitment on HIV/AIDS." Adopted by the General Assembly special session on HIV/AIDS. New York.

UNAIDS (Joint United Nations Programme on HIV/AIDS). 2000. "Global Summary of the HIV/AIDS Epidemic (December)." [http://www.unaids.org/]. November 2001.

———. 2001. "AIDS Epidemic Update (December)." [http://www.unaids.org/]. December 2001.

———. 2002. *Report on the Global HIV/AIDS Epidemic.* Geneva: UNAIDS.

UNAIDS (Joint United Nations Programme on HIV/AIDS), International AIDS Society, and Bill and Melinda Gates Foundation Expert Group. 2001. "AIDS: The Time to Act." Statement issued after 6–8 May meeting in Mont Pèlerin, Switzerland.

UNDESA (United Nations Department of Economic and Social Affairs). 2001. *World Population Prospects: The 2000 Revision—Highlights.* ESA/P/WP.165. Population Division. New York.

UNDP (United Nations Development Programme). 2002. "A Multifaceted Response to the HIV/AIDS Pandemic." *Essentials* No. 6. New York.

UN Economic and Social Council. 2000. "Intellectual Property Rights and Human Rights: Sub-Commission on Human Rights Resolution 2000/7." E/CN.4/SUB.2/RES/2000/7. New York.

UN Security Council. 2000. "Resolution 1308." S/RES/1308 (2000). New York.

USCDC (U.S. Centers for Disease Control and Prevention). 2001. *HIV Prevention Strategic Plan through 2005*. Atlanta, GA: U.S. Centers for Disease Control.

———. 2002. "Tuberculosis Morbidity among US-Born and Foreign-Born Populations—United States, 2000." *Morbidity and Mortality Weekly Report* 51 (5): 101–04.

WHO (World Health Organization). 1978. *Declaration of Alma-Ata*. Adopted at the International Conference on Primary Health Care, Alma-Ata, USSR, 6–12 September 1978.

———. 2000. *Overcoming Antimicrobial Resistance*. WHO/CDS/2000.2. Geneva.

———. 2001a. *Global Strategy for the Containment of Antimicrobial Resistance*. WHO/CDS/CSR/DRS/2001.2. Geneva.

———. 2001b. *World Health Report 2001: Mental Health—New Understandings, New Hope*. Geneva.

———. 2002. *Weekly Epidemiological Record* 13 (77): 97–108.

Woodward, David, Nick Drager, Robert Beaglehole, and Debra Lipson. 2001. "Globalization and Health: A Framework for Analysis and Action." *Bulletin of the World Health Organization* 79 (9): 875–81.

Woodward, David, Richard Smith, Arnab Acharya, Robert Beaglehole, and Nick Drager. 2001. "Communicable Disease Control: A GPG for Health." World Health Organization, Geneva.

Zacher, Mark W. 1999. "Global Epidemiological Surveillance: International Cooperation to Monitor Infectious Diseases." In Inge Kaul, Isabelle Grunberg, and Marc A. Stern, eds., *Global Public Goods: International Cooperation in the 21st Century*. New York: Oxford University Press.

[23]

Strengthening governance for global health research

The countries that most need health research should decide what should be funded

Kelley Lee and Anne Mills

As experts from around the world gather in Bangkok to attend the international conference for health research for development and to ponder the challenge of strengthening this research, they face a monumental task. About $56bn (£37.3bn) per year is spent worldwide on health research by both the public and private sectors; this is more money than ever before.[1] Yet far more could be done both to increase the amount spent and to improve how funds are used. The Global Forum for Health Research, one of the sponsors of the Bangkok conference, estimates that less than 10% of research funds are spent on the diseases that account for 90% of the global burden of disease. This gap is now widely quoted as epitomising the inequitable nature of health research. The consequences of this gap are profound: diseases affecting large proportions of humanity are given comparatively little attention. Similarly, simple and low cost technologies, appropriate for use in settings with few resources, are undervalued and hence inadequately researched.[1]

Much of the problem lies in how health research is governed. Governance of health research concerns the means and rules by which relevant stakeholders set and achieve their agreed research goals. This includes decisions about what kind of research should be supported, by whom, and for what ends. How good the governance of health research is can be assessed by criteria such as representativeness, transparency, and accountability.[2] Achieving good governance of health research is essential for ensuring research is ethically conducted, relevant to the people who it is targeted for, and of recognised scientific quality.

The state of global health research suggests that too often governance is not good. Imbalances in financial and intellectual resources between the wealthy and poor have contributed to the latter being the subject of health research that primarily benefits the former. How ethical is it to test drugs for AIDS in countries that cannot afford these treatments?[3] Another challenge is that the competitiveness of medical research can hamper collaborative research.[4] Money for research into tropical medicine usually comes from funding bodies such as North American and European governments, foundations such as the Wellcome Trust and the Bill and Melinda Gates Foundation, and international agencies such as the World Health Organization's tropical diseases research programme. Each funding body tends to favour commissioning research themselves, rather than supporting research initiated by investigators; this makes it hard for some countries to set their own research priorities. Although there have been some efforts to improve coordination, for example through the multilateral initiative on malaria that tries to promote collaboration in the research community, most research relations are vertical—that is, they exist between research groups in a particular country and research groups or funders in the developed world. There is little horizontal interaction between research groups within countries.[5] It is difficult to scrutinise the quality of funding decisions because of poor data on how much money is spent worldwide, by whom, and for what purposes.

A second area of concern is the role of research in health policy making as a whole. Research should have an important role in the policy process, providing the evidence for identifying issues and prioritising them, laying out the options for addressing policy problems, and feeding back the appropriateness of those decisions. Health research is thus a central component of effective health governance.

In developing countries the ability of national institutions to produce and use high-quality health research that is appropriate to their own needs can be weak at every stage of the policy process as described by Sitthi-Amorn and Somrongthong in this issue (p 813).[6]

Financial and technical support from donors to train and retain national researchers in these countries, and to build up research institutions where researchers can ply their trade, remains woefully inadequate. Without such support, developing countries will continue to struggle to define their own needs and to contribute meaningfully to research that meets those needs. This matters for global health because understanding the health needs of poorer communities is critical to the collective good of health worldwide. Health research is the starting point for achieving such an understanding.

It is on this basis that a new approach to global health research could be initiated in Bangkok. Developing countries should not be seen as recipients of charitable handouts but as partners in producing health research that is of a high quality and tackles major problems such as health inequalities, infectious diseases, and changes in the environment.[7] Such an approach should begin with larger scale commitments by funding bodies to train researchers in developing countries in areas ranging from basic to applied research. Investment in research capacity would need to be made for the middle to long term, and it should be better coordinated and strategically deployed, should be programme based rather than project based, and should make a more serious commitment to building local, national, and regional institutions. What must be different, above all, and no doubt will be most difficult for funding bodies to accept, is the need to at least share the driver's seat when it comes to making decisions. From this starting point, the governance of health research would need to be very different.

Kelley Lee *senior lecturer in global health policy*
Anne Mills *professor of health economics and policy*

Department of Public Health and Policy, London School of Hygiene and Tropical Medicine, London WC1E 7HT

1 Global Forum for Health Research. *The 10/90 report on health research 2000*. Geneva: World Health Organization, 2000.
2 United Nations Development Programme. *Reconceptualising governance*. New York: Management Development and Governance Division, 1997.
3 Tan-Torres Edejer T. North-South research partnerships: the ethics of carrying out research in developing countries. *BMJ* 1999;319:438-41.
4 Trostle J, Simon J. Building applied research capacity in less-developed countries: problems encountered by the ADDR project. *Soc Sci Med* 1992;35:1279-87.
5 Wolffers I, Adjei S, van der Drift R. Health research in the tropics. *Lancet* 1998;351:1652-54.
6 Sitthi-amorn C, Somrongthong R. Strengthening health research capacity in developing countries: a critical element of achieving health equity. *BMJ* 2000;321:813-7.
7 Lee K. Globalisation—a new agenda for health? In: McKee M, Garner P, Stott R, eds. *International co-operation and health*. Oxford: Oxford University Press (in press).

Part VII
Public Health and Human Rights

[24]

IS THERE A GOVERNMENT IN THE COCKPIT: A PASSENGER'S PERSPECTIVE OR GLOBAL PUBLIC HEALTH: THE ROLE OF HUMAN RIGHTS

Sofia Gruskin[*]

I. INTRODUCTION

Since the creation of the United Nations ("UN") over fifty years ago, the world has increasingly recognized international responsibility for both public health and human rights. Embedded within a similar state-centric view of the world, these two areas nonetheless evolved along parallel but distinctly separate tracks. Traditionally, public health and human rights have each focused on the responsibility of governments to deliver services (health and otherwise), as well as to create the enabling conditions necessary for people to make and effectuate choices, cope with changing patterns of vulnerability, and keep themselves and their families healthy.[1] Within the past twenty years, the HIV/AIDS pandemic and reproductive and sexual health concerns have been central not only in bringing attention to the intrinsic connections between health and human rights and in clarifying the legal, policy, and programmatic ways in which they connect, but also in highlighting the boundaries of state action and the roles of other actors in both assuring the conditions necessary for health and for the delivery of the needed services.[2] While still placing the ultimate responsibility for the promotion of public health and human rights with the state, the fields of public health, human rights, and health and human rights are increasingly adapting to encompass the actions of other actors, ranging from nongovernmental organizations ("NGOs") to other civil society actors, such as multinational corporations, in their legal, advocacy, and programmatic work. But to what extent are governments still in the driver's seat? The challenge is now to

---

[*] Director of the Program on International Health & Human Rights at the François-Xavier Bagnoud Center for Health & Human Rights; Associate Professor of Health & Human Rights, Department of Population & International Health, Harvard School of Public Health. M.I.A., Columbia University; J.D., Cardozo School of Law.

1. *See* Sofia Gruskin & Daniel Tarantola, *Health and Human Rights, in* OXFORD TEXTBOOK OF PUBLIC HEALTH 311, 322 (Roger Detels et al. eds., 4th ed. 2002) (describing both public health and human rights as requiring governments to address health-related issues in a human rights sensitive way).

2. *See id.* at 311 (explaining how the global response to HIV/AIDS epidemic has included the need to protect human rights to be effective).

consider the contributions of these various actors and approaches to global health governance and the places where additional attention is needed to ensure the ultimate benefits to the health of populations. This article begins with an exploration of the ways in which human rights have come to be of relevance to global public health in the past twenty years. It then goes on to provide a review of the ways in which the formal structures and systems of human rights and of global health have been set up to deal with similar areas of concern. It then surveys the variety of approaches bringing human rights and health together and ends with a discussion of current challenges, in particular those concerning the accountability of non-state actors for their work in this area.

II. SOME RECENT HISTORY: HOW DID HUMAN RIGHTS COME TO BE IMPORTANT TO PUBLIC HEALTH WORK?

A. *Global Public Health Strategies*

The first global public health strategy to explicitly name human rights was promulgated in the late 1980s, when Jonathan Mann served as director of the Global Program on AIDS at the World Health Organization ("WHO").[3] The call for human rights and for compassion and solidarity with people living with HIV/AIDS embodied in the first WHO global response to AIDS was motivated by moral outrage but also, key to any consideration of state responsibility for health, by the recognition that protecting the human rights of people living with HIV/AIDS was a necessary element of the worldwide public health response to the emerging epidemics. The fact that people living with HIV were being denied access to care, social services, housing, employment, education, and other rights because they were living with HIV was offensive to their dignity, but it was also increasingly recognized to be counterproductive to public health, to economic development, and to the structures and institutions that are necessary for societies to function.[4] Quite simply, whether those with responsibility for health were interested in human rights or not, the evidence was showing that discrimination against people living with HIV was driving people underground, creating fertile ground for people not to know their HIV status, not to be tested, and to further the spread of the virus. While the public health motivation for combating this discrimination derived not from human rights per se, the implications of an intergovernmental organization setting forth this approach were far-reaching. WHO, as an intergovernmental organization, grounded its framing of a public health strategy in international law, therefore made governments and intergovernmental organizations publicly accountable for their

3. *See Global Strategy for the Prevention and Control of AIDS*, Res. WHA40.26, World Health Organization [hereinafter WHO] World Health Assemb., 40th Sess. (1987) (urging member states to recognize the role of non-discrimination in what is needed to enable people to protect themselves from HIV/AIDS).

4. Jonathan Mann & Daniel Tarantola, *Responding to HIV/AIDS: A Historical Perspective*, 2 HEALTH AND HUM. RTS. 5, 5-8 (1998).

actions toward people living with HIV/AIDS.[5] This helped draw attention not only to the responsibility of governments, and the international organizations such as WHO that serve them, to put policies and programs into place to reduce the impact of HIV and AIDS on the lives of individuals and populations, but also to the accountability of governments and international organizations for their actions (or inactions) in this area. The groundbreaking contribution of this effort lies not only in the recognition of the applicability of international law to HIV/AIDS issues, but also in the attention this approach then generated to the ultimate accountability of the state under international law for issues relating to health and well-being.

B. *Global Conferences*

In the past decade, an important role has been played by the series of international conferences held under the UN system's auspices in further solidifying state responsibility for health issues from within an international human rights framework. While each of these conferences—ranging from the World Summit for Children (1990) to the United Nations General Assembly Special Session on HIV/AIDS (2002)—is of relevance,[6] the 1994 International Conference on Population and Development ("ICPD") was the most crucial negotiated consensus document in articulating the dual obligations of governments for health and human rights concerns. Out of each of these conference processes comes a Declaration and Program of Action reflecting the consensus of the governments of the world. The ICPD Declaration and Program of Action explicitly framed, in human rights terms, its articulation of the health issues of concern and the accountability of states for addressing that.[7] Though technically "non-binding" commitments, these documents demonstrate the consensus of the world's nations that their international political and legal obligations encompass both health and human rights concerns, and that these nation states are accountable for taking steps to advance these concerns at local, national, and international levels.

C. *The United Nations System*

In recent years, there has been a substantial increase in attention and

5. Sofia Gruskin et al., *Human Rights and Responses to HIV/AIDS, in* AIDS IN THE WORLD II 326-40 (Jonathan Mann & Daniel Tarantola eds., 1996).

6. Most relevant are: United Nations General Assembly Special Session on Children, New York, USA (May 8-10, 2002); United Nations General Assembly Special Session on HIV/AIDS, New York, USA (June 25-27, 2001); United Nations Millennium Summit, New York, USA (Sept. 6-8, 2000); World Summit for Social Development, Copenhagen, Denmark (Mar. 5-12, 1995); Fourth World Conference on Women, Beijing, China (Sept. 4-15, 1995); International Conference on Population and Development (ICPD), Cairo, Egypt (Sept. 5-13, 1994); World Conference on Human Rights, Vienna, Austria (June 14-25, 1993).

7. *See Report of the International Conference on Population and Development*, Int'l Conf. on Population and Dev., at 56, U.N. Doc. A/CONF.171/13 (1994) (advising governments to take necessary actions in both health and human rights terms to improve reproductive health worldwide).

resources devoted to programmatic action in the global health arena framed with attention to human rights. These events are linked, in many ways, to the programs of action of the international conferences on health and population. The 1997 Program for Reform set forth by UN Secretary-General Kofi Annan, which highlights the promotion of human rights as among the United Nations system's core activities, has been another crucial step in moving the UN system's rhetorical attention to human rights in the health area towards concrete implementation, action, and accountability.[8] This process of mainstreaming human rights within the UN system requires assessing the human rights implications of any planned action, including legislation, policies or programs, in all areas and at all levels. It is a strategy for making human rights an integral dimension of the design, implementation, monitoring, and evaluation of policies and programs in political, economic and social spheres.[9] Virtually all development agencies, organizations, and programs of the UN, albeit to varying degrees, now pay attention to human rights in their work in the health field, in relation both to their activities with government partners and within their own efforts more generally. Each currently has policy documents and programmatic activities at various stages of development bringing together health and human rights work, and technical staff responsible for the integration or implementation of human rights into at least some aspects of their work.[10] Two examples may serve to illustrate some of the complexities of UN partners engaging with human rights in their global health responsibilities. United Nations Children's Fund's ("UNICEF"'s) mission statement, announced in the late 1990s, explicitly named pursuit of the rights of children and of women a fundamental purpose of the organization. This attention to rights then led to a restructuring of the organization; UNICEF is, to some degree, now accountable through the UN system to its members states for ensuring that their policy and programmatic work is guided by the principles and standards established by the Convention on the Rights of the Child and the Convention on the Elimination of All Forms of Discrimination Against Women.[11] Within WHO, a similar process began in 1999, with the aim of defining the goals of human rights mainstreaming for the

---

8. *See generally Renewing the United Nations: A Programme for Reform, Report of the Secretary-General*, U.N. GAOR, 51st Sess., Agenda Item 168, U.N. Doc: A/51/950 (1997) (reorganizing administration of U.N. activities including in the area of human rights).

9. *Coordination of the Policies and Activities of the Specialized Agencies and Other Bodies of the United Nations System Related to the Coordinated Follow-Up to and Implementation of the Vienna Declaration and Programme of Action, Report of the Secretary-General*, U.N. ESCOR, 1998 Sess., Agenda Item 4, PP U.N. Doc. E/1998/60 (1998).

10. WHO, Informal Consultation on Mainstreaming Human Rights in WHO, April 3-4 (2000), Geneva (report on file with author).

11. *See generally* UNICEF, A HUMAN RIGHTS APPROACH TO UNICEF PROGRAMMING FOR CHILDREN AND WOMEN: WHAT IT IS, AND SOME CHANGES IT WILL BRING (1998) (noting importance of the Convention on the Rights of the Child and the Convention on the Elimination of All Forms of Discrimination Against Women to UNICEF's mission), *available at* http://coe-dmha.org/Unicef/HPT_Intro Reading01.htm (last visited Sept. 27, 2004); UNICEF, MISSION STATEMENT (1996) (stating that the Convention on the Rights of the Child guides UNICEF's mission), *available at* http://www.unicef.org/crc/bg016.htm (last visited Sept. 27, 2004).

organization in its national and international health work. This process followed a 1998 World Health Assembly Resolution that set out the need to "promote and support the rights and principles, actions and responsibilities enunciated in the [World Health Declaration] through concerted action, full participation and partnership, calling on all peoples and institutions to share the vision of health for all in the twenty-first century, and to endeavour in common to realize it."[12] The past few years have seen efforts towards the creation of a strategy document that will commit and support WHO operationally in respecting, protecting, and fulfilling human rights in its policy and program work. It appears, however, that concerns about the degree of accountability this would engender has greatly constrained the process. Similar efforts under way in the Joint United Nations Program on HIV/AIDS ("UNAIDS"), the United Nations Development Program ("UNDP"), and the World Bank face related challenges.[13] Because it is the UN agencies' mission to service their member states and it is the UN agencies' that are bringing human rights into their public health responsibilities, these efforts must be grounded in strict interpretations of international human rights law. While this ensures that the UN agencies are on solid footing with all governments of the world—whether sympathetic to human rights or not—this slows down the operational side of these efforts.

D. National Level Governments

At a nation-state level, in developing and industrialized countries alike, a number of governments are beginning to integrate their human rights obligations into the ways they are carrying out their health-related activities. In part, this is because the international conference process highlighted that the international human rights obligations of a government include the actions of people who are working on behalf of the state, or with the support of the state, including those within departments of health and in other sectors of government whose actions may impact on health. It is also of note that efforts in this respect can be helpful in demonstrating governmental compliance with their international human rights obligations when reporting to the international human rights treaty monitoring bodies. Some governments are also finding that, apart from their accountability for doing so, the fact that human rights obligations extend to the government as a whole makes it possible to support diverse government partners—such as Ministries of Health, Departments of Justice, Women's Affairs, Foreign Affairs, etc.—in working together on health related issues. While the implications of this approach for resource allocation and priority setting are not yet sufficiently clear, in several countries it appears that an important byproduct of the use of

12. *Health-for-All Policy for the Twenty-First Century*, Res. WHA51.7, WHO World Health Assemb., 51st Sess., 10th plen. mtg., Annex: World Health Declaration, art. V (1998).

13. *See, e.g.*, *Memorandum of Understanding Between the U.N. Development Programme and the U.N. High Commissioner for Human Rights*, U.N. Dev. Programme (1998) (illustrating recognition of need to closely integrate human rights into operations of U.N. institutions); Sophia Gruskin, *The Conceptual and Practical Implications of Reproductive and Sexual Rights: How Far Have We Come?* 4 HEALTH & HUM. RTS. 1, 1-6 (2000).

the international human rights framework is a strengthening of the reach and effectiveness of Ministries of Health, who are often perceived as a weaker leg within state structures. This approach also serves to extend government responsibility and accountability for health to other arms of government. The technical assistance of various parts of the UN system, most notably UNICEF, United Nations Population Fund ("UNFPA"), UNAIDS, and pockets within the WHO, often support governmental efforts within this area.

E. The Particular Role of the United States

It is impossible in the current political reality to avoid specific mention of the United States and its role in relation to the ways that human rights are integrated into health concerns within this country, at the global level and within countries dependent on the US for development assistance. In 1998, under then President Clinton an Executive Order was issued that obliged the United States to fully respect and implement its obligations under the international human rights treaties to which it is a party and to "promote respect for international human rights in our relationships with all other countries."[14] As a result, all U.S. federal agencies, including those with health related responsibilities, were directed to re-examine their policies and strategies from the perspective of international human rights standards. While efforts in this area continue, recent developments, supported by the current US administration, such as increasing federal funding for abstinence-until-marriage sex education programs, which limit discussion about the health benefits of contraception, including condoms, in preventing unintended pregnancy, sexually transmitted infections (STIs), and HIV/AIDS, present serious challenges to both health and human rights concerns. At the 2001 United Nations General Assembly Special Session on HIV/AIDS, governments, lead by the United States, backed away from endorsement of a human rights based approach to HIV/AIDS. At the United Nations General Assembly Special Session on Children in 2002, adolescent rights to access to appropriate and scientifically accurate reproductive and sexual health information and services was seriously challenged by a curious alliance of states—including the United States, Sudan, Iran, and the Holy See. What is at stake is not a matter of US partisanship, or only of concern to people living in the US, Sudan or Iran, the commitment to ensuring access to information and services goes to the heart of human rights based approaches to health.

III. FORMAL SYSTEMS: HOW IS THE INTERNATIONAL HUMAN RIGHTS SYSTEM SET UP TO ENGAGE WITH HEALTH?

A. Human Rights Norms, Standards and Institutions

While human rights thinking and practice has a long history, after World

14. William Jefferson Clinton, Executive Order on Implementation of Human Rights Treaties. Exec. Order No. 13,107, 3 C.F.R 234 (1998).

War II the importance of human rights for governmental actions and accountability was only widely recognized. Nation-states reached agreement that all people "are born free and equal in dignity and rights" in 1945 when the promotion of human rights was identified as a principal purpose of the newly created UN.[15] The UN Charter established general obligations that apply to all its member states, including respect for human rights and dignity.[16] In practical terms, international human rights law is fundamentally about what governments can do to us, cannot do to us, and should do for us. For example, governments obviously should not torture people, imprison them arbitrarily or invade their privacy, but should ensure that all people in a society have shelter, food, medical care, and basic education. Since its adoption in 1948, the Universal Declaration of Human Rights ("UDHR") has set a common standard of achievement for all peoples and all nations.[17] The UN has overseen the formulation of more than twenty multilateral human rights treaties since the adoption of the UDHR. These treaties create legally binding obligations on the nations that ratify them, thereby giving them the status and power of international law.

The key international human rights treaties, the International Covenant on Economic, Social and Cultural Rights ("ICESCR") and the International Covenant on Civil and Political Rights ("ICCPR") further elaborate the content of the rights set out in the UDHR and contain legally binding obligations for the governments that ratify the treaties.[18] According to the latest data available, as of November 2003, 148 countries had ratified the ICESCR and 151 had ratified the ICCPR.[19] Building upon these core documents, other international human rights treaties have focused on either specific populations, e.g., the International Convention on the Elimination of All Forms of Racial Discrimination (1965),[20] the Convention on the Elimination of All Forms of Discrimination Against Women (1979),[21] and the Convention on the Rights of the Child (1989),[22] or on specific issues, e.g., the Convention Against Torture and other Cruel, Inhuman or Degrading Treatment or Punishment (1984).[23] At this point in time, every country in the world. except the United States and Somalia. has ratified the

15. U.N. CHARTER art.1, art. 13 para. 1.b., art. 55, art. 62, art. 68, art. 73, art.76.

16. *Id.*

17. *See generally* G.A. Res. 217, U.N. GAOR, 3d Sess., pt. 1, at 71, U.N. Doc. A/810 (1948) (promoting respect for all peoples' rights).

18. G.A. Res. 2200, 21st Sess., Supp. No. 16, at 49, U.N. Doc. A/6316 (1967) (creating International Covenant on Economic, Social and Cultural Rights and International Covenant on Civil and Political Rights).

19. OFFICE OF THE U.N. HIGH COMMISSIONER FOR HUMAN RIGHTS, STATUS OF RATIFICATIONS OF THE PRINCIPAL INTERNATIONAL HUMAN RIGHTS TREATIES 12 [hereinafter RATIFICATIONS], *at* http://www.unhchr.ch/pdf/report.pdf (Jun. 9, 2004).

20. G.A. Res. 2106 (XX), Annex, U.N. GAOR, 20th Sess., Supp. No. 14, at 47, U.N. Doc. A/6014 (1965).

21. G.A. Res. 34/180, U.N. GAOR, 34th Sess., Supp. No. 46, at 193, U.N. Doc. A/34/46 (1979).

22. G.A. Res. 44/25, U.N. GAOR, 44th Sess., Supp. No. 49, at 167, U.N. Doc. A/44/49 (1989).

23. G.A. Res. 39/46, U.N. GAOR, 39th Sess., Supp. No. 51, at 197, U.N. Doc. A/39/51 (1984).

Convention on the Rights of the Child.[24] There are also regional human rights treaties, which concern essentially the same sets of rights but are only open for signature by states in the relevant region, such as the African (Banjul) Charter on Human and Peoples' Rights (1986),[25] the American Convention on Human Rights (1992),[26] and the European Convention on the Protection of Human Rights (1959).[27] Only the Asian region does not contain such a treaty.

Attention to governmental responsibility for health, means that governments are responsible, not only for not directly violating rights, but also for ensuring the conditions which enable people to realize their rights as fully as possible.[28] These treaties codify health and government responsibility for health in several ways. The right to the highest attainable standard of health appears in one form or another in most every one of them; however, governmental obligations in relation to health are understood to attach not only to the right to health, but to the whole range of rights that can be relevant to health.[29] While the U.S. government may not recognize the right to health as such, the right to health has been recognized by 148 other countries, both resource rich and resource poor. It is worth noting that every country in the world is party to at least one human rights treaty that includes attention to rights that are relevant to health; every country is therefore legally responsible and accountable under international law for human rights as they relate to health.

The bodies of the UN system with responsibility for human rights are increasingly focusing attention on the legal accountability of states for health-related concerns. This is most easily seen in changes in the efforts and reporting guidelines of the human rights treaty monitoring bodies, and the issues they are choosing to focus on in their dialogues with the State parties.[30] Countries that become party to international human rights treaties accept certain procedures

24. RATIFICATIONS at 2-11.

25. African (Banjul) Charter on Human and Peoples Rights, June 27, 1981, OAU Doc. CAB/LEG/67/3 rev. 5, 21 I.L.M. 58 (1982) (entered into force Oct. 21, 1986).

26. American Convention on Human Rights: "Pact of San José, Costa Rica," Nov. 22, 1969, 1144 U.N.T.S. 123 (entered into force July 18, 1978).

27. Convention for the Protection of Human Rights and Fundamental Freedoms, Nov. 4, 1950, 213 U.N.T.S. 222 (entered into force Sept. 9, 1953), as amended by Protocols Nos. 3, 5, 8, and 11 (entered into force on Sept. 21, 1970; Dec. 20, 1971; Jan. 1, 1990; and Nov. 1, 1998, respectively).

28. *See* Asbjørne Eide, *Economic, Social and Cultural Rights as Human Rights*, *in* ECONOMIC, SOCIAL AND CULTURAL RIGHTS: A TEXTBOOK 21, 21-40 (Asbjørne Eide et al. eds., 1995) (discussing acceptance of economic, social, and cultural rights as human rights); Gruskin & Tarantola, *supra* note 1, at 315-16 (stating requirements of governments to respect, protect, and fulfill people's right to health).

29. *See Substantive Issues Arising in the Implementation of the International Covenant on Economic, Social and Cultural Rights: General Comment No. 14*, U.N. ESCOR, 22d Sess., Agenda Item 3, at 2, U.N. Doc E/C.12/2000/4 (2000) (characterizing such rights as food, education, equality, etc., as "components of the right to health").

30. *See Compilation of Guidelines on the Form and Content of Reports to be Submitted by States Parties to the International Human Rights Treaties, Report of the Secretary-General*, Int'l Hum. Rts. Instruments, at 26, U.N. Doc. HRI/GEN/2/REV.1 (2001) (requiring member states to submit, within one year of ratification of the Covenant, a report detailing steps that the state has taken to effectuate the rights provided for in the Covenant).

and responsibilities, including periodic submission of reports on their compliance with the substantive provisions of the texts to these international treaty-monitoring bodies. The focus is on resource poor and resource rich countries alike, as the accountability framework distinguishes between government unwillingness and government incapacity. Resource rich countries must also account for their actions in relation to health beyond their own borders, for example, providing information about what they are doing in terms of technical assistance and cooperation in other countries. Each of the treaty monitoring bodies meets several times each year. The procedure for such monitoring is formal. The government under review must submit a copy of their report approximately two months before the meeting and, of relevance here, health-oriented UN institutions, such as WHO, UNAIDS, or UNICEF are invited to provide the treaty bodies with information on the state of health and the performance of health systems in the country under review.[31] NGOs can also submit informal reports (often termed shadow reports), as well as state their views on the situations and issues at stake. After review of this information and dialogue with the government in question, the relevant treaty body issues Concluding Comments and Observations which provide suggested areas of government intervention in health, development, and other related fields. [32]

While the formal human rights system was slow to take on health issues in any significant way, as the utility of these modalities for ensuring state responsibility and accountability for health has become clearer, there have been increasing efforts and resources devoted to strengthening what is being done with respect to health in recent years. Beyond the work of the human rights treaty monitoring bodies, including the adoption of the 2000 ICESCR General Comment on the Right to the Highest Attainable Standard of Health, other notable efforts under way include the work of the UN Special Rapporteur on the Right to Health, and a variety of initiatives by the other Charter-based bodies of the UN system in particular with respect to HIV/AIDS, maternal mortality, reproductive health, and the so-called "neglected diseases."[33] Governments themselves, through the creation of commissions and ombudspersons, as well as NGOs and the media, monitor government accountability for meeting legal commitments not only at the international level but also, in many places, at the national level. [34]

---

31. *See Effective Implementation of International Instruments on Human Rights, Including Reporting Obligations Under International Instruments on Human Rights, Note by the Secretariat*, U.N. GAOR, 58th Sess., Agenda Item 119(a), at 2, U.N. Doc. A/58/350 (2003) (describing meeting process).

32. *See id.* at 13-14 (listing recommendations to strengthen treaty system).

33. *See The Right of Everyone to the Enjoyment of the Highest Attainable Standard of Physical and Mental Health*, U.N. Comm'n on Hum. Rts., Res. 2002/31, 49th mtg. (2002) (appointing a special rapporteur to monitor efforts of governments in pursuing highest attainable standard of physical and mental health).

34. *See* Gruskin & Tarantola, *supra* note 1, at 317-19 (describing these institutions as a vital source for maintaining government compliance).

B. One Conceptual Point: The Protection of Public Health Within the International Human Rights Legal Framework

The international human rights framework recognizes that responsibility for public health is much broader than simply the control of infectious disease, and that the control of infectious disease is only one component of global health governance.[35] The measures needed, and taken, by governments in the context of the recent Severe Acute Respiratory Syndrome ("SARS") outbreak have, however, brought questions about the compatibility of public health and human rights approaches to health and well-being in the control of infectious disease both within countries and globally back to the fore.[36] The major human rights instruments were all developed in the post-World War II era and, in spite of the importance attached to the promotion and protection of human rights, these instruments recognize that there are situations where it is legitimate to restrict rights in order to achieve a broader public good. As described in the ICCPR, the public good can take precedence to: "secure due recognition and respect for the rights and freedoms of others; meet the just requirements of morality, public order, and the general welfare; and in times of emergency, when there are threats to the vital interests of the nation."[37] Public health is one such recognized public good. Traditional public health measures generally focused on curbing the spread of disease by imposing restrictions on the rights of those already infected or thought to be most vulnerable to becoming infected. The restrictions on rights that occur in the context of public health generally have as their first concern the protection of the public's health; coercion, compulsion, and restriction have historically been significant components of these measures.[38] Interference with freedom of movement when instituting quarantine or isolation

---

35. Article 21 of the WHO's Constitution states:

> The Health Assembly shall have authority to adopt regulations concerning: (a) sanitary and quarantine requirements and other procedures designed to prevent the international spread of disease; (b) nomenclatures with respect to diseases, causes of death and public health practices; (c) standards with respect to diagnostic procedures for international use; (d) standards with respect to the safety, purity and potency of biological, pharmaceutical and similar products moving in international commerce; (e) advertising and labeling of biological; pharmaceutical and similar products moving in international commerce.

36. *See generally* David P. Fidler, *Constitutional Outlines of Public Health's "New World Order,"* 77 TEMP. L. REV. 247 (2004); Jason W. Sapsin et al., *SARS and International Legal Preparedness*, 77 TEMP. L. REV. 155 (2004).

37. *See International Covenant on Civil and Political Rights*, G.A. Res. 2200, 21st Sess., Supp. No. 16, at 49, 53, 55 (stating in Article 4 that "[i]n time of public emergency which threatens the life of the nation and the existence of which is officially proclaimed, the States Parties to the present Covenant may take measures derogating from their obligations under the present Covenant to the extent strictly required by the exigencies of the situation, provided that such measures are not inconsistent with their other obligations under international law and do not involve discrimination solely on the ground of race, colour, sex, language, religion or social origin.")

38. *See, e.g.*, Stephen Smith, *The Powers and Duties of the Board of Health*, 2 SOC. DISEASES 18, 18-24 (1911) (describing broad powers available to Department of Health of New York City to act during public health emergencies); T.A. Schmidt, *When Public Health Competes with Individual Needs*, 2 ACAD. EMERGENCY MED. 217, 217-22 (1995).

for a serious communicable disease—for example typhoid or untreated tuberculosis—is an example of a restriction on rights that may, within a specific set of facts, be necessary for the public good and therefore could be considered legitimate under international human rights law. It is nonetheless also true that measures taken in the name of public health are often excessive, and that a check on potential abuse is of utmost importance.

Certain rights are absolute, which means that restrictions may never be placed on them, even if justified as necessary for the public good. These include such rights as the right to be free from torture, slavery, or servitude; the right to a fair trial; and the right to freedom of thought. Paradoxically, the right to life, which might at first glance appear to be inalienable, is not absolute; what is forbidden is the arbitrary deprivation of life. It is possible to justify interference with most rights as necessary under narrowly defined circumstances.[39] Limitations on rights, however, are considered a serious issue under international human rights law, regardless of the apparent importance of the public good involved. When a government limits the exercise or enjoyment of human rights, it must do so only as a last resort and this limitation will only be considered legitimate if it meets the following criteria:

1. The restriction is provided for and carried out in accordance with the law;
2. The restriction is in the interest of a legitimate objective of general interest;
3. The restriction is strictly necessary to achieve the objective;
4. There are no less intrusive and restrictive means available to reach the same objective; and
5. The restriction is not unreasonable or otherwise discriminatory in the way it is written in law or policy or in the way it is applied.[40]

This framework, although still rudimentary, may be helpful in identifying actions that are abusive, whether intentionally or unintentionally. Restrictions on rights in the context of the SARS outbreak last year, as well as now, would require rigorous examination under these criteria by the government officials charged with responsibility for determining the course of action to follow. Relevant considerations would include the legal and political context within which the outbreak is happening and the current state of knowledge about the virus and its spread. The burden of proof falls on those who want to restrict rights, and it is in genuinely responding to these criteria, in particular the final three, that public health evidence is needed and that the utility of bringing public health and human rights tools and approaches together becomes clear.

The international legal human rights framework does not, in and of itself,

---

39. See *supra* note 36 and accompanying text for a discussion of Article 4 of the International Covenant on Civil and Political Rights, which provides that even during public health emergencies, certain defined rights shall not be restricted.

40. *See generally Siracusa Principles on the Limitations and Derogation Provisions in the International Covenant on Civil and Political Rights*, U.N. ESCOR Sub-Comm'n on Prevention of Discrimination and Protection of Minorities, Annex, 41st Sess., Agenda Item 18, U.N. Doc. E/CN.4/1985/4 (1985) (setting out analytical framework).

conflict with restrictions on rights as long as both the objectives and the process used to make the decision to restrict rights are clear, and it does not privilege protection of individual rights over the "public good." The focus is on processes, not the imposition of any preordained results.[41] A health and human rights approach mandates, however, that the adoption of any public health strategy be informed by evidence and debated openly and that public health decisions, whether or not rights are to be restricted, are made through transparent and accountable processes. This is necessary to protect against the imposition of unproven and potentially abusive and counterproductive strategies, even if they are motivated by genuine despair and fear, for example, in the face of the emerging threat that SARS was/is assumed to present. While it is possible to use the international human rights system to hold public health authorities accountable for measures that restrict rights and fail to consider other valid alternatives, not only of human rights norms but also of public health "best practice," the frameworks of accountability within the global public health system are very different.

IV. More Formal Systems: How Is the International Health System Set Up to Engage with Accountability and the Protection of Human Rights?

A. *Norms, Standards, and Institutions*

The World Health Assembly ("WHA") of the WHO is the forum where the governments of the world formulate and debate international public health policies. This policy work is done primarily through World Health Assembly Resolutions, enforcement of the International Health Regulations, and now includes also attention to the Framework Convention for Tobacco Control. The 193 Member States of the WHO adopt WHA Resolutions on policy and administrative matters through the World Health Assembly, or its Executive Board.[42] Almost every issue in global health, from approaches to disease prevention and control to compliance with the Millennium Development Goals, is debated through the WHA process. Although in recent years, NGOs, professional groups, manufacturers and distributors of health goods, consumer organizations, academia, and other institutions have contributed to the debates, the resolutions are only open to governments for adoption. Member States generally pass these resolutions by consensus, with any reservations being stated for the record. Resolutions are not considered to be legally binding, with the exception of those resolutions that approve the scale of assessed contributions and regulations adopted pursuant to Article 21 of the WHO Constitution.[43] The level of accountability for the decisions taken by the WHA is unfortunately fairly

---

41. Sofia Gruskin & Bebe Loff, *Do Human Rights Have a Role in Public Health Work?*, THE LANCET, Dec. 7, 2002, at 1880.

42. WHO CONST. arts. 19, 21, 28.

43. WHO CONST. art. 21.

limited in that the interest of Member States to revisit an issue is required for any sustained engagement.

In one form or another, the International Health Regulations ("IHR") have been in place since 1951, and even then they were replacing sanitary treaties that had been in existence since the early twentieth century.[44] The IHR are legally binding on all WHO Member States unless they register reservations within six months of adoption, or reject them in their entirety.[45] In addition to currently requiring reporting of three infectious diseases (cholera, plague, yellow fever), the IHR emphasize epidemiological surveillance for communicable disease recognition and control and outline the maximum protective measures acceptable for use by Member States in order to prevent disproportionate action by one Member State against another.[46] At the level of accountability, governments are expected to provide this disease reporting information to the WHO Secretariat. Beginning with a 1995 resolution of the WHA, the WHO has been revisiting IHR to expand their scope to include diseases of current importance and define new approaches towards control of these diseases.[47] The WHA has scheduled a review of the revised IHR in May 2005 and the WHO Member States will need to vote before any changes can be made to the form, content, or approach of the IHR. The fears of new threats to health because of terrorism and the rapid international spread of SARS seem to have inspired a shift in the attitude of Member States, as reflected in a 2003 Resolution, from a primary concern with national sovereignty in health matters to greater global accountability and transparency.[48] However, it appears that while Member States will agree to consider information provided outside formal government processes, for example by media and NGOs, they will insist that any actions taken as a result of this information be done only in close consultation with the government in question.[49] It is therefore likely that the framework of accountability under the IHR will largely remain the same even as the

---

44. *See International Health Regulations*, WHO, *at* http://www.who.int/csr/ihr/en/ (last visited Sep. 20, 2004) (stating history of IHR from first International Sanitary Conference in 1851).

45. *See* WHO CONST. art. 22 (allowing WHO members to notify Director-General of any rejections or reservations regarding regulations adopted by the Health Assembly pursuant to Article 21).

46. *International Health Regulations*, WHO World Health Assemb., 22d Sess., pt. II, arts. 2-11 (1969), *amended in* 1973 and 1981.

47. *See* Res. WHA56.28, WHO World Health Assemb., 56th Sess. (2003) (creating committee to recommend revisions to International Health Regulations); Res. WHA55.16, WHO World Health Assemb., 55th Sess. (2002) (recommending enhanced global surveillance of infectious diseases); Res. WHA54.14, WHO World Health Assemb., 54th Sess. (2001) (calling on member states to maintain up-to-date information regarding control of infectious diseases); Res. WHA48.13, WHO World Health Assemb., 48th Sess. (1995) (requesting creation of means to better identify emerging diseases); Res. WHA48.7, WHO World Health Assemb., 48th Sess. (1995) (urging revision of International Health Regulations).

48. *See* Res. WHA56.28, *supra* note 46 (expressing concern over both threats to health from terrorist attacks and spread of SARS).

49. WHO Exec. Board Mtg., January 19-24, 2004, *at* http://www.who.int/gb/e/e_eb113.html (last visited Sep. 20, 2004).

Regulations themselves may take a very different form.

In 1996, the WHA requested the "development of a framework convention (on tobacco control) in accordance with Article 19 of the WHO Constitution."[50] This was the first time WHO used its constitutional mandate to elaborate and adopt an international convention. The framework convention is a legal instrument in the form of an international treaty to which signatory states agree to pursue broadly stated goals and, over time, to elaborate specific protocols. It is meant to build incrementally, building on international consensus and scientific knowledge. The WHA began working on the Convention in 1999 and it was adopted unanimously by the 56th World Health Assembly on May 21, 2003.[51] The Framework Convention on Tobacco Control becomes law for individual Member States only after signature and ratification. While similar to international human rights treaties in that it is open for ratification by Member States, there is no international monitoring body in place to ensure accountability, although signatory governments are meant to provide periodic reports to the WHA regarding their efforts towards compliance.

B. One Conceptual Point: Explicit Attention to Human Rights by the International Health System

The 1946 Constitution of the WHO projected a vision of health as a state of complete physical, mental, and social well-being—recognizing that the enjoyment of the highest attainable standard of health was one of the fundamental rights of every human being and that governments have a responsibility for the health of their peoples, which can be fulfilled only through the provision of adequate health and social measures.[52] This definition of health was an important step in helping to move global health actions beyond more limited biomedical and pathology-based perspectives towards the more positive domain of well-being. Nonetheless, when the WHO was created it was hoped that within the foreseeable future that antibiotics and the progress achieved in vaccines and biomedical technology would provide sufficient tools to enable individuals everywhere in the world to reach the highest attainable standard of physical, mental, and social health.[53] The public health world has since recognized that regardless of the effectiveness of technologies, many of the major determinants of better health are outside the health system. The underlying civil, cultural, economic, political, and social conditions at both a global and local level also have to be addressed. Better education and information must be provided, as well as fulfillment of an array of rights, which are relevant to, but not intrinsically connected to, the right to health. Both the Declaration of Alma-Ata (1978), and the Ottawa Charter for Health Promotion

---

50. Res. WHA49.17, WHO World Health Assemb., 49th Sess. (1996).

51. Res. WHA56.1, WHO World Health Assemb., 56th Sess. (2003).

52. WHO CONST. pmbl.

53. *See* Katarina Tomasevski, *Health*, *in* 2 UNITED NATIONS LEGAL ORDER 859, 901-05 (Oscar Schachter & Christopher C. Joyner eds., 1995) (noting this history including WHO's reluctance to advocate for changes in law to promote good health throughout the world).

(1986), while not naming human rights per se, emphasized these dimensions of health. The Alma-Ata Declaration describes health as a social goal whose realization requires the action of many social and economic sectors in addition to the health sector.[54] The Ottawa Charter proposes the fundamental conditions and resources for health to be peace, shelter, education, food, income, a stable ecosystem, sustainable resources, social justice, and equity.[55] In 1998, the World Health Assembly reaffirmed the commitment of nations to strive towards these goals in a WHA Resolution that stressed the "will to promote health by addressing the basic determinants and prerequisites for health" and the urgent priority "to pay the greatest attention to those most in need, burdened by ill health, receiving inadequate services for health or affected by poverty."[56] The current Director-General of the WHO has reaffirmed the Organization's commitment to Alma-Ata and has linked this to promotion and protection of human rights.[57]

An understanding has developed that responsibility for global public health requires attention to the increasingly complex relationship of people to their environment. Work by the international health system to integrate human rights is primarily driven by the recognition that the respect, protection and fulfillment of civil, political, economic, social, and cultural human rights, is necessary not because they are the binding legal obligations of governments but because they are critical to improving the health status of individuals and populations. This recognition helps to set the frame for a careful examination of the role of governments and of other actors in delivering equal and equitable health services and striving to create the underlying conditions necessary for health.

V. BEYOND THE FORMAL SYSTEMS: HOW ARE HUMAN RIGHTS AND PUBLIC HEALTH APPROACHES ACTUALLY BEING BROUGHT TOGETHER?

For a variety of reasons, actors within the UN system, governments, and nongovernmental organizations are using very different approaches in bringing the language of human rights and health together in their work these days. This is the case whether organizations are working in direct service, engaged in programmatic efforts, responsible for health policy, or health advocacy. Some are using human rights in a strictly legal sense, basing their work in strictly-accepted internationally agreed to definitions, not on what they mean in any one particular country or cultural setting. Others are pushing to expand these definitions and are working to build the legal and political structures that can

---

54. Int'l Conf. on Primary Health Care, Declaration of Alma-Ata art. II (1978).

55. FIRST INT'L CONF. ON HEALTH PROMOTION, OTTAWA CHARTER FOR HEALTH PROMOTION, para. 4, U.N. Doc. WHO/HPR/HEP/95.1 (1986) (conference co-sponsored by Canadian Public Health Association, Health and Welfare Canada, and the WHO).

56. Res. WHA51.7, WHO World Health Assemb., 51st Sess. (1998).

57. *See* Lee Jong-wook, *Global Health Improvement and WHO: Shaping the Future*, THE LANCET, Dec. 20, 2003, at 2084 (suggesting adherence to Alma-Ata's missions of "equitable access, community participation, and intersectoral approaches to health improvement" as method of addressing current health inequalities).

support any expanded definitions. Others are more concerned with how notions of rights can inform their work, whether or not these rights have, per se, been legally recognized. These three frameworks are offered below in the hopes that attention to their similarities and differences may help to clarify the different ways in which human rights are currently engaged with global health work. These frameworks represent different paradigms and the hope here is to draw attention to where they connect, where they conflict, and where they overlap. Different approaches have their place at different times and in different situations, but explicit acknowledgement of these differences is imperative to our ability to consider the roles of various actors and approaches in global health and human rights work now and in the future.

A. *The Law and Policy Framework*

This approach to health and human rights is grounded in international human rights law at international and national levels and is focused on relating these norms, standards, and accountability mechanisms to health related efforts. This includes not only engaging with law in the formal sense, but also employing human rights norms and standards in the work of global and national health, economic and development policy-making bodies, in relation to the specifics of the underlying determinants of health as well as to the availability, acceptability, accessibility, and quality of health systems, including their outcomes among different population groups. Some of this work includes building on the consonance between national law and international human rights norms, for example, to promote and protect the rights of people living with HIV/AIDS through litigation. Increasingly, efforts here also include working with human rights structures within countries, such as national government human rights commissions to bring health concerns more substantially into their work. At the international level, this includes working with and through the international human rights bodies and mechanisms to promote the accountability of governments for their health related actions. There is a strong focus on the laws, policies, and formal systems described earlier in this article; there is also attention given to how and if human rights have been incorporated by governments in their actions which impact on health. This includes paying attention to what systems are in place to promote and to protect health related rights. This framework is premised on the legal and political responsibility and accountability of states under international law for doing this work. The actors engaged in this work include governments, the UN system, and NGOs, and while there are differences in emphasis, there is a great deal of commonality in the conceptual approach to doing this work.

B. *The Advocacy Framework*

Efforts from this perspective are focused on mobilizing for change. This includes recognizing and exposing governmental obligations, determining the level of government action or inaction that contributes to the fact that violations exist, looking at how a government deals or does not deal with these issues once they are identified, and providing recommendations and approaches as to what can be done. There is a focus on transparency, accountability, and functioning norms and systems to promote and protect health related rights, whether of individuals or of communities. This also means linking with and supporting activists working on related issues (such as groups focused on violence against women, poverty, and global trade issues), translating international human rights norms to the work and concerns of local communities, and supporting the organizing capabilities of affected communities. Advocacy is a key component of most organizations' work in health and human rights, whether government, UN system, or NGO. NGOs are not as constrained by the strict interpretation of international human rights law that is required of UN system partners and governments in how they work with human rights in their health related advocacy. These NGOs have far more flexibility to push the legal and political boundaries of health and human rights work—but until recently were fairly reluctant to do so. Hearteningly, NGOs with a human rights focus such as Amnesty International and Human Rights Watch are now significantly increasing their concerns for health in the human rights work they do.[58] One may cite a number of reasons for this increase, ranging from the call to action required by the catastrophic proportions of the HIV/AIDS pandemic, to more mundane organizationally driven motives, such as a move beyond a tight focus on civil and political rights to attention to economic, social, and cultural rights—including the right to health. These developments are not only helping to shape new forms of advocacy but are also bringing increased attention to government responsibility for the health of their populations.

C. *The Programmatic Framework*

This approach is concerned with the implementation of human rights in health programming and includes also operationalizing human rights work within an organization's individual programs and departments. Here the focus is less on international legal norms and more on the effectiveness of interventions for health, including the design, implementation, monitoring, and evaluation of health programs. This perspective requires explicit consideration of the civil,

58. There is an emerging focus on health in human rights endeavors. *See, e.g.*, Amnesty International, *Rwanda: "Marked for Death," Rape Survivors Living with HIV/AIDS in Rwanda*, *at* http://web.amnesty.org/library/Index/ENGAFR470072004?open&of=ENG-RWA (Apr. 6, 2004) (reporting on situation of persons who have contracted HIV/AIDS as a result of sexual assault); Amnesty International, *Harming the Healers: Violations of the Human Rights of Health Professionals* 1-18, *at* http://web.amnesty.org/library/index/engact750022000 (May 22, 2000) (reviewing cases of mistreatment of health care workers and the responses by NGO's and professional bodies); Human Rights Watch, *Unprotected: Sex, Condoms and the Human Right to Health*, 16 HUM. RTS. WATCH No. 6 (2004) (discussing government inaction in the face of HIV/AIDS in the Philippines), *available at* http://hrw.org/reports/2004/philippines0504/ (last visited Sept. 26, 2004); Human Rights Watch, *Locked Doors: The Human Rights of People Living with HIV/AIDS in China*, 15 HUM. RTS. WATCH No. 7 (2003) (describing situation of HIV positive persons in China, including those who contracted the disease from government blood plasma drives), *available at* http://www.hrw.org/reports/2003/china0803/ (last visited Sept. 26, 2004).

political, economic, social, and cultural factors that surround the studies and interventions that are carried out. Concerns with discrimination and inequality, and consciously taking into account such factors as gender relations, religious beliefs, homophobia, and racism, that individually, and in combination, influence the extent to which individuals and communities are protected from discrimination, inequality, and exclusion and their ability to access services and to make and carry out free and informed decisions about their lives are key to this approach. The programmatic approach often also includes attention to ensuring the participation of affected communities at every stage of work.

Bringing human rights into public health programming also raises a number of questions including: what information, education, health and social services are being provided to what populations and in what ways? Who and what is being left out and in what ways? How are decisions being made about the types of studies and interventions that are being formed and conducted? Who is making these decisions, and according to what criteria? Were affected communities a part of these processes? Have they been able to meaningfully participate in the decisions that will potentially affect their health? The application of human rights norms and standards to public health programming does not necessarily change the results, but it brings a conscious focus to transparency and accountability in how these questions are answered. Work in this area varies widely in that there is no definitive way in which human rights norms and standards are being applied to public health programming efforts, and these efforts are still new enough that any sort of "compendium of best practice" remains elusive.[59] NGOs that focus on health or development issues, many of which previously saw human rights as having little relevance to their work, are increasingly using the rhetoric of human rights and their methods of analysis to help shape their interventions.[60] While governments and the UN system must work within accepted legal definitions, the lack of constraint on the work of NGOs in this respect is helping to give some perspective to how human rights may most effectively be used in programming efforts in the coming years.

VI. A Note on Accountability: State and Non-State Actors

Globalization and the direct and indirect impacts of intensifying global flows of money, trade, information, culture, and people on health and related

59. *See, e.g.*, Emma Harris-Curtis, *Rights-based Approaches–Issues for NGOs*, 13 DEV. IN PRAC. 558, 558-64 (2003) (analyzing various issues involving NGO's and rights-based approaches, including the role of the state and issues of faith); *Report of the Second Interagency Workshop on Implementing a Human Rights-Based Approach in the Context of UN Reform*, (May 5-7, 2003) (outlining recommendations for organizations to follow in implementing human rights based approaches), *available at* http://www.humanrights.se/svenska/Common%20Understanding%20FN%202003.pdf; U.N. High Comm'n on Human Rights, *Human Rights in Development: Rights Based Approaches*, *at* http://www.unhchr.ch/development/approaches-04.html (last visited Sept. 12, 2004) (describing methodology of human rights based approaches to international development work).

60. *See, e.g.*, David Patterson, Statement of ICASO to the United Nations Commission on Human Rights International Council of AIDS Service Organizations (Apr. 16, 1999) (addressing human rights in HIV/AIDS prevention context).

aspects of human development have brought out new sets of issues and concerns for both health and human rights. The process of globalization has proceeded at a much faster pace than the development of governmental policies and programs aimed to maximize globalization's benefits to human development and to prevent or mitigate its harmful effects. The international human rights framework draws attention to the legal obligation of the state to ensure that all human beings are guaranteed their basic human rights, whether this obligation is fulfilled directly through government-run services or through private intermediaries.[61] Governmental roles and responsibilities are increasingly being delegated to non-state actors (e.g., private foundations, biomedical research institutions, health insurance companies, health management organizations, and the pharmaceutical industry). Political and social forces are increasingly calling on these institutions to create and operate alternative mechanisms to extend health and social services and to make available new and affordable vaccines and drugs.[62] These requests highlight the roles of a range of actors beyond governments, the international organizations that represent them, and the NGOs that hold them accountable. Today, the places where world issues are debated have expanded from assemblies of governments, for example within the UN system, to gatherings such as the forum at Davos—demonstrating that the state and non-state actors that lead the world economy have become inseparable partners. From a health and human rights perspective, the desirable forms and extent of responsibility for these non-state actors within the international legal system have yet to be defined in ways that help to ensure their accountability for what they do, do not do, or should do about people's health. The role of these non-state actors is thus poorly defined and inadequately monitored.

The use of human rights norms and processes to hold the private sector accountable and to directly make claims against them at the national level has been effective within some legal systems, but current structures are generally insufficient to effectively monitor and hold these actors accountable, even those operating on a national scale.[63] This problem is compounded when these companies or foundations are multinational, in that because they are multinational, they largely escape the realm of legal accountability within states.

61. Gro Harlem Brundtland, *Fifty Years of Synergy Between Health and Rights*, 3 HEALTH AND HUM. RTS. 21, 21-5 (1998).

62. *See, e.g.*, The Bill And Melinda Gates Foundation, *at* www.gatesfoundation.org (last visited July 24, 2004) (stating their purpose of work); The Global Alliance for Vaccines and Immunization, *at* http://www.vaccinealliance.org (last visited July 24, 2004) (stating purpose to expand use of vaccines and introduce new ones); The Global Fund to Fight AIDS, Tuberculosis and Malaria, *at* www.theglobalfund.org/en (last visited July 24, 2004) (focusing on managing and disbursing resources).

62. *See generally* Kamal Hossain, *Globalization and Human Rights: Clash of Universal Aspirations and Special Interests, in* THE FUTURE OF INTERNATIONAL HUMAN RIGHTS 187, 187-99, (Burns H. Weston & Stephen P. Marks eds., 1999); Res. 2001/03, U.N. OHCHR Sub-Comm'n on the Promotion and Protection of Human Rights, 53rd Sess., ¶4, U.N. Doc. E/CN.4/Sub.2/2001/03 (2001) (renewing for three-years a sessional working group to examine the working methods and activities of transnational corporations); *Report of the Chairpersons of the Human Rights Treaty Bodies on their Fifteenth Meeting*, U.N. GAOR, 58th Sess., at 10-11, U.N. Doc. A/58/350 (2003) (noting intersection of globalization and human rights).

And while they may choose to adopt ethical guidelines and codes of conduct, there is no international human rights law that directly applies to them or to their actions.[64] However, the options for increasing their accountability must be examined with care. For example, opening human rights treaties to them for ratification could on the one hand increase their legal accountability, but on the other could well serve to increase their power—by de facto giving them the powers of a state. The lack of clarity in this area regarding how the limits can be defined and according to what criteria—for example whether it could be argued that this would then give a corporation a state's powers to declare war—requires careful exploration.

VII. Conclusion: Current Challenges and Opportunities

The translation of the obligations of health-related human rights into guidelines and other tools useful to national and international monitoring of governmental, intergovernmental, and civil society accountability remains in its infancy. The work of the international human rights system, for example, in relation to the ICESR General Comment on the Right to the Highest Attainable Standard of Health, is beginning to provide some useful guidance.[65] In parallel, the tools and recommendations being developed by WHO to redirect the monitoring of global health towards indicators that are more reflective of the degree to which health and human rights principles are respected, protected, and fulfilled, deserves attention.[66] The human rights bodies and international organizations concerned with health are engaged in an open dialogue and a degree of collaboration that greatly exceeds the level and quality of interagency collaboration traditionally observed within the UN machinery. This includes the sharing of goals and collective technical cooperation in defining obligations and monitoring methods and standards relevant to health and human rights. The linkages in the work of the formal human rights system, the UN specialized agencies, and NGOs to articulate health and human rights concerns is not only useful at the global level, but is also beginning to contribute directly and concretely to enhancing implementation of human rights and health at the national level. In several countries, including Brazil, Thailand, and South Africa, human rights principles relevant to health have found their way into court cases and national legislation, thereby using national juridical means to ensure, for example, a national legal right to care and treatment.[67] As the methods and

---

64. Gruskin & Tarantola, *supra* note 1, at 322.

65. *Substantive Issues Arising in the Implementation of the International Covenant on Economic, Social and Cultural Rights*, U.N. ESCOR Comm'n on Econ., Soc. and Cultural Rights, 22d Sess., Agenda Item 3, at 1, U.N. Doc. E/C.12/2000/4 (2000). *See, e.g., Provisional Agenda*, U.N. ESCOR Comm'n on Econ., Soc. and Cultural Rights, 32d Sess., U.N. Doc. E/C.12/2004/1 (demonstrating that states and NGOs are providing information under the right to health).

66. *See, e.g.*, WHO, *Consultation on Indicators for the Rights to Health: Draft Meeting Report* (2004) (emphasizing right to health indicators), *available at* http://www.who.int/hhr/activities/indicators/en/ (last visited August 24, 2004).

67. *See, e.g.*, Government of South Africa & Pharmaceutical Manufacturers Association of South Africa, Text of Agreement in PMA v. Republic of South Africa, *at*

tools for monitoring and accountability of health related issues mature, it is likely that cases of human rights violations related to health will increasingly be heard both within countries and at the regional and international level. Various groups are also taking steps to build national and international capacity to develop and reform public policy and laws in line with international human rights norms and standards as they apply to health.[68] This work requires institutional change, as well as capacity building within governmental systems, international organizations, NGOs, and other civil society actors. The state remains ultimately responsible for the promotion of public health and human rights, but as we welcome the involvement of other actors in these efforts, their accountability for their actions must also be increased. Not only is this required for effective global health governance, it is necessary to ensure the health and well-being of populations in the years to come.

---

http://www.aidslaw.ca/Maincontent/issues/cts/agreementSA.htm (last visited Sept. 12, 2004) (issuing joint statement after withdrawal of PMA and 39 pharmaceutical companies from suit to prevent South Africa from implementing Medicines and Related Substances Control Amendment Act); Minister of Health and others v. Treatment Action Campaign, 2002 (5) SA 721, *75 (CC) (holding South African Constitution requires government to act to prevent mother-to-child HIV transmission), *available at* http://www.concourt.gov.za/judgment.php?case_id=11915; Hurst Hannum, *The UDHR in National and International Law*, 3 HEALTH AND HUM. RTS. 145, 145-58 (1998) (stating importance of Universal Declaration of Human Rights as a model for states' laws around the world); Paulo R. Teixeira et. al., *The Brazilian Experience in Providing Universal Access to Antiretroviral Therapy*, at www.iaen.org/files.cgi/11066_part_1_n2_Teixeira.pdf (last visited Sept. 12, 2004) (describing Brazilian response to HIV/AIDS).

68. *See generally* Mahesh Patel, *Human Rights as an Emerging Development Paradigm and Some Implications for Programme Planning, Monitoring and Evaluations* (UNICEF ed., 2001); Fabio Sabatini, *Programming with a Human Rights Approach: An Experience in Operational Practice: UNICEF Zimbabwe 1998-2003* (UNICEF ed., 2003); WHO, *Transforming Health Systems: Gender and Rights in Reproductive Health, A Training Manual for Health Managers* (2003); WHO & Francois-Xavier Bagnoud Center for Health and Human Rights, Program on Int'l Health and Human Rights, *Using Human Rights for Maternal and Neonatal Health: A Tool for Strengthening Laws, Policies and Standards of Care* (forthcoming 2005) (providing approaches to integrating human rights into health work).

[25]

Medicine and Public Health, Ethics and Human Rights

by Jonathan M. Mann

There is more to modern health than new scientific discoveries, the development of new technologies, or emerging or re-emerging diseases. World events and experiences, such as the AIDS epidemic and the humanitarian emergencies in Bosnia and Rwanda, have made this evident by creating new relationships among medicine, public health, ethics, and human rights. Each domain has seeped into the other, making allies of public health and human rights, pressing the need for an ethics of public health, and revealing the rights-related responsibilities of physicians and other health care workers.

The relationships among medicine, public health, ethics, and human rights are now evolving rapidly, in response to a series of events, experiences, and struggles. These include the shock of the worldwide epidemic of human immunodeficiency virus and AIDS, continuing work on diverse aspects of women's health, and challenges exemplified by the complex humanitarian emergencies of Somalia, Iraq, Bosnia, Rwanda, and now, Zaire.

From among the many impacts of these experiences, three seem particularly salient. First, human rights thinking and action have become much more closely allied to, and even integrated with, public health work. Second, the long-standing absence of an ethics of public health has been highlighted. Third, the human rights-related roles and responsibilities of physicians and other medical workers are receiving increased attention.

Public Health and Medicine

To explore the first of these issues—the connections between human rights and public health—it is essential to review several central elements of modern public health.

Jonathan M. Mann, "Medicine and Public Health, Ethics and Human Rights," *Hastings Center Report* 27, no. 3 (1997): 6-13.

A version of this paper was presented in plenary session at the III World Congress of Bioethics, San Francisco, 20 November 1996.

Medicine and public health are two complementary and interacting approaches for promoting and protecting health—defined by the World Health Organization (WHO) as a state of physical, mental, and social well-being. Yet medicine and public health can, and also must be differentiated, because in several important ways they are not the same. The fundamental difference involves the population emphasis of public health, which contrasts with the essentially individual focus of medical care. Public health identifies and measures threats to the health of populations, develops governmental policies in response to these concerns, and seeks to assure certain health and related services. In contrast, medical care focuses upon individuals—diagnosis, treatment, relief of suffering, and rehabilitation.

Several specific points follow from this essential difference. For example, different instruments are called for: while public health measures population health status through epidemiological, survey, and other statistically based methods, medicine examines biophysical and psychological status using a combination of techniques, including dialogue, physical examination, and laboratory study of the individual. Public health generally values most highly (or at least is supposed to) primary prevention, that is, preventing the adverse health event in the first place, such as helping to prevent the automobile accident or the lead poisoning from happening at all. In contrast, medicine generally responds to existing health conditions, in the context of either secondary or tertiary prevention. Secondary prevention involves avoiding or delaying the adverse impact of a health condition like hypertension or diabetes. Thus, while the hypertension or insulin deficiency exists, its effects, such as heart disease, kidney failure, or blindness, can be avoided or delayed. So-called tertiary prevention involves those efforts to help sustain maximal functional and psychological capacity despite the presence of both the disease, such as hypertension, and its outcomes, heart disease, stroke, or kidney failure.

Accordingly, the skills and expertise needed in public health include epidemiology, biostatistics, policy analysis, economics, sociology, and other behavioral sciences. In contrast, medical skills and expertise center on the exploration, analysis, and response to the biophysical status of individuals, based principally on an understanding of biology, biochemistry, immunology, pharmacology, pathology, pathophysiology, anatomy, and psychology.

Naturally, the settings in which public health and medicine operate also differ: governmental organizations, large-scale public programs, and various fora associated with developing and implementing public policy are inherently part of public health, while private medical offices, clinics, and medical care facilities of varying complexity and sophistication are the settings in which medical care is generally provided.

Finally, the relationship between the profession and the people with whom it deals differs: in a sense, public health comes to you, while you go to the doctor. And expectations associated with each domain differ: from medicine, individual care and treatment are sought; from public health, protection against broad health threats like epidemic disease, unsafe water, or chemical pollution is expected.

Therefore, public health and medicine are principally distinguished by their focus on collectivities or on individuals, respectively, with a series of subsidiary differences involving methods of work, systems of analysis and measurement, emphasis on primary versus secondary or tertiary prevention, types of expertise and relevant skill, settings in which work is conducted, and client/public relationships and expectations.

Yet obviously, there is substantial overlap. Public health requires a sound biomedical basis, and involves many medical practitioners, whose services are organized in settings such as maternal and child health clinics, or immunization programs. Also, medical practice operates within a context highly influenced and governed by law and public policy. The potentially fluid relationship between public health and medicine is further suggested by recent proposals in this country that certain traditional public health functions be delegated to the private medical sector.

Despite these many differences, people equate medical care with health. Certainly, this basic confusion has informed the recent discussions of health care in the United States; and coverage of health issues in the popular press around the world reflects this perspective, in which access to medical care and the quality of that care are seen as the principal health needs of individuals and populations.

Medicine and Health

Yet the contribution of medicine to health, while undeniably important (and vital in certain situations), is actually quite limited. For example, it is estimated that only about one-sixth of the years of life expectancy gained in this country during this century can be attributed to the beneficial impact of medicine, medical care, and medical research. And it has been estimated that only about 10 percent of preventable premature deaths are associated with a lack of medical care. Similarly, the World Bank has estimated that a lack of essential clinical services is responsible for between 11 and 24 percent of the global burden of disease. Of course, none of these data, including also the notable decline in diseases like tuberculosis well before antimycobacterial therapy became available, suggest that medical care is irrelevant; rather, they suggest its limits.

In 1988, the United States' Institute of Medicine defined the mission of public health as "ensuring the conditions in which people can be healthy." This profound definition begs the most vital question for public health, namely, what are these essential conditions in which people can best achieve the highest possible level of physical, mental, and social well-being? If not medical care—its availability and quality—then what?

The vast majority of research into the health of populations identifies so-called "societal factors" as the major determinants of health status. Most of the work in this area has focused on socioeconomic status as the key variable, for it is clear, throughout history and in all societies, that the rich live generally longer and healthier lives than the poor. Thus, in the United Kingdom in 1911, the age-adjusted standardized mortality rate among members of the lowest social class was 1.6 times higher than for the highest social class. Interestingly, following creation of the National Health Services to ensure full access to medical care, and despite a dramatic change in major causes of death (from mainly infectious to mainly chronic diseases), in 1981 this societal gradient not only persisted, but increased, to a 2.1-fold higher standardized mortality rate among the lowest compared with the highest social class.

A major question arising from the socioeconomic status-health gradient is why there is a gradient. For example, among over 10,000 British civil servants followed for many years, health status and longevity were better for each successive category of civil servants, from lowest to highest. This raises two issues: first, while we believe we can—at least intuitively—explain poor health among the destitute when compared with the rich, associated with a lack of good food, housing, and with poor sanitary conditions, even the lowest class of British civil servants cannot be considered poor. Secondly, why should the civil servants in the next-to-highest group, living in quite comfortable circumstances, experience poorer health than the highest group?

Beyond these unanswered issues, many recent studies have pointed to the limited explanatory power of socioeconomic status, generally measured in terms of current income, years of education, and job classification. Other measures, such as the extent of socioeconomic inequality within a community, the nature, level, and temporal pattern of unemployment, societal connectedness and the extent of involvement in social networks, marital status, early childhood experiences, and exposure to dignity-denying situations have all been suggested as powerful potential components of a "black box" of societal factors whose dominant role in determining levels of preventable disease, disability, and premature death is beyond dispute.[1]

An Ethics for Public Health

Public health, although it began as a social movement, has—at least in recent years—responded relatively little to this most profound and vital knowledge about the dominant impact of society on health. To illustrate: we all know that certain behaviors have an enormous impact on health, such as cigarette smoking, excess alcohol intake, dietary choices, or levels of exercise and physical fitness. How these behaviors are conceptualized determines how they will be addressed by public health. The basic question is whether and to what extent these behaviors can be considered, and therefore responded to, as isolated individual choices.

The curve represented in Figure 1 (replicable among public health practitioners in at least three countries) reflects a strong belief that important health-related behaviors are substantially influenced by societal factors and context. Yet examining public health programs designed to address the health problems associated with these same behaviors reveals that they generally consist of activities which assume that individuals have essentially complete control over their health-related behaviors. Traditional public health seeks to provide individuals with information and education about risks associated with diet or lack of exercise, along with various clinic-based services such as counseling, or distribution of condoms and other contraceptives. However, while public health may cite, or blame, or otherwise identify the societal-level or contextual issues—which it acknowledges to be of dominant importance, both in influencing individual behavior and for determining health status more broadly—it does not deal directly with these societal factors.

At least three reasons for this paradoxical inaction may be proposed. First, public health has lacked a conceptual framework for identifying and analyzing the essential societal factors that represent the "conditions in which people can be healthy." Second, a related problem: public health lacks a vocabulary with which to speak about and identify commonalities among health problems experienced by very different populations. Third, there is no consensus about the nature or direction of societal change that would be necessary to address the societal conditions involved. Lacking a coherent conceptual framework, a consistent vocabulary, and consensus about societal change, public health assembles and then tries valiantly to assimilate a wide variety of disciplinary perspectives, from economists, political scientists, social and behavioral scientists, health systems analysts, and a range of medical practitioners. Yet while each of these perspectives provides some useful insight, public health becomes thereby a little bit of everything and thus not enough of anything.

With this background in mind, it would be expected that in the domains of public health and medicine, different, yet complementary languages for describing and incorporating values would be developed. For even when values are shared at a higher level of abstraction, the forms in which they are expressed, the settings in which they are evoked, and their practical application may differ widely.

Not surprisingly, medicine has chosen the language of ethics, as ethics has been developed in a context of individual relationships, and is well adapted to the nature, practice, settings, and expectations of medical care. The language of medical ethics has also been applied when medicine seeks to deal with issues such as the organization of medical care or the allocation of societal resources. However, the contribution of medical ethics to these societal issues has been less powerful when compared, for example, with its engagement in the behavior of individual medical practitioners.

Public health, at least in its contemporary form, is struggling to define and articulate its core values. In this context, the usefulness of the language and structure of ethics as we know it today has been questioned. Given its population focus, and its interest in the underlying conditions upon which health is predicated (and

Health-Related Behaviors

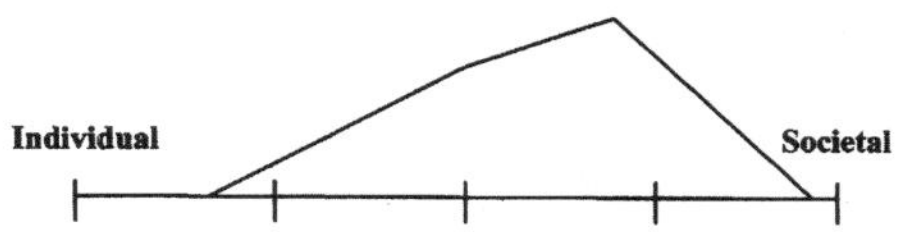

that these major determinants of health status are societal in nature), it seems evident that a framework which expresses fundamental values in societal terms, and a vocabulary of values which links directly with societal structure and function, may be better adapted to the work of public health than a more individually oriented ethical framework.

For this reason, modern human rights, precisely because they were initially developed entirely outside the health domain and seek to articulate the societal preconditions for human well-being, seem a far more useful framework, vocabulary, and form of guidance for public health efforts to analyze and respond directly to the societal determinants of health than any inherited from the past biomedical or public health tradition.

Public health has lacked a conceptual framework for identifying and analyzing the essential societal factors that represent the "conditions in which people can be healthy."

Public Health and Human Rights

The linkage between public health and human rights can be explored further by considering three relationships. The first focuses on the potential burden on human rights created by public health policies, programs, and practices. As public health generally involves direct or indirect state action, public health officials represent the state power toward which classical human rights concerns are traditionally addressed. Thus, in the modern world, public health officials have, for the first time, two fundamental responsibilities to the public: to protect and promote public health, and to protect and promote human rights. While public health officials may be unlikely to seek deliberately to violate human rights, there is great unawareness of human rights concepts and norms among public health practitioners. In stark contrast to the large number of bioethics courses available in medical educational settings, a recent survey of all twenty-eight accredited schools of public health in the United States and schools of public health in thirty-four other countries identified only seven formal courses in human rights for the presumed future leaders of public health.

Public health practice is heavily burdened by the problem of inadvertent discrimination. For example, outreach activities may "assume" that all populations are reached equally by a single, dominant-language message on television; or analysis "forgets" to include health problems uniquely relevant to certain groups, like breast cancer or sickle cell disease; or a program "ignores" the actual response capability of different population groups, as when lead poisoning warnings are given without concern for financial ability to ensure lead abatement. Indeed, inadvertent discrimination is so prevalent that all public health policies and programs should be considered discriminatory until proven otherwise, placing the burden on public health to affirm and ensure its respect for human rights.

In addition, in public health circles there is often an unspoken sense that public health and human rights concerns are inherently confrontational. At times, this has been true. In the early years of the HIV epidemic, the knee-jerk response of various public health officials to invoke mandatory testing, quarantine, and isolation did create a major clash with protectors of human rights. Even quite recently, an opinion piece in the *British Medical Journal* purports that excessive respect for human rights crippled public health efforts and is therefore responsible for the intensifying and expanding AIDS epidemic.

However, while modern human rights explicitly acknowledges that public health is a legitimate reason for limiting rights, more recently the underlying complementarity rather than inherent confrontation between public health and human rights has been emphasized. Again in the context of AIDS, public health has learned that discrimination toward HIV-infected people and people with AIDS is counterproductive. Specifically, when people found to be infected were deprived of employment, education, or ability to marry and travel, participation in prevention programs diminished. Thus, recent attention has been directed to a negotiation process for optimizing both the achievement of complementary public health goals and respect for human rights norms.

A second relationship between public health and human rights derives from the observation that human rights violations have health impacts, that is, adverse effects on physical, mental, and social well-being. For some rights, such as the right not to be tortured or imprisoned under inhumane conditions, the health damage seems evident, indeed inherent in the rights violation. However, even for torture, only more recently has the extensive, life-long, family and communitywide, and transgenerational impact of torture been recognized.

For many other rights, such as the right to information, to assembly, or to association, health impacts resulting from violation may not be initially so apparent. The violation of any right has measurable impacts on physical, mental, and social well-being; yet these health effects still remain, in large part, to be discovered and documented. Yet gradually, the connection is being established.

The right to association provides a useful example of this relationship. Public health benefits substantially—even requires—involvement of people in addressing problems that affect them. Because the ability of people concerned about a health problem to get together, talk, and search for effective solutions is so essential to public health, wherever the right to association is restricted, public health suffers. Taking a positive example from the history of HIV/AIDS: needle exchange—the trading-in of needles used for drug injection for clean needles, so as to avoid needle-sharing with consequent risk of HIV transmission—was invented by a union of drug users in Amsterdam. Needle exchange was a classic example of an innovative, local response to a pressing local problem. Needle exchange was not and would have been highly unlikely to have been developed by academics, government officials, or hired consultants! Yet the creative solution of needle exchange and respect for the right of association are closely linked. Thus, in societies in which people generally, or specific population groups, cannot associate around health, or other issues, such as injection drug users in the United States, or sex workers, or gay and lesbian people in many countries, local solutions are less able to emerge or be applied and public health is correspondingly compromised.

An exploration of the meanings of dignity and the forms of its violation—and the impact on physical, mental, and social well-being—may help uncover a new universe of human suffering, for which the biomedical language may be inapt and even inept.

A third relationship between health and human rights has already been suggested; namely, that promoting and protecting human rights is inextricably linked with promoting and protecting health. Once again, this is because human rights offers a societal-level framework for identifying and responding to the underlying—societal—determinants of health. It is important to emphasize that human rights are respected not only for their instrumental value in contributing to public health goals, but for themselves, as societal goods of pre-eminent importance.

For example, a cluster of rights, including the rights to health, bodily integrity, privacy, information, education, and equal rights in marriage and divorce, have been called "reproductive rights," insofar as their realization (or violation) is now understood to play a major role in determining reproductive health. From an early focus on demographic targets for population control, to an emphasis on ensuring "informed consent" of women to various contraceptive methods, a new paradigm for population policies *and* reproductive health has recently emerged. Articulated most forcefully at the United Nations Conference on Population and Development in 1994 in Cairo, the focus has shifted to ensuring that women can make and effectuate real and informed choices about reproduction. And in turn, this is widely acknowledged to depend on realization of human rights.

Similarly, in the context of HIV/AIDS, vulnerability to the epidemic has now been associated with the extent of realization of human rights. For as the HIV epidemic matures and evolves within each community and country, it focuses inexorably on those groups who, before HIV/AIDS arrived, were already discriminated against, marginalized, and stigmatized within each society. Thus, in the United States the brunt of the epidemic today is among racial and ethnic minority populations, inner city poor, injection drug users, and, especially women in these communities. In Brazil, an epidemic that started among the jet set of Rio and São Paulo with time has become a major epidemic among the slum-dwellers in the *favelas* of Brazil's cities. The French, with characteristic linguistic precision, identify the major burden of HIV/AIDS to exist among *"les exclus,"* those living at the margins of society. Now that a lack of respect for human rights has been identified as a societal level risk factor for HIV/AIDS vulnerability, HIV prevention efforts—for example, for women—are starting to go beyond traditional educational and service-based efforts to address the rights issues that will be a precondition for greater progress against the epidemic.

Ultimately, ethics and human rights derive from a set of quite similar, if not identical, core values. As with medicine and public health, rather than seeing human rights and ethics as conflicting domains, it seems more appropriate to consider a continuum, in which human rights is a language most useful for guiding societal level analysis and work, while ethics is a language most useful for guiding individual behavior. From this perspective, and precisely because public health must be centrally concerned with the structure and function of society, the language of human rights is extremely useful for expressing, considering, and incorporating values into public health analysis and response.

Thus, public health work requires both ethics applicable to the individual public health practitioner and a human rights framework to guide public health in its societal analysis and response.

These relationships between medicine and public health, and between ethics and human rights, can be provisionally diagrammed as in Figure 2.

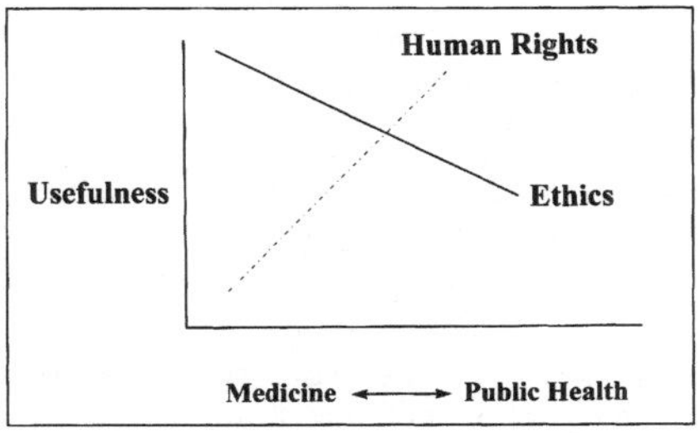

At the hypothetical extreme of individual medical care, ethics would be the most useful language. However, to the extent that the individual practitioner is cognizant of the societal forces acting upon the individual patient, societal level considerations may also be articulated in human rights terms. At the other extreme of public health, human rights is the most useful language, speaking as it does directly to the societal level determinants of well-being. Nevertheless, the ethical framework remains critical, for public health is carried out by individuals within specific professional roles and competencies. In practice, of course, positions between the hypothetical extremes of medicine and public health are more common, calling for mixtures of human rights and ethical concepts and language.

Professional Roles and Responsibilities

The placement of both human rights and ethics and public health and medicine at ends of a continuum suggests also that the interest domains of individuals and organizations can be "mapped" (as in Figure 3), and areas calling for additional attention can be highlighted.

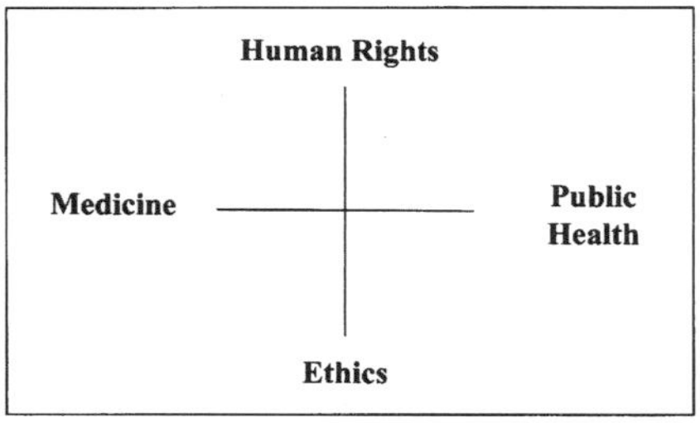

According to this mapping approach, the "French Doctors" movement can be seen as primarily medical, primarily ethics-based, yet with growing involvement in the public health dimensions of health emergencies and in human rights issues raised by these complex humanitarian crises. Similarly, many traditional, medical ethics-based institutes and centers can be placed on this map. At the Harvard School of Public Health, the François-Xavier Bagnoud Center for Health and Human Rights, along with several others, is now focusing on the health-human rights territory. This map also suggests two major gaps in current work: on the ethics of public health, and on the relationships between medicine and human rights.

Where are the ethics of public health? In contrast to the important declarations of medical ethics such as the International Code of Medical Ethics of the World Medical Association and the Nuremberg Principles, the world of public health does not have a reasonably explicit set of ethical guidelines. In part, this deficiency may stem from the broad diversity of professional identities within public health. Yet, curiously, many of the occupational groups central to public health (epidemiologists, policy analysts, social scientists, biostatisticians, nutritionists, health system managers) have not yet developed, or are only now developing, widely accepted ethical guidelines or statements of principle for their work in the public health context. Thus, while a public health physician may draw upon medical ethics for guidance, the ethics of a public health physician have yet to be clearly articulated.

The central problem is one of coherence and identity: public health cannot develop an ethics until it has achieved clarity about its own identity; technical expertise and methodology are not substitutes for conceptual coherence. Or, as one student remarked a few years ago, public health spends too much time on the "p" values of biostatistics and not enough time on values.

To have an ethic, a profession needs clarity about central issues, including its major role and responsibilities. Two steps will be essential for public health to reach toward this analytic and definitional clarity.

First, public health must divest itself of its biomedical conceptual foundation. The language of disease, disability, and death is not the language of well-being; the vocabulary of diseases may detract from analysis and response to underlying societal conditions, of which traditional morbidity and mortality are expressions. It is clear that we do not yet know all about the universe of human suffering. Just as in the microbial world, in which new discoveries have become the norm—Ebola virus, hantavirus, toxic shock syndrome, Legionnaires' disease, AIDS—we are explorers in the larger world of human suffering and well-being. And our current maps of this universe, like world maps from sixteenth century Europe, have some very well-defined, familiar coastlines and territories and also contain large blank spaces, which beckon the explorer.

The language of biomedicine is cumbersome and ultimately perhaps of little usefulness in exploring the impacts of violations of dignity on physical, mental, and social well-being. The definition of dignity itself is complex and thus far elusive and unsatisfying. While the Universal Declaration of Human Rights starts by placing dignity first, "all people are born equal in dignity and rights," we do not yet have a vocabulary, or taxonomy, let alone an epidemiology of dignity violations.

Yet it seems we all know when our dignity is violated or impugned. Perform the following experiment: recall, in detail, an incident from your own life in which your dignity was violated, for whatever reason. If you will immerse yourself in the memory, powerful feelings will likely arise—of anger, shame, powerlessness, despair. When you connect with the power of these feelings, it seems intuitively obvious that such feelings, particularly if evoked repetitively, could have deleterious impacts on health. Yet most of us are relatively privileged, we live in a generally dignity-affirming environment, and suffer only the occasional lapse of indignity. However, many people live constantly in a dignity-impugning environment, in which affirmations of dignity may be the exceptional occurrence. An exploration of the meanings of dignity and the forms of its violation—and the impact on physical, mental, and social well-being—may help uncover a new universe of human suffering, for which the biomedical language may be inapt and even inept. After all, the power of naming, describing, and then measuring is truly enormous—child abuse did not exist in meaningful societal terms until it was named and then measured; nor did domestic violence.

A second precondition for developing an ethics of public health is the adoption and application of a human rights framework for analyzing and responding to the societal determinants of health. The human rights framework can provide the coherence and clarity required for public health to identify and work with conscious attention to its roles and responsibilities. At that point, an ethics of public health, rather than the ethics of individual constituent disciplines within public health, can emerge.

Issues of respect for autonomy, beneficence, nonmaleficence, and justice can then be articulated from within the set of goals and responsibilities called for by seeking to improve public health through the combination of traditional approaches and those that strive concretely to promote realization of human rights. This is not to replace health education, information, and clinical service-based activities of public health with an exclusive focus on human rights and dignity. Both are necessary.

For example, the challenges for public health officials in balancing the goals of promoting and protecting public health and ensuring that human rights and dignity are not violated call urgently for ethical analysis. The official nature of much public health work places public health practitioners in a complex environment, in which work to promote rights inevitably challenges the state system within which the official is employed. Ethical dimensions are highly relevant to collecting, disseminating, and acting on information about the health impacts of the entire range of human rights violations. And as public health seeks to "ensure the conditions in which people can be healthy," and as those conditions are societal, to be engaged in public health necessarily involves a commitment to societal transformation. The difficulties in assessing human rights status and in developing useful and appropriate ways to promote human rights and dignity necessarily engage ethical considerations. For example, beyond accurate diagnosis, beyond efforts to cure, and even beyond the ever-present responsibility for relief of pain, the physician agrees to accompany the patient, to stand by the patient through her suffering, even to the edge of life itself, even when the only thing the physician can offer is the fact of his or her presence. Is this not as relevant to public health? For public health must engage difficult issues even when no cure or effective instruments are yet available, and public health also must accompany, remain with, and not abandon vulnerable populations.

That this work—added to, not substituted for, the current approach of public health—will require major changes in public health reflection, analysis, action, and education, is clear. That it is urgently required, in order to confront the major health challenges of the modern world, is equally clear.

Physicians and Human Rights

Finally, turning to the third issue raised by new challenges to the domains of public health, medicine, ethics, and human rights: what about the human rights role and responsibilities of medicine and the medical professional? To what extent and in what ways are—or might, or should—medicine generally and physicians in particular be involved in human rights issues?

Physicians have developed important roles in the context of human rights work. This work generally started from a corporatist interest in the fate of fellow physicians suffering human rights abuses, and then expanded in four directions. First, physicians created the "French Doctors" movement, providing medical assistance to populations in need, across borders. This dramatic and catalyzing work, including the concept of the right to assistance and the duty to intervene, expressed—in medical terms—the same transnational, universalist impulse as the modern human rights movement. Then, groups such as Physicians for Human Rights applied medical methods and analysis to detect and document torture, executions, and other similar human rights violations. In this manner, credible documentation, necessary also for redress and prosecution, has increasingly been made available. Meanwhile, Amnesty International has been concerned with the participation of physicians in human rights violations, usually in the context of torture and imprisonment under inhumane conditions. Finally, at a global level, physicians have articulated a role in seeking to prevent health catastrophes, exemplified by the Nobel Peace Prize-winning organization, International Physicians for Prevention of Nuclear War.

These historic and often courageous engagements with human rights issues have carried physicians to the frontiers of new challenges, exemplified by complex humanitarian emergencies, efforts to identify the full range of health consequences from human rights violations, and further struggle with societal issues inextricably linked with the health dimensions of conflict, economic consumption, and the degradation of the global environment. Increased physician participation and concern with these issues will inevitably blur pre-existing boundaries between public health and medicine and create new interactive configurations between human rights and ethics.

Yet for individual medical practitioners, how is a human rights perspective relevant? Human rights and dignity will be engaged to the extent that the physician seeks to go beyond the usual, limited boundaries of medical care. Take two examples: a child with asthma, or a woman seeking emergency room care for injuries inflicted by her spouse. In each case, the limited medical perspective is vital. For the precipitating factors for asthma, and the likelihood of seeking early care as asthmatic attacks begin, lead directly to environmental conditions, economic issues, and discrimination. Similarly, domestic violence invokes, necessarily, societal issues in which the human rights framework will be useful, if not essential. Whether considering cancer, heart disease, lead poisoning, asthma, injuries, or infectious diseases, while the medical professional may start from a context dominated by individual relationships, a larger, societal set of issues will inevitably exist. The question then becomes, To what extent is the physician responsible for what happens outside the immediate context and setting of medical care? To what extent is a physician responsible for assuring access to care of marginalized populations in the community, or helping the community understand the medical implications of public policy measures, or identifying, responding to, and preventing discrimination occurring within medical institutions?

Where, that is, does the boundary of medicine end? This seems a uniquely rich context for ethical discussion, at the frontiers of human rights and public health.

Of course, for those interested in the human rights dimensions of medicine, many may accuse physicians of "meddling" in societal issues that "go far beyond" their scope or competence. Also, issues of human rights inherently and inevitably represent a challenge to power—and health professionals are often part of, or direct beneficiaries of, the societal or institutional status quo that is challenged by the claims of human rights and dignity.

In conclusion, there is more to modern health than new scientific discoveries, or development of new technologies, or emerging or re-emerging diseases, or changes in patterns of morbidity and mortality around the world. For we are living at a time of paradigm shift in thinking about health, and therefore about medicine and public health. Health as well-being, despite the World Health Organization's definition, lacks more than rudimentary definition, especially regarding its mental and societal dimensions. The universe of human suffering and its alleviation is being more fully explored. Awareness of the limits of medicine and medical care, growing recognition of the health impacts of societal structure and function, globalization and consequent interdependence, and the sometimes active, sometimes ineffectual actions of nation-states, all intersect to lead toward a new vision of health.

We are living at a time of paradigm shift in thinking about health, and therefore about medicine and public health.

In the ongoing work on values and their articulation, we must acknowledge the provisional, untidy, and necessarily incomplete character of our understanding of the universe of health. In this context, medicine need not compete with public health, nor ethics with human rights; the search for meaning deserves to draw on all, as new constellations emerge and new relationships evolve.

Yet at such times of profound change, another kind of value becomes all the more vital. To build bridges—between medicine and public health, and between ethics and human rights—the critical underlying question may be, Do we believe that the world can change? Do we believe that the long chains of human suffering can be broken? Do we agree with Martin Luther King that "the arc of history is long, but it bends towards justice?" Bioethical pioneers at the frontier of human history, we affirm that the past does not inexorably determine the future—and that it is precisely through this historic effort to explore and promote values in the world for which we share responsibility, articulated in philosophy and in action—that we express confidence in our own lives, in our community, and in the future of our world.

Reference

1. N. E. Adler et al., "Socioeconomic Status and Health: The Challenges of the Gradient," *American Psychologist* 49, no. 1 (1994): 15-24.

CORRECTION

There is an error on page 13 of the Center's *1996 Annual Report.* The reference to the amicus brief in support of reversal of *Compassion in Dying v. Washington* should read: Brief of the American Suicide Foundation, Amicus Curiae, to the United States Supreme Court, Supporting Reversal of Compassion in Dying v. Washington (12 November 1996), EH Moskowitz, Counsel of Record, ER Grant and JF Cannon, Of Counsel.

[26]

Global Disparities in Health and Human Rights: A Critical Commentary

Solomon R. Benatar, MBChB, FRCP

ABSTRACT

Widening disparities in health and human rights at a global level represent the dark side of progress associated with escalation of economic and military exploitation and exponential population growth in the 20th century. Even the most basic universal human rights cannot be achieved for all under these circumstances. The goal of improved population health will be similarly elusive while medical care is commodified and exploited for commercial gain in the marketplace. Recognition of the powerful forces that polarize our world and commitment to reversing them are essential for the achievement of human rights for all, for the improvement of public health, and for the peaceful progress required to protect the "rational self-interest" of the most privileged people on earth against the escalation of war, disease, and other destructive forces arising from widespread poverty and ecological degradation. (*Am J Public Health.* 1998;88:295–300)

Introduction

Global challenges at the millennium's end call for deep introspection by the people of the nations that have been most privileged to benefit from scientific and economic progress and for reevaluation of the costs of such progress for those less fortunate. In this regard, we should consider how progress is linked to exploitation of people and nature and how it contributes to the widening national and global disparities (in health, wealth, and human rights) that now jeopardize human health and survival. Such threats to billions of marginalized people can be addressed only through a long-term perspective acknowledging that the self-interest of wealthy and powerful nations will be optimized through the pursuit of policies that foster all human well-being. Failure to respond to such global challenges can only lead to greater poverty and deprivation, continuing conflict, escalating migration of "asylum seekers" from poor to rich countries, and the spread of new and recrudescing infectious diseases (for example, drug-resistant tuberculosis) and ecologic damage that will harm all nations individually and the world collectively.

Consider, for example, that in the 1960s the richest quintile of the world's population was 30 times richer than the poorest 20% and that this gap had increased to over 60 times by the 1990s. An analogy can be drawn between this global scenario and the problems faced in delivering health care, sustaining medical professionalism, and improving public health. Here the challenge is to find ways of providing greater equity in access to health care for individuals within constrained budgets and the means for improving population health within nations and globally. If the annual per capita expenditure of $3500 on health care in the United States (10 times the total annual per capita gross national product [GNP] of half the world's population) is not enough to ensure access to a decent level of health care for all US citizens, we must ask what implications this has for US citizens and for the structure of health care systems and health care delivery in poor countries.

I should like to offer here a synoptic (and therefore necessarily incomplete) perspective on such complex global problems. My hope is that a perspective that acknowledges the complex roots of global disparities while seeking resolutely to ensure more widespread realization of human rights can refocus attention on these issues and lead to more open scholarly debate and new commitments to finding solutions that may influence the future. Imaginative, global thinking and visionary actions specific for particular societies are the seeds for initiating and propagating qualitative and quantitative changes that could have major long-term advantages for humankind.

Man's Exploitation of Man and the Creation of Two Worlds

The Western world view has been shaped over centuries through the power of the scientific method, analytical philosophy, industrialization, urbanization, democratization, liberalism, and capitalism. The modern perspective emphasizes capitalism, the pursuit of rational economic self-interest, and the nation-state framework of international relations.[1,2] These scientific, industrial, and economic developments, much cherished in the Western world, have eman-

The author is with the Department of Medicine, University of Cape Town, and Groote Schuur Hospital, Cape Town, South Africa.

Requests for reprints should be sent to Solomon R. Benatar, MBChB, FRCP, Department of Medicine, University of Cape Town, Observatory 7925, Cape Town, South Africa.

cipated human life and fostered unprecedented human progress. However, the application of a somewhat libertarian version of liberal political philosophy,[3] with overemphasis on economic thinking (and underemphasis on social and economic rights), has also been associated with erosion of spirituality, loss of a sense of community, and division of the world (and many countries) into a small, rich core and a large, poor periphery.[4] Growing polarization between these worlds as they drift apart threatens the future of both wealthy and poor countries. The failure of socialism, as implemented under communist rule in the Soviet Union, has seemingly vindicated the "capitalist" world view. However, celebration is premature, because the crisis of liberal internationalism must now be faced, particularly in regard to the competing elements of the liberal agenda—human rights and the expansion of free trade.[2] While the liberal vision has been effectively focused on limiting excessive and arbitrary state power, it has neglected the other great enemy in today's world: violence among the poor and dispossessed and the disintegration of power leading to millions of refugees fleeing poverty and disaster.[2,5]

Human domination and subordination of others in the understandable (perhaps inevitable) pursuit of self-interest has long been clearly evident. However, more recently the scientific credibility given to a form of rationality based on economics that has fostered the growth of powerful and unaccountable multinational corporations has led to the evolution of less obvious exploitative behavior. It is less widely appreciated how these more sophisticated and more covert means of achieving short-term economic self-interest cast a shadow over a broader moral conception of life.[1–13]

Fortunately, our consciences can be reawakened through critical thinking and social activism. For example, a 50-year program against slavery ultimately led to its delegitimation; the implications of destructive uses of nuclear power are increasingly being counteracted through endeavors to delegitimate nuclear testing and prevent the further development of weapons of mass destruction; the degradation of human dignity inflicted through colonial imperialism in Africa (and elsewhere) is being more widely appreciated; there is a deeper understanding that nazism in Germany reflected submission to authority and that such submission to authority also occurs with different implications in other countries; and the adverse effects of neocolonialism resulting from the collusion of superpowers with despotic leaders in developing countries are being exposed. Lessons learned from these adverse experiences increase awareness of the need for attention to a conception of human rights that goes beyond civil and political rights.

The International Bill of Human Rights (which includes the United Nations Charter [1945], the Universal Declaration of Human Rights [1948], and the International Covenant on Civil and Political Rights [1976], with its optional protocol) was a global expression of the rejection of human domination and exploitation of fellow humans, a dedication to the need for respecting individual human dignity, and an attempt to foster this through development of international law. Nations that refused to identify with the Universal Declaration of Human Rights (for example, the Soviet Union and South Africa) and placed what they perceived to be their own self-interest above high aspirations delayed their own progress toward peaceful democracies. The failures of socialism under communist rule and of apartheid provide powerful messages in favor of valuing human dignity and human rights. But less obvious human exploitation persisted and grew within and between even those nations that aspired to be the international guardians of human rights. Sophisticated forms of exploitation, propagated through cultural imperialism, militarism, and devastating wars intimately linked to economic power struggles that shaped a globalized economy, inexorably widened the gap between rich and poor peoples and nations and prevented the widespread access to education, employment, and other opportunities required to foster the realization of human rights.

A brief overview of some demographic data and of wasted resources on armed conflict will vividly portray the consequent predicament of the world's poor. In the 1990s, 77% of the world's population lives in developing countries. The 85%:15% distribution of global GNP between industrialized and developing nations reflects respective average annual per capita GNPs of $12 510 and $710[10] (Table 1). In 1986, 50% of the world's rapidly growing population lived in countries where the annual per capita GNP was less than $270.[10] Poverty is increasing in most parts of the world, and this is a major factor preventing sustainable control of population growth, which in turn threatens physical and mental health as the prerequisites for a decent human life and global survival.

In addition, modern international economic policies have resulted in the extraction of vast quantities of material and human resources from poor developing countries to rich industrialized nations.[1,4,9–15] Total developing country world debt in 1990 was $1.3 trillion (double the level in 1980), and it had grown further to $1.9 trillion by 1995.[1] The net transfer of resources from developing to industrialized nations between 1983 and 1989 was $241 billion[10]: "a kind of colonial tribute extracted by the rich nations from the poorest people on earth"[11] to service the industrial world's deficits and growth rates.[10] Thus, "the debt burden is a scandal which in numerical terms makes the international slave trade of the nineteenth century look like a petty crime."[15] Trade protectionism in industrialized countries costs developing countries a further $150 billion annually in lost export earnings.[10] Finally, the losses incurred through the "brain drain" are incalculable.

The world spends almost $1 trillion a year (according to 1990 figures) on military goods and services.[12,16] About 20% of the world's 2.5 million research scientists and engineers (50% of physicists and engineering scientists) work entirely on military research and development.[17] Approximately $340 billion worth of military arms were sold or given to developing countries between 1981 and 1988, most of which were produced by the Soviet Union or the United States.[12] The value of arms produced in developing countries (under the influence of superpowers' expansion of their military industrial complex) increased 500-fold between 1950 and 1980 (from $2 million to $1.1 billion).[12] Such militarization and the associated militarism have compromised the health of individuals and nations through many mechanisms: killing, maiming, torture, refugeeism, destruction of livelihoods, diversion of resources, crime, terrorism, black markets, poverty, starvation, environmental damage, and destabilization within developing countries.

Industrialized countries spend an average 5.4% of GNP on the military and only 0.3% on aid to developing countries. The Nordic countries admirably contribute 0.9% of their GNP to developing countries, most for social development, whereas the United States focuses most of the 0.15% of its GNP it donates on defense support for Egypt, Israel, Turkey, Pakistan, and the Philippines.[10] In 1990, British aid fell by two thirds of its 1979 value to the lowest ever, 0.27% of GNP.[15]

Despite Henry Kissinger's statement at the World Food Conference in 1974—"The profound comment of our era is that for the first time we may have the technical capacity to free mankind from the scourge of hunger"—up to 1 million people died in the Ethiopian famine,[18] the specter of Somalia

TABLE 1—Disparities between "Worlds Drifting Apart." (Data for 1988 from Human Development Report 1991[10])

	Industrialized World	Developing World
Population % total	23	77
Global GNP %	85	15
GNP per capita	$12 510 (USA $19 840)	$710
Population growth rate %	0.8	2.3
Population poor	0.3 billion	1.2 billion
Maternal mortality: 100 000	24	290
Life expectancy yr	74.5	62.8
Under 5 mortality: 1000	18	116
Annual urban population growth rate 1960–1990	1.4	4.0
Population below poverty line %	2%	32%
Share of world trade 1968	84.8%	15.2%
Share of world trade 1988	87.1%	12.9%
Annual per capita utilisation of energy (kilowatts per year)	3.2 (USA 9)	0.28
Losses from trade protectionism/yr		
Agriculture		$100 billion
Textiles		$50 billion

and Rwanda haunts us today, and the industrialized world continues to impose austere structural adjustment programs that divert resources away from food, education, health, and welfare in poor countries to repay debts that can in reality never be repaid.[13,15]

The wealthy, productive, and fortunate in the world cannot be burdened with all of the blame for the complex series of historical developments that polarize the world. However, insight is required into the complex adverse social forces initiated and sustained over centuries,[4,10,14,19,20] which, with destabilizing effects of "independence" under adverse conditions,[21,22] distanced and further separated many developing countries from the industrialized world.[4] Regrettably, disparities between rich and poor within industrialized nations have essentially similar causes,[4,9,14] highlighting the pervasiveness of adverse economic policies and the need to ameliorate these policies to improve social stability.[23]

Ecological Implications

Domination and subordination through exploitation of people is not the whole story. For centuries, the goals of philosophy and science had been the search for wisdom in understanding the natural order and endeavoring to live in harmony with it. Since the scientific revolution, this integrative approach to nature has shifted toward an aggressive quest to dominate nature in pursuit of economic growth that has, until recently, included little concern for its profound ecological and, hence, evolutionary consequences. "We are destroying the life support systems of this planet and threatening not only civilization as we know it, but also the survival of our species. . . . Cumulative use of fossil fuels has doubled every twenty years since 1890."[24] The world has lost 500 million acres of trees since 1972 (roughly one third the area of the continental United States). Lakes, rivers, even whole seas have been turned into sewers and industrial swamps.[25] The 1 billion people residing in industrialized countries use 10 times the resources and produce 10 times the waste per capita of the 4 billion people residing in developing countries.[24] What is needed now, as never before, is a major shift in our way of thinking about the future.[24–26]

Africa

The African continent has been most severely affected by the temporal relationship of the powerful social forces described earlier to its economic and political development.[18,21,27–30] The desperate condition of Africa has recently been reviewed from differing but complementary perspectives.[31,32] The withdrawal of industrialized nations from even attempting to deal with the dire condition of the African continent is reflected in the writings of political scientists. "The crisis is so diffuse and of such magnitude that the United States and the world at large shrink from engaging it."[30] "In fact, history mocks the very idea of an international coalition to save Africa."[27] Economic analysts now suggest that "with the end of the Cold War, Africa has lost whatever political lustre it may once have had."[27] Southern countries are weaker individually and collectively than 15 years ago, and the debt crises have reduced their control over their own economic destinies.[33] International affairs in the 1990s are increasingly dominated by economic affairs. As the Cold War recedes, there is the danger that it will be replaced by trade wars between the three major northern economic blocks and that increased competition between southern countries may extend to armed (even nuclear) conflict.[33]

Deeply troubling questions persist and cannot be ignored. As Gill has asked in his powerful account of Africa: Whose industries benefit from continuing underdevelopment in the Third World? Whose consumers benefit from primary products that keep African producers just above the bread line? Whose bankers benefit from Third World indebtedness? Whose arms manufacturers benefit from African arms races? Whose delicate consciences are soothed by the giving of modest gifts?[18] Hancock has documented these concerns in a devastating critique of the inefficiency, inadequacies, and corruption associated with many official international development aid projects.[13]

Human Rights and International Ethics

The Universal Declaration of Human Rights has no enforcement machinery, yet as a statement of aspirations it has served as the basis for constitutions and bills of rights in many countries. Regrettably, worldwide paper support for such human rights is frequently not followed in practice.[7,8] In a discussion of such widespread violations of the declaration, a South African activist,[34] outspokenly critical of industrialized nations' morality, has suggested that the statement "All human beings are born free and equal in dignity and rights" is not a social fact either in any liberal democracy rooted in the laissez-faire principles of capitalism or in socialist countries.

> There is no equality between the peoples of the First and the Third Worlds and there is no equality between a child born in an African township and one born in a white suburb. The child in the slum is born neither within dignity nor in dignity and he or she is born with practically no rights. . . . Theologically, we are born free and equal, sociologically we are born into differential socio-economic-emotional situations; and in the world in which we live sociology defines our reality. . . . On a global level the [Universal Declaration of Human Rights] fails because of the ethnocentric satisfaction of developed countries with their own state of freedom and their general unconcern for the freedom of others. . . . Those under their jurisdiction, as colonized or, in the sense of capitalistic exploitation, continue to be treated as lesser people, deserving of lesser rights whatever the noble articulations of the First World. . . . Self interest and expediency, and not mutual concerns for each other's freedom and dignity, govern international relations.[34]

The depressing reality of this view is intensified by the despicable attitude that two thirds of all of the people in the world are "superfluous from the perspective of the market. By and large we do not need what they have; they can't buy what we sell."[35] Inconsistencies in human rights standards demanded of other nations by powerful nations, the lack of self-assessment regarding rights that a monitoring country itself violates, and the consequent influence on human rights elsewhere should also be noted.[36,37] Human rights are most at risk when political, military, and economic considerations become the overwhelming preoccupation of governments.[8]

These concerns should not be misinterpreted as a "collectivist" critique of Western liberal values; rather, they underscore the clash between competing elements of the liberal agenda: human rights and the expansion of free trade.[2] The financial revolution that has been associated with massive expansion of the world economy since the Second World War, together with the revolution in communications that encourages international speculation and instantaneous transfers of vast sums of money, has fostered the growth of an integrated global economy. This has allowed multinational corporations, unfettered by the democratic requirement of accountability, to wield great economic and political power. Through such processes, the combined assets of the top 300 firms in the world now constitute roughly 25% of the world's productive assets. Their formidable economic power and transnational mobility increasingly undermine the ability of national governments to provide the legal, monetary, or protective functions necessary for a well-working national economy. The trillion-dollar-a-day market for foreign exchange effectively places the valuation of any nation's currency at the pleasure of the "market" rather than at the discretion of its monetary authorities, thus disrupting the relationship between the economy and the state. Less than 10% of the trillions of dollars transacted across financial networks are for trade in goods and services. Of the 5.6 billion people in the world, about 3.6 billion have no cash or credit with which to make purchases, and more and more people are clamoring to get into the global labor pool. The naive view that these trends can only be beneficial has been contested, and some of the adverse implications of such "irresponsible forces" (both for industrialized democracies and for developing countries) have been described.[38–40]

Overemphasis on market forces and on civil and political rights has eclipsed the need to affirm the associated social and economic rights that foster essential community values.[39,41] A broader formulation of human rights must include state and corporate duties to avoid depriving, duties to protect from deprivation, and duties to aid the deprived.[42] Articulating the problems of living in the modern world and vigorously proposing possible solutions to the appalling conditions confronting humanity today must become intellectual and political priorities if human rights are to be more widely achieved.[39,41,43] The challenges involved in redistribution of wealth, propagation of the education and skills required to sustain development, and reparations for centuries of human and environmental exploitation are fraught with difficulty.[40,44,45] They are, however, surely essential both within nations (as in the new South Africa) and at the global level to ensure that progress since the scientific revolution is not limited to the rich at the increasing expense of the poor.[4,14,38–40,44–46]

Medical Practice and Health for All

The foregoing suggests an analogy between global trends and Western medical practice. Advances in medicine and technology have provided many with much celebrated relief from suffering, hope for cure, and additional years of productive and satisfying lives but, through overaggressive approaches to transplantation and use of technology, have also inflicted intense suffering on others in the quest for new knowledge.[47,48]

The progressively dominating influence of "economic rationality" (with money as the bottom line) in medical care and its bureaucratic implementation by powerful multinational drug companies, insurance companies, and managers are also impoverishing the concept of medicine as a caring profession. "Increasingly, physicians find themselves engaged in bureaucratic and political struggles that sap their time and energy, exhaust their patience for treating uninsured people, and erode their dignity."[49] Impressive scientific and medical advances with profound impacts on human well-being have, regrettably, become associated with an inequitable, costly "medical industrial complex" within the most powerful nation on earth.[50]

Market-driven health care in a powerful nation has profound symbolic and material effects on health services worldwide. Health care delivery is being transformed from a professional service delivered with dedication, concern, and compassion within mutually rewarding and trusting healing relationships[49–51] toward the sale of a commodity in an adversarial marketplace in which professional satisfaction from patient care is being eroded and increasingly replaced by rewards external to the professional service: satisfying health service bureaucrats and acquiring wealth, scientific fame, and prestige among peers. Legitimation of this transition transmits a powerful message that gravely undermines the will and ability of other nations to develop and sustain equitable access to affordable health care. Established national health systems (for example, those in Canada and the United Kingdom) are fracturing under the influence of the market model, and health care reform in the new South Africa is being largely confined within a shrinking and weakened public sector while a bloated private sector continues largely unaffected.[52]

Efforts to reverse these trends by dedicated and enlightened physicians[50,51,53–55] are supported by professional organizations in the United States[56,57] and through changes in medical education that incorporate education in the humanities into the medical curriculum.[58,59] However, health care reform in the United States, and elsewhere, remains an elusive goal. Debate must go beyond medical education and the physician/patient relationship to include consideration of macro-allocation of resources, the structure of health care systems, and ways to deliver health care that will enhance the dignity and lives of individual patients and advance population health. Recognizing international disparities in health and health care provision as the single gravest problem of medical ethics challenges physicians, lawyers, and ethicists to become involved in global aspects of justice, human rights, and health care.[60–67]

The Future

Complex interlocking contributions to the emergence of an unequal world need to be openly acknowledged and addressed if progress is to be made toward widespread achievement of human rights and improved population health.[3,4,10,42–44,63–71] Sustaining human development requires a much more sophisticated approach than can be achieved through paternalistic dispensation by well-intentioned but largely unaccountable aid agencies[13,18] or through World Bank loans.[71] The 1991 Human Development Report describes a human development index (calculated on the basis of literacy and life expectancy, as well as per capita GNP) that goes beyond economic considerations alone and suggests linking financial aid to human development rather than merely to consumption, as a strategy to accelerate human development as a unifying concern for both industrialized and developing countries.[10]

There is now also growing acknowledgment of the enormous disparity between expenditure on military endeavors and on sustainable development and of the potential for the diversion of resources to the latter in order to foster self-actualization and self-sufficiency, which could help spread respect for and achievement of human rights.[72,73] Linkage of economic growth with human rights through human wellbeing is the key to progress and is a unifying concern for developing and industrialized countries.[10,44]

The operationalization of such processes through (1) cancellation of some of the unpayable debt accumulated by some of the poorest countries in the world,[15,32] (2) continuing attempts to redirect military expenditures toward social development,[72] (3) taxation on electronic financial transactions, and (4) suggestions such as those by Susser[65] and others[66,67] to advance the achievement of global health and human rights are the challenges of the future. These challenges, it is hoped, will be advanced through linkage with the planned World Health Organization proposal for a global health charter.[74]

There is also a need for us to begin to understand diverse world views and value systems.[75] Progress lies not in propagating false dichotomies but, rather, in working to acquire deeper understandings of differences and the willingness to create solidarity through greater identification with common human attributes and aspirations.[68,69] Wealthy nations that show concern largely for their own short-term economic self-interest could consider whether they are unintentionally behaving like countries that failed to identify with the Universal Declaration of Human Rights in 1948. The credibility of their commitment to contributing to achieving a broad range of human rights for all is now in the world's spotlight. Their ability to acknowledge and act on their awesome responsibility to humanity will shape the world's future.

The universal humanistic ideals for which medicine strives are, like human rights for all, unattainable without serious attention to the concept of international interdependence and the consequent restructuring of health care systems, especially those in powerful and wealthy nations that serve as role models for the world.[57,76,77] The American Association for the Advancement of Science has demonstrated vision and admirable moral responsibility in its call for a human rights approach to health care reform.[57] Further support could be provided through forging closer links between the bioethics movement and the promotion of human rights.[65–67,78–80] These ideas, like the call for transnational actions by physicians and lawyers,[66,67] are embryonic but are increasingly widely shared[73,74] and in need of much hard work to be developed into action plans.

The complexity of these tasks should not be a deterrent. As the celebrated Nigerian author Chinua Achebe has stated, despair should not eclipse hope: "neither history nor legend encourages us to believe that a man who sits on his fellow will some day climb down on the basis of sounds reaching him from below. And yet we must consider how so much more dangerous our already very perilous world would become if the oppressed everywhere should despair altogether of invoking reason and humanity to arbitrate their cause."[81] □

Acknowledgments

I am grateful to Professors Heribert Adam, Kogila Moodley, H.C.J. van Rensburg, Peter Folb, and Fredrik Barth; Dr Elena Nightingale; and the anonymous reviewers for their constructive assistance and encouragement and to Harvard University for a Fellowship in the Program in Ethics and the Professions in 1994/95, during which this project was further developed.

References

1. *Our Global Neighbourhood: Report of the Global Commission on Global Governance.* Oxford, England: OUP; 1995.
2. Hoffman S. The crisis of liberal internationalism. *Foreign Policy.* 1995;98:159–177
3. Rosenblum N, ed. *Liberalism and the Moral Life.* Cambridge, Mass: Harvard University Press; 1989.
4. Gilbert A. *An Unequal World: The Links between Rich and Poor Nations.* 2nd ed. London, England: Nelson; 1992.
5. Fuller G. The next ideology. *Foreign Policy.* 1995;98:145–157.
6. Schwartz B. *The Battle for Human Nature: Science Morality and Modern Life.* New York, NY: WW Norton & Co; 1986.
7. Vincent RJ. *Human Rights and International Relations.* Cambridge, England: Cambridge University Press;1986.
8. Donnelly J. *Universal Human Rights in Theory and Practice.* Ithaca, NY: Cornell University Press; 1989.
9. Massey DS, Denton NA. *American Apartheid: Segregation and the Making of the Underclass.* Cambridge, Mass: Harvard University Press; 1991.
10. *Human Development Report 1991.* New York, NY: Oxford University Press Inc; 1991.
11. Summerfield D. Western economics and Third World health. *Lancet.* 1989;2:551–552.
12. Kiefer CW. Militarism and world health. *Soc Sci Med.* 1992;34:719–724.
13. Hancock G. *Lords of Poverty.* London, England: Macmillan Publishing Co Inc; 1989.
14. Wallerstein I. America and the world: today, yesterday and tomorrow. *Theory Soc.* 1992;21:1–28.
15. Logie D. The great exterminator of children. *BMJ.* 1992;304:1423–1426.
16. Zwi AB, Ugalde A. Military expenditure and foreign aid: should they be linked? *BMJ.* 1992;304:1421–1422.
17. *The World Armaments and Disarmament SIPRI Yearbook 1983.* London, England: Taylor & Frances Ltd; 1983.
18. Gill P. *A Year in the Death of Africa: Politics, Bureaucracy and the Famine.* London, England: Paladin Grafton Books; 1986.
19. *World Population: Fundamentals of Growth.* 2nd ed. Washington, DC: Population Reference Bureau; 1990.
20. Ransford O. *The Slave Trade: The Story of Transatlantic Slavery.* London, England: John Murray Publications; 1971.
21. Boahen AA. *African Perspectives on Colonialism.* Baltimore, Md: Johns Hopkins University Press; 1987.
22. Ray JL. *Global Politics.* 4th ed. Boston, Mass: Houghton Mifflin; 1992.
23. Wilkinson RG. *Unfair Shares: The Effect of Widening Income Differences on the Welfare of the Young.* Brighton, England: Trafford Centre for Medical Research, University of Sussex; 1994.
24. *Blue Planet: Now or Never.* Ottowa, Ontario, Canada: Blue Planet Group; 1991.
25. Last J. Redefining the unacceptable. *Lancet.* 1995;346:1642–1643.
26. Potter VR. Global bioethics facing a world in crisis. *Global Bioethics.* 1992;5:69–76.

Health Law and Ethics

27. Chege M. Remembering Africa. *Foreign Aff.* 1992;71:146–163.
28. Davidson B. *The Black Man's Burden: Africa and the Curse of the Nation-State.* London, England: James Currey; 1992.
29. Ayittey GBN. African Rights. *Policy Rev.* 1986;35:8–9.
30. Marcum JA. Africa: a continent adrift. *Foreign Aff.* 1989;68:159–179.
31. Elmoore-Meegan M, O'Riorden T. Africa on the precipice: an ominous but not yet hopeless future. *JAMA.* 1993;270:629–631.
32. Benatar SR. Africa and the world. *S Afr Med J.* 1994;84:723–726.
33. Ravenhill J. The north-south balance of power. *Int Aff.* 1990;66:731–748.
34. Meer F. The Universal Declaration of Human Rights and the Freedom Charter—similar or apart? *J Hum Rights Trust.* 1988;71–74.
35. Gardels N. The post-Atlantic capitalist order. *New Perspect Q.* Spring 1993:2–3.
36. Howard RE. Monitoring human rights: problems of consistency. *Ethics Int Aff.* 1990;4:33–51.
37. Wipfler WL. Human rights violations and US foreign assistance: the Latin American connection. In: Brown G, Maclean D, eds. *Human Rights and US Foreign Policy.* Lexington, Mass: Lexington Books; 1979.
38. Kennedy P. *Preparing for the Twenty First Century.* New York, NY: Random House; 1993.
39. Teeple G. *Globalization and the Decline of Social Reform.* Atlantic Highlands, NJ: Humanities Press; 1995.
40. Heilbroner R. *Twentieth Century Capitalism.* New York, NY: WW Norton & Co; 1993.
41. Howard RE. Human rights and the search for community. *J Peace Res.* 1995;32:1–8.
42. Shue H. *Basic Rights.* Princeton, NJ: Princeton University Press; 1980.
43. Vincent RJ. The idea of rights in international ethics. In: Nardin T, Mapel DR, eds. *Traditions of International Ethics.* Cambridge, England: Cambridge University Press; 1992.
44. Young M. Sustainable investment: the economic challenge. *Impact Sci Soc.* 1992;116: 111–119.
45. Moll P, Nattrass N, Loots L. eds. *Redistribution: How Can It Work in South Africa?* Cape Town, South Africa: David Philip Publications;1991.
46. Hosle V. The Third World as a philosophical problem. *Soc Res.* 1992;59:227–262.
47. Fox R, Swazey J. *Spare Parts: Organ Replacement in American Society.* New York, NY: Oxford University Press Inc, 1992.
48. Rothman DJ. *Strangers at the Bedside.* New York, NY: Basic Books; 1991.
49. Iglehart J. The American health care system. *N Engl J Med.* 1992;326:962–967.
50. Relman AS. Shattuck Lecture. The health care industry: where is it taking us? *N Engl J Med.* 1991;325:854–859.
51. Lundberg GD. Countdown to millennium—balancing the professionalism and business of medicine: medicine's rocking horse. *JAMA.* 1990;263:86–87.
52. Benatar SR. Health care reform in the new South Africa. *N Engl J Med.* 1997;336: 891–895.
53. Pellegrino ED. The medical profession as a moral community. *Bull N Y Acad Med.* 1990;66:221–232.
54. Pellegrino ED, Thomasma D. *For the Patient's Good: The Restoration of Beneficence in Health Care.* New York, NY: Oxford University Press Inc; 1987.
55. Bulgar RE, Reiser SJ, eds. *Integrity in Health Care Institutions: Humane Environments for Teaching, Enquiry and Healing.* Iowa City, Iowa: Iowa Press; 1990.
56. Access to health care. *Ann Intern Med,* 1990;112:641–661.
57. Chapman A, ed. *Health Care Reform: A Human Rights Approach.* Washington, DC: Georgetown University Press; 1994.
58. White KL, Connelly JE, eds. *The Medical School's Mission and the Population's Health.* New York, NY: Springer-Verlag; 1992.
59. *Healthy America: Practitioners for 2005. An Agenda for Action for US Medical Schools.* Durham, North Carolina: Pew Health Professions Commission; 1991.
60. Attfield R. The global distribution of health care resources. *J Med Ethics.* 1990;16:153–156.
61. Gellert GA. Global health interdependence and the international physicians movement. *JAMA.* 1990;264:610–613.
62. Lanza R, ed. *Medical Science and the Advancement of World Health.* New York, NY: Praeger; 1985.
63. Holdstock P. Arms or health: a role for medical colleagues. *J R Coll Physicians Lond.* 1989;23:185–188.
64. Grant JP. From cell to society: public health in the next millennium. Presented at the 75th Anniversary Meeting of The Johns Hopkins School of Hygiene and Public Health, April 1992, Baltimore, Md.
65. Susser M. Public health as a human right: an epidemiologist's perspective on the public health. *Am J Public Health.* 1993;83:418–426.
66. Grodin MA, Annas GJ, Glantz LH. Medicine and human rights: a proposal for international action. *Hastings Cent Rep.* 1993;4:8–12.
67. Grodin MA , Annas GJ. Legacies of Nuremberg: medical ethics and human rights. *JAMA.* 1996;276:1682–1683.
68. Urevbu AO. Impact of science and technology on everyday life: an African perspective. *Impact Sci Soc.* 1992;161:69–77.
69. Kung H. *Global Responsibility: In Search of a New World Ethics.* New York, NY: Continuum; 1993.
70. The public duty of the professions. *Hastings Cent. Rep.* 1987;17(suppl):1–20.
71. Broad R, Cavanagh J. Don't neglect the impoverished south. *Foreign Policy.* 1995;101: 18–35.
72. Sivard RL. *World Military and Social Expenditures 1996.* 16th ed. Washington, DC: World Priorities; 1996.
73. Benatar SR. War, or peace and development: South Africa's message for global peace and security. *Med Conflict Survival.* 1997;13: 125–134.
74. *Equity in Health and Health Care: A WHO/SIDA Initiative.* Switzerland: World Health Organization; Geneva, 1994.
75. Smart N. *World Views: Cross-Cultural Explorations of Human Beliefs.* 2nd ed. Englewood Cliffs, NJ: Prentice Hall; 1995.
76. Loewy EH. *Suffering and the Beneficent Community: Beyond Libertarianism.* Albany, NY: State University of New York Press; 1991.
77. Mechanic D. America's health care system and its future: the view of a despairing optimist. *Med Care Rev.* 1992;50:7–48.
78. *Medical Ethics and Human Rights: Report of the Commonwealth Medical Association Project on "The Role of Medical Ethics in the Protection of Human Rights."* London, England: British Medical Association; 1994.
79. Heggenhougen HK. The epidemiology of functional apartheid and human rights abuses. *Soc Sci Med.* 1995;40:281–284.
80. Benatar SR. World health report: some millennial challenges. *J R Coll Physicians.* 1997;31: 156–157.
81. Achebe C. *Hopes and Impediments.* New York, NY: Doubleday; 1989:175–176.

Part VIII
Surveillance and Privacy

[27]

The Limits of Privacy: Surveillance and the Control of Disease

RONALD BAYER and AMY FAIRCHILD
Center for the History & Ethics of Public Health, Department of Sociomedical Sciences, Mailman School of Public Health, Columbia University
Address for correspondence: 722 West 168th Street, 9th Floor, New York, New York 10032 (E-mail: rb8@columbia.edu)

Abstract. What justified the Center for Disease Control's 1999 determination to require HIV case reporting? Why were names necessary? Why did opponents view the reporting of names with such alarm? This paper retells the history of the encounters over HIV reporting that had occurred since the mid 1980s. In placing HIV reporting within a larger context, however, we understand the clash between privacy and public health necessity as a complex issue, both in historical and contemporary practice. By underscoring the similarities and differences with the histories of surveillance for other infectious diseases, vaccination, occupational diseases, cancer, and birth defects, and HIV reporting internationally, we can better understand the implications of the HIV debate for an ethics of surveillance more generally.

Key words: birth defects, cancer, ethics, HIV/AIDS, name-based reporting, occupational disease, surveillance, tuberculosis, vaccination

On December 10, 1999 the Center for Disease Control made final and formal a policy it had sought to impose for some years. That new policy required of states that they adopt a system of HIV case reporting. While the CDC left open the possibility of using coded unique identifiers, it was clear that the federal health officials favored the use of names (CDC, 1999). In adopting this stance the CDC brought to closure a debate that had raged for 15 years, that had pitted advocates of comprehensive public health surveillance against AIDS advocates, gay organizations, civil libertarians, and their allies in some state health departments.

What justified the Center for Disease Control's 1999 determination to require HIV case reporting? In part, it was a reflection of the triumph of tradition over privacy-focused opposition. But more it reflected a growing sense that the surveillance of the AIDS epidemic was no longer adequate to the task. The reporting of AIDS cases – universal in the United States since 1983 – represented a picture of the end stage of a disease process that commenced years earlier when HIV infection occurred. If the public health required an understanding of the contours of the epidemic of HIV transmis-

20

sion then something very different was required. Furthermore, with the advent of the era of powerful antiretroviral therapeutics in 1995–1996 the period between infection and an AIDS diagnosis had grown. And so some believed that AIDS case reporting captured the picture of events that had occurred 10 years earlier. Only HIV case reporting could remedy the situation. The availability of powerful new therapies, then, provided an incentive for testing that might well overcome whatever the putative disincentives of HIV name reporting might be.

But why were names necessary? Why did opponents view the reporting of names with such alarm? To answer these questions requires a retelling of a history of the encounters that had occurred since the mid 1980s. With an appreciation of that history it will then be possible to locate the clash between the claims of privacy and surveillance first, in the context of the history of name based reporting; second, in the context of a range of contemporary surveillance practices; and finally it will be possible to look at the matter from an international perspective.

AIDS/HIV Reporting: A Brief History

Soon after the first cases of AIDS were reported by the Center for Disease Control in June 1981, state health departments – which bear the primary responsibility for public health activities in the US – began to require physicians and hospitals to report by name each newly diagnosed case (Bayer, 1989). In so doing they were pursuing a course understood to be a public health tradition. They shared a common belief that the understanding and control of disease necessitated adequate surveillance data. In the epidemic's early years this entailed not only a matter of enumeration and mapping but of investigating the commonalties among cases for which there was no etiological explanation. If gay men were so prominent among the first cases why were they? If hemophiliacs and blood transfusion recipients fell ill why was that the case? If intravenous drug users seemed at increased risk what could account for that fact? It is remarkable that given the intensity of the opposition that would emerge to HIV reporting just a few short years later that the American Association of Physicians for Human Rights – a gay and lesbian health group – would call upon local health departments to make AIDS cases reportable by name (AAPHR, 1983).

Surveillance, in the contexts of most diseases, but not all as we will discuss below, is based on the premise that medical privacy is not an absolute. Both historically and in contemporary practice, reporting the names of those with disease to public health authorities has represented a central example of an acceptable exception to medical privacy and the confidentiality of the clinical relationship. Nevertheless, individuals whose names are placed on disease registries have a right to expect that their identities will be held in confidence, that data reported to registries would not be used in ways that pose a threat to the patient's dignity and well-being. This was done for moral as well as practical reasons. Indeed, to the extent that they do not believe that such confidentiality will prevail, they will tend to resist name-based reporting as an unacceptable intrusion on their privacy.

It was this lack of confidence that confidentiality would be respected that prevailed in the case of HIV. Once the capacity to test for the presence of the antibody to HIV became possible in 1985, it was only a matter of time before some public health official would seek to extend the reporting requirements that were in place for AIDS. The first successful effort to mandate HIV case reporting occurred in Colorado. There the health authorities presented the claims that would be made repeatedly over the next years: Reporting would alert public health officials to the presence of individuals infected with a lethal infection; would allow officials to counsel them about what they needed to do to prevent further transmission; would permit the authorities to monitor the incidence and prevalence of infection. Alert to concerns about privacy and confidentiality, Colorado health officials underscored the existence of administrative, regulatory, and statutory protections for reported names. There was no reason to believe, officials argued, that the state health department would fail to protect the identities of those with HIV when it had protected those with AIDS, tuberculosis, and other reportable infections.

To these propositions the antagonists to name-based reporting retorted that AIDS was different: social hostility and AIDS-related hysteria could lead to changes in policy, legislatively imposed, that would permit for breaches that would never occur with other conditions. And then those in registries would lose their jobs, their housing, and perhaps their liberty. The intensity of the opposition is best captured by the extent to which genocidal images were invoked. In Minnesota, which followed Colorado in making HIV reportable, one opponent declared at a public meeting, "The road to the gas chambers began with a list in Weimar Germany" (Bayer, 1989, p 131). A less extreme formulation put the issue this way: "the fear, anger, and mistrust felt by me and many other groups reflects our profound belief that the threat to our fundamental human rights posed by the existence of AIDS is an evil of equal strength to the disease itself. To ignore our feelings will only alienate the gay community thereby impeding [the health department's] often legitimate efforts to arrest this serious health problem" (Bayer, 1989).

Here then was the powerful argument against reporting that would impress many health officials in states with relatively large AIDS caseloads. Reporting would be counterproductive; it would drive people away from testing and counseling – essential control measures in the public health campaign against AIDS in the United States. It did not matter that public health departments had an exemplary record in protecting name-based reports (Gostin et al., 1997). If those most at risk for HIV had fears about what would happen to them that was all that mattered.

As therapeutic advances began to emerge in the late 1980s – as public health began to have more to offer than the perceived threat of quarantine or partner notification – fissures began to appear in the relatively broad and solid alliance against named reporting. Thus, in 1989, New York City's Health Commissioner stated that the prospects of early clinical intervention warranted "a shift toward a disease-control approach to HIV infection along the lines of classic tuberculosis practices," including the "reporting of seropositives" (Joseph, 1989). Although his proposal met with fierce and effective resistance, it is clear that his call represented part of a national trend.

At the end of November 1990, the CDC declared its support for HIV reporting, which it asserted could "enhance the ability of local, state and national agencies to project the level of required resources" for care and prevention services (MMWR, 1990). Within a week, the House of Delegates of the American Medical Association endorsed the reporting of names as well, thus breaking with the traditional resistance of medical practitioners to such intrusions on the physician-patient relationship (Bayer, 1991). In 1991, New Jersey became the first high-prevalence state to require HIV-case reporting by name (Intergovernmental AIDS Reports, 1989).

In the following years, the CDC continued to press for named reporting of HIV cases, an effort that assumed the dimensions of a campaign. During that period, it was supported by a growing number of public health officials. Indeed, the Council of State and Territorial Epidemiologists adopted resolutions in 1989, 1991, 1993, and 1995 encouraging states to consider the implementation of HIV case surveillance (CSTE, Personal Communication).

Nevertheless, resistance on the part of AIDS activist organizations and their political allies persisted, and as a consequence, HIV cases typically became reportable by name only in states that did not have large cosmopolitan communities with effectively organized gay constituencies or high AIDS case loads. By 1996, although 26 states had adopted HIV-case reporting, they represented jurisdictions with only 24% of reported AIDS cases (CDC, 1997). By October 1998, however, it was clear that opposition to name-based reporting was weakening: 32 states now reported cases of HIV by name, though 3 states reported only pediatric cases; Florida, with its large case load, had become a reporting state, and Texas – which together with Maryland, had experimented with a unique identifier system for HIV-case reporting as an alternative to the use of names – had come to the conclusion that such an approach was unworkable and adopted name-based reporting (CDC, 1998). This trend must be seen as part of the more general move away from the exceptionalism that had placed such emphasis on the privacy and social rights of people with HIV infection and that had set AIDS policy apart from the response to other communicable conditions (Bayer, 1991; Bayer, 1999).

Nothing more forcefully underscored the changes that occurred than the course of events in New York. In 1997, the state with the largest concentration of AIDS cases began, for the first time, to consider name reporting. Although a state health department task force charged with the responsibility of advising the commissioner of health on the matter remained bitterly divided, the lines of cleavage were stark. It was the representatives of community-based organizations who most adamantly opposed name reporting. Public health officials on the committee and throughout the state supported HIV-case reporting by name. Objections and disagreements notwithstanding, there was significant, broad agreement on the need for HIV surveillance data to track the HIV epidemic and on the need to bring the sexual and needle-sharing contacts of individuals with HIV into testing and treatment. Yet ultimately the deadlock between community and public health officials paved the way for final action in the legislative arena. On June 19, 1998, in the waning hours of the legislative session, the Democratic-controlled assembly voted 112 to 34 for a bill that would mandate case reporting by name and a more aggressive approach to partner notification. In so doing, it joined the Republican-dominated state senate, which had already passed the bill (1998 NY Laws, Chapter 163). For advocates of name reporting, the significance of the New York decision could not be overstated.

The New York decision is best understood in light of therapeutic advances on the national policy debate on name reporting. That impact was made clear in an editorial published in late 1997. Jointly authored by Larry Gostin, a well-known proponent of civil liberties, John Ward, MD, of the CDC, and Cornelius Baker, the African American President of the National Association of People With AIDS, the editorial represented a new alliance. Locating the argument for named reporting in the context of the remarkable therapeutic achievements represented by the protease inhibitors and the advent of triple-combination antiretroviral therapy, the authors declared:

> We are at a defining moment of the epidemic of HIV infection and AIDS. With therapy that delays the progression to AIDS, mental illnesses, and death, HIV infection or AIDS is becoming a complex clinical disease that does not lend itself to monitoring based on end stage illness. Unless we revise our surveillance system, health authorities will not have reliable information about the prevalence of HIV infection. To correct these deficiencies, we propose that all states require HIV case reporting.

24

Among the additional advantages of HIV-case reporting, they asserted, was that it would give public health authorities a greater ability to "ensure timely referrals for health and social services" (Gostin et al., 1997, pp 1162–1167).

Although many, if not most, AIDS-service organizations remained adamantly opposed to name reporting, arguing instead for the use of unique identifiers, the public health community, with the CDC in the lead, concluded that such an approach would simply impede the adoption of an effective system of surveillance. Nevertheless, marking the extent to which political factors shape decision-making in public health, the CDC, in its 1999 recommendation, opened the way to the use of unique identifiers in those states that preferred an anonymous reporting course, provided states could radically limit the error rates associated with such an approach.

It was in trying to place HIV reporting within a larger context that we came to understand that the question of public health surveillance is a much more complex issue, both in historical and contemporary practice. Indeed, it was as a result of our ongoing study of this issue that we came to recognize the need for an analysis of the broad history of public health surveillance. Without such an analysis, it becomes impossible to understand that the HIV reporting controversy was radically affected by the circumstances under which it emerged, that is, the existence of a transformed conception of the rights of privacy, constitutional limits on state authority exercised for benevolent purposes, the development of a vigorous debate about medical ethics, and the emergence of patient advocacy as a potent social force. Indeed, without underscoring similarities and differences with the histories of surveillance for other infectious diseases, vaccination, cancer, occupational diseases, and birth defects, the ability to understand the implications of the HIV debate for surveillance more generally becomes impossible.

Case Reporting in Historical and Contemporary Contexts

Although the quantification of disease and concerns with health statistics have origins in the era of sanitary reform, it was not until the late nineteenth century – in the period in which the new science of bacteriology identified germs that could be transmitted from person to person as the cause of disease – that most nations began systematic reporting of infectious disease among individuals by name, often but not exclusively for the purpose of initiating quarantine, isolation, or vaccination and for epidemiological reasons, as well (Eyler, 1979).

The new public health practices that were linked to the bacteriological revolution, however, were also linked to a heightened public and professional concern about such practices. Notification by name for infectious diseases in many western nations followed on the heels of a period of public protest over compulsory or coercive health policies associated with the bacteriological revolution. Physicians, too, on occasion, challenged the scientific authority of public health officials to intervene in the doctor-patient relationship. In New York City for example, physician outrage over mandatory tuberculosis reporting beginning in 1897 resulted in the development of an essentially voluntary reporting system in which physicians withheld the names of their private patients and reported the names of their poor, dispensary cases (Fox, 1975, 1986).

Despite such opposition and some anticipation of what might follow the extension of the reporting requirement, public health officials began to argue in the second decade of the twentieth century that "All the general arguments for complete reporting of other communicable diseases apply with equal force to venereal disease" (Snow, 1917). But they appreciated the various factors influencing the potential for venereal disease reporting. They most often opted to forego name-based notification – remaining content with an inadequate surveillance system focused on public clinics. Although it was ultimately unsuccessful, public health officials in New York requested that physicians report cases of venereal disease by code beginning in 1912. A 1911 California system, which required physicians to report cases of venereal disease by code to protect patient confidentiality, served as their model (Brandt, 1987). Similarly, although it ultimately opted for name reporting, Massachusetts also considered adopting a laboratory-based coded system for tracking syphilis cases in 1916. Allan Brandt has underscored the point: "Although anonymous reporting precluded rigorous case-tracing, officials hoped it would deflate the possible objections of practitioners." How opposition to name-based reporting could vary and how such opposition was often linked to the way in which reports could trigger public health interventions that could be coercive is demonstrated by the early history of polio reporting.

The New York City Department of Health declared polio a communicable disease and made it mandatory for physicians to report all cases in 1910. During 1916 the epidemic became a public affair. Newspapers reported cases amongst the most prominent in the City. The City's health commissioner published a daily tally of new cases and deaths by name and street address in local newspapers. Homes with a sick child displayed a placard warning of the presence of disease (Emerson, 1917).

What is astonishing is that while polio primarily struck the middle class, in sharp contrast to the history of reaction to tuberculosis reporting discussed above, reporting elicited no objection from physicians or the private patients they served in large measure due to the differential nature of departmental intervention, particularly in the case of quarantine. Families with a private

26

toilet for the patient, separate dining facilities, and a private nurse could maintain a domestic quarantine. Children of those who lived in tenements or other types of multi-family dwellings were taken, sometimes by force, to public hospitals. Similarly, tenement homes and the children living in them were subject to unannounced inspections. As a consequence resistance to reporting and the interventions that followed has been documented only amongst poor, working class, or immigrant families. An analysis of the period recounts that during the epidemic of 1916 one mother warned that she and her child would disappear by morning if her doctor reported the case to health authorities. The Department of Health nurse assigned to inspect tenement houses received a letter promising, "If you report any more of our babies to the Board of Health we will kill you and nobody will know what happened to you. Keep off our streets and don't report our homes and we will do you no harm" (Rogers, 1992, p. 54).

The point here is to underscore the fact that opposition to name based reporting is not new. Although it is important to note that as part of the tradition of public health practice it had gone largely unquestioned in recent years – until AIDS. While infectious disease reporting represents the oldest example of public health surveillance, the creation of vaccine registries – designed to prevent infectious disease by tracking the vaccination history of children by name of the child and parents and following them across states and over time – represents the most recent effort. Development of vaccine registries began in the 1970s, but only recently have federal efforts to coordinate and link these registries begun. On January 12, 1999, in response to sporadic disease outbreaks, poor coverage in urban, inner-city communities, increasingly complex vaccine schedules, family mobility, and poor provider and patient awareness of immunization coverage levels, the National Vaccine Advisory Committee (NVAC), as part of the federal Initiative on Immunization Registries, recommended creation of a nationwide network of state and community immunization registries (NVAC, http://www.cdc.gov/nip/registry/i_recs.htm).

The federal initiative to register immunization coverage put a premium on community participation and cooperation, principally because of the fears of immigrant communities (worried that registry information would be a means of alerting the Immigration and Naturalization Service to their status), parents (those who opposed vaccination for their children feared that they would be harassed and discriminated against), and providers (those with low immunization rates were concerned that they would be "punished" in some fashion).

Central to the recommendations of the National Vaccine Advisory Committee was the protection of patient confidentiality. Registry developers were to give careful consideration to privacy and confidentiality issues in a way that reflected the values and special needs of the communities they served. The committee's analysis of confidentiality highlighted the fact that a tension existed between a need for the completeness of data and risks of unacceptable disclosure. The committee thus adopted as a guiding principle a commitment to direct, active parental notification that the registry exists and to parental choice in participation: "Parents," said NVAC, "must be given the option to decide whether or not their children will participate in a registry." Remarkably, despite these recommendations, the most recent survey of immunization registries has found that 35 rely on implied consent to participation in registries and that 12 states did not notify parents of their child's participation.

Cancer registries in the United States provide the primary example of a surveillance regime that has not produced ethical or political controversy (Tigerstrom, et al., 2000 and Cavoukian, 1992). Nevertheless such registries, by their very definition, represent an ongoing intrusion on privacy and confidentiality. Proposals to make cancer reportable date back more than 70 years (Wood, 1930). Cancer registries have been in existence for 60 years and, outside of infectious disease reporting, represent one of the most substantial efforts of the public health and medical communities to trace patterns of morbidity and mortality and evaluate therapeutic interventions. In 1971 the National Cancer Act mandated that collection and analysis of data on cancer be undertaken to assist in the prevention, treatment, and diagnosis of cancer. The Surveillance, Epidemiology, and End Results program at the National Cancer Institute was organized to take advantage of cancer data already being collected at several population-based tumor registries. Some 20 years later, Congress enacted the Cancer Registries Amendment Act (1992), which authorized the CDC to establish a national program in support of cancer registries. The goal of the program was to enhance existing registries and to help establish new ones so that all states would have registries that met minimum standards for completeness, timeliness, and quality.

Despite the wide array of medical information to which cancer registries are linked or linkable and the duration of surveillance for each case – from the first pathology report through death – few patients are ever told that they will be reported and followed over time.

Although cancer is historically a highly stigmatized disease and registration of cases in Western Europe has in recent years been the subject of strict regulation, the necessity for reporting and tracking those with cancer without consent has almost never been challenged in the United States. For example, in Rhode Island there is an exception to the confidentiality statute, which permits reporting of health care information on an individual to the state's central cancer registry (R.I. GEN. LAWS, 1987). While professionals often note the importance of preserving patient confidentiality, the focus of their concern has been on enhancing the reliability and usability of the registries as part of follow-up research (Hermeren, 1988).

When issues of privacy and confidentiality have been addressed, those most committed to cancer registries have argued strongly for the necessity of using names as the basis for linking records, grounding their arguments in the demands of surveillance accuracy. For example, researchers assert, "The incontrovertible fact is that linkage of individual records is essential if cancer is to be measured accurately, the causes ascertained at minimum expense, and the effect of control measures assessed. This is an issue that has to be faced squarely: one cannot have both absolute secrecy and rational cancer control" (Muir et al., 1985, p. 21). The North American Association of Central Cancer Registries has declared, "The public health surveillance system must be exempted from restrictions on collection and retention of personal identifying information in medical privacy legislation. Personal identifiers ... must be collected ... without individual consent" (North American Association of Central Cancer Registries, 1999).

In a climate where privacy and confidentiality concerns have become so salient, the status and function of cancer registries has become a matter of consternation. In 1999 the National Cancer Institute (NCI) noted, "Unfortunately, in the current concern about confidentiality protections, the needs of clinical research are not often explicitly addressed. Some of the contemplated or actual legal remedies, or their interpretation, seriously threaten the conduct of important medical research." The NCI explained, "One of the difficulties in the formation of policy to cover a broad and complex area like health care is that laws or regulations designed to protect against worst-case scenarios may exert unintended and highly adverse consequences on the conduct of medical research, which depends on access to and exchange of information" (National Cancer Institute, http://www.nci.nih.gov/confidentiality.html).

It was not however only public health agencies that were concerned with how privacy standards could effect registries. In sharp contrast to the events that surrounded AIDS, breast cancer advocates urged the maintenance of reporting requirements. The National Breast Cancer Coalition, in their February 2001 "Position Statement on Medical Privacy" (NBCC, http://www.natlbcc.org/bin/index.htm) stressed, "The fundamental right to privacy must include the right to keep one's health information confidential and control the flow of and access to this information," but noted, "Privacy protections should ensure that health information remains private but should not impede the progress of medical research." The statement continued, "Specific authorization to disclose health care information should be required for uses that are not directly related to treatment, payment, or health care operations. A trustworthy system with a proper informed consent process should create an environment where most people would not object to sharing health care information for the purpose of research. With large studies," the NBCC noted, "there are legitimate and serious questions about the feasibility of seeking individual authorizations, because sometimes the research involves thousands of individuals. In cases where it is not possible or feasible to obtain individual consent, there should be clear, consistent and transparent criteria for determining when individual authorization should be waived." The statement acknowledged, "While data can be encrypted, researchers need to link this data back to individuals in order to generate meaningful conclusions." This commitment to research was put to the test in Massachusetts, where an effort to make cancer registration voluntary was opposed by breast cancer advocates who declared: "To have that kind of requirement would certainly undermine 100 percent ascertainment" (NBCC, 2001, http://www.natlbcc.org/bin/index.htm). This encounter underscores the fact that there are occasions when those whose privacy will be compromised view such limits not as a burden but as serving their interests. This pattern could also be seen in the context of occupational disease reporting.

Although sixty thousand people die each year of occupational diseases and the federal government has borne primary responsibility for the surveillance of occupational diseases and injuries, advocates of workers' health argue that such diseases and injuries are under-recognized (Rosenman et al., 1997). Advocates have accordingly urged that occupational diseases be made reportable for purposes of epidemiological surveillance and, significantly, intervention to protect workers' health.

It was the relative inadequacy of existing reporting mechanisms that ultimately led the National Institute for Occupational Safety and Health (NIOSH) to develop the Sentinel Event Notification System for Occupational Risks in 1987 (SENSOR). SENSOR helps 20 state programs expand their reporting capacity and develop standardized case definitions. The program initially focused on six targeted conditions (silicosis, occupational asthma, pesticide poisoning, lead poisoning, carpal tunnel syndrome, and noise-induced hearing loss) and has since expanded to include accidental amputation, work-related dermatitis, and injuries to minors. But the full range of occupational disease surveillance supported by NIOSH is much broader.

Infectious disease surveillance and its role in guiding public health efforts have also served as a model for those concerned about birth defects. In 2000, the Pew Environmental Health Commission declared, "The United States has an adequate network to capture data on infectious disease in order to spot dangerous outbreaks before they spread. Certainly, we know how to build an effective mechanism that provides the consistency of reporting data and privacy protections." What is needed, however, "is a national policy to guide state implementation of a comprehensive, modern tracking program that will help identify environmental and other preventable factors that contribute to birth defects and other disabilities and chronic diseases" (Pew Environmental Health Commission, 2000).

Although New Jersey required the reporting of birth defects in 1928, the modern era of birth defects registries did not begin until the 1960s, when the Thalidomide disaster and growing concern over addressing environmental and teratogenic hazards to the fetus in utero sparked new interest in surveillance (Hogan, 1994). The Metropolitan Atlanta Congenital Defects Program was the first new state-based registry, established in 1967. The pace of development was slow, however. The CDC began its own Birth Defects Monitoring Program using hospital discharge data in 1974 and became the largest source of birth defects information in the nation. But by 1978, only two states (Nebraska and Florida) had established registries. As of the mid-1980s, 14 additional states had developed registries. By the year 2000, 42 states had done so. In 1999, following a congressional mandate to develop a clearing house of birth defects surveillance, the CDC was given appropriations to establish or improve state-based surveillance.

Advocates for birth defects reporting note the importance of using names. For instance, CDC states, "the use of personal identifiers facilitates follow-up studies and allows investigators to link infant, maternal, and paternal records" (Lynberg and Edmonds, 1992).

This brief historical and contemporary review has sought to demonstrate that the move toward HIV name-based reporting must be viewed as entailing an effort to integrate HIV/AIDS into the broad system of public health surveillance in the United States, to end the exceptionalism that had characterized AIDS policy in the epidemic's formative period.

Nonetheless it is instructive to note that with its emphasis on name reporting, the United States sets itself apart from the practice common in Europe. In February 1998, a meeting of European experts convened under the auspices of the European Centre for the Epidemiological Monitoring of AIDS concluded:

> At the European level AIDS case reporting, introduced in 1984, has been the principal means of monitoring the epidemic. ... However, in the changing epidemiological context [AIDS case reporting] is no longer sufficient. HIV case reporting is a key element for HIV surveillance. ... It should be continued where it exists and, where necessary, developed. At a country level, confidentiality should be guaranteed and elimination of duplicate reports should be ensured. HIV case reports should be linkable with AIDS case reports (Hammers, 1998, p. 51).

All of this, the experts concluded, could be achieved without the use of names. The commitment to linkable records without the use of names reflected the professional concerns of epidemiologists troubled by the existence of reporting systems that failed to meet the highest statistical standards or accurate surveillance.

These recommendations reflected current practice regarding HIV reporting in Europe. A 1998 study found that 36 countries, including 9 European Union countries, had nationwide HIV reporting systems. Reporting was mandatory in 27. Notification was by name in 10 countries, by code in 20, and without unique identifiers in 6. Strikingly, the use of names was almost exclusively restricted to the former Communist nations. As in the United States, AIDS-related organizations in Europe have tended to support coded HIV reporting but oppose the use of names as a threat to privacy and human rights. Thus, in Spain, which approved a national anonymous registry of people with HIV using a 15-digit code, the Movimiento Cuidado Antisida supported the new registry, but expressed its opposition to the name-based approach adopted in the region of Asturias. "We do not agree with a [name-containing] registry since names of persons have nothing to do with the epidemiologic knowledge of the infection and, in addition, may seriously harm the confidentiality of a given person" (Bosch, 1999, p. 977).

Conclusion

The central ethical question posed by HIV name reporting indeed of all disease reporting is: When do the claims of public health legitimately trump the claims of privacy and confidentiality in the context of disease surveillance? A subsidiary question is: Do the claims of privacy carry sufficient weight to make reporting systems that are less accurate, but that are nevertheless adequate more compatible with ethical standards?

While these questions have, in some way, been at the heart of disease reporting for more than a century, with the exception of HIV/AIDS, despite almost three decades of systematic discussion of the ethics of human subjects research, no sustained discussion of the ethics of public health reporting has been undertaken. In the 1970s, Leon Gordis, Alexander Capron, and others began to discuss whether the emerging rules and regulations for human subjects research would apply to epidemiological studies, whether the principle of informed consent for the use of records was necessary, and whether such requirements would render epidemiological research virtually impossible (Gordis et al., 1977; Gordis and Gold, 1980; Gostin, 1991; Capron, 1991; Cann and Rothman, 1984; Hershey, 1985; Rothman, 1981).

32

Yet that discussion has not extended to public health surveillance. While research, including epidemiological research, has been the subject of IRB review, public health surveillance has not been subject to similar oversight. Indeed, dispute exists over the boundary distinguishing research – that must be subject to review – from public health practice – such as case identification and treatment (Snider and Stroup, 1997; Mariner, 1997).

Surveillance stands at the boundary of public health practice and research. Surveillance data is not collected toward the end of research, though it is clear that it serves those ends. Austin, for example, refers to cancer registries as "a tool in epidemiology" (Austin, 1983, pp. 119–140). And while Meriwether argues that research should not be confused with surveillance, she does acknowledge its critical role in the generation of research hypotheses (Meriwether, 1996). Finally, in the one chapter dealing with ethical issues in Teutsch and Churchill's *Principles and Practice of Public Health Surveillance*, Hahn states, "although several features may distinguish surveillance related ethical issues from ethical issues in other areas of epidemiology and public health, many of the ethical issues confronting public health surveillance are similar to those of epidemiology" (Hahn, 1994, pp. 175–189).

Surveillance, undertaken for public health purposes rather than epidemiological research, carries the risk, however small, that information might be inadvertently disclosed despite the best efforts to keep it confidential. It also may trigger public health intrusions, such as, in the case of HIV/AIDS, partner notification. Notifying the sexual partners of people with HIV may place them at risk of domestic violence, of losing housing, or of losing employment. Yet the consequences and risks change over time. As we have seen in the prior discussion, they vary by both the nature of the disease in question and the social perception of it. They also vary in terms of those who bear the burden of disease and their own sense of social vulnerability. Thus, as we noted, breast cancer advocates have proven adamantly opposed to the notion of requiring informed consent for registration of cases.

The case of HIV dramatically underscores the limits of considering ethical questions regarding surveillance out of political and social context, in a way that does not account for the characteristics of the people affected by disease including their agency and vulnerability, the cultural perception of the disease in question, and the public health consequences of disease. Fairness requires that equals be treated equally. It also requires that where morally relevant differences exist, they be taken into account. In short, we must begin to account for those factors – such as race, gender, and class that clinical medical ethics needed to elide to prevent researchers from capitalizing on social or political vulnerability in designing and conducting studies – in a systematic yet not rigid fashion.

What then can be said about how the confrontation over the limits of privacy and confidentiality should have gone forward in the case of HIV and should go forward in other instances of surveillance? What standards should govern decision-making? The following might serve as principles worthy of consideration.

1. Wherever the state seeks to breach confidentiality for purposes of the surveillance it bears the burden of demonstrating that such an intrusion on privacy is critical for the ends of protecting the public health.
2. When the state breaches confidentiality in the name of surveillance it must demonstrate that it has taken all necessary steps to protect the confidentiality of the names it will collect; that it has in place mechanisms that will preclude the possibility or unwarranted intrusions upon its records; that it has promulgated regulations and laws that will penalize unwarranted intrusions.
3. When those whose names are to be reported express fears about how they will suffer as a consequence of notification the state must seek to address their concerns directly and respectfully in a process of an open consultation.

But, though officials and even some advocates may prize the demands of public health over those of privacy, in the end it is clear that there is an inherent tension between public health and the claims of privacy, though the response to the tension may vary over time and place. What we have a right to expect is that the balance struck will be fair, judicious, and carefully wrought. To believe, however, that we can escape the tension is a dangerous illusion.

References

Austin D. (1983) Cancer Registries: A Tool in Epidemiology. *Reviews in Cancer Research* **2**, 119–140.

Bayer R. (1989) *Private Acts Social Consequences: Aids and the Politics of Public Health.* New Brunswick: Rutgers University Press.

Bayer R. (1991) Public Health Policy and the AIDS Epidemic: an End to HIV Exceptionalism? *N Eng J Med* **324**, 1500–1504.

Bayer R. (1999) Clinical Progress and the Future of HIV Exceptionalism. *Arch Intern Med* **159**, 1042–1048.

Bosch. (1999) Confidential Spanish Registry of HIV-infected Individuals. *JAMA* **281**, 977.

Brandt A. (1987) *No Magic Bullet*. New York: Oxford University Press.

Cann C. and Rothman, K. (1984) IRBs and Epidemiologic Research: How Inappropriate Restrictions Hamper Studies. *IRB: A Review of Human Subjects Research*, July/August: 5–7.

34

Capron A. (1991) Protection of Research Subjects: Do Special Rules Apply in Epidemiology? *Law, Medicine, and Health Care* **19**, 184–90.

CDC (1990) Update: public health surveillance for HIV infection – United States, 1989 and 1990. *MMWR* **39**, 861.

CDC (1997) HIV/AIDS Surveillance Report. Atlanta: CDC 8.

CDC (1998) Evaluation of HIV case surveillance through the use of non-name unique identifiers: Maryland and Texas, 1994–1996. *MMWR* **46**, 1254–1258.

CDC (1999) *Guidelines for national human immunodeficiency virus case surveillance.* Atlanta: CDC, pp. 1–28.

Eyler J. (1979) *Victorian Social Medicine: the Ideas and Methods of William Farr.* Baltimore: Johns Hopkins University Press.

Emerson H. (1917) *A Monograph on The Epidemic of Poliomyelitis [Infantile Paralysis] in New York City in 1916. Based on the Official Reports of the Bureaus of the Department of Health* New York: Department of Health.

Fox D. (1975) Social Policy and City Politics: Tuberculosis Reporting in New York, 1889–1900. *Bulletin of the History of Medicine* **49**, 169–195.

Fox D. (1986) From TB to AIDS: Value Conflicts in Reporting Disease. *Hastings Center Report*, December, 11–17.

Gordis L., Gold E. and Seltzer R. (1977) Privacy Protection in Epidemiologic and Medical Research: A Challenge and a Responsibility. *American Journal of Epidemiology* **105**, 163–168.

Gordis L. and Gold E. (1980) Privacy, Confidentiality and the Use of Medical Records in Research. *Science* **207**, 153–156.

Gostin L. (1991) Ethical Principles for the Conduct of Human Subject Research: Population-Based Research and Ethics. *Law, Medicine, and Health Care* **19**, 191–201.

Gostin L., Ward J. and Baker C. (1997) National HIV case reporting for the United States: a defining moment in the history of the epidemic. *N Engl J Med.* **337**, 1162–1167.

Hahn R. (1994) Ethical Issues. In: S. Teutsch and R. Elliott (Eds.) *Principles and Practice of Public Health Surveillance* (pp. 175–189). New York: Oxford University Press.

Hammers F. (1998) Recommendations for HIV Surveillance in Europe. *Eurosurveillance* **3**, 5, 51.

Hershey N. (1985) IRB Jurisdiction and Limits on IRB Actions. *IRB: A Review of Human Subjects Research* March/April, 7–9.

Hermeren G. (1988) Ethical Problems in Register Based Medical Research. *Theoretical Medicine* **9**, 105–116.

Hogan J. (1994) The Michigan Birth Defects Registry: Development and Operation. *Journal of AHIMA* **65**(6), 38–40.

Intergovernmental Health Policy Project (1989) HIV Reporting in the states. *Intergovernmental AIDS Reports* November- December.

Joseph S. (1989) Remarks at the 5th International Conference on AIDS. (June 5) mimeo.

Lynberg M. and Edmonds L. (1992) Surveillance of Birth Defects. In: W. Halperin and E.L. Baker (Eds.), *Public Health Surveillance.* New York: Nostrand Reinhold, pp. 157–177.

Mariner W. (1997) Public confidence in public health research ethics. *Public Health Reports* **112**, 33–36.

Meriwether R. (1996) Blueprint for a National Public Health Surveillance System for the 21st Century. *Journal of Public Health Management Practice* **2**(4), 16–23.

Muir C., Demaret E. and Boyle P. (1985) The Cancer Registry in Cancer Control: An Overview. *The Role of the Registry in Cancer Control.* IARC Scientific Publications, 21.

35

National Vaccine Advisory Committee Report of the National Vaccine Advisory Committee (NVAC), Development of Community-and State-Based Immunization Registries. http://www.cdc.gov/nip/reistry/i_recs.htm.

National Breast Cancer Coalition, www.natlbcc.org/bin/index.htm. National Cancer Institute. Confidentiality, Data Security, and Cancer Research: "Perspectives from the National Cancer Institute," http://www.nci.nih.gov/confidentiality.html.

North American Association of Central Cancer Registries (1999) Policy Statement 99–01: Confidentiality. November 17.

Pew Environmental Health Commission (2000) Healthy from the Start: Why America Needs a Better System to Track and Understand Birth Defects and the Environment.

Rhode Island General Laws. 5–37. 3–4(b) (18) 1987.

Rogers N. (1992) *Dirt and Disease: Polio Before FDR* (pp. 54). New Brunswick: Rutgers University Press.

Rosenman K., Reilly M. and Kalinowski D. (1997) A State-Based Surveillance System for Work-Related Asthma. *JOEM* **39**(5), 415–425.

Rothman K. (1981) The Rise and Fall of Epidemiology, 1950–2000 A.D. *NEJM*, March 5, 600–602.

Snider D. and Stroup D. (1997) Defining research when it comes to public health. *Public Health Reports* **112**, 29–32.

Snow W. (1917) Public Health Measures in "Relation to Venereal Diseases," *Proceedings of the Second Pan American Scientific Congress*, 1915–1916, Section 8, Part I (Washington, D.C.) 9: 491.

Von Tigerstrom B., Deschenes M., Knoppers B. and Caulfield, T. (2000) Legal Regulation of Cancer Surviellance: Canadian and International Perspectives. *Health L J* **8**, 1.

Wood F. (1930) Need for Cancer Morbidity Statistics. *AJPH*, 11–19.

Part IX
Prevention and its Limits

[28]

INDIVIDUAL AND COLLECTIVE CONSIDERATIONS IN PUBLIC HEALTH: INFLUENZA VACCINATION IN NURSING HOMES

MARCEL VERWEIJ

ABSTRACT

Many nursing homes have an influenza vaccination policy in which it is assumed that express (proxy) consent is not necessary. Tacit consent procedures are more efficient if one aims at high vaccination rates. In this paper I focus on incompetent residents and proxy consent. Tacit proxy consent for vaccination implies a deviance of standard proxy consent requirements. I analyse several arguments that may possibly support such a deviance. The primary reason to offer influenza vaccination is that vaccinated persons have a significantly reduced risk of getting the flu. This reason however cannot support the assumption that each nursing home resident is 'better off' if she is vaccinated. Neither can it support tacit proxy consent policies. More promising are arguments that take the collective nature of infectious diseases into account. A potentially strong, but ultimately insufficient, argument for non-express consent is that vaccination contributes to prevention of harm to others. Other arguments emphasise the importance of group protection: herd immunity. I discuss three collective reasons for aiming at herd immunity: solidarity, a common interest in reducing the risk of illness, and a common interest in the prevention of an influenza outbreak. The latter argument appears to be most important. An outbreak is not just detrimental to the health of residents; it is detrimental to their everyday social life as well. Outbreaks can be seen as a collective evil. My analysis shows that there are valid (though not necessarily sufficient) moral arguments for a tacit proxy consent policy.

INTRODUCTION

Public health and preventive medicine are relatively neglected areas in bioethics. This may be partly due to the focus of bioethics on interests, rights, and obligations of individual persons. Ethical issues in preventive medicine on the other hand require a shift of attention to collective interests and values. In public health, collective interests and community values are often considered as outweighing individual interests and rights.[1] Such a view is however too crude. Collective reasons are diverse and not all are equally strong and overriding. A fruitful public health ethics at least requires a taxonomy of collective values and interests. In my paper I focus on one example of preventive medicine: influenza vaccination in nursing home practice. I discuss several arguments that may or may not support a strong preventive policy, going from 'simple' arguments about the good of individuals to various types of collective reasons.

INFLUENZA VACCINATION AND TACIT CONSENT

In the Netherlands, persons who belong to certain risk groups are invited once a year to visit their family physician in order to get influenza vaccinations. Participation is voluntary; only persons who want vaccinations will respond and get them. The case is different for elderly persons living in nursing homes, especially for persons who are not fully competent to consent. Often, nursing homes do not require explicit consent for vaccination against influenza, although, presumably, if a person or her proxy refuses vaccination, this refusal will be respected. In other words, at least a number of institutions follow a 'tacit consent' procedure.[2,3] Such a procedure diverges from normal

[1] Cf. D.E. Beauchamp. Community: the neglected tradition of public health. *Hastings Center Report* 1985; 15: 28-3-6; S.A. Hall. Should public health respect autonomy? *Journal of Medical Ethics* 1992; 18: 197–201; and, notably, M. Lappé. 1986. Ethics and public health. In: *Maxcy-Rosenau Public Health and Preventive Medicine.* J.M. Last, ed. Norwal. Appleton: 1867–77.

[2] The first results of a survey we are carrying out in the Netherlands give us reason to believe some 50% of all nursing homes follow a tacit proxy consent procedure with respect to vaccination of incompetent residents.

[3] Beauchamp and Childress (1994. *Principles of Biomedical Ethics.* New York. Oxford UP: 128–130) distinguish several forms of consent which diverge from express consent: tacit consent, implicit consent, and presumed consent. Tacit consent involves information disclosure and opportunity for the person to object or refuse. If the person does not object, this is interpreted as consent. Presumed consent is a bit different: normally, patients do not have to give

requirements of (proxy) consent and one may question whether this divergence is morally justified.[4] I think there are some valid reasons for a tacit consent procedure, but suspect that these differ from the justifications in current nursing home policies. I will focus on vaccination of decisional incompetent residents and on the reasons for following a procedure of *tacit proxy consent.*

TWO INSUFFICIENT ARGUMENTS FOR TACIT CONSENT

Why follow a tacit consent procedure? The obvious answer is that this is an efficient way to realise a high vaccination rate in the nursing home, and hence a reduced morbidity and mortality.[5] Moreover, one may expect that, if requested, almost all proxies would consent to vaccination and only a few would not. Therefore it is more efficient to inform about the intention to vaccinate all residents and give proxies the opportunity to object. Objectors will probably respond rather promptly, so reminders are not necessary and the whole procedure of information and consent will only take a limited amount of time. In this way vaccination procedures can be completed before the influenza season dawns.

Both arguments offer insufficient support for a tacit consent vaccination policy. This is because, apparently, both arguments start from a strong *presumption* in favour of vaccination. They only offer support as far as it is justified to presume that vaccination of nursing home residents serves an uncontroversial and obvious interest of the residents as individuals or as a group. Such a justification should not remain implicit, especially because the presumption aims to support a policy that diverges from standard

consent for each part of a medical procedure. If they have consented to a treatment plan, they are often presumed to have consented to parts or implications of the treatment plan as well.

[4] In this paper I take the legal assumption for granted that in case a person is incompetent for decision making, health care providers have obligations of informed consent towards the person's (legal) representative. The representative 'observes' the patient's rights to informed consent, hence the requirements of informed consent do not change. I am not certain about this assumption. However, justifying and/or adjusting this assumption would require a theory of (proxy) informed consent; developing such a theory is not my aim in this research project.

[5] See, for example, K.L. Nichol, M.B. Grimm, D.C. Peterson. Immunizations in long-term care facilities: policies and practice. *J Am Geriatr Soc.* 1996; 44: 349–55; N. Arden, A.S. Monto, S.E. Ohmit. Vaccine use and the risk of outbreaks in a sample of nursing homes during an influenza epidemic. *Am J Public Health* 1995; 85: 399–401.

informed proxy consent procedures. Therefore, some questions need to be answered: (1) Why is a high vaccination rate important? (2) Does this importance yield a valid argument for a non-express proxy consent policy? And finally, (3) are the arguments sufficient to justify non-express consent? My primary interest is in the first two questions and especially in answers that refer to collective reasons.

THE BENEFIT FOR INDIVIDUALS

However, the most important reason to offer persons vaccination is not a collective reason. Vaccinated persons have a considerably reduced risk of getting the flu. Influenza may be rather harmless for persons who are otherwise healthy, but, especially among the elderly, there is a serious risk of complications requiring hospitalisation and which may result in loss of functions and even death. So there is an important reason to vaccinate nursing home residents: vaccination protects their health, and hence their well being. As the side-effects of the influenza vaccination are generally considered rather mild, this argument about the medical benefit of vaccination for individual residents seems strong enough to support the presumption in favour of vaccination, and possibly the choice for a tacit consent policy. Is this latter conclusion justified? Moreover, is it justified, in nursing homes, to adopt a 'tacit consent' procedure for medical interventions that have proven to be effective and that do not involve serious side-effects? I am not sure about that. At least I would hold that such justification would require that the intervention contributes in a rather uncontroversial, 'evident' way to the person's good. (For example, if a resident suffers from a fierce headache, presumed consent for a therapy that relieves the pain, e.g. paracetamol, seems perfectly justified.)

Does influenza vaccination involve such an obvious good to individual nursing home residents? There is a controversial reason to reject this general claim. Frail elderly persons who get the flu may develop serious, even fatal complications, notably pneumonia. Vaccination reduces these risks. Normally, avoidance of such illnesses and complications can be considered a benefit. For some old persons however, this is not necessarily the case. Pneumonia is sometimes considered 'an old man's friend'.[6] This is not to say that it is a good thing if old persons die

[6] See for example, W.A. Hensel. The old man's friend. *JAMA* 2000; 283: 1793–4.

of pneumonia. Yet pneumonia may result in a relatively mild process of dying: sometimes this 'premature death' is less tragic and painful than a slowly devastating disease, for example Alzheimer's. This consideration challenges the thought that health professionals may safely *presume* that the medical benefits of influenza vaccination contribute to a good life of frail elderly persons.[7] Instead, it makes sense to discuss the meaningfulness of influenza vaccination with residents or proxies.

Of course, influenza vaccination protects the health of each vaccinated resident, and this is the most important reason to have a vaccination policy in the first place. Yet I have argued that this interest of individual persons provides insufficient support for a tacit proxy consent procedure. However, the interests involved in a nursing home vaccination policy go beyond the private interests of each resident. In the remainder of this paper I distinguish some collective reasons that may (or may not) provide for additional support for vaccination policies. Do these reasons support a non-express consent policy?

VACCINATION PREVENTS HARM TO OTHERS

Vaccination not only reduces the risk of becoming ill, it thereby also reduces the chance that one person will infect others. Hence it may be argued that vaccination prevents harm to others. This argument, if successful, would not only support the presumption in favour of vaccination, but also give direct support to a non-express consent policy. After all, in a liberal democratic society, the prevention of harm to others is generally considered a legitimate cause for constraints on autonomy. Now, if prevention of harm to others justifies constraining autonomy and even the use of force or compulsion, it may certainly justify a policy which resumes to a weak version of consent, viz. tacit proxy consent.

This argument faces at least two problems, a medical and a philosophical one. First, if vaccination prevents persons from getting the flu, it seems awkward and medically inefficient to vaccinate person A in order to protect B; after all, B is best protected if she is vaccinated herself, hence the intention to prevent contamination from A to B seems rather superfluous. This objection however is not fully justified. Vaccination does protect against influenza, but it is not a guarantee against the disease. It is notably less effective in persons whose immune system is compromised. So, the weakest, bedridden residents are still at risk of getting the flu,

[7] The same holds for pneumococcal vaccination.

even though they may have been vaccinated themselves. Moreover, these people probably run an increased risk of disabling, even fatal complications of influenza. Hence, vaccination may indeed prevent residents from infecting other residents.

The philosophical objection is, however, more serious. The argument about prevention of harm to others only succeeds if contamination with the flu can be considered as a case of *harm*. Now if the influenza virus passes from me to you, can it be said that I harmed you? Contamination may imply a setback of your interests, but that is not sufficient to see it as a case of harm. According to Joel Feinberg, harm occurs when a setback to interests results from an action (or omission) that is *wrong*.[8] Now, first it is far from clear that influenza contamination can be considered as springing from my actions or omissions. Apart from epistemic problems (how can we know that it was me who brought you the flu?), it seems awkward to analyse contamination in terms of the actions of me. My body may have hosted the influenza virus, and the virus may have struck you because I had a talk with you, but it was not *me* who made you ill. It may be argued that I had a possibility to prevent contamination, either by having myself vaccinated, or by staying out of your neighbourhood. The latter possibility only makes sense if I know that I host the virus (for example because I am ill myself). What about the former: vaccination? Can it be possible that I wronged you because I forwent vaccination? Probably, foregoing vaccination will only be considered morally wrong if such foregoing involved considerable risk to others, and if the vaccination of a person would significantly reduce these risks to others. Both premises are questionable. If few residents are vaccinated, then *my* vaccination will have little effect on your risk of becoming ill. Of course, my vaccination contributes to your protection. But my contribution is only significant if there is already a strong *protection within our whole group*. If it is difficult to see foregoing vaccination as a case of wrongful harm, the argument of harm to others is not a convincing justification for a non-express consent vaccination policy.

THE COLLECTIVE NATURE AND VALUE OF HERD IMMUNITY

The justifying idea behind a tacit consent procedure is that either vaccination belongs to 'standard due care' (involving an evident

[8] J. Feinberg. 1984. *Harm to Others. The Moral Limits of the Criminal Law I.* Oxford University Press: 36.

benefit for persons) – this is what I have rejected earlier – or that, from a collective point of view, a high vaccination rate is a good thing to aspire to. This latter aim finds support in the ('surplus') benefits of a strong herd immunity. Vaccination of some residents will have little effect on the *spread* of a virus, especially if there are many contacts between many persons within the population. Yet if many residents are vaccinated, this will result in an increased protection, due to the emerging 'herd immunity'. The more people who are immune, the fewer hosts there are for the virus. Hence reproduction and spreading of the virus will become more difficult. As a result, the risk of infection will decrease, both for vaccinated and non-vaccinated members of the population. Herd immunity only emerges if a population's vaccination rate is high. Evidently, establishing herd immunity requires a collective effort and participation. What kind of (collective) values and interests support this quest for a *high* (adequate) vaccination rate, and may these values support tacit consent procedures?

HERD IMMUNITY PROTECTS THE MOST VULNERABLE RESIDENTS AGAINST ILLNESS

If the vaccination rate is high enough to result in a 'herd immunity' this implies that all residents have a reduced chance of coming into contact with the influenza virus. Especially persons who are not vaccinated and persons for whom vaccination offers inadequate protection will benefit from herd immunity. Now the aim to protect these vulnerable persons is worthwhile, but is it strong enough to justify a policy in which residents are vaccinated on the basis of non-express consent? Such an argument may be valid if some sort of solidarity among residents can be assumed. Solidarity involves a collective value.[9] In our case, solidarity implies that residents would think it important to protect the weakest persons among them, and therefore consider it important to, and are prepared to contribute to a high vaccination rate. If this were true, then it could be reasonable to choose for a non-express consent vaccination policy, because it would be the most efficient means to realise the shared goal: optimum vaccination rates. However, it will be difficult to justify the thought that the incompetent residents on which we are focusing would be *willing* to share certain burdens in order to

[9] See for example G. Postema. Collective Evils, Harms, and the Law. *Ethics* 1987; 97: 414–440.

contribute to protection of co-residents. Hence, the collective value of solidarity cannot serve to justify policies that aim at optimum vaccination rates, and, consequently, it cannot justify a non-express consent policy either.

ALL RESIDENTS HAVE A COMMON INTEREST IN A STRONG HERD IMMUNITY

Instead of appealing to the value of solidarity, one may propose a weaker claim to support the aim to realise herd immunity. Especially residents whose physical health is compromised will benefit from herd immunity. Now, many if not all residents are frail and face the possibility that their health will decline for some reason (for example the common cold). Given this uncertainty, all have an interest in collective protection against influenza. Hence, all residents, in their capacity of persons at risk, have an interest in vaccination but also in a policy that aims to increase vaccination rates in order to realise herd immunity. Is this common interest in a vaccination increasing policy a strong argument in favour of non-express consent procedures?

To get the argument clear we should analyse in which sense this argument involves a collective type of interest. First, one may hold that most if not all residents share an interest in protection against influenza, hence they have an interest in common. This *common* interest however does not yet make clear why some sort of pressure or instigation in the form of non-express consent could be justified.[10] The crucial element of the argument is that it is about protective *herd* immunity. This goal is necessarily a collective goal; it can only be realised if enough members of a group participate, i.e. are being vaccinated. If most residents share an interest in such a collective goal, this may be a good reason to rule out frustration of the goal as a result of the forgetfulness or indecisiveness of proxies who do not reply to a vaccination offer. Nursing home residents have a common interest in a collective goal and to establish this collective goal some 'pressure', viz. a tacit consent procedure, may be necessary.

The argument however is not yet fully convincing. This is because it rests on the assumption that the nursing home residents, as persons at risk of getting ill, do have an important interest in protection against the flu. Above I have pointed out

[10] Analogously, if all persons in a conference session share an interest in extending the discussion for two hours, this is still not a valid reason for making it more difficult to leave the room.

that this assumption is not self-evident. Of course, probably all will have a stake in avoiding the burdens of illness (fever, fatigue, pain, etc.) But to some residents, influenza with its possible lethal effects could be considered a 'friend' rather than a 'foe'. They will have an interest in protection against the burdens of illness, but, at the same time, *not* have an interest in protection against the flu because this disease may stop a long lasting process of deterioration and suffering. It is an open question as to how these interests are to be weighed, or, in other words, what the *net* interest is of these residents.

Anyhow, the argument of this section can be put forward as one valid reason to support a tacit consent procedure for influenza vaccination. Residents have a shared interest in a policy that aims to establish the collective goal of herd immunity. Tacit consent procedures may help to prevent that this goal is frustrated as a result of negligence or forgetfulness of proxies. This shared interest of residents in establishing herd immunity however does not imply that *all* have a *net* interest in such a policy.

There is also a second way in which this argument requires qualification. The weight of this argument in a justification of tacit consent procedures depends on the difference herd immunity makes for persons who are vaccinated anyway. What is the marginal benefit of a herd immunity for individual (vaccinated) members of the group? This question requires epidemiological expertise, yet it seems clear that from the perspective of a vaccinated individual, the establishment of a herd immunity may make relatively little difference to one's personal risk of getting ill.

ALL RESIDENTS SHARE AN INTEREST IN THE PREVENTION OF AN INFLUENZA OUTBREAK

The latter consideration however does not downgrade the importance of herd immunity. Herd immunity is not just important because it reduces the health risks of (all) individual persons. A strong herd immunity is also important because it reduces the chance of a large outbreak of influenza within the institution. The detrimental effects of such an outbreak exceed the influenza morbidity and mortality. If many residents become ill, this may have tremendous effects on the daily life of residents and the workload for nurses and other caregivers. Ill patients will require the most attention and care and this may reduce the resources for daily care, visits, talks, walks and other activities of all residents. Hence, an influenza outbreak may have a grave impact on social life and the quality of care in the institution.

Given these non-health effects, all residents regardless of their vaccination status, health, or risk of becoming ill, or other particular capabilities, have a common interest, in policies that reduce the risk of influenza outbreaks. This common interest is not just shared by persons who opt for vaccination (either by themselves or through their proxies). All, including the persons for whom pneumonia could be considered 'a best friend', share this interest simply because all live in the institution and because outbreaks will affect social life and institutional care.

If one focuses not just on the effects of outbreaks on the health of individuals, but also on the effects on their social life and on the care they are given, then a policy which prevents outbreaks could well serve a *net* interest of all residents.

This argument appeals to the collective on three different levels. First, it refers to a *common* interest of all residents in a vaccination policy. But, as explained above, the fact that residents have a common interest in a vaccination policy is not as such a good reason for following a tacit consent procedure. Second, there is a goal (herd immunity) which can only be attained if *enough* residents are vaccinated. This at least can be considered a valid reason for a tacit consent procedure. However, one may question the strength of this argument. If herd immunity is only aimed for because it further reduces each person's risk of getting ill, then the argument depends on the marginal benefits of herd immunity for individual persons, above the benefit they receive from personal vaccination. The third 'level' of collectiveness strengthens the case for tacit consent procedures. An outbreak in a long term care institution can be considered a 'collective evil'. If many residents fall ill in the same period, this may have a negative impact on the normal care each person receives and hence on each person's social life and well being. This argument supports the idea that the value of collective health, hence the importance of a reduction of morbidity, exceeds the aggregate value of the health of individuals.

To conclude, are arguments as explained strong enough to justify a tacit consent procedure? I cannot answer this question by now, as my analysis only concerned one tier of the pair of scales. In my introduction I assumed that tacit consent procedures in medicine do not fully satisfy standards of informed consent. Hence it seems as if tacit consent procedures do violate (though possibly in a justified way) a principle of respect for autonomy. This assumption may be correct in 'normal cases' of medical treatment for competent persons. But what about incompetent persons and their proxies? Evidently, the justification, meaning and weight of consent standards will differ if they apply to patients themselves or to their proxies. I will not go into this complex subject. If tacit proxy consent is to be regarded a non-optimal form of proxy consent, this divergence requires justification. I rest my case with the conclusion that there are valid collective reasons that support such a 'violation' in a nursing home influenza policy; whether these are strong enough remains an open question.

Marcel Verweij
Centre for Bioethics and Health Law, Utrecht University
Heidelberglaan 2, NL 3582 CZ Utrecht, The Netherlands
mverweij@theo.uu.nl

[29]

The Precautionary Principle, Epidemiology and the Ethics of Delay

Elihu D. Richter and Richard Laster (with comment by Colin Soskolne)
Unit of Occupational and Environmental Medicine, Hebrew University-Hadassah School of Public Health and Community Medicine, Jerusalem, Israel

ABSTRACT

Ethics tells us: do good and do no harm and invokes the norms of justice, equity and respect for autonomy in protecting and promoting health and well-being. The Precautionary Principle, a contemporary re-definition of Bradford Hill's case for action, gives us a common sense rule for doing good by preventing harm to public health from delay: when in doubt about the presence of a hazard, there should be no doubt about its prevention or removal. It shifts the burden of proof from showing presence of risk to showing absence of risk, aims to do good by preventing harm, and subsumes the upstream strategies of the DPSEEA (Driving Forces Pressure Stress Exposure Effect Action) model and downstream strategies from molecular epidemiology for detection and prevention of risk. The Precautionary Principle has emerged because of the ethical import of delays in detection of risks to human health and the environment. Ethical principles, the Precautionary Principle, the DPSEEA model and molecular epidemiology all imply re-emphasizing epidemiology's classic rôle for early detection and prevention. Delays in recognizing risks from past exposures and acting on the findings (e.g., cigarette smoking and lung cancer, asbestos, organochlorines and endocrine disruption, radiofrequency, raised travel speeds) were examples of failures that were not only scientific, but ethical, since they resulted in preventable harm to exposed populations. These may delay results from, among other things, external and internal determinants of epidemiologic investigations of hazard and risk, including misuse of tests of statistical significance. Furthermore, applying the Precautionary Principle to ensure justice, equity, and respect for autonomy raises questions concerning the short-term costs of implementation to achieve long-term goals and the principles that guide compensation.

Key Words: Precautionary Principle, epidemiology, ethics, delay.

This article is reprinted with permission from the *European Journal of Oncology Library*, vol. 2, 2003, with which the copyright resides.
Address correspondence to Prof. Elihu D. Richter, Unit of Occupational and Environmental Medicine, Hebrew University-Hadassah School of Public Health and Community Medicine, POB 12272, Jerusalem, Israel. E-mail: elir@cc.huji.ac.il

"The time is short, the work is great, the master of the house is waiting, the workers are lazy, and it is not for you to finish the job, but you are not exempt from beginning"
"If not now, when?"

The Talmud[3]

"Epidemiology is merely a tool for helping people in trouble"

Irving J. Selikoff

INTRODUCTION

Ethics tells us: do good and do no harm. It invokes the norms of justice, equity, and respect for autonomy as values governing relationships between human beings as individuals[1,2] (Table 1). The preservation, protection and promotion of life is the norm by which we judge the worth of all activities (Talmud).[3] It follows that we endorse activities that bring us closer to this norm and reject activities that do not—a viewpoint common to classic theologic and humanistic traditions.[4] These traditions exhort us to protect the weakest and most vulnerable. Social contracts and laws seek to translate these ethical norms into systems of justice, laws and social organization. Right to know, right to act, informed consent and compensation are some of legal tools these systems use. Failure to use these tools leads to abuse of these ethical norms.[5,6]

The Precautionary Principle restates common sense rules for doing good by preventing harm: "better to be safe than sorry" or "when in doubt about the presence of a hazard, there should be no doubt about its prevention or removal."[7] Bradford Hill's term—the case for action—the need for intervention when there is uncertainty concerning definitive proof of causation, anticipated the Precautionary Principle.[8]

The Precautionary Principle repudiates waiting for result of complete assessment of past risk, especially when the results are severe, and not doing everything possible to anticipate future risk, so as narrow the time gap between suspicion and verification.[9] In other words, time is of the essence.

The major components of the Precautionary Principle are: defining the risk to be prevented, shifting of the burden of proof from demonstration of risk to demonstration of absence of risk, reducing risk through substitute technologies or

Table 1. Ethics, norms, and legal tools

Ethics
Do good
Do no harm
Norms
Justice
Equity
Respect for autonomy.
Legal tools
Right to know
Right to act
Informed consent
Compensation

Table 2. Precautionary Principle.

Aim:	Do good by preventing harm
Implication:	When in doubt (about the presence of a hazard), there should be no doubt (about its prevention or removal)
Redefinition:	Bradford-Hill's case for action
Ethical Issues:	Delay, benefits vs. risks, risks vs. risks

removal or modifying a hazardous technology exposure at the source, and promoting modal shifts and substitution, and using interventions proportionate in cost to the costs of the prevented hazards and risks. There is also emphasis on rigorous evaluation of the efficacy of interventions, in terms of benefits versus the risks, or the risks of doing something as opposed to waiting and doing nothing[9–12] (Table 2).

The strategies of the Precautionary Principle mesh with those of the World Health Organization (WHO) model for DPSEEA for doing good by preventing harm. The DPSEEA model is utopian; it promotes "upstream" change in social, economic and technological systems to prevent creation of hazard and risk in the first place in a time line going from driving force → pressure → stress → exposure → effect → action.[11] But the Precautionary Principle also subsumes molecular epidemiology, which though it restricts itself to the "downstream" detection of effects of exposures inside living systems, offers promise of preventing delay by earlier—i.e., faster—detection of risk.[13,14]

Epidemiology's missions are the early detection and prevention of risk and the study of the distribution and determinants of disease.[15] The first mission tells us time is short and the message is to hurry up. The second tells us not to rush into premature conclusions. The two missions are based on contrasting interpretations of the adage "better to be safe than sorry"; the first from the risks of delays from doing nothing and accepting a false negative, the second from the risks of prematurely doing something and accepting a false positive (Figure 1).

Epidemiology and risk assessment, because they deal with public health, are not ethically neutral disciplines in the same way that mathematics, musicology, and archeology are. No human lives were lost because mathematicians required 300 years to solve Fermat's theorem. In public health and environmental epidemiology, delay in identifying and acting to reduce risks itself may create risks to health and

DPSEEA: "Upstream": Before The Black Box
("Fixing the System"):

Driving Force ---> Pressure ––> Stress ––> **Exposure ––> Effect ––>** Action

Molecular Epidemiology – "Downstream": Inside the Black Box:
("Finding the victim")

Exposure ––> Absorption ––> Internal Dose ––>
Biologically Effective Dose ––> Early Response ––>
Altered Structure Function ––> **Effect**

Figure 1. Time lines of DPSEEA and molecular epidemiology.

environment. Is the precautionary principle the *deus ex machina* for rescuing public health from delays in recognizing risk and our inability to deal with uncertainty?

ETHICS, THE PRECAUTIONARY PRINCIPLE, EPIDEMIOLOGY AND THE DIMENSION OF TIME

Ethical imperatives for preserving, protecting and promoting life and preventing damage, depletion or destruction of life-support systems in our environment drive us towards use of what some call the Precautionary Principle and others call precautionary strategies. In public health, delay in recognizing risk is of ethical import, and therefore, in the broadest sense, indicates negligence. We suggest that delay too often derives from a disproportionate emphasis on the use of epidemiology as an instrument for definitive proof of the distribution and determinants of disease rather than as a tool for early detection and warning of preventable risk.

The most extreme recent example of the acutely catastrophic human cost of delay comes from the epidemiology of genocide.[16] In Srbnice, officials ignored early warnings and interventions that would have prevented the massacre of 8,000 Bosnians—in one day in 1995—which came one day too late; the resignation of the Dutch Government seven years later, in 2002, was seven years and one day too late.

The very title of the Document of the European Environmental Agency—*Late Lessons from Early Warnings*, and the timelines for its case studies underscore the ethical import of delay for public heath.[17] The 50 to 100 year delays in assimilating, accepting and acting on the early evidence on risks from ionizing radiation, benzene, asbestos, DES, and sulfur dioxide and mad cow disease were catastrophic, even if not in an acute manner.[17] Our own work on health risks from lead,[18,19] asbestos,[20] solvents, and cancer in university laboratory workers,[21] cancer in naval divers with underwater exposures to toxicants[22] and increased speed limits[23] documents examples of epidemiologic delay and their human costs in occupational medicine and public health in Israel. More recently, proposal to remove chalk containing silica, arsenic, cadmium and chromate from classrooms following presentation of sentinel cases of lung cancer and impairment of pulmonary diffusion in school teachers is an example of the application of the Precautionary Principle in the face of uncertain and preliminary knowledge about possible risk, resulting mainly from rapid delivery of information of concern to the population at risk.[24]

If the ethical case for the Precautionary Principle is the human cost of delay, then the time interval between emergence of risk and its detection and removal is a surrogate measure of this cost of delay. Conversely, saving time by shortening this interval saves lives. But saving time is what drives much technological change and brings innovations that sometimes create new risks. For example, promoting increased speeds of vehicular travel, which means time saved, was the pretext for one of the worst decisions against public health in the 20th century: the addition of lead to gasoline, to make motor vehicles go faster. This step, which in its day was promoted as "progress" in saving economic time, not only produced massive neurotoxic damage to tens of millions of children,[25] but even worse, resulted in increases in road deaths owing to the exponential relationship between the fourth power of increases in speed and road deaths and emissions of pollutants. Here we have an example of how an econometric definition of progress through time saved

Table 3. Barriers to detection of risk.

External
Suppression
Repression bias
Funding bias
Lamppost epidemiology
Not asking the right questions

was catastrophic as defined by criteria derived from classic theologic and humanistic traditions—and could have been prevented if society had applied the Precautionary Principle.

THE EPIDEMIOLOGY OF DELAY

The determinants of delay in epidemiology are two-fold: external barriers and methodologic errors of commission and omission (Table 3).

Elsewhere, we have commented on the external determinants (suppression, repression, funding, and publication bias), proposed institutional reforms to reduce their occurrence[26] and reported on a mechanism for protection of investigators subject to pressures that produce these biases.[27]

Table 4 lists some errors of methodologic commission inherent to epidemiologic studies that are reasons for lateness.

Table 5 lists errors of commission associated with ignoring biologic evidence and divorcing epidemiology from collateral information on biologic plausibility.

Table 6 list errors of omission that derive from not going beyond the rigid structures of hypothesis testing confined to case control and cohort studies. The other papers in this conference address most of these issues.

External pressures on the content and direction of epidemiologic research produce delays in recognition of risk, as does an excessive preoccupation with statistical modes of reasoning divorced from the ABC's of biologic plausibility. These trends accounted for resistance of Ronald Fisher, the greatest biostatistician of his time—and a consultant for the British Tobacco Trust, to recognizing the cause-effect relationship

Table 4. Why epidemiology is late: some errors of commission: methodologic reasons.

- Small studies → low power
- Large studies→big numbers→exposure misclassification → bias towards null (radar studies?)
- Looking for grey hair in third graders: truncated follow-up of outcomes ("Small is not beautiful")
- Dismissing effects associated with $P > 0.05$ from small studies and clusters Chance does not favour the prepared mind: Bonferroni vs Pasteur: automatic dismissal of positive findings on sub-groups hypothesized to be at special risk; phantom confounding
- Failing to correct for the healthy worker effect

Table 5. Why epidemiology is late: some errors of commission: ignoring the biologic sentinels.

Underuse of ecological markers:
– Organophosphates and bee mortality[28]
– DNA changes, endocrine disrupters and developmental defects in fish[22]
– Herbicides and lymphomas in dogs[29]
– Electrical and magnetic fields from high tension lines and milk productivity in cows[30]

between cigarette smoking and lung cancer.[37] As Bradford Hill himself noted, the failure to use collateral lines of evidence, and the inherent delays and uncertainties associated with discovering new knowledge, are other reasons for delay.

HOW TO SPEED UP EPIDEMIOLOGY'S RESPONSE TIME

Ethical principles, the Precautionary Principle, the DPSEEA model, and molecular epidemiology all imply re-emphasizing and strengthening epidemiology's classic rôle for early detection and prevention. Can we reduce the time lag between suspicion of risk and intervention, in keeping with the principle of the case for action? Strategies for enhancing epidemiology's effectiveness for earlier detection and prevention of risk or avoidance of Type II errors involve addressing the errors of commission and omission we have just listed in Tables 4–6. The first strategy is to address the distortions in direction and content of epidemiologic research resulting from external pressures associated with repression, suppression, and funding biases. The other strategies include: investigating sentinel events and cancer cases with short latent periods, recognizing that certain exposures (single or mixed) produce multiple outcomes (e.g., cancer, reproductive, neurotoxic), using partial data sets when there are barriers to access to data, and making greater use of ecologic comparisons of time trends on population-wide impacts. Finally, there is the issue

Table 6. Why epidemiology is late: errors of omission.

Non-use, underuse or non-investigation of
– Sentinel events → groups at risk[31]
– Early cases of cancer with short induction periods[32]
Increases in case fatality
– Early effects of raised speed limit on deaths[23]
– Increased case fatality from leukemias in residents near radio and TV antennae[33]
– Non-use of proportional incidence and mortality when denominators not available
– Ignoring disproportionate number of multiple primaries[34]
– Failure to assess natural experiments from ecological associations
– Road deaths: 40% drop in UK vs absence of drop in USA during 1990s[35]
"Fallacy of ecological fallacy"[36]

of greatest substantive and symbolic importance: abandoning the *routine* use of $p < 0.05$ as a criterion for not making a Type I error when outcomes are catastrophic.

ETHICS OF DELAY AND THE CONTEXT OF TESTS FOR SIGNIFICANCE TESTING

Bradford Hill, when he invented the term, the case for action, warned against the dangers of misusing tests for statistical significance as pretexts for delay:

"The χ^2 test is an excellent servant and a bad master."

"No formal tests of significance can answer those questions [regarding causality]. . . they contribute nothing to the "proof" of our hypothesis."

"To decline to draw conclusions without standard errors can surely be . . . silly . . . we waste a great deal of time, we grasp the shadow and lose the substance, we weaken our capacity to interpret data and to make reasonable decisions whatever the value of P. And far too often we deduce "no difference" from "no significant difference."[6]

Tests of statistical significance are criteria for judging the reproducibility of an experimental association between exposure and risk. They are not guides for making decisions about life and death under conditions of uncertainty for assessing either rare catastrophic events or long-term large population risks. For rocket science, we want a p of zero in estimating error of a landing site on the moon; for deciding whether or not to close a shaky bridge, any p value short of 1.00 carries unacceptable risk. The decision to operate on a patient with RLQ pain, nausea, vomiting, fever, tenderness at McBurney's point and rebound is not guided by significance testing, but a weighing of the benefits and risks of operating versus not operating dictated by the diagnosis of appendicitis, a potentially fatal medical emergency.

ETHICAL CONSTRAINTS

Invoking the Precautionary Principle is, by itself, not an exercise in validation of efficacy of an intervention for doing good, preventing harm and not causing harm. We can ask: does applying the Precautionary Principle ensure justice, equity and respect for autonomy? How is good defined? Who decides? And for whom? And who pays the short-term costs of implementation to achieve long-term goals? All environmental dilemmas can be reduced to several bottom-line principles: everything is interrelated, everything has to go somewhere, there is a cost to everything, and someone has to pay, in one form or another (Table 7).

THE SOCIAL COSTS AND DANGERS OF THE PRECAUTIONARY PRINCIPLE

Implementation of the Precautionary Principle means there will be social costs associated with turn-arounds. For example, terminating many industrial processes, and substitution, and therefore, the loss of work and livelihood for large cohorts of workers, produces a scenario of better public health for many and worse social stress for some. If doing no harm and promoting equity are two principles of environmental ethics, then it follows that policies to apply the Precautionary

Table 7. Ethical constraints: principles: justice, equity, respect for autonomy of individual.

Questions:
Who decides?
For whom?
Good for all?
Costs: who pays and how?
Justice?
Protection of weakest → protect all
Greatest good for greatest number?
Abuse: casting as susceptibles
Costs of preventing false positives

Principle presuppose compensation of those worker populations deprived of employment by its application.[1] The attached commentary, prepared by Colin Soskolne, defines the ethics of distributive justice and compensation of those losing work as a result of application of the Precautionary Principle.

Furthermore, as Goldstein has shown,[38] there is a need to apply a precautionary strategy in evaluating the impact of intervention strategies that themselves can produce risk. Invoking the Precautionary Principle to do no harm means that when there is an intervention to prevent a health risk, its effect must be evaluated. It therefore follows that if to predict is to prevent, then the use of the Precautionary Principle to explicitly repudiate risk assessment—the everyday tool for practicing public health—carries the potential for doing harm.

Above all, equity, justice, and respect for individual autonomy dictate against invoking the Precautionary Principle to misuse molecular epidemiology—the major danger from its misapplication. Its capacities for the early detection of special risks in sub-groups should not mutate into search for susceptible sub-castes. As Geoffrey Rose has shown, such strategies presuppose acceptance of low-level exposures with lower risks, but more victims in the larger group.[39]

CONCLUSION

Is the move to the precautionary principle driven by a sense that epidemiology has lost its soul? But at the same time, are there dangers from using the Precautionary Principle to ignore or discredit evidence-based risk assessment when it is properly carried out in a transparent and open manner.

The lag time between preventable risk and the discovery of its cause measures the gap between the Precautionary Principle and certainty of proof. Ethics suggests that time and delay equate with harm, and medicine tells us, above all, to do no harm. Irving Selikoff, on his deathbed, confessed his regret over waiting so many years before he worked to get asbestos banned—and wondered whether the years he spent in research were misspent: "I could have saved a lot of those boys instead of waiting."[40]

COMMENT: ETHICS AND THE PRECAUTIONARY PRINCIPLE: THE ETHICS OF DISTRIBUTIVE JUSTICE (BY COLIN SOSKOLNE)

Compensation for those people suffering untoward side effects from the application of any new approved substance or technology ought to be built into the notion of precaution. We protect all by protecting the most vulnerable. But it is the most vulnerable who are often those first or most harmed. While the herd is protected or enjoys the benefits of new technologies, should the herd not compensate the vulnerable or susceptible minority that experiences some ill effect, and provide them with, say, access to free health care and compensation for lost income? The rationale underlying an affirmative response to this question is that if the vast majority enjoys benefits, then those enduring harms should be compensated, because it is at their expense that the herd will have derived its benefits. This rationale fits well with the ethical core principle of "distributive justice."[41]

The notion of whether compensation would be acceptable under the Precautionary Principle is very much a matter of context. If the principle is applied in a context of "egalitarian theory/values," as in Canada, then compensation would likely be acceptable. However, in the context of "libertarian theory/values," as exists in the USA, compensation likely would not be favoured. Finally, there is the utilitarian principle of "the greatest good for the greatest number." This ethically problematic theory guides much of every day public health. Under "utilitarian theory," the intent of any public health action is to achieve the greatest good for the greatest number. This theory accepts that some will be harmed. Distributive justice would require that those harmed deserve to be compensated by those not harmed. Under the Precautionary Principle, one aims to reduce the risk of harm to zero, or more practically speaking, to minimize as far as possible harm in the presence of uncertainty.

ACKNOWLEDGEMENTS

I thank Sheldon Samuels for his sage advice, but the responsability for errors in this paper is ours.

REFERENCES

1. Soskolne C. 1983. In Weed DL. Ethics and chemoprevention research. Semin Oncol X; 355–9
2. Richter ED, Barach P, Berman T, *et al.* 2001. Extending the boundaries of the Declaration of Helsinki: a casestudy of an unethical experiment in a non-medical setting. J Med Ethics 27(3):126–9
3. Talmud. Soncino Press, Brooklyn, New York
4. Encyclopedia Britannica. Christianity
5. Gauthier D. 1986. Morals by Agreement. Oxford, UK: Clarendon Press
6. Lessnoff M. 1986. Social Contract. Hampshire, UK: Macmillan
7. Goldberg E. Knesset hearings on State Controller Committee's report on exposures to non-ionizing radiation. Knesset Committee on Governmental Operations, Government of Israel, Nov. 2001 (Hebrew). www.Knesset.gov.il
8. Hill AB. 1965. The environment and disease: association or causation? Proc Royal Soc Med 58:295–300

9. Kriebel D, Tickner J, Epstein P, *et al.* 2001. The precautionary principle in environmental science. Environ Health Perspect 109(9):871–6
10. European Commission. 2000. Communication from the Commission on the Precautionary Principle, COM 1, Brussels
11. Sanderson H. 2002. International summit on science and the precautionary principle. Lowell Center for Sustainable Production, University of Massachusetts, Lowell. September 20-22, 2001. Environ Sci Pollut Res Int 9(2):155–6
12. Raffensperger C, Schettler T, and Myers N. 2000. Precaution: belief, regulatory system, and overarching principle. Int J Occup Environ Health 6(4):266–9
13. http://www.who.dk/eprise/main/who/progs/ehi/indicators/20020320_1
14. Richter ED and Peretz T. 2003. Ethical issues in molecular epidemiology in Molecular Epidemiology in Preventive Medicine, ed. Jedrychowski W, Perera F, Maugeri U, 381–96
15. http://www.pitt.edu/~super1/lecture/lec8011/001.htm Supercourse on Epidemiology, Paneth N. Introduction
16. Richter ED and Berman T. Jul 2–3 1999. Genocide, ecocide, Public health and ecology: commentary on workshop on global ecological integrity and human health at the World Health Organization, European Centre for Environment and Health, Rome Division, December 3–4, 1998. Proc Conf: Challenges to Epidemiology in Changing Europe, ed. Jedrychowski W, Vena J, Maugeri U, Krakow 213–9
17. European Environmental Agency. 2001. Late lessons from early warnings: the precautionary principle 1896-2000: Report no. 22, Luxembourg
18. Richter ED, Yaffe Y, and Gruener N. 1979. Blood and air lead levels in a battery factory. Environ Res 20(2):87–98
19. Richter ED. 1992. "Acceptable" levels of lead exposures in Israel: Do they lower childhood IQ and damage workers' health? (Editorial) Isr Journ Med Sci 28:81–4
20. Tulchinsky TH, Ginsberg GH, Iscovich J, *et al.* 1999. Cancer in ex-asbestos cement workers in Israel. Am J Ind Med 35(1):1–8
21. Richter ED, Gordon M, and Westin JB. 1996. Cancer clusters in university laboratory workers and students: zebras or horses with stripes? A case study in epidemiologic delay. Epidemiology 7(4):Supplement S 41
22. Richter ED, Ben-Michael D, Berman T, *et al.* 2003. Cancer risks in naval divers with multiple exposures to carcinogens. Environ Health Perspect 111(4):609–17
23. Richter ED, Barach P, Ben-Michael E, *et al.* 2003. Raised speed limits, speed spillover, case fatality and road deaths in Israel: a five-year follow-up. Am J Publ Health (in press)
24. Westin J, Bitchachi E, and Richter ED. Oct 2002. Classroom chalk: a possible new source of exposure to crystalline silica. Abstract Second International Conference on Silica, Italy
25. Richter ED and Berman T. 2001. Speed, air pollution and health (editorial). Arch Environ Health 56(4):296–9
26. Richter ED, Soskolne C, LaDou J, *et al.* March 2002. Whistleblowers in environmental science, prevention of suppression bias and the need for a code of protection. Proc Conference of Office of Research Integrity
27. The International Society for Environmental Epidemiology (ISEE) Research Suppression and Research. http://www.iseepi.org/index1.htm Repression
28. Richter ED, Chuwers P, Levy Y, *et al.* 1992. Health effects from exposure to organophosphate pesticides in worker and non-worker groups in Israel. Isr J Med Sci 28: 584–97
29. Hayes HM, Tarone RE, and Cantor KP. 1995. On the association between canine malignant lymphoma and opportunity for exposure to 2,4-dichlorophenoxyacetic acid. Environ Res 70(2):119–25
30. Burchard JF, Nguyen DH, Richard L, *et al.* 1996. Biological effects of electric and magnetic fields on productivity of dairy cows. J Dairy Sci 79:1549–54

31. Richter ED and Barach P. 1995. Occupation and environment in internal medicine: sentinel events and trigger questions. Mt Sinai Journ Med 62(5):390–400
32. Richter ED, Berman T, and Levy O. 2002. Brain cancer with induction periods <10 y in military workers exposed to radar. Arch Env Health 57(4):270–72
33. Hocking B, Gordon I, and Hatfield GE. 1999. Childhood leukaemia and TV towers revisited. Aust N Z J Public Health 23(1):104–5
34. Begg CB. 2001. The search for cancer risk factors: when can we stop looking? Am J Public Health 91(3):360–4
35. Richter ED, Barach P, Ben-Michael E, *et al.* 2001. Death and injury from motor vehicle crashes: a public health failure, not an achievement. Injury Prevention 7(3):176–8
36. Schwartz S. 1994. The fallacy of the ecological fallacy: the potential misuse of a concept and the consequences. Am J Public Health 5:819–24
37. Terris M. 1993. The Society for Epidemiologic Research and the future of epidemiology. J Public Health Policy 14(2):137–48.
38. Goldstein B. 2001. The precautionary principle also applies to public health actions. Am J Public Health 91(9):1358–61
39. Rose G. 1981. Strategy of prevention: lessons from cardiovascular disease. Br Med J (Clin Res Ed). 282(6279):1847–51
40. Richter ED, Gasteyer S, El Haj S, *et al.* 1997. Agricultural sustainability, pesticide exposures, and health risks: Israel, the Palestinian National Authority and Jordan. Ann NY Acad Sci 837:269–91
41. Soskolne CL. 1991. Ethical decision-making in epidemiology: the case study approach. J Clin Epidemiol 44(Suppl 1):1255–305.

[30]

The Precautionary Principle Also Applies to Public Health Actions

| Bernard D. Goldstein, MD

The precautionary principle asserts that the burden of proof for potentially harmful actions by industry or government rests on the assurance of safety and that when there are threats of serious damage, scientific uncertainty must be resolved in favor of prevention. Yet we in public health are sometimes guilty of not adhering to this principle.

Examples of actions with unintended negative consequences include the addition of methyl tert-butyl ether to gasoline in the United States to decrease air pollution, the drilling of tube wells in Bangladesh to avoid surface water microbial contamination, and villagewide parenteral antischistosomiasis therapy in Egypt. Each of these actions had unintended negative consequences. Lessons include the importance of multidisciplinary approaches to public health and the value of risk-benefit analysis, of public health surveillance, and of a functioning tort system—all of which contribute to effective precautionary approaches.

PUBLIC HEALTH ADVOCATES around the world have increasingly invoked the precautionary principle as a basis for preventive actions.[1–9] This has been particularly true for environmental and food safety issues, in which the precautionary principle has moved from being a rallying cry for environmental advocates to a legal principle embodied in international treaties.[2,6,8–11] Definitional issues have become more important as the term has made the transition from a noble goal to a component of legal requirements. For the purposes of this commentary, a useful definition is one that is contained in the 1989 Rio Declaration[12]: "Nations shall use the precautionary approach to protect the environment. Where there are threats of serious or irreversible damage, scientific uncertainty shall not be used to postpone cost-effective measures to prevent environmental degradation."

The upsurge in use of the term "precautionary principle" has been relatively sudden. For example, changes in the approach to hazardous air pollutants in the 1990 US Clean Air Act Amendments embody the precautionary principle. Until then, control of individual air pollutants in this category depended on a risk-based approach in which the burden of proof was on the US Environmental Protection Agency (EPA) to demonstrate that environmental levels of the air pollutant were likely to produce adverse effects. Further, the extent of imposed control measures was based on the feasibility of reducing risk. Instead, the 1990 amendments state that maximal available control technology is to be used on each of more than 180 pollutants unless the pollutant can be clearly shown to be harmless.

Shifting the burden of proof and moving away from risk science to a technology-based approach were much debated at the time, but the term "precautionary principle" was not part of the debate. Now it certainly would be, although whether this precautionary approach will be more successful than the previous risk-based approach is still open to debate. For example, germane to the broader issue of the value of the precautionary principle is the question of whether regulating specific air pollutant emission control technology will stifle the invention and application of newer, more effective technology.

At its core, the precautionary principle contains many of the attributes of good public health practice, including a focus on primary prevention and a recognition that unforeseen and unwanted consequences of human activities are not unusual. Yet there are at least 3 recently reported examples of actions taken in the name of improving public health that would better have been avoided or at least considered more carefully beforehand. I argue that the precautionary principle needs to be applied to public health actions as well as to actions pursued by government and industry for competitive and economic reasons. It is not my intention to provide a well-rounded critique of the precautionary principle, which is discussed by Kriebel and Tickner[13] and by Jamieson and Wartenburg[14] in this issue of the Journal.

MTBE AIR AND GROUNDWATER CONTAMINATION

The 1990 US Clean Air Act Amendment also contained requirements for the use of oxygenated automotive fuels, both to decrease carbon monoxide emissions and to lessen oxidant air pollutant precursors. Unfortunately, these requirements were implemented without a thorough evaluation of the potential human health and environmental consequences. As many as 100 million Americans were exposed to fuel oxygenates in air. Almost immediately, a controversy developed concerning symptomatic responses among exposed individuals, as well as animal data suggesting that methyl tert-butyl ether (MTBE), the major fuel oxygenate, might be a carcinogen. However, there was no retreat from MTBE use until there was belated recognition of MTBE's contamination of water supplies, a recognition that appears to have been anticipated by industry.

This episode vividly illustrates how failure to act in a precautionary manner can inappropriately shift the burden of proof. Once MTBE became a major part of the nation's gasoline supply, the appropriate question—whether there was sufficient assurance about the safety of MTBE to expose humans and the environment—became moot, and the question asked by regulators was whether there was sufficient evidence of harm to remove MTBE from gasoline. EPA responded by conducting repeated reviews of the existing evidence while providing only a meager amount of support for obtaining new evidence. This resulted in an 8-year delay in making the appropriate decision.[15] Even now, MTBE remains in use, although in substantially decreasing amounts.

Perhaps most distressing is that US environmental authorities appeared to have learned little from the MTBE debacle. Oxygenated fuels continue to be required by EPA, resulting in the replacement of MTBE by compounds such as tertiary amyl methyl ether, for which even less toxicological and environmental information is available than for MTBE.

ARSENIC IN BANGLADESH AND WEST BENGAL, INDIA

Diarrheal infectious diseases caused by human consumption of sewage-contaminated surface waters have long been a major public health problem in Bangladesh and the adjacent West Bengal area of India. Tapping into sterile subsurface water supplies would seem to be an obvious solution to this problem. The use of relatively low-technology approaches to drill local tube wells has been advocated by many international agencies, including UNICEF.

Encouragement and assistance by these agencies and local health authorities have led to the drilling of a few million wells, of which perhaps as many as 2 million are contaminated with arsenic levels above drinking water standards. Arsenic toxicity is now evident in large numbers of individuals in these villages. In a study of 11 180 randomly selected individuals from affected areas in Bangladesh and 29 035 from affected areas in West Bengal, Chowdhury et al. reported the incidence of arsenic-induced skin lesions as 24% and 15%, respectively.[16] They also found arsenical neuropathy in 37% of 413 arsenicosis patients. Significant increases are anticipated in the incidence of cancer of the skin and internal organs, and in diabetes and vascular disease, now that the latency period for these disorders is approaching.[17–19]

How could the rationale of improving public health lead to 100 million people's being put at risk for arsenic toxicity, including cancer? Arsenic contamination of well water with significant resultant toxicity was not unknown and in fact had been reported, primarily in Asia. Although testing for arsenic is not part of routine practice, high levels of arsenic in water could readily have been detected more than a decade before there were overt and unmistakable signs of arsenic toxicity in the population. The precautionary principle can be defined in terms of not undertaking activities about whose impact there is scientific uncertainty. With a minimum of precaution, arsenic toxicity in Bangladesh and West Bengal could have been averted, or at least minimized.

HEPATITIS C IN EGYPT

Egypt has an exceptionally high prevalence of hepatitis C infection, with correspondingly high morbidity and mortality due to cirrhosis and hepatocellular carcinoma. This high prevalence has been traced to transmission of the hepatitis C virus during campaigns of mass inoculation with antimony compounds for the treatment of endemic schistosomiasis, campaigns that continued until the early 1980s.[20,21] In areas of Egypt where the schistosomiasis treatment campaigns were concentrated, such as the Nile Delta, the prevalence of hepatitis C virus antibodies is higher than 50% among persons of an age to have received those injections.[21,22] Although oral therapy has replaced parenteral therapy, the high rate of persistence of hepatitis C means that these individuals provide a reservoir for continued transmission. There is evidence that parenteral antischistosomiasis therapy was a factor in hepatitis B transmission as well.

Schistosomiasis has been a major public health problem in Egypt for millennia.[23] The Egyptian public health community has been justifiably proud of its ability to mobilize to combat schistosomiasis through a wide range of activities. It has been joined in this effort by international public health organizations and by the academic public health community. The centerpiece of this public health campaign was administration of a series of 12 to 16 intravenous injections of potassium antimony tartrate in high-risk villages. Frank et al. point out that a major change in the time course of the injections occurred in 1960, when they were spaced out to once weekly rather than given more intensively over a 2- to 3-week period.[21] This may have contributed to the likelihood of hepatitis C virus transmission, given that observed sterilization procedures were improper or nonexistent. The risk of transmission of bloodborne pathogens through improper sterilization of needles was certainly appreciated before the 1960s.

There were undoubtedly great exigencies requiring mass campaigns against the major public health threat of schistosomiasis in a developing country. But the adverse public health legacy in Egypt is substantial and will continue.

LESSONS

The need for a breadth of outlook that goes beyond the initial problem is an obvious lesson from these examples. Perhaps the most egregious example is the most recent. Because of a lack of communication within a single federal agency, the EPA, those responsible for protecting the nation's water paid no attention to what their colleagues in the air pollution office in the same building were doing to that water. All 3 of these examples point up the need for multidisciplinary and multiorganizational approaches to public health problems. They also argue for the routine use of the framework for risk assessment and risk management advocated by the Presidential/Congressional Commission of Risk Assessment and Risk Management.[24]

Multidisciplinary approaches are not easy to accomplish, particularly in government and academia, which, far more than industry, have inherent difficulties in fostering and rewarding any but the narrower approaches to problem solving. The MTBE fiasco, for example, occurred in a federal agency whose leadership has repeatedly recognized the importance of multimedia approaches to environmental regulation and which, during the last 2 administrations, has made great strides in this direction. And it occurred despite warnings from the EPA's own scientists.[15,25] Perhaps a major contributing factor is that the EPA inherently has difficulties in acting as a public health agency,[24] although in the other 2 examples described here there was major input from public health organizations.

RISK–BENEFIT CONSIDERATIONS

Public health actions should always consider risks as well as benefits. In all 3 cases described above, it is conceivable that even with complete foreknowledge of the adverse consequences, the public health action would be seen as beneficial overall. The best case for this can perhaps be made for the drilling of wells in Bangladesh and West Bengal, where the adverse consequences of possible arsenic contamination might have been balanced against the undoubted benefit of a cleaner water supply. The benefits of MTBE are far more controversial.[27] Of note is that the petrochemical industry has written off perhaps a billion dollars in investments for a problem it could have anticipated and avoided.[15]

The core maxim of the precautionary principle is that an action should not be taken when there is scientific uncertainty about its potential impact.

SURVEILLANCE

We frequently speak about the importance of surveillance as a public health tool. Yet too often we do not advocate surveillance in relation to public health activities to ensure both that the intended beneficial effect does occur and that there are no unforeseen adverse consequences. In all 3 of the examples given here, the assumption was that benefit would accrue and that there was no need to install a surveillance system capable of early detection of adverse consequences. Public health agencies in each case initially expressed disbelief or surprise when early signs of an adverse consequence began to appear.

The precautionary principle provides an additional rationale for public health and environmental surveillance activities. Surveillance is needed to detect threats of adverse consequences as early as possible to maximize the value of precautionary activities. Surveillance also helps to put threats in perspective. For example, it could be argued that the mostly decreasing levels of DDT and other persistent organic compounds in human fat tissue and biota make such compounds less of a concern for precautionary action than global climate changes that appear to be increasing over time and for which the maximum adverse impact is far less certain.

TOXIC TORTS AND THE PRECAUTIONARY PRINCIPLE

The toxic tort system in the United States is in disarray. Yet to the extent that it makes an industry think twice before introducing a chemical into commerce, it functions in a manner consistent with the precautionary principle. Plaintiffs' lawyers for individuals claiming adverse health effects due to MTBE and for municipalities whose water sources have been affected are seeking to sue the petrochemical industry. Meanwhile, lawyers for MTBE-producing companies are working hard on a defense that to a large extent consists of hiding behind the federal government, although there is evidence suggesting the companies' own culpability as well. Had MTBE been a newly patented fuel additive distributed on the basis of a single petrochemical company's claims, this company would now be seeking the protection of a bankruptcy court. In Bangladesh, whose toxic tort system is not as fully evolved as that of the United States, there has been an attempt to sue UNICEF for the damage caused by arsenic contamination.

The precautionary principle is still evolving and does not have a firm operational definition. To some, the precautionary principle is already included in the usual risk-assessment approaches to environmental health and food safety; to others, it transcends these approaches; to still others, it is antithetical to risk assessment.[8,28–31] There are issues related to the legal definition of the term, to the role of science, to its use as a justification for economically motivated trade barriers, and to whether it will stifle innovation or interfere with a true understanding of the cause of problems.[32–37] In public health policy, Wainwright has used the term "precautionary principle" as a negative, blaming the stifling of innovative change in the British National Health Service on the desire to avoid adverse consequences.[38]

No matter how the precautionary principle evolves, the value of acting in a precautionary manner is obvious to those in public health. It is a form of primary prevention, avoiding problems by not engaging in activities until it is reasonably certain that they will not produce harm.

The core maxim of the precautionary principle is that an action should not be taken when there is scientific uncertainty about its potential impact.[39] We in public health must recognize that the precautionary principle applies to our own actions, that when a public health action is proposed, the burden of proof—to ensure that all risks and consequences are taken into account—rests on us just as surely as it rests on others. ■

About the Author

Bernard D. Goldstein is with the University of Pittsburgh Graduate School of Public Health, Pittsburgh, Pa.

Requests for reprints should be sent to Bernard D. Goldstein, MD, University of Pittsburgh Graduate School of Public Health, 130 DeSoto St, Pittsburgh, PA 15261 (e-mail: bdgold@pitt.edu).

This commentary was accepted May 25, 2001.

References

1. Davis DL, Axelrod D, Bailey L, Gaynor M, Sasco AJ. Rethinking breast cancer risk and the environment: the case of the precautionary principle. *Environ Health Perspect.* 1998;106:523–529.

2. Horton R. The precautionary principle. *Lancet.* 1998:252.

3. Krimsky S. The precautionary approach. *Forum for Applied Research and Public Policy.* 1999;13:34–37.

4. Mahoney RJ. Opportunity for agricultural biotechnology. *Science.* 2000; 288:615.

5. Raffensperger C, Tickner J, eds. *Protecting Public Health and the Environment. Implementing the Precautionary Principle.* New York, NY: Island Press; 1999.

6. deFur PL. Guest perspectives: an environmental scientist's view of the precautionary principle. *Risk Policy Rep.* 2000:7:44–46.

7. Graham JD. Making sense of the precautionary principle. *Risk in Perspective.* 1999;7:1–6.

8. Commission of the European Communities. *Communique on the Precautionary Principle.* Brussels, Belgium: European Commission; 2000.

9. Cameron J, Abouchar J. The precautionary principle: a fundamental principle of law and policy for the protection of the global environment. *Boston College International & Comparative Law Review.* 1991;14(1):1–27.

10. Hey E. The precautionary concept in environmental policy and law: institutionalizing caution. *Georgetown International Environmental Law Review.* 1992; 4:303–318.

11. Cartagena Protocol on Biosafety. Available at: http://www.biodiv.org/biosafety/protocol.asp. Accessed June 29, 2001.

12. *Rio Declaration on Environment and Development.* Stockholm, Sweden: United Nations; 1992. Publication E.73.II.A.14.

13. Kriebel D, Tickner J. Reenergizing public health through precaution. *Am J Public Health* 2001;91:1351–1355.

14. Jamieson D, Wartenburg D. The precautionary principle and electric and magnetic fields. *Am J Public Health* 2001:91:1355–1358.

15. Erdal S, Goldstein BD. MTBE: a policy review. *Annual Review of Energy and the Environment.* 2000;25:765–802.

16. Chowdhury UK, Biswas BK, Chowdhury TR, et al. Groundwater arsenic contamination in Bangladesh and West Bengal, India. *Environ Health Perspect.* 2000;108:393–397.

17. Smith AH, Lingas EO, Rahman M. Contamination of drinking-water by arsenic in Bangladesh: a public health emergency. *Bull World Health Organ.* 2000;78:1093–1103.

18. Tseng CH, Tai TY, Chong CK, et al. Long-term arsenic exposure and incidence of non-insulin-dependent diabetes mellitus: a cohort study in arseniasis-hyperendemic villages in Taiwan. *Environ Health Perspect.* 2000;108:847–851.

19. Pearce F. Danger in every drop. *New Scientist.* 2000;165:16–17.

20. El-Sayed NM, Gomatos PJ, Rodier GR, et al. Seroprevalence survey of Egyptian tourism workers for hepatitis B virus, hepatitis C virus, human immunodeficiency virus, and *Treponema pallidum* infections: association of hepatitis C virus infections with specific regions of Egypt. *Am J Trop Med Hyg.* 1996;55: 179–184.

21. Frank C, Mohamed MK, Strickland GT, Lavanchy D, Arthur RA, Magder LS. The role of parenteral antischistosomal therapy in the spread of hepatitis C virus in Egypt. *Lancet.* 2000;355: 887–891.

22. Darwish MA, Faris R, Clemens JD, Rao MR, Edelman R. High seroprevalence of hepatitis A, B, C, and E viruses in residents in an Egyptian village in the Nile Delta: a pilot study. *Am J Trop Med Hyg.* 1996;54:554–558.

23. Deelder AM, Miller RL, de Jonge N, Krijger FW. Detection of schistosome antigen in mummies. *Lancet.* 1990;335: 724–725.

24. Omenn GS. Putting environmental risks in a public health context. *Public Health Rep.* 1996;111:514–516

25. *Alternative Fuels Research Strategy. Interim Draft 4.* Washington, DC: US Environmental Protection Agency; 1989.

26. Goldstein BD. EPA as a public health agency. *Regul Toxicol Pharmacol.* 1988;8:328–334.

27. *Achieving Clean Air and Clean Water: The Report of the Blue Ribbon Panel on Oxygenates in Gasoline.* Washington, DC: US Environmental Protection Agency; September 1999. EPA420-R-99-021.

28. Bishop WE. Guest perspectives: risk assessment vs the precautionary principle: is it really either/or? *Risk Policy Report.* 2000;7(3):35–38.

29. Cap AP. The chlorine controversy. *Int Arch Occup Environ Health.* 1996; 68:455–458.

30. Food & Agriculture Organization of the United Nations/World Health Organization. US comments responding to European position on precautionary principle: Codex Alimentarius Commission. *Inside Washington Publishers.* 2000;6(12):1–5.

31. Pugh DM. The precautionary principle and science-based limits in regulatory toxicology: the human experience, individual protection. *Arch Toxicol Suppl.* 1997;19:147–154.

32. Goldstein BD. Guest perspectives: use and abuse of the precautionary principle. *Risk Policy Report.* 2000;7(3): 39–40.

33. Holm S, Harris J. Precautionary principle stifles discovery [letter]. *Nature.* 1999;400:398.

34. Carpenter RA. Precautionary principle [letter]. *Chemical and Engineering News.* 1998;8(15):6–8.

35. Foster KR, Vecchia P, Repacholi MH. Risk management. Science and the precautionary principle. *Science.* 2000; 288:979–981.

36. Hodgson J. National politicians block GM progress. *Nat Biotechnol.* 2000;18:918–919.

37. Miller H, Conko G. The protocol's illusionary principle. *Nat Biotechnol.* 2000;18:360.

38. Wainwright D. Disenchantment, ambivalence, and the precautionary principle: the becalming of British health policy. *Int J Health Serv.* 1998; 28:407–426.

39. Duvick DN. How much caution in the fields? *Science.* 1999;286:418–419.

Part X
Confinement and Liberty

[31]

Cuba's Quarantine of AIDS Victims: A Violation of Human Rights?

David W. Johnston

Introduction

In 1987, the Cuban regime became the first government in the world to implement a strict quarantine for all individuals infected with the Human Immuno-deficiency Virus (HIV).[1] To detect carriers of the virus, a precursor to Acquired Immuno-deficiency Syndrome (AIDS), Cuba instituted a national mandatory testing program.[2] The program required infected individuals to move to a former sanitarium outside of Havana for an indefinite period of time.[3] Contrary to the recommendations of the United Nations World Health Organization (WHO),[4] the policy continues today.[5]

The implementation of the quarantine policy raises a number of human rights issues. Foremost among them is the concern that the detention is arbitrary.[6] Most international scholars agree that an arbitrary detention constitutes a violation of international human rights law. Whether a particular detention is arbitrary, however, may be open to debate.[7] Some scholars, for example, believe education alone can halt the spread of AIDS.[8] Thus, a quarantine

---

[1] Joseph B. Treaster, *Havana Reports 3 Cubans Dead of AIDS and Sets Up Isolation Unit*, N.Y. Times, Apr. 18, 1987, at A2.

[2] *See infra* text accompanying notes 97–107.

[3] *See infra* text accompanying notes 108–23.

[4] The World Health Organization (WHO) is a specialized agency of the United Nations with primary responsibility for international public health matters. *See generally* World Health Organization, Basic Documents (1990). Created in 1948, 166 countries, including Cuba, are now WHO members. The objective of WHO is stated in article I of its Constitution as "the attainment by all peoples of the highest possible level of health." *Id.* at 2.

[5] *See infra* text accompanying notes 73–74; Jonathan M. Mann et al., *Global Coordination of National Public Health Strategies*, 18 Law, Med. & Health 20, 22 (1990); World Health Organization, Guideline for Nursing Management of People Infected with Human Immunodeficiency Virus (HIV) 41 (1988) [hereinafter Guidelines for Nursing].

[6] *See infra* text accompanying notes 66–68. *See also* Ernesto F. Betancourt, *Cuba's Callous War on AIDS*, N.Y. Times, Feb. 11, 1988, at B2; M.D. Kirby, *AIDS Strategies and Human Rights Obligations*, 42 Int'l Commission of Jurists Rev. 42, 49 (1989).

[7] *See infra* notes 35, 92 and accompanying text.

[8] *See infra* text accompanying notes 75–76.

policy would be a disproportionate response to the AIDS threat and, therefore, arbitrary.[9] Others suggest that the international community must examine any policy designed to combat AIDS in light of a country's particular demographic, economic, political, and cultural composition before passing judgment.[10]

This Comment attempts to determine whether Cuba's quarantine program violates international human rights law. In order to establish that a body of international law exists upon which critics of the quarantine can base their claim, Part I provides an overview of the sources and development of internationally recognized human rights. Part II discusses the international response to AIDS and the impact of that response on the development and scope of human rights law as it applies to AIDS victims. Part III describes the Cuban quarantine policy, while Part IV analyzes the policy—and criticisms of it—in light of those political, social, and economic factors that are unique to Cuba. This Comment concludes that, considering the nature of the policy and Cuban society in general, its quarantine does not violate international human rights law.

I. THE DEVELOPMENT AND SOURCES OF INTERNATIONAL HUMAN RIGHTS LAW: AN OVERVIEW

A. *The Development of Human Rights Law*

The idea that there exist certain immutable human rights which transcend national boundaries, and which all states must respect, is a relatively new phenomenon within the international community.[11] Prior to discovery of the Nazi atrocities inflicted upon millions of people, the only rights afforded individuals were those their national governments provided.[12] Documents such as the Magna Carta, the Bill of Rights, and the Charter of Privileges

---

[9] *See* Kirby, *supra* note 6, at 50. Kirby argues: "The derogation from the human rights of persons compulsorily detained because of HIV infection is completely disproportional to the benefits secured thereby." *Id.*

[10] *See, e.g.*, Maria Paalman, *Epidemic Control Through Prevention*, *in* THE GLOBAL IMPACT OF AIDS 215, 216–17 (Alan F. Fleming et al. eds., 1988); *infra* notes 87–88 and accompanying text.

[11] *See* Richard B. Bilder, *The Status of International Human Rights Law; An Overview*, *in* INTERNATIONAL HUMAN RIGHTS LAW AND PRACTICE 1, 1 (1978).

[12] *See id.*; A.M. Stuyt, *Human Rights Sources–An Outline*, *in* INTERNATIONAL LAW AND ITS SOURCES 165, 165 (Wybo P. Heere ed., 1988).

address the rights of citizens living within a society as distinct from the rights of individuals as human beings.[13] Protecting the rights of individuals was not a traditional function of international law.[14]

The limited international concern for individuals which existed prior to the Second World War found expression in various treaties between states banning slavery and protecting certain ethnic minorities.[15] The individual, however, only found protection as a member of a group and exclusively through the establishment of treaties between states.[16] With the creation of the United Nations came the articulation of a principle upon which *individuals* could assert rights.[17] That principle, contained within the Preamble of the Charter of the United Nations (U.N. Charter or Charter), is that respect for the "human dignity" of individuals must be maintained by all states.[18] This essentially means that individuals no longer need rely on treaties between states to assert a right—the simple fact that they are human beings grants them that privilege.[19]

International human rights law is not as developed and coherent as other areas of international law, but it has "clearly reached a stage where it deserves and has received recognition as a specialized field of its own."[20] The number of specialized organizations, conferences, journals, academic literature, and courses devoted to furthering and defining international human rights law provides ample evidence of its legitimate standing in the wider sphere of international law.[21]

---

[13] *See* Stuyt, *supra* note 12, at 165.

[14] *See* Bilder, *supra* note 11, at 1.

[15] *Id.* Governments used treaties to protect Jews in Russia, and Armenians in the Turkish empire, as well as to ban slavery. *See, e.g.*, International Convention to Suppress Slave Trade and Slavery, Sept. 25, 1926, 46 Stat. 2183, 60 L.N.T.S. 253.

[16] *See* Bilder, *supra* note 11, at 1.

[17] *See* U.N. CHARTER pmbl.

[18] *Id.* The preamble states in part that one of the aims of the United Nations is "to reaffirm faith in fundamental human rights, in the dignity of worth of the human person . . . ." *Id.* For a partial list of subsequent important documents which reaffirm the principle of inherent human dignity, see Stuyt, *supra* note 12, at 169.

[19] *See* Stuyt, *supra* note 12, at 168–69. For a discussion of methods by which individuals may attempt to remedy an abuse of their rights, see generally RESTATEMENT (THIRD) OF THE FOREIGN RELATIONS LAW OF THE UNITED STATES § 703 (1987) [hereinafter RESTATEMENT].

[20] Bilder, *supra* note 11, at 3.

[21] *Id.*

B. *The Sources of Human Rights Law*

International law is derived from three principal sources: international treaties, international custom, and the general principles of law recognized by "civilized nations."[22] Judicial decisions and the treatises of the most qualified scholars serve as secondary sources.[23] Because the scope of international human rights is still evolving, various human rights treaties, declarations, and instruments provide the most useful means for determining the extent of those rights.[24]

1. Treaties

The substantial number of human rights treaties currently in force, when viewed together, place a significant number of legal obligations upon states.[25] The most important treaty, to which most states are parties, is the U.N. Charter.[26] Nevertheless, while the Charter is legally binding on all U.N. members, its human rights provisions are too broad for use in defining the scope of those rights.[27] There are two conventions in force, however, which enlarge into detailed treaty form not only the skeletal human rights provisions of the Charter, but many provisions of the Universal Declaration of Human Rights (Universal Declaration).[28] These conventions are the International Covenant on

---

[22] *See* Statute of the International Court of Justice, Oct. 24, 1945, art. 38, 59 Stat. 1055, T.S. No. 993 [hereinafter I.C.J. Statute]. *See also* JOHN HUMPHREY, NO DISTANT MILLENNIUM: THE INTERNATIONAL LAW OF HUMAN RIGHTS 156 (1989).

[23] *See* I.C.J. Statute, *supra* note 22, at art. 38.

[24] *See* Bilder, *supra* note 11, at 4. It is not practical to examine in detail the full range of international human rights rules, procedures, and precedents that may affect the Cuban quarantine policy. Instead, it is more useful to focus on those instruments used by opponents of the policy to substantiate their contention that quarantine is a violation of international human rights.

[25] *See id.* at 4, 7. For a listing of U.N. human rights treaties in force see RESTATEMENT, *supra* note 19, at Part VII Introductory Note.

[26] *See* Bilder, *supra* note 11, at 7.

[27] *See* U.N. CHARTER art. 55(c). Article 55(c) of the U.N. Charter contains its most explicit reference to human rights, stating that "the United Nations shall promote . . . universal respect for, and observance of, human rights and fundamental freedoms for all without distinction as to race, sex, language, or religion." *Id.*

[28] *See* JOSEPH M. SWEENEY ET AL., THE INTERNATIONAL LEGAL SYSTEM 632 (3d ed. 1988). *See also infra* text accompanying notes 42–45.

Economic, Social, and Cultural Rights[29] and the International Covenant on Civil and Political Rights (Covenants).[30]

The importance of the Covenants in regard to Cuba's quarantine policy rests in the assertion that they are binding on Cuba even though it is not a signatory.[31] According to some commentators, the provisions of the Covenants represent international customary law.[32] This argument, however, is subject to debate.

The Covenants became effective in 1976, and approximately ninety nations have ratified them.[33] Portions of the Covenants, such as provisions banning slavery, torture, and systematic racial discrimination, represent international customary law and are, therefore, binding on all states regardless of whether they signed the Convention.[34] The international community, however, recognized these compelling provisions as customary law prior to, and not as a result of, ratification of the Covenants.[35] Less com-

---

[29] International Covenant on Economic, Social, and Cultural Rights, *opened for signature* Dec. 19, 1966, 993 U.N.T.S. 3 (entered into force Jan. 3, 1976) [hereinafter ICESCR].

[30] International Covenant on Civil and Political Rights, *opened for signature* Dec. 19, 1966, 999 U.N.T.S. 171 (entered into force, Mar. 23, 1976) [hereinafter ICCPR].

[31] *See* Kirby, *supra* note 6, at 48.

[32] *Id.* Kirby states: "For all countries, whether they have ratified these international instruments or not, the International Covenants . . . provide statements of rules which are legally binding because they are now part of international law." *Id.*

[33] *See* RESTATEMENT, *supra* note 19, at Part VII Introductory Note.

[34] *See* B. G. RAMCHARAN, THE CONCEPT AND PRESENT STATUS OF THE INTERNATIONAL PROTECTION OF HUMAN RIGHTS 59 (1987). *See also* HUMPHREY, *supra* note 22, at 156. There is little agreement regarding the meaning or character of custom in international law. Nevertheless, a precise definition of the concept is not necessary in the context of this Comment. Any references to standards of conduct as customary international law are made only when those standards have been widely recognized as such. *See, e.g., infra* note 35 and accompanying text.

[35] *See* LOUIS B. SOHN & THOMAS BUERGENTHAL, INTERNATIONAL PROTECTION OF HUMAN RIGHTS 518–19 (1973). The international community recognized such provisions as part of customary international law following the adoption of the Universal Declaration of Human Rights. *Id. See also* RESTATEMENT, *supra* note 19, at § 702. The American Law Institute takes the position that there are certain fundamental human rights that are now part of customary international law. A violation occurs if a state practices, encourages, or condones (a) genocide; (b) slavery or slave trade; (c) the murder or causing disappearance of individuals; (d) torture or other cruel, inhuman, or degrading treatment or punishment; (e) prolonged arbitrary detention; (f) systematic racial discrimination; or (g) a consistent pattern of gross violations of internationally recognized human rights.

The customary international law of human rights creates obligations by each state for all other states. Thus, every state may, in principle, pursue remedies against any other state that violates the human rights of those individuals subject to its jurisdiction. In practice, however, states will usually attempt to vindicate only those wrongs committed against individuals in whom the vindicating state has a special interest—that is, their own nationals. *See* RESTATEMENT, *supra* note 19, at § 701.

pelling provisions of the Covenants, which quarantine critics use to attack the policy, include the "right to gain a living by work freely chosen."[36] The status of such provisions is widely debated, but it may be premature to claim that they constitute customary international law.[37] At most, they represent an ideal which non-signatories should consider when formulating national policies.[38]

2. Declarations

Along with international treaties, there exist a large number of international declarations that the United Nations or other international organizations have adopted.[39] While not drafted in binding language, these declarations contribute to the establishment of minimal standards of conduct for all peoples and all nations.[40] Human rights activists often invoke various provisions of these declarations as expressions of international law.[41] This is especially true of the Universal Declaration, which the U.N. General Assembly adopted in 1948.[42]

While the drafters of the Universal Declaration expressly denied that it represented a binding international document, it eventually acquired a moral and political authority equal to that of the Charter.[43] Not only has the Universal Declaration inspired a large number of international conventions, but it is reflected in national constitutions, legislation, and in the decisions of national

---

[36] Kirby, *supra* note 6, at 51; ICESCR, *supra* note 29, at art. 6(1).

[37] *See* RESTATEMENT, *supra* note 19, at § 702 cmt. a. The American Law Institute does not include the "right to gain a living by work freely chosen" among those rights considered part of customary international law.

[38] *See* RAMCHARAN, *supra* note 34, at 59. Ramcharan states: "The International Covenants are, in principle, legally binding only upon the States which have expressly ratified or acceded to them except to the extent that some provisions of the Covenants might represent international customary law." *Id.*

[39] *See* Bilder, *supra* note 11, at 5.

[40] *Id.*

[41] *Id. See also* RESTATEMENT, *supra* note 19, at § 701; PAUL SIEGHART, THE INTERNATIONAL LAW OF HUMAN RIGHTS 53–55 (1983); Robert M. Jarvis, *Advocacy for AIDS Victims: An International Law Approach*, 20 INTER-AM. L. REV. 1, 9–11 (1988). *See also infra* note 42 and accompanying text.

[42] Universal Declaration of Human Rights, G.A. Res. 217 A (III), U.N. Doc. A/810 (1948) [hereinafter Universal Declaration]. Sieghart asserts: "Between 1958 and 1972, references to [the Universal Declaration] were included in 25 new national constitutions and 8 domestic legislative acts." SIEGHART, *supra* note 41, at 53 n.9.

[43] HUMPHREY, *supra* note 22, at 154.

and international tribunals.[44] Contrary to the drafters' stated intentions, many of the Declaration's provisions are now part of customary international law.[45]

3. Decisions, Resolutions, and Recommendations

Another category of instruments which contribute to the body of international human rights law are those decisions, resolutions,[46] and recommendations generated by various U.N. organs or international agencies that deal with human rights problems.[47] There are essentially three points of view regarding the impact of resolutions on international law: a resolution's provisions (1) are legally binding on states; (2) possess only political and moral significance; or (3) contain a legal element, but are not legally binding.[48]

The most widely accepted position is that resolutions have only political and moral force.[49] To the extent that a single resolution has any bearing on international law, it is that it gives a state the right to act in ways consistent with that resolution.[50] Actions states take in accordance with such resolutions, therefore, cannot be legally challenged.[51]

While a single resolution may be relatively insignificant, some commentators believe that several identical resolutions can, taken as a whole, provide evidence of customary law.[52] However, "[r]esolutions, as a rule, do not result from state practice; they are recommendations for the future."[53] The resolutions become

---

44 *See id.* at 155.

45 *Id.*; SIEGHART, *supra* note 41, at 54–55.

46 The U.N. General Assembly's adoption of a resolution concerning AIDS makes resolutions—as opposed to decisions and recommendations—particularly relevant. *See infra* text accompanying notes 78–80.

47 *See* Bilder, *supra* note 11, at 5. For a detailed discussion of the impact of resolutions and recommendations on international law, see generally G.I. Tunkin, *The Role of Resolutions of International Organisations in Creating Norms of International Law*, *in* INTERNATIONAL LAW AND THE INTERNATIONAL SYSTEM 5 (W. E. Butler ed., 1987); Ingrid Delupis, *The Legal Value of Recommendations of International Organisations*, *in* INTERNATIONAL LAW AND THE INTERNATIONAL SYSTEM 47 (W. E. Butler ed., 1987).

48 *See* Tunkin, *supra* note 47, at 5.

49 *See id.* at 7.

50 *Id.* at 8.

51 *Id.*

52 *See* Delupis, *supra* note 47, at 47.

53 Tunkin, *supra* note 47, at 13.

binding only when, in the course of practice, states gradually recognize them as binding.[54]

II. THE INTERNATIONAL RESPONSE TO AIDS

A. *The U.N. Charter, the Universal Declaration, the Covenants, and AIDS*

Some opponents of AIDS quarantine programs like Cuba's support their contention that the policy violates international human rights law by citing various articles of the U.N. Charter, the Universal Declaration, and the Covenants.[55] The Charter's human rights provisions, however, are too broad to add significant weight to anti-quarantine arguments. Thus, critics rely chiefly on the Universal Declaration and the Covenants.[56]

The most important articles of the Universal Declaration used to support claims of human rights violations address the right to freedom of movement,[57] the right to be free from arbitrary detention,[58] the right to privacy,[59] and the right to marry.[60] Because these "rights" are contained within the Universal Declaration, it is possible to argue that they have obtained the force of customary international law.[61] With the exception of the right to be free from arbitrary detention, however, they merit only a brief examination where quarantine is concerned.[62]

---

[54] *Id.* at 14.

[55] *See, e.g.*, Kirby, *supra* note 6, at 48–51; Jarvis, *supra* note 41, at 8–13.

[56] For a discussion of quarantine critics' use of the Covenant, see *supra* text accompanying notes 29–38.

[57] *See* Universal Declaration, *supra* note 42, at art. 13. Article 13 states: "(1) Everyone has the right to freedom of movement and residence within the borders of each State. (2) Everyone has the right to leave any country, including his own, and to return to his country." *Id. But see* ICCPR, *supra* note 30, at art. 12(3). Article 12(3) provides a number of exceptions permitting restrictions, including restrictions to protect public health.

[58] *See infra* text accompanying note 66.

[59] *See* Universal Declaration, *supra* note 42, at art. 12. Article 12 states: "No one shall be subjected to arbitrary interference with his privacy, family, home or correspondence . . . ."

[60] *See id.* at art. 16 ("Men and women of full age . . . have the right to marry and to found a family.").

[61] *See* SIEGHART, *supra* note 41, at 54; *supra* text accompanying note 57.

[62] The rights to privacy and marriage do not belong to that category of rights that are never subject to derogation. *See* RESTATEMENT, *supra* note 19, at § 702, note 11. The Universal Declaration states that rights may be limited by law for purposes of meeting "the just requirements of morality, public order and the general welfare . . . " of the state. Universal Declaration, *supra* note 42, at art. 29(2). Infringement on the rights to privacy

The right to freedom of movement is set forth in article 13 of the Universal Declaration.[63] Opponents of quarantine policies argue that this gives AIDS victims the right to leave a country to avoid detention.[64] While this argument bears some merit, it is less compelling in a country such as Cuba where no one is afforded freedom of movement.[65] Restrictions on the freedom of movement out of the country have no special applicability to AIDS patients. Such policies are essentially unrelated to the AIDS quarantine, and therefore are beyond the scope of this Comment's analysis.

Article 9 of the Universal Declaration states: "[n]o one shall be subjected to arbitrary arrest, detention or exile."[66] Most scholars agree that this article represents customary international law.[67] If the quarantine policy is arbitrary, it would, therefore, constitute a human rights violation. On the other hand, if the detention is not arbitrary, the policy is legitimate, and there is no need to examine the claims of a right to privacy or a right to marry. These individual rights may be restricted for legitimate reasons.[68] The dispositive question, then, is whether the AIDS quarantine is an arbitrary detention.

B. *WHO's View of Quarantine Policies*

In 1985, as the global scope of the AIDS crisis became apparent, WHO drafted a global strategy for the prevention and control of AIDS.[69] Its objectives are threefold: "(a) to prevent HIV

---

and marriage, then, would be acceptable for maintaining public health if it represents the only means to do so.

Quarantine critics might also argue that it constitutes cruel, inhuman, and degrading treatment, a more serious violation of international human rights law. *See supra* note 35 and accompanying text. Critics could not persuasively argue that the policy is, by definition, cruel or degrading if it is not arbitrary, or, stated positively, if it is legitimate. A stronger argument would focus on the way the interned are treated. Even such an approach, however, would probably not reveal a violation of human rights law given Cuba's apparent effort to treat the interned humanely. *See infra* text accompanying notes 114–18. For a discussion of what constitutes cruel, inhuman, and degrading treatment, see generally *Ireland v. United Kingdom*, 2 Eur. H.R. Rep. (ser. A) at 25 (1978).

63 *See supra* text accompanying note 57.

64 *See, e.g.*, Jarvis, *supra* note 41, at 10; Kirby, *supra* note 6, at 50–51.

65 *See* HUGH S. THOMAS ET AL., THE CUBAN REVOLUTION 50 (1984).

66 Universal Declaration, *supra* note 42, at art. 9.

67 *See* RESTATEMENT, *supra* note 19, at § 702.

68 *See supra* note 62 and accompanying text.

69 *See* World Health Organization, *Fortieth World Health Assembly, Geneva, 4–15 May 1987, Resolution and Decisions, Annexes* (WHA.40/1987/REC/1); Mann et al., *supra* note 5, at 20.

infection; (b) to reduce the personal and social impact of HIV/AIDS; and (c) to unify national and international efforts against AIDS."[70] A number of guidelines determine the manner in which states can realize the objectives, including assertions that education is the key to AIDS prevention, that public health must be protected, that human rights must be respected, and that discrimination must be prevented.[71]

WHO has directly addressed the social aspects of AIDS prevention and control in its publications.[72] WHO's literature states that no public health rationale justifies quarantine or any discriminatory measures based solely on the fact that a person is known to be HIV-infected.[73] WHO further asserts that "persons suspected or known to be HIV-infected should remain integrated within society to the maximum possible extent. . . ."[74] Thus, WHO strongly discourages the methods used by Cuba to prevent the spread of AIDS.

Dr. Jonathan M. Mann, former Director of WHO's Global Program on AIDS, has advanced at least two reasons why AIDS-infected people should remain in society.[75] First, the AIDS virus is not dangerous, provided society is educated about the means of transmission.[76] Second, the threat of quarantine will drive the problem "underground," effectively thwarting testing strategies and educational efforts.[77]

In 1987, the U.N. General Assembly adopted a resolution commending WHO for its efforts toward global AIDS prevention and control.[78] Moreover, the resolution confirms that WHO should direct and coordinate the global battle against AIDS and

---

[70] Mann et al., *supra* note 5, at 20.

[71] *Id.* at 21.

[72] *See* GUIDELINES FOR NURSING, *supra* note 5, at 41–42. *See generally* WORLD HEALTH ORGANIZATION, AIDS PREVENTION AND CONTROL (1988).

[73] GUIDELINES FOR NURSING, *supra* note 5, at 41.

[74] *Id.* at 42.

[75] *See* Jonathan M. Mann, *A Global Strategy for a Global Challenge*, WORLD HEALTH, Mar. 1988, at 4.

[76] *Id.*

[77] *Id.*

[78] *See Prevention and control of acquired immune deficiency syndrome (AIDS)*, G.A. Res. 42/8, U.N. GAOR, 42d Sess., Supp. No. 49, at 19, U.N. Doc. A/42/49 (1987) [hereinafter Resolution]. The Resolution recognizes the "established leadership and the essential global directing and coordinating role of . . . [WHO] in AIDS prevention, control and education . . . ." *Id.*

it commends those governments whose AIDS programs are in harmony with WHO's strategy.[79] The General Assembly reaffirmed in 1988 and 1989 "the established leadership and the essential role of . . . [WHO] in the global direction and coordination of AIDS prevention . . . ."[80] Statements from various international assemblies also support WHO's efforts.[81]

The international support shown for WHO's strategy has led some commentators to argue that the strategy amounts to a requirement under international human rights law.[82] This is a tenuous assertion, however, considering that many of the countries supporting the General Assembly resolution have adopted the same preventative measures WHO discourages.[83] As indicated above, General Assembly resolutions may impose on U.N. members an "obligation to take [the resolution] into consideration."[84] Such resolutions, however, would not bind states to introduce specific legislation even if they had voted for the resolution. This is not to say that the position concerning quarantine expressed by WHO is without significance. It is simply not the *sole* approach to AIDS prevention consistent with international human rights.

C. *Individual State Considerations*

A fundamental concern expressed in WHO's AIDS program is that states should protect human rights and preserve the dignity of those who have the disease.[85] Almost all states would agree that these goals are of prime importance.[86] Deciding how best to achieve them is another matter. As Maria Paalman, Director of the Dutch Foundation for STD Control, has written, "[o]ne global

---

[79] *Id.*

[80] *See* Mann et al., *supra* note 5, at 22.

[81] *See id.* at 20. The strategy has been approved and adopted by the World Health Assembly (May 1987), the Venice Summit of the Heads of State of Government (June 1987), the Economic and Social Council of the United Nations (July 1987) and the World Summit of Ministers of Health on Programmes for AIDS Prevention (London, Jan. 1988).

[82] *See, e.g.*, Kirby, *supra* note 6, at 48.

[83] *See* Michael Micklin & David F. Sly, *International Population Movements and AIDS: Patterns, Consequences, and Policy Implications*, *in* THE GLOBAL IMPACT OF AIDS 67, 76 (Alan F. Fleming et al. eds., 1988) (pointing out the large number of countries which have some form of mandatory AIDS screening contrary to WHO's policy recommendations). *See also* Jarvis, *supra* note 41, at 1009–11.

[84] *See* Delupis, *supra* note 47, at 52.

[85] *See* Mann et al., *supra* note 5, at 21.

[86] *See generally* Resolution, *supra* note 78.

strategy for AIDS prevention is neither possible nor desirable."[87] Common sense dictates that there is a need to consider state-specific factors when designing a prevention strategy.[88] Thus, determining whether Cuba's quarantine policy is consistent with international human rights law requires viewing it not only in light of WHO's guidelines, but against factors particular to Cuba. These factors include Cuba's political structure and principles, its educational and cultural environment, the prevalence of the HIV virus, and the strengths and weaknesses of Cuba's national health care system.[89]

Examination of Cuba's quarantine program in light of the above factors permits testing of the premises behind the assertion that no public health rationale exists to justify the policy.[90] If, for example, most Cubans would not heed warnings of infection even if informed, then one of the underlying reasons for WHO's strategy is lost.[91] Studying the performance of the Cuban education system and its impact on Cuban society should help determine whether AIDS can be successfully fought through education. In essence, analyzing Cuba's quarantine policy in this manner will provide a means by which to determine whether the detention is arbitrary.[92]

---

[87] Paalman, *supra* note 10, at 218. *See also* Robert J. Earickson, *International Behavioral Responses to a Health Hazard: AIDS*, 31 SOC. SCI. & MED. 960 (1990).

[88] *See* Earickson, *supra* note 87, at 960. Earickson states: "Differences have been documented in individual responses to natural hazards in developing and developed countries. Similarly, there are different cultural responses to AIDS in these nations." *Id.*

[89] The factors selected do not exhaust the possibilities. Nevertheless, they represent factors likely to influence the effectiveness of the AIDS prevention program employed.

[90] *See* Mann, *supra* note 75, at 4.

[91] *Id.* Some individuals will fail to act responsibly even if they know the risks. *See, e.g., infra* note 147 and accompanying text. Failure to reach a few individuals through education does not, however, make reliance on education as a means of preventing AIDS unsound. Yet, if the number of individuals ignoring the message becomes significant, then it would be irresponsible to continue making education the sole element of the anti-AIDS strategy.

[92] In its treatment of article 9 of the Universal Declaration, the American Law Institute offers a definition of arbitrary, but only as it pertains to the detention of alleged criminals. *See* RESTATEMENT, *supra* note 19, at § 702 cmt. h. The U.N. Commission on Human Rights has also studied the concept of arbitrary detention, but its study is also largely concerned with criminal detention. *See generally* UNITED NATIONS, STUDY OF THE RIGHT OF EVERYONE TO BE FREE FROM ARBITRARY ARREST, DETENTION AND EXILE, 1964 [hereinafter STUDY]. The study only briefly discusses detention of persons afflicted with infectious diseases, concluding that detainees must be treated with dignity. *Id.* at 182. Thus, for the purposes of this Comment, an arbitrary health policy will be defined as one that will not work, or if it does work, is more restrictive or harsh than is necessary.

III. CUBA'S QUARANTINE

Prior to 1986, Cuba had no program designed to address the AIDS crisis.[93] In fact, Cuban authorities thought of AIDS as a "Western" disease, the result of decadent behavior.[94] By mid-1986, however, Cuban authorities began to formulate a concerted plan of action against the AIDS problem.[95] Part of the program is designed to educate the public about the dangers of AIDS, but it is not the crux of the strategy.[96]

By early 1987, the Cubans made the focus of their strategy known. The government announced that it would test Cuba's entire population.[97] Consequently, all Cubans returning from visits abroad, all Cubans admitted to any hospital for any reason, and all Cubans likely to have contact with foreigners are tested for HIV infection.[98] In addition to testing its own population, the government requires foreigners planning to stay in the country for more than three months to have a blood test upon entering Cuba.[99] The government does not, however, plan to test vacationing tourists who enter the country.[100]

As with other public health campaigns in Cuba, these efforts enlist the help of "mass organizations" such as the Committees for the Defense of the Revolution, the Women's Federation, and various trade unions.[101] Cuban officials state that it is unnecessary to test people through coercion because all Cubans come into contact with the medical system, whether through the workplace, at school, or for medical treatment.[102] Additionally, informed consent is not required. According to Dr. Hector Terry, Cuban

---

[93] *See* Nick Caistor, *Treatment for Life*, NEW SCIENTIST, Feb. 18, 1989, at 65; Anne McElvoy, *Soldiers of Misfortune*, THE TIMES (London), Nov. 10, 1989, at 14E.

[94] *See* OFFICE OF RESEARCH & POLICY RADIO MARTI PROGRAM, CUBA ANNUAL REPORT: 1986 481 (1990) [hereinafter RADIO MARTI].

[95] Caistor, *supra* note 93, at 65.

[96] *See* Ronald Bayer & Cheryl Healton, *Controlling AIDS in Cuba*, 320 NEW ENG. J. OF MED. 1022, 1022 (1989).

[97] *See* Treaster, *supra* note 1, at A2.

[98] *See* N.Y. TIMES, Jan. 22, 1989, at E24, col. 5; Bayer & Healton, *supra* note 96, at 1022.

[99] Caistor, *supra* note 93, at 65.

[100] Eliseo J. Perez-Stable, *Cuba's Response to the HIV Epidemic*, AM. J. OF PUB. HEALTH, May, 1991, at 565.

[101] *See* Bayer & Healton, *supra* note 96, at 1022. These organizations are called upon to help perform various non-specialized functions, such as compiling lists of persons who have served outside of Cuba since 1975.

[102] *Id.* at 1022–23.

Vice-Minister of Health,[103] "[p]hysicians undertake the tests that they consider crucial. It is not for patients to make such determinations."[104]

The Cuban government uses a variety of testing methods similar to or the same as those used by other countries.[105] Despite the medical system's best efforts, however, both false positive and false negative readings are possibilities.[106] The consequence of a false positive, if authorities do not later discover the error, is quarantine.[107]

Once AIDS carriers are identified, cases come under the jurisdiction of the Ministry of the Interior.[108] Anyone who tests HIV positive is "asked" to move to Finca Los Cocos, a former plantation and sanitarium outside of Havana.[109] Some reports indicate that those who refuse to go are brought by force, although this has not been confirmed by any human rights organizations.[110] According to Rodolfo Rodriguez, head of the AIDS testing program, doctors and nurses are sent to convince AIDS carriers that "it is better to go . . . ."[111] While he denies that force or coercion is used, the fact that everyone depends on the state for their livelihood is likely to induce cooperation.[112]

Given the controlled nature of Cuban society, it is difficult to determine effectively the nature of the care AIDS patients re-

---

[103] *Id.* at 1023.

[104] *Id.*

[105] *Id.*

[106] *Id. See also* Perez-Stable, *supra* note 100, at 564. Cuba's testing program identifies AIDS carriers through the use of domestically developed enzyme-linked immonosorbent assay (ELISA), Western blot assay, and antigen tests. The Cuban tests meet international standards, according to Cuban authorities. Nevertheless, even if the tests meet international standards and stringent laboratory procedures are maintained, approximately one in every 135,000 persons will, at least initially, receive a false positive test result.

[107] Perez-Stable, *supra* note 100, at 565. Cuban authorities are aware of the possibility of false positive and negative results. To guard against internment of uninfected persons, multiple screening tests are conducted on individuals who test positive. It is impossible to know, however, how carefully the tests are performed.

[108] *See* Betancourt, *supra* note 6, at 2.

[109] Caistor, *supra* note 93, at 65.

[110] *See* Bayer & Healton, *supra* note 96, at 1024; Betancourt, *supra* note 6, at 2; *infra* note 123 and accompanying text.

[111] Caistor, *supra* note 93, at 65.

[112] *Id.* On the other hand, the Cuban people, including those who are often critical of the government, seem to accept the quarantine policy, and patients may indeed believe it is best to separate themselves from society. *See* Perez-Stable, *supra* note 100, at 566.

ceive.[113] A number of U.S. health professionals have visited Los Cocos, however, and report that living conditions, by Cuban standards, appear clean and humane.[114] Patients questioned generally spoke as though they were willingly cooperating with the authorities, although they made their statements in the presence of sanitarium staff members.[115] A doctor at the sanitarium said that the patients receive the wages they did previous to their internment.[116] The authorities allow visits to local shops in the company of an attendant, and patients with families can visit them for up to five days, again with a chaperone, if they sign a promise to abstain from any sexual relations.[117] The Cuban doctor also said that the staff provides both medical treatment and psychological counseling to the patients.[118]

With no cure for AIDS in sight, Cuba's isolation of AIDS carriers is indefinite.[119] Naturally, this has resulted in escape attempts, reportedly leading to massive man-hunts.[120] Dr. Terry stated that there had been escapes from the sanitarium, but that the fugitives returned after recognizing their need for care at the center.[121] Other sources report that the treatment of escapees is harsh, and includes imprisonment.[122] Again, independent human rights organizations have been unable to confirm the allegations.[123]

---

113 Foreigners who were allowed to visit Los Cocos were accompanied by authorities. *See* Bayer & Healton, *supra* note 96, at 1023–24. Nevertheless, considering the world-wide attention AIDS is receiving and the desire of the Cuban government to present its medical system in the best possible light, it is doubtful that the government would allow the patients to be mistreated. *See infra* note 172 and accompanying text.

114 *See* Betancourt, *supra* note 6; Bayer & Healton, *supra* note 96, at 102; N.Y. TIMES, *supra* note 98, at E24, col. 5. The officials who visited Cuba include two medical doctors and two public health specialists from Columbia University.

115 *See* Bayer & Healton, *supra* note 96, at 1023.

116 Caistor, *supra* note 93, at 65.

117 *Id.*

118 *Id.*

119 "Indefinite" does not necessarily mean "until a cure is found." Cuban authorities are exploring the possibility of allowing individuals to return to their families in certain cases. *See* Bayer & Healton, *supra* note 96, at 1024; Perez-Stable, *supra* note 100, at 566. *See also infra* note 183 and accompanying text.

120 *See* Betancourt, *supra* note 6, at 2; Bayer & Healton, *supra* note 96, at 1024.

121 *See* Bayer & Healton, *supra* note 96, at 1024.

122 Betancourt, *supra* note 6, at 2.

123 Bayer & Healton, *supra* note 96, at 2. Americas Watch, a human rights group concerned about Cuban prison conditions, has been unable to substantiate the allegations. Telephone Interview with Mary-Jane Camejo, Americas Watch (Oct. 8, 1991).

IV. FACTORS INFLUENCING THE CHOICE OF STRATEGY: IS THE DETENTION ARBITRARY?

A. *The Political System and Ideology*

Cuba's political system is decidedly Marxist-Leninist.[124] As such, individual rights are subservient to the needs of the state.[125] While this does not eliminate individual rights, it does mean that collective interests weigh heavily in the event that the two require balancing.[126]

Marxist-Leninist ideology makes government actions relatively easy to justify on grounds of the "collective good." This, in turn, makes individual human rights violations difficult, though not impossible, to establish in Communist countries.[127] Cuba is known to have perpetrated human rights abuses on individuals in the name of state interests.[128] The concern about Cuba's quarantine policy is that the government is using the "public good" to justify what is actually an arbitrary detention.

Critics of the quarantine policy may point to past oppressive treatment of homosexuals as proof that the Cuban government is using public health and safety as a pretense for continued persecution. In the early 1970s, the government began a campaign designed to eliminate homosexuality because it represented Western decadence and was, therefore, counter-revolutionary.[129] Homosexuals were "arrested in the streets, seized from their homes, and sent to reeducation camps."[130] While the repression lasted only two years, the attitudes reflected in the policy may still be held by members of government, if not society as a whole.[131]

---

[124] *See* THOMAS ET AL., *supra* note 65, at 48.

[125] *Id.*

[126] *See* Bayer & Healton, *supra* note 96, at 1024. In the context of AIDS prevention, this philosophy favors public health over individual freedom.

[127] *See, e.g.*, Rosalyn Higgins, *Conceptual Thinking About the Individual in International Law*, *in* INTERNATIONAL LAW: A CONTEMPORARY PERSPECTIVE 476, 486–87 (R. Falk et al. eds., 1985) (referring to the Soviet Union's use of an *order public* caveat in the ICCPR to justify strict emigration restrictions).

[128] *See* THOMAS ET AL., *supra* note 65, at 48–49 (discussing political prisoners who are classified as "counterrevolutionaries"); *infra* note 129 and accompanying text.

[129] THOMAS ET AL., *supra* note 65, at 48–49. *See* JACOBO TIMERMAN, CUBA: A JOURNEY 57 (1990). Timerman states: "The problem of homosexuals was always linked in revolutionary morality and political analysis to the relations existing between prostitution and corruption as controlled by the U.S. East Coast Mafia." TIMMERMAN, *supra*, at 57.

[130] TIMERMAN, *supra* note 129, at 58.

[131] *Id.*

This might be a powerful argument except for the fact that the majority of all internees are not homosexual.[132] Educational pamphlets and materials distributed by the government "stress that AIDS is not a disease exclusively of homosexuals and can affect any person."[133] Additionally, initial government claims that AIDS is a "Western" disease have ceased.[134]

B. *Education and Culture*

At first glance, Cuba would appear to have the very kind of education system needed for an effective fight against AIDS.[135] Cuba has reportedly excelled in education.[136] In 1961, the government stunned the world when it announced a reduction in illiteracy to just 4 percent from a rate of 25 percent in 1957.[137] In the 1958–1959 school year there were 17,355 teachers in Cuba. Ten years later the number had risen to 47,876. The number of primary school students jumped from 700,000 to 1.4 million during the same period. Despite these achievements, however, there are serious problems with the system.

While school enrollment during the 1960s increased dramatically, in the 1970s over 70 percent of elementary and 85 percent of high school age students dropped out of school.[138] There is a lack of teaching materials, graduation requirements are substandard, and behavioral problems are extensive.[139] Academic fraud and cheating is widespread, involving both students and teachers.[140] Frustration with the education system is expressed at the highest levels of government.[141]

---

[132] *See* Bayer & Healton, *supra* note 96, at 1023. Authorities stated that approximately one-third of the 171 male residents at Los Cocos were homosexual or bisexual.

[133] *Id.* at 1022.

[134] *See* Betancourt, *supra* note 6, at 2.

[135] Given Cuba's 94 percent literacy rate, dissemination of AIDS information should not be a problem. For a comparison of Cuba's literacy rate with that of other Latin American countries, see SANDOR HALEBSKY & JOHN M. KIRK, TRANSFORMATION AND STRUGGLE: CUBA FACES THE 1990s 144 (1990).

[136] *See* THOMAS ET AL., *supra* note 65, at 42.

[137] *Id.* at 41.

[138] *Id.* at 51.

[139] *See* RADIO MARTI, *supra* note 94, at 108.

[140] THOMAS ET AL., *supra* note 65, at 42. According to official sources, 34 percent of all secondary schools were involved in fraud or cheating.

[141] *See* RADIO MARTI, *supra* note 94, at 108. Castro himself has described the shortcomings of the Cuban system: "The quality of our education still leaves much to be desired. Some classes are still mediocre or poor; notes rather than textbooks, are often relied upon

Adding to this frustration may be the Cuban government's inability to re-shape "unhealthy" Cuban societal and cultural practices through "re-education" campaigns.[142] One of these campaigns was aimed at reducing or eliminating prostitution in Cuba.[143] Despite extensive government efforts, prostitution remains prevalent.[144]

The failure of the Cuban education system may have contributed significantly to the government's decision to employ quarantine as the primary means of controlling AIDS. The government simply has no faith in the ability of its educational system to change undesirable behavior.[145] Cuba is concerned that even those who know they have the disease might not alter their behavior.[146] Considering that such irresponsibility is not uncommon, their concern is not unfounded.[147]

On the other hand, Cubans arguably might respond differently if confronted with a sexually transmitted disease that causes death. As indicated above, however, Cubans are frustrated with and unresponsive to their educational system.[148] While the government is reluctant to acknowledge the possibility, it may fear

. . . . Problems persist in the cultivation of proper social conduct, even in the case of teachers as [with] some young people." *Id.*

[142] *See* TIMERMAN, *supra* note 129, at 57.

[143] *Id.* at 92.

[144] *Id.* Timerman, who traveled extensively throughout Cuba with the government's permission, writes: "I don't understand why Castroism insists that the Revolution has eliminated prostitution through a reeducation campaign . . . . In Cuba you encounter prostitutes everywhere." *Id. See also* MAX AZICRI, CUBA: POLITICS, ECONOMICS AND SOCIETY 161–62 (1988).

[145] *See* Bayer & Healton, *supra* note 96, at 1024; TIMERMAN, *supra* note 129, at 88. Timerman states that while government ideology has altered many elements of Cuban culture, "[t]he Revolution could do nothing to steer or rechannel the energy which Cubans assign to eroticism." TIMERMAN, *supra* note 129, at 88. *See also* Perez-Stable, *supra* note 100, at 564. The Interior Ministry's greatest concern is "that of irresponsible sexual behavior among men characterized by the machismo cultural trait who are likely to seek extramarital sexual partners." Perez-Stable, *supra* note 100, at 564.

[146] *See* Caistor, *supra* note 93, at 65. This is amply illustrated by Cuba's use of chaperones and written promises to abstain from sexual relations whenever AIDS patients leave Los Cocos.

[147] *See* Earickson, *supra* note 87, at 957. Earickson states: "It is clear that some people are reluctant to alter their behavior even when damage to property or a threat to life is at stake." *Id.* The number of documented cases of informed AIDS carriers behaving irresponsibly is not insignificant. For a brief discussion of international reaction to such cases, see Robert M. Jarvis, *AIDS: A Global View*, 12 NOVA L. REV. 979, 1007–08 (1988).

[148] *See supra* text accompanying notes 138–41.

that society will perceive its warnings concerning AIDS as nothing more than Revolutionary rhetoric.[149]

Given the failure of the Cuban education system to curb undesirable and risky social behavior,[150] it seems inappropriate to fault the government for having little faith in education as a means to prevent the spread of AIDS. Nevertheless, even if education efforts would not effectively halt the spread of AIDS in Cuba, questions surrounding the efficacy of its quarantine remain.[151]

C. *The Prevalence of AIDS and the Health System's Capabilities*

Critics argue that quarantine is ineffective because people will avoid testing out of fear.[152] They also argue that mandatory testing will not guarantee prevention of the spread of the disease for two reasons. First, they argue that transmission may occur after testing, and second, that the tests may yield false negative readings. Finally, they claim that the costs of quarantine will be prohibitive.[153] These blanket predictions are unconvincing. Cuba's method of coping with the medical challenge of AIDS must be analyzed in light of the prevalence of the disease and the capabilities of its medical system.

The prevalence of the AIDS virus in Cuba is difficult to measure because only tightly controlled government statistics are available.[154] The government asserts that it has completed mandatory testing of more than 90 percent of its 10.4 million citizens.[155] Over 400 Cubans have tested HIV positive,[156] and as of December 31, 1990, seventy-three Cubans had contracted AIDS.[157] The number of AIDS cases per capita is far lower than the figures reported by other Caribbean nations, a fact the Cu-

---

149 *See* THOMAS ET AL., *supra* note 65, at 51.

150 *See supra* notes 141, 145 and accompanying text.

151 *See infra* text accompanying notes 152–53.

152 *See* Mann, *supra* note 75, at 4.

153 Mass HIV testing costs the Cuban government about $2 million per year. Perez-Stable, *supra* note 100, at 564.

154 *See* Treaster, *supra* note 1, at A2. *See also infra* note 158 and accompanying text.

155 *See* McElvoy, *supra* note 93, at 14E.

156 *See* Perez-Stable, *supra* note 100, at 563.

157 *See* World Health Organization, WEEKLY EPIDEMIOLOGICAL RECORD, July 5, 1991, at 198.

bans attribute to their health care system generally and, specifically, their quarantine policy.[158]

The Cuban government is said to have made extraordinary gains in health care since Fidel Casto seized power in 1959.[159] The health care system is extensive and still growing. By the year 2000, Cuba plans to have one doctor per 173 inhabitants, the highest ratio of doctors per capita in the world.[160] Cuba recently instituted a new family physician program which places a general practitioner and nurse in offices located on every city block and in every rural neighborhood.[161] In addition to creating an extensive medical system, utilizing the most advanced medical technology is a priority in Cuba. The government is allocating resources to such activities as genetic engineering, basic biological research, and specialized training in advanced diagnostic and research techniques.[162] The government expects accomplishments in these areas to reinforce the image of a Cuba so advanced that it can provide excellent medical care to its entire population.[163]

Although the government is promoting Cuba as a major medical power, it is failing to meet some of its society's basic health needs.[164] The quality of health care is affected by the unavailability of even basic medical supplies, the poor maintenance of equipment, and the substandard hygienic conditions existing in some facilities.[165]

Such conditions reveal the underlying fragility of the Cuban medical system. A large scale outbreak of AIDS, such as that experienced by other Carribean nations, could strip Cuba of the resources needed to preserve its medical achievements and ad-

---

[158] *Id.*; *See also* THE WORLD ALMANAC AND BOOK OF FACTS 688–716 (1990). Cuba has acknowledged 73 AIDS cases in a population of 10.4 million. By comparison, the Dominican Republic has 1,506 cases in a population of 7.2 million; Haiti has 3,086 cases in a population of 6.4 million; and Jamaica has 201 cases in a population of 2.5 million. Some Cuban observers have questioned the accuracy of the Cuban government's figures. *See* Antonio M. Gordon & Reinaldo Paya, *Controlling AIDS in Cuba*, 321 NEW ENG. J. MED. 829 (1989). The Pan American Health Organization has, however, confirmed the government's accuracy in reporting on other diseases. Some view this as evidence that the government is honest in reporting AIDS cases. *See* Perez-Stable, *supra* note 100, at 564.

[159] *See* Bayer & Healton, *supra* note 96, at 1022; THOMAS ET AL., *supra* note 65, at 44.

[160] *See* RADIO MARTI, *supra* note 94, at 263.

[161] *See* HALEBSKY & KIRK, *supra* note 135, at 253.

[162] *See id.* at 257, 260.

[163] *See* RADIO MARTI, *supra* note 94, at 616.

[164] *Id.* at 107. *See also* TIMERMAN, *supra* note 129, at 117.

[165] *See* RADIO MARTI, *supra* note 94, at 107.

dress its failures.[166] The Cuban government has, therefore, attacked the threat of AIDS through methods that the medical system can handle without undue strain.[167]

The mandatory testing program is relatively inexpensive and easy.[168] While Cuban officials recognize that some individuals will try to avoid testing, the highly controlled nature of the society makes avoidance difficult.[169] There is every indication that the Cuban health care system can effectively account for all of its citizens.[170] While the system is in a state of material disrepair, it is still extensive.[171] High level attention and support for the program is virtually guaranteed by the high profile nature of the disease and the government's desire to be a "medical power."[172] Moreover, because it is an island, the government can easily limit unmonitored travel in and out of the country.[173]

Cuban health officials are presumably aware of the possibility of infection after testing and false negative readings.[174] Whether they plan to periodically re-test the population is uncertain.[175] There is strong consensus among health care experts that mandatory testing must continue for the program to work.[176] Given

---

[166] The costs of AIDS are high. In the United States the costs of health care and lost income were estimated at over $6 billion for the first 10,000 cases. *See* John C. Moskop, *Restrictive Public Health Measures and AIDS: An Ethical Analysis*, *in* THE MEANING OF AIDS 119, 119 (Eric T. Juengst & Barbara A. Koenig eds., 1989).

[167] *See infra* note 168 and accompanying text.

[168] A routine HIV antibody screening test costs about $6.00 in the United States. *See* Lorraine Day, *What the Government Doesn't Tell You About AIDS*, NEW DIMENSIONS, Feb. 1991, at 75. In Cuba, however, voluntary help received from various "mass organizations" such as the Committees for the Defense of the Revolution probably reduce the cost significantly. *See* Bayer & Healton, *supra* note 96, at 1022.

[169] *See* THOMAS ET AL., *supra* note 65, at 48–49.

[170] *See* Bayer & Healton, *supra* note 96, at 1022.

[171] *See* HALEBSKY & KIRK, *supra* note 135, at 253.

[172] *See* RADIO MARTI, *supra* note 94, at 616. Cuba uses its medical accomplishments to try to reinforce its image as a country which takes a rigorous scientific approach toward public health.

[173] The fact that Cuba is an island is an important factor lending credibility to the mandatory testing program. If persons infected with AIDS were able to enter the country by land—that is, relatively easily—the effectiveness of the mandatory testing program would be significantly degraded.

[174] *See* Day, *supra* note 168, at 76. A person may test negative for months or sometimes years after becoming infected.

[175] Cuban officials are aware that false negative readings occur, but they have not indicated how they plan to deal with the problem. *See* Bayer & Healton, *supra* note 96, at 1023.

[176] *See* Caistor, *supra* note 93, at 65; Bayer & Healton, *supra* note 96, at 1024.

that the apparatus is in place, it is hard to believe that the government would leave the task half finished.[177]

The monetary costs of quarantine are not prohibitively high. If the number of AIDS patients remains low, the government will be able to finance the cost of housing and medical care without excessive strain.[178] Moreover, the government would probably argue that by taking action now it is saving itself enormous financial outlays in the future.[179] Ultimately, there is no decisive way to determine how much money is saved or lost through quarantine. It is notable, however, that most observers admit that the Cuban policy to date has significantly reduced the threat of an epidemic.[180]

D. *Less Restrictive Measures*

It is arguable that less restrictive measures than strict quarantine could effectively stop the spread of AIDS. One suggested alternative to quarantine involved placing a discreet tattoo on the AIDS carrier to alert potential partners of the carrier's infection.[181] Certainly, there are moral and ethical problems with such a measure. Additionally, it would not be difficult for a carrier to hide the tattoo, especially considering the circumstances under which many sexual encounters take place.[182]

Another less restrictive measure might be quarantine of only those carriers who knowingly engage in risky sexual behavior.[183] The risks inherent in this option, however, are unacceptably high

---

177 The Cuban government is not impervious to criticism. *See infra* note 188 and accompanying text. In light of the embarrassment that failure of the policy would bring, it is unlikely that the authorities will disregard the need for re-testing. *See supra* note 172 and accompanying text.

178 *See supra* note 153 and accompanying text. Housing and medical care are socialized, thus the quarantine itself probably adds little to the overall budget. The government will lose money, however, by paying salaries to the interned if they are not employed in some capacity. On the other hand, jobs within the compound could defray these costs.

179 *See* Pramilla Senanayake & Anthony Klonda, *AIDS and Family Planning Programs, in* THE GLOBAL IMPACT OF AIDS 107, 115 (1988). The costs of medical treatment for patients is proportionally higher in developing countries than it is in developed countries.

180 Bayer & Healton, *supra* note 96, at 1024.

181 *See* William F. Buckley, *Crucial steps in combatting the AIDS epidemic: Identify all the carriers*, N.Y. TIMES, Mar. 18, 1986, at A27.

182 For other criticisms of this suggestion, see Moskop, *supra* note 166, at 126.

183 *See* Jarvis, *supra* note 147, at 1007–09.

to the Cuban government.[184] Halting the spread of the disease would not be possible until carriers are identified. Considering the prevalence and acceptance of prostitution in Cuba, the time required to identify carriers could render the policy ineffective.[185] Thus, alternative policies are unlikely to be as successful as the current policy.[186]

E. *Continuing Efforts*

Potential for success of the quarantine policy does not negate concern for the welfare of those interned. International human rights law requires respect for their dignity.[187] By providing humane living conditions and health care for the interned, the Cuban government is fulfilling this responsibility.[188]

There are problems with the Cuban program, for example, the government's decision not to test tourists. Unless recurrent testing is conducted in those areas that tourists frequent, quarantine could be rendered ineffective and, thus, arbitrary. It remains to be seen how the government will address this problem.

Despite such concerns, the Cuban quarantine policy does not appear, at this time, to constitute an arbitrary detention. Whether the policy remains legitimate depends on future decision-making. The government must maintain humane treatment of AIDS patients. It must continue to test the general population and continue to explore less draconian alternatives. Finally, it must ensure, through multiple tests, that no one who is uninfected is mistakenly interned.

---

[184] *See* Bayer & Healton, *supra* note 96, at 1024. The justification for quarantine "assumes that since it is impossible to determine which infected persons can be trusted to behave in a responsible way sexually, they all have to be restricted and treated as a hazard." *Id.*

[185] *See supra* note 144 and accompanying text.

[186] This does not mean that variations of a strict quarantine cannot be explored. *See* Bayer & Healton, *supra* note 96, at 1024. For example, if after observation and counseling at Los Cocos, doctors determine that a patient would not engage in risky behavior, the patient should be allowed to live at home. Cuban authorities say they are exploring such possibilities.

[187] *See* Stuyt, *supra* note 12, at 169; STUDY, *supra* note 92, at 182.

[188] *See* Caistor, *supra* note 93, at 65; Bayer & Healton, *supra* note 96, at 1024. Cuban authorities are well aware of the criticism their policy has provoked. They insist that they are exploring less extreme measures, but that for the present they have chosen the best course.

CONCLUSION

Cuba's response to the AIDS epidemic warrants strict scrutiny. As implemented to date, however, it is not a violation of international human rights law. The strong potential for rapid spread of the disease, the likelihood that educational efforts will be ignored, the policy's likely success, and the overall humane treatment carriers receive are factors which, taken together, legitimize the detention. Certainly quarantine would not work and would thus be arbitrary if employed in most nations. Cuba presents a unique situation, however, which for now, justifies its unique approach to the AIDS crisis.

David W. Johnston

[32]

CONTROLLING AIDS IN CUBA

The Logic of Quarantine

Ronald Bayer and C Healton

UNLIKE any other nation, Cuba has embarked on a program to control the acquired immunodeficiency syndrome (AIDS) that is designed to limit the spread of infection with the human immunodeficiency virus (HIV) by invoking the compulsory elements of the public health tradition. Widespread screening for HIV infection began in Cuba three years ago, and persons identified as infected have been sent to a sanatorium located in a Havana suburb. This unique reliance on a modified quarantine extends to all HIV-infected persons. A recent visit to Cuba as guests of the Ministry of Health permitted us to talk with Cuban officials about the logic of the program and observe some of its elements. Although many questions remain unanswered, our journey did permit us to characterize the broadest features of the challenge posed by the Cuban response to the AIDS epidemic.

From its inception, Cuban health officials have viewed the AIDS-control program as an extension of the postrevolutionary health care system, which stands as a visible accomplishment of the Cuban regime. The program also reflected concern over the dramatic rise in prevalence of sexually transmitted diseases. With a relatively young, sexually active population and a rising incidence of syphilis and gonorrhea, Cuba appeared ripe for HIV diffusion on the eve of the AIDS epidemic.[1]

A Limited Role for Education

In the absence of effective forms of therapeutic intervention, the Cuban Ministry of Health cautions in posters and pamphlets: "AIDS is not curable today, but it is preventable." Like those in other nations, the materials designed to provide broad preventive education about AIDS are careful to warn readers of the risks of promiscuous sexual relations, but they also stress the danger to Cubans from intimate relations with foreigners. Given the predominant role of heterosexual transmission in Cuba, the educational efforts stress that AIDS is not a disease exclusively of homosexuals and can affect any person. As elsewhere, condoms are recommended for protection from the threat of HIV. Like other AIDS campaigns around the world, the Cuban effort seeks not only to inform but to prevent panic.

However, in contrast to virtually every other nation, Cuba has not made education the central or dominant element in its anti-AIDS strategy. Doubts about the efficacy of mass persuasion and a low tolerance for the potential costs of relative failure have created a setting in which education has been relegated to a marginal role in the campaign against AIDS. In Cuban policy, identifying infected persons and bringing them under medical control are central.

Screening for HIV Infection

From the outset, Cuba was determined that its HIV screening program would be mandatory, ultimately including the entire population. Like other nations, Cuba sought to protect its blood supply through antibody testing. Ironically, Cubans with hemophilia were spared by an American blockade that has made access to medical supplies and products all but impossible.

To identify persons who could transmit HIV infection sexually, the first screening efforts were targeted at groups defined as being at high risk. Of primary concern were the more than 380,000 Cubans who had traveled abroad, as soldiers in Africa, or as advisers, diplomats, or participants in cultural-exchange programs. All state agencies were instructed to compile lists of persons who had served outside Cuba since 1975. The Committees for the Defense of the Revolution — ubiquitous block-level political bodies — were called on to compile a similar census. In addition, Cubans who regularly worked with foreign visitors were classed as being at high risk, as were the thousands of foreign students who came to the country to study, among them many Africans. Ultimately, mandatory testing was extended to all persons admitted to hospitals, pregnant women, patients treated for sexually transmitted diseases, and the sexual contacts of persons found to be infected with HIV. Some effort has been made to conduct screening on the basis of residence. Like other mass public health campaigns in Cuba, such efforts have enlisted the help of "mass organizations" such as the Women's Federation and the trade unions, as well as the Committees for the Defense of the Revolution.

Asked how they responded to persons who refused to participate in such "open population" testing, officials replied that no coercion was necessary, since eventually all Cubans come into contact with the medical system in the workplace, at school, or during treatment for disease. Blood drawn for other purposes would be subjected to HIV testing as well. Informed consent for such testing was deemed unnecessary. According to Dr. Hector Terry, vice-minister of health, "Physicians undertake the tests that they consider crucial. It is not for patients to make such determinations."

Cuba's HIV surveillance program has been carried out with use of an enzyme-linked immunosorbent assay (ELISA), Western blot assay, and antigen tests that have been developed domestically. Only once, with the assistance of a foreign government, have public health authorities had the opportunity to validate their testing procedures against an international standard. At present, HIV-positive persons are identified through an elaborate combination of ELISA and Western blotting, using multiple serum samples. Although the tests are numerous, they necessarily have deficiencies in quality control.

According to Dr. Francisco A. Machado Ramirez, director of the Cuban AIDS Investigations Laboratory, nearly 3 million Cubans have been tested — more than a quarter of the population. The groups tested include foreign students (infection rate, 0.44 percent in foreign students), persons with hemophilia (infection rate, 0.3 percent in persons with hemophilia), those who have lived outside Cuba since 1975 (0.025 percent), patients with sexually transmitted diseases (0.010 percent), the general population of resort areas (0.005 percent), pregnant women (0.0037 percent), blood donors (0.0017 percent), and a residual category including prisoners (0.014 percent) and the sexual contacts of seropositive persons (4.6 percent). The total seroprevalence since testing began three years ago is 0.0089 percent (259 persons). If 140 seropositive foreign students are included, the rate is 0.013 percent (399 persons).

Do the results reported by the Cuban authorities include false positives? We believe so. With infection rates of 0.01 percent or less, even when stringent laboratory standards are maintained, 1 in 135,000 persons tested would be mistakenly designated as positive.[2] More typical laboratory standards could produce much higher false positive rates.[3] We estimate that among the seven low-infection groups tested in Cuba, between 21 and 53 persons may have been inaccurately considered positive as a result of testing.

The added benefit in accuracy of the multiple screening tests used in Cuba, designed to prevent the internment of uninfected persons, is unknown. But the Cuban authorities with whom we spoke were concerned over the possibility of both false positive and false negative findings. They expressed great interest in obtaining commercially available HIV screening kits — both ELISA and Western blot assays — as a standard against which to measure their own test. In view of the low levels of infection in Cuba and the determination to screen the entire population, it is inevitable that some false positive results will be generated, and in Cuba the consequence — quarantine — is grave.

Quarantine

For the past 30 months, persons identified as infected with HIV have been sent to a sanatorium outside Havana. The importance of providing ongoing clinical evaluation and support to such persons is one justification given for quarantine. More important is the belief that only by the separation of infected from uninfected persons can the Cuban people be protected. Dr. Terry told us, "We have an opportunity to stop the disease in our country. It would be irresponsible if we didn't face the situation with courage, knowing we could stop it. We have an epidemiologic opportunity that we are not going to lose."

For that challenge to be met, infected persons must leave home, uninfected family members, friends, and jobs — though, according to Cuban officials, their salaries are maintained by the government to protect their economic security and that of their families. Persons whose homes are not too distant from the sanatorium are given weekend passes so that they may visit their families and friends, under the watchful eye of a chaperone. Those who must travel greater distances may visit their homes only every four to six weeks, but for somewhat longer periods. Married couples, we were told, are permitted passes under more liberal conditions, including unchaperoned excursions.

We were shown selected living quarters provided for the residents of the sanatorium. In one location, new housing had been built in line with a planned expansion of the facility from the current census of 240 to 300. There is a possibility that the new housing will also be used to relocate their seropositive inhabitants, who until now have lived in what some have reported to be a barracks or dormitory-like setting.

We were also shown the homes of three heterosexual couples — small three-room apartments housing two couples each. The quarters were simple but adequate. Each contained a large television, and in at least one bedroom an air conditioner was visible. Were these residences typical? It is impossible to know, of course. But it is reasonable to assume that what we were shown was the best of what is being provided.

Were the residents we met typical? It is clear that they were not. They were all married, although the authorities had told us that about a third of the 171 male residents were homosexual or bisexual. Furthermore, although one woman said that she missed her family, others spoke in a way that suggested they were being especially cooperative with the authorities. One man told us, "By being here I am protecting my daughter and the daughters of many people in Cuba." Another told us that by being at the sanatorium he was doing his part "to defend the revolution." These statements were made in the presence of Dr. Terry and the staff of the sanatorium.

What do we know about refusals to enter the sanatorium? About the consequences of escape attempts? Not very much. Questioned on these matters, the vice-minister of health asserted that if people refused to enter the sanatorium, every effort was made to convince them of their obligation to do so and of their need for medical supervision. Friends, family, and neighbors were enlisted to help with the effort. Offered an opportunity to acknowledge that coercion was necessary at times, Dr. Terry demurred, noting that one woman had refused adamantly to enter the quarantine and that he had chosen not to invoke sanctions.

On the other hand, a source admittedly hostile to the Cuban regime asserted on the basis of émigré accounts that there were "dozens" of reports of the use of aggressive methods to incarcerate recalcitrants against their will. Nylon bags have been pulled over the heads of those refusing to cooperate as they were hauled into custody, stated the executive director of Radio Martí, which is funded by the U.S. government.[4] How much credence to give such accounts is difficult to know. However, it is doubtful that a potentially lifelong quarantine could be sustained if it were widely known that the refusal to cooperate would be greeted passively.

There was also disagreement over how the authorities respond when a resident escapes from the sanatorium. Dr. Terry told us that there had been escapes, but that all fugitives eventually returned because they recognized their need for the care provided in the quarantine center. On the other hand, Radio Martí officials report that a harsh response — in some cases, imprisonment — awaits those who flee. Americas Watch, which monitors human rights violations in Latin America and has been especially interested in conditions in Cuban prisons, could not confirm these allegations.

The realities of living conditions at the sanatorium, refusals to accept quarantine, and the response to escape attempts can be studied carefully only if, in a spirit of candor, the Cuban authorities permit future studies. Opportunities for such studies would be enhanced if the U.S. government relaxed its bilateral travel restrictions.

There is no debate over a more fundamental issue — the justification for the internment policy. On this matter, Cuban officials and their critics agree. The rationale for quarantine assumes that since it is impossible to determine which infected persons can be trusted to behave in a responsible way sexually, they all have to be restricted and treated as a hazard. Education was considered unreliable as a means of modifying behavior — either in infected persons, who posed a threat, or uninfected persons, who might otherwise learn to protect themselves.

From the Cuban perspective, risks must be resolved in favor of safety and public health. There can be no presumption in favor of freedom. Here lies the fundamental difference between the path Cuba has chosen and that taken by public health officials not only in the West but in other socialist countries. The authorities in Havana are aware of the criticism their approach has provoked from health officials as well as from defenders of civil liberties. They told us of a constant search for less harsh alternatives — such as permitting children to reside with their parents, allowing family members to assume responsibility for surveillance in some instances, and building new facilities more accessible from other parts of the country. In the end, however, they believe they have chosen the proper course. It is a course that health officials in countries with a very low prevalence of HIV infection may find appealing.

The Effectiveness of the Cuban Model

Without question, a system that systematically seeks to identify persons with HIV infection and then imposes a modified quarantine on them can radically alter the threat of an epidemic. It is doubtful, however, whether such a system can halt the spread of infections entirely, since, unless the campaign of mass education is fully effective, some persons will become infected or seroconvert after testing and go on to infect others. As a consequence, it will be necessary to test all Cubans — not only those who have contact with foreign visitors or travel abroad — repeatedly and often.

Despite the inevitability of continued viral transmission, Cuban policy will certainly limit the toll of HIV infection in Cuba dramatically. The Cuban achievement comes at a great price, however. We may never know how the reduction will compare with what might have been achieved through a campaign of mass education undertaken within the highly structured health care system. The benefits and costs are those that accompany any system of preventive detention, whether justified in terms of defending society against criminal behavior or against pathogens.

A nation's response to AIDS must be informed by epidemiologic, economic, and technological factors. But the course nations choose to pursue within these constraints can vary and will be profoundly influenced by political and moral values. The Cubans have made their orientation clear. It stands as a counterpoint to those of nations for which the imperatives of prevention, however important, are not the only values to be considered in the struggle against AIDS.

Columbia University
School of Public Health
New York, NY 10032

Ronald Bayer, Ph.D.
Cheryl Healton, M.P.A.

We are indebted to Dr. Hector Terry and his staff for their willingness to examine the Cuban approach to AIDS with us.

We dedicate this article to our esteemed colleague Dr. Rafael Tavares, who was unable to join us in Cuba. He died November 8, 1988.

References

1. Public health in figures: statistical summary. Havana: Republic of Cuba. Ministry of Public Health, 1986:5.
2. Burke DS, Brundage JF, Redfield RR, et al. Measurement of the false positive rate in a screening program for human immunodeficiency virus infections. N Engl J Med 1988; 319:961-4.
3. Barry MJ, Cleary PD, Fineberg HV. Screening for HIV infection: risks, benefits and the burden of proof. Law Med Health Care 1986; 14:263.
4. Betancourt E. Cuba's callous war on AIDS. New York Times. February 11. 1988:A35.

[33]

The Politics of AIDS: Compulsory State Powers, Public Health, and Civil Liberties

Larry Gostin*

Table of Contents

I. Introduction

The politics of AIDS is moving steadily in the direction of the use of compulsory powers of the state. Some politicians have demanded isolation and criminal confinement of "recalcitrant" AIDS carriers.[1] An ever increasing number of state

---

* J.D., Duke University. Executive Director of the American Society of Law and Medicine and Adjunct Associate Professor, Harvard School of Public Health. The author recently completed a global survey of AIDS legislation for the World Health Organization and a legal and policy analysis of U.S. legislation for the U.S. Secretary for Health and Human Services. The author would like to thank Rebecca Hanson (Sarah Lawrence College), Jennifer Klein (Columbia Law School), and Richard Timmel (Harvard Law School) for their research and editorial assistance.

1. Some politicians and commentators have called for isolation of persons with HIV who persist in spreading the infection. *See* Grutsch & Robertson, *The Coming of AIDS: It Didn't Start with the Homosexuals and It Won't End with Them*, 19 Am. Spectator 12 (1986); *Florida Considering Locking Up Some Carriers of the AIDS Virus*, N.Y. Times, Jan. 27, 1988, at A15, col. 1 (state officials proposing "special lock-up wards" for AIDS virus carriers); Boodman, *Idaho's Drive to Stop AIDS at the Border Arouses Doubts*, Wash. Post, Nov. 10, 1987, at 4, col. 1; Lewin, *Rights of Citizens*

legislatures have considered or enacted statutes authorizing the exercise of compulsory public health powers.[2]

Political advocacy for a "tougher" approach to the AIDS epidemic needs to be understood. The widespread publicity given to the potential for continued spread of the epidemic[3] has charged political debate. In an atmosphere of public health crisis, and with little early prospect of an effective scientific intervention,[4] there grows an impatience with voluntary measures focused on education and counseling.

The fact that the epidemic is growing relentlessly is not the only thing that fuels calls for coercive state action. It is also that the human immunodeficiency virus (HIV) is spread predominantly through volitional behavior[5] such as sodomy, prostitution,

---

and Society Raise Legal Muddle on AIDS, N.Y. Times, Oct. 14, 1987, at A1, col.1 (Sen. Jesse Helms and Pat Robertson suggesting "quarantine may become necessary"). Support for criminal law sanctions has been even more vocal. *See* Sixteenth Conference of European Ministers of Justice, Resolution No. 1 (Lisbon June 22, 1988) (recommending use of criminal law to combat AIDS as a last resort); Sullivan & Field, *AIDS and the Coercive Power of the State*, 23 Harv. C.R.-C.L. L. Rev. 139 (1988); Squires, *Spreading AIDS on Purpose*, Wash. Post, Apr. 19, 1988 (Health), at 6; Boorstin, *Criminal and Civil Litigation on Spread of AIDS Appears*, N.Y. Times, June 19, 1987, at 1, col. 3.

2. *See infra* notes 71, 72, 125–27, & 148 and accompanying text.

3. On December 18, 1987, the U.S. Centers for Disease Control (CDC) published a full report of the Domestic Policy Council containing an extensive review of published and unpublished data on the prevalence and incidence of HIV infection. *Human Immunodeficiency Virus Infection in the United States: A Review of Current Knowledge*, 36 Morbidity & Mortality Weekly Rep., (Supp. 6) 1 (1987) [hereinafter *Review of Current Knowledge*]. By June 6, 1988, a total of 64,506 cases of AIDS had been reported in the United States; over 14,000 of these had been reported since Jan. 1, 1988, and 36,255 cases had resulted in death. In the previous twelve months, 23,200 cases were reported, representing an increase of 58% over the year before. CDC, Weekly Surveillance Rep.June 6, 1988; *Quarterly Report to the Domestic Pol'y Council on the Prevalence and Rate of Spread of HIV and AIDS in the United States*, 259 J. A.M.A. 2657 (1988). By the end of 1991 it is projected that there will be more than 270,000 cases, with more than 74,000 of those occurring in 1991 alone. *Confronting AIDS: Directions for Pub. Health, Health Care and Research*, 1986. Inst. of Med., Nat'l Acad. of Sciences, 8–9, 85–89. *Confronting AIDS: Update* 1988, 1988 Inst. of Med. Nat'l Acad. of Sciences 51–52 [hereinafter Update 1988]. These are all cases of AIDS as defined by the *Revision of the CDC Surveillance Case Definition for Acquired Immunodeficiency Syndrome*, 36 Morbidity & Mortality Rep. 35 (1987); *Human Immunodeficiency Virus (HIV) Infection Codes Official Authorized Addendum ICD-9-CM (Revision No.1)*, 36 Morbidity & Mortality Weekly Rep. (Supp. 7) 1S (1987). Cases of CDC-defined AIDS are only the surface of the epidemic. There is a second epidemic of persons who harbor the virus and who show few or no symptoms. The number of persons infected with HIV in the United States is estimated to be between 945,000 and 1.4 million people. Update 1988, at 49–50. *See* Harris, *The AIDS Epidemic: Looking into the 1990s*, 90 Technol. Rev. No. 5, at 58 (July 1987). These two pandemic epidemics are connected by a towline of time—the time between infection and subsequent disease. *See generally* Mueller, *The Epidemiology of the Human Immunodeficiency Virus Infection*, 14 Law, Med. & Health Care 250 (1986). This time link between infection and disease can be measured in months or many years. It is now thought that the overwhelming majority of infected individuals will develop serious symptomology. Update 1988, at 35–36; Foreman, *Virus 'Inexorably' Leads to AIDS, U.S. Study Says*, Boston Globe, June 2, 1988, at 1, col. 1.

4. Development of a preventative vaccine for HIV is fraught with difficulty. Frances & Petricciani, *The Prospects for and Pathways Toward a Vaccine for AIDS*, 313 New Eng. J. Med. 1586 (1985); Gostin, *Vaccination for AIDS: Legal and Ethical Challenges from the Test Tube, to the Human Subject, Through to the Marketplace*, 2 AIDS and Pub. Pol'y J. 9 (1987); Mariner & Gallo, *Getting to Market: The Scientific and Legal Climate for Developing an AIDS Vaccine*, 15 Law, Med. & Health Care 17 (1987). Prospects for treatment appear more likely. *See* Yarchoan & Broder, *Development of an Antiretroviral Therapy for the Acquired Immunodeficiency Syndrome and Related Disorders: Progress Report*, 316 New Eng. J. Med. 557 (1987). Yet, the only approved treatment, azidothymidine (AZT) is not intended to be curative and can be highly toxic. Its purpose is to help prevent the occurrence of opportunistic infections in patients who are immunocompromised. *See A Ray of Hope in the Fight Against AIDS*, Time, Sept. 29, 1986, at 60.

5. Of the cumulative total of AIDS cases reported to the CDC, 63% were homosexual and bisexual men and 19% were heterosexual men and women with a history of intravenous drug use. Approximately 4% of cases were attributed to heterosexual transmission. CDC, Weekly Surveillance Rep., June 6, 1988. *See also*, Curran, Morgan, Hardy, Jaffe, Darrow & Dowdle, *The Epidemiology of AIDS: Current Status and Future Prospects*, 229 Science 1352 (1985) [hereinafter Curran & Morgan]; Gostin, *Acquired Immune Deficiency Syndrome: A Review of Science, Health Policy, and Law*, in AIDS and Patient Management: Legal, Ethical and Social Issues (M. Witt, ed. 1986). The pattern of "high risk groups" is considerably different in other parts of the world. *See* Panos Institute, AIDS and the Third World (1988); Goldsmith, *AIDS Around the World: Analyzing Complex Patterns*, 259 J. A.M.A. 1917 (1988) (predominance

and the use of intravenous drugs, which are widely regarded as immoral, even criminal. Because the virus is primarily transmitted by intentional behavior that is within the control of the carrier, it is seen as susceptible to a legal, rather than a public health, solution.

The use of compulsory public health powers can be a visible political symbol of seriousness of purpose in controlling AIDS. Public opinion polls consistently show some support for coercive action, with a significant proportion of respondents favoring "quarantine" of people with AIDS "in special places to keep them away from the general public."[6] A majority of respondents also favor governmental restrictions on the sexual activities of known AIDS carriers.[7]

Public health authorities have resisted political and public pressure for the use of coercive powers.[8] Instead, they have relied upon education and counseling of high risk groups to encourage behavioral changes. Experience with hepatitis B has demonstrated that voluntary compliance can reduce the spread of a virus with an analogous pattern of transmission,[9] and emerging evidence on AIDS shows significant alterations of high risk behavior.[10] Furthermore, experience with the use of coercive measures in venereal disease control shows that they can be ineffective, discriminatory, and invidious.[11] Absent evidence that personal control measures change behavior more effectively than voluntary education and counseling, government cannot justify their use. The behaviors sought to be controlled or punished are highly ingrained, intimate, and deeply human activities. Coercive state action is a particularly crude tool to compel change in these behaviors.

Compulsory public powers are justified only if they meet the following criteria: there is a significant risk of transmission of the AIDS virus; the public health response is efficacious in preventing a primary mode of transmission of the virus; the

---

of heterosexual transmission in Africa); *Update: Acquired Immunodeficiency Syndrome (AIDS)—Worldwide*, 259 J. A.M.A. 3104 (1988).

6. In five national opinion polls conducted between Sept. 1985 and Jan. 1986, between 28% and 51% of respondents said "[p]eople with AIDS should be put into quarantine in special places to keep them away from the general public." Singer, Rogers & Corcoran, *The Polls—A Report: AIDS*, 51 PUB. OPINION Q. 580, 591–92 (1987). *See Growing Concern, Greater Precautions*, NEWSWEEK, Nov. 24, 1986, at 30, 32; *Poll Indicates Majority Favor Quarantine for AIDS Victims*, N.Y. Times, Dec. 20, 1985, at A24, col. 1.

7. Two national opinion polls conducted in Nov. 1985 and Jan. 1986 found that 58% and 51%, respectively, of the respondents believed that "governmental restrictions should be placed on the sexual activities of people who are known carriers of AIDS." Singer, Rogers & Corcoran, *supra* note 6, at 592.

8. The United States Public Health Service relies on public education and counseling to encourage behavior change and has not advocated the use of compulsion. *See* PHS Task Force on AIDS, *Public Health Service Plan for the Prevention and Control of Acquired Immune Deficiency Syndrome (AIDS)*, 100 PUB. HEALTH REP. 453 (1985); U.S. Dep't Health & Human Services, Guidelines for AIDS Prevention Program Operations (1987); *Accord*, WORLD HEALTH ORGANIZATION, GLOBAL PROGRAMME ON AIDS, GUIDING OBJECTIVES AND PRINCIPLES FOR THE COMPREHENSIVE COORDINATION OF GLOBAL AND NATIONAL AIDS ACTIVITIES, GPA/ER/88.2 (1988).

9. Blumberg & Fox, *The Daedalus Effect: Changes in Ethical Questions Relating to Hepatitis B*, 102 ANNALS INTERN. MED. 390 (1985).

10. Becker & Joseph, *AIDS and Behavioral Change to Reduce Risk: A Review*, 78 AM. J. PUB. HEALTH 394 (1988); *Self Reported Behavioral Change Among Gay and Bisexual Men—San Francisco*, 34 MORBIDITY & MORTALILTY WEEKLY REP. 613 (1985); Weller, Hindley & Adler, *Gonorrhea in Homosexual Men, and Media Coverage of Acquired Immune Deficiency Syndrome in London* 1982–83, 289 BRIT. MED. J. 1041 (1984).

11. *See* A. BRANDT, NO MAGIC BULLET: A SOCIAL HISTORY OF VENEREAL DISEASE IN THE UNITED STATES SINCE 1880, at 84–97, 156–60 (1985, Rev. Ed. 1987); Brandt, *AIDS: From Social History to Social Policy*, 14 LAW, MED. & HEALTH CARE 231, 231–33 (1986); Brandt, *AIDS in Historical Perspective: Four Lessons from the History of Sexually Transmitted Diseases*, 78 AM. J. PUB. HEALTH 367, 369–70 (1988).

economic, practical, or human rights burdens are not disproportionate to the public health benefits; and the public health power is the least restrictive alternative that would prevent viral transmission.[12]

These proposed criteria are intended to demonstrate two realities in public health. First, a compulsory power needs vigorous justification and should not be imposed merely because it is dressed in the guise of public health. Thus, there must be reliable epidemiologic evidence that the virus can, and probably will, be transmitted by the person's behavior; and that the exercise of the power will prevent the transmission of the virus. Second, while the health of the community is often an overriding public value, it is not absolute. In each case the public good to be achieved must be balanced against the costs of the policy. If the invasion of human rights, the financial cost, or the practical burdens of the policy are wholly disproportionate to the benefits, it should not be adopted. There are instances where compulsory powers are necessary to prevent a clear likelihood that the virus will be transmitted. However, I will demonstrate that many compulsory powers have been, and will be, exercised in cases where they serve no overriding public purpose.

In the following section I carefully examine the levels of risk posed by behavior which can potentially transmit HIV. It is essential to understand the relative risks of such behavior as a foundation for the rest of this Article, which analyzes two major proposals for coercive state action: isolation of carriers of HIV and criminal prosecution for transmission of HIV.

This Article will demonstrate that these compulsory state powers have little place in fighting a disease epidemic.

II. A Significant Risk of Transmission

A threshold question in assessing the value of a compulsory public health power is whether there is a significant risk of transmission of the AIDS virus. Public health powers have been advocated or used in cases where the person's behavior was highly unlikely to transmit the AIDS virus—biting, spitting, splattering of blood, or donating blood.

The imposition of compulsory powers in these types of cases is misplaced for two reasons. First, the compulsory powers will have little public utility if the risk posed by the person's behavior is exceedingly small. The resources placed into preventing low risk behavior are not well spent, for even if the behavior can be prevented, it is unlikely to have any effect on the spread of the epidemic. Second, focusing on low risk behaviors of AIDS carriers is iniquitous, for society already tolerates other activities that pose equal or greater risks. It is important to examine the relative risk when assessing sanctions against AIDS carriers. For example, a decision to incarcerate an AIDS carrier for biting or spitting ignores the fact that this behavior poses a much lower risk of serious harm than other behavior, such as dangerous driving, for which there is often no significant criminal liability.

12. *See generally*, Gostin, Curran & Clark, *The Case Against Compulsory Casefinding in Controlling AIDS—Testing, Screening and Reporting*, 12 Am. J. L. & Med. 7, 21–24 (1986).

The concept of "significant risk" is well recognized in public health law. Modern courts have consistently required a clear public health justification for any personal control measure.[13] Yet the concept of "significant risk" has never been clarified or defined. It should be based upon epidemiologic evidence of the gravity of the harm and the probability of the harm occurring. A risk is significant only if the mode of transmission is scientifically well established, there is a reasonable likelihood that viral transmission will take place, and the potential harm is serious. Below I examine the various modes of transmission of the AIDS virus and the level of risk posed.

A. *Risk of Sexual Transmission*

Sexual intercourse is a primary mode of transmission of HIV.[14] HIV is much less easily communicated than other sexually transmitted diseases, such as hepatitis B, syphilis and gonorrhea.[15] The range of the risk of transmission of HIV in a prolonged sexual relationship is 7 to 68% that the virus will be transmitted.[16] Transmission through anal-receptive intercourse is considered more efficient,[17] although it is thought that individual host susceptibility[18] and variations in infectivity[19] among different people may be additional factors. Transmission from male-to-female is well

13. *See* School Bd. of Nassau County v. Arline, 480 U.S. 273, 288 (1987) *reh'g denied*, 107 S.Ct. 1913 (1987) (school teacher with tuberculosis could not be fired unless she posed a "significant risk" to health); New York State Ass'n for Retarded Children v. Carey, 612 F.2d 644 (2d Cir. 1979) (mentally retarded children who were carriers of serum hepatitis could not be excluded from regular public school classes because the health hazard was only a remote possibility); District 27 Community School Bd. v. Board of Educ., 130 Misc. 2d 398, 502 N.Y.S. 2d 325 (Sup. Ct. 1986) (the automatic exclusion of school children with AIDS would effect a purpose having no adequate connection with public health).

14. *See* UPDATE 1988, at 38–45; Friedland & Klein, *Transmission of the Human Immunodeficiency Virus*, 317 NEW ENG. J. MED. 1125, 1128–1130 (1987); Peterman, Stoneburner, Allen, Jaffe & Curran, *Risk of Human Immunodeficiency Virus Transmission from Heterosexual Adults with Transfusion—Associated Infections*, 259 J. A.M.A. 55 (1988); *Review of Current Knowledge*, *supra* note 3, at 2–4.

15. Peterman & Curran, *Sexual Transmission of Human Immunodeficiency Virus*, 256 J. A.M.A. 2222 (1986) (Transmission rate of *Neisseria gonorrhoeae* after a single sexual exposure is 22–25% for a man and 50% for a woman).

16. *See generally* Allain, *Prevalence of HTLV-III/LAV Antibodies in Patients with Hemophilia and in their Sexual Partners in France*, 315 NEW ENG. J. MED. 517 (1986); Fischl, Dickinson, Scott, Klimas, Fletcher & Parks, *Evaluation of Heterosexual Partners, Children, and Household Contacts of Adults with AIDS*, 257 J. A.M.A. 640 (1987) [hereinafter Fischl & Dickinson]; Kreiss, Kitchen, Prince, Kasper & Essex, *Antibody to Human T-Lymphotropic Virus Type III in Wives of Hemophiliacs: Evidence for Heterosexual Transmission*, 102 ANNALS INTERN. MED. 623 (1985); Mann, Quinn, Francis, Nzilambi, Bosenge, Bila, McCormick, Ruti, Asila & Curran, *Prevalence of HTLV-III/LAV in Household Contacts of Patients with Confirmed AIDS and Controls in Kinshasa, Zaire*, 256 J. A.M.A. 721, (1986) [hereinafter Mann & Quinn]; Redfield, Markham, Salahuddin, Sarngadharan, Bodner, Folks, Ballou, Wright & Gallo, *Frequent Transmission of HTLV-III Among Spouses of Patients with AIDS-Related Complex and AIDS*, 253 J. A.M.A. 1571 (1985) [hereinafter Redfield & Markham].

17. Goedert, Sarngadharan, Biggar, Winn, Greene, Mann, Gallo, Sarngadharan, Weiss, Grossman, Bodner, Strong & Blattner, *Determinants of Retrovirus (HTLV-III) Antibody and Immunodeficiency Conditions in Homosexual Men*, 2 LANCET 711 (1984); Kingsley, Kaslow, Rinaldo, Jr., Detre, Odaka, Van Raden, Detels, Polk, Chmiel, Kelsey, Ostrow & Visscher, *Risk Factors for Seroconversion to Human Immunodeficiency Virus Among Male Homosexuals*, 1 LANCET 345 (1987); Winkelstein, Lyman, Padian, Grant, Samual, Wiley, Anderson, Lang, Riggs & Levy, *Sexual Practices and Risk of Infection by the Human Immunodeficiency Virus: The San Francisco Men's Health Study*, 257 J. A.M.A. 321, 325 (1987).

18. Eales, Nye, Parkin, Weber, Forster & Harris, *Association of Different Allelic Forms of Group Specific Component with Susceptibility to and Clinical Manifestation of Human Immunodeficiency Virus Infection*, 1 LANCET 999, 999, 1001–02 (1987).

19. Dahl, Martin & Miller, *Differences Among Human Immunodeficiency Virus Strains in their Capacities to Induce Cytolysis or Persistent Infection of a Lymphoblastoid Cell Line Immortalized by Epstein-Barr Virus*, 61 J. VIROLOGY 1602 (1987).

documented,[20] but female-to-male transmission is more controversial. Clearly female-to-male transmission occurs, but it has been less frequent in the United States.[21]

The level of risk of contracting HIV from one unprotected sexual contact with an infected partner is thought to be low. One study placed the seroconversion rate at approximately 1/1,000.[22] While the use of barrier contraception is not entirely safe, it does provide important protection.[23] Frequent and appropriate use of barrier protection clearly attenuates the rate of seroconversion.[24] The risk of contracting HIV in a single sexual encounter while using a condom (assuming 90% effectiveness of such a barrier) is estimated to be 1/10,000.[25]

Prostitution is a major target of coercive AIDS legislation.[26] Yet the primary risk factor for HIV infection in prostitutes in the United States is not sexual practice but intravenous drug use.[27] Further, prostitutes often seek to use protection against exchange of body fluids. Their clients appear to pose as significant a health threat to the prostitutes as the prostitutes to their clients. "Scientists are not certain how frequently prostitutes have been infected because of their multiple sexual contacts, or how often they have infected their customers, although the available evidence . . . indicates that this has not occurred on a large scale."[28]

B. *Risk of Transmission by Intravenous Drug Use*

Intravenous drug use has a major role in the transmission of HIV.[29] IV drug users can spread HIV through their practice of sharing drug "paraphernalia" or "works" (needles and syringes). Sharing of works often occurs in "shooting galleries" where addicts purchase their drugs and rent needles and syringes. The

---

20. The majority of cases of heterosexual transmission in the United States are women. *Review of Current Knowledge*, *supra* note 3; Friedland & Klein, *supra* note 14, at 1129. HIV is found in semen in relatively large concentrations. *See generally* Ho, Schooley, Rota, Kaplan & Flynn, *HTLV-III in the Semen and Blood of a Healthy Heterosexual Man*, 226 SCIENCE 451 (1984).

21. In Africa, female-to-male transmission has been well documented. Quinn, Mann, Curran & Piot, *AIDS in Africa: An Epidemiologic Paradigm*, 234 SCIENCE 955 (1986). But the frequency in the U.S. is much less clear. Friedland & Klein, *supra* note 14, at 1129–30.

22. Padian, Wiley & Winkelstein, *Male to Female Transmission of Human Immunodeficiency Virus: Current Results, Infectivity Rates, and San Francisco Population Seroprevalence Estimates*. Presented at the Third International Conference on AIDS, Washington D.C., June 4, 1987. *See* Padian, Marquis, Francis, Anderson, Rutherford, O'Malley & Winkelstein, *Male-to-Female Transmission of Human Immunodeficiency Virus*, 258 J. A.M.A. 788 (1987).

23. Gostin & Curran, *Response from Gostin & Curran*, 77 AM. J. PUB. HEALTH 1553 (1987).

24. Conant, Hardy, Sernatinger, Spicer & Levy, *Condoms Prevent Transmission of AIDS—Associated Retrovirus*, 255 J. A.M.A. 1706 (1986); Fischl & Dickinson, *supra* note 16, at 641; Voeller & Potts, *Has the Condom Any Proved Value in Preventing the Transmission of Sexually Viral Disease—for Example Acquired Immune Deficiency Syndrome*, 291 BRIT. MED. J. 1196 (1985).

25. Hagen, Myer & Pauker, *Routine Preoperative Screening for HIV: Does the Risk to the Surgeon Outweigh the Risk to the Patient?*, 259 J. A.M.A. 1357, 1358 (1988).

26. *See supra* notes 8–11 and accompanying text for comments on the use of coercive powers.

27. *See* Rosenberg & Weiner, *Prostitutes and AIDS: A Health Department Priority?* 78 AM. J. PUB. HEALTH 418 (1988); *Antibody to Human Immunodeficiency Virus in Female Prostitutes*, 36 MORBIDITY & MORTALITY WEEKLY REP. 157 (1987) (Table 2); *Review of Current Knowledge*, *supra* note 3, at 8.

28. Altman, *U.S. Study Examines Prostitutes and AIDS Virus*, N.Y. Times, March 27, 1987, at A14, col. 1.

29. Twenty-five percent of all AIDS cases in the U.S. have occurred in IV drug users, and 17% have occurred among those in whom IV drug use is the only risk factor. Friedland & Klein, *supra* note 14, at 1127; *Review of Current Knowledge*, *supra* note 3, at 14.

sharing experience is often part of the culture of the drug dependent population, indicating a sense of camaraderie. Drugs are injected into a suitable vein and thus, when the needle is shared, it is likely to have traces of blood.[30] Studies have documented needle sharing as a method of transmission of HIV.[31] However, it is likely that the amount of blood on the needle is minute.[32] Accordingly, the rate of seroconversion in any single case of percutaneous exposure to the needle is likely to be small—ranging from a rate of .03-.09%.[33] However, episodes of injections by individual drug users may number in the thousands, so the cumulative risk of IV drug use is high.[34]

C. *Saliva as a Route of Transmission: Biting and Spitting*

HIV has been isolated from saliva.[35] The isolation of virus from a body fluid does not necessarily mean that the fluid is a significant mode of transmission. Transmission by biting or spitting, however, continues to be a societal concern, one which has resulted in the filing of criminal charges.[36]

There are strong grounds for believing the risk of transmission by saliva to be exceedingly low, approaching zero. First, HIV has been isolated in saliva only rarely and in very small amounts.[37] It is thought that the risk of transmission from a small inoculum of virus in a single event is remote.[38] Second, experiments indicate that both whole saliva and saliva filtrates contain components that inactivate HIV in vitro.[39] Third, there has never been a documented case of transmission by saliva, despite close observation and follow-up investigations of cases of biting, spitting, deep kissing, and intimate caring activities.[40] There has been one report, for example, of an adult patient with AIDS who bit thirty health care workers without any transmission of the virus.[41] Several other follow-up studies of biting have revealed no

30. Friedland & Klein, *supra* note 14, at 1127–28; Ginzburg, *Intravenous Drug Abusers and HIV Infections: A Consequence of Their Actions*, 14 LAW, MED. & HEALTH CARE 268, 269–70 (1986).

31. *See generally* Chaisson, Moss, Onishi, Osmond & Carlson, *Human Immunodeficiency Virus Infection in Heterosexual Intravenous Drug Users in San Francisco*, 77 AM. J. PUB. HEALTH 169 (1987); Des Jarlais, Friedman & Stoneburner, *HIV Infection and Intravenous Drug Use: Critical Issues in Transmission Dynamics, Infection Outcomes and Prevention*, 10 REV. INFECT. DIS. 151 (1988); Friedland, Harris, Butkus-Small, Shine, Moll, Darrow & Klein, *Intravenous Drug Abusers and the Acquired Immunodeficiency Syndrome (AIDS): Demographic, Drug Use, and Needle-Sharing Patterns*, 145 ARCHIVES INTERN. MED. 1413 (1985).

32. Friedland & Klein, *supra* note 14, at 1128.

33. *Id.* at 1126.

34. *Id.* at 1128.

35. Groopman, Salahuddin, Sarngadharan, Markham, Gorda, Sliski & Gallo, *HTLV-III in Saliva of People with AIDS-Related Complex and Healthy Homosexual Men at Risk for AIDS*, 226 SCIENCE 447 (1984); Hoe, Byington, Schooley, Flynn, Rota & Hirsch, *Infrequency of Isolation of HTLV-III Virus from Saliva in AIDS*, 313 NEW ENG. J. MED. 1606 (1985) [hereinafter Hoe & Byington].

36. *See infra* note 117 and accompanying text.

37. Lifson, *Do Alternative Modes of Transmission of Human Immunodeficiency Virus Exist?* 259 J. A.M.A. 1353 (1988). In one study of men infected with HIV, the virus could be isolated in 28 of 50 samples of blood but in only 1 of 83 samples of saliva. Hoe & Byington, *supra* note 35.

38. Friedland & Klein, *supra* note 14, at 1126–27.

39. Fultz, *Components of Saliva Inactivate Human Immunodeficiency Virus*, 2 LANCET 1215 (1986).

40. *See* Friedland & Klein, *supra* note 14, at 1132–33; Lifson, *supra* note 37, at 1353–54.

41. Tsoukas, Hadjis, Theberge, *et al.*, *Risk of Transmission of HTLV-III/LAV from Human Bites*, presented at the Second International Conference on AIDS, Paris, June 23–25, 1986.

evidence of HIV transmission.[42] There are also no documented cases of HIV transmission through kissing or insertive oral-genital contact.[43] Fourth, there have been major population studies of households, dentists, and healthcare workers in intimate contact with HIV infected persons, without viral transmission.[44] Households with an HIV infected member have been studied over a period of years. In these families there were repeated exposures to saliva. They shared eating utensils, plates, drinking glasses, and toothbrushes; towels, linens, and clothes were sometimes soiled with saliva; family members helped patients to eat and drink; and they kissed on the cheek and on the lips. These studies involved nearly five hundred members of various families, yet failed to find a single case of a family member who contracted HIV who did not have an additional exposure through a blood transfusion, sexual relations, or perinatal transmission.[45]

The risk of transmission by saliva has also been studied among dental workers who have had repeated exposure to saliva as well as blood. In one study of 1309 dental professionals (72% of whom treated high risk patients and 94% of whom reported accidental puncture wounds), only one had HIV.[46] This one report is thought to have been from blood exposure. Other studies have not found another case of transmission to a dentist.[47]

Similar studies have been done with health workers who care for HIV-infected patients.[48] These studies also have failed to document a case of HIV transmission with parenteral, mucous membrane, or open wound exposures to saliva;[49] cardiopul-

42. Drummond, *Seronegative 18 Months After Being Bitten by a Patient with AIDS*, 256 J. A.M.A. 2342 (1986). *But see* Wahn, Kramer, Voit, Bruster, Scrampical & Scheid, *Horizontal Transmission of HIV Infection Between Two Siblings*, 2 LANCET 694 (1986) (Authors conclude one plausible, though unlikely, route of transmission between brothers was through a bite, even though it did not break skin or result in bleeding.).

43. Lifson, *supra* note 37, at 1353–54.

44. These studies are reviewed in: Friedland & Klein, *supra* note 14, at 1131–33; Gostin, Curran & Clark, *supra* note 12, at 22 n.3.

45. Fischl & Dickinson, *supra* note 16; Friedland, Saltzman, Rogers, Kahl, Lesser, Mayers & Klein, *Lack of Transmission of HTLV-III/LAV Infection to Household Contacts of Patients with AIDS or AIDS-related complex with Oral Candidiasis*, 314 NEW ENG. J. MED. 344 (1986); Jason, McDougal, Dixon, Lawrence, Kennedy, Hilgartner, Aledort & Evatt, *HTLV-III/LAV Antibody with Immune Status of Household Contacts and Sexual Partners of Persons with Hemophilia*, 255 J. A.M.A. 212 (1986); Lawrence, Jason, Bouhasin, McDougal, Knutsen, Evatt & Joist, *HTLV-III/LAV Antibody Status of Spouses and Household Contacts Assisting in Home Infusion of Hemophilia Patients*, 66 BLOOD 703 (1985); Mann & Quinn, *supra* note 16; Redfield & Markham, *supra* note 16.

46. Klein, Phelan, Freeman, Schable, Friedland, Trieger & Steigbigel, *Low Occupational Risk of Human Immunodeficiency Virus Infection Among Dental Professionals*, 318 NEW ENG. J. MED. 86 (1988). (Several letters to the editor in response to this article are in 319 NEW ENG. J. MED. 112–14 (1988).).

47. Gerberding, Bryant-LeBlanc, Nelson, Moss, Osmond, Chambers, Carlson, Drew, Levy & Sonde, *Risk of Transmitting the Human Immunodeficiency Virus, Cytomegalovirus, and Hepatitis B Virus to Health Care Workers Exposed to Patients with AIDS and AIDS-Related Conditions*, 156 J. INFECT. DIS. 1, 4 (1987) [hereinafter Gerberding & Bryant-LeBlanc].

48. Gerberding & Bryant-LeBlanc, *supra* note 47; Henderson, Saah, Zak, Kaslow, Lane, Folks, Blackwelder, Schmitt, LaCamera, Masur & Fauci, *Risk of Nosocomial Infection with Human T-Cell Lymphotropic Virus Type III/Lymphadenopathy-Associated Virus in a Large Cohort of Intensively Exposed Health Care Workers*, 104 ANNALS INTERN. MED. 644 (1986) [hereinafter Henderson & Saah]; Hirsch, Wormser, Schooley, Ho, Felsenstein, Hopkins, Joline, Duncanson, Sargadharan, Saxinger & Gallo, *Risk of Nosocomial Infection with Human T-Cell Lymphotropic Virus III (HTLV-III)*, 312 NEW ENG. J. MED. 1 (1985); McCray & The Cooperative Needlestick Surveillance Group, *Occupational Risk of the Acquired Immunodeficiency Syndrome Among Health Care Workers*, 314 NEW ENG. J. MED. 1127 (1986) [hereinafter McCray & Needlestick Group]; Weiss, Saxinger, Rechtman, Greico, Nadler, Holman, Ginzburg, Groopman, Goedert, Markham, Gallo, Blattner & Landsman, *HTLV-III Infection Among Health Care Workers: Association with Needle-Stick Injuries*, 254 J. A.M.A. 2089 (1985).

49. McCray & Needlestick Group, *supra* note 48.

monary resuscitation;[50] and performance of invasive procedures with direct exposure to saliva.[51] Nearly all documented cases of occupational transmission of HIV in health care settings have been attributed to accidental needlestick injuries or mucous membrane exposure to large amounts of blood.[52]

Of more than 60,000 cases of AIDS reported to the Centers for Disease Control, none have implicated saliva as a likely cause of transmission.[53] One recent reviewer of the medical literature noted that, given these data, the risk of transmission by saliva is still only "theoretical" or "negligible."[54]

D. *An Inoculum of Blood as a Method of Transmission: Hitting, Kicking, Splattering of Blood*

HIV has been isolated in blood.[55] Blood represents a significant method of transmission when there is a large inoculum.[56] Thus, transfusions of blood and blood products have been implicated as major routes of transmission.[57] It is the importance of blood transmissions as a risk factor for AIDS that has worried policy makers about scrapes, bruises, and bleeding occurring while there is physical contact with HIV infected persons. Thus, aggressive acts such as hitting, kicking, or splattering of blood by HIV infected people have been viewed as much more serious than the same behavior by non-infected persons.

These aggressive behaviors, however, do not involve a large inoculum of HIV infected blood into the body. Rather, they often involve either a small inoculum of blood or, more likely, no exposure to blood inside the body.[58] This shows that a single event of this kind poses a very low, or negligible, risk. The risk of transmission of HIV even after a deep parenteral exposure to infected blood is estimated to be in the range of .03-.09%.[59]

---

50. Saviteer, White, Cohen & Jason, *HTLV-III Exposure During Cardiopulmonary Resuscitation*, 313 NEW ENG. J. MED. 1606 (1985).

51. Gerberding & Bryant-LeBlanc, *supra* note 47.

52. *See supra* note 48; Allen, *Health Care Workers and the Risk of HIV Transmission*, HASTINGS CEN. REP. 2–5 (April, May 1988); *Recommendations for Prevention of HIV Transmission in Health Care Settings*, 36 MORBIDITY & MORTALITY WEEKLY REP. (Supp. 2) 35 (1987) [hereinafter *Recommendations*, 36, 1987].

53. *Review of Current Knowledge*, *supra* note 3.

54. Lifson, *supra* note 37, at 1354.

55. Barre-Sinoussi, Chermann, Rey, Nugeyre, Chamaret, Gruest, Dauguet & Axler-Blin, *Isolation of a T-Lymphotropic Retrovirus from a Patient at Risk for the Acquired Immune Deficiency Syndrome (AIDS)*, 220 SCIENCE 868 (1983); Gallo, Salahuddin, Popovic, Shearer, Kaplan, Haynes, Palker, Redfield, Oleske, Safai, White, Foster & Markham, *Frequent Detection and Isolation of Cytopathic Retroviruses (HTLV-III) from Patients with AIDS and at Risk for AIDS*, 224 SCIENCE 500 (1984).

56. Friedland & Klein, *supra* note 14, 1126–27.

57. Approximately 3% of adults and 13% of children have acquired AIDS through transfusions. CDC, WEEKLY SURVEILLANCE REP., July 4, 1988. Most transfusion-related cases occurred before screening for HIV antibody was technically possible. It is thought that, with current screening programs, the incidence of transfusion-related infections are low. *See* Gostin, Curran & Clark, *supra* note 12, at 13–17.

58. Friedland & Klein, *supra* note 14.

59. *See* Friedland & Klein, *supra* note 14, at 1127 (1987) (placing the average level of risk of HIV transmission at 0.76%). *See also* Gerberding & Bryant-LeBlanc, *supra* note 47 (a study of 270 health care workers found no evidence of HIV transmission from occupational exposure); Henderson & Saah, *supra* note 48, at 647. McCray & Needlestick Group, *supra* note 48, at 1131; McEvoy, Porter, Mortimer, Simmons & Shanson, *Prospective Study of Clinical, Laboratory, and Ancillary Staff with Accidental Exposures to Blood or Body Fluids from Patients Infected with HIV*, 294

There have been only sixteen reported cases of occupational exposure to HIV.[60] This appears insignificant, given the frequency of contact between health care workers and infected patients.

The spillage of blood on skin surfaces is not thought to pose a significant risk. But two cases of seroconversion of health care workers from mucous membrane exposures to infected blood[61] raised the level of public anxiety. The fact that these cases occurred demonstrates that HIV can be transmitted through a non-parenteral exposure to blood. However, the two cases involved virtual soaking in blood, without adequate precautions taken such as use of gloves. In each case the health care worker also had significant breaks in the skin allowing access to the virus; blood also soaked through mucous membranes. There is no data quantifying the risk of surface skin exposure to blood. However, it is reasonable to assume the risk is less than that caused by an injection of blood from a contaminated needle. This would place the risk of surface skin exposure even to a large amount of blood well below 1%.[62]

E. *Conclusion on Risks of Transmission*

There is a strong consensus in the scientific literature that transmission of HIV occurs only through an inoculation of blood, sexual intercourse, or perinatally. The law should carefully reflect this scientific understanding by focusing its interventions on those behaviors which pose significant risks. Even in the area of greatest concern—sexual transmission—the risk of a single event (particularly if barrier protection is utilized) is very low, and probably comparable to other risks which are well accepted in society.

Public concern has often focused on the aggressive behavior of "recalcitrants" who bite, kick, spit, or splatter their blood, because of the theoretical possibility that HIV can be transmitted. Scientists cannot rule out the possibility that these alternative modes of transmission may occur in the future. An unrealistic requirement for absolute certainty persists, despite the knowledge that it is impossible scientifically to prove that an event cannot occur. Society seems prepared to deprive HIV-infected persons of their liberty, under the mantle of public health, for taking remote risks. The exercise of compulsory powers is based upon unproven fears, perhaps prejudices, and not upon rational assessment of scientific facts.

III. Isolation

Infection control measures have long rested on the assumption that disease carriers must be physically separated from the rest of the population to prevent

---

Brit. Med. J. 1595 (1987) (less than 1% chance of developing HIV from a single exposure); *Recommendations* 36, 1987, *supra* note 52, at 3.

60. *See generally id.* (This is a composite total from all of the sources cited.).

61. Barnes, *Health Care Workers and AIDS: Questions Persist*, 241 Science 161 (1988). *See* Gostin, *Hospitals, Health Care Professionals and AIDS: The "Right to Know" the Health Care Status of Patients and Professionals*, Md. L. Rev. (in press); and *Update: Human Immunodeficiency Virus Infections in Health-Care Workers Exposed to Blood of Infected Patients*, 36 Morbidity & Mortality Weekly Rep. 285 (1987).

62. *See* Friedland & Klein, *supra* note 14, at 1126–27 1131–33.

transmission of the infectious agent. Although the terms "isolation" and "quarantine" are often used interchangeably, both in public health statutes and in common parlance, there is a technical distinction between them. "Isolation" is the separation of infected persons from others during the period of communicability so as to prevent transmission of the infectious agent; "quarantine" is the detention of persons who are healthy, but have been exposed to a communicable disease, to prevent contact with persons not exposed.[63] Since proposals for confining persons with AIDS tend to target persons who already exhibit symptoms of the disease or who demonstrably have been exposed to the virus, the term "isolation" is more appropriate.

Isolation is a particularly antiquated public health notion. It was designed in a very different era and intended for diseases of a character wholly different from that of AIDS. At the time most of these public health statutes were written, the sciences of virology and epidemiology were in their infancy.[64] A crude tradition of isolation and quarantine of real and suspected cases was the rule, sometimes involving separation of an entire geographic area, although there was no understanding of the mechanism by which the disease spread or how to interrupt it.[65]

Modern public health interventions are founded upon a more sophisticated understanding of disease processes. Science more precisely understands the etiological agents of infectious diseases, the most likely harborers of the agent, the most efficient modes of its transmission, and the methods of modifying behaviors or environments in order to interrupt its spread.

Accordingly, modern measures for reducing the spread of disease are predominantly based upon research, education, and counseling, specifically targeted to groups at risk of spreading or contracting the disease. Public health statutes and judicial review of public health action should reflect these scientific realities by requiring public health measures to interrupt only the most efficient modes of disease transmission. The public health benefit is thus maximized, while restrictions of individual liberty remain limited to those clearly necessary for community health.[66]

AIDS does not display the paradigmatic conditions that call for isolation. HIV is not transmitted by casual contact with others; it is not an airborne disease which is spread by coughing or sneezing; and it is not transmissable by touching, kissing, or other social activities.[67] AIDS is transmitted only by specific, conscious behavior. Therefore, to isolate those who are infected with HIV, yet who do not engage in this behavior, lacks any useful purpose.

At present, few state public health statutes authorize the isolation of persons with AIDS. Many states authorize the isolation of persons infected with venereal or sexually transmitted diseases, but for the most part AIDS is not so classified.[68]

---

63. *See, e.g.*, CAL. HEALTH & SAFETY CODE §§ 2520, 2525 (West 1976).

64. *See generally*, Gostin, *The Future of Public Health Law*, 12 AM. J. L. & MED. 461, 463–65 (1986); Parmet, *AIDS and Quarantine: The Revival of an Archaic Doctrine*, 14 HOFSTRA L. REV. 53 (1985).

65. *See, e.g.*, Jew Ho v. Williamson, 103 F. 10 (C.C.N.D. Cal. 1900) (court found that quarantine area was too large and unrelated to effective disease control).

66. *See* Gostin, *supra* note 64, at 464–65.

67. *See supra* notes 14–62 and accompanying text.

68. W. CURRAN, L. GOSTIN & M. CLARK, ACQUIRED IMMUNODEFICIENCY SYNDROME: LEGAL AND REGULATORY POLICY ANALYSIS i–ii, 204–07 (1986, republished by U.S. Dep't of Comm. 1988).

Although AIDS is classified as a communicable disease in many states,[69] that designation alone does not provide a legal basis for the imposition of personal control measures. Similarly, the fact that all states require that AIDS cases be reported to public health officials does not, in and of itself, provide legal justification for isolating infected persons.[70]

To be sure, many state legislatures have considered bills to make AIDS, and even HIV infection, isolable conditions.[71] A number of these states have already enacted statutes authorizing the isolation of persons with HIV. Some of these statutes do not mention the AIDS virus specifically, but would probably justify the detention of AIDS virus carriers.[72]

Two different kinds of isolation statute exist: those which authorize confinement on the basis of disease status alone, and those which authorize confinement of infected persons who engage in dangerous behavior. The distinction between antiquated disease-based isolation and more modern behavior-based isolation is pivotal, because one is concerned with an immutable health status, while the other is more directly targeted to prevent dangerous acts.

Isolation, whether disease- or behavior-based, is a uniquely serious form of deprivation of liberty because it can be utilized against a competent and unwilling person without criminal conviction.[73] It fully restricts the personal liberty of a rational adult, not out of concern for that person's welfare, but out of concern for the welfare of others. Furthermore, it is a form of preventive confinement based upon what a

---

69. *Id.* at ii. *See generally id.* at 1–208.

70. *Id.* at ii, 204 (summarizing findings presented at 1–179).

71. Some states specifically mention HIV in the statute, making it an isolable condition. *See, e.g.*, COLO. REV. STAT., §§ 25-4-1401 to -1410 (Bradford Supp. 1987). (When a person is or is reasonably believed to be infected with HIV, the state or local health department may order the person to be examined and tested, to visit a health worker's office for counseling, or to cease and desist from specified dangerous conduct. If a person violates a cease and desist order, personal restrictions can be imposed as necessary to prevent dangerous conduct. A person's failure to comply with the statute can result in a criminal penalty.); 1987 MINN. SESS. LAW SERV., § 209 S.F. No. 1048 (West). Other states simply add HIV to the list of communicable diseases which are isolable, *see, e.g.*, IDAHO CODE § 39-601 (1988), or classify HIV as a sexually transmitted disease subject to isolation, *see, e.g.*, KY. REV. STAT. ANN. § 214.410 (Michie/Bobbs-Merrill 1988). Finally, some states have only considered proposals for making AIDS an isolable disease. These states include Hawaii, South Carolina, and Washington. Virginia and Pennsylvania have both passed gentle probing measures authorizing investigations into the adequacy of existing state laws and regulations for disease control. *See generally* Gostin & Ziegler, *A Review of AIDS-Related Legislative and Regulatory Policy in the United States*, 15 LAW, MED. & HEALTH CARE 5 (1987); Curran, Clark & Gostin, *AIDS: Legal and Policy Implications of the Application of Traditional Disease Control Measures*, 15 LAW, MED. & HEALTH CARE 27 (1987); R. MERRITT, C. THOMAS & A. ZIEGLER, AIDS-RELATED BILLS CONSIDERED IN THE 1986 LEGISLATIVE SESSION (1987); C. THOMAS, A SYNOPSIS OF STATE RELATED LEGISLATION (1987); Sullivan & Field, *supra* note 1, at 144 n.18.

72. *See, e.g.*, 1987 ALA. CODE § 22-11A-18 (Supp. 1988) (authorizes public health officials to isolate persons with sexually transmitted diseases if they may expose others to the disease and confinement is necessary to protect the public health); CONN. GEN. STAT. ANN. § 19a-221 (West 1986) (authorizes each health director to order an individual confined if there are reasonable grounds to believe he or she is infected with a communicable disease and is unwilling or unable to act in a manner so as not to expose others); FLA. STAT. ANN. § 384.28 (West Supp. 1988) (authorizes public health authorities to isolate a person to prevent the "probable spread of a sexually transmitted disease, until such time as the condition can be corrected or the threat to the public health is eliminated or reduced.") IND. CODE ANN. § 16-1-9.5-4 (West Supp. 1988) (allows the secretary for health or local health officers to restrict people who have a communicable disease and who may be endangering the public health).

73. *See generally*, Curran, Clark & Gostin, *supra* note 71; Ford & Quam, *AIDS Quarantine: The Legal and Practical Implications*, 8 J. LEGAL MED. 353 (1987); Gostin, *Traditional Public Health Strategies*, in AIDS AND THE LAW: A GUIDE FOR THE PUBLIC 47 (H. Dalton & S. Burris eds. 1987); Merritt, *Communicable Disease Control and Constitutional Law: Controlling AIDS*, 61 N.Y.U. L. REV. 759 (1986); Parmet, *supra* note 64; Sullivan & Field, *supra* note 1.

person *might* do rather than what he or she has already done. Isolation, therefore, relies upon predictions of dangerousness. The law is usually loath to confine individuals for acts they have yet to commit,[74] especially when these individuals are rational and competent adults, and their behavior is assumed to conform to legal standards. Even more telling is the fact that isolation has no temporal limitation; indeed, inasmuch as seropositive people are presumed to be infectious for the rest of their lives, isolation amounts to a kind of civil life sentence. Unlike a criminal sentence, however, the duration of isolation is not necessarily proportionate to the gravity of the behavior. Rather, consensual sexual behavior (or even less serious acts such as spitting or biting) could result in lifelong confinement. State legislators and public health authorities ought to consider these adverse consequences before they adopt isolation.

Next, I review two legal prerequisites for any program of isolation—that procedural due process must be afforded before exercising a power to isolate an individual, and that the place of isolation should do no harm to the subject. I will then further consider the constitutionality and merits of programs for disease-based and behavior-based isolation.

A. *Procedures for Fair and Impartial Decision Making*

In addition to specifying standards for restraining individuals, a scheme for the control of communicable disease must identify the decision makers and describe a process for gathering information and making fair and correct decisions. Most state statutes delegate wide discretion to public health officials without carefully considering procedural safeguards designed to achieve both a more accurate fact finding process and greater fairness to the individual whose liberty is to be restrained.

Many public health statutes are either silent or wholly inconsistent in their provision of procedural due process protections to subjects of compulsory powers. California law, for example, authorizes the California Department of Health Services to identify and then quarantine or isolate individuals having a communicable disease whenever, *in its judgment*, such action is necessary to protect or preserve the public health.[75] Similar language is found in many public health statutes across the country.[76]

A few statutes do mandate application to a judge or magistrate for an order of isolation or quarantine, but fail to specify any other procedural requirements.[77] Even

74. The U.S. Supreme Court has upheld preventive detention of persons charged with offenses. United States v. Salerno, 107 S. Ct. 2095, 2101–02 (1987) (preventive confinement for persons on bail); Schall v. Martin, 467 U.S. 253 (1984) (preventive confinement of persons charged with juvenile offenses). It has also repeatedly upheld the detention of persons who are mentally ill and thought dangerous. *See, e.g.*, Youngberg v. Romeo, 457 U.S. 307 (1982); O'Connor v. Donaldson, 422 U.S. 563, 575 (1975). But barring such special circumstances the Court has traditionally been suspect of preventive confinement.

75. CAL. HEALTH & SAFETY CODE § 3051 (West 1979).

76. *E.g.*, FLA. STAT. ANN. § 384.28(1) (West Supp. 1988); N.J. STAT. ANN. § 26:4-2 (West 1987). *But see* CONN. GEN. STAT. ANN. § 19a-5 (West 1986) (duties of Public Health Commissioner more detailed).

77. *See, e.g.*, N.Y. PUB. HEALTH LAW § 2301 (McKinney 1985). For example, the court in State v. Snow, 230 Ark. 746, 324 S.W. 2d 532 (1959) was able to thwart a state effort to quarantine an individual for tuberculosis only because initial judicial approval was required by the authorizing statute before enforcement could take place.

statutes recognizing the importance of an impartial fact finder for an order of isolation or quarantine do not provide procedural safeguards prior to the exercise of other compulsory powers, such as mandatory physical examination, treatment, or contact tracing. Several statutes originating in the 1940s identify specific categories of individuals who may be required to undergo venereal disease examination by a public health officer.[78] The applicable New Jersey statute, for example, presumes that a prostitute "or other lewd person" may reasonably be suspected of having a venereal disease and may therefore be subjected to examination at any time without a hearing.[79]

These statutory provisions survive only because they have yet to be challenged in the courts. In contrast, mental health statutes before the 1970s which failed to require rigorous due process procedures were found to violate the due process clause of the fourteenth amendment.[80] Since then, mental health cases have required notice and a hearing before a judge and have established a right to counsel.[81] The standard of proof constitutionally required at civil commitment hearings is more than a preponderance of evidence; rather, it must demonstrate "clear and convincing evidence."[82]

Courts in the current process-oriented era of constitutional review would most likely require procedural safeguards prior to or—in an emergency—immediately after the exercise of personal control measures. In determining the kinds of procedures required under the fourteenth amendment, the courts balance the interests of the state with those of the individual.[83]

The state's interest in protecting the public from serious harm is compelling. The interest of the individual grows in proportion to the level of coerciveness of the public health measure to be applied. When a control measure, such as isolation, infringes upon liberty, the courts will likely require strict procedural due process safeguards in light of the deep invasion of personal rights, the risk of erroneous fact-finding, and the importance of avoiding confinement of nondangerous persons.

The West Virginia Supreme Court reasoned in *Greene v. Edwards*[84] that there is little difference between loss of liberty under mental health and public health rationales. In each instance, the exercise of police power and the subsequent loss of the individual's freedom are justified by the protection of the common good. Prospective subjects of isolation or quarantine are therefore entitled to the same procedural safeguards as persons facing civil commitment: written notice, counsel,

78. *E.g.*, N.J. STAT. ANN. §§ 26:4-32 (West 1987) (applicable to prostitutes), *id.* § 26:4-49.6 (applicable to migrant workers).

79. *Id.* § 26:4-32 (West 1987).

80. *See, e.g.*, Suzuki v. Yuen, 617 F.2d 173, 178 (9th Cir. 1980); Colyar v. Third Judicial Dist. Court, 469 F. Supp. 424, 429–30 (D. Utah 1979); Lessard v. Schmidt, 349 F. Supp. 1078 (E.D. Wis. 1972); *In re* Seefeld, 2 MENTAL DISABILITY L. REP. 363 (Wis. Cir. Ct. 1977) (sequel to *Lessard* in which the Wisconsin statute enacted in response to *Lessard* was held unconstitutional).

81. Vitek v. Jones, 445 U.S. 480, 488 (1980) (inmate has liberty interest in preventing transfer from prison to mental institution).

82. Addington v. Texas, 441 U.S. 418, 431–33 (1979) ("clear and convincing proof" may be required for indefinite involuntary commitment).

83. Mathews v. Eldridge, 424 U.S. 319, 334–35 (1976).

84. 263 S.E.2d 661 (W. Va. 1980).

presentation of evidence, cross examination, a "clear and convincing" standard of proof, and a verbatim transcript for appeal.

The state need not, however, go so far as to provide the procedural safeguards of a criminal trial.[85] Rather, the foregoing procedural requirements should be built into public health statutes. Prior to or—in cases of urgent necessity—immediately after the imposition of personal control measures, an impartial decision maker should hear the case. This function belongs within the jurisdiction of the courts. The states should bear the burden of providing a hearing, and the potential subject of control measures should have the right to be represented by counsel to examine critically the grounds and evidence upon which decisions are made. The individual should not be left to discover after-the-fact remedies such as habeas corpus.

State legislatures should give careful thought to these procedural safeguards designed to achieve both a more accurate fact-finding process and greater fairness to the individual whose liberty is to be restrained. Procedural due process does not merely protect the individual; it also ensures high quality decision making where a complete and structured body of information is presented to a dispassionate decision maker. Such hearings provide an opportunity for public health officials to review their general strategy for controlling disease epidemics and to apply that strategy in particular cases.

Society has yet to employ its legislature to delimit the circumstances under which important public health decisions should be made. Because public health is one of the very few reasons for which individual liberty can be restricted absent the commission of a criminal offense, it is essential that legislatures guide officials to understand clearly, and to apply fairly, decision making criteria and procedures.

B. *Safe Environment for Isolation*

Even if otherwise constitutional, the question arises whether isolation measures may themselves be allowed to pose a health risk to their subjects. Although the court in *Kirk v. Board of Health*[86] was quite prepared to uphold an isolation scheme despite the absence of proof that the form of leprosy from which Mary Kirk was suffering was contagious, it nevertheless refused to subject her to an environment it considered unsafe. Public health officials had planned to quarantine Kirk in a pesthouse, "a structure of four small rooms in a row, with no piazzas, used heretofore for the isolation of negroes with smallpox, situated within a hundred yards of the place where the trash of the city . . . is collected and burned." The court concluded that "even temporary isolation in such a place would be a serious affliction and peril to an elderly lady enfeebled by disease, and accustomed to the comforts of life."[87] The public health department was compelled to delay isolating her until it had finished building Kirk a "comfortable cottage" outside the city limits.

A more modern court, however, was less rigorous in reviewing the conditions

85. *See id.* at 662.
86. 83 S.C. 372, 65 S.E. 387 (1909).
87. *Id.*, 65 S.E. at 391.

of isolation. In *Ex parte Martin*,[88] a 1948 California case, county officials had elected to isolate people with venereal disease in a jail, despite uncontested evidence that the jail was overcrowded and had been condemned by a legislative investigating committee. The court supported the attorney general's position that "[w]hile jails, as public institutions, were established for purposes other than confinement of diseased persons, occasions of emergency or lack of other public facilities for quarantine require that jails be used."[89]

The use of the jail as a place of isolation and the absence of any rigorous demonstration that the persons isolated were actually infected with venereal disease imply that punishment was an underlying purpose in *Martin*. Punishment, however, is not an appropriate public health goal. Public health departments have an obligation not to do unnecessary harm, and that extends to avoiding unsafe or punitive environments for subjects of an isolation. Indeed, those who must forego their individual rights for the collective good should receive the best possible care and conditions. While no recent case tests the issue of a safe environment for isolation, the general trend towards insisting that health-law measures be rooted in medical considerations strongly suggests that courts will reject any isolation scheme which, like that in *Martin*, has punitive overtones.

The requirement to provide a safe and humane environment for isolation poses special problems in the AIDS context. The two options are to provide separate facilities or to integrate individuals in currently existing prisons, hospitals, mental hospitals, or other health care or criminal justice facilities. Providing separate facilities for infected persons sends a harmful message to the general public that the state is establishing "AIDS colonies." This gives the wrong impression that AIDS is transmitted from simple association with infected persons and that segregation from other populations is desirable.

Segregated facilities must also be built or re-adapted, and adequately financed and staffed. It would be difficult to recruit guards, health care and social workers, and counselors to designated AIDS facilities. Segregated facilities must be clean, sanitary, and otherwise provide a healthful, nonviolent environment. If, for example, segregated individuals are exposed to violence, sexual advances, or drug use in the facility, it could be harmful to their future health. Scientists do not entirely understand the means by which a person progresses from HIV-positivity to AIDS-related complex to AIDS. It is certainly possible that re-infection with the AIDS virus will increase the progression from dormancy of the virus to serious symptomology and death.

Use of integrated facilities would pose different problems. Residents and staff of hospitals, mental hospitals, nursing homes, and even prisons often do not want to be integrated with persons with HIV. This is particularly so if such individuals have been selected because of their irresponsible behavior. Many will rightly argue that their facilities have limited resources and training to deal with HIV infected patients.

88. 83 Cal. App. 2d 164, 188 P.2d 287 (1948).

89. *Id.* at 170, 188 P.2d at 291 (quoting 4 Op. Att'y Gen. 146, 148).

Furthermore, the facilities may argue that they were not designed or intended for this purpose. Prison authorities believe they have insufficient medical and nursing resources to treat terminally ill and infectious inmates; hospitals and nursing homes argue that they should not have a social control role of confining aggressive persons; mental hospitals argue that they cannot provide effective treatment for AIDS dementia.

If a policy of coercive action is socially beneficial, then government will engage in effective planning and resource allocation to solve many of these significant practical problems. However, given the antipathy of public health authorities toward coercive action to control a disease epidemic, it is unlikely that any of these pragmatic issues will be resolved. This places a large question mark over any program seeking systematic application of criminal or civil sanctions for AIDS transmission.

C. *Disease or Status-Based Isolation*

A disease, or status-based, isolation would reach all those who test positive for HIV or have CDC-defined AIDS.[90] Such an isolation would cause unimaginable hardship, dislocation, and human, as well as social, cost. No state has seriously proposed a general isolation, and it is highly unlikely to take place in the United States. However, disease-based isolation has already occurred in Cuba[91] and is a seriously considered option in other countries.

Traditionally, the courts have been highly deferential to public health measures, including isolation and quarantine.[92] However, it is widely agreed that a disease-based isolation would most probably be held unconstitutional under modern doctrine.[93]

Isolation impacts on liberty and travel, rights which the Supreme Court has held to be fundamental.[94] The Court would therefore evaluate an AIDS isolation statute under strict scrutiny. While the Court's strict scrutiny analysis often signals its intent to hold the measure unconstitutional, that need not always be the case. The Court requires the state to have a compelling interest,[95] and to achieve that interest by means which are narrowly tailored and minimally restrictive.[96] Impeding the spread

90. The eighth amendment's ban on cruel and unusual punishment forbids criminal punishment for the status of being ill. Robertson v. California, 370 U.S. 660, 666 (1962). But the eighth amendment would not apply to isolation, civil commitment, or preventive detention because they are regarded as regulatory, not punitive. *See* Sullivan & Field, *supra* note 1, at 146.

91. Betancourt, *Cuba's Callous War on AIDS*, N.Y. Times, Feb. 11, 1988, at A35, col. 2. *See* S. Fluss, Tabular Information on Legal Instruments Dealing with AIDS and HIV Infection, SPA/HLE/87.1 (Available from WHO, Geneva).

92. *See* Burris, *Fear Itself: AIDS, Herpes, and Public Health Decisions*, 3 Yale L. & Pol'y Rev. 479 (1985); Curran, Clark & Gostin, *supra* note 71, at 32; Gostin, *The Future of Communicable Disease Control: Toward a New Concept in Public Health Law*, 64 Milbank Memorial Fund Q. (Supp. 1) 79, 85–88 (1986) [hereinafter Gostin, *Future Communicable Disease*]; Gostin, *supra* note 64, at 464–68; Merritt, *supra* note 73, at 776–83; Parmet, *supra* note 64.

93. Gostin, *supra* note 64, at 468–71; Merritt, *supra* note 73 at 778–83; Parmet, *supra* note 73; Sullivan & Field, *supra* note 1, at 146–52; Note, *The Constitutional Rights of AIDS Carriers*, 99 Harv. L. Rev. 1274, 1281–84 (1986).

94. Addington v. Texas, 441 U.S. 418, 425 (1979) (standard of proof for civil commitment for the mentally ill); Shapiro v. Thompson, 394 U.S. 618, 629–30 (1969) (citing United States v. Guest, 383 U.S. 745, 757–58 (1966)).

95. *See* Korematsu v. United States, 323 U.S. 214, 218 (1944) (only the gravest imminent danger to public safety can justify forced removal from one's home).

96. *See* Note, *Developments in the Law—Equal Protection*, 82 Harv. L. Rev. 1065, 1084–86 (1969).

of AIDS is certainly a state interest which is sufficiently strong to survive heightened judicial scrutiny.[97]

But a status-based isolation would be substantially overinclusive. It would indiscriminately sweep in its wake not only those who spread the disease, but also many who do not. Screening of low-risk populations can generate significant numbers of false positives[98]—*i.e.*, persons who test positive but who do not harbor the virus. In addition, some individuals who do harbor the virus are no longer infectious because the virus has eliminated its host cells.[99] Even for those who are truly infectious, the great majority will not be dangerous. Some are children. Some are involved in monogamous relationships, and would inform their partners and use barrier protection against the exchange of body fluids. Still others are too debilitated or demoralized to engage in any high risk activity. To assume that all persons who test positive for HIV antibodies are dangerous, and to confine them, potentially for life, would be a substantially overbroad policy.

Status-based isolation could also be substantially underinclusive. In order to reach everyone capable of transmitting the AIDS virus, public health authorities would have to test the entire population periodically.[100] This would be such a costly policy that politicians would more narrowly draw the boundaries of coercive action. These boundaries might be based on having CDC-defined AIDS, or on membership in a high risk group. Targeting persons with AIDS or in high risk groups for special treatment would exclude growing numbers of people with infection who are heterosexual, blood transfusion recipients, hemophiliacs, and others.[101]

The courts do not always view underinclusiveness as a serious constitutional flaw.[102] Nothing prevents a state from devising a public health solution which is only partially effective. But sometimes the courts find that underinclusiveness is so arbitrary as to deny equal protection.[103] As one commentator observes, underinclusiveness casts doubt on the sincerity of the public objective: "Where a quarantine is mapped out along the boundaries of a group that is independently the object of fear, prejudice and hatred, there is reason for skepticism."[104] The fact that status-based isolation would impact exclusively or disproportionately on IV drug users, gays, and

97. *See* Jacobson v. Massachusetts, 197 U.S. 11, 25 (1905).

98. The ELISA test for HIV antibodies produces false positive results ranging from 1/3 to 2/3 of all cases in a low risk population. This figure can be substantially reduced with confirmatory testing. *See* Barry, Cleary & Fineberg, *Screening for HIV Infection: Risks, Benefits and the Burden of Proof*, 14 LAW, MED. & HEALTH CARE 259, 262–63 (1986); Cleary, Barry, Mayer, Brandt, Gostin & Fineberg, *Compulsory Premarital Screening for the Human Immunodeficiency Virus: Technical and Public Health Considerations*, 258 J. A.M.A. 1757, 1758 (1987); Gostin, Curran & Clark, *supra* note 12, at 11–13.

99. Leeson, *HTLV-III Antibody Tests and Health Education*, 1 LANCET 911 (1986).

100. Since so many persons infected with HIV and capable of transmitting the virus are symptomless, the only systematic method of identifying them would be widespread population screening. This would be a highly costly and fruitless public health intervention. *See* Cleary, Barry, Mayer, Brandt, Gostin & Fineberg, *supra* note 98, at 1761; Gostin, *Screening for AIDS: Efficacy, Cost and Consequences*, 2 AIDS AND PUB. POLICY J. 14 (1987); Gostin, Curran & Clark, *supra* note 12, at 19–24.

101. *See Review of Current Knowledge*, *supra* note 3.

102. *See* Note, *supra* note 96, at 1065, 1084–86.

103. *Id.*

104. Sullivan & Field, *supra* note 1, at 149.

racial minorities[105] who are independently disfavored communities calls into question whether the true reason for this isolation is public health at all. The suspicion would persist whether the same policy of deprivation of liberty on a massive scale would be applied to more favored social groups.[106]

There are numerous public policy reasons against a disease-based isolation which can be added to the constitutional arguments. These policy reasons flow from the unique combination of scientific findings relating to HIV. First, the sheer number of people capable of transmitting the virus, estimated at up to 1.4 million and growing,[107] would make a general isolation prohibitively expensive and wholly unmanageable. Huge practical problems would arise in identifying infected persons with initial and confirmatory tests, and then housing and caring for them, all at public expense. Second, retroviruses like HIV usually live in the carrier for life. There is no finite incubation period, so carriers of the virus are presumed chronically infectious.[108] Confinement of carriers, if it is to be truly effective, must be indefinite. A program of confinement of a person with HIV, therefore, must count on the fact that it can be potentially life-long. Such extensive restriction of personal liberty for behaviors which are part of the human biological function appear excessive. Third, there is no preventive or curative treatment for HIV infection. Those whose liberty is infringed, therefore, would have no way to restore themselves to normal conditions in order to re-join the community. Finally, because casual contact does not spread the virus, segregation from society is unnecessary and, by definition, overly restrictive. Taken together, these factors set AIDS apart from other communicable diseases that have been the subject of traditional personal control measures and make status-based isolation a singularly inappropriate policy.

---

105. The cumulative incidence of AIDS cases is disproportionately high among blacks (3.0 to 1) and Hispanics (2.6 to 1) compared with whites. When homosexual and bisexual men with AIDS are excluded, the ratio of AIDS case incidence is 12.0 to 1 for blacks, and 9.3 to 1 for Hispanics as compared with whites. *Review of Current Knowledge*, *supra* note 3, at 36. The reasons for this recurring racial disproportion of infection, whether behavioral or biological, are not yet apparent. The higher rate of IV drug use among black and Hispanic groups may be a factor, but there remains a racial disproportion even among IV drug users. *See* Greaves, *The Black Community*, in AIDS AND THE LAW: A GUIDE FOR THE PUBLIC 281–82 (H. Dalton & S. Burris eds. 1987); *Acquired Immunodeficiency Syndrome (AIDS) Among Blacks and Hispanics—United States*, 35 MORBIDITY & MORTALITY WEEKLY REP. 655, 666 (1986).

106. There are several significant reasons why a court might not find under-inclusion unconstitutional in the AIDS context. The argument that isolation denied equal protection of the laws to gays or IV drug users falters on the Supreme Court's jurisprudence refusing to find either group to be a suspect class. In Bowers v. Hardwick, 478 U.S. 186 (1986), the Supreme Court held that the states could constitutionally criminalize sodomy. The Court found no privacy interest in homosexual relations and no reason to use heightened scrutiny because of the traditionally disfavored status of gays. For strong arguments in favor of making homosexuality a suspect classification, see Note, *The Constitutional Status of Sexual Orientation: Homosexuality as a Suspect Classification*, 98 HARV. L. REV. 1285 (1985); Note, *An Argument for the Application of Equal Protection Heightened Scrutiny to Classifications Based on Homosexuality*, 57 S. CAL. L. REV. 797 (1984). In New York City Transit Authority v. Beazel, 440 U.S. 568 (1979) the Court upheld a transit authority decision to exclude methadone users from employment. The Court found no reason to find drug users as a suspect class despite the fact that they are often poor and black or Hispanic. Finally, the Supreme Court has been loath to find that disproportional representation of minority groups is a reason for special scrutiny. So long as the class is not drawn on racial lines the court has looked the other way despite overwhelming evidence of disproportionate impact on minorities. *See* McCleskey v. Kemp, 107 S. Ct. 1756 (1987) (upholding death penalty despite the fact that it was used in many more cases of black offenders).

107. *See supra* note 3.

108. *See* Curran & Morgan, *supra* note 5, at 1354; Fauci, *The Human Immunodeficiency Virus: Infectivity and Mechanisms of Pathogenesis*, 239 SCIENCE 617, 621 (1988).

D. *Modified Isolation Based upon Behavior, not Disease Status*

The terms "incorrigible" and "recalcitrant" have been used to refer to persons who are aware that they have been exposed to the AIDS virus, yet continue to engage in high-risk activities that expose others to the disease, despite warnings by doctors and health officials to modify their behavior. Numerous cases have been publicized of individuals brazenly announcing their intentions to continue to infect others through prostitution, sexual intercourse, needle sharing, or donating blood.[109] Those who engage in such seriously dangerous behavior are often well aware of the consequences of that behavior, and can be predicted to continue it. These people are widely regarded as blameworthy. If confinement is the only way to prevent an unmistakable risk to the public, then no one could reasonably deny the state's right to intervene.

The rationale for behavior-based isolation is a mix of prevention and retribution. Like traditional isolation, it is designed to be forward-looking in preventing future disease transmission. But its reliance upon past dangerous behavior has an element of retribution similar to that found in the criminal law. Apart from its purported objective of slowing the spread of AIDS, behavior-based isolation offers society an outlet for its frustration and anger towards AIDS carriers by restricting the liberty of a few individuals who are visibly evil and worthy of condemnation for fueling the epidemic. In truth, as we shall see, it will have very little positive effect on the epidemic.

Recognizing the practical and legal problems with general isolation, state authorities have begun to revise their isolation proposals to encompass only incorrigible cases. This is politically much easier because it is far less expensive, and targets only individuals who are universally seen as culpable.

While general isolation measures would be deemed unconstitutional by the courts, most commentators agree that a narrowly drawn behavior-based isolation would probably be upheld.[110] Modified isolation, unlike general isolation, does not focus on a person's health status, but upon his or her behavior. It is aimed at a small number of individuals rather than a sizeable class of persons united by a common characteristic. It is difficult to envisage a court striking down a well-focused public health measure, when there is clear evidence available that an individual is likely to engage in behavior leading to transmission of a potentially lethal virus.

The courts have consistently upheld civil confinement of persons shown to be dangerous in the public health[111] and mental health[112] contexts. Such statutes, while

109. Stephanie Smith, for example, was shunned by her drug treatment facility when it discovered she was HIV positive. She dropped out of treatment. She told public health officials that she was sharing her needles without cleaning them and engaging in prostitution without taking precautions or informing her clients. Lewin, *supra* note 1. *See* Squires, *supra* note 1; Boorstin, *supra* note 1.

110. *See* Sullivan & Field, *supra* note 1, at 152–56; Merritt, *supra* note 71; Parmet, *supra* note 64; Gostin, *Future Communicable Disease*, *supra* note 92, at 91–95. *But see* Note, *supra* note 93.

111. *See, e.g.*, Greene v. Edwards, 261 S.E.2d 661 (W. Va. 1980); State *ex rel.* Kennedy v. Head, 182 Tenn. 249, 185 S.W.2d 530 (1945); *In re* Caselli, 62 Mont. 201, 204 P. 364 (1922); Crayton v. Larabee, 220 N.Y. 493, 116 N.E. 355 (N.Y. 1917), *aff'd* 147 N.Y.S. 1105; Kirk v. Wyman, 83 S.C. 372, 65 S.E. 387 (1909); Hurst v. Warner, 102 Mich. 238, 60 N.W. 440 (1894). *See also*, Merritt, *supra* note 73, at 776–78.

112. *See, e.g.*, O'Connor v. Donaldson, 442 U.S. 563 (1975).

attracting heightened scrutiny, would achieve a powerful state interest in a way which focuses only on the dangerous and not on those unlikely to engage in high-risk behavior. The dangerous acts, moreover, are often criminal in themselves—prostitution, sodomy, or drug use.

Even if courts were to uphold limited behavior-based isolation, distinct public policy reasons make them weak candidates for implementation. Behavior-based isolation suffers from some of the same defects as does general isolation. If the target is unable to alter his or her behavior, modified isolation is likely to mean permanent confinement. Further, isolation is far more intrusive and restrictive than would be the provision of drug treatment (where appropriate), physiological or medical treatment, counseling, or economic assistance designed to alleviate or alter the conditions that lead to "incorrigible" behavior.

The objective of isolation is to prevent future risky behavior. It may do so in individual cases, but will probably have an overall adverse impact on the wider high risk populations. Isolation statutes would discourage members of high risk groups from seeking testing or treatment, or speaking honestly to counselors concerning their behavioral intentions. If the certain legal consequence of a person confiding his future intentions is loss of liberty, then individuals would avoid contact with health care professionals and public health programs. The cost, therefore, of preventing a few cases of HIV transmission through isolation may be to undermine public health efforts for broad population changes in behavior. While the objective is to impede the spread of HIV, coercive measures could drive the epidemic underground, thereby defeating the purpose.

Objective statutory and psychological criteria are inadequate to determine accurately enough who is "recalcitrant" or to predict behavior. Even for those who are mentally ill, psychiatrists are still unable to predict dangerous behavior with anything better than random accuracy.[113] There is no reason to believe that behavioral scientists could predict future behavior in the public health context any better. In other words, individuals who declared an intention to engage in high-risk behavior could not be reliably distinguished from those who forswore unsafe conduct.

Those who come to the attention of public officials as candidates for isolation are a small fraction of the total infected population. This small part of the total at-risk population is likely to be the poorest, least articulate of those harboring the virus. Such a skewed "lottery" would have a negligible impact on the spread of the disease because the vast majority of instances of transmissions would continue to go unnoticed. While isolation would lead to the impression that the state was "getting tough" on AIDS transmission, in reality it would not scratch the surface of the epidemic.

This may well lead authorities to widen the net of those subject to behavior-

113. *See, e.g.*, E. MONAHAN, PREDICTING VIOLENT BEHAVIOR: AN ASSESSMENT OF CLINICAL TECHNIQUES (1981). In Barefoot v. Estelle, 463 U.S. 880 (1983), the Court upheld the death penalty based upon a psychiatric prediction of dangerousness. This provoked Justice Blackmun to observe in dissent, based upon an amicus brief from the American Psychiatric Association, that predictions of dangerousness are wrong "two out of three" times. *Id.* at 920. "In the present state of psychiatric knowledge this is too much for me." *Id.*

based isolation. Public health authorities may seek to sweep in HIV-infected persons attending bathhouses or gay bars, prostitutes, and IV drug users attending shooting galleries. Large numbers of unpopular individuals are perceived, but not proved, to be dangerous. If a public place such as a bathhouse is demonstrated to be a public health hazard, the state can exercise its regulatory power to closely supervise its activities or close it down. But a decision to confine all those who attend such facilities would be overly restrictive and prejudicial to the nondangerous.

State intervention to prevent seriously dangerous behavior of "incorrigibles" through isolation measures appears justified. However, the policy would be ineffective, perhaps counterproductive, in controlling the AIDS epidemic, and may easily include a wider net of nondangerous persons. Below, I explore the efficacy and fairness of using a retributive criminal law model to deal with a public health problem.

IV. Criminalization of HIV Transmission

There is a powerful appeal in using the criminal law as a method of containing the spread of AIDS. The criminal law is well used to sanctioning blameworthy individuals for their dangerous acts. The justification of the criminal law is commonly understood to be retribution for past behavior. Yet, one of the principal objectives of the criminal law is the prevention of future acts. By establishing explicit penalties, the criminal law seeks to deter individuals from engaging in certain clearly specified behavior. The transmission of a potentially lethal infection with forethought or recklessness is just as dangerous as other behavior the criminal law already proscribes. It is not unreasonable for society to establish clear parameters as to the behaviors it will not tolerate. By drawing a bright line around the behaviors that pose serious public health risks, the law gives clear notice of the conduct which will be subject to criminal penalty.

This approach can hardly be considered unfair to those individuals in high-risk groups for AIDS because it protects these groups against the spread of infection. Nor can it be considered unfair to the few whose behavior subjects them to criminal penalties, for it is better to give clear forewarning of unacceptable conduct rather than to confine a person who might engage in that behavior in the future.

The criminal law has many advantages over the personal control measure most likely to survive judicial scrutiny—behavior-based isolation. Whereas isolation statutes employ such general terms as "incorrigibility" and "recalcitrance," criminal statutes must specify the behavior that is prohibited. If its language is vague, a criminal statute fails to forewarn, and is for that reason unconstitutional. Whereas isolation statutes arise from predictions about the future, criminal statutes focus on behavior that has already occurred. Whereas "incorrigibility" and "recalcitrance" need only be proved by clear and convincing evidence, each element of a crime must be proved beyond a reasonable doubt. Whereas the period of isolation is usually indefinite, the period of criminal confinement is usually finite and proportionate to the gravity of the offense. As a deterrent, the period of confinement should not last longer than necessary to discourage future reckless behavior, both by the person detained and by others who take note of his or her plight. The longer the period of confinement, the more it smacks of retribution, a goal inconsistent with the mission of public health authorities.

There is an attraction based upon clarity, objectivity, and sufficient safeguards which makes the criminal law a good candidate for public health consideration. This attraction of the criminal law has not escaped policy makers. The Presidential Commission on the Human Immunodeficiency Virus Epidemic noted that "[e]xtending criminal liability to those who knowingly engage in behavior which is likely to transmit HIV is consistent with society's obligation to prevent harm to others and the criminal law's concern with punishing those whose behavior results in harmful acts."[114]

The Presidential Commission report has been published in a political climate which has already heavily utilized the general criminal law in combatting the spread of AIDS. A conservative estimate is that there have been fifty to one hundred criminal cases brought relating to HIV transmission, which vary greatly in gravity.[115]

First, many cases have been brought against individuals who knew they were infected with HIV and had sexual intercourse without informing their partner. Several

---

114. REPORT OF THE PRESIDENTIAL COMMISSION ON THE HUMAN IMMUNODEFICIENCY VIRUS EPIDEMIC 130–31 (U.S. Gov't Printing Off., June 24, 1988) [hereinafter PRESIDENTIAL COMM'N REP.]. The Commission does not favor use of the general criminal law, but adoption of an AIDS-specific criminal statute. *See infra* notes 115–34 and accompanying text. The Presidential Commission was established under Exec. Order No. 12,601, 3 C.F.R. 238 (1987), amended by Exec. Order No. 12,603, 3 C.F.R. 238 (1987). The American Medical Association and the Institute of Medicare have also recommended the rare use of coercive powers. American Medical Association, Council on Ethical and Judicial Affairs, *Ethical Issues Involved in the Growing AIDS Crisis*, 259 J. A.M.A. 1360, 1361 (1988) [hereinafter A.M.A. Council] (recommendation 17—given the risk of infection being transmitted sexually, and given the dire potential consequences of transmission, serious consideration should be given to sanctions for past dangerous sexual acts); UPDATE 1988, *supra* note 3, at 83 (the use of the criminal law will not address the core problems, but in "rare instances" the state should restrict personal liberties).

115. *See*, W. CURRAN, L. GOSTIN, & M. CLARK, *supra* note 68, at 344–48 (in which are discussed People v. Richards, 85-1715 FG, where HIV- infected person charged in Flint, Michigan with assault and intent to commit murder after he spat on four police officers; People v. Prairie Chicken, CRE-77357, where person suspected of having AIDS in El Cajon, California pleaded guilty to a felonious assault for biting an officer; People v. Julius, 761210, where a person suspected of carrying HIV pleaded guilty to a misdemeanor assault in San Francisco after prosecutor abandoned plans to file felony charges over another police biting incident); Lacayoh, *Assault with a Deadly Virus*, TIME, July 20, 1987, at 63 (reporting several cases of criminal charges relating to AIDS transmission); *New Charges Possible in AIDS Assault Case*, U.S. Med., June 1987, at 8 (Pfc. Jane Doe charged with having sex without informing her partner that she was HIV infected); Squires, *supra* note 1 (citing numerous cases of courts martial or criminal charges brought against HIV-infected individuals for sexual relationships or biting); *Soldier with AIDS Virus to be Imprisoned for Sexual Contacts*, N.Y. Times, Dec. 4, 1987, at B5, col. 1 (first conviction); *Medical Specialist Faces AIDS Related Court-Martial*, Am. Med. News, Oct. 16, 1987, at 12 (case against Sgt. Richard W. Sargeant, similar to Pfc. Morris); Weisehaus, *AIDS Criminal Laws, Cases Rise*, Nat'l L.J., July 20, 1987, at 3, col. 1 (Minnesota prisoner convicted of assault with a deadly weapon for biting a guard. The conviction was upheld in United States v. Moore, 669 F. Supp. 289 (D. Minn. 1987)); Cummings, *Charges Filed Against Blood Donor in AIDS Case*, N.Y. Times, June 30, 1987, at A18, col. 1 (Joseph Markowski was charged with attempted murder for selling his blood to a private collection center; later the charges were dropped for lack of evidence. Pristin, *Charges of Attempted Murder Voided in Case of AIDS-Tainted Blood*, L.A. Times, Dec. 2, 1987 Part II (Metro), at 1, col. 1); *Deadly Weapon in AIDS Verdict is Inmate's Teeth*, N.Y. Times, June 25, 1987, at A18, col.6; Boorstin, *supra* note 1 (citing 30 cases being filed); *HIV Positive Private Charged with Assault*, Am. Med. News, May 22/29, 1987, at 1 (case of Army Pfc. Adrian Morris, Jr., who faced a court-martial for sexual relationships while infected with HIV); Testimony of Major Paul A. Capofari, Office of the Judge Advocate General, Department of the Army, Pentagon, to Presidential Commission on the Human Immunodeficiency Virus Epidemic, Interstate Commerce Commission Bldg. Hearing Room B, April 6, 1988 (reporting several more cases of HIV infected soldiers facing courts-martial).

The only reported criminal case outside of the United States occurred in the case of Linwood B., an employee of a U.S. Military Base in Nuremberg, West Germany. The man is a private U.S. citizen who was convicted by a Bavarian Court for sexual intercourse, knowing he had HIV. *See* E. Drucker, The Case of Linwood B., Preliminary Report to Medicins du Monde, Paris, France (Unpublished December 25, 1987) (on file at the Ohio State Law Journal); Schmemann, *Bavarian Court Convicts American in AIDS Case*, N.Y. Times, Nov. 17, 1987, at A5, col. 1.

of these cases have involved military personnel. The Department of Defense orders HIV-infected personnel to refrain from unprotected sex and to inform their partners of their condition. Violation of a "safe sex" order can result in charges ranging from disobeying a military order to assault with a dangerous weapon and attempted murder.[116]

Second, criminal charges have been brought in connection with biting, spitting, kicking, or splattering of blood by an HIV-infected person.[117] In *United States v. Moore*[118] a federal district court upheld the conviction of a prisoner for "assault with a deadly or dangerous weapon" for biting two federal corrections officers. The "weapon" was HIV. In *State v. Haines*,[119] an Indiana Superior Court judge sentenced a person with AIDS-related complex to six years imprisonment after he was convicted by a jury on three counts of attempted murder of a police officer and emergency technicians for splattering his blood at them.[120]

Finally, cases have been brought for knowingly donating or selling blood contaminated with HIV. The most celebrated of these cases was Joseph Markowski who was charged with attempted murder for selling his HIV-infected blood to a Los Angeles blood company.[121] The charges were subsequently dropped for lack of evidence on intent to murder,[122] but legislators have since developed an interest in specifically criminalizing such activity.[123]

These cases point out the inadequacy of applying a general criminal law theory

---

116. The military distinguishes between married and unmarried personnel. The spouses of married personnel are officially informed of the serological status of their spouse. A married couple then is permitted to have unprotected sex. The military will not inform a nonmarried sexual partner. But it has implemented a regulation effective April 1, 1988, requiring a commander to discuss a written counseling statement with any soldier who has tested positive and has received medical counseling. The form says that the commander is "imposing the following restrictions: 'You will verbally advise all prospective sexual partners of your diagnosed condition prior to engaging in any sexual intercourse. You are also ordered to use condoms should you engage in sexual intercourse with a partner . . . . [Failure] to adhere to your previous medical counseling or the counseling I have just given you will subject you to administrative separation and/or punishment under the Uniform Code of Military Justice as I see fit.'" *See* N.Y. Times, July 10, 1988, at A19, col. 1; *See also* Squires, *supra* note 1; Turner, *The Military Battles a New "Biological" Weapon: AIDS*, Nat'l L.J., May 11, 1987, at 6, col. 1. The first military conviction resulted from a guilty plea in a court-martial to adultery, sodomy, and disobeying an officer by Sergeant Richard W. Sargeant; Testimony of Major Paul A. Capofari, *supra* note 115; *Soldier with AIDS Virus to Be Imprisoned for Sexual Contacts*, N.Y. Times, *supra* note 115. A guilty plea for aggravated assault and absence from the post in a similar case resulted in two years imprisonment. *Army Sergeant Pleads Guilty of Infecting a G.I. with AIDS*, N.Y. Times, Dec. 17, 1987, at B25, col 1.

117. *See, e.g.*, Squires, *supra* note 1; Boorstin, *supra* note 1.

118. 669 F. Supp. 289 (D. Minn. 1987).

119. Cause No. S-5585 (Super. Ct., Tippecanoe County, Indiana 1987 Term).

120. *Id. See* Gostin, *AIDS and Safety*, Boston Globe, Feb. 22, 1988, at 19, col. 4 (Letter to the Editor); Gostin, *Emgergency Workers and AIDS*, N.Y. Times, Feb. 14, 1988, § 6 (Magazine), at 10, col. 2 (Letter to the Editor).

121. Cummings, *supra* note 115. *See* Gostin, *Criminal Law Won't Stop AIDS*, L.A. Times, July 6, 1987, Part II, at 5, col. 3.

122. Pristin, *supra* note 115.

123. A Bill by Senator Jesse Helms, for example, would make it a crime to donate blood, semen, or organs by anyone who is HIV positive or is a member of a high risk group. S.1352, 100th Cong. 1st Sess., 133 CONG. REC. S7989–91 (1987). Up to 1.4 million people are estimated to be silently harboring the virus, and many more are in high risk groups. *See supra* note 3. The great majority of these individuals are of sexually active age. An unknown number of these individuals will either know, or reasonably should know, they are at risk for HIV. We can conservatively assume that there will be hundreds of thousands of incidents each year where these individuals will engage in sexual relations or needle sharing. Should all of these incidents be defined as unlawful and subject to societal retribution? What moral or public health differences are there between the so-called "recalcitrant" prostitute or drug abuser and the rest of the many thousands who will silently engage in the same kind of behavior?

to an infectious disease. In the overwhelming majority of cases the prosecutions were dropped or individuals were acquitted. In none of these cases was there evidence that HIV had actually been transmitted. The general criminal law has sought to punish risk taking, sometimes of a very low level.

Partly in frustration with the difficulty in obtaining convictions under the general criminal law, policy makers have sought other avenues to criminalize the risk of AIDS transmission such as creating public health or AIDS-specific offenses. Approximately half the states have public health laws which designate engaging in sexual intercourse while knowingly infected with a sexually transmitted disease as a public health offense.[124] These public health statutes were created to control the spread of syphilis and gonorrhea. Most of these statutes, however, do not apply to HIV because AIDS is not usually classified as a sexually transmitted disease.[125] In response to this perceived "gap" in the law, some state legislators are moving toward re-classifying AIDS as a sexually transmitted disease.[126]

Several states have enacted AIDS-specific statutes.[127] These statutes are based on the model of older public health offenses, except that they apply solely to HIV transmission. These AIDS-specific statutes differ in scope, but all make it an offense for a person to knowingly engage in some type of behavior which poses a risk of transmission of HIV—sexual intercourse, needle sharing, donating blood, or, more broadly, attempting to transfer any "body fluid." The elegance of such statutes from the prosecutor's perspective is usually there is no need to prove any specific intent. The elements of the crime are usually straightforward: the person knew he was infected with HIV, engaged in well-defined, risky behavior, and failed to inform his partner of the risk.

The haste to criminalize the risk of AIDS transmission ignores the failure of previous attempts to control venereal disease,[128] as well as the considerable jurisprudential and public health problems that would arise. Below I enumerate those

---

124. Gostin, *supra* note 64, at 477; Sullivan & Field, *supra* note 1, at 170.

125. W. Curran, L. Gostin & M. Clark, *supra* note 68. A few public health statutes are not solely applicable to venereal diseases but cover any act where the person knowingly transmits a communicable disease. *See* Okla. Stat. Ann. tit. 21 § 1192 (West 1983); Tex. Rev. Civ. Stat. Ann. art. 4419b-1 (Vernon Supp. 1987).

126. *See, e.g.*, Fla. Stat. Ann. § 384.25(2) (West Supp. 1988).

127. *See, e.g.*, Fla. Stat. Ann. §§ 384.24, .34(1) (West Supp. 1988) (criminal offense for person with HIV to knowingly have sexual intercourse with another person, unless he first informs that person); Idaho Code § 39-608 (Supp. 1988) (makes it a felony for any person to expose another with intent to infect or knowing he has HIV, including sexual or shared needle transmission as well as donative gifts); 1987 La. Sess. Law Serv., extraordinary session 663 H.B. no. 1728 (West) (criminalizes intentional, sexual transmission of HIV without partner's informed consent); 1988 Wash. Legis. Serv. 206 S.B. 6221 (West Supp.) (a person who with intent to inflict bodily harm or "causes to be taken" by another HIV or exposes or transmits HIV is guilty of assault). There are many other bills which have been proposed which would create AIDS-specific offenses. *See also* H. R. 345, 100th Cong. 1st Sess. (1987) (would make it a crime if a federal employee with HIV knowingly or recklessly attempts to transfer any of his body fluids).

128. Experience with these public health offenses shows that the laws are now very rarely enforced. When they have been enforced on a wide scale, there has been no perceptible impact on the rate of transmission of sexually transmitted diseases. *See* Brandt, *supra* note 11, at 239; Merritt, *supra* note 71. The most extensive use of coercive powers have often been against vulnerable and visible populations such as prostitutes. *See, e.g.*, *HIV Tests Ordered for Prostitutes, Their Clients*, 31 Med. News 39 (Feb. 12, 1988). Indeed, some public health statutes now specifically target this population. Fla. Stat. Ann. § 796.08(4) (West Supp. 1988) (any person who commits prostitution knowing that she or he has a sexually transmitted disease is guilty of an offense); Nev. Rev. Stat. Ann., 1987 Cum. Supp. (Michie, 1987) tit. 15, chap. 201, § 201.443 (any licensed prostitute who practices with knowledge of a positive HIV test result is guilty of a felony).

problems in relation to general criminal law theory and AIDS-specific criminal statutes.

A. *General Criminal Law Theory*

Acts which pose a risk of HIV transmission have resulted in criminal charges ranging from simple or aggravated assault to attempted homicide or homicide.[129] The objective of this section is to demonstrate the difficulty of proving that a crime has been committed under general criminal law theory; and, where it can be proved, to show that often it achieves no important public purpose.

Depending upon the charge, there are three possible mental states required to prove an offense. The HIV-infected person can be accused of an act of transmission which is intentional, knowing, or reckless.[130]

1. *Intentional or Knowing Transmission*

A person acts purposefully if his conscious objective is to cause a harmful result such as death.[131] The Model Penal Code uses a subjective standard for criminal attempts so that if the facts were as the person believes them to be, it is an offense.[132] This is important in the AIDS context because a person could be convicted of attempted murder if his intent is to kill, regardless of whether or not the method used poses a real risk of viral transmission.[133] For example, if a person spits at an enemy intending to kill him by transmitting AIDS, he has in theory committed attempted murder.

If an HIV-infected person plans to kill out of a motive such as revenge or greed, and uses a means which has some reasonably significant chance of killing such as sexual contact or needle sharing, that person should bear full responsibility under the criminal law. Yet, it would be unfair and contrary to public policy to punish acts which a person falsely believes to be dangerous. This is tantamount to punishing evil beliefs, while the law should be concerned with punishing and preventing truly dangerous acts. The criminal law achieves no valid purpose by punishing the nondangerous.[134]

---

129. It would be highly unlikely for a homicide or manslaughter charge to be relevant because the victim must already have died. There is a period of five years or longer from the time HIV is contracted to development of serious symptomology. *See* Fauci, *supra* note 108, at 621. In most cases the person accused would have pre-deceased the victim.

130. *See* MODEL PENAL CODE § 210.2(1) (1980) (defining murder as the killing of a human being purposely, knowingly, or recklessly "under circumstances manifesting extreme indifference to the value of human life."). For a perceptive discussion of the application of the Model Penal Code to HIV transmission, see Sullivan & Field, *supra* note 1, at 162–69.

131. MODEL PENAL CODE § 2.02(2)(a) (1980) (defining a purposeful act).

132. *Id.* at § 5.01(1)(a).

133. Impossibility or low likelihood is not a defense to an attempted murder charge. *See, e.g.*, Rex v. White [1910] 2 K.B. 124 (C.A.) (low dose of poison insufficient to cause death resulted in conviction for attempted murder). The reason such cases are attempted murder is that, according to Justice Holmes, they address "an evil which threatens death, according to common apprehension." Commonwealth v. Kennedy, 170 Mass. 18, 22, 48 N.E. 770, 771 (1897). *See also* E. MEEHAN, THE LAW OF CRIMINAL ATTEMPT—A TREATISE 165–66 (1984). Compare such low dose poison cases with an HIV-infected person who enters into a long sexual relationship, intending to kill. While a single sexual encounter has a low chance of viral transmission, a longer relationship raises the probabilities considerably.

134. There is strong legal support for this conclusion in a number of jurisdictions which employ a "dangerousness test"–*viz*, acts which are "directly dangerous" to society, or any interest protected by the criminal law, should be an

Irrespective of the dangerousness of an act, intentionality is exceedingly difficult to prove. One commentator illustrates the rarity of such cases by observing that "[h]aving sex or sharing needles is a highly indirect modus operandi for the person whose purpose is to kill."[135]

"Knowing" transmission of HIV is also difficult to prove. A person acts knowingly if he is aware or is "practically certain" that his conduct will cause harm or death.[136] In the AIDS context, the person must have tested positive for HIV and must know that the particular act would almost certainly transmit the virus. Knowledge of seropositivity, however, is difficult to prove because many individuals are tested anonomously at "alternative test sites," or decline to be tested at all. In the event that such knowledge can be proved, the prosecution must show further that the person understood the conduct was an almost certain method of viral transmission. But epidemiological studies have demonstrated very low probabilities of HIV transmission in a single incident. The press, moreover, has given contradictory messages about the communicability of HIV. Some reports, for example, have minimized the risk of heterosexual transmission,[137] while others have emphasized it.[138] Given these ambiguities, it is doubtful that the prosecution could show that the defendant "knew" his conduct would be infectious.

Charges of attempted murder have been brought in cases where it is barely conceivable that any "purposeful" or "knowing" state of mind could reasonably be established.[139] Such cases often reflect either a politically motivated eagerness to be seen to be combatting AIDS or a misunderstanding of how it is transmitted. Unfortunately, many juries will labor under the same misapprehensions or have the same kinds of prejudices against groups most vulnerable to HIV.[140]

a. *Sexual Intercourse*

Numerous cases have been brought against HIV-infected persons for knowingly or intentionally seeking to harm his or her partner through sexual intercourse.[141] People enter sexual relationships with many different intentions, passions, desires,

---

attempted offense. *See* Sayre, *Criminal Attempts*, 41 HARV. L. REV. 835, 845 (1928). This is also referred to as the "dangerous proximity" test. Hyde v. United States, 225 U.S. 347, 388 (1912). Justice Holmes explained the rationale by stating that public policy is at the "bottom of the matter; the considerations . . . being the nearness of the danger, the greatness of the harm, and the degree of apprehension felt." O. HOLMES, THE COMMON LAW 68 (1881).

135. Sullivan & Field, *supra* note 1, at 163.

136. MODEL PENAL CODE, § 2.02(2)(B)(II) (1980). "Knowledge is established if a person is aware of a 'high probability' of a particular fact." *Id.* § 2.02(7).

137. Gould, *Reassuring News About AIDS: A Dr. Tells Why You May Not Be At Risk*, Cosmopolitan Magazine, Jan. 1988, at 146.

138. W. MASTERS, E. JOHNSON & R. KOLODNY, CRISIS: HETEROSEXUAL BEHAVIOR IN THE AGE OF AIDS (1988).

139. *See supra* notes 115–123, and *infra* notes 140, 147–151 and accompanying text.

140. In the *Haines* case, for example, the jury took barely two hours to convict the defendant of attempted murder on all three counts, despite the paucity of any evidence that he intended to kill a police officer and emergency technicians. Mr. Haines had never seen his victims before. They found him unconscious, face down in a pool of blood after a serious suicide attempt. When he was revived by the emergency workers, his first words were "let me die, I have AIDS." A superior court judge in Lafayette, Indiana substituted a conviction for battery in place of the jury's finding of attempted murder. Mr. Haines was sentenced to six years imprisonment. State v. Haines, No. S-5585 (Super. Ct., Tippecanoe County, Indiana 1987 Term). *See also supra* note 120 and *infra* notes 160–61 and accompanying text.

141. *See supra* note 115 and accompanying text.

and fears. Causing harm through sexuality is seldom consciously planned. Often the relationship involves love, affection, or passion, where neither partner wants to harm the other, but is willing to take risks. In order to establish beyond a reasonable doubt what the person knew or intended, it is often necessary to discuss what went on and what was said, in the privacy of a sexual encounter. That encounter may have taken place years ago, or it may be part of an ongoing relationship where much was discussed. Did the person know he harbored the virus? Did he inform his sexual partner? Did they engage in protected sexual intercourse? Did the partner assume the risk of HIV transmission in many other sexual encounters or IV drug experiences? Such issues as consent or assumption of risk may not be defenses to a charge of attempted homicide. But all these questions can be probative in establishing whether the person's intention was in fact to kill. A person whose purpose is homicide is unlikely to inform a consenting partner of the risk or to use barrier protection.

The criminal law is ill suited to deal with intimate sexual relationships. Transmission of a virus does not fit neatly into the model of a guilty offender and an innocent victim. Both parties engaged in a relationship can, and are advised to, take precautions to avoid exchange of body fluids. It is usually problematic to allocate blame to one of the partners. For example, many targets of criminal prosecutions are prostitutes,[142] who often try to use barrier protection despite client objections. If a man seeks out and pays a prostitute, and refuses to use protection, is the woman the only culpable party? Yet, in most such cases, only the prostitute is charged with a serious criminal offense.[143]

Sexual intercourse is a primary mode of transmission of HIV. A knowing decision by an HIV-infected person to endanger an unsuspecting partner is blameworthy. But balanced against this undoubted fact is the relatively low likelihood of HIV transmission in a single incident (estimated at 1/1,000 or 1/10,000 if a condom is used appropriately).[144]

Serious criminal sanctions to prevent relatively low risks may not be worth the costs. Attempts to criminalize sexual behavior are notoriously problematic. Sexuality and prostitution are highly complex human and biological behaviors which are resistant to change. Sexual intercourse is an integral part of human gratification and reproduction. Prostitution is a profession which has resisted societal efforts to prohibit it for millennia.

The criminal law, moreover, does not simply require high-risk groups to change a single act for a specific period of time. They are required to alter their behavior over

142. *See generally* A. Brandt, *supra* note 11.

143. In an analagous case at Fort Sam Houston in Texas, an Army serviceman tested positive for HIV and was ordered by his company commander to inform his sexual partners of the test results and to take precautions. According to the charges against him, he continued dating and having sexual relations with three people. He confessed to his commander that while he took precautions to protect his sexual partners, he never informed them of his HIV status. Squires, *supra* note 1.

144. *See* Boorstin, *supra* note 1; *supra* notes 22–25 and accompanying text. Compare the relatively low risk of sexual intercourse with the much more significant risk of an HIV-infected mother having a seropositive baby. Here the risk is approximately 50% or greater. Yet, the criminal law would not establish a penalty on the mother for conceiving and failing to abort.

a lifetime. We already know from other health-related behavior such as smoking and diet how difficult such alterations are.

High-risk groups, then, are required, under pain of law, to alter their social behavior, not necessarily for their own good, but for the welfare of others. This is tantamount to asking individuals to behave at the highest stages of moral development. Reaching a high level of moral development is a goal most of us will not attain,[145] and it may be particularly unrealistic to expect vulnerable groups such as drug users or prostitutes to do so. Society creates harsh legal penalties, disproportionately applied to vulnerable risk groups, for failure to attain such lofty behavioral ambitions. Consequently, the law appears unrealistic and inequitable.

The creation of sexual offenses invites intrusion into the private lives of persons, particularly if they are gay or drug users. It legitimizes the state's interests in the intimate relations of adults in their homes, hotels, social clubs, and places of entertainment. It also allows utilization of the numerous components of the criminal justice system—police surveillance, grand jury investigations, and search warrants. Enforcement of sexual offenses is controversial not only because of the intimate behaviors involved, but also because the persons who are most likely to be affected have a disfavored, sometimes minority, status. The potential for selective and discriminatory enforcement against certain individuals and groups, and overzealous intrusion into their lives, is substantial.

A strong campaign of education and counseling to encourage monogamous relationships, avoidance of prostitutes, and use of barrier protection is likely to accomplish the public health objective more effectively and equitably.

b. *Donation of Blood*

Approximately 2% of all cases of HIV are attributable to transfusions of contaminated blood.[146] This mode of transmission has particularly interested prosecutors[147] and federal[148] and state legislators[149] in the use of coercion, because it directly affects heterosexual men, women, and children. When the behavior of a disfavored group such as gays or IV drug users has the potential for seriously harming a favored group such as heterosexuals and children, calls for compulsion are likely to be louder.

145. *See* R. KEAGAN, THE EVOLVING SELF (1982); L. KOHLBERG, THE PHILOSOPHY OF MORAL DEVELOPMENT (1981); Kohlberg, *Moral Stages and Moralization: The Cognitive-Developmental Approach*, in MORAL DEVELOPMENT AND BEHAVIOR: THEORY, RESEARCH AND SOCIAL ISSUES (T. Lickona ed. 1976).

146. *See* CDC, *Weekly Surveillance Rep.*, June 6, 1988.

147. The most celebrated case is Joseph Edward Markowski. Mr. Markowski, who had AIDS, sold his blood to a Los Angeles blood company, Plasma Production Associates. His case was discovered when he approached a bank security guard, tried to grab his gun and yelled "kill me, kill me, I have AIDS." He told police he had donated his blood on 23 other occassions, but this was never confirmed. He was charged with attempted murder. His case was later dropped for lack of evidence on intent, but not before receiving widespread publicity. *See* Gostin, *supra* note 121.

148. *See* S. 1352, 100th Cong., 1st Sess., 133 CONG. REC. S7989-91 (1987) (bill to make it a criminal offense to donate blood, semen, or organs by a person who knows he is HIV positive or in a high risk group).

149. *See, e.g.*, IND. CODE § 16-8-7-6 (Supp. 1988) (knowing donation of blood is a felony); Ky. Reg. Sess. 1988 New Laws 557 HB 50 (persons in risk groups who donate or sell blood commit a class D felony); TENN. CODE ANN. § 68-32-104 (1987) (offense to knowingly donate HIV positive blood). California has considered a similar statute. Cummings, *supra* note 115.

The issue of criminalization for intentional donation of infected blood first emerged in the nationally publicized case of Joseph Markowski, who the prosecution claimed willingly received a small sum of money in return for a donation to a private blood collection agency.[150] Proving intent in cases of donation of blood is problematic. It is usually impossible, for example, in the case of a person who is destitute and gives blood for money, to prove a specific intent to cause death.[151] The motive may well be to obtain a sum of money to buy food, drugs, or alcohol, rather than to harm others. Difficulties of proving that a person fully understood the consequences of his act and intended to kill some unknown blood recipients are potentially insurmountable. The circumstances lack a conceivable motive to kill.

The concern with blood donations as a mode of transmission of HIV are exaggerated. Since 1985 the U.S. blood supply has been screened for HIV antibodies using an Enzyme Linked Immunosorbent Assay (ELISA).[152] The ELISA is very sensitive and is highly likely to detect contaminated blood.[153] From 1985 to 1987, only two cases of HIV-infected blood had escaped detection. During that time twenty-four million units of blood were screened.[154] The act of selling blood for which individuals are charged with attempted murder has a minuscule risk of causing harm.

If the real objective of such prosecutions were to protect the blood supply there would be many more effective ways to do so. In most of the known cases of intentional donations of contaminated blood, payments were involved. Indeed, some private blood collection agencies have shown a blatant disregard for public health. They often recruit donors in poor, minority areas where there are high incidences of IV drug use and sexually transmitted diseases. These areas have a disproportionately high seroprevalence of blood-borne diseases such as AIDS and hepatitis B.[155]

Private blood collection agencies are largely unregulated and often do not actively seek to weed out individuals with infection by rigorous questioning and medical examination. Joseph Markowski, for example, had full-blown AIDS,[156] and was an IV drug user. Either of these conditions probably could have been discovered if the agency were taking reasonable care.[157]

In effect, private blood collection agencies offer a monetary incentive to donate blood among the poorest members of the community; and because they are commercial entities interested in buying blood they may take less care in screening donors. Prohibition or direct regulation of private blood collection enterprises would

150. *See supra* note 147.

151. Mr. Markowski was reported to say, "I was so hard up for money that I didn't give a damn." Gostin, *supra* note 121.

152. *See* Gostin, Curran & Clark, *supra* note 12, at 13–17.

153. *Id.* at 11–13.

154. *See* Cummings, *supra* note 115 (quoting Terry Gautier of the American Red Cross).

155. The prevalence of HIV in large, usually poor, urban areas like the Bronx, Newark, or Miami is disproportionately high. *See A Review of Current Knowledge*, *supra* note 3, at 10–11.

156. *See supra* note 121.

157. IV drug use can be readily detected from examination of the person's arm. Manifestations of symptomatic carriers of HIV can be detected from examination of swollen glands, rashes, or an emaciated state.

be more beneficial to the public health than imposing harsh criminal penalties on HIV-infected donors.[158]

c. *Spitting, Biting, and Splattering of Blood*

Spitting, biting, or splattering blood at a person in anger can be a serious assault. But prosecutors across the country are viewing the same behavior among persons with HIV as attempted murder or assault with a deadly weapon.[159] By viewing assaultive behavior as much more serious when exhibited by AIDS patients, prosecutors make two fundamental errors in judgment: they wrongly assume that persons with HIV have a desire to kill when they behave irresponsibly, and they significantly overestimate the danger presented by the behavior.

Many of the cases reported to date involve HIV-infected persons biting, spitting, or splattering blood during the course of a medical emergency such as following a suicide attempt.[160] Their intent to murder is supposedly established by words such as "I want you to know what it is like to die of AIDS."[161] Such outbursts are not uncommon for persons in emergency rooms, hospitals, or closed institutions such as prisons. The person's behavior can just as easily be attributed to human despair and frustration, as to the desire to kill. In most cases the police officer, emergency physician, or medical technician is not even known to the defendant. Those who truly plan to kill, moreover, do not use the highly indirect means of spitting, biting, or splattering their blood.

It must also be remembered that in these cases the defendant has a terminal illness. The hopelessness of the person's condition and the anger involved in contracting a lethal virus relatively early in life can result in irrational behavior. Equally important is the fact that HIV has profound neurological effects which can develop before immunological deterioration can be detected.[162] However, the extent

---

158. In many European countries, private blood collection agencies are banned. Another way to help protect the blood supply would be to develop a verifiable deferral list. Once a person donates positive blood, he would be informed that he was being placed on a list circulated to all blood collection centers.

159. *See supra* notes 115–16, 127.

160. The most illuminating case is State v. Haines, cause No. S-5585 (Super. Ct., Tippecanoe County, Indiana 1987 Term). On August 6, 1987, Joseph Haines, having discovered he had an advanced case of AIDS-related complex, tried to kill himself in his apartment. Police Officer John Dennes entered the apartment and found Haines unconscious, lying face down in a pool of blood. Two emergency medical technicians arrived, Rodney Jewell and Daniel Garvey. They were applying pressure to his severely cut wrists when Haines jerked away screaming, "let me die, I have AIDS." He then got up off the floor, advanced toward them, shouting that he wanted them to know what it was like to have AIDS. He thrust his arms forward, spraying his blood toward them. None of the emergency personnel has tested positive for HIV. On January 14, 1988, Haines was convicted on three counts of attempted murder. Circuit Court Judge Vincent F. Grogg set aside the jury's verdict because Haines' assault "could not constitute a substantial step toward killing." Grogg found Haines guilty of simple assault and sentenced Haines to three consecutive two year prison terms. *See*, Gostin, *When AIDS is a Weapon*, L.A. Daily Journal, March 3, 1988, at 4, col. 3; Gostin, *AIDS and Safety*, *supra* note 120.

161. *See* State v. Haines, *supra* note 160. But note the equally important first words in the Haines case, "Let me die, I have AIDS." Similar expressions of a wish to die are found in other cases. *See supra* note 147; Squires, *supra* note 115.

162. Levy & Bredesen, *Central Nervous System Dysfunction in Acquired Immunodeficiency Syndrome*, 1 J. Acquired Immune Deficiency Syndrome 41 (nearly 40% of AIDS patients develop neurological complications, and about 10% experience neurological symptoms as the initial manifestations of AIDS). *See generally* Fauci, *supra* note 108, at 621 (neurologic abnormalities occur in at least 60% of AIDS patients); Ginzberg & Gostin, *Legal and Ethical Isues Associated with HTLV-III Diseases*, 16 Psychiatric Annals 180, 182 (1986); Ho, Rota, Schooley, Kaplan, Allan, Groopman, Resnicke, Felsenstein, Andrews & Hirsch, *Isolation of HTLV-III from Cerebrospinal Fluid and Neural*

to which intentional or aggressive behavior can be associated with the neurological defects caused by HIV is not fully understood.

Theoretically, a person could be convicted of attempted murder under the Model Penal Code if the prosecution successfully proves that he believed his behavior could kill, and that he intended that result.[163] Although the risk of HIV transmission from spitting, biting, or splattering of blood is exceedingly remote,[164] the law will treat it as a seriously dangerous act. Of course prosecutors are concerned with evil intentions of aggressors and the apprehension of victims. But where the behavior is truly not dangerous, application of the criminal law appears unjust and unnecessary.[165] It is unjust because a person should not face serious punishment for a belief which will cause no harm.[166] Individuals should not be imprisoned for misguided beliefs, but for seriously dangerous acts. It is unnecessary because the acts which society seeks to prevent are futile and pose no significant risks to the community. The principal purpose of the criminal law when applied to a disease epidemic is prevention. Because this spontaneous, highly emotional behavior is fundamentally irrational, it is unlikely to be deterred by the criminal law. But even if the criminal law could prevent such minor assaultive behavior it would have no impact on the epidemic, because HIV will almost never be transmitted by such behavior.

While transmission of HIV through saliva has never been reported,[167] there have been two cases of transmission of HIV to health care workers who were soaked with contaminated blood.[168] It is, therefore, a valid goal for public health authorities to seek to minimize the risk of exposure to contaminated blood. There are more effective and less restrictive ways to accomplish this objective besides the use of the criminal law.

The most efficient method of preventing exposure to HIV-infected blood is for police, corrections officers, firefighters, emergency medical workers, and others to use rigorous precautions. The Centers for Disease Control (CDC) have issued detailed guidelines on prevention of HIV transmission in various settings such as the workplace,[169] schools,[170] and health care facilities.[171] CDC guidelines for health care workers include all persons whose activities involve contact with patients or with blood or other body fluids. The CDC recommends universal precautions whenever a

---

Tissues of Patients with Neurologic Syndromes Related to Acquired Immunodeficiency Syndrome, 313 NEW ENG. J. MED. 1538 (1985).

163. *See supra* notes 129–136 and accompanying text.

164. *See supra* notes 36–40 and accompanying text.

165. *Cf. supra* note 133.

166. Should a person be prosecuted for a criminal attempt because of a harmless belief? "Even though a 'voodoo doctor' just arrived here from Haiti actually believed that his malediction would surely bring death . . . I cannot conceive of an American Court upholding a conviction . . . ." Commonwealth v. Johnson, 312 Pa. 140, 152–53, 167 A. 344, 348 (1933) (Maxey, J., dissenting). If the means used are so ineffective, a conviction is often thought inappropriate. *See* A.G. v. Sillem, 133 Rev. Rep. 731 (Ex. Ch. 1863). *See also* E. MEEHAN, *supra* note 133, at 172–74.

167. *See supra* notes 35–54 and accompanying text.

168. *See supra* note 61 and accompanying text.

169. *Recommendations for Preventing Transmission of Infection with Human T-Lymphotropic Virus Type III/Lymphadenopathy-Associated Virus in the Workplace*, 34 MORBIDITY & MORTALITY WEEKLY REP. 681 (1986).

170. *Education and Foster Care of Children Infected with Human T-Lymphotropic Virus Type III/Lymphadenopathy-Associated Virus in the Workplace*, 34 MORBIDITY & MORTALITY WEEKLY REP. 517 (1985).

171. *Recommendations*, 1987, 36 (Supp.), *supra* note 52, at 2S.

person is likely to have contact with blood or body fluids, whether or not the fluid is known to be contaminated with HIV. It also urges particular care in emergency settings "in which the risk of blood exposure is increased and the infection status of the patient is usually unknown."[172]

The Departments of Labor and Health and Human Services are developing a far reaching plan to prevent the transmission of blood-borne diseases. First, these Departments issued a Joint Advisory Notice on occupational exposure to HIV and hepatitis B virus (HBV).[173] The Notice is applicable to any worker who has a "predictable job-related requirement" that may involve exposure to blood or body fluids, such as health care workers, law enforcement officers, firefighters, and other "first response" emergency wokers.[174] Second, the Occupational Safety and Health Administration (OSHA) has announced a targeted inspection program to examine actual workplace compliance with the guidelines.[175] Third, OSHA has given advanced notice of proposed rulemaking in order to protect workers from the risk of blood-borne diseases.[176] OSHA purports to act under the "general duty clause" of the Act, and the existing requirement for personal protective equipment whenever necessary to control environmental or other workplace hazards.[177]

OSHA requirements include the development of special operating procedures that must be followed in all cases of expected exposure to body fluids. Each worker must receive education and training on special procedures to be followed and the use of protective clothing, including gloves, overalls, and eye and face protection.

Many police stations, prisons, and emergency departments across the country have not implemented OSHA requirements.[178] In the *Haines* case, police and emergency personnel responded to a suicide call, knowing the patient was HIV positive, without any protective clothing or equipment.[179] They applied pressure to a severely bleeding artery without any covering for their hands or face. Compliance with CDC guidelines and OSHA requirements would be more effective in preventing the transmission of blood-borne diseases than prosecutions under the criminal law.

An alternative to a charge of attempted murder is aggravated assault. In *United States v. Moore*[180] a federal district court upheld a conviction of assault with a "deadly" or "dangerous" weapon in connection with the biting of two federal correctional officers. The court decided there was sufficient evidence to sustain the

---

172. *Id.* at 5S.

173. Dep't of Labor and Dep't of Health & Human Services, Joint Advisory Notice, Protection Against Occupational Exposure to Hepatitis B and Human Immunodeficiency Virus, (Oct. 19, 1987).

174. *Id.* at 5.

175. 52 Fed. Reg. 41818 (1987) (proposed Oct. 30, 1987).

176. Occupational Exposure to Hepatitis B Virus and Human Immonodeficiency Virus, 52 Fed. Reg. 45438 (1987) (codified at 29 C.F.R. 1910) (proposed Nov. 27, 1987).

177. Occupational Safety and Health Act 1970, § 654(a)(1), 29 U.S.C. § 654 (1982) (requires each employer to furnish a place of employment which is "free from recognized hazards that are causing or are likely to cause death or serious physical harm to his employees.").

178. *See, e.g.*, Judis, *An AIDS Nightmare*, N.Y. Times, Jan. 17, 1988, 6 (Magazine), at 32 (police and emergency workers soaked in blood when handling a brutal murder).

179. *See supra* note 140. The rescue workers covered the wound with their bare hands.

180. 669 F. Supp. 289 (D. Minn. 1987).

conviction because the defendant tested positive for HIV, HIV could be transmitted through bodily fluids, and blood was sometimes present in the mouth.

The reasoning in *Moore* is flawed. A dangerous or deadly weapon is an object that is "used in a manner likely to endanger life or [cause] serious bodily harm."[181] Scientific evidence clearly shows the absence of any "likelihood" that a human bite would endanger life or cause serious physical harm through transmission of HIV. Systematic epidemiologic investigations of persons exposed to small amounts of HIV infected saliva or blood demonstrate that there have been no documented cases of transmission from biting; that saliva may block transmissibility; and that even sustained exposures do not result in serological conversion.[182] The federal district court, then, accepted evidence of a theoretical possibility of serious harm as sufficient to prove a likelihood. The Supreme Court, in a related context, has stressed the importance of basing legal decisions on scientific probabilities rather than remote, unforeseeable risks.[183]

In a charge of assault with a dangerous weapon, the weapon is a potentially lethal microbe. Because that microbe can potentially be isolated in most, if not all, bodily fluids, prosecutors wrongly assume that a person's saliva, blood, and mucous are deadly. It follows that what would ordinarily be regarded as minor assaultive behavior such as spitting, biting, kicking, or splattering blood becomes a felony if the person harbors the human immunodeficiency virus. The mischief of this approach is that the same behavior which many people exhibit in anger, frustration, or despair becomes a potentially serious crime because of the person's health status. Such minor assaultive behavior can be witnessed almost daily in hospital emergency rooms, closed and overcrowded institutions such as prisons or hospitals for the mentally ill or retarded, and on sports fields when a player is angry with another player or the umpire.

A human bite is clearly a battery and the law can and should prevent such crimes. But to raise this behavior to a very serious offense because of the person's health status is misguided. I suggest that the reason for the new spate of charges of aggravated assault in relation to HIV has more to do with misbelief and prejudice than any clearly thought out position on culpability or degree of danger involved. The same minor assaultive behavior of persons with other blood-borne diseases such as hepatitis B (HBV) occurs with equal regularity. Transmission of HBV is much more efficient and is likely to result in higher overall morbidity and mortality from a bite or splattering of blood;[184] yet, no prosecutions for deadly assault have been reported against HBV carriers.

The reason for the differences in society's treatment of these two comparable

181. United States v. Hollow, 747 F.2d 481, 482 (8th Cir. 1984).

182. *See supra* notes 35–54 and accompanying text.

183. School Bd. of Nassau County v. Arline, 480 U.S. 273, 288 (1987) *reh'g denied*, 107 S.Ct. 1913 (1987). *See supra* note 13 and accompanying text.

184. *See, e.g.*, Lettau, Smith, Williams, Lundquist, Cruz, Sikes & Hadler, *Transmission of Hepatitis B with Resultant Restriction of Surgical Practice*, 255 J. A.M.A. 934 (1986) (Five patients contracted HBV after surgery, directly attributable to surgeon. Surgeon still permitted to practice using infection control until a further case of HBV transmission was discovered.).

diseases is that AIDS has developed a special mystique. Public apprehension of transmissibility from aggressive behavior is out of proportion to the real risks involved.

2. *Reckless or Negligent Transmission*

One of the principal difficulties with criminalization of intentional or knowing transmission of HIV is that the requisite mental states often cannot be proved. Criminal charges can also be brought against an individual for recklessness, or even negligence, in connection with HIV transmission. The problem here is not so much inadequate proof, but that too many people would be swept into the criminal justice system.

A person acts recklessly under the Model Penal Code when he "consciously disregards a substantial and unjustifiable risk"[185] and a person acts negligently when he "should be aware of a substantial and unjustifiable risk."[186] Disregarding that risk for a reckless or negligent act must involve "a gross deviation from the standard of conduct that a law-abiding"[187] or "reasonable"[188] person would observe in a similar situation.

Crimes involving recklessness or negligence cast a very wide net. They could include not only persons who test positive for HIV, but also people in high risk groups. The criminal law could, therefore, impact on a very large population engaging in sexual activity.[189]

The great majority of the population is aware that AIDS is a sexually transmitted disease and that it is lethal.[190] If a person knows he is seropositive and, nonetheless, engages in sexual intercourse, he is consciously disregarding a known risk, which can be considered reckless behavior. At the very least he should be aware of that risk, which can be negligent behavior.

Opinion polls also show that most of the population knows that gays and IV drug users are at high risk for AIDS.[191] It is conceivable that the criminal law would hold gays and IV drug users accountable not only for what they know, but also for what they reasonably should know. If a person has engaged in high risk behavior and failed to be tested,[192] the courts could put him in the same position as if he knew he were seropositive. Any other rule of law would provide an incentive to avoid being tested or counseled.

Thus, if a person tests positive for HIV or knows he is in a high-risk group, and

---

185. Model Penal Code § 2.02(2)(c).

186. *Id.* § 2.02(2)(d).

187. *Id.* § 2.02(2)(c).

188. *Id.* § 2.02(2)(d).

189. *See generally* Sullivan & Field, *supra* note 1, at 164.

190. Polls consistently show that 98–99% of the public know about AIDS, and up to 93–95% know it is sexually transmitted. Singer, Rogers & Corcoran, *The Polls—A Report, AIDS* 51 Pub. Opinion Q. 580, 584, 588 (1987).

191. *Id.* at 586.

192. The Centers for Disease Control strongly advises persons in high risk groups to be tested. *Additional Recommendations to Reduce Sexual and Drug Abuse-Related Transmission of Human T-Lymphotropic Virus Type III/Lymphadenopathy-Associated Virus*, 35 Morbidity & Mortality Weekly Rep. 152 (1986) [hereinafter *Additional Recommendations*].

has sexual intercourse, he is potentially committing a criminal offense under a recklessness or negligence standard. The question will arise whether sexual intercourse by a person who knew, or reasonably should have known, he was HIV positive is always reckless or negligent. Put in terms expressed by the Model Penal Code, is sexual intercourse by a person at risk always a "gross deviation" from the standard of conduct a law abiding or reasonable person would observe?[193] Public health options for persons at risk for HIV are not limited to abstinence. Health education efforts acknowledge that it may be reasonable for a person at risk to have sex, provided he discloses the risk to his partner and engages in "safer sex" practices.[194] A strong argument could be made that no crime is committed if public health advice is followed, because the person has not grossly deviated from acceptable societal standards.

There are two major problems with using a recklessness or negligence test for criminalizing HIV transmission. First, there are potentially millions of people who come within recognized risk groups who could be susceptible to criminal charges.[195] There is no clear advance notice given to these individuals as to what behavior will be treated as an offense; the prospect exists that any sexual or needle sharing behavior of persons in these groups would be viewed as a criminal act, at least by some prosecutors and juries. The potential for widespread use of the criminal law would chill cooperation with public health programs, and legitimize prejudice and moral disapproval of already disfavored populations.

Second, an approach based upon recklessness or negligence would fail to target only those who engage in truly blameworthy behavior. For example, a person engaging in a long-term, loving relationship could "recklessly" or "negligently" transmit HIV to his partner, even though he had no intention whatsoever of causing him harm. Using a vague and far-reaching standard of recklessness or negligence could punish individuals who have no evil or antisocial intentions.

B. *Public Health or AIDS-Specific Offenses*

The substantial difficulties involved in prosecuting AIDS cases under the traditional criminal law have led state legislators to consider specific public health offenses. Criminal offenses are commonly found in old infectious disease and venereal disease statutes. Some statutes create an offense for transmission of any communicable disease, while others are limited only to specified sexually transmitted diseases. Many venereal disease statutes do not apply to HIV because of the way AIDS is classified.[196]

---

193. Model Penal Code § 2.02(2)(c), (d).

194. *See Additional Recommendations, supra* note 192.

195. The CDC lists a wide range of groups that are at high risk for HIV including homosexual and bisexual men, past and present IV drug users, persons with signs or symptoms of AIDS or ARC, persons born in Haiti and countries in Central America where heterosexual transmission has occurred, male and female prostitutes, sex partners of infected persons, hemophiliacs who have received blood-clotting products, and children of infected mothers. W. Curran, L. Gostin & M. Clark, *supra* note 68, at 224–25. Are all of these individuals obliged in law to be tested? If they are not tested and have sexual intercourse, is that sufficient to establish recklessness or negligence?

196. *See supra* notes 68–71 and accompanying text.

One commentator has criticized the old public health laws as ineffective, unusable, and punitive (targeting "easy" populations such as prostitutes).[197] Such statutes have rarely been used. Undaunted by this historical perspective, state legislators are reclassifying HIV to include the virus within existing public health law offenses or are enacting new AIDS-specific statutes. The new statutes follow the same model as old public health law offenses, but many authorize more restrictive sentencing. While the old statutes tended to have a mild "public health" sanction,[198] levying a fine or a very short prison sentence, modern AIDS-specific offenses make HIV transmission a felony.[199]

The numerous problems of prosecuting under the traditional criminal law have been reviewed.[200] Is it possible to prove that a person intended to kill a partner through the indirect method of sexual intercourse or sharing a needle? How real a possibility of transmission must exist before a prosecution can be successful? Does it matter if the virus is not actually transmitted and the "victim" is left unharmed? Is the fact that the person disclosed his HIV status and/or used a condom relevant? Can a person's mouth or teeth be regarded as a "deadly" weapon? What behavior is "reckless" or "negligent?" Should all high risk groups be included whether or not they actually test positive for HIV? Many, if not all, of these "nice" jurisprudential questions can be avoided by using statutes which clearly define the behavior they seek to punish. By creating a specific statute, legislators make it easier to convict in cases in which the individual is engaging in truly dangerous behavior and also give clearer notice to persons about the behavioral norms to which society expects them to conform.

In formulating a specific public health statute, legislators should inquire what behavior may reasonably be proscribed as criminal by society. Such a statute would not be concerned with particular levels of mental intent and culpability.[201] Rather, it would narrowly target those behaviors which were truly dangerous and which the criminal law might reasonably be expected to deter. Accordingly, the statute would be concerned only with the two primary modes of HIV transmission—sexual intercourse and the sharing of contaminated needles. It would not ban all sex and drug use of HIV- infected people. Such a course would be unrealistic and unfair. It would be unrealistic to expect individuals to forego all sexual contacts and use of drugs for their entire lives. Society has never had success in enforcing similar outright bans in the past.[202]

Banning all sex and drug use would also be unfair because sexuality is necessary

---

197. *See supra* note 11 and accompanying text.

198. *See* Curran, Gostin & Clark, *supra* note 12.

199. *See, e.g.*, IDAHO CODE § 39-608 (Supp. 1988) (any person exposing another intentionally or knowingly commits a felony punishable by up to 15 years in prison, a fine of up to $5000 or both).

200. *See supra* notes 131–195 and accompanying text.

201. It has been proposed that AIDS-specific statutes should follow a classic culpability approach. Robinson, *AIDS and the Criminal Law: Traditional Approaches and a New Statutory Proposal*, 14 HOFSTRA L. REV. 91 (1985). But such a statute would retain virtually all of the problems with a traditional criminal law approach. *See* Sullivan & Field, *supra* note 1, at 178–82.

202. *See supra* notes 141–45 and accompanying text; Fineberg, *Education to Prevent AIDS: Prospects and Obstacles*, 239 SCIENCE 592, 596 (1988).

for human contentment and gratification and because persons who use drugs are often physically dependent on them.[203] Further, such a ban would not be narrowly tailored to combat the harm intended under the statute. Sharing a needle after it has been sterilized with bleach and having sexual intercourse using barrier protection are not highly dangerous acts, although they do pose a lower level risk.

Finally, where a partner is informed of the person's HIV status and consents, there should be no criminal penalty for sexual intercourse or needle sharing. Criminal statutes should not unnecessarily restrict sexual freedoms and should criminalize only culpable acts. Society may well believe that interference with an intimate relationship where both partners give a fully informed consent is unnecessary and unjust.

A specific public health statute, therefore, would seek to change behavior of people who were infected with HIV by requiring them to give certain information and take certain precautions before engaging in well-defined dangerous behavior. A statute, following this conception, would make it a criminal offense only if *all* of the following elements were present: 1) the person knows he is HIV positive and has been apprised by a health care professional or public health official not to engage in unsafe sexual or needle sharing behavior; 2) the person does not notify his partner of his HIV status or does not use barrier protection against exchange of body fluids; and 3) the person engages in sexual intercourse or needle sharing. To establish the offense, it would not be necessary to prove either an intent to harm or that HIV was actually transmitted.

The proposed test is the most acceptable formulation of a criminal standard for HIV transmission: it is based upon objective fact and not moral judgment, it is narrowly targeted to the most dangerous modes of transmission, and it allows vulnerable risk group members to engage in their private lives without state interference provided they obtain an informed consent from their partner or use barrier protection.

Several recent public health acts authorize substantial prison sentences for breach of the statute.[204] Such draconian measures are wholly inconsistent with the goal of a public health statute. Since those statutes appear in public health, not penal codes, their rationale should be different. The objective should not be retribution and sentences should not appear punitive.[205] Mild public health sanctions such as fines, supervision, or attendance orders or, as a last resort, short prison sentences are more appropriate to the public health objective. The reasons are threefold. First, the state's purpose is to set a behavioral boundary to prevent transmission of disease, not to be overly concerned with culpability and moral judgment. The public health statute says nothing about whether the person deserves punishment because of his evil intentions. Where such evil intentions can be proven, and a retributive sentence is justified, the state should be required to bring a traditional criminal law prosecution such as attempted murder. Retribution is only justified if the sufficient criminal intent can be proven.

---

203. *See supra* notes 141–145 and accompanying text.

204. *See supra* notes 140, 199 and accompanying text.

205. *See infra* notes 207–209 and accompanying text.

Second, there is no evidence that the imposition of a stiff criminal penalty will be more effective in preventing dangerous behavior. Most defendants will be terminally ill themselves, and are unlikely to be deterred by a potential felony, as opposed to a misdemeanor, conviction. Nor would there be much public support for harsh sentences of terminally ill individuals.

Finally, the state ought to tread carefully in applying harsh criminal sentences in the deeply private sphere of sexuality or in the underground world of shooting galleries. These are activities which do not respond well to a punitive approach because they are, in part, biologically driven or habitual.[206]

There is a growing consensus among public health authorities that if coercion is to be used at all in the AIDS epidemic, a narrowly focused, nonpunitive approach such as the one proposed would be preferable.[207] To be sure, such a statute would not address the core problems of the spread of HIV, but the inability or unwillingness of authorities to deal with such hard cases may undermine confidence in those who are entrusted with the protection of public health.[208]

The best case for criminalization of HIV, then, would be a specific public health statute. But it may well be a mistake to venture into any criminal law solution to a disease epidemic. The fundamental error of a specific criminal statute lies in the fact that it specifically addresses a subject (sexuality) which is deeply private and sensitive, and targets unpopoular populations (prostitutes, gays, and IV drug users). By doing so, society risks significant abuse of the organs of law enforcement and criminal justice. A statute addressing sexually transmitted disease legitimizes police interest in intimate sexual activities: how partners are chosen, what was said, what precautions were taken. Such a statute also provides an outlet for society's moral distaste for prostitution, drug abuse, and homosexuality. Entrusting police, prosecutors, and juries to detect, enforce, and adjudicate these laws invites unwarranted intrusions into privacy, and victimization of unpopular groups.

An AIDS-specific statute also has the effect of separating HIV from the mainstream of communicable disease control. HIV is a virus which has many unique features. But public health measures designed to impede the spread of HIV should not be fundamentally different from those aimed at other viral infections.[209] Risking transmission of HIV is no more dangerous than risking transmission of many other serious communicable diseases. By enacting laws which apply only to AIDS, legislators will further stigmatize carriers and raise apprehension among the public.

The central question of whether the criminal law, in any form, should be applicable to HIV transmission is whether any legitimate societal goal would be served.

---

206. *See supra* notes 141–145 and accompanying text.

207. *See* PRESIDENTIAL COMM'N REP., *supra* note 114; A.M.A. Council, *supra* note 114.

208. UPDATE 1988, *supra* note 3, at 83.

209. *See* Gostin, *The Future of Public Health Law*, 12 AM. J. LAW & MED. 461 (1986).

C. *Goals of the Criminal Law*

The overarching policy question in determining whether the criminal law is an appropriate model to apply to the AIDS epidemic is whether it serves some important public purpose. Each of the usual rationales for the criminal law—retribution, incapacitation, and deterrence—appear ill-suited to deal with a disease epidemic.

There is an understandable outrage when any citizen acts maliciously to place another's life in jeopardy. But apart from those rare cases where a person consciously decides to use the virus to kill, there would be little public support for retribution for transmission of a virus. Persons who transmit HIV are also infected themselves and will probably die from AIDS. Thus, if punishment were to be sought, it would be directed against a terminally ill patient. Sometimes, if a person has only a short time to live, it can even provide a justification for discontinuing a prosecution.[210] Further, in the overwhelming majority of cases, it is very difficult to establish that the accused had evil intentions deserving punishment. It is more often the case that the person took unreasonable risks motivated by sexual passions, physical dependence on drugs, or both. The application of a retributive criminal law model to a disease epidemic would likely be strongly opposed by public health authorities and distrusted by persons most vulnerable to infection.

Even those responsible for prosecuting cases of HIV transmission reject retribution as a rationale.[211] Instead, they argue for incapacitation. Incapacitation can be defined as the right or duty of society to incarcerate a dangerous individual to prevent him from doing harm, at least while he is deprived of liberty. It is certainly understandable to seek to isolate an individual engaging in dangerous behavior. But the danger is caused by a retrovirus that will remain in his body potentially for life. Any incapacitation during the period of "danger," therefore, can be lifelong. This potential life sentence is unjust when directed against an individual for public health "crimes" such as having sex or sharing needles. More importantly, because the person continues to be infectious once he is imprisoned, he is not incapacitated at all. The decision to incarcerate only shifts the risk to a new, probably more vulnerable, population. The problem of homosexuality, rape, and drug use in prisons may make it more, not less, likely that the virus will be transmitted.

Probably the most important goal of the criminal law in the context of a disease epidemic is deterrence. The best that can be hoped for is that the threat of criminal sanctions will prevent people from taking unreasonable risks that could trasmit the virus. The criminal law is not a likely vehicle for deterring such behavior. In most cases where the criminal law has been used against AIDS carriers there was no motive or advanced planning. Spontaneous behavior driven by human anguish, despair, or passion is difficult to prevent. Further, persons infected with HIV are dying, and a long prison sentence is unlikely to be a deterrent. It is hard to envisage that a person who only has months or years to live would fundamentally alter enjoyable behavior

210. *See* New York v. Camargo, 135 Misc. 2d 987, 516 N.Y.S.2d 1004 (N.Y. Sup. Ct. 1986) (N.Y. criminal court ruled that in the interests of justice it was discontinuing the prosecution of a defendant charged with the sale of cocaine because he was bedridden with AIDS and had only months to live).

211. *See* Squires, *supra* note 1.

because of the threat of a criminal prosecution. The person might be just as likely to continue the risky practices, but be certain not to confide in his physician, counselor, or sex partner. Use of the criminal law in cases of AIDS transmission, then, is unlikely to serve a valid public purpose.

V. Summary

This Article has examined the charged issue of whether a person who risks AIDS transmission should be subject to coercive state action. This is not simply an academic question, for state legislators have already enacted laws which authorize isolation and criminal prosecution of "recalcitrant" AIDS carriers, and prosecutors have already filed criminal charges in numerous cases.

The reasons society has been attracted to coercive measures are understandable. A deliberate or reckless decision to endanger another person's life is deplorable. Public health officials have sometimes appeared uncaring or impotent in dealing with highly visible cases of persons who act in wilful disregard of the value of human life. The use of compulsion provides an outlet for the rage and frustration society has for these "hard" cases.

The use of coercive powers, far from accomplishing its mission of impeding the spread of the AIDS epidemic, could well fuel it. Coercive powers would not go to the core of the problem. The overwhelming majority of cases of HIV transmission are outside the reach of legal control mechanisms and will go unnoticed. Those who do come to the attention of the police and public health officials are likely to be the poorest, least articulate of those harboring the virus. Indeed, there is ample historical evidence to demonstrate that coercive powers have almost exclusively been used against unpopular targets such as prostitutes; and even when used against large numbers of subjects, compulsory powers have not altered the course of disease epidemics.[212]

The reasons coercive powers are inappropriate to control the spread of disease are that they often fail to discriminate between unsubstantiated fears, or even loathing, of high-risk groups, and truly dangerous behavior; they are unlikely to deter highly ingrained human sexual or needle sharing behavior; and they cause a loss of trust and confidence by vulnerable populations who will not cooperate with essential public health programs of education, counseling, and treatment.

Most compulsory powers do not focus narrowly on significant health risks. They sweep in nondangerous behavior such as spitting, biting, or splattering of blood, along with more dangerous behavior such as sexual intercourse and needle sharing. Prevention of very low risk behaviors will not have any effect on the AIDS epidemic, even assuming that such spontaneous behavior could be prevented by the threat of coercive action.

Compulsory public health powers are unlikely to be efficacious in preventing even dangerous acts such as unprotected sexual intercourse and needle sharing. Both are highly resistant to change. Sexuality, including prostitution, is driven by a

212. *See supra* note 11 and accompanying text.

complicated set of biological, psychological, and social forces, and drug use is often physically addicting. Prostitution, drug use, and often sodomy are already unlawful, and it is doubtful whether new criminal offenses or isolation for HIV transmission would serve as a deterrent. The value of coercive laws as a deterrent is diminished further by the fact that AIDS is a terminal condition. Persons with catastrophic illnesses may be just as likely to continue their enjoyable activities quietly as they would be to give them up for fear of punishment.

Indeed, there is good reason to believe that widespread use of coercion against AIDS carriers would make it more difficult to combat the disease. The argument that coercion will drive the epidemic underground is well rehearsed. But it may be one thing to require a person to be tested, and quite another to deprive a person of his liberty for having sexual intercourse or sharing a needle—behaviors he, and others, have engaged in throughout adulthood. It will very much be in the interests of risk group members not to know if they have the virus and not to discuss their sexual or needle sharing contacts with counselors or physicians. The last thing that public health officials want is a population that is frightened of punitive solutions to their health problems.

The use of compulsion, then, is unlikely to be effective in impeding the spread of HIV, and may even exacerbate public health problems. Balanced against the marginal benefit of compulsion are the potential intrusions into the private lives of vulnerable populations. If persons at risk for HIV are prohibited from engaging in unprotected sex or drug use, then police and public health authorities have a corresponding duty to enforce these prohibitions. Isolation or criminal statutes open the door to surveillance of intimate relationships where there is an expectation of privacy.

The concern is not only that compulsory measures are directed at intensely private affairs. It is also that the primary targets of coercion are traditionally unpopular groups—gays, drug users, and prostitutes, disproportionately represented by racial minorities. Police, prosecutors, and juries may base their decisions, in part, on "vague, undifferentiated fears" or on "irrational prejudice."[213] Worse, they may succumb to a "bare . . . desire to harm a politically unpopular group."[214]

Public policy aimed at isolating or criminalizing AIDS transmission may appear to be getting tough with the disease. But they divert our attention and resources from the policies that would make a real difference—focused education, testing, counseling, and treatment for drug dependency.

213. City of Cleburne v. Cleburne Living Center, 473 U.S. 432, 449 (1985).
214. United States Dep't of Agriculture v. Moreno, 413 U.S. 528, 534 (1973).

Name Index